WHAT IS AN *Aspen RoadMap*?

Aspen RoadMaps™ are comprehensive course outlines that lead you, step by step, through your law school courses—helping you prepare for class and study for exams. With a clean, modern design that is as easy to use as it is visually appealing, you'll be guided from the "big picture" to the details you need to know.

WHAT MAKES THE *ASPEN ROADMAP*™ FOR CONTRACTS THE BEST?

The Aspen RoadMap™ *for Contracts:*

- Represents the newest, most up-to-date outline available, brought to you by the publishers of the successful *Examples and Explanations Series.*

- Is informed by the insights and teaching methods of Michael Kelly, one of America's best classroom teachers in Contracts.

- Provides easy access to all the significant rules of Contracts you might need.

- Illustrates how the rules apply, defines key terms, and reveals traps and other intricacies that may crop up on an exam.

- Offers the most complete set of study tools available to help you reinforce your learning and prepare for exams.

THE PRACTICAL COMPONENTS OF YOUR *ASPEN ROADMAP*™

- **The Casebook Correlation** *Chart* helps you match sections of your casebook to this *RoadMap*.™

- **The RoadMap**™ **Capsule Summary**, cross-referenced to the outline text, provides a "big picture" view anytime you need it.

- **Chapter Overviews,** each no more than two pages long, highlight key concepts.

- **Minority Positions** are clearly explained and the effects of rival approaches clarified.

- **Hypotheticals** are interwoven throughout to help further clarify important concepts.

- **Examples**—complete with accompanying analyses—are included in each chapter to provide lively and memorable illustrations of key points.

- **Chapter Review Questions**—complete with answers—reinforce your understanding.

- **Exam Tips** help you target what you really need to know in order to maximize your study time and do well on exams.

- **Sample Exam Questions**, presented as short essays, are accompanied by model answers.

Dear Student,

I'd like to take this opportunity to welcome you to the *Aspen RoadMap*™ for Contracts. I am Michael Kelly, Professor of Law at the University of San Diego School of Law—where I have taught Contracts for more than nine years.

During my years in the classroom and in the many hours I've spent talking with students outside of class, I have come to learn when and why you, as a student, might have difficulty in this course. From what other students have told me, I have developed specific approaches and effective techniques that can help you navigate your way around potential problems.

Contracts is the basis for many upper level law school courses—Insurance Law, Labor Law, Family Law, Banking Law, and Health Law, to name a few. A mastery of your first course in Contracts may well be critical to your success in law school, if not in your legal career.

Have no fear! With your *RoadMap*™ in hand, you won't get lost. Your *RoadMap*™ presents the rules succinctly. And it offers more than just the rule; it illustrates how the rule applies, defines key terms, and gives you practice examples and lots of hypotheticals to guide you every step of the way.

While the law of Contracts is comprised of a multitude of rules and codes, contracts themselves are really fundamental: they form the basis of a vast number of relationships. It's easy, however, to get bogged down in details, to feel overwhelmed, and to overlook the more interesting "big picture" nuances of contracts as a cornerstone of society. Your *RoadMap*™ can help you put the details in context and give you a more confident perspective from which to venture into your reading, your classroom, and your exams.

Good luck, and please remember that this book is not intended to replace your casebook and assigned primary material, but rather to help you orient yourself in your reading, as well as in the classroom and at exam time. With your *RoadMap*™ in hand, I think you will find Contracts a worthwhile (and possibly even enjoyable) journey.

Sincerely,

Michael B. Kelly

Michael B. Kelly
Professor of Law

P.S. I'd welcome your suggestions for making the *RoadMap*™ even more useful. Please write to me at Aspen Law & Business, Law School Division, One Liberty Square, 10th floor, Boston, MA 02109 or e-mail us at j.barmack@aspenpubl.com

Aspen Publishers, Inc. A **Wolters Kluwer** Company

1185 Avenue of the Americas, New York, NY 10036

Contracts

Michael B. Kelly

Professor of Law
University of San Diego School of Law

ASPEN LAW & BUSINESS
A Division of Aspen Publishers, Inc.

Copyright © 1997 by Aspen Law & Business
A Division of Aspen Publishers, Inc.
A Wolters Kluwer Company

Printed in the United States of America

Library of Congress Cataloguing-in-Publication Data
Kelly, Michael B., 1953–
    Contracts / Michael B. Kelly.
      p.   cm. — (Aspen roadmap)
    Includes index.
    ISBN 1-56706-472-8
    1. Contracts—United States—Outlines, syllabi, etc.   I. Title.
II. Series.
KF801.Z9K45   1997
346.7302—dc21
                                                97-15536
                                                CIP

SUMMARY OF CONTENTS

CONTENTS

3 CONSIDERATION AND ITS ALTERNATIVES 101

4 THE ROLE OF WRITINGS: STATUTES OF FRAUDS

5   INTRODUCTION TO DEFENSES: FACTORS THAT INTERFERE WITH ARM'S-LENGTH BARGAINING   185

9 MISTAKE OF BASIC ASSUMPTION   237

10   UNCONSCIONABILITY: EFFORTS TO AVOID UNFAIR CONTRACTS

11 PUBLIC POLICY LIMITS ON CONTRACTS   263

14 · PAROL EVIDENCE: LIMITATIONS ON INTERPRETATION AND GAP FILLING

16   MATERIAL BREACH: DOES NONPERFORMANCE JUSTIFY TERMINATION?   345

17 EXCUSABLE NONPERFORMANCE: DOES NONPERFORMANCE JUSTIFY DAMAGES?

18   REPUDIATION: CAN BREACH OCCUR BEFORE PERFORMANCE IS DUE?

22   REMEDIES AGREED ON BY THE PARTIES

23   RESTITUTION AND UNJUST ENRICHMENT   471

CASEBOOK CORRELATION

Aspen RoadMap	Dawson, Harvey & Henderson, **Cases and Comments on Contracts** (6th ed. 1993)	Farnsworth & Young, **Cases and Materials on Contracts** (5th ed. 1995)	Knapp & Crystal, **Problems in Contract Law: Cases and Materials** (3d ed. 1993)	Murphy, Speidel, Ayus, **Studies in Contract Law** (5th ed. 1997) *References are to chapters (c) and to sections (§).*
1. INTRODUCTION TO CONTRACT LAW				
A. Sources of Contract Law			4-9, 15-23	c1, §1; c2, §1
B. Overview of Contract Doctrine			9-12, 36-55	c1, §2
C. Framework for Analyzing the Enforcement of Promises	11-22, 26-35	20-22	81-82	c1, c2
2. FORMATION: PROMISES, ASSENT (OFFER AND ACCEPTANCE), AND DEFINITENESS				
A. Promise	300-312	116-137	87	c1, §2; c3
B. Definiteness (or Certainty)	300-303, 353-361	279-285		c3, §2
C. Overview of Assent	328-340	138-152	36-37	c1, §2; c3
D. Identifying an Offer	340-349	153-168	52-55	c3, §1
E. Special Problems with Offers	349-353	165-168	55	c3, §1
F. The Duration of an Offer	374-375, 384-425	188-190, 198-211, 217-219	61-81, 234-272	c3, §1
G. Acceptance	370-384, 425-452	161, 212-217, 219-248	55-61, 272-307	c3, §1; c3, §1(c)(1)
H. Preliminary Agreements	353-355, 361-364	248-279	251-260, 307-350	c3, §2
3. CONSIDERATION AND ITS ALTERNATIVES				
A. Rationale for the Bargain Requirement	193-199, 203-205	44-47, 52-54	90-96	c1, §2; c2, §1
B. Elements of Consideration: Bargained-for Exchange	205-208, 210-211, 217-219	51-52, 54-60	96-104	
C. Common Misconceptions	208-210, 211-213, 216-217, 219-227, 293-300, 576-582	47-51, 52	83-90, 92, 104-118	c1, §2; c2, §1; c2, §1(B)(1); c2, §1(3)
D. Exception for Delivered Gifts	213-215			c1, §2
E. Exception for Past Consideration and Moral Obligation	228-231, 233-248	62-73, 79	118-129, 165-179	c2, §1(B)(1); c2, §2
F. Preexisting Duty	227-228, 286-293, 577-596, 603-615	352-364, 371-374	788-793	c2, §1(2); c5, §4(D)

Aspen RoadMap	Dawson, Harvey & Henderson, **Cases and Comments on Contracts** (6th ed. 1993)	Farnsworth & Young, **Cases and Materials on Contracts** (5th ed. 1995)	Knapp & Crystal, **Problems in Contract Law: Cases and Materials** (3d ed. 1993)	Murphy, Speidel, Ayus, **Studies in Contract Law** (5th ed. 1997) *References are to chapters (c) and to sections (§).*
G. Exception for Action in Reliance (or Promissory Estoppel)	249-293	84-116	180-228, 230-260	c1, §2; c2, §1; c2, §3
H. Formality as an Exception to the Consideration Requirement	199-203	209	102-104	c2, §4
4. THE ROLE OF WRITINGS: STATUTES OF FRAUDS 　A. Rationale 　B. Statutes of Frauds 　C. Writings Required by the Parties	457, 507 95-98, 270-275, 278-281, 957-974 508-516	286-288 288-323	351-354, 371-372 354-371, 372-381, 384-412	c2, §4(B)(1)
5. INTRODUCTION TO DEFENSES 　A. Framework of Defenses 　B. Procedural Framework 　C. Terminology: Void vs. Voidable	98-100, 104-105, 237, 296-298, 563-573, 579-580, 583, 588-589 296-298, 546-577, 615-630, 658-663	171-178, 354-361, 502-505, 672 326-327		
6. INCAPACITY 　A. Rationale 　B. Infancy: Until the Day before a Person's Eighteenth Birthday, any Contract She Enters is Voidable 　C. Mental Illness or Defect 　D. Intoxication	546-551 552-563	324-326 326-329 329-336 325	585-586 171, 586-591 591-601	c4 c4, §1(A) c4, §1(B) c4, §(B)
7. IMPROPER PRESSURE 　A. Duress 　B. Undue Influence	570-582, 596-603 563-569	349-371	601-614, 805-806 614-622	c4, §2(c) c4, §2(c)
8. MISREPRESENTATION 　A. Rationale 　B. Fradulent or Material Misrepresentation 　C. Nondisclosure and Concealment 　D. Misrepresentation Concerning the Content of the Agreement	615-621 647-658 283-284, 484-489, 494-495	382-385 383-385 374-382 382-386	622-624 624-634 634-660 624-632	c4, §2(B) c4, §2(B)
9. MISTAKE OF BASIC ASSUMPTION 　A. Mutual Mistake 　B. Unilateral Mistake	364-369, 621-634 634-641	795-804 801	730-742 742-751	c3, §2; c4, §2 c4, §2

Aspen RoadMap	Dawson, Harvey & Henderson, **Cases and Comments on Contracts** (6th ed. 1993)	Farnsworth & Young, **Cases and Materials on Contracts** (5th ed. 1995)	Knapp & Crystal, **Problems in Contract Law: Cases and Materials** (3d ed. 1993)	Murphy, Speidel, Ayus, **Studies in Contract Law** (5th ed. 1997) *References are to chapters (c) and to sections (§).*
10. UNCONSCIONABILITY: EFFORTS TO AVOID UNFAIR CONTRACTS				
A. Unconscionability in Context		386-388	660-661	
B. Contracts of Adhesion: The Role of Form Contracts	510-522, 542, 723-726	394-408, 413-415, 423-426	661-667, 668-669	c5, §2
C. Judicial Treatment of Form Contracts	522-526, 538-545, 723-726	388-394, 398, 415, 416-418	667-668, 669-670	
D. Elements	707-713	336-348, 426-436, 438-441	671-694	c4, §2(b)
E. Alternative Views	526-537, 700-707, 714	408-413, 415-416, 418-420	694-698	
F. Putting the Rhetoric in Perspective: Procedural Unconscionability vs. Substantive Unconscionability	722	420-421	665-669	
11. PUBLIC POLICY LIMITS ON CONTRACTS				
A. In General		467-482	698-705	c4, §3
B. Contracts Within a Family: Status vs. Contract	453-457, 614-615	83-84, 149, 455-456	151-165, 181-190, 721-724	c4, §3
C. Contracts in Restraint of Trade	176-184	456-467	698, 705-721	c4, §3
12. INTERPRETATION: WHAT DOES THE CONTRACT REQUIRE?				
A. General Techniques of Interpretation			413-417, 424-432	
B. Inferences	498-505, 769-770	609-611, 613-615, 650-663, 694		
C. Canons of Construction	499	606-608	422-432	
D. Filling Gaps in the Agreement		611-650	499-584	c5, §4
13. EFFECT OF PARTIES' MISTAKES ON INTERPRETATION: MISUNDERSTANDING AND MISTAKE OF INTEGRATION				
A. Misunderstanding	364-369	592-595	415, 417	
B. Mistake of Integration and Reformation	495-500	578-579	729-738	
14. PAROL EVIDENCE: LIMITATIONS ON INTERPRETATION AND GAP-FILLING				
A. Rationale	457, 507	565-566	413-417, 451-454	c5, §1

Aspen RoadMap	Dawson, Harvey & Henderson, **Cases and Comments on Contracts** (6th ed. 1993)	Farnsworth & Young, **Cases and Materials on Contracts** (5th ed. 1995)	Knapp & Crystal, **Problems in Contract Law: Cases and Materials** (3d ed. 1993)	Murphy, Speidel, Ayus, **Studies in Contract Law** (5th ed. 1997) *References are to chapters (c) and to sections (§).*
B. The Basic Rule	457-464	566-570	417-422, 454-461	c5, §1
C. Integrated Writings	464-476	570-578, 580-581	430-432, 458	c5, §1
D. Conditional Contracts	477-483			c5, §1
E. Interpretation	498-507	581-611, 650-663	476-493	c5, §1(B)
F. Exception for Torts	483-489	578-580	459-460	c5, §1(B)
G. Exception for Contract Defenses	489-498	617-620, 678-680	460	
H. Exception for Modification	583-589	353, 580-581	461, 786-807	c5, §4(c)
15. IS PERFORMANCE DUE?				
A. Condition Defined	727-729	672-677, 739	866-870	c5, §2
B. Effect of Conditions	729-738, 762-765	665-672, 677-690		c5, §4
C. Excusing Conditions: Waiver, Modification, and Estoppel	591-596, 755-761, 765-770	681, 693-698	825-844	c5, §2
D. Classifying Conditions	734-750, 761-762, 770-773	665-698	811-825	c5, §2
16. MATERIAL BREACH: DOES NONPERFORMANCE JUSTIFY TERMINATION?				
A. Rationale: Why Allow Termination for Material Breach?	773-785	735-739	848-849, 857-870	
B. The Rule			854-857	
C. The Order of Performance	786-825	699-707		c5, §2; c5, §4
D. Factors Affecting Materiality of a Breach	818-823	735-741	854, 857-862	c5, §2
E. Suspension or Termination? Time for Cure	844-856	740-745	855-857	c5, §2
F. Examples: Balancing Forfeiture with Parties' Expectations	826-842	707-720	849-854, 862-863	
G. Divisibility: Mitigating the Harshness of Material Breach	823-825, 857-859	720-724, 732-734	865-866	c5, §2
17. EXCUSABLE NONPERFORMANCE: DOES NONPERFORMANCE JUSTIFY DAMAGES?				
A. Impracticability	658-686	745-747, 805-834, 853	751-753, 754-759, 769-784	c5, §3
B. Frustration	686-700	834-851	753-754, 759-761	c5, §3(c)
C. Mistake, Reprised		851-862	765-769	c5, §3
18. REPUDIATION: CAN BREACH OCCUR BEFORE PERFORMANCE IS DUE?				
A. Repudiation	53-57	755-788	870-878	c6, §1; c6, §2(c)

Aspen RoadMap	Dawson, Harvey & Henderson, **Cases and Comments on Contracts** (6th ed. 1993)	Farnsworth & Young, **Cases and Materials on Contracts** (5th ed. 1995)	Knapp & Crystal, **Problems in Contract Law: Cases and Materials** (3d ed. 1993)	Murphy, Speidel, Ayus, **Studies in Contract Law** (5th ed. 1997) *References are to chapters (c) and to sections (§).*
B. Reasonable Grounds for Insecurity	856-857, 859-867	788-794	878-889	c6, §1
C. Events after Repudiation: Retraction and Mitigation	38-51, 71-73	760-763, 783-786	878	c6, §1
19. EQUITABLE RELIEF				
A. Specific Performance: Compelling the Breaching Party to Perform	151-158, 162-174, 187-188, 700-707	22-38	1074-1093	c6, §4
B. Enforcing Negative Convenants	174-187	33-41	1093-1107	c6, §4
20. EXPECTATION INTEREST: THE NORMAL RECOVERY RULES				
A. Basic Principle: The Financial Equivalent of Performance		7-14, 74-76, 483-486	892-898, 1001-1008	c6, §2
B. Value of the Promised Performance	35-38, 53-60	27, 34-38, 486-494	898-902	c6, §2(B)
C. Avoiding Undercompensation: Incidental Losses, Consequential Losses, and Prejudgment Interest	60-80		902-903	v6, §2
D. Avoiding Overcompensation: Reasonable Cover, Losses Avoided, and Costs Avoided	11-22, 60-65	22-28, 494-505, 514-519	1009-1023	c6, §2(B); c6, §2
E. Limitations on Expectation Recoveries	38-53, 65-80	14-20, 43-44, 505-514, 519-552, 745-754	908-939	c6, §2
21. THE RELIANCE INTEREST				
A. Appropriate Cases for the Reliance Interest	29-31, 80-89	7-14	1033, 1035-1036	
B. Calculating Reliance Recoveries	35-38, 89-92	501-505	1025-1032, 1037-1038	
C. The Reliance Interest Cannot Exceed the Expectation Interest	92-93		1033-1035	
22. REMEDIES AGREED ON BY THE PARTIES				
A. Types of Agreed Remedies			1107-1109, 1119-1121	c6, §5(B)
B. Agreements Excluding Consequential Damages	145-150	534-544, 893-894	1119-1120, 1129	c6, §5(B)
C. Agreements Specifying an Exclusive Remedy	98-100			
D. Liquidated Damages and Penalties	26-28, 133-145, 150-151	553-564	1109-1119, 1121-1131	c6, §5
E. Agreed Remedial Procedures: Choice of Law and Forum Selection		441-450		

Aspen RoadMap	Dawson, Harvey & Henderson, **Cases and Comments on Contracts** (6th ed. 1993)	Farnsworth & Young, **Cases and Materials on Contracts** (5th ed. 1995)	Knapp & Crystal, **Problems in Contract Law: Cases and Materials** (3d ed. 1993)	Murphy, Speidel, Ayus, **Studies in Contract Law** (5th ed. 1997) *References are to chapters (c) and to sections (§).*
F. Arbitration	189-192	41-43, 450-451	1131-1134	c6, §6
23. RESTITUTION AND UNJUST ENRICHMENT				
A. Terminology	106-109	76-84	135-138	
B. Restitution When the Contract Was Not Enforceable	102-104, 126-132	74-84	138-165	
C. Restitution as a Remedy for Breach of Contract	98-100	502-505	1051-1057	
D. Calculating the Benefit Bestowed	100-102, 119-124		1068-1072	
E. Restitution to the Breaching Party	109-114, 115-126, 842-843	724-735	1057-1068	
24. ASSIGNMENT, DELEGATION, AND THIRD PARTY BENEFICIARIES				
A. Third Party Beneficiaries	877-917	863-912	1197-1231	c7, §2
B. Assignment of Rights	917-932, 942-956	913-943	1231-1238, 1258-1259	c7, §1(A)
C. Delegation of Duties	932-942	438-439, 944-992	1238-1258	c7, §1(B)

Capsule Summary

Don't use this summary instead of the outline itself. Use it for review.

 INTRODUCTION TO CONTRACT LAW

A. SOURCES OF CONTRACT LAW

One of your tasks this year is to learn how to find law. (In the long run, your course in research and writing is more important than any substantive course, such as Contracts.) Contract law will be easier to understand once you appreciate the relationship between the different kinds of materials you will read in the process of finding the law.

1. Uniform Commercial Code (UCC)

a. **UCC governs in 49 states.**

b. **Article 2 of the UCC governs sales of goods.**

c. **Goods are movable things.** An item that is movable at the time it is identified to the contract is a good. Goods include crops to be sold after harvest and the unborn young of animals. They exclude, however, money, securities, and other intangible items (e.g., insurance policies or lawsuits). See UCC §2-105. Real estate and service contracts are not governed by the UCC.

2. Restatements and Other Secondary Sources

a. **Restatements.** The Restatement (Second) of Contracts was compiled by a foundation composed of prominent judges, attorneys, and professors who identified the dominant doctrines in state common-law decisions and summarized them in a succinct form. The result resembles a statute: a straightforward statement of a rule. The Restatement is not a statute. It is persuasive but not binding.

B. FRAMEWORK FOR ANALYZING THE ENFORCEMENT OF PROMISES

Contracts is two courses, not one. One course identifies how to win a suit for breach of contract and the remedies available when you do. But another course, hidden in the first, deals with other remedies, available to parties who cannot prove the other party breached an enforceable contract. These remedies (usually called restitution) come into play throughout the course. Thus, in studying contracts, the significant issue often revolves around **which** remedy to apply more than around **whether** to apply a remedy at all. This outline discusses remedies in detail in later chapters.

1. Possible Responses to Broken Promises

This section introduces the various options courts have and summarizes how they use those options.

   a. **Specific performance: Compelling the breaching party to perform.**   Specific performance is an injunction, a court order requiring a person to do specified things, such as deliver goods or finish construction.

   b. **Expectation damages: The financial equivalent of performance.** Damages based on the expectation interest seek to put the nonbreaching party, usually the plaintiff, in the position she would have occupied if the defendant had performed the contract. As with all damage remedies, the court accomplishes this goal by awarding the plaintiff money.

   c. **Reliance damages: Compensating for the detriment of breach.** Damages based on the reliance interest in theory seek to put the plaintiff in the position she would have occupied if the defendant had not made the promise at issue.

   d. **Restitution: Preventing unjust enrichment.**   Restitution seeks to restore the defendant to the position she would have occupied if she had not made the promise in the first place.

PART 1 WHICH PROMISES SHOULD THE LAW ENFORCE?

 2 FORMATION: PROMISES, ASSENT (OFFER AND ACCEPTANCE), AND DEFINITENESS

A. PROMISE

A contract is a promise the law will enforce or the performance of which the law recognizes as a duty.

1. Promise Defined

The Restatement (Second) of Contracts §2 defines promise as "a manifestation of intention to act or refrain from acting in a specified way, so made as to justify a promisee in understanding that a commitment has been made." This definition includes several components.

 a. **Promises must be manifest.** Words and actions can constitute promises; unexpressed intentions cannot.

 b. **No magic words.** Words that indicate a commitment to act are a promise, even if not preceded by the incantation "I promise."

2. Jest

A party would not be justified in believing a commitment had been made if she understood that the promisor spoke in jest.

 a. **Promisee understood or should have understood.** If a reasonable person observing the transaction would have believed that the promisor was serious, not jesting, a promise exists: The promisee justifiably could understand that a commitment had been made. The fact that the promisor **intended** to jest does not negate a promise. The promisor must include in her words or actions some indication that should alert the promisee to the jest.

 b. **Promisee's failure actually to understand may not matter.** If a reasonable person would have understood that the promisor was joking, the fact that a dense or inattentive promisee did not discern the jest will not convert the jest to a promise. The promisee would not be **justified** in understanding that a commitment had been made even though she sincerely may believe that the promisor made a commitment.

   c.   **Restitution.**   A promisee who acts in reliance on an unjustified belief that the promisor made a commitment may be entitled to restitution.

3.   **Illusoriness or Conditional Promises**

Some promises contain conditions that negate commitment (e.g., a promise to perform "if I feel like it"). This is not a promise; the words create the illusion of a promise.

   a.   **Illusoriness defined: Unbridled discretion to withdraw.**   If the promisor remains completely free to change her mind about the deal, any commitment is illusory and no promise exists. A promise involves commitment. A promisor who can withdraw from the transaction on a whim without paying damages for breach has made no commitment.

      i.   **Conditional promises generally bind.**   Almost any limit on the promisor's ability to change her mind may satisfy the requirements of a commitment. If the promisor remains bound to perform under some circumstances, the fact that other circumstances would permit the promisor not to perform does not negate the commitment.

      ii.   **Implied promises and illusoriness.**   If an implied promise, such as the duty to act in good faith, limits a party's ability to change her mind, commitment exists and the agreement is enforceable even if the expressed words, standing alone, were illusory.

   b.   **Effect of illusoriness.**   Illusoriness prevents enforcement of duties under an agreement. If defendant's "promise" is illusory, there is no promise to enforce. If plaintiff's promise is illusory, it cannot serve as consideration for defendant's promise. If plaintiff gave things in addition to the illusory promise, the other things still might be consideration.

4.   **Requirements and Output Contracts**

Contracts may specify a quantity measured by the amount buyer's requirements or the seller's output. These promises are not illusory, even though a buyer may require none or a seller may produce none. The buyer and seller must determine their requirements or output in good faith. Thus, they cannot withdraw at will. Nor can they deal with others if they in fact have some requirements or some output.

a. **Excessive requirements.** A buyer in a requirements contract cannot pretend to need a huge amount of the goods, hoping that the seller cannot meet the demand and will breach. A request that exceeds the amount that the buyer really needs breaches the promise to act in good faith.

b. **UCC prohibits excessive demands.** A party need not perform if the other tenders or demands a quantity grossly disproportionate either to estimates or to prior performance under the contract. UCC §2-306. The test is objective, not dependent on good faith.

c. **Best efforts.** An exclusive dealing contract makes at least one party dependent on the other party's efforts. If the other fails to produce sufficient business, the party who cannot deal with anyone else suffers. In these circumstances, the UCC assumes that the contract requires more than good faith; it requires best efforts. UCC §2-106(2).

B. DEFINITENESS (OR CERTAINTY)

Courts will not enforce an indefinite contract. But courts have ways to find definiteness when the parties themselves have left matters open. Few contracts actually fail for want of definiteness.

1. The Rule

Terms are definite if they provide a basis for determining whether a breach has occurred and for giving an appropriate remedy. Restatement (Second) of Contracts §33(2). The rule has two rationales.

2. Identifying the Performance Required by the Contract

When the parties' words or actions signify that they intended a contract, modern courts will do all they can to discover the terms of the contract and to enforce those terms.

a. **Interpreting the agreement.** Often, a little effort to discern the parties' meaning will permit the court to identify the promises made.

b. **Supplying missing terms.** On some occasions, uncertainty arises because the parties omitted a term. Courts (often encouraged by legislation) may fill these gaps in the contract.

    i. **UCC default terms.** The UCC specifies a number of default terms: terms that apply to all contracts for the sale of goods unless the parties specify a different term.

3. Identifying an Appropriate Remedy

This is almost the same as identifying a breach. If you know what the defendant promised, you usually can ascertain what position the plaintiff would have occupied if the defendant had performed the promise. That is the definition of the expectation interest, the usual remedy in breach-of-contract suits.

C. OVERVIEW OF ASSENT

Unless both parties want to make the exchange, at least at the time they enter the contract, the law will not treat the promises as enforceable.

1. Problems with Assent

Such problems usually involve one of three questions.

a. Did the party assent at all?

b. When did the assent occur?

c. To what terms did the parties assent?

2. The Structure of Assent

Assent has evolved from rather rigid common-law rules concerning **offer** and **acceptance** to a more open-ended inquiry into all the facts and circumstances that might indicate agreement between the parties. Because that evolution is incomplete, your course probably will address both approaches.

a. UCC approach. The UCC explicitly recognizes that almost any method of signifying agreement can create a contract. Thus, words, actions (e.g., performance or reliance), or (in some cases) even silence can communicate a commitment to perform according to the terms of an agreement.

b. Common-law approach.   The common law assessed assent according to a fairly rigorous paradigm: One party made an **offer** to the other; the other then either gave an **acceptance** or did not. Acceptance marked the moment a contract became binding. Up to that point, each party remained free to change her mind and withdraw from the transaction.

D. IDENTIFYING AN OFFER

"An offer is a manifestation of willingness to enter into a bargain, so made as to justify another person in understanding that his assent to that bargain is invited and will conclude it." Restatement (Second) of Contracts §24.

1. **Manifestation**

   An offer must be manifest.

2. **Promise**

   Usually, an offer takes the form of a conditional promise: I promise to perform x if you promise to do y in return. You must identify a promise within an offer to find a promise to enforce if the offer is accepted.

3. **Invitation to Accept**

   Some expressions may imply willingness to enter a bargain without inviting assent (e.g., "For two cents I'd sell that cat!").

4. **Conclusiveness**

   An offer gives the other party the power to conclude a deal by accepting.

5. **Bargain**

   An offer must propose a bargain. Including a bargain in the definition of an offer unnecessarily complicates matters. Discuss bargains under consideration.

E. **SPECIAL PROBLEMS WITH OFFERS**

   1. **Advertisements**

      Typically, ads are **not** offers. They invite others to make offers.

      a. **Ads can be offers.** An ad that contains words of commitment and all necessary details of the bargain may be an offer.

   2. **Infelicitous Offers**

      Courts sometimes rescue a party who intended to seek bids but used language others could see as inviting acceptance.

   3. **Auctions**

      Some items placed for auction have a reserve price; only bids above that price will be accepted, effectively specifying a minimum bid. Some items are placed for auction without reserve; that is, they will be sold to the highest bidder, no matter how low the bid.

      a. **Auctions with reserve invite offers.** Putting an item up for auction invites others to make offers. Bids are offers. Bidders can revoke offers before accepted by the auctioneer. Each bid terminates the offer of any prior bid.

b.   Auctions without reserve are offers.   The offer is made to the highest bidder. The highest bid accepts the offer, forming a binding contract.

F.   THE DURATION OF AN OFFER

If an offer terminates before it has been accepted, no assent exists.

1.   Methods of Terminating an Offer

a.   Lapse of time.   The offer may specify the time it expires. If it does not, the offer expires after a reasonable time has passed. Reasonableness depends in part on how quickly values change.

b.   Rejection.   Rejection terminates an offer, unless the offeror agrees to leave the offer open despite the rejection. Equivocal words are a rejection, unless the offeree indicates she continues to consider the offer.

c.   Counteroffer.   A response that proposes new or different terms rejects the original offer and puts a different offer on the table. As with rejections, the offeror can allow the offer to remain open despite the counteroffer, and the offeree may indicate that the original offer remains under consideration.

d.   Death or incapacity of either party.   An offer cannot be accepted after either the offeror or the offeree dies or suffers incapacity.

e.   Nonoccurrence of conditions.   If an offer specifies conditions on the ability of others to accept, the offer ends when the conditions cannot occur.

f.   Revocation.   An offeror usually remains free to revoke an offer any time before acceptance. Revocation is effective when communicated to the offeree, either by the offeror or by another. Offers made to the public can be revoked by giving equal publicity to the revocation.

2.   Firm Offers

An offeror may relinquish the right to revoke an offer. When the power to revoke is effectively waived, the offer is called a firm offer.

a.   Statutes enforcing firm offers.   The most significant example is UCC §2-205, which makes an offer **by a merchant** irrevocable if a **signed writing** ensures that the offer will be held open. If the offer does not specify when it expires, it remains open a reasonable time, up to 90 days.

3. Options: Bargains to Keep an Offer Open

If one party pays the other consideration for a promise to keep an offer open, the promise to keep the offer open is enforceable. This is called an option contract.

a. Creating an option. An option is created in the same way as any other contract: by assent to a definite bargain.

b. Exception for reliance. As with other promises, exceptions to the requirement of a bargain also may make enforceable the promise to keep an offer open. As it applies to options, the reliance exception requires that:

- The offeror **promised** to keep the offer open for a time;
- The offeror **reasonably should have expected that the offeree would rely** on that promise;
- The **offeree did rely** in a way the offeror should have expected; and
- Enforcement will be necessary to avoid injustice (because the **offeree will be harmed** unless the promise to keep the offer open is enforced).

c. Reliance without a promise. Reliance can create an option even if the offeror does not promise to keep the offer open.

   i. An offer must exist.

   ii. The offeror reasonably should have expected reliance of a substantial character before acceptance. This differs from the preceding test by requiring **substantial** reliance **before** acceptance.

   iii. The offeree actually relies in a way the offeror should have expected.

   iv. The option exists to the extent necessary to avoid injustice. This implies that a revocation may be effective, at least in part, if injustice is limited or nonexistent.

4. Breach of an Option Contract

An offer held open by an option contract can be accepted at any time until the option expires, **even if the offeror tries to revoke the offer earlier.**

5. **Unilateral Contracts**

Offers may require a party to accept by completing performance. If so, no other form of acceptance will work.

　　a.　**Complete performance is acceptance.**　No contract exists until performance is complete. The offeree could stop performing at any time, without any liability to the offeror.

　　b.　**Beginning performance creates an option.**　The offeror cannot revoke the offer after the offeree begins the requested performance (or tenders the performance or a beginning of it).

　　c.　**Reliance before performance begins.**　An option does not arise based on preparations to perform. Actual performance must have begun.

6. **Bilateral Contracts: Reliance When Promises Can Constitute Acceptance**

Usually, an offer can be accepted either by performance or by a promise (or can only be accepted by a promise). These offers are bilateral.

　　a.　**Beginning performance is acceptance.**　The court infers that beginning to perform is a promise to finish performance. The promise is acceptance.

　　b.　**Failure to complete performance is breach.**

　　c.　**Performance without acceptance.**　An offeree who begins performance can avoid accepting the contract by notifying the offeror that she does not accept the offer.

G.　ACCEPTANCE

A contract requires mutual assent. An offer represents the assent of one party. A promise becomes binding only when the offer has been accepted.

1. **Acceptance Defined**

Acceptance is a manifestation of assent made in a manner that the offeror invited or required.

　　a.　**Only the offeree may accept.**

　　b.　**Assent must be manifest.**　Thinking that you plan to assent is insufficient to create a contract. The offeree must express assent by words or actions.

c. **Acceptance must conform to offeror's requirements.** If the offeror specifies a method of acceptance, the offeree must accept in that manner. Some specifications in an offer may be suggestions rather than requirements.

d. **Offeree must have knowledge of the offer.** An offeree who does not know of an offer cannot accept it even if her conduct otherwise would constitute an acceptance.

2. **Acceptance by Silence**

An offer may indicate that, if the offeree does not respond, the offeror will interpret the failure to object as assent to the terms of the offer. The offeror specifies silence as a manner in which the offeree may assent. With a few exceptions, **silence is not acceptance**. The exceptions generally try to protect people who rely on the existence of a contract accepted by silence.

a. **Accepting offered services.** An offeree who, despite an opportunity to reject services, accepts the benefit of the offeror's services knowing the offeror expects compensation will be held to have accepted the offer.

b. **Intent to accept.** Silence is acceptance if an offeree intends her silence to accept the offer.

c. **Inferences from prior dealings.** When parties deal repeatedly, patterns of behavior may develop that make silence seem like acceptance.

d. **Exercise of dominion.** When an offeree obtains possession of the offeror's property and treats it as her own, silence indicates acceptance.

3. **Mirror Image Rule**

Traditionally, an acceptance must echo the terms of the offer. If the acceptance differs from the offer, even in a minor way, the terms of the contract are not agreed. Rather, the response is taken as a counteroffer. Since the adoption of the UCC, some courts have relaxed this rule.

4. **Additional or Different Terms under the UCC: The Battle of the Forms**

In business, each party often has a printed form it uses in commercial transactions. The seller's terms often do not match the buyer's. The mirror image rule would preclude many contracts. The UCC adopted a different approach.

a. Acceptance despite different or additional terms.   The UCC treats writings that purport to accept offers or to memorialize oral contracts as acceptances, not counteroffers, even if the terms differ. The acceptance agreed to all terms of the offer. The different or additional terms were an offer to modify the contract.

b. Avoiding unwanted terms.   An offeree can avoid accepting the offeror's terms by explicitly making the acceptance "expressly conditional on assent to the additional or different terms." UCC §2-207(1).

c. Additional terms may be accepted.

  i. Explicit acceptance will modify the agreement.

  ii. Between merchants, silence may constitute acceptance.

  iii. Even between merchants, silence might not accept the modifications.

  (a) Material change.   New terms that materially alter the contract are not accepted by silence.

  (b) Objection.   Terms to which the offeror objects or has objected do not become part of the contract by silence.

  (c) Limitations in the offer.   If the offer "expressly limits acceptance to the terms of the offer," no changes will be accepted by silence.

  iv. These rules apply to confirmations as well as to acceptances.   When assent becomes binding during a phone conversation, a writing may confirm the agreement, filling in details not discussed on the phone. Each party's writing proposes a modification, which the other party might accept by silence.

d. Contracts that arise by conduct.   If these rules do not produce assent, but the parties' conduct shows they have made an agreement, the court will enforce the agreement using any terms **agreed** plus **default terms** from the UCC.

e. Common-law reaction.   Courts have relaxed the mirror image rule.

  i. Counteroffer.   A response that makes assent to a new or different term a condition of acceptance is still a counteroffer.

ii. **Acceptance and proposal to modify.**   A response that accepts all terms of the offer but proposes a new term or a changed term as a modification to the original transaction is an acceptance. The contract is formed on the offeror's terms.

iii. **Accepting modification.**   If the offeror accepts the proposal for change, the modification becomes binding. Acceptance of the modification can occur in any normal manner—including, if appropriate, by silence.

5.   When Acceptance Takes Effect: The Mailbox Rule

When an offer permits acceptance by mail (or other media in which the acceptance is not received at the same time it is sent), an **acceptance is effective when it is sent by the offeree.** Revocation, however, usually is effective when it is received by the offeree.

a. **Notification of acceptance.**   Acceptance usually requires reasonably diligent efforts to notify to the offeror, unless the offeror waives the right to notice of acceptance.

i. **Acceptance by performance** does not require notice **unless** the offeror requests notice or the offeree has reason to know that the offeror "has no adequate means of learning of the performance with reasonable promptness and certainty."

ii. **Acceptance by silence** does not require notice.

b. **Mail might constitute reasonable diligence.**   The offer expressly may allow acceptance by mail. If the offer is made by mail, it usually may be accepted by mail. Acceptance by mail is permissible if that is customary in similar transactions.

c. **Acceptance is effective upon dispatch.**   When mail is a reasonable method of acceptance, the acceptance is effective once the acceptance leaves the offeree's possession—provided it is properly dispatched.

d. **Revocation of an offer is effective upon receipt by the offeree.**   Receipt occurs when a notice comes into the addressee's possession or the possession of someone authorized to receive it for the addressee, or it is deposited in a place the addressee authorized as a place for such communications to be left for her.

H. PRELIMINARY AGREEMENTS

1. Agreements When Parties Contemplate a Writing

Parties may agree orally but intend not to be bound until a writing is signed. If so, signing is the acceptance; everything up to that point is preliminary negotiation. If parties intend their oral agreement to be final and see the writing as a mere formality, oral assent forms a contract; the writing merely records the terms.

2. Renewal Options

Some contracts, especially leases, allow one party to renew when the contract expires. If the parties leave important renewal terms open (say, rent), it is hard to enforce the contract for the renewed term.

a. Assent clear. Renewal provisions are part of an original agreement, which is a binding contract. Assent to the renewal clause is clear. Unlike other preliminary agreements, definiteness poses a problem.

b. Definiteness problematic. When parties provide a means to determine the renewal terms, the contract is sufficiently definite to permit enforcement.

c. Underenforcement. To avoid giving too little weight to valuable renewal options, courts may resort to implied obligations. Gap filler terms may be employed. Frequently, a duty to bargain in good faith is imposed.

3. Reliance on Preliminary Negotiations

Sometimes reliance on preliminary negotiations leads a court to enforce a promise without assent. This generally requires **substantial reliance**, after a **detailed agreement** has been worked out, which makes reliance reasonable.

3   CONSIDERATION AND ITS ALTERNATIVES

A. RATIONALE FOR THE BARGAIN REQUIREMENT

Requiring a bargain limits enforcement to agreements where both parties expect to be better off after the exchange than before.

B. ELEMENTS OF CONSIDERATION: BARGAINED-FOR EXCHANGE

Consideration requires a bargained-for exchange. Bargain exists if the promisor sought something in exchange for the promise and the promisee gave that something in exchange for the promise.

1. Sought in Exchange

Usually this is easy to identify. "Sought" gets tricky if the promisor asks for something she doesn't really want. "In exchange" gets tricky if the promisor puts a condition on a gift.

    a. The thing sought must be a performance or a return promise.

       i. Performance includes an act, a forbearance, or the creation, modification, or destruction of a legal relation.

       ii. A promise is consideration if fulfilling the promise would be a performance.

    b. It does not matter who receives the consideration or who gives it. As long as the promisor seeks it, the transaction may qualify as a bargained-for exchange.

    c. Sham consideration. A party makes a gift look like consideration by requesting something trivial in exchange. If the promisor does not seek the thing in exchange, it technically is not consideration. But if the thing is part of the reason for the promise, it is consideration even if other reasons (e.g., generosity) motivated the promisor.

    d. Conditional gifts are not bargains. A promise made on the condition that a future event will occur may resemble consideration if the condition requires some action by the promisee. Some specifications merely state how the promisee may collect a gift. These requests do not seek a return and, thus, are not consideration.

2. Given in Exchange

Failure to give what the promisor sought usually prevents assent. (The promisee made no promise, so did not accept the offer.) Tricky issues arise if the promisee gives something but not in exchange for the promise.

    a. The promisee must give that which the promisor requested.

CAPSULE SUMMARY

      b. **Reciprocal gifts are not consideration.** The recipient of a promise cannot convert a gift promise into an exchange by promising a return gift.

      c. **Promisee must know of the promise.** If the promisee does not know that the promisor has made a promise or has asked a return, the promisee's performance cannot have been given in exchange for the promise.

      d. **Promisee's acts cannot be what she would have done without the promise.** If a promisee acts exactly as she would have acted even if no offer had been made, her conduct may have been mere coincidence, rather than given in exchange for the promise.

C. COMMON MISCONCEPTIONS

1. Benefit or Detriment

Consideration does not require a benefit or a detriment.

2. Mutuality of Obligation

Consideration does not require mutual obligations.

3. Adequacy of Consideration

Consideration need not be even; a party can make any exchange she desires.

4. Motivation of the Parties

Consideration depends on the parties' words and actions, not their secret intentions.

D. EXCEPTION FOR DELIVERED GIFTS

A promise, once performed, is not revocable merely because no consideration was given in exchange. Gift promises, once performed, are final.

E. EXCEPTION FOR PAST CONSIDERATION AND MORAL OBLIGATION

When a promise is made after a performance has already been received, the performance cannot have been given in exchange for the promise. Courts sometimes enforce promises despite this defect.

1. Past Consideration

When a party to a bargain has an excuse or defense against performing, a promise to perform despite the excuse or defense has no consideration. If there was consideration for the initial promise (before the excuse arose), courts may enforce the new promise based on the original consideration. In effect, the new promise waives a defense rather than creating a new obligation. A new promise waives defenses such as **bankruptcy, the statute of limitations, nonoccurrence of a condition, or factors making promises voidable**.

2. Moral Obligation

Moral obligation cases often involve acts of generosity, often when bargaining in advance was impossible. The recipient may promise to compensate for the benefits of that generosity. The justification for enforcement is based largely on restitution, though it could be based on a bargain theory.

a. Elements under the restatement.

- The existence of a **promise**;
- That **the promisor received a benefit**;
- That **the promisee provided that benefit**; and
- That failure to enforce the promise would produce **injustice**.

b. Justice may not require compensation.

i. Unsolicited benefit. No injustice would result if the benefit was a **gift** or was bestowed by an officious intermeddler.

ii. Disproportionate compensation. When the promisor has made a promise that is disproportionate to the benefit received, the courts may limit recovery to the value the promisor actually received.

c. An alternative explanation: Ill-timed bargains.
Claims based on moral obligation appeal because the parties probably would have struck a bargain if negotiating in advance had been possible. The exception may reflect desire to ignore the accident of timing and enforce an otherwise acceptable bargain.

F. PREEXISTING DUTY

A promisee may assert that she gave consideration by promising to do something that she already had an obligation to do. The promise arguably is not given **in exchange** for the promise, since the promisee had no right to refuse to perform, even if the promisor made no (additional) promise. **The preexisting duty rule has been eroded almost to the point of extinction.** The more important issue is duress.

1. **Evasions**

    a. **New consideration.** A promise to do a little more than the preexisting duty could be consideration.

    b. **Rescinding the duty.** Some parties rescind preexisting contracts and immediately enter new contracts on different terms. Rescission ended the preexisting duty.

    c. **Waiving the duty.** Some parties argued that a waiver of the right to enforce a preexisting duty constituted a delivered gift, ending the preexisting duty.

2. **Settlement of Disputes**

    When a preexisting duty is disputed, giving up the right to contest the duty is consideration if the promisee has (at least) a good faith belief that her position may be found valid. **A real bargain exists here**: The promisee gives up the right to assert a defense in litigation in exchange for additional performance by the promisor. Bargains exist in four situations:

    -   **If the claim or defense is valid** (that is, if no preexisting duty existed);
    -   If, at the time of the agreement, **the claim or defense is doubtful** because of uncertainty as to the facts or the law;
    -   If the party asserting a claim or defense **has a good faith belief that it may be held valid**; or
    -   If **a promisor seeks a written release** of claim or defense that the other party has not raised, even though the party giving the release has no belief that the claim or defense is valid.

3. **Modification of Contracts**

    A promisee's preexisting duty may arise from an earlier contract with the promisor. If parties want to change one party's duties under that contract, consideration can pose a problem—especially if neither party contends the original contract is invalid.

    a. **Cautionary note.** Modifications exist when **both parties agree to change a contract**. One party cannot modify the contract unilaterally.

    b. Concern for duress. The real issue is duress: preventing one party from using improper threats to extort a greater promise from the other in exchange for a performance she had a right to receive for less under the original contract. When changed circumstances lead parties to adjust a contract, courts prefer to enforce modifications.

    c. Modification in sales of goods: Consideration not required. The UCC abolished the requirement of consideration for modification of a contract for the sale of goods. A modification is enforceable, however, only if made in good faith, even if supported by additional consideration.

    d. Modification of other contracts. Common-law courts have enforced modifications without new consideration is some situations.

        i. Limited to executory contracts. The exceptions apply only if neither party has completed her performance.

        ii. Statutory exceptions. When a statute authorizes modification without consideration, courts follow the will of the legislature.

        iii. Exception for action in reliance. When one party has changed her position **materially** in reliance on the promise, courts may enforce the modification if justice so requires.

        iv. Exception for unanticipated circumstances. If the modification is **fair and equitable** in view of **circumstances not anticipated** by the parties when the contract was made, the modification is enforceable.

4. Accord and Satisfaction

Although courts discuss it in different terms, accord and satisfaction raise fundamentally the same consideration issues found in settlement of disputes. See the main text for details.

G. EXCEPTION FOR ACTION IN RELIANCE (OR PROMISSORY ESTOPPEL)

Often people rely on promises even if they have not given anything in exchange for the promise. Particularly when they incur substantial expense in reliance on the promise, courts see an injustice in allowing the promisor to refuse to perform. Thus, instead of denying enforcement on the ground that the promise lacked consideration, courts enforce promises if necessary to avoid injustice — that is, to prevent harm to the party who relied.

1. **Elements**

   - A **promise**;
   - The **promisor reasonably should have expected the promisee to rely** on the promise;
   - The **promisee did rely** on the promise (in a way the promisor reasonably should have expected);
   - **Injustice** can be avoided only by enforcing the promise.

2. **Applying §90**

   The elements for proving reliance, as set forth in the Restatement (Second), involve some subtleties that an exam question might attempt to probe.

   a. **Promise is vital.** Don't try to analyze reliance until you identify a promise.

   b. **Unreasonable reliance might suffice.** The issue is not whether the promisee acted reasonably but **whether the promisor had reason to believe the promisee would rely.** Where reliance is unreasonable, a promisor may have had no reason to believe that the promisee would rely in that way. But reliance cases often involve social contexts, where the parties know one another and might anticipate unreasonable reliance.

   c. **Is actual reliance necessary?** Some courts require reliance of a "definite and substantial character." Other courts do not require actual reliance at all. Actual reliance is unimportant for promises of **charitable contributions** or marriage settlements.

   d. **Injustice usually boils down to detrimental reliance.** If the promisee changed her position for the worse because the promise was made, either by acting or remaining inactive, justice probably requires enforcement of the promise.

   e. **Courts compensate for expectation, not merely reliance.**

H. **FORMALITY AS AN EXCEPTION TO THE CONSIDERATION REQUIREMENT**

One justification for the requirement of consideration is that persons making bargains realize that their promises will be taken seriously. Formal promises probably serve this **cautionary function**.

1. Seal

The act of affixing a seal to a written promise gave the promisor time to consider whether she really wanted the promise to become legally enforceable. Most states have abolished laws enforcing promises made under seal.

2. Signed Writings

The formal step of reducing a promise to writing and signing the document can serve the same function as a seal. Some states have enacted statutes enforcing signed written promises even if they lack consideration.

 4 THE ROLE OF WRITINGS: STATUTES OF FRAUDS

A. RATIONALE

A writing reduces the risk that the promisee lied about the existence or terms of a promise. **A writing does not make the promise enforceable**; the contract still needed to satisfy consideration and other requirements. **The absence of a writing makes the promise unenforceable.**

B. STATUTES OF FRAUDS

In some contexts, statutes preclude courts from enforcing a contract unless the agreement was recorded in some writing signed by the party who now disputes the existence of the agreement (usually, the defendant).

1. Agreements Unenforceable without a Writing

- **Promises in consideration of marriage**
- **Promises that cannot be performed within a year**
- **Promises conveying interests in land**
- **Promises of an executor** to pay estate's debts from executor's personal assets
- **Guaranty or suretyship**: promises to pay the debt of another
- **Goods of $500 or more**

2. Satisfying the Writing Requirement

The amount of detail necessary to satisfy the writing requirement varies between contexts and between jurisdictions.

a.   **One signature.**   A writing need not be signed by both parties. The concern is whether the party contesting enforcement actually made a promise.

b.   **Informal signature.**   Under the UCC, any mark intended to authenticate the writing is a signature, as long as the mark identifies the party to be charged. Thus, initials, a typed name, or even a company letterhead or logo might constitute a signature for these purposes. A seal or a thumbprint might suffice.

c.   **Failure to respond to a writing.**   For sales of goods, failure to respond to a writing signed by the other party may be the equivalent of signing a writing. Specifically, "**Between merchants** if **within a reasonable time** a writing in confirmation of the contract and **sufficient against the sender** is **received** and the party receiving it **has reason to know its contents**, it satisfies the [writing] requirements of subsection (1) against such party unless written notice of **objection to its contents is given within ten days** after it is received."

d.   **Partial writings.**   A writing need not contain all the terms of a contract. The amount of detail required will vary.

   i.   **Sales of goods.**   The UCC requires very little detail. As long as a writing contains the **quantity**, it will suffice — even if the writing **misstates** the quantity.

   ii.   **Other contracts.**   The Restatement (Second) requires the writing to present considerable detail, including: (I) the **subject matter** of the contract; (ii) an indication that the signor has **consented** to the deal; (iii) "the **essential terms of the unperformed promises**," stated in "reasonable detail." Restatement (Second) of Contracts §131.

e.   **Timing of signature unimportant.**

f.   **Multiple writings.**   Several writings taken together may satisfy the statute, even though none individually would suffice.

g.   **Lost or destroyed writing may suffice.**   Copies, even if unsigned, or other testimony may satisfy the court that a writing did exist. Parties who created a writing did everything the statute asked of them. Inability to produce the document does not prevent enforcement of the contract.

3.   Exceptions to the Writing Requirement

Courts have been hostile to the writing requirement. When courts are convinced that an agreement really was made, they have employed exceptions to prevent the promisor from escaping on a technicality.

a.   Generally: evidence corroborating an agreement.   The exceptions are specific, but each involves some evidence that the party **resisting** enforcement really made a promise.

b.   Admissions under oath.   Testimony that a promise existed makes a writing unnecessary to prove the promise.

c.   Full performance by both parties.   If both parties have fully performed their promises, neither can use the lack of a writing to compel the other to reconvey what she received.

d.   Full performance by one party.   Under some circumstances, one party's performance can give rise to an exception.

  i.   When one party accepts the other party's performance, this provides some indication that she promised something in return. Thus, the UCC allows enforcement without a writing when goods have been "received and accepted" or when "payment has been made and accepted."

  ii.   Contracts not performable within a year.   Full performance by one party removes a promise that could not be completed within a year from the provisions of the statute.

  iii.   Partial performance.   The UCC may allow partial enforcement based on partial performance. A contract "is enforceable . . . with respect to goods for which payment has been made and accepted or which have been received and accepted." Thus, if only part of the goods have been paid for or delivered, the agreement might be enforceable "with respect to" those goods but not with respect to other goods allegedly called for by the agreement.

4.   Restitution

A person who relies on an unenforceable oral promise may seek restitution. The recipient may be required to return any benefits received under the unenforceable contract in order to prevent unjust enrichment.

CAPSULE SUMMARY

5. **Exception for Action in Reliance**

If **a party relies** on an oral promise is a way **the promisor reasonably should have expected, injustice** might result unless the courts enforce the promise. Thus, courts have carved out an exception to the statute of frauds similar to the reliance exception to the bargain requirement.

   a. **Reliance interest only.** To give some effect to the statute of frauds, courts limit recovery under this exception to the reliance interest.

   b. **Identifying injustice.** Restatement (Second) of Contracts §139 lists factors to consider in determining when injustice requires enforcement.

      i. **The availability of other remedies,** such as restitution, may make compensation for reliance unnecessary.

      ii. **The magnitude of the reliance** relative to the remedy sought may support recovery. Reliance that is more "definite and substantial" may require more protection than insignificant reliance.

      iii. **Reliance that corroborates the existence of a promise** puts the court on firmer ground in extending a more generous remedy.

      iv. **Reasonable reliance** supports compensation.

      v. **The foreseeability of the reliance** supports compensation.

   c. **Reliance in sales of goods.** The UCC makes one special provision for reliance: the case of custom-manufactured goods. UCC §2-201(3)(a). The exception involves three elements: goods have been specially manufactured for the buyer, goods are unsuitable for resale to others in the ordinary course of seller's business, and a substantial beginning or commitment has been made.

C. **WRITINGS REQUIRED BY THE PARTIES**

Sometimes the parties themselves insist that agreements be in writing, even if the legislature and the courts would permit them to make oral commitments.

1. **Before the Contract Becomes Binding: Limiting Assent to Writings**

Some parties do not want to be bound until they have negotiated all the terms and had a chance to read and consider the final writing. The details of this issue are discussed in connection with assent. **Rule of Thumb**: If you want the binding event to be the signing of a writing, you should explicitly say so as early as practical in the negotiations.

2. Before Modifications Become Effective

Parties sometimes agree to clauses that prohibit oral modification of a contract. These clauses are enforceable. The parties may waive the requirement. Oral waivers are effective. But waivers are revocable by notifying the other party that you will insist on the terms of the contract, unless the other party has relied on the waiver to her detriment.

5 INTRODUCTION TO DEFENSES: FACTORS THAT INTERFERE WITH ARM'S-LENGTH BARGAINING

A. PROCEDURAL FRAMEWORK

Contract defenses can be raised as a defense to a claim for breach of contract or as a claim to rescind a contract and recover performance already rendered under the invalid contract.

B. TERMINOLOGY: VOID VERSUS VOIDABLE

Most defenses make a contract voidable at the option of the victim. She may elect to ratify the contract instead of disaffirming it.

6 INCAPACITY

A. INFANCY

Until the day before a person's eighteenth birthday, any contract she enters is voidable. Age, **not appearance**, defines infancy. **Marriage** may negate infancy. **Ratification** after reaching 18 waives the defense. Contracts for **necessaries** are not voidable. Statutes may **exempt transactions**, such as payment of insurance premiums and withdrawals from a bank. **Fraudulent representations of age** may negate the defense. If the defense applies, the other party may be limited to **specific restitution**, even if the thing she sold to the minor has lost value or cannot be returned.

B. MENTAL ILLNESS OR DEFECT

A contract is voidable if one party's **mental illness or defect** prevented her from **understanding the nature and consequences of the transaction** or, if the **other party had reason to know** of her condition, **prevented her from acting in a reasonable manner** in relation to the transaction. Contracts for **necessaries** may be enforceable despite mental illness. A person **unaware of the mental illness** may be entitled to enforcement if the contract was made on **fair terms** and the party has performed or otherwise **relied** to her detriment.

C. INTOXICATION

If a party **has reason to know** that the other is so **intoxicated** that she **cannot understand** in a reasonable manner the nature and consequences of the transaction or **cannot act in a reasonable manner** in relation to the transaction, the contract is voidable. **A person who induces another's intoxication** may be unable to enforce the agreement even if the intoxicated person cannot prove the inducer had reason to know of the extent of intoxication. Intoxication need not mean alcohol. Disaffirmance must occur promptly upon becoming sober.

 7 IMPROPER PRESSURE

A. DURESS

1. Elements

    a. Improper threat.

    b. Inducement. Did the threat substantially contribute to the threatened party's decision to assent to the agreement?

    c. Lack of reasonable alternatives. Did the threatened party have a reasonable alternative to assent?

2. Improper Threat

Some threats are proper. The threat not to give away your property unless paid the price you demand is not improper.

    a. Improper regardless of terms. A threat is always improper if:

        i. The threatened act is **a crime or a tort**.

ii.   The threatened act **would be a crime or a tort if the threatening party obtained property** as a result of the threat. Blackmail is illegal. Even if you have a right to publish embarrassing information, you have no right to extort payments by threatening to publish.

iii. The threatened act is **a criminal prosecution.** Criminal prosecutions serve a public purpose. It is improper for people to threaten them for private gain.

iv.   The threatened act is the **use of civil process in bad faith.** Normally, a threat to commence a civil suit is proper. But if a party knows or believes that she has no reasonable basis for such a suit, a threat to pursue a lawsuit is improper.

v.   The threatened act would **breach an obligation of good faith and fair dealing under a contract** with the threatened party. This type of threat normally arises when one party seeks to modify an existing agreement. Changed circumstances may make a threat to stop performing unless the other party agrees to modification proper. A threat made without any legitimate basis for seeking modification, however, would be improper.

b.   **Improper if terms unfair.** Some improper threats may not be easy to catalogue. Efforts to generalize what makes some other types of threats improper are vague and apply only if the terms of the agreement are unfair.

i.   The threatened act would **harm the threatened party without significantly benefiting the threatening party.** In these situations, the only reason to fulfill the threat would be vindictive, since no advantage would accrue to the threatening party.

ii. **The threat has been made significantly more effective by prior unfair dealing by the threatening party.** Weakness increases susceptibility to a threat. Where the threatener unfairly caused the weakness or susceptibility, prior unfair dealing may change the nature of an otherwise legitimate threat into an improper threat.

iii. The threatened act is a **use of power for illegitimate ends.** The legitimacy of the threatening party's ends does not offer a very clear standard for courts to apply. This is a catch-all provision.

3. **Inducement**

If the threat "substantially contributed to the manifestation of assent," the threat induced the assent. Thus, the threatened party need not prove that she would have rejected the offer if no threat had been made, as long as the threat contributed to the decision.

4. **Reasonable Alternatives**

If a party has reasonable alternatives to succumbing to the threat, courts reject the duress, expecting a threatened party to "just say no."

5. **Threats by Third Parties**

Threats by a third party will make the contract voidable unless the other party to the contract relied materially on the agreement in good faith and without reason to know of the duress.

B. UNDUE INFLUENCE

Pressure may arise from statements that may not be threats but that may exert pressure on a party who does not want to assent. When undue influence induces assent, the contract is voidable.

1. **Undue Influence**

Undue influence consists of **unfair persuasion** combined with either **domination** of the other party or a **relationship** that justifies the other in believing the party exerting influence would not act against the influenced party's interests. Clues to unfair persuasion include odd times and places for negotiations and pressure to decide quickly.

2. **Influence by Third Parties**

Undue influence by a third party will make the contract voidable unless the other party to the contract relies materially on the agreement in good faith and without reason to know of the undue influence.

 8 MISREPRESENTATION

A. FRAUDULENT OR MATERIAL MISREPRESENTATION

A contract is voidable if assent was induced by a fraudulent or material misrepresentation on which the party justifiably relied.

1. **Misrepresentation**

A misrepresentation is "an assertion not in accord with the facts." Sometimes, actions or silence can be assertions.

2. **Material**

A misrepresentation is material if (a) "it would be likely to induce a reasonable person to manifest" assent to the agreement; or (b) "the maker knows that it would be likely to induce" the other party to manifest assent.

3. **Fraudulent**

A misrepresentation is fraudulent if (a) the party **intends** [the] assertion **to induce** another party to manifest . . . assent to the agreement"; **and** (b) one of the three following conditions applies: (i) the speaker knows or believes the assertion is false; or (ii) the speaker "does not have the confidence [s]he states or implies in the truth of the assertion"; or (iii) the speaker "knows [s]he does not have the basis that [s]he states or implies for the assertion."

4. **Inducement**

"A misrepresentation induces a party's manifestation of assent if it substantially contributes to his decision to manifest his assent."

5. **Justified Reliance**

Normally, a party is justified in relying on assertions of fact by the other party, including facts implied by promises or opinions.

a. **Pure (nonassertive) opinions.**   Reliance on an opinion that does not assert facts **is not justified**, with some exceptions.

   i. **A relation of trust and confidence between parties.**

   ii. **Special expertise.**   When the deceived party reasonably believes that the other party has special skill, judgment, or objectivity that she herself does not possess, it is reasonable to rely on the opinion.

   iii. **Special susceptibility.**   When the deceived party is particularly susceptible to misrepresentation via opinion, the court may find her reliance justifiable.

b. **Deceived party's fault.**   If a deceived party knew the truth — or would have known the truth if she had acted in good faith — she cannot justifiably rely on the false assertion.

CAPSULE SUMMARY

6.   **Misrepresentations by Third Parties**

Misrepresentation by a third party will make the contract voidable **unless** the other party relied materially on the contract in good faith and without reason to know of the misrepresentation.

B.   NONDISCLOSURE AND CONCEALMENT

For purposes of analyzing the other elements of misrepresentation, **silence may be taken as an assertion that a fact does not exist**. If the fact does exist, that assertion is not in accord with the facts.

1.   **Concealment**

If a party intends or knows that her action "is likely to prevent another from learning a fact," the action is an assertion that the fact does not exist.

2.   **Nondisclosure**

Unless a party has a duty to reveal facts, her silence is not an assertion. Usually, no duty to speak exists — with some exceptions.

   a.   **Correct prior assertions.**   When a party **knows** that disclosure of a fact is necessary to prevent a prior assertion from being a misrepresentation or from being fraudulent or material, she must disclose the additional facts.

   b.   **Correct known mistake re content of writing.**   When a party knows that disclosure of a fact would correct the other party's mistake as to the contents or effect of a writing embodying the agreement, she must disclose the additional facts.

   c.   **Relation of trust.**   If a relation of trust or confidence between the parties entitles the other person to know the fact, a duty to speak arises.

   d.   **Good faith and known mistakes of basic assumption.**   "Where [s]he knows that disclosure of the fact would correct a mistake of the other party as to a basic assumption on which that party is making the contract and if non-disclosure of the fact amounts to a failure to act in good faith and in accordance with reasonable standards of fair dealing," she must disclose the additional facts.

C.   MISREPRESENTATION CONCERNING THE CONTENT OF THE AGREEMENT

Signing a document does not manifest assent to a bargain unless the signor knows or should know what the document contains. If a lie about the content induces signature, the liar cannot reasonably believe the signor assented to the deal as written. No assent exists (and the contract is void, not merely voidable) if a **misrepresentation** as to the **character or essential terms** of an agreement **induced** another to appear to manifest assent unless she had a **reasonable opportunity to know the terms** (say, by reading the agreement).

 ## 9 MISTAKE OF BASIC ASSUMPTION

A. MUTUAL MISTAKE

If both parties share a mistaken belief, courts apply rules governing **mutual mistake**.

1. Elements

Mutual mistake makes a contract voidable if:

a. **Mistake existed at time of formation;**

b. **Mistake involved a basic assumption** on which the contract was made;

c. **Mistake had a material effect** on the agreed exchange of performances; and

d. **Risk of the mistake** is not allocable to the adversely affected party.

2. Risk of Mistake

Because a loss caused by a mistake will be borne by one of two innocent parties, courts decide whether it is fair to allocate the risk to one of them.

a. **Allocation by contract.** If the agreement expressly or implicitly imposes the risk of some contingencies on one party, courts accept that allocation.

b. **Conscious ignorance.** A party who enters an agreement knowing that she lacks information must bear the risk that the facts prove adverse to her.

c. **Judicial allocation.** The court may allocate the risk to the adversely affected party if that is reasonable under the circumstances.

B.   UNILATERAL MISTAKE

If only one party was mistaken, courts may allow the mistaken party to avoid the contract if she proves **all elements of unilateral mistake** *plus* one of the following factors: (1) that enforcement would be **unconscionable**; or (2) that the other party **caused** the mistake; or (3) that the other party had **reason to know** of the mistake. As used here, unconscionability refers to substantive unconscionability — the fairness of the bargain. To meet this test, the terms must be extremely harsh (not merely less profitable) because of the mistake.

 UNCONSCIONABILITY: EFFORTS TO AVOID UNFAIR CONTRACTS

A.   UNCONSCIONABILITY IN CONTEXT

A one-sided deal may reveal that one party valued the promised performance much more than others would have. If this seems implausible, the harsh terms raise a red flag to see whether fraud, duress, or other problems with the negotiations induced assent to unfavorable terms. When all else fails, courts sometimes resort to unconscionability as a technique for refusing to enforce unjust contracts.

B.   CONTRACTS OF ADHESION: THE ROLE OF FORM CONTRACTS

Harsh terms may result when a party signed a form contract that the drafter refused to negotiate. Contracts offered on a take-it-or-leave-it basis are called contracts of adhesion. **Most adhesion contracts are enforceable**. But courts sometimes try to abate harsh results.

1.   Interpretation against the Drafter

If any contract contains ambiguous terms, courts try to interpret them. If interpretation fails, courts may interpret the term against the party who drafted it. In form contracts, courts sometimes resort to this technique even if other techniques might allow the court to interpret the term properly and, sometimes, even it the term is not ambiguous.

2.   Reasonable Expectations of the Nondrafting Party

Courts sometimes will interpret the contract to embody the reasonable expectations of the nondrafting party, without worrying about whether a term is ambiguous.

3. Public Policy

Courts may refuse to enforce harsh clauses on the ground that the clauses violate public policy.

C. ELEMENTS OF UNCONSCIONABILITY

Most courts and statutes do not define unconscionability. Its meaning must be inferred from decisions. The guidelines here are one view, not **the** view.

1. Effect of Unconscionability

If a term is unconscionable at the time the contract is made, a court may (1) refuse to enforce the contract; or (2) enforce the contract without the unconscionable term; or (3) limit the effect of the term to prevent unconscionability.

2. Identifying Unconscionable Terms

A term is unconscionable if a party is **unfairly surprised** to discover the existence or effect of the term after formation and the term is **unreasonably favorable** to the other party.

a. **Unfair surprise** helps explain how someone could agree to a term that produces such one-sided results: **The party did not know the term was there or did not know what effect the term would have.**

b. **Unreasonably favorable terms.** Even terms that are harsh or oppressive may be justified by commercial exigencies. Only **unreasonably** harsh terms justify judicial intervention.

D. ALTERNATIVE VIEWS

Other approaches place weight on additional factors. Criticism of these factors is contained in the body of the outline.

1. Unequal Bargaining Power

Although the UCC explicitly rejected unequal bargaining power as a factor in identifying unconscionability, some courts believe a powerful party can compel others to accede to terms they do not want and that courts should refuse to enforce those terms.

2. Harshness

Some cases suggest that unfair terms, without any other factor, justify a finding of unconscionability.

11　PUBLIC POLICY LIMITS ON CONTRACTS

A. IN GENERAL

Courts will refuse to enforce a contract if:

- "legislation provides that it is unenforceable"; or
- a public policy against enforcement clearly outweighs the interest in enforcement. Restatement (Second) of Contracts §178(1)

B. CONTRACTS UNENFORCEABLE BY STATUTE

Some statutes declare particular contract provisions unenforceable. Examples include **penalty clauses**, **indemnities against a party's own negligence**, and contracts by **unlicensed professionals**.

C. BALANCING COMPETING PUBLIC POLICIES

Courts balance the interest in enforcement against the public policy. The presumption lies with enforcement; unless the public policy clearly outweighs the interest in enforcement, the contract is enforceable.

1. Interest in Enforcing Promises

This interest includes a consideration of (1) the parties' justified expectations; (2) any forfeiture that would result from nonenforcement; and (3) any public interest in enforcement of a particular term.

a. Restitution is not available in most public policy cases. Courts that refuse to enforce a contract leave the parties as they find them. Thus, **forfeiture is more likely in this context** than in others.

b. Exceptions. In two situations, courts have shown some willingness to allow a plaintiff to recover restitution.

i. Excusable ignorance. Restitution is available to a party who is excusably ignorant either of **facts** or of a **minor law** that made the promise unenforceable, unless the parties to the contract were "equally in the wrong."

ii. Laudable regret. A party who has not engaged in **serious misconduct** may recover in restitution if (a) she **withdraws** from the contract before it achieves its improper purpose or (b) allowing the claim would **end a continuing violation** of public policy.

2.   Policy against Enforcement

This policy involves consideration of several factors.

a.   Strength of policy.

b.   Advancing policy goal.
Some misconduct will not be deterred by a refusal to enforce the agreement. If refusal to enforce the agreement will not further the public policy at issue, the interests in enforcement of the contract may outweigh the policy against enforcement.

c.   Severity of misconduct.
When the contract involves serious misconduct, the policy against enforcement increases. The seriousness of the misconduct may vary with the strength of the policy or with the culpability of the violator.

d.   Deliberateness of misconduct.
When misconduct was inadvertent, enforcement of the agreement may be appropriate.

e.   Connection between the contract and the misconduct.
Sometimes a contract specifically calls for misconduct (e.g., a contract for murder). But sometimes the connection is more tenuous. When the connection is remote, refusal to enforce the agreement seems less appropriate.

D.   CONTRACTS WITHIN A FAMILY: STATUS VERSUS CONTRACT

1.   Contracts between Family Members

These usually are enforceable if they are **express** and proven with **clear and convincing evidence**.

2.   Contracts Altering Status under the Law Governing Families

These usually are not enforceable. By statute, many states now allow prenuptial agreements that alter the usual terms of marriage, but the statutes limit which terms parties may alter.

3.   Contracts Creating Informal Families

Some states refuse to enforce promises made to a person who is functionally a spouse but without a recognized marriage. If **sexual relations are explic-**

itly part of the consideration, the contract is void under the public policy against meretricious relationships (money for sex). Other states are willing to enforce these promises as long as the agreements do not explicitly refer to sex as part of the consideration. Some courts will enforce express contracts but will not find implied contracts in this context.

PART 2 WHEN SHOULD THE LAW INTERVENE?

12 INTERPRETATION: WHAT DOES THE CONTRACT REQUIRE?

A. GENERAL TECHNIQUES OF INTERPRETATION

At the time of formation, the parties apparently shared common ground—they each had a reason to want to enter the transaction and they (usually) agreed on words that expressed that agreement. To the extent possible, interpretation seeks to identify and to give effect to that common ground. Secret intent plays no part in the interpretative process; words and actions are interpreted objectively.

1. Express Language

Generally, the words the parties chose to express their agreement provide the best indication of what the parties intended.

2. Agreed Meaning

If parties define terms in the contract, that definition governs.

    a. Written definitions. Careful practitioners include a section of definitions in written contracts.

    b. Oral definitions. An intention to use a word in an unconventional way must be manifest, but in some cases that manifestation may be oral.

3. Plain Meaning

When parties have not specified a different meaning, words are given their usual, or "generally prevailing," meaning (e.g., dictionary meaning).

4. Special Meaning

A term may have a technical or special meaning in some fields or localities. When used in a transaction within that field or locality, the word should be given its special meaning—unless another intent is manifest.

B. INFERENCES

Often, the parties' conduct allows inferences concerning what they intended a word or phrase to mean.

1. Usage of Trade

If a practice or meaning is understood or expected by everyone in a particular trade, courts can infer that the parties (if members of the trade) intended their agreement to be interpreted consistently with that usage of trade.

2. Course of Dealing

Parties who have dealt with one another in the past may expect words in the current contract to have the same meaning that they had in other contracts. Courts often interpret the current contract in the same way.

3. Course of Performance

Course of performance refers to the way the parties have performed in the past under the contract being interpreted. It applies only if the contract involves multiple performances (such as installments). If performance reveals what the parties intended a term to mean, courts so interpret it.

4. Priorities of Construction

a. **Specific language** deserves more weight than general language.

b. **Negotiated terms** deserve more weight than standardized terms.

c. **Express terms** deserve more weight than inferences from conduct.

d. **Course of dealing and course of performance deserve more weight than usage of trade.**

e. **Course of performance deserves more weight than course of dealing.**

C. CANONS OF CONSTRUCTION

These are rules of thumb about how parties use language. Evidence that the parties intended something different overrides them.

1. Government Regulations

When possible, interpret a contract to require performance that is consistent with the law (or public policy) rather than requiring illegal conduct.

2. Inconsistent Terms

When a term can be interpreted in a manner that is consistent with other terms in the contract, that interpretation is preferred.

3. Superfluous Terms

When a term can be interpreted in a way that gives effect to all terms in the contract, that interpretation is preferred.

4. Interpretation against Drafter

When a term is susceptible to equally plausible interpretations, the court may reject the interpretation offered by the party who drafted the contract in favor of the interpretation advanced by another party.

D. FILLING GAPS IN THE AGREEMENT

When the parties intend to make a contract, courts will enforce the contract and fill any gaps with default terms.

1. Terms Implied from Context

Often, terms the parties have agreed on will suggest other terms they intended to govern the transaction, even though those terms were not expressed.

2. Terms Implied by Good Faith

Each party's obligation to act in good faith may lead a court to infer some duties or promises not expressly stated in the agreement.

3. Terms Implied by Statute: Default Rules or Gap Fillers

    a. Time for delivery. Unless otherwise agreed, delivery must occur within a reasonable time after formation of the contract.

    b. **Place of delivery.** With some exceptions, delivery is to be made at the seller's place of business (or residence, if seller is not a business) unless the parties agree otherwise.

    c. **One lot or two?** Unless otherwise agreed, all goods must be delivered in a single delivery.

    d. **Time and place for payment.** Unless otherwise agreed, payment is due at the time and place the buyer receives the goods (which, when goods are shipped, may not be the place of delivery).

    e. **Price.** Unless otherwise agreed, the price is a reasonable price at the time for delivery.

4. Implied Warranties

A number of UCC default provisions deal with **warranties**: assurances regarding the quality of goods.

    a. **Warranty of title.** Unless specifically disclaimed, every sale includes a warranty that the seller has title to the goods and that they are conveyed free of any liens.

    b. **Warranty of merchantability.** Unless specifically disclaimed, every sale **by a merchant** includes a warranty that the goods are merchantable. Merchantable means that the goods would pass without objection in the trade, are of average quality, "are fit for the ordinary purposes for which such goods are used," are of roughly even quality, are adequately packaged, and conform to the label.

    c. **Warranty of fitness for a specific purpose.** Unless specifically disclaimed, a contract includes a warranty that the goods are fit for the buyer's purpose if (1) the seller has reason to know the particular purpose for which buyer wants the goods; and (2) the seller knows the buyer is relying on the seller's skill to select suitable goods.

EFFECT OF PARTIES' MISTAKES ON INTERPRETATION: MISUNDERSTANDING AND MISTAKE OF INTEGRATION

A. MISUNDERSTANDING

Misunderstanding exists when parties enter an agreement, each believing that a term has a meaning different from the meaning the other party attaches to the term.

1. **Misunderstanding as Aid to Interpretation**

    If parties claim they intended different meanings when they entered an agreement, a court may enforce one meaning if the party who did not intend that meaning **knew or had reason to know** the other did intend that meaning (and the other did not know or have reason to know of the first party's intent).

2. **Misunderstanding as Negating Assent**

    If both meanings are plausible and the court cannot select one, it may hold that the parties never assented to a contract. This occurs if **neither** party knew or had reason to know of the other's intended meaning or if **both** parties knew or had reason to know of the other's intent.

B. MISTAKE OF INTEGRATION AND REFORMATION

If the writing the parties sign differs from the agreement the parties made, a court may correct the mistake via **reformation**. Reformation is a court order effectively rewriting contract documents to correct mistakes. It may require clear and convincing evidence to persuade a court that the writing is wrong. It does not matter who made the mistake. If third parties have relied on the written agreement, unaware of the inaccuracy, the court may limit or deny reformation.

14   PAROL EVIDENCE: LIMITATIONS ON INTERPRETATION AND GAP FILLING

A. THE BASIC RULE

When parties have reduced their agreement to an **integrated writing**, the court will not allow **extrinsic evidence** of **prior or contemporaneous discussions** for the purpose of **varying**, **contradicting**, or (in some cases) **supplementing** the terms of the writing.

B. INTEGRATED WRITINGS

The parol evidence rule applies only if **the parties intend their writing(s) to express the final term(s) of their agreement**. Often contracts include a clause stating they are integrated. Courts also consider the completeness of the writing, usage of trade, or extrinsic evidence of intent in deciding whether the writing is integrated.

1.   **Partially Integrated Writings**

If parties adopt a writing as the **complete statement of the terms it contains** but do not intend for it to exclude other agreements, it is partially integrated. If an agreement is partially integrated, extrinsic evidence is admissible to show the existence of a separate oral agreement but not to vary or contradict the terms in the writing. In deciding whether an agreement is partially integrated, courts consider whether the alleged side agreement involved **separate consideration** and whether it would be **natural to omit** the side agreement from the writing.

2.   **Completely Integrated Writings**

If parties adopt the writing as **the complete and exclusive agreement** between them, it is a completely integrated agreement. If so, extrinsic evidence is not admissible to show side agreements.

C.   WORKING AROUND THE RULE

Courts admit extrinsic evidence for many purposes, either because it does not violate the rule or because it fits an exception to the rule.

1.   **Conditional Contracts**

Extrinsic evidence may be introduced to show that the parties intended no assent unless a condition occurred.

2.   **Interpretation**

To decide whether extrinsic evidence varies or contradicts the written terms, the court must know what the written terms mean. Extrinsic evidence may be admissible to help interpret a term.

a.   **Traditional hostility: The plain meaning approach.**   Extrinsic evidence is admissible to help interpret an ambiguous term but not to help interpret a term that seems clear on its face. Courts usually admit evidence of usage of trade and course of dealing.

b.   **Modern relaxation.**   If a contract term is "fairly susceptible" to either of the interpretations proposed, extrinsic evidence is admissible to support either interpretation. Often courts admit extrinsic evidence to show that a contract term is fairly susceptible to either of the interpretations proposed—even if the term seems plain on its face.

3. Torts

The parol evidence rule does not apply to torts, even the tort of fraudulently making an oral side promise.

4. Contract Defenses

The parol evidence rule does not preclude evidence introduced to prove a defense to the contract. Evidence seeks to establish a right to avoid a contract, not to contradict the terms of the contract.

5. Reformation

Extrinsic evidence may be admitted to establish reformation despite the parol evidence rule. Although the parties may have intended an integrated writing, they also intended the writing to include the terms to which they actually agreed. Thus, before the writing gains preclusive effect, it may need to be reformed to comport with the parties' agreement.

6. Remedial Discretion

Extrinsic evidence may be introduced to influence the court's equitable discretion to grant such remedies as specific performance or reformation.

7. Modification

The rule precludes evidence of prior or contemporaneous negotiations, not subsequent discussions that may have led to a modification.

 ## 15   CONDITIONS: IS PERFORMANCE DUE?

A.   CONDITION DEFINED

A condition is "an event, not certain to occur, which must occur, unless its non-occurrence is excused, before performance under a contract becomes due."

1. Conditions versus Promises

Conditions and promises have different effects. The failure to fulfill a promise is a breach of contract (unless excused). The nonbreaching party may sue for damages. The failure to fulfill a condition means performance does not become due. The failure is not breach and no damage action arises. Some language may create both a promise and a condition. The nonoccurrence would both excuse the other party's performance and allow suit for breach.

2.   Identifying Conditions

Usually, words such as "if" or "unless" introduce conditions.

3.   Interpretation as a Promise Preferred

If contract language is uncertain, courts prefer to interpret the language as creating a promise rather than a condition.

4.   Satisfaction as a Condition

Some contracts specify that a party's duty to perform arises only if she is satisfied with the other party's performance. If a party pretends dissatisfaction, her lack of good faith will excuse the condition, making her fail to perform breach. Where performance can be subjected to an objective test, an unreasonable claim of dissatisfaction might excuse the condition.

B.   EXCUSING CONDITIONS: WAIVER, MODIFICATION, AND ESTOPPEL

Courts have found ways to minimize the harsh consequences of conditions even when the parties clearly intended to create a condition.

1.   Waiver

The party for whose benefit the condition was specified may waive it. Waiver of a condition is revocable unless another has relied to her detriment on the waiver.

2.   Modification

Parties may modify a contract to delete the conditional term.

3.   Estoppel

A party is estopped to insist on a condition if other parties have **relied** on a **waiver** of the condition.

4.   Disproportionate Forfeiture

When a condition produces "disproportionate forfeiture," courts may excuse the condition "unless its occurrence was a material part of the agreed exchange." Forfeiture usually involves amounts a party has irretrievably invested before nonoccurrence of the condition excused the other party's performance.

16   MATERIAL BREACH: DOES NONPERFORMANCE JUSTIFY TERMINATION?

A. THE RULE

One party's **substantial performance** is a **condition** of the other party's duty to perform. That is, a party's performance is excused if there is an earlier **uncured material nonperformance** by the other party. When nonperformance is relatively minor, the nonbreaching party may collect damages but must continue to perform her part of the contract. She can terminate the agreement only if breach is material.

B. THE ORDER OF PERFORMANCE

Courts must decide who needed to perform first to decide whether one party's failure to perform excused the other's refusal to perform.

1. Contract Provisions

A contract may specify which party shall perform first.

2. Simultaneous Performance

When the contract is silent, the parties should perform simultaneously, if possible. Each party's duty to perform is conditioned on the other's **tender** of substantial performance. Tender is an offer to perform immediately, combined with a manifest ability to perform immediately. Upon tendering performance, a party need not complete performance unless the other tenders the return performance.

3. Prolonged Performance First

If one party's performance must be rendered over time, that performance is due first. Thus, employers pay at the end of the week.

C. FACTORS AFFECTING MATERIALITY OF A BREACH

Five factors influence decisions regarding whether a breach is material. No one factor is determinative, though in any given case one factor might outweigh the others.

1. Amount of Benefit Lost

When the breach deprives the nonbreaching party of a substantial part of the benefit expected under the contract, it is more likely to be material.

2.   Adequacy of Compensation

When damages or restitution can compensate for the losses caused by the breach, the breach is less likely to be material. Compensation makes up for some of the benefits lost, minimizing the first factor.

3.   Amount of Forfeiture by the Breaching Party

Forfeiture refers to wasted expense preparing to perform or performing prior to the breach. Forfeiture does **not** mean the breaching party will lose the benefit of the bargain. If the breaching party has relied significantly on the contract, suspension or termination may produce significant waste. Forfeiture makes a breach less likely to be material.

4.   Likelihood of Cure

If the breaching party will cure (correct any shortcomings in performance), termination may be unnecessary to provide the nonbreaching party with the benefit to which she is entitled. If cure is uncertain, the breach is more likely to be material.

5.   Breaching Party's Good Faith

A party's lack of good faith and fair dealing increases the likelihood of a finding of material breach.

D.   SUSPENSION OR TERMINATION? TIME FOR CURE

If a breach is material, the nonbreaching party immediately may **suspend** performance until the other party cures. Eventually, the party may want to **terminate** the contract and make other arrangements for the performance (or even live without it). Termination requires an additional inquiry.

1.   The Rule

A party has no further obligation to perform once a condition of her performance "can no longer occur." Substantial performance by the other party is one such condition. If the breach would still be material even if the breaching party cured, the nonbreaching party's performance is discharged and she may terminate the contract.

2.   Time for Cure

The time for cure is governed by a set of factors similar to those for determining materiality.

a.   Five factors governing materiality.   These factors will not be repeated here.

    b.   **Amount of harm from delaying substitute arrangements.**   When delay will prevent or hinder efforts to make substitute arrangements (e.g., cover), discharge will occur sooner.

    c.   **Agreement that time is of the essence.**   The contract may require timely performance, either expressly or by implication. An agreement that timely performance is important makes immediate discharge more likely.

E.   SALES OF GOODS: THE PERFECT TENDER RULE

In sales of goods, any breach, no matter how trivial, once permitted immediate termination. The rule remains but has eroded slightly.

1.   Timely Cure

If the time for performance has not yet expired, the seller may cure by tendering conforming goods.

2.   Untimely Cure

Even if the time for performance has expired, the seller is allowed a chance to cure within a reasonable time if she had reason to believe the goods tendered would be acceptable to the buyer.

3.   Accepted Goods

If buyer accepts nonconforming goods, she may later revoke the acceptance only if "the non-conformity substantially impairs" the value of the goods.

4.   Multiple Lots

If performance involves a series of installments, the buyer cannot reject future installments unless the nonconformity in the current installment "impairs the value of the whole contract."

F.   DIVISIBILITY: MITIGATING THE HARSHNESS OF MATERIAL BREACH

If material breach occurs after the breaching party has performed part (or even most) of the contract, compensation is required for that partial performance. The issue is whether to allow compensation under the **contract** or to limit the breaching party to a claim for **restitution**.

1.   Effect of Divisibility

If a breaching party has performed all duties of a divisible portion of a contract, the court will allow that party to recover the contract price (or other return performance) for that part of the contract—even though the party breached other portions of the divisible contract.

2. Identifying Divisible Contracts

When the contract can be divided into **pairs of part performances that are agreed equivalents**, the court may treat the contract as if it was two or more contracts, each involving a pair of part performances. Divisibility usually requires a contract that specifies a price for each part of performance. If a term regulates the timing of payments, it may not reflect an intent that each payment compensates for the work done so far.

17   EXCUSABLE NONPERFORMANCE: DOES NONPERFORMANCE JUSTIFY DAMAGES?

A. IMPRACTICABILITY

If the nonoccurrence of an event is a basic assumption on which the contract was made, the occurrence of that event excuses a party's nonperformance if, without the nonperforming party's fault, the event makes performance impracticable—unless the contract or other circumstances indicate that the party agreed to perform despite the event.

1. Basic Assumption

The nonoccurrence of an event must have been a basic assumption on which the contract was made. The continued **life or capacity** of a person critical to performance is one such basic assumption. So is the continued **existence of property** critical to performance. The **nonexistence of laws preventing performance** also is a basic assumption.

2. Performance Becomes Impracticable

Impracticability requires more than just reduced profitability or even losses under the contract. "Extreme and unreasonable difficulty, expense, injury or, loss" is required. An increase in cost that "alters the essential nature of the performance" may support impracticability.

3. Without a Party's Fault

When a party's own act makes performance impractical, her performance is not excused. For sales of goods, absence of fault is not required by the UCC, but good faith is required.

4. **Agreement to Assume Greater Obligations**

When parties can foresee events, they may provide for them in the contract. If a party agrees to perform in spite of an event that would make performance more burdensome, impracticability will not excuse nonperformance.

5. **Remedial Concerns**

Impracticability may excuse performance when uneven partial performance makes it necessary to award a remedy to one party or the other. The usual tools are available. If the contract is divisible, the portion performed so far may be compensated at the contract rate. Restitution for benefits bestowed also remains available.

6. **Temporary Impracticability**

If events do not make performance impracticable forever, performance is suspended until performance is practicable, with two exceptions.

a. **Party facing impracticability.**   If performance after the impracticability ends would be "materially more burdensome" than it was if the impracticability had not occurred, the duty is discharged.

b. **Other party.**   When impracticability delays performance, rules on material nonperformance govern the other party's ability to terminate the contract and make substitute arrangements.

7. **Partial Impracticability**

Events may reduce a party's ability to perform without preventing all performance. In these situations, a party usually must allocate the performance reasonably among customers.

B. **FRUSTRATION**

If the nonoccurrence of an event is a basic assumption on which the contract was made, the occurrence of that event excuses a party's nonperformance if, without that party's fault, the event substantially frustrates the party's principal purpose—unless the contract or other circumstances indicate that the party agreed to perform despite the event.

1. **Sales of Goods**

The UCC does not mention frustration. In that silence, "the principles of law and equity . . . supplement [the UCC's] provisions," presumably including frustration.

2. Principal Purpose of the Contract

The frustration must effect the essence of the contract: an object "so completely the basis of the contract that, as both parties understand, without it the transaction would make little sense."

3. Substantially Frustrated

Events that make the contract less valuable do not substantially frustrate the contract. The effect must be extreme, much the way the effect of impracticability must be extreme.

18 REPUDIATION: CAN BREACH OCCUR BEFORE PERFORMANCE IS DUE?

A. REPUDIATION

Repudiation can consist of either a statement or actions. An **unequivocal** statement that a party will not perform when due is an **express repudiation**. Action that makes it appear impossible for a party to perform when due is an **implied repudiation**. In either case, a repudiation exists only if the statement or action indicated that the party will commit a **material breach**.

B. REASONABLE GROUNDS FOR INSECURITY

If a party has reasonable grounds to believe that the other will commit a material breach, she may (1) **demand adequate assurance of due performance**; (2) if reasonable, **suspend performance** (except to the extent she has already received compensation for the performance); and (3) treat the failure to provide adequate assurance within a reasonable time as a **repudiation** of the contract. This helps protect a party when statements or actions that are equivocal but suggest nonperformance are likely.

C. EVENTS AFTER REPUDIATION: RETRACTION AND MITIGATION

1. Responding to Repudiation

After a repudiation, a party may (1) accept the repudiation as final and proceed to make other arrangements; (2) urge the other party to retract the repudiation and perform; or (3) do nothing and hope the other party performs.

    a. Terminating the contract. Repudiation discharges the other party's duty to perform under the contract. Thus, the other party may accept the repudiation as final and make substitute arrangements immediately.

b. Urging performance.   If substitute arrangements will be unsatisfactory, a party may urge the other party to retract the repudiation and to perform. A party should suspend performance anyway. If continued performance causes damages to mount unreasonably, those damages are recoverable. Urging retraction does not limit the right later to make substitute arrangements—though retraction could make these duplicative.

2. Retraction by the Repudiating Party

As the time for performance has not arrived, cure (by performing when due) is inherently possible. Retraction requires actual notice to the nonrepudiating party. Retraction is too late if (a) the other party has **relied** on the repudiation; or (b) the other party has **indicated** to the repudiating party that **she considers the repudiation final**.

PART 3   HOW SHOULD THE LAW RESPOND?

 19   EQUITABLE RELIEF

A. SPECIFIC PERFORMANCE: COMPELLING THE BREACHING PARTY TO PERFORM

Specific performance is an **injunction** ordering a party to perform as promised under a contract.

1. Inadequate Remedy at Law (the Irreparable Injury Rule)

Courts will deny injunctions if the remedy at law is adequate. A remedy at law is inadequate if it is not as complete, practical, and efficient as injunctive relief. That is, **unless damages are just as good as an injunction, the court will grant the injunction.**

a. **Uniqueness.** Most courts will grant specific performance if the promised performance is unique. A remedy at law is not as good as an injunction because you could not take the money and use it to buy a suitable substitute for performance.

    i. **Land generally is held to be unique.** No two pieces of land are located in exactly the same place.

    ii. **Art often is unique.** So is any tangible item to which sentimental value might attach.

    iii. **People are unique.** Even those with no special skills are a unique assortment of attributes—at least as different as parcels of land in a modern subdivision.

    iv. **Money is not unique.** Specific performance of a promise to pay money is very rare.

    v. **Goods usually are not unique.** Most of the goods we buy are fungible: there are others just like them available elsewhere. Custom made goods may be unique.

b. **Shortage.** The ability to use money damages to buy the same performance elsewhere may be limited by scarcity. If there are few of the things available, money may not be as good as specific performance.

c. **Difficult damage remedies.** Sometimes damage remedies will be difficult to use. If so, preventing the loss by ordering specific performance may be more practical than relegating plaintiff to a damage action. When damages are uncertain, precluded by other rules, or uncollectable due to insolvency, the remedy at law is inadequate.

2. **Other Limitations on Injunctions**

Even when the remedy at law is inadequate, courts may deny injunctions for other reasons.

a. **Undue hardship.** If the harm an injunction does to defendant greatly exceeds the benefit to the plaintiff, a court may deny the injunction and award damages instead.

b. **Excessive judicial supervision.** Courts deny injunctions if the burdens of enforcement exceed the benefits an injunction has over the damage remedy.

c. **Compelling individuals to perform personal services.** Courts refuse to order individuals to perform personal service contracts.

B. ENFORCING NEGATIVE COVENANTS

A promise to work for one employer implicitly includes a promise not to work for any other employer at the time. Courts sometimes order employees not to work for any other employer even though they cannot be ordered to perform for the plaintiff.

 ## 20 EXPECTATION INTEREST: THE NORMAL RECOVERY RULES

A. BASIC PRINCIPLE: THE FINANCIAL EQUIVALENT OF PERFORMANCE

The expectation interest seeks to place the nonbreaching plaintiff in the position she would have occupied if the breaching defendant had performed the contract.

1. Fundamentals

To calculate expectation, you need two numbers:

(a) How much wealth (money or property) **should** the plaintiff have received (i.e., how much would she have if defendant had performed)?

(b) How much **did** she receive (i.e., how much does she have despite the breach)?

Subtract the second from the first. That is the expectation interest.

B. VALUE OF THE PROMISED PERFORMANCE

The central component of all damage calculations is the value (or price) of the thing promised.

1. Market Value

If a performance is available in the market, the price set by the market is the value of that performance. Awarding the plaintiff this amount of money will allow her to go into the market and buy the same performance from another supplier. Market value is calculated at the place performance was to occur at the time plaintiff learned of the breach. For items rarely traded, experts can testify about how much an item would fetch in a market.

2. Cover Price or Resale Price

Sometimes a plaintiff will make her own arrangements for substitute performance: She will sell the performance to a different buyer or buy a substitute from another seller. The actual transaction provides a convenient alternative to a hypothetical market price.

a. Plaintiff's option. The UCC allows the plaintiff to recover based on an actual transaction at her option.

b. Commercially reasonable transactions. Only commercially reasonable transactions (sometimes called bona fide arm's-length transactions) can substitute for market price. Paying more (or accepting less) than a reasonable buyer (or seller) would have paid (or demanded) deprives the cover (or resale) transaction of its validity as a proxy for market price (or even of subjective value).

C. AVOIDING UNDERCOMPENSATION: INCIDENTAL LOSSES, CONSEQUENTIAL LOSSES, AND PREJUDGMENT INTEREST

A breach may involve more costs than just the loss of the promised performance. Additional costs also require compensation.

1. Incidental Losses

Such losses involve additional costs incurred because the deal fell through, including the cost to locate a substitute buyer or seller or to make do in the meantime.

2. Consequential Losses

Such losses involve the way the plaintiff intended to use the performance, usually in ways that would have generated a profit.

3. Prejudgment Interest

This is a special example of consequential losses. If breach postpones the receipt of money (or property she could have sold to obtain money), the plaintiff loses the use of that money (or property) for the period of time. Interest compensates for the lost opportunity to use (invest) the money.

D. AVOIDING OVERCOMPENSATION: REASONABLE COVER, LOSSES AVOIDED, AND COSTS AVOIDED

Plaintiff cannot keep gains caused by the breach and still collect all costs from the defendant, if that leaves her better off than she would have been if defendant had performed.

1. Substitute Goods of Superior Quality

The buyer is entitled to cover with a performance equal to the one defendant promised. If she substitutes a better performance, her recovery is limited to the amount required to obtain an equal performance.

2. Costs Avoided

If, after the other party's breach, a plaintiff avoids some costs by stopping her performance, she cannot recover costs she avoided.

3. Losses Avoided

A plaintiff cannot recover for losses she avoids as a result of the breach (often by shifting resources that would have been used in one contract to another profitable use, she cannot recover for the losses avoided).

4. Losses Not Really Avoided: The Lost Volume Seller

Sometimes a party can enter more than one contract, earning profits on each. The fact that the party earned a profit on a second contract, then, does not necessarily mean that she has avoided the loss of profit on the contract defendant breached. Before treating losses as avoided, consider whether plaintiff could have entered both contracts.

E. LIMITATIONS ON EXPECTATION RECOVERIES

1. Avoidable Consequences (or Mitigation of Damages)

Sometimes plaintiffs do not avoid costs following the breach, even though they should have avoided them. Courts subtract the costs a plaintiff **should have avoided** anyway, just as if the plaintiff actually had avoided them.

a. **Preventing losses.** Plaintiff cannot recover for any loss that she could have avoided without undue risk, burden, or humiliation.

b. **Defendant's burden.** The defendant must prove the amount that could have been avoided by reasonable efforts.

c. **Plaintiff's reasonableness precludes reduction.** As long as the plaintiff's efforts to minimize the loss are reasonable, damages will not be reduced by amounts that could have been avoided by other (reasonable) methods.

d. **Unavoidable losses.** Any portion of the loss that could not be avoided is recoverable.

e. **Costs of minimization recoverable.** Any costs incurred to pursue reasonable efforts to minimize the loss are recoverable from the defendant.

2. **Foreseeability**

A plaintiff can recover damages if either (a) the loss flows **naturally** from the breach; or (2) the defendant, at the time the contract was made, **had reason to know** that losses of this type probably would from a breach. Where the consequences of breach are unusual, defendant may have no reason to know about them unless plaintiff tells her about the likely consequences of breach.

a. **Buyer's losses.** Foreseeability problems usually involve buyers seeking damages from sellers for the project in which they would have used the seller's performance.

b. **Common errors.** Foreseeability requires **reason to know**, not actual knowledge. Foreseeability, at least in theory, does not require that defendant have reason to know the amount of damages, only that **damages of that type** probably will result.

3. **Certainty**

Plaintiff cannot recover damages unless she can prove them with reasonable certainty. If the breach may not have caused any loss at all, courts typically refuse any recovery. If the **existence** of a loss is certain, courts allow juries to make a reasonable estimate of the **amount** of the loss.

a. **New businesses typically have trouble proving lost profits.**

b. **Reliance interest.** If profit cannot be proven with reasonable certainty, courts generally award the reliance interest: the costs incurred so far in an effort to make profits. To avoid paying expenditures, defendant must prove the venture would not have broken even — that expenses would have exceeded revenues. If so, any actual losses will be deducted from the expenses recovered.

4. **Emotional Distress**

Damages for emotional distress usually are not recoverable in contract actions. Exceptions exist if a breach of contract causes **physical injury** or if **severe distress was particularly likely** as a result of the breach.

5. Attorneys' Fees

Attorneys' fees usually are not recoverable as an element of damages in a contract action. If the **contract allows** recovery of attorneys' fees as part of the damages, that provision of the contract usually is enforceable. If defendant's breach of a contract forces the plaintiff to incur attorneys' fees in **collateral** litigation (against third parties), those fees are recoverable as consequential damages. A few statutes also allow recovery of attorneys' fees.

6. Punitive Damages

Punitive damages are not recoverable in contract actions except for **breach of promise to marry** (generally unenforceable today) and a **breach of good faith by an insurer**. For punitive damages, attorneys try to characterize the wrong as a tort.

 21 THE RELIANCE INTEREST

A. APPROPRIATE CASES FOR THE RELIANCE INTEREST

Reliance damages are available when expectation damages are uncertain. Reliance damages may be available when a contract is unenforceable but restitution provides an inadequate remedy. In a few cases, courts award reliance damages when they concluded the full expectation interest allowed too great a recovery in proportion to the wrong committed.

B. CALCULATING RELIANCE RECOVERIES

The reliance interest seeks to put the plaintiff in the position she would have occupied if the defendant had not made the promise. Reliance primarily involves reimbursing the plaintiff for any expenditures made in reliance on defendant's promise, especially for partial performance or for preparations to perform.

1. Entire Venture

If the defendant's performance is part of a larger venture, expenditures include other expenses incurred to pursue that venture.

2. Lost Opportunities

In theory, the reliance interest also requires the defendant to compensate the plaintiff for any opportunities lost as a result of the promise, such as the opportunity to enter a similar contract with a different promisor. Courts rarely include lost opportunities in reliance recoveries.

C. THE RELIANCE INTEREST CANNOT EXCEED THE EXPECTATION INTEREST

In losing contracts, reliance technically would exceed expectation. Reliance would allow recovery of all expenditures. Thus, plaintiff would break even on the project even though she would have incurred losses had the contract been performed. If the defendant can prove that plaintiff would have suffered a loss even if defendant had performed, the amount of losses will be subtracted from the total expenses. Thus, recovery is limited to the expectation interest.

 ## 22 REMEDIES AGREED ON BY THE PARTIES

A. AGREEMENTS EXPANDING THE RECOVERY AVAILABLE

The parties may agree to allow recovery of elements of damage not usually allowed by the courts, such as attorneys' fees.

B. AGREEMENTS EXCLUDING CONSEQUENTIAL DAMAGES

A contract explicitly may disclaim any liability for consequential damages. Agreements excluding consequential damages are **enforceable** unless **unconscionable**. A clause excluding consequential damages for personal injuries caused by consumer goods is prima facie unconscionable. A clause excluding consequential damages when the loss is commercial is not prima facie unconscionable.

C. AGREEMENTS PROVIDING AN EXCLUSIVE REMEDY

Sellers may exclude potentially large recoveries by providing alternative remedies, such as limiting remedies to repair or replacement of the item sold. The alternative is optional unless explicitly stated to be the exclusive remedy. These provisions usually are enforceable unless the remedy **fails of its essential purpose**.

1. Failure versus Undercompensation

A limitation that prevents complete relief does not fail of its essential purpose merely because the law would provide additional compensation that the limited remedy excludes. All limitations will prevent recourse to some options that the law would have allowed.

2. Worthless Remedy

When a limited remedy cannot be implemented, it becomes worthless. For example, when an item cannot be repaired or replaced, a clause limiting the remedy to repair or replacement fails to provide any relief at all. In these situations, the remedy fails of its essential purposes.

3. Independent Limitations

Some contracts contain multiple limitations. The unenforceability of one limitation may not preclude enforcement of other limits.

D. LIQUIDATED DAMAGES CLAUSES

If parties wish to avoid the expense of litigating over the amount of damages, they may specify the amount of damages recoverable for breach in the contract.

1. Basic Rule

Courts enforce liquidated damage clauses but refuse to enforce penalties.

2. Reasonable Estimate of the Loss

Parties may agree on any amount of damages that is reasonable in light of the anticipated **or** actual loss caused by the breach and the difficulty of proving the loss.

E. ARBITRATION AND SIMILAR PROCEDURAL CLAUSES

The parties may seek to specify the way in which disputes are resolved by specifying a particular court in which to litigate, specifying the state law that governs the dispute, or requiring that disputes be submitted to arbitration.

1. Choice of Law

Contracts are governed by state law, which may vary on some points. Parties may specify the body of law they wish to govern their agreement and may negotiate with that law in mind. The provisions usually are enforceable unless unconscionable.

2. Forum Selection

For their own convenience (and to keep costs down), parties may agree to require suits against a party to be filed in a particular state. These clauses are generally enforceable, as long as the forum chosen has some connection to at least one party or to the dispute. An unconscionable clause would not be enforceable.

F.   ARBITRATION

By statute or decision, most American jurisdictions now recognize arbitration as a legitimate method to reduce the burden on courts and shift the cost of litigation from the taxpayers (who pay judges) to the parties (who pay arbitrators). Because arbitrators have no official power to enforce their judgments, arbitration awards still come to court for review.

1.   Fighting Arbitration

Despite an agreement to arbitrate, a party may seek to avoid arbitration by **filing suit** despite the clause or by **challenging an arbitration award in court**.

2.   Suits Stayed Pending Arbitration

If one party sues in court instead of initiating arbitration, the court usually will stay proceedings pending the outcome of arbitration — if the other party requests a stay.

3.   Review after Arbitration

If one party objects to the arbitration award, a court may review it and, in an appropriate case, set it aside. The grounds for setting aside the decision of an arbitrator are fairly narrow.

   a.   Exceeded authority.   Parties may agree to submit only some disputes to arbitration. If the arbitrator decides a matter that the parties have not agreed to allow her to decide, the court cannot bind a party to the arbitrator's decision on that point.

   b.   Serious misconduct.   A court will not defer to arbitration proceedings infected by fraud, bribery, corruption, or other difficulties that undermine the fairness of the hearing.

   c.   Complete irrationality.   A court will not enforce a decision that falls outside the realm of any reasonable result. An arbitrator need not apply the law the way a court would. Arbitrators are not bound by judicial rules and precedent.

   d.   Public policy.   If an arbitration award contravenes public policy, a court will not enforce it. The bounds of this requirement are not well defined. For example, courts are split on whether (and under what

CAPSULE SUMMARY

circumstances) public policy precludes arbitrators from awarding punitive damages in contract actions.

 ## 23 RESTITUTION AND UNJUST ENRICHMENT

A. RESTITUTION WHEN THE CONTRACT WAS NOT ENFORCEABLE

Unjust enrichment is a separate cause of action, fully equal to breach of contract and the various torts. Thus, even when conduct does not breach a contract or commit a tort, recovery may be justified to prevent unjust enrichment.

1. Elements of an Action for Unjust Enrichment

To establish entitlement to recover for unjust enrichment, a plaintiff must prove that (a) the defendant received a **benefit** from the plaintiff's (partial) performance; and (2) it would be unfair to allow the defendant to retain that benefit without compensating the plaintiff.

   a. Benefit received. Restitution seeks to deprive the defendant of benefits she cannot, in fairness, retain. Expenditures made by a plaintiff that did not benefit the defendant do not give rise to a cause of action for restitution.

   b. Injustice. People may give benefits that others have no obligation to return, such as gifts. Only when circumstances make it unjust to allow the defendant to keep the benefit without compensating the plaintiff will an action for unjust enrichment lie.

2. Situations Requiring Restitution

If parties discover that a contract is unenforceable after performance has already begun, restitution is necessary. The contract is unenforceable, so a party cannot reclaim her performance (or its value) by suing for breach of the contract.

3. Public Policy

Restitution generally is not available when a contract is declared void because of public policy. Courts prefer to leave the parties where they are, ordering neither to pay the other. Exceptions were discussed above.

B. RESTITUTION AS A REMEDY FOR BREACH OF CONTRACT

"Give me my money back!" may be the most intuitive response to a breach of contract. Essentially, that is a restitution recovery: The defendant must return any benefit she received under the contract. Because other contract remedies (e.g., expectation) usually are more generous than a refund, restitution is not the most commonly requested remedy — at least not once suit is brought. Nonetheless, restitution remains a plausible alternative to the expectation interest.

1. Motivation to Seek Restitution

Most plaintiffs seek restitution when they wish they had made a better contract. Getting their money back allows them to go out and make a better deal elsewhere — or, in the case of losing contracts, to avoid the losses they would have suffered if they had needed to complete performance. In these situations, restitution can exceed expectation.

C. CALCULATING THE BENEFIT BESTOWED

If it would be unjust for the defendant to keep the benefit without compensating the plaintiff, courts must decide how to calculate the amount of compensation required. Restitution seeks to restore the defendant to the position she would have occupied if the contract had not been made.

1. Specific Restitution

The easiest cases involve specific restitution: returning to the plaintiff exactly what she gave the defendant.

2. Cost to Obtain Similar Performance

When an item cannot be returned specifically, its value can be measured by deciding how much it would have cost to obtain that performance from another party. The plaintiff is entitled to recover the **amount that a third party would have charged to perform the same services** at the time the plaintiff performed the services. The contract price is not the measure of restitution. Maybe other persons would have charged the same amount specified in the contract. But this must be proven. The contract price itself is relevant only if it helps establish what other people would have charged.

3. Value to Recipient

Sometimes services will increase the value of defendant's assets. The plaintiff is entitled to recover **the amount by which the defendant's property increased in value** because of the services rendered.

4. Limitation of Availability

If a plaintiff has fully performed and the defendant's only remaining duty is to pay money, the plaintiff may not recover for restitution. Courts will award the amount promised (plus interest) rather than try to recalculate the value of the performance differently from the parties' calculation in the contract.

D. RESTITUTION TO THE BREACHING PARTY

Because unjust enrichment is a separate cause of action, to recover the plaintiff need not prove that the defendant breached a contract. Thus, a party who breached a contract can seek restitution against a party who did not breach the contract.

1. Situations in Which Breaching Parties May Recover in Restitution

Sometimes one party (call her *A*) must perform first. The other party (*B*) receives the benefit of her performance before paying for it. If for any reason *A* does not complete performance, *B* retains a benefit. *B* may be entitled to keep that benefit as damages for *A*'s breach of contract. But if the benefit she receives is larger than the damages she suffers, *A* may claim restitution for any benefit *B* received in excess to the damages to which *B* was entitled.

2. Limitations on Remedies to the Breaching Party

The same two techniques for measuring the benefit can be used regardless of whether the plaintiff is the breaching or nonbreaching party. But a breaching plaintiff may not recover the full amount of the benefit bestowed if one of the following limitations applies.

a. Pro rata share of the contract price.   A party who breaches can never recover more than she would have received if she had performed the contract. The most a breaching plaintiff can recover is a percentage of defendant's performance equal to the percentage of performance actually rendered by the plaintiff (often called a pro rata share of the contract price).

b. Defendant's damages for breach of the contract.   A breaching party may owe the other damages caused by the breach. A breaching party may recover restitution only if the benefit bestowed exceeds the amount of damages she owes the other party.

PART 4 WHO CAN INVOKE THE LAW? RIGHTS AND OBLIGATIONS OF THIRD PARTIES

 24 ASSIGNMENT, DELEGATION, AND THIRD-PARTY BENEFICIARIES

A. THIRD-PARTY BENEFICIARIES

Some contracts include promises that benefit third parties—people other than those who actually enter the contract. A third party may acquire rights under the contract—including the right to sue if performance is not received as promised.

1. **Intended Beneficiaries**

   Intended beneficiaries may sue to enforce a contract even though they are not parties to the contract. Incidental beneficiaries gain no such rights.

   a. **Identifying intended beneficiaries.** Three things must be true for a person to assert claims as a third-party beneficiary.

      i. **Benefit.** She must be a beneficiary of the contract. That is, she must be able to identify some benefit that would have flowed to her if the contract had been performed; and

      ii. **Intent.** Recognition of rights must be appropriate to effectuate the intention of the parties. The agreement must reveal a purpose to benefit another, not merely knowledge that another would be benefitted if the contract is performed; and

      iii. **Debt.** The promisee owes money to the beneficiary and performance will satisfy that debt; or

      iv. **Gift.** The promisee intends to give the benefit of the contract to the third party.

   b. **Identity immaterial.** As long as a beneficiary can be identified with some certainty at the time of enforcement, it does not matter that a beneficiary is not specifically identified in the contract.

2. **Effect of Defenses**

    When sued by a beneficiary, the promisor may seek to plead various defenses to performance under the contract.

    a. **Promisor's defenses against promisee.** If the contract was unenforceable, the promisor's duty to perform cannot be binding, even though the beneficiary rather than the promisee seeks to enforce the agreement. **Thus, most defenses against the promisee are fully effective when asserted against a third-party beneficiary.**

        i.   **Void.** A beneficiary cannot recover on a contract that was not formed (say, because it lacked consideration or assent).

        ii. **Voidable.** A beneficiary cannot recover on a contract that was voidable or unenforceable, provided the promisor has standing to avoid the agreement.

        iii. **Discharge or excuse.** A beneficiary may not recover on a contract if the promisor's duty to perform has been discharged or excused by events occurring after formation.

        iv. **Other defenses.** Other defenses against the promisee may not be asserted by the promisor against the beneficiary. Few contract defenses remain, so you may not encounter this situation.

    b. **Promisor's defenses against beneficiary.** The promisor may assert any defense that arises from the conduct of the beneficiary, such as an offset of amounts the beneficiary owes the promisor.

    c. **Promisee's defenses against the beneficiary.** The promisor cannot avoid liability to the beneficiary by arguing that the promisee could have refused to provide the benefits.

    d. **Promisee's power to vary the beneficiary's rights.** Sometimes the promisor and promisee modify the contract in ways that alter (or even eliminate) the beneficiary's rights.

        i.   **Contractual limitations.** A contract provision prohibiting the promisor and promisee from altering the beneficiary's right is enforceable.

        ii. **Permissible modification.** If the contract does not preclude the parties from altering the beneficiary's rights, the parties may modify or discharge the contract **before the beneficiary relies on it**.

   iii.   **Notice.** For modification or discharge to be effective, the parties must notify the beneficiary of the changes before she does one of the following:

- **Relies** justifiably on the promise.
- **Sues** to enforce the promise.
- **Manifests assent** to the agreement at the request of one of the parties to the contract.

3. Special Problems with Intent: Government Contracts

A beneficiary cannot assert rights against a promisor who made a contract with the government unless one of the following occurs:

(a) The contract **expressly** provides for liability to third parties; or

(b) The **government could be sued by the beneficiary** for failing to provide the benefit and a direct action against the promisor is consistent with both the terms of the contract and the law authorizing the contract.

B. ASSIGNMENT OF RIGHTS

A right to receive performance under a contract is valuable. A party may try to realize this value before the other party has performed by selling the right to receive that performance (or giving it away). Transferring the right to receive performance is called **assignment**.

1. Limitations on Assignment

An obligor may prevent an assignment of rights on several grounds.

   a.   **Limits imposed by contract.** A contract may limit the ability of the parties to assign their rights under the contract. Because assignment generally is favored, courts make it somewhat difficult for parties to prevent assignment.

      i.   **Delegation only.** A clause that prevents assignment of the contract may be interpreted to preclude only delegation of duties.

      ii.   **Assignment of damages.** A clause prohibiting assignment does not preclude assignment of a right to damages for total breach.

      iii. No specific enforcement. A clause prohibiting assignment gives rise to an action only for damages. The obligor must perform for the assignee and sue the assignor for damages, if any, caused by the assignment.

      iv. Waiver. The obligor can waive the clause that precludes assignment.

      v. Consent provisions. Some contracts, instead of prohibiting all assignments, prohibit assignment without the obligor's consent. When an obligor withholds consent, litigation may erupt over the reasons for withholding consent.

         (a) Arbitrariness. Arguably, the obligor may withhold consent for any reason, even an arbitrary one. Although many courts accept this position, it seems to undermine the requirement that parties to a contract act in good faith.

         (b) Good faith. Some courts uphold any objection the obligor makes in good faith.

         (c) Commercial reasonableness. At least one court has required a commercially reasonable reason for the refusal to accept the assignment, apparently willing to reject an unreasonable decision even if made in good faith.

b. Limits imposed by public policy. A few express statutes preclude assignment of rights under a contract. Absent an express statute, courts may weigh policies contravened by the assignment with the policy favoring its enforcement.

    i. Wages. Statutes commonly prohibit assignments of wages due under employment contracts or limit them to 10% or 25% per paycheck.

    ii. Pensions. Assignment of rights to receive pension benefits may be ineffective.

c. Limits imposed by contract law. Although assignments generally are favored, contract law recognizes that some assignments may impose hardship on the obligor.

    i. Duty changed materially. An assignment that materially changes the duty of the obligor is not valid. Often assignment has little effect on the obligor's duty. If performance varies significantly with the identity of the assignee, the assignment may be invalid.

ii. **Burden increased materially.** An assignment that materially increases the burden on the obligor is not valid. Materially increasing the cost of performance increases the burden.

iii. **Risk increased materially.** An assignment that materially increases the risk to the obligor is not valid. This provision seems broad enough to encompass another often stated limitation: when the assignment **materially impairs the obligor's chance of obtaining return performance.** That is one of the risks that an assignment might materially affect.

iv. **Value materially decreased.** An assignment that materially reduces the value of the return performance to the obligor is not valid.

C. DELEGATION OF DUTIES

Delegation of duties often accompanies an assignment of rights but poses more problems. An assignment does not change what the obligor receives or from whom she receives it but merely gives her performance to a different person than she anticipated. Delegation involves receiving what she expected from a different person—a fact more likely to change significantly the value of the performance.

1. Terminology

A delegation again involves three persons. The **delegating party** is an **obligor**, one who owes duties under a contract with an **obligee**, who is entitled to receive the performance. Instead of performing those duties personally, the **delegating party** agrees with a **delegated party** that the **delegated party** will perform them. Thus, the **obligee**, without being consulted, may receive performance from the **delegating party**, someone with whom she has no contract.

2. Delegation Permissible

Normally, delegation is allowed. That is, a person who owes a duty may perform that duty personally or via an agent. Delegation is not permitted if the **contract prohibits delegation**, delegation **contravenes public policy**, or if the **obligee has a substantial interest in having the delegating party perform or control the performance** of the duties.

a. **Imposed by contract.** A contract validly can prohibit delegation of duties. In fact, a contract clause that prohibits assignment will be interpreted as prohibiting delegation of duties but allowing assignment of rights.

b. **Imposed by public policy.** As with assignment, public policy might prevent delegation.

   i. **Alienability favored.** To some extent, public policy is more likely to favor delegation. Limiting delegation limits the alienability of property. Public policy generally opposes unreasonable restraints on alienability.

   ii. **Duties to the government.** Delegation of duties owed to the government probably violates public policy.

c. **Imposed by contract law.** When the obligee has a substantial interest in having the obligor (delegating party) perform or control the performance, the delegation is forbidden by contract law, even if neither the contract nor public policy is at stake.

   i. **Personal services.** A substantial interest almost always exists in personal service contracts. Thus, a person hired to teach school (including law school) could not delegate the duties to another. The school, not the individual, has the authority to choose who may represent the school in the classroom.

   ii. **Other services.** Some service contracts are not personal service contracts. A person who enters a contract with a business entity rather than an individual may not have a substantial interest in having the work performed or supervised by any individual.

   iii. **Corporations.** Even when a company, rather than an individual, is hired to perform services, a court may find a substantial interest in having that company (or its key personnel) perform or supervise the services.

3. **Effects of Delegation**

Delegation does not alter the underlying contract; it simply changes the identity of the person who must perform certain duties. Thus, issues surrounding performance and breach remain unaffected.

a. **Sue the delegating party.** If the delegated party does not perform, the obligee may sue the delegating party. Unless the obligee releases the delegating party from her obligations, the delegating party remains liable for any breach by the delegated party.

b. Sue the delegated party.   If the delegated party does not perform, the obligee may sue the delegated party. The obligee is an intended third-party beneficiary of the contract between the delegating party and the delegated party.

c. Request assurance of performance.   The obligee may treat the delegation as reasonable grounds for insecurity and demand adequate assurances of performance from the delegated party. Any change in the identity of the party who will perform gives the obligee this right — even if she does not have sufficient interest in the identity of the performing party to prevent the delegation.

4. Novation: Obligee's Agreement to Excuse Delegating Party

The delegating party may want to eliminate its liability to the obligee. The obligee may agree to release the delegating party and look only to the delegated party for performance. Such a release is called a **novation**. In effect, the obligee agrees to rescind the contract with the original (delegating) party and replace it with a new (usually identical) contract with the new (delegated) party.

a. Release versus acquiescence.   Agreeing to accept performance from the delegated party does not establish a novation. The essence of a novation is a release of the delegating party. Simply agreeing to accept performance from the delegated party does not establish such a release.

b. Discharge of delegating party.   A novation ends any liability of the delegating party. If the obligee releases the delegating party, her only recourse in the event of breach is against the delegated party.

INTRODUCTION TO CONTRACT LAW

CHAPTER OVERVIEW

Contracts is a hard subject to begin. It easily divides into topics. But to understand any one topic, you need to know something from another topic first. Thus, no starting point is perfect — which may explain why you are looking for outside guidance in the first place. This section is intended to introduce you to contract law. It lays the groundwork necessary to help you understand the detailed discussion of each doctrine that follows. The introduction includes three different components: an introduction to the **sources** of contract law you will study this year; an introduction to the legal rules and **doctrines** courts apply to contract disputes; and one **approach** that may help you put these elements into perspective.

A. SOURCES OF CONTRACT LAW

One of your tasks this year is to learn how to find law. (In the long run, your course in research and writing is more important than any substantive course, such as Contracts.) Contract law will be easier to understand once you appreciate the relationship between the different kinds of materials you will read in the process of finding the law.

1. Contract Is Governed by State Law

The United States Constitution gives the federal government a limited number of powers. Regulating contracts was not included among the Congress's powers, at least under nineteenth-century interpretations of the Constitution. Thus, contract law was created by the states. Each state was free to develop its own rules. This has several implications.

a. Rules vary from state to state. States have evolved very similar rules governing contract law. But the exact content of any given doctrine may vary from state to state. Thus, your contracts course (and this outline) can present only the general principles of contract law, not the precise details of every doctrine in every state.

    i.   **Don't exaggerate the differences.** At times the differences among states are small or even meaningless. The duress defense may have the same content even if called coercion or menace. Slight differences in the words used to declare a rule may not affect the outcome except in unusual cases. Thus, even the bar exam tends to focus on general principles, not idiosyncratic details, of contract law.

    ii.   **Don't ignore the differences.** One lesson you learn this year is to recognize how subtle changes in the statement of a rule might lead to different outcomes. Thus, when your casebook or other materials identify different ways to state the rule, pay attention. Materials gloss over many differences. When they identify a difference, it probably deserves your attention.

b.   **Federal decisions have less weight.** In many settings, federal decisions take precedence over state decisions. In contracts, state decisions often take precedence. To decide contract cases, federal courts often must interpret and apply state law. Their opinions about state law are not the final word; the state supreme court has final power over the interpretation of state law. There are exceptions.

    i.   **Contracts with the federal government.** The federal government has the power to make laws governing its own contracts. In fact, government contracts — federal, state, and local — are so different from private contracts that many law schools offer separate courses in that subject. Contracts courses usually focus on private contracts.

    ii.   **Federal statutes.** Modern interpretation of the Constitution has expanded the ability of Congress to regulate contracts. Thus, many newer statutes affect the validity of private contracts. When a federal statute is at issue, the interpretation of a federal court takes priority over that of a state court.

    iii.   **The U.S. Constitution.** Federal courts take priority in interpreting the United States Constitution. If a private contract raises a constitutional concern, federal courts have the final say.

2. Most Contracts Are Governed by Common Law

For centuries, legislatures paid relatively little attention to the way courts decided contract cases. The courts, not the legislatures, created rules governing private contract disputes and enforced those rules. Although legislatures recently have assumed a greater role, the common-law nature of contract law remains significant.

a. Judicial decisions are the law. Except when a statute has replaced the common law, judicial decisions **are** the law. Judges create the rules — or apply rules created by earlier judges. Judges can amend these (judge-created) rules when appropriate. Thus, the official statement of doctrine is a judicial opinion — either the one you read or one it cited as authority.

b. Legislation can supplant the common law. American government places the primary lawmaking power in the legislative branch of government. Common law does not alter legislative supremacy. Although courts have the authority to act without legislative guidance, the legislature gets the final say. **Once a legislature acts, the statute is the law.** Of course, a court must interpret the statute in order to apply it.

3. Uniform Commercial Code and Codification Generally

In the twentieth century, legislatures have increasingly codified the law. They have taken areas of law once governed by common-law judicial decisions and enacted statutes — sometimes endorsing, but often revising, the rules judges created. Statutes have become increasingly important in the law generally and contract law in particular. Article 2 of the Uniform Commercial Code (UCC) is the most important example of codification in contract law.

a. UCC governs in 49 states. Every state but Louisiana has adopted the UCC — though some states amended it in the process. The UCC is neither uniform nor universal. Nonetheless, the UCC has achieved such widespread and nearly uniform adoption that it is a very important statute — one studied (to some extent) in almost every course in contracts.

b. Article 2 of the UCC governs sales of goods. Most of the provisions studied in contracts courses come from Article 2 of the UCC. That article governs **one type of contract**: sales of goods.

    i. Goods are movable things. An item that is movable at the time it is identified to the contract is a good. This includes crops to be sold after harvest and the unborn young of animals. It excludes, however, money, securities, and other intangible items (e.g., insurance policies or lawsuits). See UCC §2-105.

    ii.   **Real estate and service contracts do not involve goods.** Article 2 does not apply to these two significant types of contracts. They remain subject to the common law. Thus, in some doctrines, different rules may apply depending on the nature of the transaction.

    c.   **State codification.**   Some state legislatures have enacted additional statutes. Some modify judicial decisions they find imperfect. Others, like California, enact statutes codifying the entire range of contract law. Thus, you will occasionally encounter statutes other than the UCC. These statutes, too, take priority over judicial decisions (at least in theory).

    d.   **International sales of goods.**   The United States has ratified the Vienna Convention on Contracts for the International Sale of Goods. That international treaty takes priority over the UCC or any federal statute. The treaty codifies rules that govern sales of goods whenever the parties' places of business are located in different countries. This treaty does not often arise in first-year contracts courses.

4. Restatements and Other Secondary Sources

Judicial decisions can be an unwieldy source of law. They require you to read a large number of pages to identify a rule that sometimes can be stated rather succinctly. (You need to read cases anyway, because they also show how courts apply the rule.) Secondary sources try to simplify the process by distilling succinct statements of law from judicial decisions.

    a.   **Secondary sources are not law.**   Secondary sources are efforts by learned people to present the law in a more accessible and coherent way. They try to repeat the law as accurately as possible. But they are not law. The statute or the judicial opinion is the law.

    b.   **Restatements.**   The most important secondary source for contract law is the Restatement (Second) of Contracts. This outline frequently cites it as authority, as do many casebooks. Restatements are compiled by the American Law Institute, a foundation composed of prominent judges, attorneys, and professors. These jurists identify the dominant doctrines (and sometimes trends) in state common-law decisions and summarize them in a succinct form. The result resembles statutes: a straightforward statement of a rule. The commentary and illustrations accompanying each section help explain the workings of the rules stated in the text of each section.

c. **Treatises.** Some prominent authors compile works that attempt to summarize and explain an entire field of the law. (Hornbooks are treatises prepared with law students in mind.) Treatises share the value of Restatements: the author has read the judicial opinions for you and distilled the rules. They differ from Restatements in several ways.

    i. **Treatises present the view of the author(s).** Restatements reflect the collective judgment of the American Law Institute. Treatises may reflect more idiosyncratic views. Authors can be more efficient or more insightful than committees. Authors can have blind spots or pet theories that committees or courts might not share.

    ii. **Treatises can present multiple views.** Restatements present the rule in each section. Authors can describe the differences among approaches, without endorsing any one approach.

    iii. **Treatises explain the rules more fully.** Restatements offer some historical and theoretical explanations for the rules they identify. Treatises tend to offer more thorough explanation and background of the doctrines they discuss.

d. **Outlines.** Outlines are secondary sources aimed exclusively at law students. They differ from treatises primarily in length. Outlines focus on classes, not practice; they focus on the approach most likely to be helpful in class discussion or on an exam.

e. **Primary sources are important.** You should learn the skill of identifying these rules without help from secondary sources. For your career, that skill is vital.

    i. **Gaps in secondary sources.** In practice, you frequently must address questions that secondary sources do not resolve, such as: issues too detailed for an overview; novel issues not yet resolved; issues related to a single state, not the general trend of American law; or topics on which no one has written a treatise. In these situations, you will need to discern the rule on your own. Secondary sources will be of little help.

    ii. **Persuasiveness of primary sources.** Courts find primary sources more persuasive than secondary sources. They rely more heavily on the law than on someone's description of the law.

Thus, when possible, you should cite the primary source (even if you read the rule and the citation in a secondary source).

f.   Secondary sources can be perilous.   Even the best secondary sources can be inaccurate. In repeating the rule, a source may alter it in a way that creates misimpressions. Statements intended to be read in many states cannot capture the idiosyncracies of every state. The author's perceptive insights may turn out to be poor predictions. Thus, recourse to the original material is vital to check the accuracy of the secondary source.

g.   Secondary sources are ubiquitous.   This outline, which is a secondary source, relies heavily on the Restatement (Second) of Contracts, another secondary source. The Restatement probably is the best effort at generalizing about contract law across the 50 states. Casebooks and professors rarely focus on the law of a single state. They, too, rely heavily on the Restatement. Knowing how the Restatement resolves an issue can be important at exam time.

B.   OVERVIEW OF CONTRACT DOCTRINE

This section provides a thumbnail sketch of contract law. It is not intended as a complete summary of the law. For review purposes, you should rely on the **Capsule Summary**. This section introduces contract concepts, providing background necessary to understand the doctrines as later chapters present them in detail.

1.   Contract Defined

A contract is a promise that the law will enforce (or that the law recognizes as creating a duty). Restatement (Second) of Contracts §1.

a.   Promise implies future conduct.   Contract law involves enforcing promises that have not yet been performed. Thus, when no time elapses between making a promise and performing it, contract law has little to say about that promise. But when a person changes her mind after making a promise, contract law governs whether that refusal to perform has legal consequences.

b.   Promise defined.   A promise is a manifestation of intention to act in a particular way, made in a manner that justifies another's belief that the promisor has committed herself to act in that way. Restatement (Second) of Contracts §2.

i.   No magic words.   A promise can exist without any formal invocation, either in words (such as ''I promise'') or form (such as a writing). Any words or conduct that signify a commitment will suffice.

ii. **Objective manifestations.** Contract law focuses on objective manifestations of intent—words or actions that others can observe. When words or actions differ from private thoughts (subjective intent), the objective manifestations usually take priority.

c. **Some promises are unenforceable.** As implied by the definition of contract, some promises will not be enforceable. Much of the course explores the circumstances in which a promisor should be allowed to refuse to perform without paying damages for the breach.

2. Contract Formation: Assent, Definiteness, and Consideration

Courts generally require assent, definiteness, and consideration before they will enforce a promise. Each serves a different purpose.

a. **Consideration.** Consideration limits enforceability to promises that are part of a bargained-for exchange. Thus, whereas business deals are enforceable many gift promises are not enforceable.

i. **Bargain requires an exchange.** Consideration exists when the promisor seeks something in exchange for the promise and the promisee gives that something in exchange for the promise.

(a) The something sought can be a promise or a performance. Thus, giving a promise in exchange for a promise makes both promises enforceable.

(b) A performance can be almost anything: action (e.g., delivering goods or performing services), inaction (e.g., refraining from a lawsuit), or changing a legal relationship (e.g., becoming the guardian of another).

ii. **Exceptions (reliance).** There are several exceptions to the bargain requirement, but reliance is the most important. People sometimes rely on promises even though the promises were not part of a bargain. Promisors sometimes should realize that others will rely on their promises. If the promisor can refuse to perform, the party who relied may suffer significant harm. When these three facts come together (**reliance** the promisor **should have expected** and that **harms the promisee**), courts often enforce the promise despite the lack of a bargain.

b. **Assent.**   Exchanges involve two (or more) parties. Assent limits en-
    forceability to situations in which both (or all) parties agree to the terms
    of the exchange. One party alone cannot create a legally enforceable
    contract without the agreement of all other parties to that contract.

    i.   **Offer and acceptance.**   Any manner of expressing assent usu-
         ally suffices. Traditionally, courts try to identify an offer by one
         party that the other party accepted.

    ii. **Mirror-image rule.**   Assent requires that the offer and accep-
         tance involve the same terms. If they differ, the parties have not
         yet assented to the same deal.   .

    iii. **Exceptions (reliance).**   Sometimes parties agree to some terms
         but continue to disagree on others. Courts sometimes enforce the
         agreement reached so far, especially if a party has begun per-
         forming or otherwise relied in a way that makes nonenforcement
         harmful to that party.

    iv. **Too late to change your mind.**   Much of assent concerns
         whether a party changed her mind before or after the contract
         was formed. Changing your mind before assent, if communi-
         cated, ends negotiations without a contract. Changing your mind
         after assent is a breach of contract, which was formed when the
         parties assented. Thus, the timeliness of an acceptance or a revo-
         cation can be critical.

c. **Definiteness.**   Definiteness limits enforceability to promises whose
    terms are clear enough for a court to enforce. If a court cannot tell
    what was promised, it cannot determine whether a party performed or
    breached (and probably cannot identify an appropriate remedy). Prom-
    ises too vague to permit these determinations are unenforceable.

d. **Requiring a writing: Statutes of fraud.**   Generally, **oral contracts are
    enforceable.** But for some important promises (e.g., sales of land),
    statutes prohibit enforcement unless the party who refused to perform
    has signed a writing that evinces the existence (and perhaps the terms)
    of the agreement. This rule makes it harder for a party to pretend a
    contract existed in the hope of misleading a jury. Problems with the
    statute have led courts to recognize numerous exceptions to the rule.

3. **Defenses: Unenforceable Bargains**

A number of promises are unenforceable even if they are part of a clearly
expressed bargain to which all parties assented. These defenses reflect cir-

cumstances under which the law concludes that at least one party should be allowed to change her mind after the fact. In most cases, the agreements are voidable, not void; that is, if the victim wants to enforce the contract instead of rescinding it, she may ratify the contract instead of disaffirming it.

a. **Incapacity.** Courts refuse to enforce contracts made by people who probably lack the mental acumen to make their own judgments about whether a contract will serve their interests. Thus, minors, the mentally ill, and the intoxicated receive special protection.

b. **Duress.** An agreement is unenforceable if obtained by use of improper threats that left the victim no reasonable alternative but to succumb to the pressure.

c. **Undue influence.** An agreement is unenforceable if obtained by the use of unfair persuasion — usually by one upon whom the victim depends, such as a relative or caretaker.

d. **Misrepresentation.** A victim need not perform a contract obtained by fraud and can recover any performance already given or rendered under such a contract. Statements that were innocent but incorrect may be so important that, despite the absence of fraud, courts will not enforce an agreement.

e. **Mistake.** Where one party enters an agreement because of a mistaken belief about a basic assumption of the transaction, the agreement is unenforceable unless that party bore the risk of the mistake. (That is, sometimes you must live with your mistakes, but sometimes courts will come to the rescue.)

f. **Unconscionability.** Some contracts are so unfair that courts cannot enforce them in good conscience. Usually, these agreements involve surprising terms to which a party did not realize she had agreed.

g. **Public policy.** Some contracts are unenforceable because they call for performances that violate public policy. For example, a party who paid a contract killer cannot sue for damages if the killer breaches the contract.

4. Performance and Breach

The existence of an enforceable promise is only the first step to establishing a right to recover damages for breach of contract. Disputes may arise concerning whether the performance lives up to the requirements of the contract. This will raise additional issues.

a. **Interpretation.** To decide whether a party breached or performed, a court must decide what a contract required. Although some contracts will be crystal clear, others may require recourse to various aids.

    i. **Express language** of a contract controls — including a provision in the contract concerning how the language is to be interpreted.

    ii. **Inferences regarding usage** may arise from the way the parties have used the language in the past or the way others in the same business use the language.

    iii. **Canons of construction.** These rules of thumb provide useful guidelines for how most parties use language. Courts resort to them if necessary.

    iv. **Gap fillers.** Courts sometimes fill gaps in a contract with terms of their own choosing **if** convinced that the parties really intended to enter a binding contract but simply failed to specify some detail of the performance.

    v. **Parol evidence rule.** Courts confronted with a clear and complete written agreement prefer to enforce the agreement as written. Thus, extrinsic evidence — particularly promises that were discussed during negotiations but not included in the final writing — may be excluded from consideration when interpreting the agreement.

b. **Conditions: Is performance due?** Some promises are conditional; that is, the promisor must perform only if a specified event happens. In deciding whether the failure to perform is a breach, courts must decide whether the condition occurred. If not, the time for performance has not yet arrived (or may never arrive). Failure to perform early is not breach; failure to perform when performance is due is a breach.

    i. **Express conditions.** The parties agree to some conditions in a contract. For example, a fire insurer agrees to pay the cost to repair or rebuild your home, but only if you suffer fire damage — a condition. Similarly, a wheat dealer may agree to pay for wheat, but only after delivery.

ii. **Implied conditions.** Courts treat some things as conditions even if the parties do not specify them in the agreement. For example, substantial performance and good faith are conditions upon the duty to perform. Thus, if the other party does not act in good faith (say, by interfering with your efforts to perform on time), your duty to perform may not arise.

c. **Material breach.** One implied condition is the other party's substantial performance. If, instead, the party commits a material (significant) breach of the contract, your duty to perform is suspended and may never arise.

   i. **Every breach allows a damage award.** Material breach helps decide whether you are allowed to stop performing and cancel the contract. It has nothing to do with your right to collect damages for a breach. Even if a breach is minor, you have a right to sue and to collect damages caused by that breach.

   ii. **Minor breaches do not justify cancellation.** When a party suffers no serious harm from a breach, she must continue to perform and satisfy herself with the right to collect damages later.

   iii. **Material breach justifies cancellation.** A party who wants to cancel a contract (perhaps to deal with another, more reliable (or cheaper) provider), may do so if the breach is material.

d. **Excusable nonperformance.** Courts recognize some legitimate excuses for the failure to perform when performance is due. Thus, even when a contract is valid and the performance is due, nonperformance may not equal breach.

   i. **Impracticability** recognizes that some intervening circumstances (such as fires, wars, or changed laws) may make performance so difficult that the parties probably would not have intended the contract to apply under these circumstances. Unless the agreement indicates otherwise, courts will excuse performance under these extenuating circumstances.

   ii. **Frustration** recognizes that some intervening circumstances (e.g., fires, wars, or changed laws) may make a performance so worthless to the recipient that the parties probably would not have intended the contract to apply under these circumstances. Unless the agreement indicates otherwise, courts will excuse performance under these extenuating circumstances.

e. **Repudiation.**   Sometimes, words or conduct may constitute a breach even before performance is due.

   i. **Express repudiation.** Statements constitute an immediate breach of the contract if they unequivocally indicate that a party intends to commit a material breach of the contract when performance is due. Instead of waiting helplessly for date of performance to arrive, a party may protect herself from the consequences of breach immediately.

   ii. **Implied repudiation.**   Conduct constitutes an immediate breach of contract if it makes performance on the date due seem impossible (e.g., selling the promised property to someone else). Instead of waiting helplessly for date of performance to arrive, a party may protect herself from the consequences of breach immediately.

C. FRAMEWORK FOR ANALYZING THE ENFORCEMENT OF PROMISES

The preceding overview does not include a discussion of the remedies available to a party who wins a lawsuit against a breaching party. These remedies were reserved for last because they are the most important part of this introduction. Remedies drive litigation: They are the destination, the rest of the lawsuit merely the route taken. You cannot plot a course until you determine the target. For students, however, remedies reveal an even more important fact. **Contracts is two courses, not one**. One course identifies how to win a suit for breach of contract and the remedies available when you do. But another course, hidden in the first, deals with other remedies, available to parties who cannot prove the other party breached an enforceable contract. These remedies (usually called restitution) come into play throughout the course. Thus, in studying contracts, the significant issue often revolves around **which remedy** to apply more than around **whether to apply a remedy** at all. This outline discusses remedies in detail in later chapters. The discussion here is introductory, not exhaustive.

1. Structure of Remedies

In almost every case of a broken promise, the law identifies an ideal situation (the rightful position the law seeks to restore), contrasts it with the existing situation, and imposes whatever remedy is appropriate to move from the existing situation to the ideal situation. Usually, the ideal situation is the situation that would have existed if the contract had been performed. But sometimes courts decide a party had a right not to perform the promise. In these situations, the ideal situation may be the situation that would have existed if the parties had never made the agreement at all. Once a court identifies the rightful position — the position that it feels should have resulted—it enters an award designed to move parties from the position they actually occupy to the rightful position. Note: The term "rightful position" is not intended to denote any sense of moral probity. It simply reflects the position the court believes should have come about if the dealings with regard to the contract had not been undermined—by breach, by fraud, or by other problems that led the relationship to break down.

2. Possible Responses to Broken Promises

This section introduces the various options courts have and summarizes how they use those options.

a. **Specific performance: Compelling the breaching party to perform.** Specific performance is an injunction, a court order requiring a person to do specified things, such as deliver goods or finish construction. Orders for specific performance require a party to perform as promised in the contract. A party who fails to comply with the court order can be held in contempt of court. Courts can punish contempt severely, including the imposition of prison terms, punitive fines, and coercive sanctions (e.g., fining the party, say, $1,000 per day until she performs as ordered or even jailing her until she performs as ordered).

 # EXAMPLES AND ANALYSIS

B promises to pay S $500,000 in exchange for a parcel of land on which S grows grapes and operates a winery. On the agreed date, B tenders the price, but S refuses to deliver a deed to the property. (B and S are common initials in contract hypotheticals. B often stands for buyer and S for seller. Although most professors do not try to confuse matters by reversing these initials, you should be careful not to assume that a person referred to as B [or whose name begins with B] is the buyer when the facts given on a problem indicate otherwise.)

If B sued S for breach of contract and requested specific performance, a court could order S to give B a deed to the property. S would need to pay for the property to receive the deed. If S refused to deliver the deed despite a court order, the court could send S to jail until she performed. (In practice, a court may sign a deed for S and order it recorded, without jailing S until she signed the deed.)

b. **Expectation damages: The financial equivalent of performance.** Damages based on the expectation interest seek to put the nonbreaching party, usually the plaintiff, in the position she would have occupied if the defendant had performed the contract. As with all damage remedies, the court accomplishes this goal by awarding the plaintiff money. Under the expectation interest, the amount of money awarded is calculated to allow the plaintiff to obtain the equivalent of the performance the defendant would have provided — though some limitations on remedies (studied later) may leave the plaintiff somewhat short of this ideal. In some cases, money will be exactly what the plaintiff would have received, as when the plaintiff was selling something to the defendant for money. In other cases, money will permit the plaintiff to buy a substitute for defendant's performance from some other provider, as when other goods of equal quality can be obtained in the market. **The promise made by the defendant provides the measure of relief. Damages should allow the plaintiff to obtain neither more nor less than what the defendant promised.**

i.   **Note on terminology.** This outline generally uses the word "plaintiff" to refer to the nonbreaching party and the word "defendant" to refer to the breaching party. In practice, the defendant may prevail on a counterclaim alleging that the plaintiff actually breached the contract. Acknowledging that possibility every time the word "plaintiff" appeared would complicate discussion without increasing the value of the lessons here. On an exam, you might need to consider whether the breaching party is the plaintiff or the defendant, depending on how the case arose in particular fact patterns. In this outline, however, the breacher will always be referred to as the defendant.

 # EXAMPLES AND ANALYSIS

B promises to pay S $500,000 in exchange for a parcel of land on which S grows grapes and operates a winery. On the agreed date, S tenders the deed, but B refuses to pay the agreed price. S puts the property back on the market, eventually selling it for $475,000.

S can recover $25,000 from B. That amount plus the $475,000 she received on the sale give her a total of $500,000 in exchange for the land — the amount B promised. This puts S in the position she would have occupied if B had performed. B may have incurred other losses that could be included in the recovery — for example, the cost to advertise the property for an additional few weeks. The details of calculating damages will be addressed in Chapters 20 and 21.

c. **Reliance damages.** Compensating for the detriment of breach. Damages based on the reliance interest in theory seek to put the plaintiff in the position she would have occupied if the defendant had not made the promise at issue. The amount of money awarded is calculated to compensate the plaintiff for anything she has lost because she relied on the defendant to perform. This may include amounts she paid to the defendant, amounts she paid to other people in preparation for the defendant's performance and (in theory but rarely in practice) opportunities that she could have accepted but did not accept because she believed the defendant would perform as promised. The goal is to compensate the plaintiff for the things she lost because of the promise rather than to provide the plaintiff with the benefit she expected if the promise had been performed. **Thus, the promise itself is not the measure of recovery. Recovery depends on what the defendant would have received or would not have lost if the defendant had not made the promise.**

EXAMPLES AND ANALYSIS

1. B promises to pay S $500,000 for two machines. In preparation for the arrival of the machines, B spends $5,000 to construct a stable platform on which to install the machines. S fails to deliver the machines.

B can recover the $5,000 she spent on construction. If S had not promised to sell the machines, B would not have spent $5,000 to build a foundation for them. The reliance interest often consists of adding up the expenses plaintiff incurred in pursuance of the contract; if no contract had been made, she would not have incurred those expenses.

2. R Co. promises to pay E $24,000 per year plus 10 percent of all sales made to work for the company as a sales agent. E quits her job with T Co. (which paid her $36,000 per year with no commission) and spends $3,000 to move to the city where R wants her to work. R refuses to honor the contract. E is unemployed for two months before finding another job on terms equal to those promised by R Co.

E can recover the $3,000 she spent moving to a new city. This assumes that if R had not promised her a job, E would not have moved. In addition, E probably can recover $6,000, two months' salary at the job she left in reliance on R's promise. If R had not promised her a job, E probably would have remained employed by T for those two months. This is one of the rare cases in which lost opportunities may be recoverable in addition to expenses incurred.

d. **Restitution: Preventing unjust enrichment.** Restitution seeks to restore the defendant to the position she would have occupied if she had not made the promise in the first place. Awards based on the restitution interest generally are <u>not referred to as damages at all</u>. Recovery does not depend on the amount that the plaintiff lost (the damage she suffered) but on the amount the defendant gained. The defendant must return any benefit she received because of the promise. Commonly, this amounts to returning to the plaintiff any money or other property that the plaintiff gave to the defendant. Sometimes the amount returned will exceed the amount originally given, as when the defendant managed to profit by holding, investing, or reselling money or property she received from the plaintiff. **The measure of recovery does not focus on the promise but on the defendant's enrichment, if any.** Plaintiff receives that amount as restitution even if it is more or less than the amount she lost or the amount that she would have received under the contract.

EXAMPLES AND ANALYSIS

1. B promised to pay S $1,000 for a television set, giving S $200 as a down payment. S sells the television to someone else and cannot obtain a substitute television satisfactory to B.

B can recover at least the $200 paid as a down payment. If the contract was enforceable, B might recover more under the expectation interest (for instance, if she spent more than $1,000 to buy a suitable television from another dealer). Restitution is limited, on these facts, to a refund. Restitution, however, would be available even if the promise was not enforceable. S may not need to deliver the television, but cannot keep the $200 down payment.

2. B promises to pay S $15,000 for flour to be delivered in New Orleans. B pays S $5,000 as a down payment. S fails to deliver the flour. On the day of delivery, B could go purchase flour from other vendors in New Orleans for $12,000.

B may recover the $5,000 down payment in restitution. B's expectation interest is only $2,000. If B purchased substitute flour for $12,000 and S paid B $2,000, B would be in the same position she would have occupied if S had performed. B, however, can recover the full $5,000 down payment under the restitution interest. *Bush v. Canfield*, 2 Conn. 485 (1818).

---

e. **Efficient breach versus disgorgement: Confiscating the benefits of breach.** In theory, a court could seek to restore the defendant to the position she would have occupied if she had performed the contract. This would require the court to calculate how much the defendant would have lost by performing the contract and to award that amount to the plaintiff. That basis for recovery has not been explicitly acknowledged by the courts. Nonetheless, some cases arise in which the disgorgement interest appears to explain the recovery better than any of the other interests described previously. *See* Examples and Analysis immediately following. More often, however, when the benefit to the defendant of breaching a contract is so great that the defendant would prefer to breach and to pay damages rather than to perform, courts award expectation damages to make the plaintiff whole and allow the defendant to keep any excess benefit. *See* the second Examples and Analysis that follows. Breaches of this nature have been called "efficient breaches," because the plaintiff is no worse off than if the contract had been performed (assuming courts measure damages appropriately) but the defendant is better off.

 # EXAMPLES AND ANALYSIS

1. W agrees to grow 100 acres of Sunflower seeds and deliver them to X for $10 per hundredweight. X promises to deliver to Y all the seeds X receives from W, at $11 per hundredweight. The price of sunflower seeds increases to $18 per hundredweight. W breaches and sells the seeds to Z at $18 per hundredweight.

The formula usually used to measure expectation—market price minus contract price plus incidental and consequential losses—would allow X to recover $8 per hundredweight from W. In this situation, that remedy seems excessive—more consistent with disgorgement than expectation. X's expectation interest appears to be limited to $1 per hundredweight—the profit it would make by reselling to Y. *See Tongish v. Thomas*, 840 P.2d 471 (Kan. 1992).

2. B promises to pay S $1,000 in exchange for a machine S will manufacture. S starts building the machine in its workshop but discovers that the machine will not fit through the door. S can deliver the machine only by tearing down a wall which will cost $2,000 to replace. B, however, can purchase an equally good machine from another shop for $1,200. S breaches.

S must pay B $200. B can buy the machine it needs at the same cost to B ($1,000 + $200 provided by S), while S saves $1,800 (minus expenses already incurred to start work on the machine) because S does not need to rebuild the wall. The court will not award B an additional $1,800 as disgorgement.

f. **Nominal damages.** In some cases, a breach of contract may leave the plaintiff no worse off than she would have been if the contract had been performed. In these situations, the law need not award any remedy at all to restore the plaintiff to her rightful position. Nonetheless, if the defendant breached a contract without excuse, the law will award a symbolic recovery — often one dollar — to the plaintiff. This recovery, called nominal damages, vindicates the plaintiff's meritorious claim but limits recovery to avoid enriching her (i.e., making her better off than if the contract had been performed).

3. **Choosing the Appropriate Response**

Courts apply the various remedies to different situations, depending on a number of factors. The most important factor is the enforceability of the promise. If a promise is enforceable, courts may employ any of the remedies noted previously. If a promise is not enforceable, courts generally limit themselves to restitution, though some award a reliance remedy.

a. **Action for breach of contract: Expectation interest and injunctive relief.** When a promise is enforceable, the plaintiff is entitled to receive what was promised. That usually means either specific performance — an injunction ordering performance — or the expectation interest — damages designed to give the plaintiff enough to replace the performance elsewhere. To establish an enforceable promise, the plaintiff must prove the elements of a cause of action for breach of contract. That requires plaintiff to establish the following:

   i. **The existence of a binding promise.** This element involves inquiries into mutual assent, consideration, and various defenses to contract formation that the parties might raise.

   ii. **That defendant, without excuse, failed to perform when performance was due.** This element involves inquiries into whether the defendant broke the promise at all and, if so, whether society should excuse the breach.

   iii. **The amount of loss plaintiff suffered as a result of the breach.** The plaintiff must demonstrate a loss caused by the breach. Usually this means showing that she would have been better off if the contract had been performed, establishing the expectation measure. But a plaintiff may elect to prove reliance damages by proving expenditures made in reliance on the contract or to seek a restitution recovery by showing the amount of unjust enrichment the defendant received under the contract.

b. **Recovery without an enforceable agreement: The restitution interest.** If a promise is not enforceable, damages based on expectation are not available. Because the defendant had no legal obligation to perform, she has no legal obligation to pay damages that are the equivalent of performance. In some of these cases, however, people have performed part of the promises before the unenforceability of the promise became apparent. In those cases, the refusal to grant any remedy might leave one party enriched at the expense of the other. When that enrichment would be unjust, courts intervene to prevent windfall gains by either party. In deciding whether unjust enrichment requires restitution, courts consider the following two elements:

i. **Did the defendant benefit from the promise or performance?** Benefits often involve defendant's receipt of partial performance from the plaintiff. Sometimes, however, promises can produce benefits that take more subtle forms — for example, when defendant's promise to buy certain property prevents a competitor from buying it or affects the market for defendant's stock.

ii. **Would it be unjust to allow the defendant to keep the benefit without paying for it?** Some benefits are justly retained — as when plaintiff intended the benefit as a gift to defendant or when plaintiff bestowed a benefit the defendant neither wanted nor requested. (If tomorrow morning you discovered someone painting your house, you should not be required to pay for that uninvited benefit.) In other situations, however, it may be unjust for the defendant to retain a benefit without paying for it.

 # EXAMPLES AND ANALYSIS

1. E agrees to work for R on a farm for one year, in exchange for $1,200 to be paid at the end of the year. After nine months, E quits without excuse. E can recover the value of any benefit bestowed on R during the nine months she worked there — minus any damages that R can recover because E breached the contract. R would be unjustly enriched if allowed to keep all the benefits of E's labor without paying something for the services. *Britton v. Turner*, 6 N.H. 481 (1834).

2. S threatens to harm B's family unless B promises to sell stock to S at a steep discount. B, unable to protect her family any other way, agrees to the terms. B delivers the stock to S and S pays for it. Later, after protecting her family, B sues S

seeking a return of the stock (or its value in money, if S no longer has the stock). B can recover the stock. Note: B must return the price S paid for the stock. B would be unjustly enriched if she could have both the stock and the money she received in exchange for the stock.

---

     c.   Imperfect actions for breach of contract: The reliance interest. Some cases fall between these two extremes. The case for enforcing the promise is imperfect, often because a close issue on some defense makes an award of the expectation interest seem excessive. On the other hand, a simple refund may not adequately protect a party who relied on a promise. In these in-between cases, the apparent justice of the plaintiff's claim leaves the court willing to allow some recovery, despite the court's unwillingness to allow the full expectation interest. These cases vary too much to allow any succinct statement of elements. However, two situations recur that can introduce the concept.

          i.   Uncertain expectation damages. Sometimes a plaintiff cannot demonstrate the amount of loss with sufficient certainty to allow the court to assess the expectation interest with any confidence. The plaintiff, however, usually can demonstrate the amount of her **expenses** with certainty. These expenses, made in reliance on the contract, offer a compromise between awarding full expectation and limiting recovery to restitution. Note: **The promises involved here are fully enforceable**. The defense does not negate defendant's obligation to perform the promise but challenges the value of that promise to the plaintiff.

 # EXAMPLES AND ANALYSIS

C, a construction contractor, promises to build a restaurant for R, who has never operated a restaurant before. B breaches the contract by finishing the building three months late. R spent $3,000 advertising the planned opening. That expenditure was wasted because of the delay. R, however, cannot prove how much, if anything, she would have earned during those three months or how much sooner the business would have become profitable if it had opened three months earlier.

R may recover the $3,000 wasted on advertising (plus any other demonstrable expenses wasted because of the delay). Courts do not allow speculation on the amount of lost profit, but will allow recovery of the relatively certain expenditures.

ii.   **Exceptions based on reliance.**   In several defenses, courts recognize exceptions when one party has relied on the promise. For example, even when a statute makes a promise unenforceable unless in writing, a court may enforce an oral promise if the plaintiff has relied on the promise. Similarly, courts enforce some promises without consideration if a party has relied on them. In each case, the promise does not fit the ideal of a legally enforceable promise. In deciding to enforce the promise anyway, courts sometimes limit the award to the reliance interest. This avoids the harm to the plaintiff who relied on the promise without fully requiring the defendant to perform or pay the equivalent in damages.

 # EXAMPLES AND ANALYSIS

1. O orally promised to sell O's home to B. In reliance on that promise, B paid a civil engineer $500 to inspect the home for defects and spent $300 for a fire insurance policy on the property. O, before signing any writing that mentioned the promise to sell the home, changed her mind and refused to sell to B.

B cannot recover the expectation interest; sales of land are unenforceable unless evinced by a writing signed by O — the party resisting enforcement. Nor has O received any benefit under the promise that would justify restitution. Courts, however, sometimes enforce promises despite the Statute of Frauds if one party has relied on the promise. Thus, a court probably would award B the $800 wasted because O refused to complete the transaction.

2. E moved to Hawaii because R allegedly promised him a job for one year. No writing signed by R mentioned the promise. R breached the contract by firing E after three months.

E cannot recover the salary promised for the rest of the year because the promise was not in writing — as required for promises that cannot be performed within a year. The court allowed E to recover the cost of moving to Hawaii, because E would not have relocated but for R's promise. E's reliance on the promise justified recovery, even though the statute precluded full enforcement of the promise (by awarding the expectation interest). *McIntosh v. Murphy*, 469 P.2d 177 (Haw. 1970).

PART 1 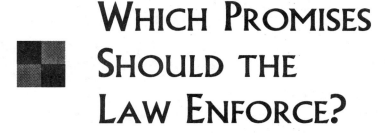 WHICH PROMISES SHOULD THE LAW ENFORCE?

Before addressing how the law selects which promises to enforce, you should focus on two assumptions embedded in this question.

First, contract law involves the enforcement of promises. This is inherent in the definition of a contract: "a promise or set of promises for the breach of which the law gives a remedy, or the performance of which the law in some way recognizes as a duty." **Restatement (Second) of Contracts §1.** This reveals two important aspects of contract law. Contract law revolves around people who (1) once wanted to do something, but (2) no longer want to do it. Immediate exchanges, such as buying a newspaper at a newsstand, pose little problem for contract law. No time elapses between the commitment to make an exchange and the completion of the exchange. Promises, however, involve a commitment to act in the future, leaving time in which one party may change her mind. The promise indicates that the defendant once wanted to act in a particular way. The fact that she has not performed suggests that she no longer wants to perform or, sometimes, cannot perform. Thus, the selection of which promises to enforce often involves societal decisions about when people should be allowed to change their minds without government intervention.

Second, the law enforces some, but not all, promises. Sometimes, society may believe that a person has a right to change her mind, that failing to perform a promise is acceptable behavior. Other times, society might disapprove of the breach but nonetheless conclude that the government should not intervene to enforce the promise. Part 1 of this Outline identifies those circumstances in which society believes a person should perform and is willing to stand behind that judgment with government intervention to correct matters if the person fails to perform.

FORMATION: PROMISES, ASSENT (OFFER AND ACCEPTANCE), AND DEFINITENESS

CHAPTER OVERVIEW

- A **contract** is a **promise** the law will enforce.
- A **promise** is an expression of intention to act made in a way that justifies others in believing the promisor is committed to perform.
    - Words spoken in **jest** can be promises if a reasonable observer would not recognize the lack of commitment.
    - Words that retain unbridled discretion for the party to refuse to perform are not a promise but are **illusory**.
    - Conditional promises are enforceable, not illusory, if they limit a party's discretion to withdraw from the transaction.
- Bargains are enforceable from the time both parties **assent** to the agreement.
    - **Assent** consists of an **offer** made by one party and **accepted** by another.
    - Offers may be accepted only while they remain **open**.
- An **offer** terminates (and can no longer be accepted):
    - At the time specified in the offer or after a reasonable time lapses;
    - When the offeree rejects the offer or makes a counteroffer;
    - When either the offeror or the offeree dies or becomes incapacitated; and
    - When the offeror revokes the offer — even if she promised to keep the offer open longer — except:
- Revocation of an offer is ineffective if the offeror promised to keep it open and:
    - The offeree gave consideration for the promise, creating an **option** contract;
    - A statute makes the promise irrevocable without consideration; or
    - The offeree relied on the promise in a way the offeror should have expected and justice requires treating the offer as irrevocable.
- Only the offeree may accept an offer.
    - An offeree can accept an offer only if she knows of its existence.

- Acceptance must comply with the requirements of the offer:
  - — The offer may specify the manner in which the offeree must signify acceptance. For instance, some offers (called **unilateral contracts**) can be accepted only by full performance.
  - — Acceptance may be ineffective if it alters or supplements any term of the offer (the **mirror-image rule**).
  - — Some acceptances varying the terms of an offer are valid acceptances containing proposals for modifying the contract.
- A contract must contain terms that are sufficiently **definite** to allow the court to identify a **breach** and formulate an appropriate **remedy**.
- When the parties intend a binding agreement but omit a term, a court may **fill the gap** in the agreement by supplying a **default term**.
- Negotiations leading up to a formal agreement can produce binding **preliminary agreements**.
- Parties who enter an agreement may be bound even if they intended to memorialize an agreement in writing but never finished the writing.

A.   PROMISE

A contract is a promise the law will enforce. Naturally, identifying the promise is the first step in deciding whether an enforceable promise exists. Before evaluating assent to a promise, one must identify a promise.

1.   Note re Consideration

A party may challenge the existence of a promise in either of two settings. A defendant may claim that she made no promise and, thus, did not breach a promise. Alternatively, a defendant may admit that she made a promise but may claim that her promise was not enforceable because the plaintiff made no promise in exchange. (As noted in the introductory chapter, consideration is either a promise or a performance. If the plaintiff has not performed, only a promise to perform would constitute consideration.) **The rules defining a promise are the same in each context.** They are addressed here (even though you have not yet had a chance to study consideration in detail) because promise is the foundation of contract law. Having read the first chapter's introduction to consideration, you should be able to follow the discussion without difficulty.

2.   Promise Defined

The Restatement (Second) of Contracts §2 defines promise as "a manifestation of intention to act or refrain from acting in a specified way, so made as to justify a promisee in understanding that a commitment has been made." This definition includes several components.

a. **Promises must be manifest.**   Words and actions can constitute promises; unexpressed intentions cannot.

b. **No magic words available.**   Children often say they will do something, but when necessary plead "I didn't **promise**." The law does not draw this distinction. Words that indicate a commitment to act are a promise, even if not preceded by the incantation "I promise." An offhand remark, however, may not indicate commitment.

c. **Words resembling promises may fall short.**   Some words and actions superficially resemble promises but fail to express commitment. Generally, two situations arise in which the promissory effect of the words may be negated by other circumstances: when the promisee should realize that the words are spoken in jest and when conditions on the promise negate commitment.

3. Jest

A party would not be justified in believing a commitment had been made if she understood that the promisor spoke in jest. Words, taken literally, might constitute a manifestation of assent. But tone of voice, facial expressions such as winks, and gestures such as crossing one's fingers may affect the reasonable interpretation of the words. **If these indications would warn a reasonable observer that the promisor did not intend a commitment, the words or actions do not constitute a promise.**

a. **Promisee understood or should have understood.**   The fact that the promisor **intended** to jest does not negate a promise. The promisor must include in her words or actions some indication that should alert the promisee to the jest. **If a reasonable person observing the transaction would have believed that the promisor was serious, not jesting, then a promise exists: The promisee justifiably could understand that a commitment had been made.**

b. **Example (Lucy v. Zehmer, 84 S.E.2d 516 (Va. 1954)).**   Lucy offered to buy a farm from the Zehmers for $50,000. The Zehmers, apparently believing Lucy was bluffing, agreed. Mr. Zehmer wrote the agreement on the back of a receipt from the bar where they were drinking; both he and his wife signed it. Lucy took the writing and offered the Zehmers $5 to seal the deal. Zehmer then realized Lucy was serious and told Lucy that he had no intention of selling the farm. Lucy sued. The trial court dismissed the suit. The appellate court reversed, ordering the trial court to grant Lucy specific performance of the contract. Because Zehmer's conduct did not give Lucy any reason to know that Zehmer was joking (until after the agreement was concluded), Lucy justifiably believed Zehmer entered a commitment to sell the farm.

    i.   **Was Lucy joking?** The court did not discuss Zehmer's belief that Lucy was joking. This would be important if Zehmer sued to collect the $50,000 and Lucy claimed to have entered the agreement in jest. Lucy, however, made no effort to avoid performing his promise.

    ii. **A consideration argument.** The Zehmers could have argued that they received no consideration for their promise because Lucy made no promise. If they had, it would matter whether the Zehmers had reason to believe Lucy was joking. (If Lucy was joking and the Zehmers had reason to know of the jest, Lucy's words would not constitute a promise and, thus, could not be consideration.) The Zehmers' lawyers may have overlooked this characterization of Lucy's conduct. Alternatively, maybe Lucy's conduct would not have led a reasonable person to believe that he was joking. If so, the Zehmers' contention that they thought Lucy was joking may resemble a desperate attempt to escape from an agreement they now regret by recharacterizing Lucy's words as jest, even though Lucy made no indication that he was jesting.

 # EXAMPLE AND ANALYSIS

Suppose the Zehmers had accepted $5 from Lucy before they realized he was serious. Would the outcome be any different?

Once accepted by Zehmer, the $5 payment would be part performance by Lucy. Full performance can be consideration even without a promise. Starting performance can be interpreted as a promise to complete performance—a point discussed later in this chapter. *See* 2.F.6. The issue will turn on how a reasonable person would have interpreted the ambiguous act of paying $5. Paying $5 could be an extension of the jest (let's watch him squirm if he thinks we might have been serious!) or it could be evidence that Lucy was in fact serious all along.

    c. **Promisee's failure actually to understand may not matter.** If a reasonable person would have understood that the promisor was joking, the fact that a dense or inattentive promisee did not discern the jest will not convert the jest into a promise. The promisee would not be **justified** in understanding that a commitment had been made, even though she sincerely may believe that the promisor made a commitment. The promisor whose conduct would alert a reasonable person to the jest has done all that she reasonably needed to do to avoid making an enforceable promise.

    i.   **Objective standards common.**   What an individual subjectively believed often will not matter if the party should have realized the truth based on objective manifestations sufficient to dispel the belief in a reasonable person. This distinction will recur throughout contract law.

    ii.   **Subjective knowledge affects the objective standard.** The promisee cannot justifiably rely on the existence of a commitment when she actually knows the other party is jesting. Her knowledge may derive from clues too subtle for a reasonable observer to recognize or from the promisee's personal knowledge about the promisor's idiosyncracies that an observer might not share. Still, a promisee who actually recognizes the jest cannot justifiably rely on the existence of a commitment.

d. **Restitution.** A promisee who acts in reliance on an unjustified belief that the promisor made a commitment may be entitled to restitution. For example, in *Keller v. Holderman*, 11 Mich. 248 (1843), defendant gave plaintiff a check for $300 in exchange for a watch worth $15. The check bounced but defendant kept the watch. Defendant successfully argued that the agreement had been a jest, not a serious agreement to pay $300 for the watch. Plaintiff was entitled to the return of the watch.

e. **Evidentiary obstacles.** Some of the subtle issues raised by jest can pose severe evidentiary obstacles. Only the person actually knows whether she was in fact jesting or in fact recognized the jest. But at the time a lawsuit arises, that person's testimony may be shaded by self-interest, either intentionally or unintentionally (via selective perception or selective retention).

    i.   If Lucy really was jesting when he offered to buy a farm from the Zehmers, he might not admit it in court now that he wants to enforce the agreement. Without Lucy's admission, the Zehmers will have difficulty proving that Lucy really was jesting.

ii. If a promisee with personal knowledge of a promisor's quirks recognizes a jest when any other observer would believe the promisor was serious, the promisee who wants to enforce the promise might not admit that she actually knew the promisor was jesting. Without an admission, the promisor may have difficulty proving that the promisee actually recognized the jest.

iii. **Evidentiary difficulties help explain why the law prefers to consider the objective manifestations of intention.**   The problems would be compounded if the outcome turned on what the promisor actually intended instead of what the promisee justifiably believed the promisor intended based on her words and actions. Actual intent is even harder to prove than the manifestations of intent. Nonetheless, the objective rules described here may not avoid all difficulties of proof that can arise in arguing about the effect of a jest—or any other doctrine where intention is at issue.

4. Illusoriness or Conditional Promises

Some promises contain the seeds of their own negation. For example, a promisee hearing the words "I promise to buy your property if I still feel like it when the time comes" could not understand that a commitment had been made—at least not justifiably. The problem stems from the condition placed on the promise: The words following "if" (or, in other circumstances, "unless") indicate that, under some circumstances, the promisor will not perform in the manner specified in the promise. Some conditions—but not all conditions—negate commitment.

a. **Effect of illusoriness.**   Illusoriness prevents enforcement of duties under an agreement. The party whose words were illusory made no promise, so there is no promise to enforce. The other party received no promise, thus no consideration existed that would justify enforcing her promise. Thus, either party could refuse to perform and defend a suit for breach on the ground that illusoriness defeated the contract.

i. **Illusoriness may frustrate expectations.**   Some parties who intend to enter binding contracts may create illusory promises instead of actual promises. This can happen by inartful drafting or by including conditions that, although sensible for some purposes, are stated too broadly. If the agreement later proves disadvantageous to one party, she may try to escape from her obligations by raising illusoriness as a defense. Refusing to enforce the agreement may deny the other party the benefits she realistically expected under the transaction.

   ii. **Inconsistent cases.** Courts walk a tightrope. No enforceable contract can exist without a promise. But overzealous application of illusoriness might prevent enforcement of agreements that seem to deserve enforcement. Thus, courts often are reluctant to deny enforceability on the ground of illusoriness — particularly when a party who intended to make a binding commitment tries to use a technical defect in the promises to avoid the transaction.

  b. **Illusoriness defined: Unbridled discretion to withdraw.** If the promisor remains completely free to change her mind about the deal, any commitment is illusory and no promise exists. A promise involves commitment. A promisor who can withdraw from the transaction on a whim without paying damages for breach has made no commitment.

EXAMPLE AND ANALYSIS

Mr. Sheffield, the husband of Strong's niece, bought Strong's business on credit but failed to make payments when due. Strong obtained a promissory note from the Sheffields in which Mrs. Sheffield (who owned her own successful business) agreed to pay the debt if Mr. Sheffield defaulted. In return, Strong promised "I will not pay that note away; I will not put it in any bank for collection, but I will hold it until such time as I want my money." After a time, Strong sued Mrs. Sheffield on the guaranty. *Strong v. Sheffield*, 39 N.E. 330 (N.Y. 1895).

 1. **The issue involved consideration.** Mrs. Sheffield argued that her promise to pay could not be enforced because Strong made no promise in exchange for it.
 2. The court held that Strong's promise not to demand payment "until I want my money" did not limit his discretion at all; he could have demanded payment and sued on the note the day it was signed. Although a promise to forbear would constitute consideration, Strong did not **promise** forbearance and, thus, did not make any commitment that could serve as consideration for Mrs. Sheffield's promise as guarantor.

   i. **Value of conditional promises.** Conditions can serve useful business purposes: They allow parties to consider the possibility that circumstances might change in unexpected ways and to specify whether the contract should be performed if those changes occur. If conditions always negated commitment, the parties could not provide for these contingencies; including a condition would make the agreement unenforceable even if the condition occurred.

ii.   **Conditional promises generally bind.**   Almost any limit on the promisor's ability to change her mind may satisfy the requirements of a commitment. As long as the promisor remains bound to perform under some circumstances, the fact that other circumstances would permit the promisor not to perform does not negate the commitment.

iii.   **Promisor's control over condition.**   Few cases of illusoriness involve obvious reservations of a right to withdraw at will. Rather, the promises contain conditions that seem reasonable but that may allow a party to withdraw from the deal by exerting control over whether the condition occurs. When the promisor cannot cause the condition to occur or prevent it from occurring, the promisor lacks any ability to change her mind. The more control the promisor retains over the occurrence of the condition, the more scrutiny you need to use in deciding whether a commitment ever existed.

(a)   **Contingencies outside parties' control.**   When the contingency is outside the influence or control of both parties, neither can use the contingency to avoid performing merely because she changed her mind. For example, a fire insurer promises to pay the insured's loss if a fire damages her home. The promise is conditional; the insurer will pay if and only if a fire occurs. Even if the insurer changes her mind, there is little she can do to prevent a fire (and thus prevent her obligation to pay from arising). The promisee justifiably can understand that the insurer is committed from the moment the agreement is made.

(b)   **Contingencies parties may influence.**   A contingency within the influence, but not the control, of at least one party poses a closer case but usually will not be illusory. For example, if a farmer promised to sell wheat to a silo "unless the government lifts the embargo on sales of wheat to Iraq," either party could write to Congress in an effort to influence legislation on the embargo. A buyer or seller with significant influence might even affect the outcome. Still, the promisor cannot simply change her mind and withdraw from the deal. She will be bound unless the condition occurs, an event she cannot control at will.

(c) **Contingencies promisor may control.** Some conditions allow the promisor considerable control over whether the condition occurs. In these situations, the promisor who changes her mind can simply cause the condition to occur and, thus, prevent any duty to perform from arising.

 ## EXAMPLE AND ANALYSIS

De Los Santos entered into a "hauling contract" in which he promised to haul "such tonnage of beets as may be loaded by the Company" at rates and for a period of time specified in the agreement. Before the period expired, Great Western told De Los Santos that they no longer required his services. De Los Santos sued for breach. The court held that there was no contract because the company retained absolute discretion whether to load beets on the plaintiff's trucks, never committing to load any particular quantity. *De Los Santos v. Great Western Sugar Co.*, 348 N.W.2d 842 (Neb. 1984).

1. **Identify the condition.** Great Western promised to pay De Los Santos for hauling beets, but **only if** it loaded beets on De Los Santos' trucks. Great Western could choose not to load beets at whim. The lack of commitment negated the existence of a promise — though once beets were loaded, mutual promises existed regarding those beets.
2. De Los Santos was not bound by the contract either; he could quit at any time (between loads). Because Great Western had made no promise, there was no consideration to make a promise by De Los Santos binding.

      iv. **Oxymoron: partial illusoriness.** If part of an agreement was not illusory, courts could enforce that part. A promise existed: The law can enforce it and treat it as consideration for a return promise.

 ## EXAMPLE AND ANALYSIS

O agrees to sell a building to B in exchange for $50,000 plus one-third of the rent received during the first five years after sale. B decides not to rent any space in the building during that five years.

The contract is not illusory. B arguably retained complete discretion to prevent any rents from accruing to O. That part of the promise arguably is illusory. (O still has a card to play; keep reading.) But B's promise to pay $50,000 is an unconditional commitment; B has no ability to withdraw from that part of the deal. Thus, a promise exists. The law can enforce it and can treat it as consideration for O's promise.

    c.   **Implied promises and illusoriness.**   Courts often find that agreements include more promises than those expressly stated by the parties. Some statutes impose additional duties, even if the parties did not agree to them expressly. When an implied promise creates a commitment, the agreement is enforceable even if the expressed words, standing alone, would have been illusory.

        i.   **Obligation of good faith and fair dealing.**   The UCC and the common law both infer that every contract includes a promise to act in good faith. UCC §1-203; Restatement (Second) of Contracts §205. The obligation to act in good faith may limit a party's ability to withdraw from the transaction, despite a condition that arguably would permit the party to withdraw at will.

EXAMPLE AND ANALYSIS

Plaintiff wanted to buy defendant's land for a shopping center. Defendant agreed to sell under a contract that contained a condition allowing plaintiff to back out of the transaction if unable to locate "satisfactory" leases. Defendant later reneged, arguing that the satisfaction clause gave plaintiff the right to change his mind at will. *Mattei v. Hopper*, 330 P.2d 625 (Cal. 1958).

The court held that the agreement included a promise by plaintiff to use good faith in deciding whether the leases were satisfactory. If the plaintiff refused to go forward even if he found leases that satisfied his good faith requirements, that would constitute breach. Because plaintiff did not have complete discretion to change his mind, a commitment existed that served as consideration for the defendant's promise.

        ii.   **Reasonableness versus good faith.**   The *Mattei* court noted an alternative test when goods can be evaluated according to an objective standard. Evidence that a reasonable merchant would have found the goods satisfactory might suffice to hold that rejection by the plaintiff constituted breach, not the failure of the condition. The court did not apply this test to leases because they contain many variables to which different landlords reasonably may attach different degrees of importance. The satisfaction clause permitted the plaintiff to use his own judgment (in good faith); it did not require him to accept unsatisfactory leases merely because some other developers might have found them satisfactory.

iii. **Other implied promises.** Sometimes the parties' agreement contains terms that, taken together, clearly indicate that an additional promise was part of their bargain: not the bargain the court wishes the parties had made but the bargain the parties actually made (but did not completely express in writing).

 # EXAMPLES AND ANALYSIS

Lady Duff-Gordon gave Wood an exclusive license to place her endorsement on fashions. In exchange, Wood was to receive half of all revenues from endorsements. Lucy breached by placing endorsements herself or through other agents. Wood sued for half of the revenues from those other endorsements. Lady Duff-Gordon argued that because Wood had not promised to seek or to obtain any endorsements, he had made no commitment that would serve as consideration to make her promise enforceable.

The court held that the agreement included an implicit promise by Wood to make reasonable efforts to obtain endorsements for Lady Duff-Gordon. By interpreting the agreement this way, the court found that Wood had made a commitment and, therefore, that Lady Duff-Gordon's promise was enforceable. *Wood v. Lucy, Lady Duff-Gordon*, 118 N.E. 214 (N.Y. 1917).

5. Illusoriness in Requirements and Output Contracts

Some contracts contain imprecise specifications of the quantity involved. Requirements contracts specify that one party will purchase all its requirements for a certain item from the other party (and that the other party will supply as much as the first requires). Output contracts specify that one party will sell the entire quantity that it produces of an item to the other party (and that the other party will buy all that the first produces). These are useful for producers who want a guaranteed supplier or buyer but who cannot predict their requirements or output with certainty. For example, agricultural contracts often specify "all of the [crop] grown on 175 acres" (specifically identified in the contract). Coal mines may promise to supply all the coal the power plant needs (or the plant promises to buy all the coal the mine can produce). These contracts arguably produce a problem with illusoriness. Today, their enforceability has been recognized.

a. Requirement contracts.   A buyer agrees to buy all of a particular good or service that she needs from one seller. That promise implicitly includes a promise not to buy the good from any other seller. Because the quantity is not specified, **the buyer arguably retains the right to buy none of the good**. This is true if the buyer actually needs none of the good. But the buyer cannot pretend not to need the good to avoid the contract, because she cannot buy the good from others. If she does, she has breached a promise to buy all of her needs from this seller.

b. Output contracts.   A seller agrees to sell all of a particular good or service that she produces to one buyer. (Lawyers hired by a law firm typically promise the firm all the legal work they do; thus, they cannot siphon off clients for their own private account.) The **seller appears to retain discretion not to perform simply by not producing any of the good involved**. But the seller cannot produce the good and sell it to anyone else, because all that she does produce has been promised to the buyer. Because the seller's discretion is limited, she is committed and the promise is not illusory.

c. Good faith.   In either situation, courts could interpret the agreement to include a promise to make production or requirement decisions in good faith. See UCC §2-306.

  i. Application.   If the buyer (in a requirements contract) or the seller (in an output contract) decided on a quantity of zero, the court could inquire whether the decision was made in good faith. A buyer who really does not need any of the good or a seller who really does not want to produce any of the good has not breached. But a party who really needs or wants to produce the good cannot escape the contract (and thus deal with a different contract partner) by pretending she has no needs or no output.

EXAMPLE AND ANALYSIS

Seller promised to provide all of buyer's requirements of cardboard used for boxes in which to ship its glass. Buyer stopped producing glass because uneconomical.

Thus, it did not need cardboard for shipping glass. The court held the requirements were zero and did not permit an inquiry into the buyer's reasons for closing the factory except to determine whether it was a ruse to evade the contract. Once it determined that buyer had no need for boxes, it did not inquire into whether buyer should have continued to produce glass so that it could continue to buy seller's boxes. *Fort Wayne Corrugated Paper v. Anchor Hocking Glass*, 130 F.2d 471 (3d Cir. 1942).

---

ii. **Excessive requirements.** Good faith has more bite when a party demands too much performance. A buyer in a requirements contract might pretend to need a huge amount of the good, hoping that the seller cannot meet the demand. Seller's breach might allow the buyer to cancel the contract and buy its supply elsewhere. A request that exceeds the amount that the buyer really needs breaches the promise to act in good faith.

   (a) **Excessive output rarer.** This problem is possible, but less likely, in an output contract. Rarely will a seller be able to pretend that she has a huge output, hoping the buyer will refuse to accept delivery, a breach that might justify cancellation. (If other buyers will pay more for the goods — the primary reason a seller would want to cancel the contract — this buyer might accept them, planning to resell them. Thus, the bluff may backfire. The same problem could affect requirements contracts, but a buyer can get a loan to pay for the excessive output more easily than a seller can increase production dramatically.) The reciprocal problem — pretending that output is very low — is similar to pretending the output is zero. If seller sells any goods to another buyer, she breaches the promise to sell the entire output to this one buyer.

   (b) **UCC prohibits excessive demands.** A party need not perform if the other tenders or demands a quantity grossly disproportionate either to estimates or to prior performance under the contract. UCC §2-306. The test is objective, not dependent on good faith.

   (c) **Not illusory.** The ability to produce or to demand too much is not the ability to back out of the deal. Thus, the absence of a specific quantity would not make the agreement illusory.

EXAMPLE AND ANALYSIS

M owns a paper factory. P, a printer, agreed to buy all the paper it required from M and M agreed to sell all the paper P required at a specified price. In the third year of the contract, P's business experienced a tremendous increase in its need for paper. P thus asked M to supply four times as much paper as P had ordered in the previous year. M agreed to deliver 120 percent of last year's deliveries but refused to deliver the full amount P ordered. May P sue M for breach?

Under the UCC, P cannot demand a grossly disproportionate deliveries, even though P really needs the entire amount ordered. Four times previous deliveries is so disproportionate that M's failure to deliver that amount cannot be taken as a breach. Thus, P cannot cancel the contract. Nonetheless, P probably can fill any needs that M fails to fill by buying paper from other sources, despite the promise to buy only from M. P must continue to buy from M as much as M can supply. But if M cannot meet the need, P probably is free to fill additional needs elsewhere.

---

    d.   Best efforts.   An exclusive dealing contract makes at least one party dependent on the other party's efforts. If the other fails to produce sufficient business, the party who cannot deal with anyone else suffers. In these circumstances, the UCC assumes that the contract requires more than good faith; it requires best efforts. UCC §2-306(2).

       i.   Exclusive dealings.   An agreement that requires one person to buy or sell exclusively to another requires the exclusive agent to use her best efforts—unless the agreement expressly provides otherwise. Thus, if a buyer agrees to purchase exclusively from the seller, the seller must use best efforts to supply the goods. If a seller agrees to sell exclusively to (or through) the buyer, the buyer must use best efforts to promote the sale (or resale) of the goods.

       ii.   One-way exclusivity.   Exclusivity need not work both ways. For instance, a small buyer might agree to buy exclusively from a large seller. The seller could retain the right to sell to others, even though the buyer had no right to buy from others. Similarly, a small seller might sell exclusively to one large buyer, even though the buyer purchased from many such small suppliers.

       iii.   Protection for the limited party.   The rule protects the party who must deal exclusively with the other. Because that party cannot deal with anyone else, her benefits under the contract depend on the other party's efforts. See, e.g., *Tigg v. Dow Corning*, 962 F.2d 1119 (3d Cir. 1992).

 # EXAMPLE AND ANALYSIS

G, who owns a gasoline station, promises to buy all its gasoline from M, a major oil company. M, which sells to many other stations, does not promise to sell exclusively to G. M has a duty to use best efforts to supply fuel to G, even if the contract does not mention this duty. G has an obligation to act in good faith but would not owe M a duty to use best efforts to promote the sale of gasoline (unless the contract mentioned that duty).

Contracts of this sort can be exclusive in both directions if M promises not to sell its gasoline to anyone else in the same territory as G. (The contract would define the territory—for instance, a two-mile radius of G's location.) If so, G also would owe M a duty to use her best efforts to promote the sale of M's gasoline within that territory.

---

    iv. **Two-way protection.** Some courts impose an obligation of best efforts on both parties if either one has an obligation to deal exclusively with the other. This effectively requires **both** parties in **every** requirement or output contract to use best efforts.

 # EXAMPLES AND ANALYSIS

Seller promised to sell all the bread crumbs it produced to buyer. The seller discontinued production of bread crumbs as "uneconomical." The court held that the seller still could be liable for breach if its decision was not made in good faith. *Feld v. Henry S. Levy & Sons*, 335 N.E.2d 320 (N.Y. 1975). Smaller profits than expected would not justify discontinuance; actual losses would, if "more than trivial." Thus, seller might need to continue to produce crumbs at a loss (or pay buyer's damages for having to pay more to other sellers). While the result is defensible, the court took odd steps along the way.

    1. The court cited UCC §2-306 as if seller had an obligation to use its best efforts to supply buyer with bread crumbs. The output contract precluded

seller from selling crumbs to others; it did not prevent buyer from buying crumbs from others. Thus, poor efforts by buyer would leave seller with no market; poor efforts by seller would not prevent buyer from obtaining a supply elsewhere. The court's reasoning purports to apply a good faith test—the proper standard. Mentioning the best efforts test is odd.

2. The court noted that seller took no steps to obtain more economical equipment for producing crumbs. This is pertinent under a best-efforts test but good faith requires an honest decision (under UCC §1-201(19)) that comports with reasonable commercial standards of the trade (UCC §2-103, applicable here because seller was a merchant). Not buying new equipment hardly seems dishonest or a breach of trade standards. The court, however, did not rely on this fact in its conclusion.

3. The court did not evaluate the seller's decision against the definition of good faith: honesty and reasonable commercial standards. That may be proper because the court merely denied summary judgment and remanded the case for trial. Yet without mentioning the standard, it is hard to see how the court could decide that an issue of fact remained for the jury to resolve.

4. The contract provision allowing cancellation may imply the parties really intended to limit the seller's ability to shut down an unprofitable part of its business while the contract remained in force. The court's reliance on good faith, however, is harder to endorse.

B. DEFINITENESS (OR CERTAINTY)

Definiteness is a requirement of a contract, technically equal to assent and consideration. This exaggerates the practical importance of definiteness. **Courts will not enforce an indefinite contract. But courts have developed many ways to find definiteness even when the parties themselves have left matters open.** These techniques mean that few contracts actually fail for want of definiteness.

1. Terminology: Definiteness versus Certainty

Sometimes people say a contract must be certain, rather than definite. This risks confusion with the damage rule requiring that losses be proven with reasonable certainty. See 20.E.4. These rules are quite different and should be kept distinct. "Definiteness" is a more useful word in discussing the terms proposed or agreed. On an exam, however, use the language that your professor prefers.

2. The Rule

Terms are definite if they provide a basis for determining whether a breach has occurred and for giving an appropriate remedy. Restatement (Second) of Contracts §33(2). The rule has two rationales.

a. **No offer.** Indefinite terms make it seem unlikely that the parties had concluded their negotiations. An offer may not exist if the terms are vague; because important points remain unsettled, a reasonable person could hardly believe that her assent would conclude the transaction. (For the definition offer, see 2D.) Thus, indefinite terms make the talks seem more like preliminary negotiations, where the other party expects to have a further opportunity to assent before a deal is concluded.

b. **No possible solution.** As a practical matter, a court cannot resolve a controversy unless the contract offers some guidance regarding what the parties promised. Even if the parties clearly intended the vague terms to be a contract, the court cannot enforce it unless it can tell the difference between performance and breach. Thus, when no basis for identifying a breach or a remedy exists, courts cannot act.

3. **Identifying the Performance Required by the Contract**

When the parties' words or actions signify that they intended a contract, modern courts will do all they can to discover the terms of the contract and to enforce those terms. Courts are reluctant to allow one party to withdraw from what the parties believed was a contract by arguing that some obscure term had not been settled completely. Thus, when reasonable means exist to identify the parties' obligations, even when the agreement is silent or obscure, courts employ them.

a. **Interpreting the agreement.** Often, a little effort to discern the parties' meaning will permit the court to identify the promises made. The specific techniques of interpretation are discussed in subsequent chapters. See Chapters 12–14. They include resolving ambiguities by examining how the parties (or other parties in the same trade) have acted under similar contracts in the past.

b. **Supplying missing terms.** On some occasions, uncertainty arises because the parties omitted a term. For example, the parties might specify price and quantity but neglect to state when delivery or payment should occur. These terms may not negate the existence of assent. Conduct or fair inference from the language may show that the parties intended a fully binding agreement. But the court nonetheless must decide whether delivery or payment is late — or, in some cases, which should occur first. Though initially reluctant to make a contract for the parties, courts (often encouraged by legislation) have begun to fill these gaps in the contract.

   i. **UCC default terms.** The UCC specifies a number of default terms: terms that apply to all contracts for the sale of goods unless the parties specify a different term. See UCC §2-204; see also UCC §§2-305 to 2-315 (specific default terms). The drafters chose terms commonly used by businesses, thus minimizing surprises. Default terms can simplify contract drafting. Parties need not specify every detail; they can rely on the default terms unless they dislike them. The UCC can provide almost any term, including price. See UCC §2-305. The UCC, however, has no default provision for quantity.

ii.   **Common-law default terms.**   The common law provided some terms long before the UCC was drafted. For example:

(a)   **Impracticability.**   When war or natural disasters precluded performance, the common law often excused performance on the ground that the parties would not have intended to require performance under those circumstances. See 17.A. (The impracticability excuse evolved from impossibility, a less lenient common-law doctrine.)

(b)   **Good faith.**   Courts occasionally held that good faith required the party to act in ways that the contract did not explicitly mention. This rule basically added obligations to the contract—but usually conformed to what the parties probably would have agreed if they had discussed the matter before the dispute arose.

4.   Identifying an Appropriate Remedy

This is almost the same as identifying a breach. If you know what the defendant promised—as you must to identify a breach—you usually can ascertain what position the plaintiff would have occupied if the defendant had performed the promise. That is the definition of the expectation interest, the usual remedy in breach-of-contract suits. Other remedies, such as reliance or restitution, usually provide an even easier (but less generous) way to measure the remedy. Thus, this provision rarely adds anything to the analysis.

 # EXAMPLE AND ANALYSIS

Sun ordered paper from Remington. Price was specified for the first four months. For the remaining 12 months of the contract, price and the period to which the price applied was left to future negotiations, with a price cap. (That is, a price the parties set for January could apply for February and March, before renegotiating again in April.) Remington refused to deliver after the first four months. Sun tendered the maximum price the cap allowed each month. *Sun Printing & Publishing v. Remington Paper & Power*, 139 N.E. 470 (1923).

Held: No contract due to indefiniteness. The maximum price each month might not be the right price, because the parties could have agreed that a price would last for several months. The dissent identified three ways the contract could have been interpreted to provide a remedy. The majority felt unable to choose one of these approaches to fill in the gap for the parties.

1. **Remedy, Not Promise, Unclear**. The case is exceptional but not unique. Defendants promise was clear: provide paper. Plaintiff's promise — the price — was not. Plaintiff's loss depended on the difference between the contract price and the price it had to pay elsewhere. See 20.A, 20.B.1. Thus, the remedy could not be ascertained without knowing plaintiff's promise.
2. **Alternative View**. The court could have adopted Sun's approach. Because prices rose during this period, monthly adjustment offered Remington the greatest possible price. (If prices had fallen, a longer term would have benefitted Remington, fixing a higher price for several months.) For purposes of proving damages with reasonable certainty, Sun's method seems adequate. By selecting the largest possible price they would have paid, it provides the smallest possible loss they suffered. The court, however, found no assent to this price. It was not required by the contract. Thus, indefiniteness of the contract left the agreement unenforceable. It is not clear whether courts would follow this stiff approach today.

---

5. **Tentative Generalizations**

    It is hard to generalize about gap filling in the common law. A few tentative pointers may help.

    a. **UCC versus common law.**   Courts applying the common law are less willing to fill gaps in the contract than courts applying the UCC. Statutory authority makes courts bolder.

    b. **Creating assent versus filling in terms.**   Courts are less willing to fill a gap to create a contract than they are to fill a gap when the parties clearly intended a contract (for example, where both parties have performed, but dispute the quality of one party's performance). Thus, where one party denies a contract existed, courts require a strong showing in order to fill a gap that would create a contract.

EXAMPLE AND ANALYSIS

Lucy promised Wood the exclusive right to place her endorsements on fashion articles. Lucy also promised Wood half the revenues on her endorsements. Lucy breached Wood's exclusive right by placing endorsements herself. Wood sued for half the revenue on these endorsements, per the agreement. Lucy contended that she had received no consideration for the promise, as their written agreement did not require Wood to do anything. *Wood v. Lucy, Lady Duff-Gordon*, 118 N.E. 214 (N.Y. 1917).

Held: For Wood. The court carefully read the agreement, noting several clauses that showed the parties intended obligations to arise on both sides. It decided the contract implicitly required Wood to make efforts to place endorsements. Careful analysis of the contract, the negotiations, and the context produced the result, not a cavalier declaration that the parties must have intended whatever the court felt was fair for them to intend.

---

c. **Specifying the term.**   When they fill gaps, courts impose terms that are reasonable under the circumstances. Restatement (Second) of Contracts §204. This includes considering whether the parties would have agreed on a term if they had considered this problem originally. Although scholars often favor the latter formulation, the Restatement emphasizes the fairness of the term, not its appeal to the parties.

   i. **Generality may suffice.**   Sometimes, as in *Wood*, the content of a missing term seems easy to determine. The parties would have agreed that Wood owed a duty to seek endorsements. Because any duty on Wood satisfied the consideration requirement, the court did not get more specific.

   ii. **Specific terms more difficult.**   If Lucy had sued Wood for breach, a court might have needed to define the duty more clearly. Would Wood and Lucy have required "good faith efforts," "reasonable efforts," or "best efforts"? Good faith efforts might tolerate unreasonably little effort, if Wood subjectively thought the measures were sufficient. Best efforts might require Wood to do more than a reasonable person would have done, if he was capable of more. (The court in *Wood* mentioned reasonable efforts. For sales of goods, the UCC now specifies best efforts. See UCC §2-306(2).)

C. OVERVIEW OF ASSENT

The law enforces contracts because society benefits from mutually agreed exchanges. The requirement of consideration, discussed in the next chapter, seeks to limit the law's attention to exchanges. The requirement of assent limits the law's attention to mutually agreed exchanges. Unless both parties want to make the exchange, at least at the time they enter the contract, the law will not treat the promises as enforceable.

1. Problems with Assent

Such problems usually involve one of three questions.

a. Did the party assent at all? One party may claim that she never said or did anything that could be taken as assent. This is the most obvious objection to assent, but also the rarest. Absent fraud, such as forged signatures or lies about what was said during negotiations, words or actions rarely produce such ambiguity that one party believes assent exists whereas the other does not. Doctrines such as jest and illusoriness deal with these ambiguous situations but are not among the key problems for determining assent.

b. When did the assent occur? One party may claim that although she manifested a willingness to enter a contract, she changed her mind and terminated negotiations before the agreement became final and binding. In these circumstances, you must identify when assent occurred. If assent had not occurred at the time she effectively withdrew from the transaction, no agreement arose. If, however, assent occurred before the party effectively withdrew, a refusal to go forward would be called breach. Many problems involving assent center on the timing of assent.

c. To what terms did the parties assent? Often both parties admit that they entered a binding contract but disagree about what terms the contract contained. Sometimes the disagreement focuses on interpretation, the subject of a later chapter. See Chapter 12. At other times, however, the parties disagree about whether a particular term ever became part of the agreement in the first place. This situation arises, for example, when parties use their own standard forms, each ignoring conflicting terms on the other's form. In these circumstances, the problem is to determine which terms, if any, the parties' assent included.

2. Assent as a Subterfuge

Parties rarely refuse to perform **because** they did not assent to the bargain. Rather, they refuse to perform because the bargain would produce unfavorable results. They use problems of assent as a rationale for refusing to perform, but the decision was reached for different reasons. Assent, then, is a technicality often deployed to avoid terms that may once have seemed favorable but now seem undesirable. It is an important technicality. Without assent, there is no voluntary obligation for the law to enforce. But in many cases assent is not the core of the problem. Rather, parties seek any means possible to avoid a bad bargain, even if they tried to assent (and, in some cases, did assent) before they realized the danger of the bargain.

3.   The Structure of Assent

Assent has evolved from rather rigid common-law rules concerning **offer** and **acceptance** to a more open-ended inquiry into all the facts and circumstances that might indicate agreement between the parties. Because that evolution is incomplete, your course probably will address both approaches.

a.   UCC approach.   The UCC explicitly recognizes that almost any method of signifying agreement can create a contract. See UCC §2-204. Thus, words, actions (such as performance or reliance), or (in some cases) even silence can communicate a commitment to perform according to the terms of an agreement. The statute, while designed to produce fair results, does not offer students much insight into how courts address the problems that make assent questionable in a given case. Thus, it can be hard to predict how a dispute might be resolved. For this reason, many casebooks focus the discussion of assent on the common-law rules.

b.   Common-law approach.   The common law assessed assent according to a fairly rigorous paradigm: One party made an **offer** to the other; the other then either gave an **acceptance** or did not. Acceptance marked the moment a contract became binding. Up to that point, each party remained free to change her mind and withdraw from the transaction. Everything that occurred before the offer (including prior offers) is shuffled aside under the rubric **preliminary negotiations**. Negotiations that continue after acceptance become negotiations to **modify** the contract — which may produce a modification if the parties assent via a new offer and an acceptance of it.

c.   Convergence.   Common-law rules have slowly evolved toward the UCC. The common law recognizes silence or action in reliance as assent in appropriate circumstances. Some rigid concepts, like the mirror-image rule, have relaxed. Some preliminary negotiations produce enforceable preliminary agreements. Common-law courts, however, still address issues in terms of offer and acceptance.

D. IDENTIFYING AN OFFER

"An offer is a manifestation of willingness to enter into a bargain, so made as to justify another person in understanding that his assent to that bargain is invited and will conclude it." Restatement (Second) of Contracts §24. This definition contains or implies several attributes of offers.

1. Manifestation

An offer must be manifest. An uncommunicated offer is an oxymoron. No offer exists unless expressed to another.

2. Promise

Usually, an offer takes the form of a conditional promise: I promise to perform x if some contingency occurs. (The contingency typically specifies a form of acceptance, such as "if you promise to do y in return.") You must identify a promise within an offer to find a promise to enforce if the offer is accepted.

3. Invitation to Accept

Some expressions may imply willingness to enter a bargain without inviting assent. The easiest examples are words addressed to someone else. I may offer to sell my car to my daughter on terms that I would not offer to a stranger. See also Restatement (Second) of Contracts §52 (Who May Accept an Offer).

Other expressions may not invite anyone's assent. "For two cents I'd sell that cat!" is an expression of annoyance. No one should understand this as an invitation to enter a bargain for the sale of a cat. (Fang would have been through dozens of owners by now if this were not true.) The issue depends on what listeners reasonably believe the speaker intends, not on what the speaker actually intended.

4. Conclusiveness

An offer gives the other party the power to conclude a deal by accepting. Offerees hold all the cards: They are not yet bound themselves, but they can bind the offeror (and themselves) with a word. To create that power, the offer must contain indications that acceptance will conclude the deal. If the other party has reason to know that the offeror expects not to be bound until she has made some further expression of assent, the words are not an offer but preliminary negotiations. Restatement (Second) of Contracts §26.

 # EXAMPLES AND ANALYSIS

1. S, while talking to F, a friend, mentions that she is thinking of selling her old sofa because she needs $400 but is torn because she is fond of the old sofa, which is more comfortable than her new one. F plausibly could understand S's words to invite an offer of $400. But F's response will not conclude the transaction. S's words reveal uncertainty regarding the sale. S expects a chance to signify assent (or not) before the deal is complete.

2. Brown made a machine for Hercules. Brown's quote included a term requiring Hercules to indemnify Brown if anyone (especially Hercules's employees) sued Brown for injuries caused by the machine. Hercules's purchase order did not include an indemnity clause. To decide whether the clause was part of the contract, the court had to decide whether Brown's quote was an offer that Hercules accepted (by phone, before it sent the purchase order). Because the price quote specifically stated that the sale would not become final until acknowledged by Brown, no offer existed. Hercules's assent was invited but would not conclude the transaction until Brown made a further indication of assent. *Brown Machine v. Hercules, Inc.*, 770 S.W.2d 416 (Mo. Ct. App. 1989). (**Note:** Results may vary depending on the language of the documents. See *Idaho Power v. Westinghouse Elec.*, 596 F.2d 924 (9th Cir. 1979) (price quote was an offer, accepted by a purchase order).)

5. **Bargain: A Cautionary Note**

Including bargain in the definition of an offer unnecessarily complicates matters. Unless your professor insists otherwise, ignore that portion of the definition of an offer that refers to a bargain.

a. **Technical reading of the Restatement.** The Restatement (Second) of Contracts §24 defines an offer to include "willingness to enter into a **bargain**." Thus, a proposal that does not specify a bargain is not an offer. Offers **usually** specify bargains. The contingencies specified in an offer usually identify the consideration sought in return for the promise. Thus, contingencies often take the form of "if you will perform *y* in return." (A promise to fulfill the contingencies, such as by performing in return, is an acceptance.)

b. **Inconsistency within the Restatement.** Restatement (Second) of Contracts §17(2) states that contracts can exist without bargains under some circumstances. That language would be meaningless if the assent rules preclude formation of a contract without a bargain. Exceptions to the consideration requirement specify when a promise is enforceable despite the absence of a bargain. The definition of offer should not override these rules.

 # EXAMPLES AND ANALYSIS

D, a wealthy person, promises to give $100,000 to C, a major charity, if C will accept. C agrees to accept the donation. Has D made an offer?

D's promise specifies a contingency but not a **bargain**, because nothing is sought or given in exchange for the promise. Restatement (Second) of Contracts §71(2). Thus, there is no consideration for the promise. The law, however, will enforce promises to make charitable donations without consideration. Restatement (Second) of Contracts §90(2). Thus, this promise is enforceable if an offer has been accepted.

But arguably no **offer** has been made. An offer requires "willingness to enter into a **bargain**." Restatement (Second) of Contracts §24 (emphasis added). Because no bargain has been proposed, D has not manifested a willingness to enter a bargain and, hence, has made no offer C can accept. Without assent, the promise cannot be enforced.

This analysis, although technically tight, is crazy. The parties clearly assented to the terms proposed. The absence of a bargain affects consideration, not the existence of an agreement. The example demonstrates the dangers of overreliance on the language of the Restatement.

c. **Undue reliance on the Restatement.** Contracts casebooks are sold in every state; they cannot focus on the law of any one state. Books and professors tend to rely on the Restatement for a general view of the common law. This is useful, but can be carried to extremes.

i. **The Restatement is not law.** It is not a statute. It is not a court decision. It is a (very good) summary of court decisions in 50 different states. States differ on the wording and even the substance of some rules. Seeking definitive answers in the details of the language of the Restatement is deceptively reassuring. But it can produce some absurd results, like the one identified here.

ii. **The Restatement is a very good summary of the common law.** It is the best summary available to most students and (more important) most professors. Thus, professors often rely on the Restatement for guidance (for example, when grading exams). This outline, like most casebooks, relies heavily on the Restatement. But keep a grain of salt handy.

E. SPECIAL PROBLEMS WITH OFFERS

Usually, offers are easy to recognize. Casebooks, however, include some borderline examples.

1. Advertisements

Typically, ads are **not** offers. An ad manifests a willingness to enter into a bargain with readers. But in many cases the seller may have a limited supply and be unable to satisfy all customers. If customers generally are aware of this possibility, they cannot justifiably believe that their assent will conclude the deal. Thus, courts call ads "invitations to treat"; they invite customers to make an offer that the seller can accept or reject.

a. **Ads can be offers.** The more detail an ad contains, the more likely a court is to find it was an offer. A general ad is viewed as publicity, informing the public of what they may find in the store without committing to the terms mentioned in the ad. An ad that contains words of commitment, however, invites acceptance and indicates that acceptance will conclude the deal. *See* Restatement (Second) of Contracts §26 comment b.

 EXAMPLES AND ANALYSIS

A fur store advertised a black lapin stole for $1, "first come, first served." Plaintiff was first in line that day, but the store refused to sell him the stole. The court awarded damages to the plaintiff. The words "first come, first served" made the ad "clear, definite, explicit, and [left] nothing open for negotiation." The court treated the ad as an offer that plaintiff accepted before the store revoked it. *Lefkowitz v. Great Minneapolis Surplus Store*, 86 N.W.2d 689 (Minn. 1957).

b. **Law versus custom.** The Restatement expresses concern that it may be unreasonable to understand an ad as inviting acceptance or that acceptance will conclude the deal. Restatement (Second) of Contracts §26 comment b. This seems an anachronism. Today, many people probably believe ads are binding on a store. If the law declares that ads are not offers, that belief may be unreasonable. That point, however, is circular.

    c. **Carelessly drafted ads.** Cases seem to express concern that advertisers may be disadvantaged if bound to perform according to the terms of an ad. They might receive more acceptances than they can fill. They might receive acceptances long after the ad was published, when they are no longer willing to sell on these terms. Most of these problems, however, can be cured by carefully drafting the ad. The treatment of ads seems designed to protect careless drafters from the consequences of failing to say "supplies limited" or "for a limited time only" in their ad.

2. Infelicitous Offers

Occasionally, a party carelessly communicates willingness to enter a bargain. Although intending to invite bids, the language may reasonably be understood to invite acceptances. Where a party cannot perform if she gets too many acceptances, treating the communication as an offer would pose problems. Courts sometimes rescue persons who make infelicitous offers of this sort.

    a. **Example (Nebraska Seed Co. v. Harsh, 152 N.W. 310 (Neb. 1915).** Defendant sent plaintiff (and perhaps others) a letter announcing willingness to sell "about 1800 bu[shels]" of millet seed for "$2.25 per hundredweight." Plaintiff wired acceptance of 1,800 bushels. The defendant sold the seed to another. The jury found for plaintiff, but the state Supreme Court reversed.

    b. **Analysis.** The court's reasons for refusing to find an offer are questionable.

        i. **Magic words.** Defendant's letter said "I want to sell" instead of "I offer to sell." But contract law does not require magic words, such as "I promise" or "I offer." Offer turns on what the plaintiff reasonably could have understood from the words used.

        ii. **Open terms.** The letter "as a whole shows that it was not intended as a final proposition, but as a request for bids," particularly as it did not fix a time for delivery, thus leaving a term open for further negotiation. Although open terms might make it unreasonable for the plaintiff to understand that its acceptance would conclude the deal, the jury was better situated to decide what it was reasonable to understand from this language. The court did not explain why it rejected the jury's verdict — an unusual oversight.

iii.   **Mirror-image rule.**   The court's invocation of the mirror-image rule (see 2.G.4) is also somewhat crabbed but does not belong at this point in the outline.

iv.   **Implied clause.**   Reading between the lines, the court seems concerned that the defendant probably sent this notice to several possible buyers and might face big damages if each of them could accept. One would get the seeds; the others could collect expectation damages. Plaintiff probably should have qualified the letter with a clause such as "subject to prior sale" or "best offer accepted." The court seems to read such a clause into the letter to save the plaintiff from his own careless drafting.

c.   **Comparing *Lefkowitz* and *Harsh*.**   Taken together, these cases suggest that courts will find an offer when the advertiser (or writer) includes sufficient provisions to protect itself from acceptances it did not really want but will refuse to find an offer when the advertiser has left herself open to unwanted acceptances. Thus, a qualified ad was an offer, but an unqualified letter was not.

3.   Auctions

Which is the offer: putting an item up for auction or making a bid? The answer depends on whether the item is placed for sale without reserve.

a.   **Reserve defined.**   Some items placed for auction have a reserve price; only bids above that price will be accepted, effectively specifying a minimum bid. Some items are placed for auction without reserve; that is, they will be sold to the highest bidder, no matter how low the bid.

b.   **Auctions with reserve invite offers.**   Putting an item up for auction invites others to enter a bargain, but bidders cannot reasonably understand that their bid will conclude the transaction. Thus, putting an item up for auction generally is not an offer.

c.   **Bids are offers.**   Bids express willingness to enter into a bargain and invite the auctioneer to conclude the sale by accepting the bid. A bid, then, is an offer.

      i.   A bidder may revoke the offer at any time prior to acceptance by the auctioneer. See 2.F.1.f.

      ii.   Each bid serves to terminate the offer made by prior bidders. (In effect, the auctioneer tacitly rejects all preceding bids as each new bid comes in.) Thus, if a bid is revoked, the preceding bid is **not** revived. Restatement (Second) of Contracts §28(c). Thus, any bid would be in order (at least until the preceding bidder reiterated her bid).

  d. **Auctions without reserve are offers.** The offer is made to the highest bidder. Bidders reasonably understand that if their bid is the highest, it will conclude the transaction. The auctioneer cannot withdraw the item from the sale because the highest bid accepted the auctioneer's offer, forming a binding contract.

F.   THE DURATION OF AN OFFER

Assent may depend on whether one party withdrew from the transaction before or after the other assented to the bargain. That often means deciding whether the offer was still open at the time the offeree tried to accept it.

1.   Methods of Terminating an Offer

Offers do not endure forever. If they did, we would rarely make offers, for fear they might be accepted decades later. The question of how long an offer stays open is usually simple—but a few doctrines aimed at limiting the ability to terminate an offer complicate matters. See 2.F.2, 2.F.3.

  a. **Lapse of time.** Restatement (Second) of Contracts §41.

      i.   **Specified in the offer.** An offer may specify the time it lapses. After that time, the offer is not operative.

      ii.   **Reasonable time.** An offer that does not specify how long it remains open lapses after a reasonable time.

      iii.   **No formula.** There is no formula for determining a reasonable time. As a guide, the more volatile the price, the shorter the time the offer will remain open.

          (a) An offer to sell **stock** at a set price may expire within moments. Stock prices change constantly. A party should not be allowed to see how the market price changes before deciding to accept the offer — unless she pays for that right by buying an option.

(b) An offer to sell a **home** may remain open a few days. Home prices usually do not vary rapidly and time to inspect the home or the competition may be reasonable. On the other hand, when other buyers are negotiating for the house, an offer might lapse within moments to allow the seller to deal with other buyers.

iv.   New offers.   Often lapse of an offer will not prevent formation of a contract. If both parties still want to deal, one will make a new offer and the other will accept. Thus, few offers need to stay open very long. Lapse of an offer matters when one party (usually the offeror) no longer wants to deal on those terms. That usually means something significant has changed (if only the party's mind), making renegotiation in light of changed circumstances preferable.

b.   Rejection.   When an offeree responds to an offer, the response usually terminates the offer. Response by acceptance terminates the offer by converting it to a contract. Other responses leave further negotiation possible.

i.   Rejection terminates offer.   Once the offeree rejects an offer, she cannot later accept it. Restatement (Second) of Contracts §38.

ii.   Waiver.   An offeror may waive the benefit of this rule. Either in the offer or after rejection, the offeror may indicate that the offer remains open.

iii.   Implied rejection.   Rejection includes any "manifestation of intention not to accept."

(a)   Equivocal words.   Words such as "I don't think I can afford it right now" may operate as a rejection. The offeror reasonably would understand she is free to deal with others instead of waiting for the offeree to change her mind.

(b)   Reserving judgment.   Words that indicate an intention to consider the offer further are not a rejection. For example, "I don't think I can afford it right now, but I'll let you know after I check with my spouse" indicates that a rejection or acceptance will be forthcoming. The offeror knows she is not free to deal with others until the offeree decides.

c. **Counteroffer.** Counteroffers are simply a special kind of rejection. A response that proposes new or different terms rejects the original offer and puts a different offer on the table. Restatement (Second) of Contracts §39. After making a counteroffer, the offeree cannot later accept the original offer.

   i. **Small differences.** Any offer relating to the same matter as the original offer is a counteroffer, no matter how small the differences.

   ii. **Waiver.** As with rejections, the offeror can allow the offer to remain open despite the counteroffer.

EXAMPLES AND ANALYSIS

Defendant offered to sell plaintiff land for $1,800. Plaintiff responded, "Send lowest cash price. Will give $1,600 cash. Wire." Defendant refused the counteroffer, wiring, "Cannot reduce price." Plaintiff then accepted the original offer. Defendant, who had already sold the land to another, resisted. *Livingstone v. Evans*, [1925] 4 D.L.R. 769 (Sup. Ct. Alta. 1925).

Held: For plaintiff.

1. The court acknowledged the general rule. The counteroffer by plaintiff ended the original offer. The original offer, therefore, could not be revived by the plaintiff.
2. The court held that defendant's reply, "Cannot reduce price," implicitly **renewed** the original offer. Because plaintiff promptly accepted the renewed offer, a contract was formed (negating the contract with the other buyer, as defendant no longer had the right to sell the property). [The court expressed some uncertainty concerning whether, on the facts, the defendant's language really renewed the offer. I would echo that uncertainty.]

   iii. **Reserved judgment.** Similarly, a counteroffer may indicate that the original offer remains under consideration. If so, either party can create a contract by accepting the others' terms.

EXAMPLE AND ANALYSIS

S offers to sell B a used car for $1,500. B says, "I'd take it for $1,200, but I can't pay $1,500 without more thought. I'll let you know tomorrow morning." B has made a counteroffer that S could accept. But B's words indicate she is still considering S's original offer rather than rejecting it via the counteroffer.

d. **Death or incapacity of either party.**   An offer cannot be accepted after either the offeror or the offeree dies or suffers incapacity. Restatement (Second) of Contracts §48. The rule sounds absolute, but exceptions seem likely.

   i.   **Voidable contracts.**   A person under an incapacity may have the power to make voidable contracts. Thus, not every incapacity will prevent formation of a contract. An offer need not terminate upon the onset of an incapacity that would not prevent the contract from being effective.

   ii. **Intoxication.**   Such a condition does not seem to fit the rule. Although it might prevent acceptance while the offeree is intoxicated, an offer made by a sober person and accepted by a sober person need not terminate simply because one party got drunk in the interim. (The same might be said of temporary mental disease or defect, though the offer seems likely to lapse during the recovery period more often than it will lapse while someone sobers up.)

   iii. **Agents.**   Some offers may allow acceptance by a personal representative of the offeree if the offeree dies or loses capacity to assent.

   iv. **Option contracts.**   Such contracts remain open for the period specified, regardless of incapacity or death of either party. (Options are discussed in detail shortly. See 2.F.3.

e. **Nonoccurrence of conditions.**   An offer may specify conditions on the ability of others to accept. When these conditions cannot be satisfied, the offer terminates.

EXAMPLE AND ANALYSIS

P, a parent, tells C, P's child, that if C is admitted to AMU, P's alma mater, in the fall of 1997, P will sell C a car at a steep discount. Admission is a condition on C's ability to accept. If it becomes impossible for C to be admitted to AMU that term (say, C misses the application deadline), the offer lapses.

f.   **Revocation.**   An offeror usually remains free to withdraw the offer at any time prior to acceptance. Just as the offeree is not bound until she accepts, the offeror is not bound until the offeree accepts. Once the offeror revokes an offer, no acceptance is possible. Exceptions for firm offers and option contracts will be discussed shortly. See 2.F.2, 2.F.3.

   i.   **Communication necessary.**   A revocation, to be effective, must be communicated to the offeree. A revocation is effective only when the offeree receives it. *See* Restatement (Second) of Contracts §42.

 EXAMPLES AND ANALYSIS

1. Recall *Lefkowitz v. Great Minneapolis Surplus Store*, 86 N.W.2d 689 (Minn. 1957). The fur store offered a lapin stole for $1, first come, first served. When the plaintiff appeared to accept the offer, the store informed him that the offer was open only to women. This language could revoke the offer. But the plaintiff accepted the offer before the store announced the limitation. Thus, the revocation was ineffective. This result applied even though plaintiff knew the store meant to limit a previous offer to women. The new offer did not mention the limitation and the store did not communicate the revocation until after plaintiff had accepted.

2. Defendant offered to sell plaintiff a house for £750. The next day, defendant wrote a letter to plaintiff revoking the offer and sold the property to another for £760. That same day, before the revocation arrived, plaintiff accepted the offer (by mail). The acceptance created a contract because the revocation was ineffective until received by the offeree. *Henthorn v. Fraser*, 2 Ch. 27 (Eng. Ct. App. Ch. Div. 1892). (Under the mailbox rule, discussed at 2.G.6, the offeree's acceptance was effective the moment it was posted.)

ii.   **Indirect communication sufficient.**   An offeree may receive notice of a revocation from persons other than the offeror. Indirect notice is sufficient if the information received by the offeree is reliable and indicates that the offeror has taken "definite action inconsistent with an intention to enter into the proposed contract." Restatement (Second) of Contracts §43.

 # EXAMPLES AND ANALYSIS

The classic example is *Dickinson v. Dodds*, 2 Ch. D. 463 (1876). Dodds offered to sell some land to Dickinson, indicating that Dickinson must accept by Friday morning. On Thursday, Dickinson heard that Dodds had offered the land to another buyer at the same price. Dickinson accepted the offer either late Thursday or early Friday, within the time allowed by the offer.

Held: The offer had been revoked before the acceptance. Because Dickinson knew that Dodds was offering the land to another, he knew that Dodds no longer wanted to sell to him, and therefore knew that the offer had been revoked.

1. Is *Dickinson v. Dodds* consistent with the Restatement? Could you use the Restatement rule to argue for a different result?

Offering to sell the land to another is not necessarily inconsistent with a willingness to sell the land to Dodds. It might indicate a willingness to sell the land to either party at the proposed price. Thus, Dodds reasonably could believe the offer remained open for the stated period — or, at least, that it remained open if he accepted before the land was sold to the other.

As for the second question, unless Dickinson knew the terms of the other offer, he could not know whether it was inconsistent with the offer to sell to him. The offer to another may have been contingent on his own refusal. ("I will sell you the land on Friday if Dickinson does not accept my offer.") Thus, he may have had no reliable information that the new offer was inconsistent with the offer to him.

2. What if Dickinson heard that Dodds had sold the land to another, rather than just offered it? (Note: the facts of *Dickinson* may support this inference, though the judges do not rely heavily on this interpretation.)

A sale to another clearly would be inconsistent with the intention to sell to Dickinson. Thus, this information would constitute a revocation of the offer. But the information would need to be **reliable**. Varying the credibility of the source could still produce different results.

iii. **Revoking general offers.** Some offers are made to the general public (e.g., posters offering rewards). Revoking such an offer would be nearly impossible if actual notice to each offeree were necessary. When other means of revocation are impossible, the law permits **revocation by a notice that receives publicity equal to that of the offer**. Restatement (Second) of Contracts §46.

   (a) **Prior acceptances.** Revocation by publicity may take time. Acceptances received before the notice of revocation has received as much publicity as the original offer may be effective.

   (b) **Timing questions.** Uncertainty surrounds when the revocation becomes effective. The amount of publicity required may not be quantifiable. The time the publicity takes effect is open to argument: when the publication hits the streets or after a reasonable time for people to read it? How long is reasonable?

   (c) **Notice to individuals.** Sometimes notifying individuals is possible. For instance, a store might post a revocation notice prominently on the entrance, alerting offerees to the revocation before they enter. This may speed revocation, at least for people who visit the store.

iv. **Promises not precluding revocation.** With few exceptions, a promise to keep an offer open for a specified period of time **does not** prevent the offeror from revoking the offer before the time expires. If the offeree does not provide any consideration for the promise to keep the offer open, the promise to keep the offer open is unenforceable. (The next few sections discuss the exceptions.)

EXAMPLE AND ANALYSIS

In *Dickinson v. Dodds*, the offer stated, "This offer to be left over until Friday, 9 o'clock," A.M. The court interpreted this language as a promise not to revoke the offer until Friday morning. Dickinson accepted before 9 A.M. Friday. Yet the court held the offer was revoked on Thursday. Because no consideration had been given for the promise to keep the offer open, Dodds could breach the promise freely by revoking the offer earlier.

2.   Firm Offers

An offeror may relinquish the right to revoke an offer. When the power to revoke is effectively waived, the offer is called a firm offer.

a.   Statutes enforcing firm offers.   Some states have passed laws enforcing promises to keep offers open even without consideration. The most significant example is UCC §2-205, which makes an offer **by a merchant** irrevocable if a **signed writing** gives assurances that the offer will be held open.

   i.   Merchants.   The rule only applies to merchants—generally, people engaged in the business of selling goods and who, therefore, probably know about the rule. See UCC §2-104 (defining "merchant").

   ii.   Sales of goods.   As with any aspect of the UCC, the rule applies only to sales of goods. Some states may have passed similar laws for other types of contracts. Occasionally, courts will adopt an approach endorsed by the UCC into the common law.

   iii.   Writing necessary.   The rule requires a signed writing, minimizing the difficulty of proving what was said.

      (a)   Forms.   If a standardized form includes assurance that an offer will remain open, the term must be separately signed by the offeror. The rule protects merchants from terms an offeree might try to slip into a form it supplied.

      (b)   Signature.   The UCC takes a fairly broad view of what qualifies as a signature. See UCC §2-205 comment 2; 4.B.5.b.

   iv.   Open time.   The rule does not require the party to specify how long the offer will remain open. When a time is specified, the offer remains open for that period. Otherwise, the offer must remain open for a reasonable time.

   v.   90-day limit.   The statute allows revocation after three months, regardless of the terms of the writing or how long a reasonable time might be.

3.   Options: Bargains to Keep an Offer Open

An option is a contract to keep an offer open. When consideration is given for a promise to keep an offer open, the promise becomes enforceable. The option contract is separate from the contract being negotiated: The promise to keep the offer open is accepted and paid for independently. The offer then becomes irrevocable for a period of time. If the offer is accepted within that period, a second contract is formed. But the option contract is complete—and must be paid for—even if the offeree decides not to accept the offer that has been kept open under the option contract.

a.   Creating an option.   An option is created in the same way as any other contract: by assent to a definite bargain.

 ## EXAMPLE AND ANALYSIS

Suppose Dickinson had paid Dodds 1 shilling in exchange for the promise to keep the offer to sell land open until Friday at 9 A.M. Dodds nonetheless revoked the offer on Thursday. Dickinson accepted the offer before Friday at 9 A.M. Did this acceptance create an enforceable contract for the sale of the land to Dickinson?

Dodds could not revoke on Thursday. Dodds did not **lose** the power to revoke, he **sold** it. The revocation is a nullity; the offer to sell the land remained open until Friday at 9 A.M. Because Dickinson accepted the offer before that time, a contract for the sale of the land existed. [What if poor Dodds already had sold the land to another? One gets the land and the other gets damages. Dodds shouldn't sell the same property twice.]

b.   Exception for reliance.   Some promises are enforceable without consideration, based on an exceptions to the bargain requirement. A promise to keep the offer open for a specific time may fit one of these exceptions—particularly the exception for action in reliance on a promise. The details of these exceptions are discussed in the chapter on consideration. See 3.D–3.H. The exception for action in reliance, however, must be introduced here. It provides the foundation for a specific exception relating to options, which is addressed below.

i.   Elements.   An exception to the consideration requirement exists if:

- A promise has been made;
- The promisor reasonably should expect a promisee to rely on that promise;
- The promisee does rely in a way the promisor should have expected; and
- Injustice can be avoided only by enforcing the promise.

ii.   Application.   As applied to options, the exception exists if:

- The offeror promised to keep the offer open for a time;
- The offeror should have realized that the offeree would rely on that promise—say, by making other related contracts because she believed the offeror could not revoke the offer;
- The offeree did rely in a way the offeror should have expected; and
- The offeree will be harmed unless the promise to keep the offer open is enforced—for instance, because the other related contracts are useless or onerous without a contract with the offeror.

c.   Reliance without a promise.   Reliance can create an option even if the offeror does not promise to keep the offer open. Restatement (Second) of Contracts §87(2). The requirements to establish reliance are similar, but not quite identical, to the elements of reliance under §90. See 2.F.3.b.i.

i.   An offer must exist.   Reliance based on hope does not create an option. An offer to enter a contract must exist.

ii.   The offeror reasonably should have expected reliance of a substantial character before acceptance.   The requirement that the offeror should have anticipated the reliance is discussed in connection with §90. See 3.G. This provision adds two new components.

(a)   Substantial reliance.   The anticipated reliance must be of a substantial character. An offeror who reasonably expects minor reliance may revoke the offer. But an offeror who should expect significant action or forbearance may lose the power to revoke.

(b)   Reliance before acceptance.   The offeror should have anticipated reliance before acceptance. In many situations, an offeror reasonably will expect the offeree to accept before relying on the offer. Only if the offeror should know that the offeree will rely before accepting will she lose the power to revoke the offer.

iii.   The offeree actually relies in a way the offeror should have expected.   See 3.G.

> iv.   **The option exists "to the extent necessary to avoid injustice."**   Restatement (Second) of Contracts §87(2). This implies that the power to revoke the offer may not be completely lost. A revocation may be effective, at least in part, if injustice is limited or nonexistent.

 # EXAMPLES AND ANALYSIS

1. S, a construction subcontractor, submits a bid to G, a general contractor preparing a bid for a large building for O, the owner of land. S knows that if her bid is the lowest, G will rely on the bid in preparing her own bid to O. G cannot accept the bid until G finds out whether she received the contract from O. (If G does not get the job, she will not have any use for S's services on that job.) G in fact uses S's bid and gets the job from O. G promptly calls S to accept S's bid, but S revokes the bid before G can speak. G accepts the bid despite S's revocation. Is the acceptance effective?

The acceptance can be effective only if the offer was irrevocable. No statute, consideration, or express promise to keep the offer open appear in the facts. But S reasonably expected G to rely on the bid before accepting the bid. The reliance is substantial: G's contract with O requires G to do the work S bid on at S's price, even though all other subcontractors wanted more. Thus, allowing S to revoke the bid at that point could create injustice. G's reliance on the bid created an option to accept the bid within a reasonable time after G learned O awarded her the contract. See *Drennan v. Star Paving Co.*, 333 P.2d 757 (Cal. 1958).

2. Because this problem is common in the construction trades, it seems fair to infer that every bid implicitly contains a promise to keep the offer open for a reasonable time. Simply as a matter of interpretation, the usage of trade makes it likely that all offerors intend to make such promises unless they explicitly reserve the right to revoke the offer sooner. (For a discussion of usage of trade, see 12.B.1. Thus, *Drennan* may involve reliance on an **implied** promise to keep the offer open, not reliance in the absence of a promise. Outside the construction industry, the decision to infer a promise to keep the offer open is more problematic. The Restatement, by treating the issue as reliance without a promise, may have overlooked the sounder basis usage of trade offers for justifying this result.

> v.   **Effect of an option.**   Like other options, the offeree retains power to accept or reject the bid. Reliance on the bid does not accept the bid, even conditionally.

EXAMPLE AND ANALYSIS

A general contractor relied on a subcontractor's bid and received a contract. She then hired a different subcontractor to do the work. The court held that the option created by reliance did not constitute acceptance of the subcontractor's offer. Reliance precluded the subcontractor from revoking, but the general contractor remained free to accept or reject the offer as she wished. *Holman Erection Co. v. Orville E. Madsen & Sons*, 330 N.W.2d 693 (Minn. 1983).

4. Breach of an Option Contract

An offer held open by an option contract can be accepted at any time until the option expires, **even if the offeror tries to revoke the offer earlier**. Thus, if Dickinson had paid Dodds for the promise to keep the offer open until Friday, but Dodds had explicitly revoked the offer on Thursday, Dickinson's acceptance on Friday would be timely and a contract for the sale of the property would have been formed.

a. Specific performance.   This result is unusual. Usually, a party can breach and pay damages. That would mean Dodds could revoke the offer (even though he promised to keep it open) and pay Dickinson any losses Dickinson suffered because of the breach. By declaring that the offer remained open, courts in effect make specific performance (of the option contract) automatic. Treating the offer as open is equivalent to ordering the offeror not to revoke.

b. Damages no different.   If Dickinson would have rejected the offer anyway, no damages result. But if Dickinson would have accepted the offer, the damage from revoking the offer includes all the gains Dickinson would have made by buying the land. Thus, no matter how the remedy is characterized, it will include all gains the plaintiff would have made on the underlying contract, not just on the option.

 EXAMPLES AND ANALYSIS

S offers to sell B a parcel of land. B gives S $1 in exchange for a promise to keep the offer open until Friday. On Thursday, S tells B that the offer is revoked. Believing that acceptance is futile, B does not accept the offer on Friday. One year later, B sues S for breach of the option contract. The land has increased significantly in value during that year. Can B recover damages for the breach? Can B obtain title to the land by requesting specific performance, the usual remedy in real estate contracts?

Note the danger here. What if B had decided not to buy the land that Friday but later changed his mind when he saw that it increased in value? Breach of the option did not cause B any loss, as B would not have accepted the offer even if S had left it open.

How can we tell whether B decided not to buy the land or decided to buy it but failed to accept because she thought the offer had been revoked? The only person who can tell us is B, who has a lot to gain by persuading jurors that she would have accepted but for the revocation.

If the law treats the revocation as a nullity, it can dismiss cases in which B did not accept the offer. Enforcement focuses on the contract to buy the land, not on the option. If B did not accept, the contract to buy the land was not formed, and no damages are due.

If the law treats the revocation as a breach of the option, it must determine what B would have done if S had not revoked the offer with the difficulties noted here.

Treating the revocation as a nullity also encourages B to accept even if the offer is revoked. This minimizes the problem of discerning how B would have acted but for the revocation. If B knows the law will give effect to his acceptance despite the revocation, B has a reason to accept and remove any doubt about her intentions.

---

5.   Unilateral Contracts: Reliance Creating an Option

Some offers invite a party to perform or prepare to perform before the contract becomes binding. Offers may require acceptance by completing performance. Problems can arise if the offeror attempts to revoke the offer after the other party has begun to perform.

   a.   **Terminology: Unilateral and bilateral.**   These terms are not very helpful, but you need to know them when reading older cases.

      i.   **Unilateral contracts** arise when an offer can be accepted only by performance. The offeree must perform unilaterally before the offeror is bound at all. Once the offer has been accepted, only the offeror (unilaterally) has any remaining duties. **The contract itself involves duties on both sides**; it is not truly one-sided (unilateral). But at any given point in time, only one side has any unperformed duties: Before acceptance, the offeror has no duties; after acceptance, the offeree has no remaining duties.

ii.   **Bilateral contracts** arise when an offer can or must be accepted by a promise. (That is, an offer that can be accepted either by a promise or by a performance is bilateral, as is an offer that can be accepted only by a promise.) At the time of acceptance, both parties may have some unperformed duties remaining. The remaining rules in this section involve unilateral contracts; the rules governing bilateral contracts are addressed shortly (2.F.6).

b.   **Complete performance is acceptance.**   When an offer can be accepted only by performance, no contract exists until performance is complete. Thus, the offeree could stop performing at any time without any liability to the offeror. Restatement (Second) of Contracts §45(2).

c.   **Beginning performance creates an option.**   The offeror cannot revoke the offer after the offeree begins the requested performance (or tenders the performance or tenders a beginning of it). Restatement (Second) of Contracts §45(1). The offeree is not bound to continue, but the offeror must allow her a fair opportunity to complete the performance.

d.   **Terminology: Tender.**   Section 45 deals not only with beginning performance but also with "tendering" performance or "tendering a beginning" of performance.

i.   **"Tender."**   A tender is an unconditional offer to perform immediately, coupled with the manifest ability to perform. Thus, by holding out money to another, you tender the amount. Even if they reject it, you have tendered it. If you don't let go, say because they do not tender their performance as required, you have still tendered it.

ii.   **"Tender a beginning."**   This term refers to a performance that requires several steps—for example, several payments. Tendering the first step tenders a beginning.

iii.   **Not "beginning to tender."**   The section does not refer to beginning to tender. Thus, getting ready to tender performance does not create an option under these rules.

e.   **Interrupted performance.**   The rules do not specify a time during which the option prevents revocation. This may create problems differentiating cases in which an offeree abandons performance from cases in which she suspends performance intending to come back and complete the job.

EXAMPLES AND ANALYSIS

1. O offers P $5,000 to paint O's house, acceptable only by performance. P finishes half the job but suspends performance to fill a prior commitment to paint another house. P intends to return, but in the interim O revokes the offer.

Beginning performance created an option. To exercise the option, P must complete performance before the option expires. Express options state how long the offer will stay open; O's promise did not. The court will need to supply this term, probably inferring an intent that the offer stay open for a reasonable time. If P does not complete the job within a reasonable time, O would owe nothing on the contract. (A reasonable time will vary, as discussed in 2.F.1.a.)

2. O offers P $5,000 to paint O's house by May 1, acceptable only by performance. P finishes half the job but suspends performance to fill a prior commitment to paint another house. P intends to return, but in the interim O revokes the offer.

A court **might** interpret the date to mean that once P began performance, O could not revoke the offer until May 1. (Beginning created an option; the date specified how long it must remain open.) Another interpretation seems equally plausible. O wanted the job finished by May 1. If P does not resume work in time to finish by May 1, perhaps O should be permitted to find another painter who can finish the job on time—or, at least, sooner than P can finish it.

In both hypotheticals, P will have a remedy in restitution even if P cannot press a contract claim. If P's services increase the value of O's property or save O money when she hires a painter to finish the work, O would be unjustly enriched if she could keep the services without paying their value. A restitution claim, however, will not be compensated at the contract rate. If the contract rate was good for P, P will prefer a contract claim over an unjust enrichment claim. In some situations, P may begin performance without any benefit accruing to O yet. If so, restitution would provide no alternative, making the contract issue critical.

    f. Reliance before performance begins. An option does not arise based on preparations to perform. Actual performance must have begun. Restatement (Second) of Contracts §45.

EXAMPLES AND ANALYSIS

Petterson owed Pattberg money and had given Pattberg a lien on Petterson's land to secure the debt. Pattberg offered to accept less than full payment if Petterson would (a) make the next payment on schedule and (b) pay the rest of the debt (as reduced) by May 31. Petterson made the April payment and went to Pattberg's house to give him the money, but before opening the door, Pattberg revoked the offer. *Petterson v. Pattberg*, 161 N.E. 428 (N.Y. 1928).

Held: No contract. Do not rely heavily on the majority opinion in this case. It seems to indicate that even **tendering** the money (holding it out for Pattberg to accept) would not have created an option, since full performance could occur only if Pattberg **took** the money. The Restatement rejects this result.

Gathering the money and walking to Pattberg's house arguably did not begin performance. They were necessary **preparations** for performance, but performance itself involved delivering money to Pattberg. Delivery had not begun.

Did the April payment begin performance? Perhaps. But this payment was ambiguous. Even if Petterson had no intention of paying the debt early, he would have needed to make the April payment to avoid breaching the original obligation to pay. Thus, this payment was not made in reliance on the offer. The court reasonably did not treat it as a beginning of performance under a new contract.

g. **Section 87 distinguished.**   The rule resembles other options based on reliance, such as §87(2). Two differences require note.

i.   **Preparation as reliance.**   Preparations to perform may satisfy the reliance requirement of §87(2). Relying on a subcontractor's bid is not a beginning of performance. Nonetheless, the law creates an option in those cases.

 EXAMPLE AND ANALYSIS

Return to *Petterson v. Pattberg*. Would Petterson's reliance satisfy the other aspects of §87(2)? See 2.F.3.c.

Because only performance could accept the offer, Pattberg should have known Petterson would need to rely before acceptance. But Petterson's reliance may not have been of a substantial character. If he just withdrew money from the bank, he could redeposit it immediately, without significant loss.

Suppose Petterson, in reliance on Pattberg's offer, sold the property to another free and clear of the Pattberg's lien. To perform that contract, Petterson would need to redeem the lien (at full value) from the person to whom Pattberg sold it.

That reliance is of a substantial character—and easily quantifiable. But a sale of the property may not be the kind of reliance that Pattberg reasonably should have expected. That factual issue may depend on Pattberg's sophistication and how much Pattberg knew about Petterson.

---

6. **Bilateral Contracts: Reliance When Promises Can Constitute Acceptance**

The preceding discussion focuses on situations in which only performance can constitute acceptance. Usually, an offer can be accepted either by performance or by a promise (or can only be accepted by a promise).

a. **Beginning performance is acceptance.** Restatement (Second) of Contracts §62. The court infers that beginning to perform acts as a promise to finish performance. Because a promise can accept the offer, assent is complete the moment performance begins. As with §45, tendering performance or tendering a beginning of performance also satisfies the rule. See 2.F.5.d.

b. **Failure to complete performance is breach.** Acceptance promises to complete performance. Restatement (Second) of Contracts §62(2). Thus, unlike the option created by §45, if the offeree changes her mind and stops work, the offeror can sue for breach of contract.

c. **Performance without acceptance.** An offeree who begins performance can avoid accepting the contract by notifying the offeror that she does not accept the offer. Restatement (Second) of Contracts §53.

   i. **Notice.** Actual notice is not required as long as the offeree exercises reasonable diligence to inform the offeror that she does not accept the offer (despite the part performance).

   ii. **Timeliness.** Notice of nonacceptance must be made within a reasonable time. This requirement protects reliance by the offeror. If part performance continues for a period before the offeree notifies the offeror of her intention not to accept the offer, the offeror may have relied to her detriment on the acceptance — say, by refusing deals with other people who would finish the job.

d. Difference lies in the offer.   Because the effect of part performance is different, it is important to distinguish an offer that invites only performance from an offer that invites a promise as one way to accept. Unfortunately, courts rarely discuss the factors that differentiate these two types of offers. They seem to "know it when they see it."

i. Bilateral preferred.   When in doubt, courts assume an offer can be accepted by either a promise or a performance. Restatement (Second) of Contracts §32.

ii. Advice.   If you can explain why the offeror might want a promise, probably you can persuade a court that the offer could be accepted by promise. For instance, whenever an offeror probably would like some assurance that the other party would perform, a promise seems a reasonable way to accept. Remember, if you create doubt, courts will resolve doubt in favor of acceptance by promise or performance.

iii. Fear.   Sometimes the court may decide which result seems fairest and characterize the offer in the manner that produces that result. This makes the result hard to predict based on facts that existed at the time the offer was made, because a court can use 20-20 hindsight to take subsequent facts into account.

RELATIONSHIP AMONG §§45, 62, AND 87(2)

Type of Reliance	Unilateral: Can Be Accepted Only by Performance	Bilateral: Can Be Accepted by a Promise
Preparations for performance	§45: no option; §87: maybe option, if preparations were substantial reliance that offeror should have expected before acceptance.	§53: no acceptance; §87: maybe option, if preparations were substantial reliance that offeror should have expected before acceptance.

Type of Reliance	Unilateral: Can Be Accepted Only by Performance	Bilateral: Can Be Accepted by a Promise
Performance begun **Performance tendered** **Beginning of performance tendered**	§45: option created; §87: could create option, but superfluous as §45 definitely creates option.	§62: acceptance, contract created; §87: acceptance makes option irrelevant.
Performance completed	§45: acceptance, contract created; §87: acceptance makes option irrelevant.	§62: irrelevant, acceptance complete at beginning of performance; §87: ditto.

G. ACCEPTANCE

An offer represents the assent of one party. A contract, however, requires mutual assent. Thus, a promise becomes binding only when the offer has been accepted. Some aspects of acceptance have been introduced in the context of options — particularly acceptance by beginning performance. This section defines acceptance more generally and addresses some of the problems that create doubt concerning the validity of an acceptance.

1. Acceptance Defined

Acceptance is a manifestation of assent made in a manner that the offeror invited or required. Restatement (Second) of Contracts §50. Implicit within this definition are four components.

a. Only the offeree may accept. Willingness to enter a contract may be personal. An offer made to one person is not necessarily made to anyone else. One can, of course, make an offer to the world, such as a reward for anyone who finds a lost dog. But one can also limit an offer to an individual. When your law school offered you a place in the entering class, only you could accept the offer. See Restatement (Second) of Contracts §51.

i. Careless wording. Carelessness can convert an offer intended for a limited group into an offer to others. For example, in *Cobaugh v. Klick-Lewis, Inc.*, 561 A.2d 1248 (Pa. 1989), a car dealer offered a car to anyone making a hole-in-one at a charity golf tournament. It did not remove the signs when the tournament ended. Two days later, a golfer who read the signs shot a hole-in-one. Held: The offer had been accepted.

    ii.   Objective approach at work.   This is another example of how objective manifestations (the signs, which did not limit the offer to the charity event) govern over unstated subjective intent.

b.   Assent must be manifest.   Thinking that you plan to assent is insufficient to create a contract. The offeree must express assent by words or actions that a reasonable third party could understand.

    i.   Failure to object.   This is an action that, under some circumstances, could signify assent. See 2.G.3.

    ii.   Notice.   Manifestations of assent generally are aimed at notifying the offeror of the acceptance. In three situations, however, a manifestation may be effective without notice to the offeror. Restatement (Second) of Contracts §56.

        (a)   Terms of the offer.   The offer may indicate that notice is unnecessary in order to accept. If so, the offeror cannot avoid the contract on the basis that she never received notice of the acceptance.

        (b)   Acceptance by silence.   Where silence (the failure to refuse an offer) is a legitimate form of acceptance, no additional notice is necessary. The lack of any response is the notice as well as the acceptance.

        (c)   Reasonable diligence.   An acceptance is valid if the offeree exercises reasonable diligence to notify the offeror, even if the offeror does not receive the notice. Thus, a letter lost in the mail may be a legitimate acceptance.

        (d)   Actual notice of acceptance.   Such notice is effective even if the offeree did not make reasonable efforts to communicate acceptance. An offeror who receives notice cannot complain that notice was insufficient.

    iii.   Equivocal acceptance.   Where an offeror is entitled to notice of an acceptance by promise, the law accepts any reasonable interpretation an offeror places on an equivocal acceptance. The parties' conduct can clarify equivocal conduct.

(a) Risks of uncertainty.   Equivocal responses pose dual risks for the offeror. If she ignores them, the offeree may claim a contract was formed and sue for breach. But if the offeror treats them as an acceptance, the promisee may argue she never made a promise and thus, avoid the contract.

(b) Offeror inferred no acceptance.   An offeror is entitled to an unequivocal acceptance. Given any reasonable doubt that the offeree has assented to the terms, the offeror may treat the notice as insufficient. Thus, even if the offeror would have been justified in believing the offeree had made a commitment, any uncertainty created by the offeree's words leave the offeror free to treat the deal as open rather than concluded.

(c) Offeror inferred acceptance.   If the offeror reasonably understood the words as an acceptance, courts will treat them as such. The offeree cannot use the rule requiring unequivocal notice to avoid a contract—unless her words were so equivocal that the offeror was not justified in believing a commitment had been made. (In effect, the offeree must argue she never made a promise.)

c. Acceptance must conform to offeror's requirements.   The offeror is the master of an offer. If she specifies the method of acceptance, the offeree must accept in the specified manner.

i.   Acceptance must comply with any requirements of the offer.   If the offeror specifies a manner in which the offeree must express assent, the offeree must conform to those requirements to accept the offer. Restatement (Second) of Contracts §60. Anything else would not be an acceptance.

(a) Timely acceptance.   The most common requirement involves timing. If the offeror requires acceptance by a certain date, acceptance after that date is ineffective. (Late acceptance might be a counteroffer that the original offeror could accept if it still wanted to enter the transaction.)

(b) Performance.   Unilateral contracts are examples of offerors requiring acceptance in a special way: by performing. A promise cannot accept such an offer; only performance will suffice.

(c) **Form of payment.** An offer might require acceptance by payment in a particular currency (say, yen, not U.S. dollars). Tendering the proper amount in the wrong currency would not accept the offer.

(d) **Odd requirements.** An offeror may specify odd forms of acceptance — such as standing on your head while singing the national anthem. They do not often arise in practice. One is tempted to see the form of acceptance as part of the performance the promisor seeks. (In this example, perhaps the offeror seeks the humiliation of the offeree.)

ii. **Is offeree required or invited?** Some specifications in an offer may be suggestions rather than requirements. That is, the offeror has invited the offeree to accept in that way but has not required the offeree to accept in that way. Thus, other reasonable means of signifying acceptance may be effective to create a binding contract.

EXAMPLE AND ANALYSIS

Ford purchased machines from Allied. Ford's offer specified that the contract was not binding until accepted and that "[a]cceptance should be executed on acknowledgment copy which should be returned to buyer." The agreement also required Allied to indemnify Ford for any injuries during installation. Allied began performing, but did not sign and return the contract until November. Meanwhile, an employee was injured in September during installation of the machines. Allied argued the contract was not effective until November, so the indemnity clause did not cover the accident. *Allied Steel & Conveyors v. Ford Motor*, 277 F.2d 907 (6th Cir. 1960). Held: for Ford.

The offer invited Allied to accept by returning the acknowledgment copy but did not preclude Allied from accepting in any other reasonable manner. Beginning performance was a reasonable manner of acceptance, creating a binding contract at that time.

(a) **Resolve doubts for invitation.** Courts generally seek to enforce promises, not find ways to let parties out of them. Unless an offer clearly states that the **only** method of acceptance is the one specified, a court is likely to interpret the offer as **inviting** acceptance in that mode, but not requiring that mode of acceptance. Thus, an offeree who tried to accept in a manner that seems reasonable under the circumstances probably can enforce the promise.

(b) More unusual, less enforceable. Corbin, a highly regarded writer on contract law, suggested that unusual requests are less likely to be honored by courts because there seems little legitimate purpose in requiring the offeree to accept in this way as the exclusive manner for creating the contract. To this I would add a caution: where a reason for the request appears, give it due consideration. Particularly if the method of acceptance forms part of what the offeror sought in exchange for the promise, failing to limit acceptance accordingly changes the exchange by giving the offeror less than she bargained for.

d. Offeree must have knowledge of the offer. An offeree who does not know of an offer cannot accept it, even if her conduct otherwise would constitute an acceptance. Restatement (Second) of Contracts §23.

EXAMPLE AND ANALYSIS

Veterans offered a reward for information leading to the arrest and conviction of a murderer. One suspect was the boyfriend of plaintiff's daughter. Unaware of the reward, plaintiff gave the police the address of relatives whom her daughter and the suspect might be visiting. The suspect was arrested at the first address they tried. Glover claimed the reward. *Glover v. Jewish War Veterans*, 68 A.2d 233 (D.C. Mun. Ct. App. 1949).

Held: One cannot accept an offer of which one is not aware.

i. Assent versus consideration. These cases can involve lack of consideration rather than (or in addition to) lack of acceptance. Although Glover did what the offeror specified (gave information), she did not do so in exchange for the promise. The promise was unknown to her; it could not have been even part of the reason she performed.

ii. Special case: acceptance by performance. If an offer can be accepted by performance, an offeree who learns of the offer after beginning performance can accept the offer by completing performance. Restatement (Second) of Contracts §51. The offeror can frame the offer to preclude this, either by negating acceptance by performance or by expressly limiting the offer to persons aware of it before they begin performance.

2.   Acceptance by Promise

Most acceptances take the form of promises. Even words such as "I accept," which may not sound promissory, indicate a commitment (i.e., promise) to perform whatever return the offeror requested. An express promise, in words, will be fairly easy to recognize. Promises expressed by action — such as beginning performance — have been addressed previously. See 2.F.6. The following sections address two additional problems: acceptance by silence and acceptance by words that alter the terms of the offer.

3.   Acceptance by Silence

Sometimes offers indicate that, if the offeree does not respond, the offeror will interpret the failure to object as assent to the terms of the offer. In effect, the offeror, as master of the offer, specifies the manner in which the offeree may assent. With a few exceptions noted later, **silence is not acceptance**, even when the offer tries to make it acceptance. Restatement (Second) of Contracts §69.

a.   **Rationale: Ambiguous silence.**   The rule reduces the occasions when people who never intended to make a contract are trapped into binding contracts without saying a word. Silence is ambiguous: It could mean acceptance; it could mean the offeree never received the offer; or it could mean the offeree felt no need to reply (perhaps to express contempt).

    i.   **Offeror must tolerate ambiguity.**   An offeror who permits acceptance by silence must accept the ambiguity. The rule requiring an unequivocal acceptance contains an exception for offerors who waive their right to notice of acceptance. Treating silence as acceptance certainly waives a right to any notice.

    ii.   **Offeror cannot bind unwilling offerees.**   The concern for ambiguity protects the offeree. Silence is not a sufficient manifestation of intent to commit to the deal to allow courts to enforce a contract against the offeree. The ambiguity of silence destroys any confidence that the deal was mutually agreed.

b. **Exceptions: Protecting reliance.** The exceptions try to protect offerors who reasonably believed that the other party's silence indicated assent to the transaction. This is particularly important when the offeree knows that her silence will be interpreted as assent. To allow her to refuse to perform gives her an enormous advantage: She can use hindsight to determine whether the terms are favorable or unfavorable. If the terms are unfavorable, she can back out (claiming her silence was not a promise). But if they prove favorable, she can try to enforce the transaction (because both parties intended silence to constitute assent). Silence, however, is sufficient acceptance in four situations:

- If the offeree accepts services covered by the offer;
- If the offeree intends her silence to signify acceptance;
- If previous dealings make it reasonable to expect the offeree to notify the offeror that she does not accept the offer; or
- If the offeree exercises dominion over offered property.

c. **Accepting offered services.** An offeror may rely on silence as an acceptance and perform the services offered. Unlike goods or land, services cannot be returned once performed. Silence as the offeror performs may create an injustice: The offeree should not keep the services without compensating the offeror for them. Three elements must be demonstrated to show the injustice.

i. **The offeree must know the provider expected compensation for the services.** Where the offeree believes the provider intends a gift, she has no reason to speak up and reject the services.

ii. **The offeree must have a reasonable opportunity to reject the services.** It is difficult to take silence as assent if the offeree has no opportunity to speak up and reject the services. But where an offeree watches without objection as the services are performed, inferring her assent from silence is more reasonable.

iii. **The offeree must accept the benefit of the services.** In some situations, the offeree may have an opportunity to eschew the benefit of the services even though already rendered. For example, if someone paints your address on the curb in front of you house, you could refuse the benefit of the services by painting over the numbers or washing the paint away.

iv. **Offeror has choice of remedy.** Even if silence was not acceptance, the offeror often can claim a restitution recovery based on unjust enrichment: It is unfair to allow the offeree to keep the benefit of the services without paying for them.

(a) Expectation. The elements mentioned above convert silence into acceptance. This creates a contract; the offeree effectively promised to perform on the terms specified in the offer. The offeror, thus, can recover her expectation interest in an action for breach of contract.

(b) Restitution. If no contract arises, the offeror may recover the fair market value of the benefit bestowed. This may be less (or more) than the amount sought in the offer. Even if the offeror could establish silence as acceptance, she may prefer to sue for restitution.

d. Intent to accept. Sometimes, an offeree intends her silence to accept the offer. In that case, interpreting her silence as assent poses no problems — as long as the offeror indicated that silence was an acceptable method of indicating assent.

i. Evidentiary difficulties. An offeree who intended silence as an acceptance may testify differently if sued on the contract. When evidence (such as statements to others) permits the inference that the offeree intended silence as an acceptance, a jury may find assent under this exception.

ii. Objective versus subjective approach. The objective and subjective approaches do not conflict here. The offeree subjectively intended acceptance and manifested that acceptance by conduct the offeror invited: by being silent.

e. Inferences from prior dealings. When parties deal repeatedly, patterns of behavior may develop that make silence seem like acceptance. In these situations, the offeree may bear the onus to speak up and reject the offer rather than rely on silence as a failure to accept it. For example, when your automobile insurer offers to extend your policy at the end of the term, your silence may constitute acceptance of the renewal. (The policy may give you the right to cancel at any time, but you would still owe premiums for the period before you notified the insurer that you did not want to renew.)

EXAMPLES AND ANALYSIS

Plaintiff sent defendant eel skins. Defendant kept them for several months, until they were destroyed, but refused to pay for them. On prior occasions, defendant had accepted and paid for unsolicited shipments of eelskin from the plaintiff. Defendant admitted that it would have accepted this shipment, too, if they had been of the proper length and quality. *Hobbs v. Massasoit Whip*, 33 N.E. 495 (Mass. 1893).

Held: Defendant liable for breach of contract. Casebooks use the decision to illustrate the exception for prior dealings. Because defendant had accepted plaintiff's goods by silence in the past, plaintiff reasonably could believe that if defendant did not intend to accept this shipment, it would have notified him of the rejection. Under these circumstances, inaction was a manifestation of intent, as much as words or actions.

> **f. Exercise of dominion.** When an offeree obtains possession of the offeror's property and treats it as her own, silence indicates acceptance. The conduct of exercising dominion over the goods (rather than returning them, holding them for the offeror to collect, or selling them and giving the proceeds to the offeror) provides some evidence of an intent to accept the offer.

 EXAMPLE AND ANALYSIS

Could *Hobbs v. Massasoit* be an example of this exception, too? Defendant received goods that belonged to plaintiff. (To deny they belonged to plaintiff, defendant would have to admit a contract to buy them or claim they were a gift.) It kept them, without notifying plaintiff to retrieve them. Eventually the goods were destroyed.

If defendant intentionally destroyed the goods, that act certainly would constitute an exercise of dominion. But let us assume the goods were destroyed by accident (say, a fire at defendant's plant, which may explain why defendant does not want to pay for the eel skins).

Keeping the goods arguably exercises dominion over them. Defendant could avoid exercising dominion by holding the goods for plaintiff to collect. Usually, however, that would include notifying plaintiff that the goods were being held pending instructions on how plaintiff wanted them handled. See, e.g., UCC §§2-602(1) (Manner and Effect of Rightful Rejection), 2-603 (Merchant Buyer's Duties as to Rightfully Rejected Goods). Thus, a court could apply the dominion exception, though this may not explain the opinion in *Hobbs* as well as the prior dealings.

---

i.   **Fictional intent assumed.**   The rule assumes intent even if the silent offeree did not intend to enter the contract (e.g., if she intended to keep the offeror's property without paying for it). That conduct would be conversion, a tort, for which the offeror could recover damages. Treating the silence as acceptance assumes the best motives in the offeree, sometimes unrealistically.

(a)   **Actual intent irrelevant.**   Even if the offeree argues she acted tortiously, dominion is taken as acceptance. The offeree cannot force the offeror to sue in tort.

(b)   **Remedial implications.**   Why would anyone admit an intent to convert the offeror's property? Recovery in tort depends on the fair market value of the property. Finding an acceptance would allow the plaintiff to recover the price offered. If the offered price exceeded the fair market value, admitting a tort would produce a smaller recovery than finding a contract.

(c)   **Exception for outrageous offers.**   An offer that is "manifestly unreasonable" will not be enforced despite the offeree's exercise of dominion. For example, an offer to sell goods for 100 times their value would not be accepted by silence even if the defendant exercised dominion over the goods. The offeror will need to prove a tort or make a claim for restitution. This appears to be something **akin to an unconscionability defense**: The deal is so unfair that courts will not enforce it. (Unconscionability is discussed in Chapter 10.) The Restatement, however, explains the defense in terms of offer and acceptance; the offeror (or a reasonable observer) should realize that dominion does not indicate assent to terms that are so onerous. Thus, silence does not manifest assent.

ii.   **Acceptance negates tort.**   If the property actually became the offeree's under the contract, keeping or damaging it would not be tortious. (One cannot commit a tort against one's own property.) The offeree, thus, may prefer to allege that her conduct was acceptance, avoiding tort liability. Technically, this might move the case into the exception for intent to accept. Otherwise, the offeror has the option of treating the offeree's conduct as an acceptance or as a tort.

4. Mirror-Image Rule

An acceptance must echo the terms of the offer. If the acceptance differs from the offer, even in a minor way, the terms of the contract are not agreed. Rather, the response is taken as a counteroffer. This rejects the original offer, replacing it with a new offer on amended terms.

    a. Rationale. The mirror-image rule protects parties from the formation of contracts they did not want to make. Unless the parties agree to exactly the same terms, no contract exists. The parties, not the courts, may decide how important the changes are to them.

 # EXAMPLE AND ANALYSIS

Defendant offered to sell land to plaintiff for $800 cash. Plaintiff accepted, but the acceptance specified additional terms: taking the deed to a bank in St. Paul to collect the money, delivering an abstract of title, and a period for examining title before the funds would be paid. Defendant never assented to the additional terms and did not convey the land. Plaintiff sued. *Langellier v. Schaefer*, 36 Minn. 361 (1887). Held: for defendant. The new terms included in the alleged acceptance made it a counteroffer, not an acceptance at all.

The court could have interpreted the reply as accepting the offer and proposing, but not insisting on, some of the changes. For instance, the letter suggested defendant could designate a different bank if the one plaintiff proposed was unsatisfactory. The court did not so interpret the letter. Moreover, some of the buyer's specifications could not realistically be taken as mere suggestions (such as the requirement that he be allowed to examine title before making payment).

    b. Danger. The mirror-image rule offered a possibility for abuse. A party who changed her mind about the value of a contract after formation could scrutinize the negotiations for some minor discrepancy between the offer and the acceptance. If one existed, she could refuse to perform. This would not be breach because no contract existed; the parties never assented to the same terms. The potential for such abuse — combined with the increasing use of forms that often conflicted with one another—led the drafters of the Uniform Commercial Code to handle this issue differently. That approach is detailed at 2.G.5.

 EXAMPLE AND ANALYSIS

The government sought bids on surplus raisins. Defendant offered 10 cents per pound. The government accepted the bid of 10 cents per **box** (25 lbs.)—a difference in buyer's favor of about $23,000. After discovering the mistake, the government wired a new acceptance at the correct price. Defendant refused delivery. The government sold the raisins to another for less and sued defendant for the difference. *United States v. Brauenstein*, 75 F. Supp. 137 (S.D.N.Y. 1947).

Held: For defendant. The technical reading is clear. The parties' wires did not contain the same terms. Plaintiff's reply, therefore, did not accept defendant's offer. This effectively terminated the offer (though plaintiff could not treat it as a counteroffer at a discount, because it knew the government's wire contained a mistake). The second wire could not revive defendant's offer and defendant did nothing to revive that offer: thus, no assent.

Defendant changed its mind about the sale, apparently regretting that it had bid so much. (Otherwise, it would have treated the government's second wire as an offer and accepted it.) The technical defect in the government's original wire, therefore, allows a party who intended to enter a contract but changed its mind to escape from the deal. That is not the goal of assent rules.

---

     c. **Recent changes.** The common law has changed since the adoption of the UCC. Courts in many states have applied rules similar to the UCC's treatment of the battle of the forms to other contracts. The Restatement approach will be detailed after a discussion of the UCC.

5. Additional or Different Terms: The Battle of the Forms

In business, each party often has a printed form it uses in commercial transactions. Buyers have purchase orders; sellers have invoices. Each contains a series of terms written to obtain the most advantageous deal feasible in the market. Unsurprisingly, the seller's terms do not always match the buyer's. When one party makes an offer on a form and the other accepts with a different form, the mirror-image rule implies no contract existed.

     a. **Inequity of denying contract.** Treating cases as involving no contract confronts two sources of inequity. UCC §2-207 was written to handle these problems without giving either party undue advantage.

      i.   **Reliance.** Parties may rely on the agreement, despite differences between the forms. They may forego other opportunities or may start performing. Finding no contract would harm the party who relied. She would not receive supplies she thought were promised or might find her efforts to perform wasted. The ruling would reward a party who changed her mind — sometimes for reasons unrelated to the different terms.

      ii.   **Oral contracts.**   Sometimes the parties deal by phone, then send forms as confirmation. An oral agreement clearly exists in this setting, but usually fails to specify all the terms. Thus, the court cannot easily resort to a finding that no contract existed.

b.   **Last-shot rule: Before the UCC.**   Before passage of the UCC, the party who sent the last writing before performance had an advantage. Each writing was interpreted as a counteroffer, rejecting the previous writing. But once a party accepted the goods or accepted payment, that conduct functionally accepted the terms of the last writing.

c.   **First-shot rule: Acceptance despite different or additional terms.** The UCC treated writings as acceptances, not counteroffers, even if they differed from the offer. See UCC §2-207(1). This had several consequences.

      i.   **The contract was formed on the offeror's terms.**   The acceptance agreed to all terms of the offer, giving the advantage to the party who fired the first shot.

      ii.   **The different or additional terms were treated as an offer to modify the contract.**   The terms the offeree proposed did not disappear. But they would become part of the contract only if the offeror agreed to the modification.

d.   **Avoiding unwanted terms.**   An offeree can avoid accepting the offeror's terms by making its acceptance "expressly conditional on assent to the additional or different terms." UCC §2-207(1).

      i.   **Explicit limitation.**   Courts will not assume a party rejected the offer unless changed merely because the offeree included additional or different terms in the writing. The language must "clearly reveal[ ] that the offeree is unwilling to proceed with the transaction unless he is assured of the offeror's assent to the additional or different terms." *Dorton v. Collins & Aikman*, 453 F.2d 1161, 1168 (6th Cir. 1972).

ii. **Illustrative language.** A limitation would be easy to achieve simply by saying "I reject your offer, but would agree to the following terms." The UCC does not require that formality. Words such as "I accept, but only if you agree to the following terms" make it clear that no assent is intended unless the offeror agrees to the changes.

e. **Additional terms may be accepted by silence.**   Once the acceptance has proposed a modification, the question becomes whether those changes were accepted by the offeror.

  i. **Explicit acceptance will modify the agreement.** The offeror can assent to the proposed changes. The UCC does not require consideration for modifications.

  ii. **Between merchants, silence may constitute acceptance.** The rule only applies between merchants—people who "deal[ ] in goods of the kind or otherwise . . . hold [themselves] out as having skill" regarding goods of this type. Laymen are less likely to be familiar with the UCC. They can accept modifications, but their silence will not be treated as an acceptance.

  iii. **Even between merchants, silence may not mean acceptance of the modifications.** The UCC identifies three exceptions.

    (a) **Material change.** New terms that materially alter the contract are not accepted by silence. Although minor changes will be included, significant changes require express assent. Comments 4 and 5 to the UCC give several examples of material alterations.

    (b) **Objection.** Terms to which the offeror objects do not become part of the contract by silence. This applies not only to objections sent after receiving the acceptance but also to objections sent earlier.

    (c) **Limitations in the offer.** If the offer "expressly limits acceptance to the terms of the offer," no changes will be accepted by silence. This is, in part, a special case of an objection sent before the acceptance proposed the change.

EXAMPLES AND ANALYSIS

Hercules wanted to purchase a machine made by Brown. Brown prepared a price quote, which included an indemnity clause. Hercules placed an order for the machine by phone. Hercules then sent a purchase order (p.o.) that did not include an indemnity clause but did expressly limit acceptance to the terms of the p.o. Brown acknowledged on a form that included both specifications (for the construction of the machine) and conditions of sale, including the indemnity clause. The acknowledgment stated that unless Hercules objected within seven days, Brown would assume the specifications and terms were acceptable. Hercules corrected one specification, noting that "[a]ll other specifications are correct." One of Hercules's employees sued Brown for injuries caused by the machine. Brown sought indemnification from Hercules under the clause in Brown's forms. *Brown Machine v. Hercules, Inc.*, 770 S.W.2d 416 (Mo. Ct. App. 1989). The trial court held for Brown, but the appellate court reversed.

Brown's price quote was not an offer, so the phone order did not accept that offer. See **Example and Analysis**, 2.D.4. Hercules's p.o. was an offer. Brown's acknowledgment accepted the offer, even though it contained additional terms. Brown's acknowledgment did not expressly make acceptance conditional on assent to the additional terms. Thus, at that point, a contract existed on the terms specified in Hercules's p.o.

Brown's acknowledgment proposed a modification of the contract to include the indemnity clause. Because Hercules's offer expressly limited acceptance to the terms of the p.o., additional terms in the acceptance would not become part of the contract by silence. UCC §2-207(2)(a). The court also noted the indemnity provision would materially alter the contract, which would prevent acceptance by silence even if the offer had not contained an express limitation.

Hercules's response, stating "[a]ll other **specifications** [in Brown's acknowledgment] were correct" (emphasis added), did not expressly agree to the **terms and conditions** in Brown's acknowledgment. Thus, the indemnification clause did not become part of the contract.

---

       iv.   **These rules apply to confirmations as well as to acceptances.** When assent becomes binding during a phone conversation, written forms may simply confirm the agreement, filling in details not discussed on the phone. In that case, each party's writing proposes a modification, which the other party might accept by silence. (This explains in part why the offer is mentioned separately from other writings. Confirmations that cross in the mail serve as objections to inconsistent terms in the other's confirmation, even if the offer was not expressly limited to its terms.)

 EXAMPLE AND ANALYSIS

Suppose that in *Brown*, the price quote had been the offer and the phone call the acceptance. How should the case be resolved? Cf. *Idaho Power v. Westinghouse Elec.*, 596 F.2d 924 (9th Cir. 1979) (price quote was an offer, accepted by a purchase order).

Hercules's phone acceptance would form a contract on the terms of Brown's offer, including the indemnity provision. Brown's p.o. would be a confirmation. Any different or additional terms in the p.o. would propose modifications to the contract. On these facts, Hercules's p.o. might not be held to propose deleting the indemnity clause. The p.o. did not include the indemnity clause, but also did not include any clause inconsistent with it. Thus, even if everything in the p.o. became part of the contract, the changes would not necessarily remove the indemnity clause.

Assuming the p.o. proposed deleting the indemnity clause, it would not likely become part of the contract by silence. Brown's quote may not have precluded modification, but Brown's acknowledgment reiterated the indemnity clause. This seems a fair method of objecting to the deletion of that clause. Moreover, deleting the clause seems as material a change as adding it would have been. Thus, an express acceptance by Brown probably would be required to modify the contract.

---

v. **The rule probably applies to both different and additional terms.** UCC §2-207(2) refers to additional terms. It does not explicitly state that different terms can become part of the contract by silence. The comments, however, refer to different and additional terms becoming part of the contract by silence. UCC §2-207(2) cmt. 3. Courts appear to have followed the comment.

f. **Contracts that arise by conduct.** Sometimes these rules do not produce assent. For example, each party may make its assent expressly conditional on the other's assent to the different terms. This impasse produces no verbal agreement. Despite these reservations, conduct may evince assent.

i. **Assent by conduct.** If the parties perform as if they have a contract, the UCC will enforce an agreement. Conduct, not the words, indicates assent to *some* contract. The trick is to discover the terms.

ii. **Agreed terms.** When the writings agree, those terms are part of the contract.

iii. **Gap fillers.** When the writings disagree (or when one is silent), neither party's term governs. Instead, the default terms provided in the UCC (found primarily in §§2-305 to 2-315) provide any missing terms. Specific default terms are discussed at 12.D.3.

g. **Common-law reaction.** Some state courts have tailored the common law to include elements of the UCC's approach. The Restatement (Second) of Contracts §61 now indicates that an acceptance may be effective even if it requests a change in the contract.

i. **Counteroffer.** A response that makes assent to a new or different term a condition of the acceptance is not an acceptance but a counteroffer.

ii. **Acceptance and proposal to modify.** A response that accepts all terms of the offer but proposes a new term or a changed term as a modification to the original transaction is an acceptance. The contract is formed on the offeror's terms.

iii. **Accepting modification.** If the offeror accepts the proposal for change, the modification becomes binding. Acceptance of the modification can occur in any normal manner — including, if appropriate, by silence. See Restatement (Second) of Contracts §69.

6. When Acceptance Takes Effect: The Mailbox Rule

When an offer permits acceptance by mail (or other media in which the acceptance is not received at the same time it is sent), an **acceptance is effective when it is sent by the offeree**. Revocation, however, usually is effective when it is received by the offeree.

a. **Context.** When negotiations occur face to face or over the phone, it is relatively easy to pick a point when the acceptance becomes effective. Saying "I accept" or signing a document manifests acceptance and communicates it to the offeror simultaneously. When parties negotiate over distance without the use of phones, acceptance could take effect either when sent or when received. The choice is important if the offer is revoked after the acceptance was sent but before it was received.

b.   Notification of acceptance.   Acceptance usually requires reasonably diligent efforts to notify to the offeror. Restatement (Second) of Contracts §56. Timely notice often benefits offerees. An offeror unaware of an acceptance is unlikely to perform. But an offeree who makes reasonable efforts to notify the offeror of acceptance can enforce the contract even if the offeror never actually received the notice. Notice may be completely unnecessary in some situations.

   i.   Waiver.   The offeror may waive the right to notice of acceptance. For example, an offer that provides that acceptance is complete when signed at offeree's home office specifies an event that does not require notice. The offeree need not make efforts to notify the offeror — though the offeree's performance will notify the offeror in due course.

   ii.   Acceptance by performance.   Such acceptance does not require notice **unless** the offeror requests notice or the offeree has reason to know that the offeror "has no adequate means of learning of the performance with reasonable promptness and certainty." Restatement (Second) of Contracts §54. In cases in which the offeror has inadequate means of discovering the performance, the usual rules regarding notice apply: The offeror may still waive notice; otherwise, the offeree must make diligent efforts to notify the offeror or rely on the fortuity of the offeror actually discovering the performance within a reasonable time.

   iii.   Acceptance by silence.   Such acceptance, almost by definition, does not require notice. The lack of notice — the failure to object — is the acceptance. Situations in which silence can constitute acceptance are narrowly tailored, in part to avoid injustice to an offeror who receives no notice. See 2.G.3.

c.   Reasonable diligence.   Mail sometimes constitutes reasonable diligence. Because the mail (and even the telegraph, today) is slower than other communications, it may not be a reasonable method of responding to an offer. Particularly when values fluctuate quickly, a slow response may be unreasonable. Nonetheless, some circumstances allow acceptance by mail.

i.   **Express invitation.**   The offer expressly may allow acceptance by mail.

ii. **Mailed offer.**   If the offer is made by mail, it usually may be accepted by mail. Restatement (Second) of Contracts §65. This is not true if the offeree knows circumstances that make acceptance by mail inappropriate.

iii. **Custom.**   Acceptance by mail is permissible if that is customary in similar transactions. Where customs differ, the customs at the time and place the offer is received govern.

iv. **Other media.**   References to mail in the provisions above are generic. The rule applies to any medium specified in the offer, used by the offeror, or customary in similar transactions.

d. **Dispatch.**   Acceptance is effective upon dispatch. When mail (or telegraph) is a reasonable method of acceptance, the acceptance is effective once the acceptance leaves the offeree's possession. The contract exists immediately, even if the acceptance is not received. Restatement (Second) of Contracts §63.

i.   **Proper dispatch required.**   To be effective upon dispatch, an acceptance must be properly sent. Restatement (Second) of Contracts §66. Misaddressed mail or mail without proper postage will not be effective upon dispatch.

(a)   **Improper dispatch received.**   When improper dispatch actually reaches the offeror within the usual amount of time a properly dispatched acceptance would have taken, the acceptance is effective from the time it was sent. Restatement (Second) of Contracts §67. Sometimes you get lucky.

(b)   **Improper dispatch as counteroffer.**   An ineffective acceptance may serve as a counteroffer or a new offer. Restatement (Second) of Contracts §70.

ii. **Delivery to independent party required.**   Acceptance is dispatched when delivered to a third party, such as the postal service, telegraph office, or (probably) an overnight delivery service or independent messenger. Delivery to an employee or relative to mail or deliver probably does not count. The offeree retains too much control over whether it will be delivered to conclude that the acceptance has left her possession.

iii. **Exception for options.** When an option contract guarantees that an offer will remain open until a certain time, **the offeree must give the offeror actual notice of acceptance** by that time. Restatement (Second) of Contracts §63(b). Acceptance is not effective upon dispatch. The offeree need not worry that the offeror may send a revocation of the offer before her acceptance arrives. The option precludes premature revocation. A lost or delayed acceptance, however, will not bind the offeror, no matter how reasonable the effort to have acceptance delivered on time. The exception reflects the customary language of options, specifically requiring the offeree to give **notice of acceptance** by a certain time. The exception, by extending that requirement to all options (even if the language of the option did not clearly require notice), probably accords with most parties' expectations.

iv. **Retracting an acceptance.** An offeree might change her mind after mailing an acceptance but before it is received. In theory, the acceptance is binding from the moment it was sent. Restatement (Second) of Contracts §63 comment c (supporting that result).

e. **Revocation on receipt.** Revocation of an offer is effective upon receipt by the offeree. Restatement (Second) of Contracts §42. An offeror can expressly reserve the right to revoke without notice, but this is fairly rare. Otherwise, a revocation is not effective when sent, but only when received.

i. **Receipt defined.** Receipt occurs when a notice comes into the addressee's possession, comes into the possession of someone authorized to receive it for the addressee, or is deposited in a place the addressee authorized as a place for such communications to be left for her. Restatement (Second) of Contracts §68. This rule applies to rejections and acceptances as well as to revocations. (It probably applies to counteroffers, too, though they are not specifically mentioned in the rule. Counteroffers and rejections are treated similarly in other provisions relating to receipt. See Restatement (Second) of Contracts §40.)

ii. **Receipt without notice.** Receipt does not require that anyone has read or knows the contents of the message. Once in your mailbox, the revocation is effective. An acceptance mailed is too late if the mail containing a revocation already arrived in the mail room (or at your home mailbox).

iii.   **Racing to accept.**   What if offeree sends a rejection or counteroffer, then decides she really wants to accept the offer? The rejection or counteroffer is effective only when received. Restatement (Second) of Contracts §40. If she can find a way to communicate acceptance before the rejection arrives, a contract will be formed. (It would be prudent to specify "disregard previous letter," so the offeror does not interpret the rejection as a breach or repudiation.)

H.   PRELIMINARY AGREEMENTS

Some negotiations do not neatly fit the offer-and-acceptance model envisioned by courts. They involve multiple stages, with various parts of the agreement being finalized before the bargaining proceeds to the next issue. These more complex negotiations require some additional attention.

1.   Agreements When Parties Contemplate a Writing

When parties intend to reduce the terms of an oral agreement to writing, the transaction may fall apart before the writing is signed. When this occurs, a court must decide whether the agreement was complete even without the writing. The parties may have intended not to be bound until the writing was signed. Signing is the acceptance; everything up to that point is preliminary negotiation. But sometimes parties see the preparation of a writing as a mere formality. Assent occurs orally, forming a contract; the writing merely records the terms. Courts honor the parties' intent, to the extent they can discern it.

a.   **Writing to memorialize an oral agreement.**   As long as the elements of assent are sufficient without a writing, the law will enforce the agreement. Restatement (Second) of Contracts §27. The fact that the parties expected to reduce their agreement to writing does not necessarily prevent enforcement of the oral contract. To prevent enforcement, one party must show that no assent occurred.

b.   **Writing as the manifestation of assent.**   Sometimes the parties specify that signing a final writing is their assent. Anything prior to that time is just preliminary negotiations. When that intent is clear, the court will not enforce a contract until all parties have signed the agreement.

EXAMPLE AND ANALYSIS

Plaintiff (Empro) agreed to buy defendant's company. Both parties signed a "letter of intent" setting forth the basic terms of their agreement. The letter contemplated more complete writings. It also contained several escapes for plaintiff, such as approval by the board or shareholders. Defendant became dissatisfied with the security it would receive for future payments and refused to go forward. *Empro Mfg. v. Ball-Co Mfg.*, 870 F.2d 423 (7th Cir. 1989). Held: for defendant.

The parties did not intend the original agreement to be the binding event. Escape provisions and reservations (regarding the collateral, which ultimately cratered the deal) existed when the letter was signed, making it clear that neither party expected to be bound until the final writing was executed.

---

    c. **Differentiating the two situations.**   If one party **knows or has reason to know that the other party does not intend to be bound until she has made "some further manifestation of assent,"** such as signing a writing, then discussions are preliminary negotiations and do not produce legally binding commitments. Restatement (Second) of Contracts §26.

        i. **Objective test.**   The issue turns on what the other party has reason to know. Undisclosed subjective intentions make no difference. If one party keeps its plan to wait and review the writing to itself, courts may decide the binding event occurred before the writing was signed.

        ii. **Presumption for a contract.**   When in doubt, courts **seem** to enforce contracts even without a writing. Thus, **a party who wants to remain unbound until the writing is signed should say so explicitly** early in the negotiations. Silence is not golden; it creates doubt. Parties probably can avoid inadvertent contracts by **manifesting an intention not to be bound.** Restatement (Second) of Contracts §21. Of course, at the time the preliminary agreement is made, a party may not know whether she will want to back out or go forward with the deal.

    d. **Written agreements to agree.**   The same rules apply when parties sign a written preliminary agreement that calls for further ironing out of the details into a final complete written agreement. The initial writing can be binding if the parties so intend, even if disagreements prevent completion of the final written contract.

EXAMPLE AND ANALYSIS

Plaintiff (Pennsylvania Co., a railroad) sought to buy 26 percent of the stock in another railroad from a trust which held 81 percent of the stock. The parties executed a letter that stated the basic terms but contemplated a final writing negotiated by attorneys for the parties. The letter required approval of buyer's board and the Interstate Commerce Commission, if needed. After negotiations on the final document were nearly complete (without objection to any term), the seller got a better offer. It took the better offer; the original buyer sued. *Pennsylvania Co. v. Wilmington Trust*, 166 A.2d 726 (Del. Ch. 1960). The trial court denied both parties' motions for summary judgment. The escape provisions were not so significant that they definitely prevented the letter from being the binding event. But some comments at the time of the preliminary agreement made it unclear whether the parties intended to be bound immediately. Thus, the issue required trial on the merits.

2. A Third Alternative: Duty to Bargain

Although not recognized in the Restatement, some courts have suggested that a preliminary agreement might not bind the parties to go through with the deal but might bind them to bargain in good faith until impasse occurs. That is, the party retains the right to walk away from the transaction despite the preliminary agreement if the details cannot be worked out satisfactorily while negotiating the final writing. But the party cannot walk away simply because she gets a better offer or changes her mind for reasons unrelated to the final terms. She must try to work out the details in good faith.

a. **Subjective test.** Motivation for impasse may be hard to determine. When parties cannot agree on some detail of the final writing, it may be difficult to tell whether one party really objects to the language or seeks an excuse to walk away from the deal because she has changed her mind (perhaps because she got a better offer).

EXAMPLES AND ANALYSIS

1. Butler needed a commitment of permanent financing to obtain a construction loan. TIAA made that commitment in an agreement the parties admit was binding, even

though it required a final document to be executed at closing. In the final documents, TIAA inserted a clause governing defaults that was not expressly mentioned in the original commitment letter. Butler refused to go forward unless the term was removed. *TIAA v. Butler*, 626 F. Supp. 1229 (S.D.N.Y. 1986).

Held: For TIAA. TIAA presented significant evidence that Butler did not really object to the default provision but simply wanted out of the original contract. Interest rates had fallen, so Butler could save nearly $4 million in interest if it could break the deal with TIAA and find a different lender. It was not good faith to object to the term simply as an excuse to escape from a deal to which the party, in hindsight, wished it had not agreed.

2. Parties who press what they believe are good faith objections may be found to have acted in bad faith because **fact finders cannot always determine the purity of their motives.** See *TIAA v. Tribune Co.*, 670 F. Supp. 491 (S.D.N.Y. 1987). Tribune needed a loan structured in a way that would not impede a public offering. TIAA, though aware of that need at the time the parties signed the commitment letter, refused to alter the terms of its closing documents to satisfy Tribune's needs. TIAA sued for breach of the duty to bargain in good faith and won, despite the absence of evidence that Tribune really was motivated by lower interest rates rather than legitimate concern about the terms of the final documents.

---

     b.   Unclear rules.   Unclear rules create external problems. Parties often need clear rules so they can govern their conduct accordingly. For instance, a party who receives a better offer needs to know whether it can legally accept it. More important, a party who wants to make a better offer needs a clear rule to avoid the **tort** of interference with contract. Unless the effect of the preliminary writing is ascertainable without a full trial on the merits, people may become reluctant to make better offers.

 # EXAMPLE AND ANALYSIS

Pennzoil entered a preliminary agreement with the board and shareholders of Getty Oil, whereby Pennzoil agreed to buy three-sevenths of the shares of Getty. The preliminary agreement had not been signed by all parties. Texaco made Getty a better offer, which Getty took. *Texaco v. Pennzoil*, 729 S.W.2d 768 (Tex. Ct. App. 1987). Held: Texaco committed the tort of interference with contract. The jury verdict against Texaco exceeded $10 billion.

---

3. Renewal Options

Some contracts include a provision allowing one party to renew the contract when it expires. Leases on business premises commonly contain these provisions, as do some franchise agreements or long-term sales contracts. Often, however, the parties leave important terms open—including the rent or price for the renewal term. Parties cannot always predict years in advance what the renewal terms should be. Thus, the promise to renew the lease resembles an agreement to agree.

a. **Assent clear.** Renewal provisions usually are part of an original agreement. That original is a binding contract. Thus, the parties clearly **assented** to the renewal clause—and paid for it as part of the benefits of the original lease. Unlike the preliminary agreements discussed previously, definiteness, not assent, poses the obstacle to most renewal provisions.

b. **Definiteness problematic. When parties provide a means to determine the rent, the contract is sufficiently definite to permit enforcement.** Methods that make it possible for a court to identify the appropriate rent level include a formula for determining the renewal rent or naming an arbitrator who will settle disputes about the renewal rent.

c. **Enforcement problems.** Courts often refuse to enforce the renewal option if it provides that the parties will agree on the renewal rent (and they do not reach an agreement on their own).

EXAMPLES AND ANALYSIS

1. The parties signed a five-year lease with an option to renew for an additional five years "at annual rentals to be agreed upon." Lessor demanded $900 per month rent. An appraiser hired by lessee estimated the fair rental value at $550 per month ($100 less than the rent in the fifth year of the original lease). Lessee sued, seeking enforcement of the renewal option. The trial court granted summary judgment for the lessor. The intermediate appellate court reversed. *Joseph Martin, Jr. Delicatessen v. Schumacher*, 417 N.E.2d 541 (N.Y. 1981).

Held: For lessor. Lessor had not agreed to accept any particular amount of rent for the renewal period but had reserved the right to negotiate the amount at the time of renewal. Lessee had not bargained for a right to have a court set the rent but only the right to negotiate the rent at renewal time.

2. *Walker* involved a 10-year lease at $100 a month with an option to renew for another 10 years. Renewal rent was to "be agreed upon by the lessors and the lessee" based on "the comparative basis of rental values as of the date of the renewal with rental values at this time reflected by comparative business conditions of the two periods." No agreement emerged. Lessee sued. The trial court fixed rent at $125 per month. *Walker v. Keith*, 382 S.W.2d 198 (Ky. 1964).

Held: For lessor. The terms were too vague. Although identifying factors to consider, the contract did not specify a formula the court could apply to fix the rent at any particular level.

---

    d.   Underenforcement.   The decisions give too little effect to renewal promises. Lessor's promise to renew is binding and valuable to the lessee. A lessee, especially a business, may refuse to enter a lease unless it contains a right to renew; lessee may pay more for a lease that includes a right to renew. Decisions that refuse to honor these promises deprive the lessee of an important part of the original consideration.

        i.   Gap filling.   Courts are more willing to fill gaps in existing contracts than to create new ones. By recognizing the renewal right as an important element of an existing contract, lawyers may increase a court's willingness to fill gaps.

        ii.   Duty to bargain.   Alternatively, this situation may be a perfect place to apply the duty to bargain analysis. In *Joseph Martin, Jr. Delicatessen*, why did the lessor demand $900 per month for premises worth only $550 per month? Did she really believe the property was worth that much? Or did she want to get rid of this tenant? An obligation to bargain in good faith might avoid abuses without compelling lessors to accept less than their land is worth to them — assuming a jury can recognize good faith.

4.   Reliance on Preliminary Negotiations

In some situations, parties rely on preliminary agreements, incurring substantial expenses. In these situations, courts have shown more willingness to enforce an agreement to agree.

    a.   Substantial reliance.   Most cases involve substantial reliance, not merely giving up the opportunity to seek other deals or minor expense preparing to perform.

EXAMPLES AND ANALYSIS

1. Defendant agreed to obtain a construction loan for plaintiff or, failing that, to make the loan himself. After receiving reassurances that the loan would be available, plaintiff demolished a building he intended to replace with the new construction. The trial court held the preliminary agreement unenforceable because it did not specify the interest rate or the amount of monthly payments. *Wheeler v. White*, 398 S.W.2d 93 (Tex. 1065).

Held: For plaintiff. Having encouraged the plaintiff to rely on the indefinite agreement, defendant could not now claim the indefiniteness precluded enforcement. Reliance created an estoppel.

2. Defendant owned a chain of Red Owl grocery stores. Plaintiff sought a franchise. Defendant assured plaintiff that an investment of $18,000 would be sufficient to obtain a franchise. Defendant asked plaintiff to go through a series of steps to gain experience for operating the franchise, including buying a grocery store, then selling it at a loss; moving to a new city to work at a grocery store; and selling plaintiff's bakery business. Eventually the negotiations for a franchise broke down when Red Owl required an investment of nearly $34,000 to conclude the deal. *Hoffman v. Red Owl*, 133 N.W.2d 267 (Wis. 1965).

Held: Plaintiff could recover costs incurred in reliance on Defendant's promises. *Hoffman* is quite exceptional.

   b.   **Assent usually clear.**   Cases generally involve promises the parties intended to be final and binding but which courts cannot enforce. The agreement in *Wheeler* involved a signed writing the parties thought was a final agreement. No one contended that Hoffman and Red Owl intended their oral discussions to be a binding contract.

   c.   **Detailed agreements.**   Cases generally involve fairly detailed arrangements, when courts can fill in a bare minimum number of terms. The agreement in *Wheeler* specified the amount of the loan and the length of payments but not the interest rate. Hoffman and Red Owl discussed only the most general outlines of their ultimate arrangement before the reliance occurred.

   d.   **Reasonable reliance.**   The preceding two factors, taken together, suggest reliance may be more reasonable in some situations. When assent is clear and terms are detailed, reliance is more understandable than when assent is tentative and the terms relatively unsettled.

e. **Remedial issues.** Courts may not award the expectation interest in these cases. In both *Hoffman* and *Wheeler*, the majority endorsed a reliance recovery. That is not entirely consistent with the estoppel reasoning in *Wheeler*. On the other hand, it does comport with the realization that no enforceable promise exists; compensating for actual losses seems more appropriate that requiring payment of promised benefits when the promise was not enforceable.

f. **Options distinguished.** These cases are **not** options created by reliance on an offer. An offer has enough specificity to allow the court to enforce the agreement if accepted. The option prevents revocation. Preventing revocation, however, will not provide definiteness. Even if you find a timely acceptance, you must address the definiteness and consideration requirements. This section involves negotiations that *did not* satisfy the definiteness requirement. Reliance encouraged a court to enforce the promise despite this shortcoming. Although Restatement (Second) of Contracts §87(2) governs the use of reliance to create an option, you must analyze the indefiniteness problem separately.

REVIEW QUESTIONS AND ANSWERS

Question: Under what circumstances would words that manifest an intention to act in a particular way not constitute a promise to act in a particular way?

Answer: In general: when a party hearing those words would not be justified in understanding that a commitment had been made. Specifically: when a party hearing those words should realize that they are delivered in jest or when the words contain a condition that allows the party allegedly making a promise unbridled discretion to refuse to perform it. See 2.A.2.

Question: When a party undertakes to perform in a particular way if she is satisfied with the other party's performance, is the promise illusory?

Answer: Usually not. Courts infer a term limiting the party's ability to refuse to perform based on dissatisfaction. At the least, courts hold that if the party really is satisfied with the performance but pretends to be dissatisfied to avoid performing, the party has breached an implied promise to evaluate the performance in good faith. Because the party's discretion to withdraw from the contract was limited to genuine dissatisfaction, she did not have unbridled discretion to withdraw at will. When a performance can be evaluated by reasonable commercial standards, some courts limit the discretion even further. See 2.A.4.c.

Question: When is a promise so indefinite that courts will not enforce it?

Answer: When a promise is so vague that a court either cannot tell whether conduct performed or breached the promise or cannot determine an appropriate remedy, the promise is too vague to enforce. A court often will infer certain default terms into an agreement when the parties appeared to intend to make a binding agreement but omitted some details from their expression of that agreement. See 2.B.

Question: When is an expression of willingness to enter a bargain an offer?

Answer: When the other party is justified in believing her assent to the transaction is invited and will conclude the deal. See 2.D.

Question: Is an advertisement an offer?

Answer: Usually not. But when an ad is so complete, definite, and explicit that nothing remains open to negotiation, a party may be justified in believing that her assent is invited and will conclude the deal, making the ad an offer. See 2.E.1.

Question: Is putting an item up for auction an offer?

Answer: Putting an item up for auction **without reserve** is an offer. The highest bid accepts the offer. Putting the item up for auction **with reserve** is not an offer but an invitation for bidders to make offers, which the auctioneer can accept or reject. See 2.E.3.

Question: When does an offer expire?

Answer: (1) At the time specified in the offer, if any. (2) After a reasonable time lapses, if the offer does not specify a different time. (3) When the offeree rejects the offer (with some exceptions). (4) When the offeree makes a counteroffer (with some exceptions). (5) When either party dies or suffers an incapacity (with some exceptions). (6) When the offeror revokes it, unless revocation is precluded by rules creating an option. (7) When a condition of the offer no longer can occur. See 2.F.1.

Question: Under what circumstances will an offer remain open despite a revocation by the offeror?

Answer: In general: When the offeree receives an option — a binding promise to keep the offer open for a period of time. Specifically:

1. When the offeror promises to keep the offer open for a particular time and receives consideration for that promise. See 2.F.3.
2. When a statute makes a promise (express or implied) to keep the offer open for a period of time binding. See 2.F.2.
3. When an offeree begins to perform, tenders performance, or tenders a beginning of performance under an offer that can be accepted only by performance (i.e., cannot be accepted by promising to perform). See 2.F.5.c.
4. When the offeror reasonably should expect the offeree to rely substantially on the offer before accepting the offer, the offeree does rely to his detriment, and refusing to recognize the revocation will prevent injustice. See 2.F.3.c.

Question: For contracts other than the sale of goods, when will the failure to reject an offer be taken as an acceptance of that offer?

Answer: (1) When the offer permits acceptance by silence and the offeree intends her failure to object to be acceptance; (2) when the offeree has a reasonable opportunity to reject the offeror's services but accepts them knowing the offeror expected compensation for those services; (3) when prior dealings make it reasonable to expect the offeree to notify the offeror if she does not want to accept the offer; or (4) when the offeree exercises dominion over property of the offeror, unless the offer is outrageous. See 2.G.3.

Question: In response to an offer, what is the legal effect of a response that states it accepts the offer but specifies a term not mentioned in the offer (e.g., a date or place for delivery)?

Answer: For contracts other than sales of goods, the response is a counteroffer. The counteroffer usually rejects the offer but becomes an offer the original offeror can accept or reject. See 2.G.4, 2.G.5.g.

For sales of goods, the response has two effects: (1) It accepts the offer — unless the offer explicitly stated that a response including different or additional terms would not be considered an acceptance. (2) It is an offer to modify the contract, which the original offeror can accept or reject. See 2.G.5.c.

Question: When an acceptance proposes additional or different terms, under what circumstances will they become part of the contract?

Answer: For contracts other than sales of goods, if they are explicitly accepted, including (in rare circumstances) acceptance by a failure to object to the modification.

For sales of goods, if they are explicitly accepted or, between merchants, if (1) the party does not object and has not already objected to the proposed terms; and (2) the terms do not materially alter the agreement; and (3) the original offer did not expressly limit acceptance to the terms it contained. See 2.G.5.e.

Question: When parties enter an oral agreement intending to sign a formal written agreement later, does an enforceable contract exist if the later writing is never signed?

Answer: Maybe. If the parties intended the writing to be the acceptance, the discussions are preliminary negotiations and not binding. But if the parties intended the oral agreement to be effective immediately, with a written memorandum as an aid to recollection, the agreement is binding even if the writing never is signed. Unless the parties clearly express a desire for the writing to be the binding event, courts often enforce the oral agreement. Note: The same response would apply if the initial agreement is an informal or incomplete writing, where the parties anticipate a more thorough, formal writing to follow. See 2.H.1.

3 CONSIDERATION AND ITS ALTERNATIVES

 ## CHAPTER OVERVIEW

Society cannot afford to enforce every promise made. The cost of litigation might discourage suits over unimportant promises. Most societies, however, impose additional limitations on when people can sue. Even if the litigants feel their promises are important enough to justify court proceedings, the government reserves the right to disagree. Litigation involves the use of public resources (e.g., judges and courtrooms) paid for by taxes. Thus, the public (via its representatives) can reserve those resources for disputes that involve the public interest. This chapter focuses on criteria used to separate important from unimportant promises.

- Promises are not enforceable unless supported by a **consideration** — with some exceptions.
  - Consideration consists of a **bargained-for exchange** of promises or performances.
  - Something is bargained for if it is sought by the promisor in exchange for the promise and given by the promisee in exchange for that promise.
  - The exchange need not be equal, mutual, beneficial or detrimental, or the motivation for the bargain — though many exchanges will be.
  - Net effect: Gifts are not enforceable (until delivered); exchanges are enforceable from the time the promises are made.
- Some promises are enforceable even though they are not part of an exchange.
  - **Past Consideration.** If a promisor received consideration in the past but the promise is no longer enforceable, a renewed promise without any new consideration often will be enforceable.
  - **Moral Obligation.** If a promisor received a benefit and, from a sense of moral obligation, promised to pay for that benefit, the promise may be enforceable.
  - **Preexisting Duty.** If the promisor already has the right to receive consideration from the promisee but promises to give even more in exchange for that consideration, the promise often will be enforceable.

— **Action in Reliance** (a.k.a. **Promissory Estoppel**). If the promisor reasonably should expect the promisee to rely on a promise, and the promisee does rely to her detriment, the promise often will be enforceable —but the remedy may be limited to the reliance interest.

— **Charitable Contributions.** Promises made to charitable organizations may be enforceable without consideration or reliance.

— **Formal Promises.** Promises made in a recognized formal manner (signed writings or seals) may be enforceable without consideration.

A. RATIONALE FOR THE BARGAIN REQUIREMENT

American courts use one primary requirement to distinguish important from unimportant promises: consideration. Fundamentally, consideration seeks to identify those promises that each party felt were important enough to pay for: (i.e., when each party does (or promises to do) something in exchange for the other party's performance). The elements of consideration are detailed shortly. See 3.B. Preliminarily, however, a brief description of the reasons to require consideration may help to put the legal doctrines in focus.

1. The Economic View—Identifying Promises That Benefit Society

Many theories have been put forth to explain or criticize the law's decision to rely on consideration in deciding which promises to enforce. This outline does not attempt to explore all of them. Some will become apparent as we discuss various exceptions to the doctrine of consideration. Others may already be apparent from the introductory discussion of restitution and reliance. Nonetheless, the requirement of consideration will be much easier to understand if you consider the function it serves. One function of consideration is advanced here. You may not find it completely satisfying. Scholars have been criticizing consideration for decades. You should feel free to join them. But first, consider the strongest (I think) rationale for the doctrine.

a. The value of exchange. In any voluntary exchange, both parties improve their position. That is, each party gives up something she values less in exchange for something she values more. When buying a car, the buyer reveals that she prefers having the car to anything else that she could do with the money (or credit) that she exchanges for the car. The seller reveals that she prefers having the money to anything else she could do with the car. By taking a job, an employee reveals that she prefers money (or the food, clothing, and shelter that money can buy) to anything else she could do with that portion of her time. The employer reveals that she prefers having the employee's services to anything else she could do with the money promised as wages. Under these circumstances, both parties ostensibly are better off after the exchange than they were before the exchange. The more exchanges society allows, the better off everyone becomes. Thus, societal wealth increases with each exchange, as people gain things they value more and give up things they value less. Because exchanges increase societal wealth, society has an interest in encouraging people to perform once they have promised to make an exchange. Of course, society also has reason to encourage people to commit to exchanges only when reasonably certain the exchanges will benefit them, thus minimizing the occasions when people change their minds because they committed themselves too hastily. The mere act of making some promises enforceable should serve to discourage hasty promising, though other cautionary measures are discussed later.

b.   **Gifts distinguished.**   Gifts may or may not increase societal wealth in the same way. The recipient generally values a gift more than zero; a gift that has a negative value is a curse and presumably will not be accepted by the recipient. But society cannot know whether the recipient values the gift more than the giver values it. Thus, material may flow to people who value it less. If gifts always involved items to which the giver attached no value (or negative value), even zero value to the recipient might at least equal the value to the giver. But gifts often involve items the giver values highly, not merely items worthless to the giver. Because the state cannot be sure that society would be better off if the gift is delivered to the recipient, society has less interest in intervening when a giver changes her mind and refuses to deliver the gift—unless, perhaps, the recipient is worse off if the gift is not delivered than she would have been had it never been promised.

2.   Changed Circumstances

The making of promises indicates that at the time of contract formation, both parties expect to benefit from the transaction. The breach, however, suggests that by the time of performance, at least one party believes she will not benefit from the transaction—that she would be better off to breach the contract and face a lawsuit than to perform as promised. Sometimes these decisions are strictly opportunistic; one party would rather keep the other's payment without performing in exchange. Sometimes they reflect mistakes about legal rights, such as a party believing that she need not perform because the other party already has breached the contract. Often, however, nonperformance reflects a bad deal; based on new information or changed circumstances, one party realizes that what she will receive is less valuable than anticipated or what she must give up is more valuable than anticipated. In these cases, one party benefits from performance, but the other suffers a loss. Performance may or may not increase societal wealth, depending on whether the benefit to one party exceeds the loss to the other.

a. Foresight or hindsight? Ex ante or ex post assessment of the benefits of exchange.   When one party has changed her mind, the law faces two choices: (1) accept the parties' original assessment that performance of the promises would benefit both; or (2) excuse performance if one party can prove that enforcement of the exchange really will not benefit society. The law has rejected hindsight assessment of contracts for several reasons.

  i.   Practical difficulties.   Courts cannot easily evaluate the benefit each party would receive if the contract was performed. Often these benefits are subjective, such as the utility a consumer receives from owning a television or painting. Often benefits require predictions of the future, such as the profits a company will generate using a machine defendant promised to deliver. Judges, trained in law rather than economics, cannot easily compare one party's loss with the other's gain to decide whether the net benefit of performance will in fact increase society's wealth.

  ii.   Predictability and reliance.   Hindsight would make it dangerous for parties to rely on agreements. They would never know whether the contract was enforceable until a court told them. They could not even predict what a court would say until they knew all the changed circumstances that might lead the other party to change her mind.

  iii.   Other theories.   Other theories support ex ante evaluation. Most theories of enforceability, even those that reject consideration, evaluate enforceability at the time the promise is made, not based on subsequent events. For example, some justify enforcement because a promise represents the will of the promisor, who intentionally creates an obligation to perform. Excusing performance after the fact would undermine the autonomy and free will of individuals. It deprives people of the power to make binding obligations. Reevaluating the benefits of contract performance after the fact in effect seeks to protect promisors from their own mistakes. They made promises they thought would prove beneficial; the mistake (if any) was their own. Others justify enforcement to protect reliance. People may rely on promises based on the situation at the time the contract is made, not the situation at the time one party changes her mind about performance.

b. Net result. The value of exchanges explains why society chooses to enforce promises with consideration. That is not to say that every promise for which consideration is given necessarily will produce a beneficial exchange in light of all the circumstances that may change between the time the promise is made and the time the promise is to be performed. The law, however, leaves those concerns to the parties themselves. They can make the necessary predictions and calculations to determine whether they wish to enter a contract (by exchanging promises) or remain uncommitted and, therefore, free to act as they please in the future, once new facts concerning the benefits of performance become known. The economic rationale does not prove that enforcement of all promises ultimately benefits society, only that enforcement of bargains, on the whole, benefits society. Nor does it prove that every beneficial promise will be part of an exchange — hence the exceptions discussed later in this chapter.

3. Cautionary Function

An alternative explanation of consideration rests on its cautionary function. Because the law takes any words of commitment as a promise, people occasionally may make promises casually, without reflecting on them. Allowing people some room to change their minds in these settings may be fair, limiting enforcement to serious commitments. In making exchanges, people have reason to reflect before agreeing to the transaction. They know the other party will expect performance. The bargain setting is likely to remind people of the societal taboo against breaking one's word. Thus, promises made as part of the bargain seem likely to involve reflection rather than reflex. A number of the rules below — and the exceptions to consideration — involve situations in which the promisor's opportunity to reflect before making a promise fulfills the cautionary function, making enforcement by courts seem more justifiable.

B. ELEMENTS OF CONSIDERATION: BARGAINED-FOR EXCHANGE

Because exchanges tend to increase the wealth of society, promises that are part of exchanges receive societal support in the form of judicial enforcement. Exchange is defined by two elements.

1. Terminology: Promisor and Promisee

The promisor is the party who makes a promise. The promisee is the party to whom the promise is made — usually, the person who will receive the performance if the promise is kept.

a. Source of potential confusion. In the context of exchanges, each party makes a promise to the other. Thus, either could be the promisor and either the promisee. Thus, "promisor" and "promisee" may not be a clear way to differentiate the parties.

b. Advice on usage. In litigation, usually the parties have taken on roles that make promisor and promisee clearer. One party (usually the defendant) does not want to perform. She is the promisor, the party whose promise is at issue. The other party (usually the plaintiff) wants the promisor to perform; she is the promisee, the person who would benefit from performance of the promise.

    i. Briefing or discussing cases. Follow the usage of the court. That is the way the professor and your classmates will understand the terms. For clarity, you may want to substitute a party's name or role, such as buyer or seller or employer or employee.

    ii. Evaluating consideration under a rule that refers to promisor or promisee. The following rule of thumb may help: **Treat the party who wants to avoid performing the contract (the defendant) as the promisor; treat the party who wants to enforce the contract (the plaintiff) as the promisee.** The defendant contends that there was no consideration for her promise. To find that her promise was binding, you must identify something defendant sought in exchange. The plaintiff admits that there was consideration for her promise — specifically, the defendant's promise, which she now seeks to enforce.

    iii. The reverse situation. A defendant may admit that she sought something from the plaintiff which the plaintiff gave but may contend that she did not give anything to the plaintiff in exchange. It is not useful to think of this as a consideration argument. Defendant really contends that she never made a promise to the plaintiff. If defendant never made a promise, there is no promise to enforce, quite independent of whether the defendant received any consideration for the promise. The question whether defendant ever made a promise is addressed in 2.A. Efforts to rephrase the position in terms of consideration risk becoming quite circular and ultimately miss the gist of the argument.

2. Did the Promisor Seek Something in Exchange for the Promise?

This requirement seeks to differentiate gifts from exchanges. When the promisor seeks something in exchange for the promise, she is not making a gift but proposing an exchange.

a. **Almost anything the promisor seeks in exchange for a promise can qualify as consideration.** The Restatement (Second) of Contracts §71 speaks of consideration as either "a performance or a return promise."

   i. The definition of performance is extremely broad, including:

      (a) **"An act other than a promise."** Thus, any act requested by the promisor may constitute a performance. This may include customary acts (paying money, doing work, delivering goods) or unusual acts (stop smoking, swearing, drinking, and gambling; stand on your head).

      (b) **"A forebearance."** Thus, inaction, if requested by the promisor, may constitute a performance. Often parties request others to refrain from pressing a legal claim, like a lawsuit. A promise to pay money if a suitor will stop courting one's daughter also exemplifies forebearance.

      (c) **"The creation, modification, or destruction of a legal relation."** Thus, anything that changes the rights between two people or entities may constitute a performance. A promise to rescind a contract (thus canceling the legal obligations that existed between the parties) qualifies under this heading. Accepting the role as someone's lawyer, which creates a legal relationship between the parties, also may be consideration for a promise, even if the parties do not anticipate that the relationship will involve any further work by or payments to either party. (The relationship itself would prevent the attorney from representing anyone seeking to sue the client, which may be valuable if the attorney is good.)

      (d) While the definition of performance appears broad enough to encompass anything under the sun, a few specific types of performance may not qualify as consideration. These are addressed below under the heading "Exceptions to the Bargain Requirement."

   ii. **A promise will be consideration if fulfilling the promise would qualify as a performance.** That is, anything that would be a performance if you did it will be a promise if you say you will do it. (The definition of promise requires a little more than just saying you will do something—but not much more. See 2.A.)

b.   It does not matter who receives the consideration or who gives it.   As long as the promisor seeks it, the transaction may qualify as a bargained-for exchange.

   i.   P, a parent, promises to pay L, a landlord, rent if L will lease an apartment to C, P's child. L's performance (or promise to perform) would be consideration for P's promise, even though C receives L's performance.

   ii.   R, owner of a store, promises to hire E as an employee if P, E's parent, apologizes for insulting R years ago. P's apology would be consideration for R's promise to E, even though E did not give that performance to R.

c.   Sham consideration (versus nominal consideration).   A party can dress up a gift in the clothing of consideration. By requesting something trivial in exchange (such as a peppercorn, a cliche most contracts professors cannot resist repeating), the promisor appears to make a bargain, which the law will enforce.

   i.   Officially, sham consideration is not consideration at all. The promisor did not really seek the peppercorn in exchange for the promise. Thus, no bargain really existed. Most official sources reject the enforceability of promises that involve sham consideration. See Restatement (Second) of Contracts §71 comment b.

   ii.   The rules are not entirely consistent. Official sources also reject inquiry into the promisor's motivation. See Restatement (Second) of Contracts §81; 3.C.4. Thus, if the promisor's *words* manifest a desire for a peppercorn, the fact that other motivations may co-exist with the apparent desire for the peppercorn should not prevent a promise to deliver a peppercorn from being consideration.

   iii.   In addition, courts enforce many contracts that involve *nominal consideration* — a very small amount which borders on sham consideration. Some important contracts, such as option contracts (promises to keep offers open for a period of time, see 2.F.3) often recite consideration of $1. The enforceability of these contracts is generally accepted. See Restatement (Second) of Contracts §87 comment b.

   iv.   The inconsistency here represents ambivalence over the use of formality to replace or augment consideration.

(a) At one time, promises under seal were enforceable regardless of whether the promise involved consideration. The act of affixing a seal to a paper ensured that the promisor really wanted the promise to become legally binding. The law accepted the promise as binding because the promisor wanted it to be binding, without inquiry into its importance to society. (This reflects the will theory of enforceability, an approach that would enforce more promises than the prevailing bargain theory.) Any promise important enough for the promisor to put into binding form was presumptively important enough for the law to enforce.

(b) The enforceability of options also depends on their form. A signed writing that recites nominal consideration is enforceable as an option. The acts of signing the writing and including a recitation of consideration arguably demonstrate the parties' judgment that the promise is important enough for the law to enforce.

(c) Arguably, any sham consideration could carry the same significance. If the promisor feels that enforceability is important enough to justify her going through the motions of including a consideration, even just a peppercorn, in order to secure the enforceability of a gift promise, maybe the law should accommodate the promisor by treating the promise as enforceable.

v. Some jurisdictions enforce formal promises despite a lack of consideration. This is one of the exceptions to the bargain requirement. See 3.H.

vi. Most states, however, retain some vestige of the sham consideration doctrine. Even when addressing option contracts, the Restatement (Second) of Contracts (§87 comment b) hedges on the enforceability of promises when a very small amount binds a very valuable option, suggesting that the disproportion may indicate that the payment was not sought in exchange. The form of the promise does not suffice to make it enforceable.

(a) The reluctance to reintroduce form into the law may reflect a desire by states to make their own decisions about when to employ judicial resources. If parties want to make agreements, that is fine, but the state can decide which agreements are important enough to justify supervision in the courts.

(b)   Alternatively, the reluctance may reflect concern that formalities such as sham consideration do not carry enough significance for nonlawyers, who may not understand that their actions have symbolic significance beyond the receipt of a peppercorn or $1. If so, the formalities may not reflect a genuine desire to make the promise enforceable, at least on one side of the transaction.

vii.   Sham consideration cases are fairly rare, outside the option context which the Restatement (Second) treats as sui generis.

d.   Summary.   Usually it will be fairly easy to identify what the promisor sought in exchange for the promise. Simply ask why the promisor made the promise; that should reveal the things the promisor expected to receive in exchange — particularly if the promisor actually received something. Then identify objective indications (especially in the words of the offer or promise) that the promisor actively desired that outcome.

3.   Did the Promisee, in Exchange for the Promise, Give the Thing Sought by the Promisor?

This requirement also differentiates exchanges from gifts. When the promisee did not give anything — even a promise — the transaction is one-sided. The law might conclude that the failure to give something in exchange means the promisee did not accept the offer, so no contract ever was formed. See 2.G.1. More troublesome are cases in which the promisee appears to have given something to the promisor but did not do so in exchange for the promise. In these situations, the promisee appears to have given a gift to the promisor rather than to have entered into a bargain with the promisor.

a.   The promisee must give that which the promisor requested.   The promisee cannot create a bargain by giving something other than what the promisor requested. When the promisor requests something in return for the promise, only that something will serve as consideration.

i.   This is the basis of the **mirror-image rule**, discussed earlier. See 2.G.4. Problems like this almost always involve assent more directly than consideration. Thus, it may not be necessary (or even useful) to discuss consideration if a test raises a problem of this sort. I mention the point here primarily as a prelude to the next section, when the result is not quite as intuitive.

b. Reciprocal gifts are not consideration. Sometimes people who receive a gift (or the promise of a gift) give a gift in return. Gratitude is commendable but does not create a legally binding contract. The recipient of a promise cannot convert a gift promise into an exchange by her own act or promise.

 ## EXAMPLE AND ANALYSIS

At a restaurant, B promises to give A five shares of stock. Out of gratitude, A pays for dinner. B later changes her mind about giving A the stock. A's payment is not consideration for B's promise. Thus, the promise is unenforceable (unless other facts support an exception).

B did not give A something that A sought in exchange. B gave A something of value. She probably was motivated by A's promise. But the act was independent of A's gift. Neither party indicated that A's willingness to pay for dinner to B's promise to give the stock.

There is another reason for this result. **B did not seek A's performance;** B did not ask A to pick up the check in exchange for the stock. Because B requested nothing in exchange, nothing A can give will be the thing B requested.

The alternative rationale makes it hard to illustrate the rule concerning things given in exchange. It is hard to construct cases in which B requests something in return for a promise, A gives the requested return, but A does not give the return in exchange for B's promise. Nonetheless, that is what the next two sections seek to explore.

c. Conditional gifts are not bargains. A promise made on the condition that a future event will occur may resemble consideration—particularly if the condition involves some action by the promisee. If the promisor's words **seek** the future occurrence and the promisee causes the condition to occur, the occurrence may constitute consideration. But some specifications merely specify how the promisee may collect a gift. These requests do not seek a return performance and, thus, are not consideration.

i.   Professor Williston provided a famous hypothetical on this point—one that appears in many casebooks: "A benevolent man says to a tramp: 'If you go around the corner to the clothing shop there, you may purchase an overcoat on my credit.'" 1 Williston on Contracts §112, at 232 (1920).

    (a)   If the man sought the tramp's performance (going around the corner to the store) in exchange for the promise, the promisee's performance would be consideration. Williston argued that no reasonable person would interpret the promise in this way.

    (b)   More commonly, however, a court might infer that the promisor merely intended to specify how the promisee might collect the gift. Going to the store was not sought in exchange but merely a condition on the gift. If so, no consideration exists and the court will not enforce the promise.

ii.   Benefit to the promisor may help distinguish conditional gifts from bargains. If the court can identify a reason why the promisor would desire the promisee's action **independently of the gift**, the court may find consideration. Williston saw no consideration because there appears to be no reason that the man would want the tramp to go around the corner to the store, independently of the convenience involved in delivering the gift at that time and place.

 # Examples and Analysis

1. O owns a candy store. P, who appears to be homeless, is sitting in front of the store. O believes that P's presence will deter people from entering the store to do business. O promises P that if she will go around the corner to the clothing store, P may purchase an overcoat on O's credit. If P goes around the corner to the clothing store, is that consideration for O's promise to buy the coat?

We can identify a reason O might want P to go around the corner. That act provides a (perceived) benefit for which O might be willing to pay. Under these circumstances, a court might decide that the act of going around the corner was consideration: O sought it in exchange for the coat and P gave it in exchange for the coat.

2. Porter, a real estate developer, advertised that persons who came to an auction in the park would receive an equal chance to win a car. Maughs came to the auction, received a ticket, and won the drawing. Later, Porter refused to deliver the car. The court held that attendance at the auction was sought in exchange for the chance to win a car rather than merely a condition on the manner in which people could receive a gift (a ticket for the drawing). *Maughs v. Porter*, 161 S.E. 242 (Va. 1931). (The court refused to enforce the promise as an illegal lottery.)

Again, we can identify a benefit to Porter. He realistically might want a large gathering for the auction in the park — some of whom would be potential customers, but all of whom would contribute to the atmosphere of the event. That independent benefit gives the court some confidence in declaring that the promisor sought attendance in exchange for the promise rather than simply calling it a condition on the gift.

---

    d. **Ignorance of the promise.** If the promisee does not know that the promisor has made a promise or that she has asked a return, the promisee's performance may not have been given in exchange for the promise.

 # EXAMPLE AND ANALYSIS

O offers a reward for the return of her lost dog. F does not know about the reward but finds the dog and, reading the tags, returns the dog to O. F's performance may not constitute consideration for O's promise because F did not give the performance in exchange for the promise.

The *Glover* court actually held that to accept an offer, the offeree must be aware of the offer. See 2.G.1.d. The consideration rule here follows the same logic: to give something in exchange for a promise, one must know about the promise. Cf. *Glover v. Jewish War Veterans*, 68 A.2d 233 (D.C. Ct. App. 1949) (information leading to the arrest of a murderer was given before learning about the reward).

---

    e. **Promisee acts as she would have acted without the promise.** If a promisee acts exactly as she would have acted even if no offer had been made, it is difficult to discern whether her conduct was given in exchange for the promise or whether her compliance with the offer was mere coincidence. The promisee's conduct is consistent with either interpretation.

i.   A subjective approach based on the promisee's intent poses the usual problems. The promisee's intent is hard to probe. Only she knows her thoughts and she has an incentive to report them in the light most favorable to her litigation position, even if that is not what she was thinking at the time.

 # EXAMPLE AND ANALYSIS

Plaintiff (P) was the landlord of an oil business (B). Defendant (D) supplied B with petroleum. When B had trouble paying its bills, D helped manage B's financial affairs, paying creditors from B's accounts. P claimed that D promised that if P would refrain from evicting B from its premises, D would pay P the rent B owed (**from D's own funds**, not just from B's). (D denied this promise, but the jury found for P.) P was in Florida for the winter at the time. When P returned to Minnesota a few months later, P immediately moved to evict B and sued D on its promise to pay the rent. *Baehr v. Penn-o-Tex Oil*, 104 N.W.2d 661 (Minn. 1960). **The court held** that refraining from suit while on vacation was not consideration for D's promise. Even though D requested P not to evict B, P did not refrain from suit in exchange for D's promise, but waited only for P's own convenience, to avoid interrupting the trip to Florida. **The result can be questioned** in several ways.

The court may have overestimated the inconvenience of phoning a lawyer to start proceedings. If calling a lawyer from Florida would have been relatively easy, P's decision not to do so may have been made in exchange for D's promise to pay rent.

Arguably, P's restraint might constitute reliance, even if it does not constitute consideration. See 3.G. This argument turns on the same interpretation of P's motives. If P would have stayed in Florida and not evicted B even if D never made the promise, P's decision was not made in reliance on the promise any more than it was made in exchange for the promise.

D denied ever making a promise to P. The only writing between them supported D's contention. Might the appellate court have believed D and searched for a way to overturn the verdict against D? This seems improper; the court was bound to accept the jury's finding that D made the promise. Skewing the ruling on consideration could mislead future courts if this case really turns on whether D made the promise. Probably we should not assume that the court deviated from its role in this way.

Note that P could have made the case much easier by promising not to perform (if D's offer could be accepted by either a promise or a performance. See 2.F.5. If P promised not to evict B, that promise could constitute consideration. P, however, might be accused of breaching the promise, because P did evict B. Although D allegedly breached first, that would excuse P's breach only if D's breach was material. See Chapter 16. In any event, the issue of consideration again parallels a question whether the promisee ever accepted the offer. A clearer acceptance by P also might have made consideration clearer.

C.   COMMON MISCONCEPTIONS

The concept of consideration, defined in 3.B, is quite simple. But over the years, the concept has been expressed in a number of different ways. These different attempts to say the same thing sometimes produce misconceptions about the essence of consideration. This section identifies some of the most common mistakes about consideration that students sometimes encounter.

1.   Benefit or Detriment

Consideration consists of something asked for by the party making a promise. As long as the other party gives what the person making the promise asks for, it does not matter whether receiving it benefits the recipient or parting with it is a detriment to the giver.

a.   Consideration usually is a benefit to the recipient or a detriment to the giver or both.   People tend to ask for things they consider beneficial to them. If the thing has value, the party who gives it loses that value by giving it to the party who seeks it. But neither benefit nor detriment is required. Or, more accurately, we rely entirely on the parties' assessment of benefit or detriment. As long as one seeks something in exchange, the law accepts that as a benefit even if later evidence proves that receiving what she sought leaves the party worse off than before.

b.   Benefit may help rebut other characterizations.   As noted previously, see 3.B.c.ii, the existence of a benefit may help to distinguish conditional gifts from bargains. Benefit to the promisor is not necessary, but it influences the credibility of other assertions. If the promisor will benefit from the other party's performance, it is more credible that she sought that performance in exchange for the promise. When no benefit appears, it may be credible that she did not seek the performance but merely specified the condition under which she was willing to make a gift.

EXAMPLES AND ANALYSIS

1. Defendant uncle (U) promised to give his nephew (N) $5,000 if N would refrain from drinking, smoking, swearing, and gambling until age 21. N complied with this request. U died before paying the debt. U's executor argued there was no consideration for the promise. Arguably, N suffered no detriment from performance, because N was better off for foreswearing vice than he would have been if he had indulged these vices. Arguably, U was not better off for N's performance, because all the benefit of foreswearing vice accrued to N. Nonetheless, the court held that giving what U requested satisfied the requirement of consideration. *Hamer v. Sidway*, 27 N.E. 256 (N.Y. 1891).

By giving up the liberty to smoke, etc., N arguably suffered a detriment, even if not smoking is a benefit. Some language in the opinion would support this alternative interpretation.

Similarly, one can imagine cases in which N's clean living would benefit U — say, if U was a candidate for high political office.

The case involves other issues not pertinent to the discussion of consideration: Plaintiff was N's assignee, not N; U may have paid the note before he died; N may have released the note before he sold it to the plaintiff. This is another case in which concern about poor jury fact finding may have led some appellate judges to take a creative approach to the issue of consideration.

2. Suppose O, a landowner, purchased a hideous statue for her front yard, thus reducing the value of the property and (arguably) causing no loss to the person who gave it to her (because it reduced the value of the property it was on before, too). Is delivery of the statue consideration for the purchase price?

Yes. The fact that the statue does not benefit the plaintiff (objectively) does not matter. The plaintiff received what she sought, making the promise to pay enforceable. The law accepts the plaintiff's own implicit decision about whether she benefits (subjectively) from owning the statue.

2.   Mutuality of Obligation

Because exchanges usually involve promises or performances on both sides, courts commonly referred to mutuality of obligation as a requirement for finding a binding contract. Although often accurate, the term "mutuality" adds nothing to the concept of exchange and can distract from the primary inquiry. Generally, students and lawyers are better off considering the fundamental aspects of exchange rather than being drawn off into arcane questions of mutuality. Mutuality of obligation may arise in two settings. In one it is superfluous; in the other it is misleading.

a. **Obligation.**   Questions of mutuality of obligation sometimes focus on "obligation." When words give the illusion of a promise, no obligation exists on one side. Whether viewed as the absence of a promise or absence of consideration for a promise, this lack of obligation may undermine the enforceability of an agreement.

i. **To assess the existence or sufficiency of the obligation, however, one must apply the rules governing illusoriness and conditional promises.**   Mutuality adds nothing to this inquiry.

ii. **Discussing mutuality can confuse the issue.**   Often an effort to discuss mutuality lures students and lawyers into a discussion at a very general level, overlooking the more detailed issues that may need to be resolved in assessing illusoriness. Because mutuality is superfluous, there is no need to risk superficiality by addressing it.

b. **Mutuality.**   Questions of mutuality of obligation sometimes focus on "mutuality." When one party appears to have no duties under an agreement, mutuality may seem to be absent. Here, however, the issue is consideration. As long as a bargained-for exchange exists, no additional requirement of mutuality is imposed. Thus, it may not matter that one party has no duties under the contract.

i. **Overlooking consideration.**   Discussions of mutuality sometimes focus too narrowly on the parties to the contract, causing people to overlook perfectly acceptable consideration that flows from other sources. In this way, mutuality can be misleading.

ii. **Consideration to or from third party.**   The problem usually emerges when consideration will be given to or received from a third party. As noted earlier, consideration need not flow to or from the parties to the contract. See 3.B.2.b.

3. Adequacy of Consideration

When the benefits one party receives seem far smaller than what she paid for them, the transaction may seem unfair. Adequacy of consideration — or, more accurately, inadequacy of consideration — is a term used to describe that feeling of unfairness. In effect, a party argues that even though she entered into the agreement, the other party promised so little that the promise was inadequate (or too small) to serve as consideration for her own promise. The argument has no basis in the law. The law allows parties to decide for themselves how much things are worth. As long as a party gets what she sought, the law will not second-guess her decision to pay a great deal for it. See Restatement (Second) of Contracts §79.

a. **Subjective value.**   To some extent, the rule stated here recognizes the subjectivity of value. Some things have enormous value to individuals, even though society or the market may attach insignificant value to them. The law leaves room for people to agree to pay more than an item seems to be worth to allow people to pursue idiosyncratic desires.

b. **Unfair bargaining practices.**   Other one-sided transactions may reflect unfair bargaining practices, such as fraud or coercion. When a party can establish the existence of unfair bargaining practices, the law will refuse to enforce a promise. See Chapters 5–10. **A bargain that seems one-sided can serve as a red flag that triggers lawyers and judges to examine the bargain more closely for signs of unfair bargaining practices. But the fact that a bargain seems uneven is not, in itself, a reason to refuse enforcement of a bargained-for exchange.**

c. **Sufficiency of consideration distinguished.**   Some courts still talk about the sufficiency of consideration. Sufficiency differs from adequacy.

   i. Sufficiency requires that the item identified as consideration have some objective value, however small. Thus, the warm glow in one's heart received from making a charitable gift is not consideration for a promise to make that gift.

      (a) This concept could be incorporated within the requirement that the promise give the warm glow in exchange. The warm glow arguably arises even if the promisee adamantly refuses to give it.

      (b) More commonly, however, the issue arises under questions about nominal consideration or sham consideration, addressed later. See 3.B.2.c.

   ii. Adequacy refers to the fairness of the exchange: whether the values exchanged are roughly equivalent. An item might have substantial value (and thus be sufficient consideration) even if its value is much less than the value of the promise (and thus would be inadequate consideration, if adequacy mattered).

EXAMPLE AND ANALYSIS

O, a landowner, promises to sell W, a wildcatter, the mineral rights to O's land for $50. A few years later, W discovers oil on the land and sells the mineral rights to an oil company for $500,000.

The original price ($50) was sufficient consideration: Money, even in small amounts, has objective value. The original price may not seem adequate, because the rights were worth far more — at least, after W discovered the oil. Consideration exists for O's promise, because she received what she bargained for and it was a sufficient consideration. The inadequacy has no effect unless O can demonstrate that she agreed to the bargain because of unfair bargaining practices by W.

---

4. **Motivation of the Parties**

Like other aspects of contract law, consideration depends on the parties' words and actions, not on their secret intentions. Thus, when a promisor expresses a desire for a return promise, the law does not inquire into whether the desire for the return promise really motivated the promisor to make her promise. See Restatement (Second) of Contracts §81.

a. **Mixed motives.**   Part of the problem here is mixed motives. Some promisors have more than one reason to enter into an agreement. For example, parents may sell cars to their children, not out of a desire for money but out of a desire that their children have safe transportation — and perhaps that they learn that nothing in life is free. The price they receive may be incidental to their motivations. Nonetheless, the parents sought the price in exchange for the car. The bargain is enforceable.

b. **Exception for sham consideration.**   As noted earlier, parties who intend a gift can dress up their dealings in the guise of a bargain. See 3.B.2.c. The promisor does care about the thing she requests in exchange but requests something trivial to make the gift promise enforceable. Thus, the promisor's motivation can affect the decision regarding consideration. Sham consideration doctrine, however, is in tension with the prevailing objective approach to contract law. Courts eventually may enforce promises even when the consideration is a sham, because the parties' efforts to formalize the promises evince the importance the parties attach to making enforceable promises.

D. EXCEPTION FOR DELIVERED GIFTS

The doctrine of consideration was created specifically to exclude enforcement of gratuitous promises. See 3.A.1.b. Once a gift has been delivered to the donee, however, the **promise** to make a gift loses significance. The promise has been performed; no issue of enforcing the promise can arise. Title to the property has been transferred to the donee. Property law, not contract law, governs any claim the donor may make to recover the property after she has given it away.

1. Delivered Performance

Delivery is not always final. Performance under an unenforceable contract usually is not intended as a gift. A party may recover things delivered under an unenforceable contract. For instance, if one party defrauds another into entering a contract, the victim may rescind the transaction and recover any performance she has already rendered under the unenforceable contract.

2. Restitution Rules Govern

When seeking the return of a gift or performance under an unenforceable contract, the claim arises under restitution law. These rules determine whether the title to the property actually passed to the recipient (as a delivered gift) or whether the transfer of rights in the property was ineffective. Some of the grounds for restitution are defenses to contract actions, discussed later in this outline. See Chapters 5–10.

E. EXCEPTION FOR PAST CONSIDERATION AND MORAL OBLIGATION

Some promises are made in return for performances that had already been completed before the promises were made. The promisor is not really bargaining for the past performance. Nonetheless, the promisor has received a benefit; arguably, a promise to compensate the person who provided that benefit should be enforceable. Under some circumstances courts will treat the past performance as if it was consideration for the later promise.

1. Consideration Absent

Past consideration an oxymoron. Under the definition of bargain discussed above, performance provided in the past cannot be consideration for the new promise to pay for that performance.

a. **Nothing sought in exchange.** The promisor does not seek anything in return for the later promise. She already has whatever performance the other party was supposed to provide. (That is what makes the consideration past.) The new promise, therefore, is a gift. The promise may not be motivated by generosity. Often people feel a sense of obligation to renew their commitments even if they are not legally enforceable. But the obligation (if any) is moral, not legal. The new promise is one-sided, not part of an exchange.

b.   Nothing given in exchange.   The promisee did not give anything in exchange for the new promise. The past performance was given before the promise was made. It is virtually impossible to hold that the past performance was given in exchange for the later promise. See 3.B.3.d (promisee unaware of the promise).

   i.   Promise made on account of some prior action by the promisee is never part of a bargained-for exchange.   Consideration provides no justification for enforcing these promises.

   ii.   Performance would make consideration irrelevant.   If the party performs the new promise, no problem for contract law arises. Performance, once complete, produces a delivered gift. The consideration issue, however, arises if a party changes her mind before performing the new promise.

2.   Distinguishing Past Consideration from Moral Obligation

Both involve promises that could have been made part of a bargain if the promises were made before the other party performed. Past consideration describes promises that originally were part of a bargain; a new promise became necessary, however, because the original bargain was unenforceable. Moral obligation describes promises that never were part of a bargain but could have been.

a.   Value of the distinction.   Understanding the difference can save some time on exams. Recognizing when to apply one or the other — and when neither one applies — can avoid wasting pages discussing them. For other purposes, particularly class discussion, the technical distinction may not be important. Most casebooks treat these two (very similar) topics as one.

b.   Past consideration.   Past consideration arises out of a contract that has become unenforceable. Arguments about past consideration are appropriate only if several specific circumstances exist.

   i.   The parties once made an enforceable contract, supported by consideration. A past performance that was not part of a contract is more appropriately treated as a moral obligation. The consid-

eration for the original contract technically is the **past consideration** for which this exception is named.

ii.   One party's promise became unenforceable (e.g., because the statute of limitations precludes suit on the promise after several years have passed). If the original promise is still enforceable, you need not argue about the enforceability of a later promise.

iii.   Despite the legal excuse, the party made a new promise to perform. **Focus on the new promise.** There is no point discussing past consideration unless there is a new promise to enforce—a point that some students overlook. More important, courts enforce the new promise, not the original one—which can be significant if they differ.

iv.   The promisee had fully performed under the contract before the new promise was made (usually, before the original promise became unenforceable). If the party has not fully performed, courts often can find a bargain: A promised to finish performance in exchange for your B's new promise. This bargain can raise other consideration issues (such as preexisting duty, discussed at 3.F), but does not involve past consideration. The future performance can be consideration.

 # EXAMPLE AND ANALYSIS

L loans B $5,000. B fails to make the payments. L does not sue. After five years, the statute of limitations expires, barring L from suing B for breach of the loan contract. B then makes a new promise to pay L the $5,000. B still makes no payments. L sues to enforce the new promise.

The loan is not consideration for the new promise to pay, because it was not sought in exchange or given in exchange for the new promise. The new promise must satisfy an exception to the consideration requirement in order to be enforceable.

c.   **Moral obligation.**   Moral obligation involves situations in which no contract existed before one party performed. After the performance, the other party promises compensation—sometimes out of gratitude, but perhaps out of a grudging sense of obligation. Usually, the parties could have made an enforceable exchange of promises if they had discussed the matter before the performance.

i.   Some of the limitations on past consideration are implicit here. For instance, if the promise is made before the performance is complete, it may be possible to identify a bargain (say, "I'll finish in exchange for your promise"). On the whole, moral obligation is more open-ended, covering any promise made in return for a prior performance.

 ## EXAMPLE AND ANALYSIS

H, a homeowner, hired C, a contractor, to repair H's roof. C mistakenly repaired the roof on a neighboring house instead. N, the neighbor, upon discovering the repairs, promises to pay C for the work done.

The repairs are not consideration for the promise to pay, because they were not sought in exchange or given in exchange for the promise. The promise must satisfy an exception to the consideration requirement to be enforceable.

d.   **Resemblance to reciprocal gifts.**   You may find it useful to compare these situations as mutual gifts. When someone gives you a gift, you may feel a desire or an obligation to give something in return. But what you give (or promise to give) in return also is a gift. If what you received really was a gift, you are under no legal obligation to make any return at all. What you say or do after the fact does not convert the gift you received into consideration for a promise you had not made at the time you received the gift.

i.   In past consideration cases, the party who has already performed did not intend to make a gift. She thought her performance was part of a contract. The law that made the return promise unenforceable, however, has deprived that party of any right to the promised return. Thus, before the new promise was made, the performing stood in the position of one who had made a gift: She had given up something with no legal right compensation. Her hopes depend entirely on the gratitude of the recipient.

ii.   Generally, the temptation to enforce the new promise is strongest when the characterization of mutual gifts is weakest. In many cases, the past performance cannot realistically be characterized as a gift or a charitable act. When donative purpose doesn't explain the motivations very well, courts find ways to enforce a return promise.

3. Establishing the Exception for Past Consideration

Past consideration cases vary depending on the reason the original promise became unenforceable. The Restatement (Second) of Contracts identifies separate rules for several causes, including the statute of limitations, bankruptcy, nonoccurrence of a condition, and defenses that make a contract voidable. Most first-year courses do not delve into the details of these specific provisions. The sketch that follows covers the most salient points. If your professor explored the details, see the Restatement (Second) of Contracts §§82-85.

a. **Statutes of limitations.** These statutes require a party to bring suit within a specified time after a wrong is committed. A suit brought too late will be dismissed. Thus, a creditor who waits too long to sue may find that she cannot collect a debt. (This may be a corollary of Leo Durocher's comment, "Nice guys finish last." Patient creditors don't get paid.)

  i. A subsequent promise to pay a debt will be enforceable even if the statute of limitations bars suit on the original debt. Restatement (Second) of Contracts §82.

   (a) Watch out. Once the new promise has been breached, the creditor may need to sue in a timely manner. Otherwise, the statute of limitations may run on the breach of the new promise, too.

   (b) Illustration: L loaned $5,000 to B on January 1, 1980. B breached on February 1, 1980. The statute of limitations in this state is five years. L did not sue B and the statute expired on February 1, 1985. On March 1, 1986, B made a new promise to repay the $5,000. On April 1, 1986, B breached. L must sue within five years — by April 1, 1991 — or else the statute will bar the action on the new promise.

  ii. The new promise might be made before the statute of limitations had run on the original promise. Because the new promise is enforceable, the statute of limitations for breach of the new promise will expire later than the statute for breach of the original promise.

   (a) Illustration: L loaned $5,000 to B on January 1, 1980. B breached on February 1, 1980. L did not sue B. The statute of limitations in this state is five years. On March 1, 1983, before the statute expired, B made a new promise to repay the $5,000. On April 1, 1983, B breached the new promise. The statute expired on the original promise on February 1, 1985. L has until April 1, 1988, to sue for breach of the renewed promise.

(b)   A promise made before the statute expires probably creates a bargain. L gives up the right to sue immediately (a right L still had, because the statute had not yet expired) in exchange for B giving up the right to assert the statute of limitations — at least between February 1, 1985, and April 1, 1988.

(c)   The substance of the bargain may be open to interpretation: B might waive the right to plead the statute of limitations at any time (even after April 1, 1988) in exchange for L not suing on the promise in 1983.

b.   Bankruptcy.   This is a legal proceeding that limits the rights of creditors to collect from debtors. Bankruptcy protection can take several forms, but for our purposes discharge of indebtedness is the key. Discharge means that a court declares that the debtor no longer owes money to the creditor.

i.   For purposes of contract law, a new promise made after the bankruptcy proceedings have begun is enforceable, even if the bankruptcy discharges the original debt. Restatement (Second) of Contracts §83.

ii.   The federal laws governing bankruptcy limit the usefulness of this exception. You can study those laws next year.

c.   Conditional promises.   Some promises are not absolute; a party's obligation to perform arises only if a subsequent event occurs. (For example, a promise to buy a house **if** the bank approves a mortgage loan.) If the event does not occur, the party has no obligation to perform.

i.   A promise to perform despite the nonoccurrence of a condition is enforceable unless the condition was important to the fair operation of the contract. Restatement (Second) of Contracts §84.

ii.   It is not clear why the courts allow the waiver of unimportant conditions but not important ones. The waiving party can decide whether the condition is so important that she does not want to waive it. Nonetheless, the details of the rule rarely arise in first-year courses.

d. Voidable contracts.   Some promises are unenforceable due to fraud, duress, or other defenses (discussed later in this outline). The defenses belong to the victim; if she wants to enforce the contract instead, she may do so. One way to ratify the contract is to make a new promise to perform despite the defense. Once made, that new promise is binding upon the promisor; she cannot later change her mind and again assert the defense. Restatement (Second) of Contracts §85.

e. Common elements.   The provisions covered here share some common elements. These common threads may help you apply the specific provisions or argue for the creation of new exceptions.

  i. Promises enforceable.   Past consideration deals with real bargains. The original promise, having satisfied the consideration requirement, was important enough to deserve court attention, even though other rules (technicalities?) now preclude enforcement. Usually the new promise is no different from the original promise (or the unperformed part of the original promise). When renewed, the promise retains some of the importance that it originally had.

  ii. Waiver of defenses.   The new promise in effect waives a defect in the enforceability of the first promise — a defect the party has every right not to waive, but which she can waive without consideration. By enforcing the new promise, courts basically treat the waiver as final, denying the promisor the right to withdraw the waiver.

    (a)   If we could tell when a waiver was delivered, perhaps courts could simplify matters by calling the waiver a delivered gift.

    (b)   This analysis, however, would focus attention on the original promise; waiving the defense to the original promise arguably makes it enforceable. Courts, however, enforce the new promise, not the original. The new promise shows a willingness to waive the defense. Given that willingness, courts afford the new promise the same status of enforceability that the original promise possessed.

iii. **Absence of gift.**   None of these promises seems like a gift. In each case, the promisor entered a bargain and received benefits in exchange for the original promise. The promisee expected a return at the time she performed; she had no donative intent. The new promise can be understood without recourse to generosity, gratitude, or pity, the hallmarks of gift.

4. Establishing the Exception for Moral Obligation

Moral obligation cases often involve acts of generosity — often made under circumstances that prevent bargaining in advance. The recipient, out of gratitude or pride, may promise to compensate for the benefits of that generosity. The justification for enforcing those promises under contract law is not entirely coherent. This section will both summarize and probe the most common statement of the exception.

a. **Elements under the Restatement.**   To enforce a promise based on moral obligation, the promisee must establish four things:

- **The existence of a promise** (of course);
- **That the promisor received a benefit;**
- **That the promisee provided that benefit; and**
- **That failure to enforce the promise would produce injustice.**

The details of these elements can be discussed more productively in the context of actual cases. The discussion follows at 3.E.5.

b. **Foundation in restitution.**   The elements are almost identical to those of any action for unjust enrichment — except for the existence of a promise. A person unjustly enriched may be compelled to compensate her benefactor even if she does not promise to do so. The existence of a promise here seems almost superfluous.

i. The Restatement explains the promise requirement as an effort to allow recovery in cases in which technical aspects of restitution law might preclude an independent action for unjust enrichment. This suggests that the authors see moral obligation as a way courts fill a gap in the law of unjust enrichment, not as an integral part of the way the law enforces promises.

ii. On this reading, moral obligation is less an exception to consideration and more an exception to defenses available in an action for restitution. It might properly fit within the Restatement of

Restitution more than the Restatement of Contracts. Its inclusion here evinces the inseparable nature of contracts and restitution.

c. **Example of an unenforceable promise (*Mills v. Wyman*, 20 Mass. 207 (1825)).** On returning from a sea voyage, Wyman's adult son (Levi) fell ill. Though Levi had no money, Mills provided him with care for 15 days, until Levi died. Four days later, Wyman promised to pay Mills for the expenses incurred caring for Levi. Wyman later refused to pay and Mills sued. The court refused to enforce the promise because Wyman had not requested the services from the Mills before they were performed.

   i. The court noted several exceptions for past consideration but held that they did not apply. The court preferred to leave performance to Wyman's conscience rather than make it the subject of government compulsion.

   ii. The common threads applicable to past consideration cases do not apply to Mills's generous acts. The promise never was part of an enforceable bargain. Wyman was not waiving a defense to a promise, but creating an entirely new obligation. And both Mills and Wyman seemed to be acting gratuitously, not out of some desire to exchange performances.

   iii. The promise is not too trivial to be part of a bargain. The promise would have been enforceable if made before Mills finished providing the services. But the timing of the discussions (via interstate mail in 1825) did not satisfy the bargain requirement.

d. **Example of an enforceable promise (*Webb v. McGowin*, 168 So. 196 (Ala. 1935)).** McGowin wandered into a perilous area. In saving McGowin from serious injury, Webb suffered significant permanent injuries. McGowin promised Webb $15 every other week for life and paid this amount until his own death nine years later. The executor of McGowin's estate refused to continue the payments. The court held that the promise was enforceable against the estate.

e. **Cautionary note.** Some authorities believe the *Webb* case is a unique situation, unlikely to be repeated by future courts. If true, the exception for moral obligation may be an illusion — an exception derived from a case that would not be followed. In practice, you may persuade a court not to follow *Webb*. On an exam, however, you probably need to take the exception seriously.

5.   Distinguishing *Mills* and *Webb*: The Role of Unjust Enrichment

The factors in the Restatement do a fair (but imperfect) job of explaining the results in these two cases. The basis for the distinction, however, has more to do with unjust enrichment than with bargained-for exchange.

a.   Receipt of a benefit by promisor.   The court in *Webb* distinguished *Mills* by pointing out that the promisor personally received a benefit in *Webb*, but the promisor's **son** received the benefit in *Mills*.

   i.   This difference would pose no problem if courts sought indicia of a bargain. Benefits given to a third party can be consideration. See 3.B.2.b. Thus, it would not matter who Mills cared for under a bargain approach.

   ii.   Wyman received a direct, if small, benefit from knowing his son received care in his final days. Services that provide comfort would be consideration if bargained for in advance. The *Webb* court does not explain why this direct benefit would not justify enforcement under its unjust enrichment approach.

   iii.   This requirement of direct benefit may present an unintended barrier to recovery: Unsuccessful efforts may not support an enforceable promise.

EXAMPLES AND ANALYSIS

1. M wanders into a perilous area. In an effort to save M from serious injury, W suffers significant permanent injuries. Despite these efforts, M is injured just as seriously as she would have been if W had made no effort to save her. M nonetheless appreciates W's attempt. M promises to pay W $15 every other week for life. Is the promise enforceable?

There is no bargain, because the promise was made after the services. There was no benefit to M, because the injury was just as severe as it would have been if W had made no efforts. Thus, the exception as framed in the Restatement (Second) would not apply. The promise is unenforceable.

2. Would the example change if M paid the $15 every other week until her death nine years later, but her executor refused to continue the payments after M's death?

There is still no bargain and still no benefit to M from the services. W could keep the amount already paid as a delivered gift. But the promise to make additional payments would be unenforceable.

---

      iv. Some restitution cases (not based on promises) stretch the concept of benefit to allow recovery for unsuccessful services. For example, in *Cotnam v. Wisdom*, 104 S.W.2d 164 (Ark. 1907), a doctor attempted to rescue an unconscious person. The person died without regaining consciousness. There was no promise to pay for the services and no benefit from the services. Nonetheless, the court held that the services themselves were a benefit to the deceased and allowed recovery in restitution. A similar ruling might allow the court to find a benefit in the preceding example and analysis.

  b. **The promisee must provide the benefit.** The comments to the Restatement do not explain why this requirement applies. Yet it could limit recovery oddly.

EXAMPLE AND ANALYSIS

M wanders into a perilous area. In a successful effort to save M from serious injury, W dies. M promises to pay W's widow $15 every other week for life. Is the promise enforceable?

Again there is no bargain. M received a benefit. But W's widow did not provide the benefit. M received the benefit at the expense of the promisee-widow, but did not receive it from the promisee. Courts may not apply the unjust enrichment approach this way. Because the issue does not arise often, little guidance can be offered. What guidance we have — the text of the Restatement — suggests the promise is not enforceable.

---

  c. **Enrichment will not be unjust in all cases.**

      i. **Gifts**. When the benefactor intends a gift, it is not unjust for the donee to keep the gift without compensation — even if she promises a return gift.

         (a) Many moral obligation cases involve conduct that could be treated as a gift. Neither Mills nor Webb seems to have acted with an expectation of compensation. Thus, they arguably intended gifts.

(b)   The Restatement must envision a somewhat more limited definition of gift but does not provide one.

ii.   **Other benefits.**   Some benefits are justly obtained for other reasons. For instance, a party makes a profitable contract is not unjustly enriched by receiving the benefits of a good bargain. Thus, even if the party who profited later promised to refund some of the profit to the other party, the promise would not be enforceable under this exception. While the promisor received a benefit from the promisee, no injustice exists that requires compensation.

iii.   **Officious intermeddlers.**   Restitution law does not require compensation to persons who, without justification, provide unrequested benefits. (Imagine returning from vacation to find that someone had painted your house or car and expected you to compensate them for the benefit you received.) A promise to pay compensation should not change this result. Again, the promisor received a benefit from the promisee, but no injustice would exist if compensation was not paid.

(a)   Again, both Mills and Webb could be classified as intermeddlers. Thus, the concept is not being applied too strictly.

(b)   The promise arguably could demonstrate that the promisor did not view the performing party as an intermeddler. But that would obliterate the injustice requirement entirely, because all these cases involve promises—but promises the promisor now regrets.

iv.   **Disproportionate compensation.**   When the promisor makes a promise that is disproportionate to the benefit received, the courts may limit the enforceability of the promise to the value the promisor actually received.

(a)   In bargains, the promisor may set her own value on the return she seeks, promising more than others think it is worth if she wishes. Courts generally enforce bargains as made, without questioning the amount promised.

(b) In restitution, recovery varies with the benefit bestowed on the other party. This limitation confirms that the roots of moral obligation lie in restitution, not contract. In effect, the exception includes a requirement for adequacy of consideration that does not apply to bargains.

6. An Alternative Explanation: Ill-Timed Bargains

The appeal of claims based on moral obligation often arises out of a sense that the parties would have struck a bargain if circumstances had not prevented them from negotiating in advance. The exception for moral obligation may simply reflect a court's desire to look past the accident of timing and enforce what seems to be an otherwise perfectly acceptable bargain. In answering test questions — or practicing law — you may find it useful to consider why the parties did not strike a bargain in advance and whether those reasons support enforcement of the later promise.

a.   Constructive bargains.   In moral obligation cases, it usually is plausible to assert that the parties would have entered about the same bargain if they had negotiated in advance.

   i.   The promisee, having performed without any promised return, probably would have agreed to perform for the return later offered by the promisor.

   ii.   The promisor, having made the promise after already receiving the benefit without obligation, probably would have offered the same promise in advance in order to obtain the benefit.

   iii.   This seems to satisfy one purpose of the bargain requirement: to ensure that each party valued what she received more than what she gave up.

b.   Reasons for not bargaining.   The exception seems most useful when bargaining is impossible, such as in emergency situations.

   i.   If the parties had an opportunity to negotiate in advance but failed to bargain, the court should not enforce the promise. That will encourage people to make their own deals when possible. Actual agreements are better than hypothetical agreements. The court need not guess whether the parties would have agreed because they did agree (or failed to agree) in actual negotiations. When a party bypasses an opportunity to negotiate in advance, she should not be allowed to enforce a promise made after performance.

ii. *Webb v. McGowin* is a perfect example of cases in which bargaining was not possible. Under the emergency situation, Webb had to act first; McGowin would be injured before negotiations could be conducted.

iii. An advance bargain in *Webb* would look odd. Offers to prevent injury often look like threats to cause injury, which would be voidable as coercion. The issue here, however, is consideration. Even if Webb threatened to injure McGowin and McGowin promised Webb $15 every other week to refrain, there would be consideration. The law might refuse to enforce the contract for other reasons, but the requirement of consideration would be met. The oddity of the hypothetical bargain should not impede analysis of consideration issues.

iv. *Mills v. Wyman* is harder to explain. The case may be wrongly decided. If mail between Massachusetts and Connecticut in 1825 was too slow to permit prior negotiation, perhaps the promise should have been enforceable. (Even under an unjust enrichment theory, the case may be wrong based on the comfort the father received.) If, however, Mills could have written Wyman sooner but did not, the failure to negotiate in advance may not have resulted from lack of opportunity but from lack of effort. In that case, Mills bypassed bargaining and cannot claim enforcement of the promise.

c. **Statutory support.** At least one state statute sees timing as the root of the moral obligation exception. In New York, (1) a **signed, written** promise that (2) **recites the past consideration**, will be enforced if (3) the consideration **really was given**, and (4) **would have been consideration if bargained for in advance**. N.Y. Gen. Oblig. Law §5-1105.

i. The statute does not include an exception for parties who bypassed negotiations. Thus, intermeddlers who manage to get the promise in writing can bypass negotiations and still enforce the promise. This makes the subsequent written promise conclusive on the issue of whether the bargain would have occurred if discussed in advance.

ii. The signed writing requirement may limit this effect while serving a cautionary and evidentiary function. Limiting enforcement to promises the promisor makes after appropriate reflection may reduce ill-considered promises.

> **d. Distinguishing restitution.**   Timing would reduce the significance of
> who gave or received benefits, producing different results from the pre-
> vailing approach. Consider two hypotheticals addressed earlier. See
> **Examples and Analysis** at 3.E.5.a.i, 3.E.5.b, 3.E.6.d.

 # EXAMPLES AND ANALYSIS

1. M wanders into a perilous area. In an effort to save M from serious injury, W
suffers significant permanent injuries. Despite these efforts, M is injured just as seriously as she would have been if W had made no effort to save her. M nonetheless
appreciates W's attempt. M promises to pay W $15 every other week for life. Is the
promise enforceable?

Earlier we noted that neither an actual bargain nor a benefit to M support enforceability. Yet it seems plausible that M would have been willing to pay for the efforts
to save her if asked in advance. (In advance, she would not know the efforts would
fail. She might have promised even more for the efforts.) Negotiation was impossible
because of the emergency, not because W bypassed the opportunity to bargain. The
fact that no benefit resulted would not matter; M could buy the services. (Doctors
collect fees for their services whether they cure you or not.)

2. M wanders into a perilous area. In a successful effort to save M from serious
injury, W dies. M promises to pay W's widow $15 every other week for life. Is the
promise enforceable?

Earlier we noted that the benefit did not come from the promisee-widow, thus not
satisfying the literal terms of the Restatement approach. That fact makes no difference in identifying a constructive bargain. W's performance can be consideration for
a promise that benefits a third party. See 3.B.2.b. (Again, a bargain seems absurd on
these facts. A bargain for human sacrifice almost certainly would contravene public
policy. But consideration would not be the basis for refusing to enforce such a promise.)

F. PREEXISTING DUTY

A promisee may assert that she gave consideration by promising to do something that she already had an obligation to do. The promise arguably is not
given **in exchange** for the promisor's promise, because the promisee had no
right to refuse to perform even if the promisor made no (additional) promise.
These promises come within the general classification of preexisting duty. **The
preexisting duty rule has been eroded almost to the point of extinction.** In

studying it, focus on the arguments that rebut it. Cases may remain where the preexisting duty rule defeats consideration, but they will be rare.

1. Classical View: Formalistic Analysis Denies the Existence of Consideration

A promise to do what one must do anyway was not thought to be consideration — particularly when courts defined consideration as a benefit to the promisor or detriment to the promisee. A person suffered no detriment by agreeing to do things she already had an obligation to do; any detriment was inevitable because the duty to act already existed. A person received no benefit from the renewed commitment to act, because any benefit should have been received without the new promise (when the party performed the preexisting duty). Thus, courts refused to accept a promise to perform a preexisting duty as consideration.

a. **Vestiges of the preexisting duty rule.** "Performance of a legal duty owed to a promisor which is neither doubtful nor the subject of honest dispute is not consideration." Restatement (Second) of Contracts §73. Section 74, discussed below, addresses duties that are doubtful or disputed. See 3.F.2.

b. **Concern for duress.** The classical view reflects a fear that duress, rather than a revised bargain, may explain why a promisor would agree to pay more to receive a performance she already had a right to receive for less. By refusing to enforce any promises without new consideration, courts combated duress without requiring the victim to prove duress. Consideration, however, is an awkward tool for fighting duress.

    i. The preexisting duty rule is unnecessary. Parties can avoid coerced agreements, even if they satisfy the consideration requirement. See 7.A.

    ii. The advantage of not having to prove duress is also a disadvantage. Some new promises do not involve duress. Thus, the preexisting duty rule could prevent enforcement of legitimate promises. Modern erosion of the preexisting duty limits the doctrine's overbreadth, confining it to circumstances in which duress seems most likely.

    iii. Even in its prime, parties devised ways to circumvent the preexisting duty rule in order to accommodate legitimate transactions — and courts accepted the ploys.

c. **Giving new consideration.**   A promise to do a little more than the preexisting duty could be consideration. Because there was no obligation to perform the extra component, it was an added benefit or detriment. The additional duty could be very small because the law does not question the adequacy of consideration. A minor change in one party's obligations might serve as consideration for a very large promise by the other.

   i. **Examples.**   If a preexisting duty required payment of a debt on a certain day, payment of a smaller amount a day early could be consideration for the creditor's agreement to accept the smaller amount in full payment of the debt. Similarly, payment at a different place or to a different person might constitute consideration for the agreement to accept less than the full amount. The creditor could decide whether the added convenience was worth the discount.

   ii. **Sham consideration does not avoid the rule.**   To be consideration, changes in the promisee's duty must reflect "more than a pretense of a bargain." Restatement (Second) of Contracts §73. Thus, an extorter cannot avoid the rule simply by specifying some trivial change in her own performance. Unless the promisor sought that change, the preexisting duty rule would preclude enforcement.

   iii. **Evidentiary quandary.**   Because the promisor's objective manifestations control, not her motivation, it is difficult to contest whether she sought the change. If the change was of some advantage to her, the circumvention might succeed. Of course, the promisor could raise the duress defense, but the preexisting duty rule failed to alleviate her need to prove duress.

d. **Rescinding the duty.**   Some parties rescinded preexisting contracts and immediately entered into new contracts on different terms. Once rescinded, no preexisting duty existed. Thus, a promise to do what the rescinded contract required would be consideration for any return promise. Rescission of the preexisting contract was purely fictional; at least one party had no desire to release the other from the obligations of the contract. The rescission simply cleared the way for reinstatement of the duties under a new contract, to which the preexisting duty rule would not apply. See, e.g., *Schwartzreich v. Bauman-Basch, Inc.*, 131 N.E.2d 887 (N.Y. 1921).

e. **Waiving the duty.**   Some parties argued that a waiver of the right to enforce a preexisting duty constituted a delivered gift. Gifts, once delivered, cannot be revoked even if no consideration has been paid for them. Thus, waiver of the right to receive part of the other party's duties would effectively modify the contract by reducing the other party's obligations. Once released, the party could bargain to reinstate the duties (at a greater price than originally promised) without interference from the preexisting duty rule. See, e.g., *Watkins & Sons v. Carrig*, 21 A.2d 591 (N.H. 1941).

    f.   **Preexisting duty in context.** Casebooks sometimes subdivide preexisting duty cases into several subcategories: settlement of disputes, contract modification, accord and satisfaction, and rewards. The basic principles that govern each of these subdivisions are discussed in the first two sections. Once you understand settlement of disputes and modification, you may find accord and satisfaction somewhat repetitive. For several reasons, each subcategory requires separate discussion.

        i.   The Restatement (Second) of Contracts includes separate sections for each context. Thus, your professor may expect you to recite and apply a rule specific to the context instead of applying the general principle. (If not, you can skip part of the discussion below.)

        ii.   Although accord and satisfaction are variations on the themes introduced in settlement and modification, courts use different language when discussing these variations. That, in part, is why the Restatement includes different sections. Familiarity with the different terminology will help you use it effectively, in practice or on an exam.

        iii.   The actual conclusion differs slightly from context to context. In settlement of disputes, the dispute over the preexisting duty supports the conclusion that consideration in fact existed. In modification, the absence of such a dispute precludes this rationale; courts must hold that the agreement should be enforced even though no consideration existed. **There is no difference in the effect of these two conclusions: In either event, the promise is enforceable even though the return promise appears to involve no more than the party already was obliged to do.** But the difference in rationale may be important to some professors and some courts.

2. Settlement of Disputes

If, in exchange for a promise, the promisee provides something she arguably had a preexisting duty to perform, the bargain is enforceable if the promisee disputed the existence of that preexisting duty and has (at least) a good faith belief that her position may be found valid. Restatement (Second) of Contracts §74. **A real bargain exists here:** The promisee gives up the right to assert a defense in litigation in exchange for additional performance by the promisor. This is not an exception to the bargain requirement but a more insightful application of it.

a. **Establishing a bargain despite preexisting duty.** Under the Restatement (Second), a promise not to assert a claim or defense is valid consideration under one of four circumstances:

- **If the claim or defense is valid** (i.e., if there really was no preexisting duty, the bargain is clear under Restatement (Second) of Contracts §71);
- **If, at the time of the agreement, the claim or defense "is doubtful because of uncertainty as to the facts or the law";**
- **If the party asserting a claim or defense has a good faith belief that it may be held valid; or**
- **If a promisor seeks a written release of claim or defense that the other party has not raised, even though the party giving the release has no belief that the claim or defense is valid.** Restatement (Second) of Contracts §74.

  i. **Cautionary note.** Some states apply the preexisting duty rule with classical fervor. They may insert "and" where the Restatement says "or": That is, they may require **both** that the defense be objectively reasonable **and** that the promisee have a good faith belief in the validity of the defense.

b. **Valid defense to the alleged duty.** If the claim or defense was in fact valid, no preexisting duty existed at the time of the new agreement. Thus, the preexisting duty rule does not apply. A promise to perform would create a new duty, not reiterate an existing one.

 # EXAMPLE AND ANALYSIS

M, a foreign manufacturer, promises to produce a custom-designed machine for B, an American buyer. An embargo imposed by M's government makes it impracticable for M to ship the machine to B. Because the embargo satisfies the requirements of the defense of impracticability, M's obligation to deliver the machine is excused. B promises to pay M a higher price if M will deliver the machine despite the embargo.

M's promise to deliver the machine would be consideration for the higher price. M had no obligation to deliver the machine at the time B promised to raise the price, so the preexisting duty rule does not apply. (The new promise might violate public policy, perhaps depending on the relationship between America and the foreign government. But consideration provides no basis for refusing enforcement.)

---

i. **Parties rarely rely on this line of argument because, in practice, they cannot predict whether the court will find the defense valid.** Promisees cannot know whether the new promise is enforceable until a court rules on their defense to the alleged preexisting duty. They could perform first and hope the promisor performed. But unless confident the promise is enforceable, many promisees would prefer to litigate before they perform.

ii. **A preexisting duty need not arise from an underlying contract.** Settlement agreements resolve disputes in litigation (or prospective litigation) over any subject matter.

iii. **Requiring a valid defense might prevent settlement of suits.** If courts required defendants to demonstrate that they really were not liable in order to justify enforcement of a settlement agreement, defendants might refuse to settle lawsuits. They could never receive an enforceable release in any case in which a court later decided the plaintiff had a valid claim (and, thus, defendant owed a preexisting duty to compensate plaintiff for any damages). Thus, in the cases in which settlement is most desirable (where plaintiffs' claims are valid), defendants have no incentive to settle because the agreement would not be enforceable. (If a defense is so strong a defendant **knows** a court would uphold it, the settlement would be enforceable. But a defendant who knows a defense is valid has a great incentive to litigate instead of settling.)

c. **A doubtful (but invalid) defense.** If "the claim or defense was in fact doubtful because of uncertainty as to the facts or the law," waiver of the defense (i.e., performance of the preexisting duty) is consideration for a return promise. Restatement (Second) of Contracts §74(1)(a). When a claim or defense is doubtful, each party faces litigation costs if one party asserts it instead of performing the preexisting duty. Because neither party can be sure of a victory in court, each may prefer to settle the dispute. Even if one party promises more in exchange for a performance she felt entitled to receive without the promise, she nonetheless seeks something (release from a claim or defense, thus avoiding litigation costs) that the other gives in exchange for the promise. This satisfies the bargain requirement.

>   **i.**   The merits of the claim or defense are irrelevant to enforceability of the settlement. If the outcome is objectively uncertain, an agreement between the parties resolving the dispute is enforceable, regardless of who would have won if the case had been litigated.

 # EXAMPLE AND ANALYSIS

V, owner of a seagoing vessel, promises to deliver cargo belonging to M, a manufacturer, to a buyer in India. V plans to travel through the Suez Canal and quotes a price on that basis. War in the Middle East closes the canal. V can carry the goods around the Cape, but at much greater expense. V tells M the contract is impracticable and that the vessel will return to port. M promises to pay more for the delivery of the goods and S accepts.

The promise probably is enforceable. The impracticability defense is weaker but objectively plausible. Thus, in inducing V to waive the defense and perform as originally promised, M bargained for a valuable consideration. It does not matter whether a court would have found the defense valid.

>   **ii.**   This rule will resolve most cases—particularly cases involving the settlement of litigation. Unless a claim or defense is frivolous, there will be some doubt about the outcome of the case, making a promise to settle enforceable.

>   **iii.**   **Doubt about the claim must arise from uncertainty in the law or facts, not the hope that a miscarriage of justice will occur.**   A claim or defense that has no merit can succeed if a jury misunderstands the issue or sympathizes with the party. Courts require uncertainty as to matters of law or fact, not just uncertainty as to the outcome.

>   **iv.**   **Doubt existing at the time of the agreement is sufficient to support a finding of consideration.**   Subsequent events may remove doubt. For example, scientific investigation may reveal that a particular drug could not possibly have caused the plaintiff's

injury. Nonetheless, if the claim was doubtful at the time of the settlement, subsequent events will not negate the existence of consideration.

d.   Good faith assertion of an implausible defense.   If "the forbearing or surrendering party believes that the claim or defense may be fairly determined to be valid," relinquishing the claim or defense will constitute consideration. Restatement (Second) of Contracts §74(1)(b). A claim or defense may be so weak that a reasonable observer would conclude it had no realistic chance to prevail; no uncertainty of law or fact made it doubtful at all. Still, the bargain will be enforceable if the party asserting the claim or defense honestly (though unreasonably) believed that she could prevail—not merely by prejudice or accident but by persuading a rational decision maker to see the justness of her position.

   i.   A promisee who honestly believes she is right may not give up if the promisor refuses to settle. Thus, the promisor may face significant litigation costs to prevail. She reasonably might seek to avoid the cost of litigating (despite certain victory) by settling the dispute. This satisfies the definition of bargain.

   ii.   **The party asserting the untenable claim or defense must have a good faith belief that it might prevail on the merits.**   This section is not designed to allow everyone who brings a frivolous suit to enforce a settlement. A party who has no honest belief that her claim or defense might prevail cannot enforce a settlement. Duress law explains this result better than the consideration rules.

   (a)   Promisors may seek to avoid expensive litigation if a determined plaintiff threatened a claim in bad faith. Thus, a bargain could exist in more cases than the exception here recognizes.

   (b)   The duress defense, however, allows a coerced party to avoid enforcement of a promise obtained by a threat to bring or defend a suit in bad faith. See 7.A. The preexisting duty rule produces the same effect by pretending that the promisee did not give anything in exchange for the promise under these circumstances.

   iii.   Litigants who believe their opponent has raised a claim or defense in bad faith should not rely on the preexisting duty rule in deciding to settle. Good faith is hard to challenge. When the party asserting the frivolous claim or defense testifies that she believed it might prevail, there may be little evidence to rebut this testimony. Thus, the good faith test comes very close to abandoning the preexisting duty rule altogether.

    iv. This approach helps assure a party waiving a claim or defense that the contract is enforceable. She need not worry that a court might refuse enforcement because some observer does not share her own sense what justice requires. Although mistakes about the party's good faith are possible, they seem less likely than differing views of reasonableness. (Where she lacks good faith, she also knows up front that the agreement is unenforceable — though the difficulty of challenging good faith offers some hope for the ultimate enforceability of the compromise.)

    v. Remember: Some jurisdictions require that the claim be both objectively doubtful and subjectively believed to have a chance to prevail. Thus, relinquishing even a doubtful claim is not consideration if the party believed the claim had no chance of success. Similarly, a party with a good faith belief in a frivolous defense cannot enforce the settlement.

  e. **Release of unasserted claims.**   Occasionally people want to remove any doubt concerning their rights. They may seek out people who never thought they had any claim and offer them money in exchange for a release of that claim. Written agreements of this sort are valid even if the party releasing the claim has no good faith belief that the claim or defense is valid.

 # EXAMPLE AND ANALYSIS

D, a developer, wants to build an office building on land it plans to purchase. A title search reveals a remote possibility that O, a descendant of someone who once had a claim to the property, could assert her ancestor's claim. To prevent litigation (and perhaps to satisfy a lender or insurer), D offers O $100 in exchange for a quitclaim deed conveying any interest she might have in the land. O knows that she has no claim to the land, not even a doubtful one. Nonetheless, she accepts the offer and signs the deed.

O's release is consideration for D's promise to pay $100. D really seeks something — assurance that even remote or frivolous problems will not materialize. (A corollary to Murphy's Law holds that if remote claims might materialize, they will—and at the time when the cost or inconvenience of eliminating them will be greatest.) O gives that assurance in exchange for the promise. Again, the requirements of consideration are satisfied—and problems of extortion seem remote in this setting.

3. Modification of Contracts (in General)

A promisee's preexisting duty may arise from an earlier contract with the promisor. Sometimes parties want to change their contracts. Consideration poses no problem if each party seeks a change in the other's performance —including rescission of the entire contract. Problems arise when the parties adjust only one side of the transaction—for example, the promisor agrees to pay more for work that she was already entitled to receive for less under the original contract. This does not look like a bargain.

a. **Settlement of claims distinguished.** When one party asserts that the original contract is not binding, a modification may be enforceable under the rules discussed in the previous section. See 3.F.2. A dispute over the existence of a duty may support a compromise bargain. **Modification, however, may not involve a dispute over performance under the original contract.** The parties may decide to adjust the contract, even though no plausible legal excuse exists. The method of identifying a real bargain in discussing settlement of claims may not work here. Courts enforce some modifications even though no bargain exists.

 ## EXAMPLE AND ANALYSIS

Sailors agreed to work on a ship for £5 per month. Two deserted in a foreign port, which meant more work for the hands who remained. The captain promised to divide the wages of those two among the seamen who remained. Upon return to London, the owners refused to pay the extra wages and the sailors sued. *Stilk v. Myrick*, 170 Eng. Rep. 1168 (1809).

Held: For defendant. A promise to do what they already were legally obligated to do was not consideration for the promise of additional wages. There was no dispute regarding the obligation to perform the rest of the contract. The sailor's did not walk off the job or claim to have a right to do so. Thus, the court could not find a bargain by saying they gave up a plausible defense to performance in exchange for the extra pay, even if it had been so inclined. The tenor of the decision suggests it was not so inclined.

b.   **Cautionary note.**   Modifications exist when **both parties agree to change a contract**. Occasionally, students see modifications in odd places. When one party proposes a change, that is not a modification (until the other party agrees). When one party performs in a way the other party believes is insufficient, that is not a modification (though it may be a breach). When parties dispute the meaning of a contract —that is, they disagree about what it requires one of them to do— neither party is arguing for a modification, but for enforcement of the original contract as that party interprets it. Be careful to apply rules governing modification only when a second agreement changes an original agreement.

c.   **Concern for duress.**   Again, the real issue is duress: preventing one party from using improper threats to extort a greater promise from the other in exchange for a performance she had a right to receive for less under the original contract. Alternatively, changed circumstances might make it seem unfair to insist upon the original terms, leading a party to agree to new terms. Modern courts seek to enforce legitimate adjustments without enforcing coerced agreements.

EXAMPLE AND ANALYSIS

In *Stilk*, duress seems a poor explanation for the result. The sailors had not walked off work, nor is there any mention of a threat to do so. If the captain had heard rumblings among the crew, perhaps an implicit threat existed, which might satisfy the requirements of duress. But the promise may have been motivated by the captain's sense of fair play as much as by his fear of further desertion. Much of the recent development of the law stems from efforts to permit modification in cases such as *Stilk* while preventing enforcement of modifications obtained by duress.

4.   **Modification in Sales of Goods: Consideration Not Required**

The UCC abolished the requirement of consideration for modification of a contract for the sale of goods. See UCC §2-209.

a.   **Good faith required.**   A modification is enforceable only if made in good faith—a duty the UCC imposes in the "performance or enforcement" of "[e]very contract or duty within this Act." UCC §1-203. The official comments to §2-209 clarify that this duty applies to modification of contracts. This has two implications:

    i.   **A modification obtained in bad faith will not be enforced.** Thus, modifications are not enforceable if sought to escape from an unfavorable contract or to extort additional consideration without a legitimate commercial justification.

    ii.   **Even if supported by additional consideration, a modification obtained in bad faith will not be enforced.** Under the common law, consideration posed no issue if each party's performance changed. The UCC rejects this formalistic approach. Parties cannot escape scrutiny of the commercial justification for a modification merely by including some trivial consideration for the change.

b. **Writing sometimes required.** UCC §2-209 devotes considerable attention to the circumstances in which a modification may need to be in writing. This outline addresses those issues below at 4.C.2.

5. Modification of Other Contracts

Common-law courts have not embraced the UCC's abolition of consideration in modifications. Nonetheless, they have enforced modifications despite the preexisting duty rule under some circumstances. See Restatement (Second) of Contracts §89.

a. **Limited scope of the exception.**

    i.   **Limitation to contracts without consideration.** Section 89 identifies an exception to the requirement of consideration. **A modification in which each party gives consideration for the change is binding without regard to the exception.** Thus, modifications that result from disputes over the continued enforceability of the original contract need not satisfy §89. Settlement of such a dispute constitutes consideration under §74, making analysis under §89 superfluous. (Of course, **on an exam you may want to hedge your bets** by analyzing both provisions, depending on time available and your professor's preferences.)

    ii.   **Limitation to executory contracts.** Section 89 applies only to a contract "not fully performed on either side." If either side has performed all of its duties under the original contract, §89 will not apply. Thus, a modification will require consideration unless it satisfies another exception.

b. **Statutory exceptions.** When a statute authorizes modification without consideration, courts follow the will of the legislature. UCC

§2-209 is one such statute. California enforces a written modification of an oral agreement without new consideration. Cal. Civ. Code §1697. Unless others are mentioned in your casebook or class, you probably only need to know the UCC.

  i.   **Note.**   This exception is not limited to executory contracts. A state statute that allows modification of a contract even after one party had finished performing would govern. The Restatement cannot override a statute.

c.   **Exception for action in reliance.**   When one party has changed her position materially in reliance on the promise, courts may enforce the modification if justice so requires. Restatement (Second) of Contracts §89(c).

  i.   Action in reliance is an exception to the requirement of consideration generally. See Restatement (Second) of Contracts §90; see also 3.G. The exception in §89 appears to have no independent significance. It simply reminds us that some promises (whether modifications or new promises) may be enforceable without consideration under other exceptions to the bargain requirement.

  ii.   The language of §§89 and 90 differ in two respects: (a) §89 requires a **material** change in position, whereas §90 appears to apply to any "action or forbearance"; (b) §90 requires the reliance be **foreseeable** by the promisor, whereas §89 is silent on this point. The comments to the Restatement do not explain these differences; they imply that the provision incorporates §90 into §89 to match the UCC §2-209.

  iii.   The exception for reliance may swallow the preexisting duty rule. Arguably, every promisee changes her position in reliance on the modified contract by completing her performance. The preexisting duty rule, if it survives at all, depends on either **(a)** prompt repudiation of the modification by the promisor (before the promisee relies) or **(b)** a judicial determination that justice does not require enforcement of the promise despite the reliance. The latter provision may prevent a true extorter from enforcing a coerced promise after relying on it.

d.   **Exception for unanticipated circumstances.**   When "the modification is fair and equitable in view of circumstances not anticipated by the parties when the contract was made," courts generally enforce modifications. This exception involves two inquiries: **(1) Did the parties encounter some difficulty they did not anticipate when negotiating the original contract? and (2) is the modification fair and equitable under the circumstances?**

    i.   Requiring unanticipated circumstances probably aims at the same kind of legitimate commercial reason required under the UCC good faith test. If a party had no idea circumstances would change, she can in good faith ask the other party for adjustments.

        (a)   The Restatement does not recognize any other basis for a good faith request for modification. For example, a circumstance that, although anticipated, seemed too remote to mention during negotiations does not satisfy the exception for "circumstances not anticipated by the parties." One party anticipated the circumstance, however remotely, removing the case from this exception. The Restatement seems to expect a party negotiating a contract to provide for every anticipated circumstance that might eventually arise, since a modification based on a circumstance foreseen but omitted will not be enforceable.

 ## EXAMPLE AND ANALYSIS

S promises to provide B with 100 widgets in exchange for $500,000. S considered the possibility that labor costs might increase dramatically if the union called a strike before performance was complete but thought the chances of a strike were too remote to raise during negotiations. The union did strike. After settlement, labor costs rose dramatically. Performance for the original price would devastate S's business. S asks B to modify the contract price to $1 million. B, after considering S's plea, decides that is a fair price and agrees to the modification. B later decides that it does not want to pay the higher price. Is the modification enforceable if (1) widgets are goods governed by the UCC and (2) widgets are small buildings that S would construct on B's property in a state that strictly applies the language of the Restatement (Second) of Contracts?

As to the first question, under the UCC, the modification probably is enforceable. The increased labor costs are a legitimate reason to request a price change. B could have rejected it but can hardly claim it was inappropriate for S to ask. This might legitimate the modification even if S should have discussed the strike when negotiating the original contract; the prior mistake may not undermine the good faith reason to ask for a modification after the strike. Even if S's good faith during the initial negotiations counts, her decision not to mention the possibility of a strike may reflect an honest assessment of the risks rather than bad faith.

As to the second question, under the Restatement (Second) of Contracts §89, the modification may not be enforceable. S anticipated the change in circumstances during the initial negotiations. Even if her decision not to mention it was made in good faith (or even if it was objectively reasonable), the circumstance was not unanticipated when the contract was made. Thus, unless a bargain or some other exception to the consideration requirement makes the modification enforceable, B need not perform. That B did not anticipate the changed circumstance probably is not sufficient. To satisfy the exception, the change must be "unanticipated by the parties" (plural, **both** parties). Because S anticipated the change, the exception does not apply.

(b)   Very remote possibilities may make contract defenses such as mistake and impracticability plausible. See Chapters 9, 17. If so, modification may be permissible under the rules governing settlement of disputes.

(c)   Strict reading of the Restatement produces a defensible, but not inevitable, result. The Restatement is not a statute but an effort to summarize the rulings of the courts in 50 different states. A court is more likely to resolve cases based on the reasons favoring enforcement or avoidance than to apply mechanically the language of the Restatement.

ii.   Requiring fair and equitable terms allows a court to prevent extortion — or to replace the parties' estimate of the value of performance with its own. Courts refuse to evaluate the adequacy of consideration. But the exception applies because no consideration supported the modification. Courts asked to waive the normal requirement of a bargain feel free to reserve the largesse for deals that changes that seem fair.

6.   Accord and Satisfaction

Although courts discuss it in different terms, accord and satisfaction raise fundamentally the same consideration issues found in settlement of disputes (or, less often, modification). Accord and satisfaction, however, generate some additional issues, noted below.

a.   Terminology.

    i.   An **accord** is an agreement settling a dispute concerning performance under a contract. Typically (but not inevitably), it involves one party agreeing to pay less than originally agreed in exchange for the other party's performance.

    ii.   **Satisfaction** occurs when the accord has been performed — when the party has actually paid the amount agreed under the settlement.

    iii.   Before satisfaction occurs, the settlement is referred to as an **executory accord** — an accord that has not been fully performed (or fully executed, as that term is used).

b.   Creating an accord.   The most common method for creating an accord is to send a check to the other party along with a condition that cashing the check will constitute acceptance of the amount as payment in full for a specified obligation. The recipient may reject the proposed settlement by destroying or returning the check. But if she cashes the check, she assents to the conditions placed by the sender. **Note: Payments other than a check can be used to create an accord** and to satisfy an accord. Although checks commonly appear in the cases, any agreement to accept less than full payment is an accord and any performance of the terms of an accord constitutes satisfaction.

    i.   **Effect of reservations noted on a check.**   Recipients have tried to accept payment while rejecting the condition by placing notations such as "without prejudice" or "with all rights reserved" on the check or in a letter to the sender. **In general, these reservations have not been effective.** A recipient who knows the payment or other performance was submitted on condition that it would settle the dispute cannot take the payment and reject the condition.

        (a)   At one time, the UCC seemed to require a different result. UCC §1-207(1) appeared to allow a party to keep the partial payment and reject the condition by writing "under protest" or similar words on the check.

        (b)   In 1990, the drafters of the UCC added §1-207(2), which exempted accord and satisfaction from the reach of §1-207(1).

    ii.   **Inadvertent accords.**   Organizations frequently process checks automatically, without reading conditions on them. Often checks are received by a bank, whose employees credit an account, with no employee of the organization itself ever seeing the check or the condition written on it. Under these circumstances, cashing a check could create an inadvertent accord. A provision allowing a party to cash a check under protest would not help these organizations because they process checks in bulk, without scrutinizing each check for undesired conditions.

(a)   The drafters of the UCC added §3-311 to the provisions governing negotiable instruments at the same time they revised UCC §1-207. (Checks are one kind of negotiable instrument.) This section protects parties from inadvertently accepting a check as full payment.

(b)   Organizations can avoid inadvertent accords by specifying "a person, office or place" to receive "communications concerning disputed debts" and giving "conspicuous" notice to the promisee "within a reasonable time before" she tenders the check. UCC §3-311(c)(1)(I). The notice provision probably requires periodic notice (e.g., with each bill sent or perhaps annually), rather than a single notice when opening an account. A party cannot create an accord by sending the check anywhere else. UCC §3-311(b)(1)(ii). Thus, the organization can avoid accords created by bank employees.

(c)   Anyone can avoid an inadvertent accord by tendering a return of the payment within 90 days. UCC §3-311(b)(2). However, an organization that creates an office to handle disputed debts under UCC §3-311(b)(1) cannot take advantage of this provision. If the office in charge of the disputed debts created an accord, the organization cannot change its mind later.

iii.   New provisions not adopted.   These relatively new provisions of the UCC have not been adopted by all states. Check the law of your state (or the law your professor wants you to apply on an exam) before relying on these UCC provisions.

c.   Assessing consideration.   Accord cases typically look a little different from modifications: The promisee receives exactly what she was entitled to receive but gives less (rather than gives the same and extracts more). Because her duty changes (by being decreased), it is not exactly a preexisting duty. Yet the same concern for duress arises: Why would the other party agree to accept less than she was entitled to receive under the original agreement unless coerced? (The cases transmute into a more straightforward preexisting duty case by focusing on the promisor's promise to discharge the promisee's breach by paying less than originally promised. Because the promisee has a preexisting duty to do more, there seems no consideration for the promise not to sue. An agreement to accept less seems a gratuitous promise, with nothing given in exchange by the promisee.)

i.   **Accords require consideration** unless they satisfy an exception to the bargain requirement.

ii. **Accords frequently involve disputed obligations.** A dispute over either the existence of an obligation or the amount of the obligation may lead one party to offer an accord. If the promisee offering to pay less than the original obligation required believes in good faith that she has a valid defense to the original obligation, the settlement of the dispute satisfies the bargain requirement. Similarly, changed circumstances may make it fair and equitable to modify the contract despite the absence of a dispute over the original obligation.

iii. **Disputed amounts are settled by paying undisputed amounts.** Some promisees admit that they owe a certain amount but dispute charges in excess of that amount. A check for the full undisputed amount poses a consideration issue if it pays none of the disputed amount. Partial payment of a disputed amount could settle the claim. But payment that includes none of the disputed amount looks like the performance of a preexisting duty—the duty to pay the undisputed amount. Having no good faith defense to paying the undisputed amount, the payer does not give up a right to withhold that amount. Courts differ on the appropriate result here.

(a) Some courts refuse to enforce accords if the promisee tendered only the undisputed amount. The promisee had no right to withhold the undisputed amount—and did not claim such a right, mooting concern for a good faith assertion of such a right. Thus, paying the undisputed amount cannot be consideration, despite the existence of a dispute. See *Whittaker Chain Tread v. Standard Auto Supply*, 103 N.E. 695 (Mass. 1913).

(b) **Other courts find this approach too technical.** As long as the creditor accepts the smaller payment in settlement of the entire claim, the courts enforce the agreement. The creditor can always reject the accord if she wishes to preserve the claim. Some courts, however, supported this analysis by referring to the creditor's ability to accept payment under protest, as provided in the older version of UCC §1-207. See, e.g., *Kilander v. Blickle Co.*, 571 P.2d 503 (Or. 1977). With the modification of §1-207, there is room to wonder whether these courts will reach the same conclusion.

    (c)   **When the entire amount is unliquidated, this reasoning is inapposite.** Unliquidated debts arise when the parties have not agreed on a specific amount — for example, when the contract includes a formula for calculating the price. Tendering a certain amount does not make that an undisputed amount, susceptible to the reasoning above. Rather, the entire amount may be subject to dispute and, therefore, suitable for settlement — even in jurisdictions that would not accept tender of the undisputed amount as consideration for discharge of the entire debt.

 # EXAMPLE AND ANALYSIS

Jensen hired Marton to remodel his home. The contract price was open; Jensen agreed to pay for all materials plus the time required to do the job. Marton submitted a bill for $6,538.12 but Jensen contended Marton exaggerated the number of hours worked. Jensen gave Marton a check for $5,000 as full payment; Marton cashed the check after writing "not full payment" on it. *Marton Remodeling v. Jensen*, 706 P.2d 607 (Utah 1985). The court found an accord and satisfaction.

The court rejected the argument that $5,000 was the undisputed amount, so that payment of that amount could not be consideration for waiving the balance due. The claim was **unitary**; Jensen owed Morton one amount, not two (one of which was undisputed). Thus, a dispute concerning part was a dispute concerning the entire amount due. **Query**: How could the court tell whether Jensen paid only the undisputed amount or a little more than the undisputed amount, thus offering a compromise to the dispute? When the court cannot segregate the undisputed from the disputed amounts, it cannot easily apply the rule denying enforceability of the accord when only the undisputed amount is paid.

Note: **The court refused to apply UCC §1-207(1)** to the case, even though it arose before the addition of §1-207(2). The court found the policy in favor of settling claims favored interpreting the statute narrowly—apparently, limiting its application to on-going contracts, not settlement of completed contracts.

---

7. **Accord versus Substitution**

In the check cases, accord and satisfaction occur almost simultaneously: Signing the check creates the accord; receiving the proceeds of the check satisfies the accord. Problems arise, however, when the accord has been made but not satisfied. This can occur if the check bounces after being signed. It can also happen when an accord is not created by a check—as when a party agrees to accept certain property in lieu of a debt owed. If the debtor fails to deliver the property, can the debtor sue on the original debt? Or must she accept the property (or its fair market value) instead? The result turns on whether the parties intended the settlement to create an **accord** or a **substitution**.

a. **Terminology.**

   i. A **substitute contract** arises when the parties intend the new **promise** to extinguish the original duty immediately.

   ii. When the parties intend that the new promise will extinguish the original duty only when **performed**, their agreement is an **executory accord**.

b. **Effect of a substitute contract.**

   i. If a party breaches a substitute contract, the other party may sue for enforcement of the substitute contract **but may not sue for breach of the original agreement**. Any duty that arose under the original agreement disappeared the moment the substitute contract became binding.

   ii. For example, P, a pedestrian, and D, the driver who allegedly injured her, sign a settlement agreement in which P promises to release D from liability in exchange for D's promise to pay $50,000 per year for three years. If this is a substitute contract, P could sue D for breach of the settlement agreement if D failed to make a payment. P could not, however, reinstate her tort claim and seek more than the amount of the settlement agreement.

c. **Effect of an executory accord.**

i.   If a party breaches an executory accord by failing to pay the lesser amount agreed in settlement, the other party may sue for payment of the full underlying debt. Restatement (Second) of Contracts §281(2).

(a)   This is consistent with an analysis of what the party sought by agreeing to settle the claim by accepting less than the full amount. She wanted the payment (or other performance) in hand without having to go through a lawsuit to enforce the original debt. If she does not receive the payment but must resort to litigation anyway, she does not receive what she sought. The satisfaction of the claim, rather than the promise to pay the claim, extinguishes the underlying debt.

(b)   The party may choose to sue on the accord instead of on the underlying debt if she prefers. Thus, when a party agrees (for example) to accept property instead of money, the party may sue for the property (or its market value) instead of the amount of money originally owed, at her option. The choice is especially valuable when the performance under the accord turns out to be more valuable than the original performance (say, because values changed between formation of the accord and the time for filing suit).

ii.   The party who agreed to accept a lesser performance cannot change her mind and insist on the original duty unless the other party breaches. Even though the original duty remains alive pending satisfaction, the creditor cannot refuse to accept the debtor's efforts to satisfy the accord and then claim the right to sue on the underlying obligation.

 # EXAMPLE AND ANALYSIS

The Elzas were injured in a traffic accident with Clark. The Elzas agreed to accept $9,500 in settlement of their claims. Later, they refused to accept the check or sign the release called for in the settlement. *Clark v. Elza*, 406 A.2d 922 (Md. 1979). The trial court allowed them to proceed with their tort claim against Clark. The court of appeals reversed. **The executory accord did not immediately extinguish the Elzas's tort claim. But they could not sue on that claim unless Clark breached.** Because

Clark stood ready to perform the settlement, the Elzas could enforce the accord but had no recourse to the tort claim.

1. The effect can be characterized differently. The Elzas were in breach of the accord. Clark had a cause of action for breach of the accord. The court could order specific performance of the accord — that is, it could order the Elzas to sign the release in exchange for Clark's payment of the agreed amount. That approach finds support in the Restatement (Second) of Contracts §281(3).

2. Beware of situations in which the court might find no agreement existed at all until performance. A party may offer to accept a different performance as full satisfaction in such a way that the offer could be accepted only by performance. In those circumstances, acceptance does not occur until the party performs; a promise to perform does not create a contract. See 2.F.

---

8.   Rewards

Sometimes the preexisting duty rule arises in contexts in which consideration is not really relevant, most notably in reward cases. Typically, these arise when a police officer or security guard claims a reward that has been offered for the apprehension of a criminal or the return of stolen property. Because the officer often has a preexisting duty to enforce the laws, she arguably cannot assert that she performed that duty in exchange for the reward.

a.   **Concern for duress.**   The most plausible justification for this application of the preexisting duty rule is a concern that employees or public officials might withhold performance of their duties to extract or encourage the offering of rewards. Granting a reward arguably would encourage additional efforts to enforce the law. But rewards also might create problems — such as underenforcement of laws where violations did not generate reward offers. The concern seems more appropriately addressed by internal rules adopted by law enforcement agencies. The topic is peripheral to contract law. If necessary, rules concerning duress should handle any problems that might arise. Nonetheless, courts have applied the preexisting injury rule to reward cases.

b.   **Example (*Denney v. Reppert*, 432 S.W.2d 647 (Ky. Ct. App. 1968)).** The Kentucky Bankers Association offered a standing reward of $500 (per robber) for the arrest and conviction of bank robbers. Four employees of the bank, four witnesses, two state policemen, and one county deputy sheriff claimed the reward. The employees of the bank, who gave descriptions of the criminals, had a preexisting duty of loyalty to their employer; they could not collect the reward. The four witnesses failed to comply with the procedural requirements for claiming the reward; they could not collect it. The three state policemen had a preexisting duty to enforce the law; they could not collect the reward. The deputy sheriff, however, participated in the arrest even though it occurred outside of his county. Because he had no duty to make the arrest outside his jurisdiction, he was allowed to recover the reward. (Go figure.)

G. EXCEPTION FOR ACTION IN RELIANCE (OR PROMISSORY ESTOPPEL)

Often people rely on promises even if they have not given anything in exchange for the promise. Particularly when they incur substantial expense in reliance on the promise, courts see an injustice in allowing the promisor to refuse to perform. Thus, instead of denying enforcement on the ground that the promise lacked consideration, courts enforce promises if necessary to avoid injustice — that is, to prevent harm to the party who relied.

1. Elements

Restatement (Second) of Contracts §90 sets forth the general circumstances in which courts will enforce promises based on the promisee's reliance.

- **A promise;**
- **The promisor reasonably should have expected the promisee to rely on the promise;**
- **The promisee did rely on the promise (in a way the promisor reasonably should have expected);** and
- **Injustice can be avoided only by enforcing the promise.**

2. Examples

The elements that establish action in reliance contain some subtleties that will be explored shortly. See 3.G.3. Reliance will be easier to understand, however, if you first examine a few cases that illustrate why courts feel it necessary to enforce promises even though no bargain exists.

a. **Law without the exception (*Kirksey v. Kirksey*, 8 Ala. 131 (1845)).** This case illustrates the type of injustice courts felt arose from the rigid application of consideration doctrine. Defendant promised plaintiff, his brother's widow, a comfortable house in which to raise her family if she would and her children would "come down and see me." Plaintiff moved her family to defendant's home, losing the possibility of procuring the land she then occupied. After two years, defendant compelled the plaintiff to leave the house he had allowed her to use. The court found no consideration for the promise.

i.   The author of the opinion expressed the view (not shared by the other members of the panel) that moving to defendant's home was sufficient consideration. Many reliance cases border on consideration in that the promisor appears to have sought the reliance. ("Sought" is usually the stumbling block; a promisee who actually relies gave the reliance in exchange for the promise.)

ii. The court apparently decided that the words "if you come down and see me" did not specify a performance the defendant sought but a mere condition upon the gift of a place to live. See 3.B.3.c. As a conditional gift, the promise could be revoked at any time before delivery. This analysis is plausible but not inevitable. Moving to town is a necessary step to collecting the gift — and would be even if the promisor had said nothing about coming down to see me. Whether he sought the visit depends on motivation, which is difficult to discern — especially years later, when the promisor regrets the initial promise.

iii. The court did not discuss whether allowing plaintiff to live in the house for two years constituted delivery of the gift. Apparently delivery of possession for two years did not equate with delivery for life, absent a document, such as a deed granting a life estate in the property.

b. **Reliance implicitly sought.**   Some promisors hope for a return but do not expressly ask for it. A party who recognizes the implicit request and performs as expected presents a compelling case for enforcement. The transaction has all the qualities of a bargain, except that the terms were understood without being spoken. Enforcement based on reliance allows courts to rely on observable behavior, rather than asking them to infer a request — a mind-reading task they might not handle very well.

 # EXAMPLE AND ANALYSIS

Defendant gave plaintiff, his granddaughter, a note for $2,000 at 6 percent interest, stating, "I have fixed something out that you have not got to work any more. . . .

none of my grandchildren work, and you don't have to." Plaintiff quit her employment that day. (Defendant also said, later, that he "did not think [plaintiff] ought to" work.) Defendant paid interest for one year. In the second year, with defendant's consent, plaintiff returned to work. After defendant died, plaintiff sought payment of the note from the estate. The court found that there was no consideration for the note but held that the estate was estopped to deny the existence of consideration because defendant's promise had induced plaintiff to rely to her detriment by quitting her employment. *Ricketts v. Scothorn*, 77 N.W. 365 (Neb. 1898).

Arguably, defendant really did seek the plaintiff's resignation. If he had made that request explicit, her performance would be consideration for the note. The court rejected this argument because defendant never requested the return performance. He gave the note unconditionally to plaintiff, who could then quit or not at her own will. The court did not read between the lines to find an implied request that she resign.

---

  i. Finding a bargain may impose burdens on plaintiffs. Taking the note could accept the bargain — implicitly promising to quit work and, perhaps, to remain away from work. Thus, the donee could become the breaching party if courts make gifts enforceable by finding a bargain. Consideration is a double-edged sword for enforcing gifts.

c. **Definition of estoppel.** *Ricketts*, like many early cases, refers to **promissory estoppel**. Estoppel involves a court refusing to consider an argument a party made because of the party's prior contrary statement. The party is **estopped** to raise the argument.

  i. In **equitable estoppel**, a court refuses to consider evidence presented to prove a fact because a party previously denied the fact to induce another to rely.

 # EXAMPLE AND ANALYSIS

P slips in D's store and is injured. D knows the statute of limitations is one year. Nonetheless, D tells P she has two years to file a suit. P, in reliance, delays filing suit to continue settlement negotiations. Negotiations break down more than a year after the accident. P sues and D asserts that the statute of limitations bars the action.

A court will estop D from raising the statute of limitations defense. Having told P that the statute was two years, D cannot now claim the statute is only one year.

---

ii. **Promissory estoppel** extends equitable estoppel. Promissory estoppel rests on the making of a promise, not on a statement of fact. When a party induces another to rely upon a promise, the court will not consider the argument that the promise is unenforceable for want of consideration. In effect, consideration is found to exist because the court ignores defendant's (valid) argument that consideration did not exist.

iii. Promissory estoppel is a convenient label but a poor explanation how courts operate today. You need to recognize the words "promissory estoppel" as language courts use when finding that action in reliance on a promise makes the promise enforceable even though no bargain existed.

d. **Reliance extended contract to noncommercial settings.** Contract principles evolved primarily in commercial settings, where exchanges predominate. In noncommercial settings, exchanges are not the norm — or, at least, exchanges are more subtle, involving implicit requests and performances that have value not readily measurable in money. It is not a coincidence that most reliance cases, particularly early reliance cases, involve promises within a family and gifts to charities. Reliance applied contract law to conduct not entirely contractual in nature. The reverse also is true: Reliance has extended into commercial contexts.

i. Learned Hand expressed concern that applying the doctrine of promissory estoppel to commercial contexts would make offers binding before they were accepted. In commercial settings, reliance is reasonable once a party accepts an offer. That makes the agreement binding and justifies reliance. See *James Baird Co. v. Gimbel Bros.*, 64 F.2d 346 (2d Cir. 1933). The commercial cases involving reliance, however, sometimes arise in contexts in which mere acceptance would not suffice to create a bargain — any more than Mrs. Kirksey could make her brother-in-law's promise binding by accepting it and moving to his land. (Some extensions of reliance arguments make Hand's fears more realistic. See 2.F.3.C.)

ii. Plaintiff worked for defendant company from 1910 until 1949. In 1947, the company promised her a pension of $200 per month for life upon her retirement. The company paid the pension from 1949 until 1956, when a new president stopped making payments. Plaintiff sued. *Feinberg v. Pfeiffer Co.*, 322 S.W.2d 163 (Mo. 1959). The court found no consideration, in part because plaintiff admitted she would have continued to work for the company even if no pension had been offered. The court, however, held that she relied on the pension in deciding to retire in 1949. Her reliance made the promise enforceable.

(a)   Erosion of the preexisting duty rule could produce the same result without reference to reliance. The employer can agree to modify the terms of an employment contract by promising more compensation (in this case, a pension). Continued employment, even if performance of a preexisting duty, could be consideration for that promise.

(b)   The federal Employment and Retirement Income Security Act of 1974 (ERISA) now regulates pension plans, making the specific context moot going forward. State contract law is no longer needed to make pensions enforceable.

 # EXAMPLE AND ANALYSIS

Plaintiff owned a liquor distributorship in Indiana. Defendant was one of the main suppliers for plaintiff's business. When other suppliers stopped using plaintiff as a distributor, plaintiff contemplated the sale of its business to a competitor. After obtaining an offer at a specified price, plaintiff decided that it would be better off to not to sell **if** defendant would continue to use plaintiff to distribute its products. Defendant assured plaintiff that it would continue to distribute its goods through plaintiff. Plaintiff rejected the offer to buy its business. One week later, defendant stopped distributing its goods through plaintiff. Plaintiff negotiated a new sale of the business but for $550,000 less than the original offer. *D & G Stout, Inc. v. Bacardi Imports*, 923 F.2d 566 (7th Cir. 1991). The trial court granted summary judgment to defendant. The appellate court reversed, allowing the plaintiff to recover its reliance interest.

The case is troubling. In a business context, bargains are the norm. Neither party was unsophisticated; each knew how to make a binding bargain. Enforcing promises without a bargain changes the ground rules abruptly.

Neither contract between plaintiff and defendant specified a duration. Thus, it is difficult to say that the defendant breached the promise at all, even if the promise was enforceable without an exchange.

A fraudulent promise (to continue distributing through plaintiff) would be actionable but plaintiff did not allege fraud. A promise implies a present intention to perform. The repudiation came so quickly that one might question whether defendant intended to perform at the time it made the promise. Liability might be harder to justify if the termination had occurred several months (rather than several days) later. These arguments, however, suggest the reason for finding liability has more to do with tort than with the enforcement of the promise.

---

3.   Caveats and Traps in Applying Section 90

The elements for proving reliance, as set forth in the Restatement (Second), involve some subtleties that an exam question might attempt to probe.

a.   A promise is important.   Some students try to analyze reliance without first identifying a promise. Reliance on a promise can make the promise enforceable, replacing consideration. Reliance, however, cannot replace the promise. Identify a promise before launching into an analysis of reliance on the promise.

b.   Unreasonable reliance might suffice.   As a shorthand, people often refer to reasonable reliance. That changes the emphasis in a way that might make a difference. The issue is not whether the promisee acted reasonably but **whether the promisor had reason to believe she would rely**. Thus, if a promisor knew that a promisee would act in a particular way, the reliance might permit enforcement even if a reasonable person would not have relied in that way.

   i.   When reliance is unreasonable, a promisor may have had no reason to believe that the promisee would rely in that way. Between strangers, this seems probable. But reliance cases often involve social (rather than commercial) contexts, where the parties are quite familiar with one another. In these circumstances, a promisor reasonably might anticipate unreasonable reliance.

   ii.   When reliance is unreasonable, a court might decide that no injustice would result if the promisee bore the cost of that reliance. If so, the court might refuse enforcement of the promise even though the reliance was expected by the promisor. Cases of this sort probably will be rare, because a promisor who anticipates unreasonable reliance may be no more sympathetic than the person who relies unreasonably. The promisor's conduct may verge on malicious whereas the promisee is merely unreasonable. As this language suggests, the principles at work in reliance cases border on tort.

c.   Actual reliance.   The Restatement (Second) implies that reliance must be of the kind the promisor should have foreseen. Thus, a promise may not be enforceable when the promisor should have foreseen some reliance but the promisee relied in some completely unforeseeable way.

i.   **Some courts require reliance of a "definite and substantial character."**   The first Restatement of Contracts made this requirement explicit. The Restatement (Second) treats it as a factor in assessing injustice: Insignificant reliance may mean injustice can be avoided without enforcing the promise.

ii. **Some courts do not require actual reliance at all.**   A recent survey of cases suggests that many courts enforce promises under §90 even without actual reliance, as long as the promisor reasonably should have expected reliance. This undercuts the tort-like role of reliance. The promisor's belief that the words might cause reliance justifies enforcement of the promise, even if the promisee had not (yet) been harmed by relying on it. This suggests that §90 really seeks to identify serious promises, those the promisor intends to be enforceable, rather than harmful promises.

iii. **Actual reliance is unimportant for promises of charitable contributions or marriage settlements.**   Restatement (Second) of Contracts §90(2). Although some states may not follow this rule, numerous cases suggest that actual reliance is not required in some special settings. (Thus, to get the deed to the land your in-laws promised you as a wedding gift, you may not need to testify that you never would have married your spouse but for the promised gift. But you can't refuse to pay the Red Cross the amount you pledged just because it would have engaged in its charitable acts even if you had made no promise.)

d. **Injustice usually boils down to detrimental reliance.**   If the promisee changed her position for the worse because the promise was made, either by acting or remaining inactive, justice probably requires enforcement of the promise. Some factors may limit this conclusion. If the reliance was relatively minor, perhaps no injustice would result from the refusal to enforce the promise. If the promisee can regain her former advantage at no cost (or no significant cost), perhaps breach would not create an injustice. But generally, a change for the worse will satisfy the requirement that injustice can be avoided only by enforcement of the promise.

e. **Courts compensate for expectation, not merely reliance.**   The Restatement (Second) suggests that courts may limit their remedy "as justice requires." This invites courts to compensate the party for expenses incurred in reliance on the promise instead of enforcing the promise itself. Several surveys of court decisions reveal that courts rarely limit the remedy to reliance. Instead, once they find the promise enforceable, they award the expectation interest, even ordering specific performance in some cases.

> **i.   Examination advice.**   If you conclude that reliance, rather than a bargain, justifies enforcement of a promise, **address the possibility that a court would limit recovery to the reliance interest**. Professors like the reliance interest much more than courts do.

H.   FORMALITY AS AN EXCEPTION TO THE CONSIDERATION REQUIREMENT

One justification for the requirement of consideration is that persons making bargains realize that their promises will be taken seriously. As a result, promisors will reflect on whether they really want to make the promise before they conclude the deal. This **cautionary function** of consideration can be satisfied in other ways, without requiring an actual bargain. Anything that will encourage a promisor to reflect before finally making the promise will reduce the number of ill-considered promises that the law may not want to enforce. (Recall that one justification for action in reliance is that a promisor who realizes another may rely on the promise will reflect before making the promise in the first place.) One way to encourage reflection is to require some formal step that the promisor must take in order to convert a mere promise into a legally enforceable promise.

1.   Seal

At one time, courts enforced any promise made under seal. The act of affixing a seal to a written promise gave the promisor time to consider whether she really wanted the promise to become legally enforceable. Most states have abolished laws enforcing promises made under seal.

2.   Signed Writings

The formal step of reducing a promise to writing and signing the document can serve the same function as a seal. Signed writings also allow people who do not have a family crest (for a seal) to make binding contracts. Some states have enacted statutes that make it possible to enforce signed written promises even if they lack consideration.

> **a.   California.**   Under California Civil Code §1614, a written instrument is "presumptive evidence of consideration." Thus, a plaintiff may sue

on a written promise without proving consideration. The defendant, however, may rebut the presumption by proving that no consideration was given for the promise. Cal. Civil Code §1615. Thus, the writing does not entirely replace consideration.

b. **New York.** New York General Obligations Law §5-1105 makes a written promise enforceable if it recites a past performance as consideration, as long as the consideration really was performed.

c. **UCC.** The UCC makes a written promise to keep an offer open for a period of time enforceable even without consideration. *See* UCC §2-205; 2.F.2.a.

d. **Exceptions limited.** None of these statutes makes every signed writing enforceable. Each reflects a diminished concern for consideration when the promisor clearly made a promise and had an opportunity to reflect on the decision before signing the writing.

REVIEW QUESTIONS AND ANSWERS

Question: True or false: Unless both parties undertake some duty to the other, no consideration exists.

Answer: False. Consideration can be provided by third parties.

Question: True or false: Unless the promisor receives some benefit in exchange for the promise, no consideration exists.

Answer: False. As long as the promisor receives what she sought in exchange for the promise, it does not matter whether that something is a benefit or a detriment.

Question: What two facts must exist in order to establish the existence of a bargain?

Answer: The promisor must seek something in exchange for her promise and the promisee must give that something in exchange for the promise.

Question: True or false: A promise is not enforceable unless it is part of a bargained-for exchange.

Answer: False. Several exceptions to the bargain requirement exist, including the exception for action in reliance, the exception for past consideration or moral obligation, and the exception for charitable contributions.

Question: True or false: If a promisee gives something to the promisor in exchange for the promise, consideration exists.

Answer: False. Only if the promisor sought that something would a bargain exist. A promisee cannot make the promisor's gift promise into an exchange by making a return gift the promisor did not seek.

Question: Under what circumstances will a performance rendered in the past provide consideration for a new promise?

Answer: It will never provide consideration for a promise. But sometimes courts will enforce the promise despite the absence of consideration. When the performance was part of a bargain that no longer is enforceable for various technical defects, a new promise to perform generally is enforceable, effectively waiving the defenses. When the past performance was rendered gratuitously, without any connection to a prior bargain, the promise will be enforceable only if the promisor received a benefit from the promisee and enforcement is necessary to prevent injustice. Injustice will not require enforcement when the promisee intended a gift or bestowed the benefit without request even though an opportunity to bargain existed, or when the promise greatly exceeds the value of the benefit the promisor received.

Question: When will reliance by a party justify enforcement of a promise despite the absence of a bargain?

Answer: When the promisor reasonably should have expected the promisee to rely on the promise, the promisee did rely, and injustice can be avoided only by performance.

Question: True or false: When reliance on a promise is unreasonable, the promise is unenforceable.

Answer: False as a statement of the rule but may be true in most situations. A promisee's unreasonable reliance will justify enforcement if the promisor had reason to know the promisee would rely in that way. Because promisors often have no reason to know that a promisee will react unreasonably, unreasonable reliance rarely justifies enforcement.

Question: If A already has a right to receive a performance from B, can B's renewed promise to perform be consideration for a new or different promise by A?

Answer: Yes, it can, if A truly seeks the performance he had a right to receive — or, more commonly, seeks a waiver of B's right to litigate a defense to the duty to perform. The preexisting duty rule once treated a performance the promisor had a right to receive as no consideration for a promise. Courts and legislatures have refined (or abandoned) this rule in most circumstances, absent duress.

Question: When will a promise to relinquish a claim or defense constitute consideration for a promise?

Answer: When the claim or defense is (1) valid, (2) reasonably in doubt on the merits, or (3) believed in good faith by the promisee to have a chance to succeed on the merits.

Question: Can a modification of contract in which one party's duties increase but the other's remain the same be enforceable, even when the party whose duties remained the same had no good faith belief that she had a right not to perform that duty?

Answer: Yes, in many situations. For sales of goods, as long as the parties agree to the modification in good faith, it is enforceable even if one party gives no more than she already was obligated to give. For other contracts, the modification will be enforceable if (1) neither party has completed her performance under the contract, (2) circumstances unanticipated at the time the contract was made arise, and (3) the modified terms are fair and equitable in light of those new circumstances. Even if these elements are not met, a statute or another exception to the bargain requirement (such as action in reliance) may make the modification enforceable without new consideration.

THE ROLE OF WRITINGS: STATUTES OF FRAUDS

CHAPTER OVERVIEW

Some promises are unenforceable unless evinced by a signed writing.

- Promises in consideration of **marriage**;
- Promises that cannot be performed within one **year**;
- Promises conveying an interest in **land**;
- Promises by an **executor** to pay debts of an estate;
- Promises for the sale of **goods** for more than $500; and
- Promises to pay another person's debts (**securityship**).

The writing requirement can be satisfied even if the full contract is not reduced to writing.

- For sales of goods under the UCC, the writing must:
  — Be **signed** by the party resisting enforcement of the contract;
  — Indicate that a **contract** has been made; and
  — State the **quantity** of goods to be sold.
- For other contracts, the writing must:
  — Be **signed** by the party resisting enforcement of the contract;
  — Identify the **subject matter** of the transaction;
  — Indicate that a **contract** has been made or offered by the signer; and
  — State the **essential terms** of the unperformed promises.
- A mark (e.g., initials or letterhead) intended to authenticate a writing may be a signature.

Exceptions: A contract **may be** enforceable despite the absence of a required writing if:

- The party opposing enforcement **admits under oath** that a contract was made;
- Both parties have **performed fully**;
- One party has **performed fully**;
- One party has **partially performed**; and
- In some cases, a party has **relied** on the promise in ways that make nonenforcement unjust.

The exceptions are specific, not general. They vary with the reason the writing was required.

A party who has begun performance under an unenforceable contract is entitled to **restitution.**

A party who has relied on an unenforceable contract may be entitled to recover for **reliance.**

A.   RATIONALE

In some circumstances, concern arose that courts could be made the instrument of fraud. A plaintiff could assert, falsely, that the defendant made an oral promise of significant value. If a jury disbelieved defendant's denial, the plaintiff might obtain enforcement of the promise. (Originally, defendants could not take the witness stand to deny the promise; denial was assumed from the pleadings, but the finder of fact could not hear testimony from the parties to assess their credibility.) This concern led legislatures to pass laws making some promises unenforceable unless supported by a writing. **A writing did not make the promise enforceable**; the contract still needed to satisfy consideration and other requirements. But **the absence of a writing made the promise unenforceable.**

B.   STATUTES OF FRAUDS

In some contexts, statutes preclude courts from enforcing a contract unless the agreement was recorded in some writing signed by the party who now disputes the existence of the agreement (usually, the defendant).

1.   Purpose

A writing primarily serves an **evidentiary** role. A writing signed by the promisor makes it less likely that the promisee is lying about the **existence** of the promise. A signed writing also may help resolve disputes over the **terms** of the promises if it recites those terms in some detail. Furthermore, reducing an agreement to a formal writing has a **cautionary** effect. The formality should alert the party to the serious nature of the transaction and the fact that legal consequences are likely to flow from it. Thus, requiring a writing for important contracts may afford parties one last chance to reconsider before incurring obligations that the law will enforce.

2. Useful Approach

When issues involving a statute of frauds arise, you need to address three different questions:

a. **Does the statute apply to this contract?** Many contracts are enforceable without a writing. You need not address statutes of frauds at all unless there is a plausible claim that this promise falls within one of the discrete categories in which writings are necessary.

b. **Does a writing satisfy the statute?** Most statutes do not require that the full contract be in writing. A "note or memorandum" referring to the agreement may suffice. Thus, consider whether some letter or other scrap of paper might contain enough of the terms to qualify as a signed writing.

c. **Does an exception to the statute apply?** Courts have shown some animosity to statutes of frauds. They have created a number exceptions that allow them to enforce oral contracts, even though they fall within the scope of the statute.

3. Agreements Unenforceable without a Writing

Legislatures have identified many types of agreements that fall within the statute of frauds. Statutes vary from state to state. The list here reflects some common provisions but is by no means exhaustive.

a. **Promises in consideration of marriage.** See Restatement (Second) of Contracts §124. For example, a promise to give property to another if he or she marries would be unenforceable unless evinced by a writing.

　　i. **Mutual promises to marry.** Such promises generally need not be in writing. Many states, however, have enacted statutes making promises to marry unenforceable even when written.

　　ii. **Marriage as a condition.** Marriage may not be the consideration for a promise. For example, if the bride's parents promise to give the couple property when they marry in exchange for the groom's parents' promise to give an equal amount, the promises are not within the statute. Each donation is consideration for the other; the marriage is a condition, not the consideration.

　　iii. **Prenuptial agreements.** Such agreements often fall within the statute of frauds. A promise to relinquish property rights that normally would arise from marriage is no different from a promise to give tangible property. The release may be given in con-

sideration of marriage and, therefore, fall within the statute.
Many states regulate prenuptial agreements by special statutes,
which usually contain their own writing requirements. See, e.g.,
Uniform Premarital Agreement Act §2.

b. **Promises not performable within a year.**   If a promise cannot be
performed fully within one year from the date the contract is made,
the contract falls within the statute of frauds. See Restatement (Second)
of Contracts §130. A contract that **might** be completed within one year,
however, does **not** fall within the statute. Courts often show some
creativity in identifying ways in which the promise could have been
performed within one year.

 # EXAMPLE AND ANALYSIS

Murphy hired McIntosh to work as Murphy's car dealership, allegedly for one year.
They reached agreement by phone on Saturday, April 25, 1964; McIntosh started
work on Monday, April 27. The contract was governed by the statute of frauds. By
its terms it would not be completed until April 26, 1965, more than a year after
April 25, 1964. *McIntosh v. Murphy*, 469 P.2d 177 (Hawaii 1970). The court enforced
the contract under an exception to the statute.

c. **Interests in land.**   Promises conveying an interest in land, including
easements, fall within the statute. See Restatement (Second) of Contracts §124. Some state statutes exempt leases of one year or less.

d. **Promises of an executor.**   If the executor of an estate promises to pay
the estate's debts from the executor's personal assets, the promise falls
within the statute. See Restatement (Second) of Contracts §111. This
is a special application of the next provision—promises to pay the
debt of another—and subject to all of the limitations on that provision.
See Restatement (Second) of Contracts §§112-123.

e. **Guaranty or suretyship.**   If a party promises to pay the debt of another if that other fails to pay, the promise falls within the statute. See
Restatement (Second) of Contracts §112. This is called a suretyship.
(The person who guarantees another will perform and promises to pay
if she does not is a **surety** or a **guarantor.**) The intricacies of this
provision generally do not play a role in first-year courses in contracts

and, therefore, will not be expounded here. See Restatement (Second) of Contracts §§113-123 for all the details. But don't say I didn't warn you.

f. Goods of $500.   Sales of goods for $500 or more fall within the statute of frauds under the UCC. See UCC §2-201.

4. Employment and Construction Contracts

The previous categories do not expressly include two common types of contracts: employment contracts and construction contracts. These contracts **require a writing if they cannot be performed within one year.** Often, however, these contracts will be enforceable without a writing.

5. Satisfying the Writing Requirement

The amount of detail necessary to satisfy the writing requirement varies between contexts and between jurisdictions. Some generalizations can be drawn, but in practice research will be necessary to identify the requirements more particularly.

a. One signature.   A writing need not be signed by both parties. The party seeking enforcement of an agreement admits that the agreement exists, making evidence of her consent superfluous. The concern is whether the other party, the one contesting enforcement, actually made a promise. A writing signed by the party to be charged suffices to overcome concerns for fraud.

b. Informal signature.   Under the UCC, any mark intended to authenticate the writing is a signature as long as the mark identifies the party to be charged. Thus, initials, a typed name, or even a company letterhead or logo might constitute a signature for these purposes. Nonsignatures such as a seal or a thumbprint also may authenticate a writing.

c. Failure to respond to a writing.   For sales of goods, failure to respond to a writing signed by the other party may be the equivalent of signing a writing. UCC §2-201(2). Specifically, "Between merchants if within a reasonable time a writing in confirmation of the contract and sufficient against the sender is received and the party receiving it has reason to know its contents, it satisfies the [writing] requirements of subsection (1) against such party unless written notice of objection to its contents is given within ten days after it is received." The rule contains six significant elements. Most are designed to rule out plausible explanations for why a party would ignore the communication even if it set forth a contract the parties never made.

i. **Between merchants.** Consumers might not realize the danger they faced by ignoring a false assertion of a contract. Merchants, on the other hand, can be expected to pay closer attention to both their mail and the law. If either party does not ordinarily deal in goods of the type being sold, the provision does not apply. [For a detailed definition of "merchant" and "between merchants," see UCC §2-104.]

ii. **Writing sufficient against the sender.** If the writing would not satisfy the statute if the sender raised the statute as a defense, it will not satisfy the statute when the recipient raises it as a defense. Thus, it must be signed by the sender and contain at least the quantity term. Anything less can be ignored with impunity.

iii. **Sent within a reasonable time.** A letter sent shortly after contract formation looks like normal communication about the deal. A letter sent much later looks more like an effort to create evidence useful in litigation. If the sender acts only after she realizes the other party may breach, the accuracy of the document becomes suspect — a self-serving litigation position more than an ordinary business communication. Failure to object to an inaccurate business communication tells a story about the actual business transaction; ignoring your litigation opponent's boasts tells a different story, unrelated to the statute of frauds.

iv. **Received.** The failure to object to an inaccurate writing is understandable if the writing was never received.

v. **Reason to know of its contents.** Again, a recipient who does not know the false assertion was made might not object within a reasonable time. The rule prevents senders from concealing assertions about a contract in unusual places, where the recipient might not notice them. It does not protect the recipient who fails to read her mail; she had reason to know the contents, if not actual knowledge. But a recipient may have no reason to know that, for example, a check had an unusual proviso on the back or a packing slip contained more than a list of the items in the box.

vi. **Absence of an objection.** An objection sent within 10 days negates any inference that the recipient acquiesced in the sender's version of the agreement — or even in the existence of the agreement at all. Of course, the objection itself might be a signed writing that, if it evinced an agreement between the parties on some terms, would satisfy the statute of frauds.

d. **Partial writings.**   A writing need not contain all the terms of a contract. A formal signed contract would satisfy almost any statute of frauds, but less formal writings often will serve. The amount of detail required will vary.

   i. **Sales of goods.**   The UCC requires very little detail. As long as a writing contains the **quantity**, it will suffice—even if the writing **misstates** the quantity.

   ii. **Other contracts.**   The Restatement (Second) requires the writing to present considerable detail, including (a) the **subject matter** of the contract, (b) an indication that the signor has **consented** to the deal, and (c) "the **essential terms of the unperformed promises**," stated in "reasonable detail." Restatement (Second) of Contracts §131.

   iii. **Different purposes.**   The differences here reflect different functions these statutes can serve. If concern is limited to whether the promise was made, any writing that evinces agreement suffices and the terms can be supplied later. If, however, concern exists that a party has incorrectly recounted the terms, a writing that evinces the terms may be important. A cautionary function requires a more formal writing to bring home the seriousness of the transaction. The UCC and the Restatement (Second) appear to draw different conclusions regarding the degree of evidence required.

e. **Timing of the signature is unimportant.**   A writing signed before or after formation may evince assent and terms. Similarly, a form signed before it is filled out may evince assent; signing the incomplete form implies authority for others to fill in the blanks later.

 # EXAMPLE AND ANALYSIS

Arden hired Crabtree as a sales manager. On a telephone order blank, Arden's secretary wrote the key terms, but the document was not signed. When Crabtree began work, a payroll change form was initialed by a vice president and signed by the comptroller. This later writing satisfied the statute of frauds. *Crabtree v. Elizabeth Arden Sales*, 110 N.E.2d 551 (N.Y. 1953).

f. **Multiple writings.**   Several writings taken together may satisfy the statute, even though none individually would suffice. Particularly when a signed writing refers to an unsigned writing, the unsigned writing may satisfy the statute. Similarly, when several writings each contain some of the material terms of the contract, taken together they may meet the requirements.

 # EXAMPLE AND ANALYSIS

The payroll change forms signed by defendant's agents included most terms but omitted the duration of the contract. The unsigned telephone order blank written by Arden's secretary recited all terms, including the two-year duration. The court found that the writings referred to the same contract and that the phone blank could be considered along with the other writings in deciding whether the statute had been satisfied. *Crabtree v. Elizabeth Arden Sales*, supra.

g. **Lost or destroyed writing may suffice.**   Copies, even if unsigned, or other testimony may satisfy the court that a writing did exist. Parties who created a writing did everything the statute asked of them. Inability to produce the document does not prevent enforcement of the contract.

6. Exceptions to the Writing Requirement

Courts have been hostile to the writing requirement. Although it may reduce fraud by persons who lie about the existence of agreements, it facilitates fraud by persons who really made oral agreements but now regret them. When courts are convinced that an agreement really was made, they prefer not to allow the promisor to escape based on a technicality — even a technicality created and imposed by the legislature. The result has been a number of exceptions.

a. **Generally: Evidence corroborating an agreement.**   The exceptions are specific but share a general trait. Each involves some evidence that the party **resisting** enforcement really made a promise. Remember, the party seeking to enforce the agreement may be lying; courts want corroboration that the other party really did agree. (At least one exception does not fit this general rule. See 4.B.8.)

b. Admissions under oath. Testimony that a promise existed makes a writing unnecessary to prove the promise. This is explicit under the UCC §2-201(3)(b). The comments to the Restatement (Second) imply a similar result. Restatement (Second) of Contracts §131 comment c. (However, when the statute serves a **cautionary** function, as in suretyship and marriage contexts, admissions after the fact may not suffice.)

c. Full performance by both parties. If both parties have fully performed their promises, neither can compel the other to reconvey what she received by claiming the contract was unenforceable for lack of a writing. Restatement (Second) of Contracts §145. The statute forbids courts to enforce contracts without evidence; it does not forbid parties to perform them if they so desire. Performance is fairly good evidence that the promise was made.

d. Full performance by one party. Under some circumstances, one party's performance can give rise to an exception.

    i. One party accepts the other party's performance. This provides some indication that she promised something in return. Thus, the UCC allows enforcement without a writing when goods have been "received and accepted" or when "payment has been made and accepted." UCC §2-201(3)(c).

    ii. Contracts not performable within a year. Full performance by one party removes a promise that could not be completed within a year from the provisions of the statute. Restatement (Second) of Contracts §130(2).

    iii. Partial performance. The UCC may allow partial enforcement based on partial performance. A contract "is enforceable . . . with respect to goods for which payment has been made and accepted or which have been received and accepted." Thus, if only part of the goods have been paid for or delivered, the agreement might be enforceable "with respect to" those goods, but not with respect to other goods allegedly called for by the agreement.

7. Restitution

A person who relies on an unenforceable oral promise may seek restitution. The recipient may be required to return any benefits received under the unenforceable contract in order to prevent unjust enrichment.

a. Enforcement versus restitution.   The statute of frauds prevents enforcement of a contract but does not prevent an action for unjust enrichment. Restitution does not give them the parties what was promised but returns what they had before the promises were made. Because this recovery does not literally enforce the contract, the statute has not been interpreted to preclude restitution.

b. Enforcement versus reliance.   Reliance that does not benefit the other party does not fall within this justification. Nonetheless, courts have attempted to compensate parties for their reliance on the ground that this, too, does not really enforce the contract. As the next section indicates, this line of cases creates an exception that may swallow the rule.

8. Exception for Action in Reliance

If a party relies on an oral promise in a way the promisor reasonably should have expected, injustice might result unless the courts enforce the promise. Thus, courts have carved out an exception to the statute of frauds similar to the reliance exception to the bargain requirement. Restatement (Second) of Contracts §139. The exception seriously erodes the statute of frauds. Promisees frequently can identify some way in which they relied on the promise, even though no writing existed. Arguably, the statute is designed to force these promisees to "get it in writing" before they rely. Reliance without the writing seems unreasonable. Enforcement undermines the incentive to insist on a writing, at the same time allowing fraudfeasors ample opportunity to perpetrate their deception. Nonetheless, courts convinced that they can identify fraudfeasors without a writing requirement have expanded the remedies available for parties who rely on unenforceable promises.

a. Basic elements.   The basic elements of reliance are identical under §139 and §90: The promisor reasonably should have expected reliance, the promisee did rely in that way, and injustice can be avoided only by enforcement. See 3.G. Concern for the legislature's intent to preclude enforcement of oral promises in these contexts, however, has produced some subtle differences in the language.

b.   Reliance interest only.   The remedial provision of §139 states the remedy "is to be limited as justice requires." This differs from §90's provision that the remedy "may be limited as justice requires." Thus, the Restatement (Second) contemplates only a reliance recovery; expectation damages should not be awarded because they clearly would contravene the intent of the legislature that passed the statute requiring a writing.

c.   Identifying injustice.   Section 139 offers additional guidance in determining when injustice would result if the court refused to enforce the promise. This guidance suggests that some forms of detrimental reliance will not justify enforcement, even when compensation is limited to reliance.

   i.   The availability of other remedies, such as restitution, may make compensation for reliance unnecessary. Where restitution will be adequate, the court need not stick its neck out.

   ii.   The magnitude of the reliance relative to the remedy sought may support recovery. Reliance that is more "definite and substantial" may require more protection than insignificant reliance or than action or forbearance that the promisee might have taken even if no promise had been made.

   iii.   Reliance that corroborates the existence of a promise puts the court on firmer ground in extending a more generous remedy —as does a promise demonstrated by other strong evidence.

   iv.   Reasonable reliance supports compensation. Whether it is ever reasonable to rely on an unenforceable oral promise is an open question. The cases often involve people unfamiliar with the law who make otherwise understandable decisions (e.g., moving to a new city to accept a job).

   v.   The foreseeability of the reliance supports compensation. This factor seems to repeat the basic element—that the promisor reasonably should have expected the promisee to rely. It is repeated here to emphasize the cautionary function a writing can serve. A promisor who should foresee reliance (and, therefore, liability on the oral promise) might think twice before making the promise—one of the roles a writing can serve.

EXAMPLE AND ANALYSIS

Murphy hired McIntosh to work as Murphy's car dealership, allegedly for one year. McIntosh moved from California to Hawaii to take the job. Murphy fired McIntosh less than three months later. No writing satisfied the statute. The appellate court affirmed a jury award of about $12,000 because McIntosh's reliance in moving from California to Hawaii created an exception that precluded Murphy from relying on the statute of frauds. *McIntosh v. Murphy*, 469 P.2d 177 (Haw. 1970).

Actual reliance is not clear on the facts. McIntosh decided to move to Hawaii before Murphy offered the job. The offer came when McIntosh wired Murphy that he would arrive in Hawaii on April 26. Thus, it seems McIntosh would have moved even if no job offer had been made. Therefore, the expense of moving cannot constitute an injustice that resulted from the alleged agreement. The trial court made no findings about reliance and the appellate court spent only a sentence declaring plaintiff relied.

The court appears to have awarded an expectation recovery despite the language of the Restatement. The trial court did not apply the reliance exception, so it would be unusual for it to instruct the jury in a reliance measure of loss. The jury award looks suspiciously like the salary for the rest of the year McIntosh should have worked. He was paid about $4,000 for about three months; the jury awarded about $12,000. The opinion does not reveal the amount of expense incurred moving to Hawaii. Coincidentally, moving costs could have been $12,000. But the case seems to actually enforce the contract, rather than compensate plaintiff for reliance on an unenforceable contract.

---

d. **Reliance in sales of goods.** The UCC makes one special provision for reliance: the case of custom manufactured goods. UCC §2-201(3)(a). The exception involves three elements.

i. **Specially manufactured for the buyer.** Where the goods are in stock, the argument for protecting reliance is weaker. Only specially manufactured goods are covered by the exception.

ii. **Not suitable for resale to others in the ordinary course of business.** When the goods can be resold to others, the loss resulting from breach is likely to be less severe. Reliance is more likely to give rise to injustice when the goods will need to be scrapped rather than sold to another or when resale takes the seller outside her usual business activities. The seller may suffer some loss even if goods can be resold; the resale price may be lower than the contract price. But a seller who does not get the agreement in writing must accept that portion of the loss.

iii.   **Substantial beginning.**   This provision requires not only actual reliance but significant reliance: "either a substantial beginning of their manufacture or commitments for their procurement." Once manufacture has begun, materials may have become less valuable by virtue of being incorporated into goods that cannot be sold to others. Similarly, when the seller has committed to obtain the goods from another, her contract liability to the other may be sufficiently significant that failure to enforce the agreement may create an injustice.

iv.   **Reliance before repudiation.**   Once notified that the other party does not want the goods, the seller should cease manufacture to minimize the loss. See 20.E.1. If, at that point, neither a commitment for procurement nor a substantial beginning of manufacture has occurred, reliance will not justify enforcement.

v.   **No general reliance exception.**   The UCC, by enumerating specific exceptions, rejects the general exception for reliance. Although the Restatement (Second) recognizes reliance as a general basis for enforcing oral agreements, reliance under the UCC is quite limited.

9.   **Rescission and Modification under Statutes of Frauds**

a.   **Oral rescission.**   An agreement under the statute of frauds can be rescinded by an oral agreement between the parties.

b.   **Oral modification.**   An agreement that fell within the statute of frauds originally might not require a writing if modified in a way that removed it from the reach of the statute.

c.   **Modification of oral agreements.**   An agreement that was not within the statute of frauds when originally made may require a writing if modification brings the terms within the statute. UCC §2-209(3); Restatement (Second) of Contracts §149.

 # EXAMPLE AND ANALYSIS

B agrees to buy S's old car for $450. The agreement is not within the statute and would be enforceable regardless of a writing. B later agrees to pay an additional $75

if S will include a set of snow tires. The contract may fall within the statute because the sale is for $525.

B could buy the tires later in a separate transaction without coming within the statute. But a single transaction for multiple goods normally is not divided. A promise to pay $100,000 for a large quantity of nails would be within the statute even if the price per nail or the price per box of nails was less than $500.

---

       i.   **Original remains enforceable.** If a modification is unenforceable, but the original agreement was enforceable, the original agreement remains binding despite the attempted modification.

       ii.   **Reliance on modification.** If reliance on an attempted modification makes reinstatement of the original contract unjust, courts may refuse to enforce the original contract.

C. WRITINGS REQUIRED BY THE PARTIES

Not all provisions requiring a writing are statutory. Sometimes the parties themselves insist that agreements be in writing, even if the legislature and the courts would permit them to make oral commitments. As with most other terms, the parties are free to specify the manner in which their agreements become binding. Sometimes, however, the parties disagree about whether they have required a writing. These disputes tend to arise in two contexts.

1. Before the Contract Becomes Binding: Limiting Assent to Writings

Some parties do not want to be bound until they have negotiated all the terms and had a chance to read and consider the final writing. Thus, the binding event is the signing of the written agreement. Until then, all the talk and drafts represent preliminary negotiations, with no binding effect. Other parties, however, make deals on a handshake and fill in the written terms later, often with form contracts. These parties expect the transaction to be binding immediately upon their oral assent. The writings are mere formalities confirming the oral contract they have already formed. Courts gladly accept either method of doing business but occasionally must decide which method was in play when the parties disagree about whether an oral agreement was binding.

    a.   **Rule of thumb: Expressly require a writing.** If you want the binding event to be the signing of a writing, you should explicitly say so as early as practical in the negotiations. The details of this issue have been discussed above. See 2.H.1. A brief reminder follows.

b. **Other party's awareness.** If the other party **knows or has reason to know** that you do not intend to be bound until you have made "some further manifestation of assent," such as signing a writing, discussions will be labeled preliminary negotiations and will not give rise to legally binding commitments. Restatement (Second) of Contracts §26.

c. **Silence not golden.** You can be bound without intending to be bound; subjective intentions rarely matter in contract law. But you probably will not be bound as long as you **manifest an intention not to be bound.** Restatement (Second) of Contracts §21.

2. Before Modifications Become Effective

Parties sometimes agree to clauses that prohibit oral modification of a contract.

a. **Purpose.** These clauses are particularly important to companies that have many agents dealing with the public. If they wish to keep their contract obligations reasonably uniform, they must prevent every statement made by an agent from changing their form agreements. Similarly, construction contracts frequently require changes. Insisting that changes be in writing can minimize disputes about whether particular changes were authorized and how much the price should be adjusted.

b. **Enforceability.** The UCC expressly recognizes the power of parties to require written modifications. UCC §2-209(2). When a contract contains such a clause, oral modifications are ineffective.

c. **Waiver.** Parties may waive their rights under a contract orally. An attempt to modify the contract orally might be interpreted as an oral waiver. This could have the same effect as a modification, despite a clause attempting to preclude oral modification. UCC §2-209(4).

 # EXAMPLE AND ANALYSIS

Plaintiff sold defendant a car. Defendant consistently made payments late. Plaintiff eventually repossessed the car. Defendant alleged the repossession was wrongful because the parties had orally agreed to modify the date the payments were due. If modified, defendant's payments were timely. The court did not expressly find a modification but did find that plaintiff had waived the right to insist on timely payments.

Thus, the repossession was a breach of contract. *Margolin v. Franklin*, 270 N.E.2d 1979 (Ill. Ct. App. 1971).

      d.   **Waiver revocable.**   A waiver of this sort can be revoked by notifying the other party that you will insist on the terms of the contract, unless the other party has relied on the waiver to her detriment. UCC §2-209(5).

REVIEW QUESTIONS AND ANSWERS

Question: What categories of contracts are governed by statutes of frauds?

Answer: Promises in consideration of **marriage**, promises not performable within a **year**, promises conveying an interest in **land**, promises by an **executor** to pay debts of the estate, promises for sales of **goods** of $500 or more, and promises to serve as **surety** for the debt of another. (The mnemonic device MY LEGS may help you remember these types of contracts.)

Question: True or false: In order to be enforceable, a contract governed by the statute of frauds must be in writing signed by both parties.

Answer: False. The contract itself need not be written as long as a note or memorandum evincing the contract is written and signed. A writing signed by one party — the party resisting enforcement (the party to be charged) — will suffice.

Question: What constitutes a signature?

Answer: Any mark intended to authenticate the contents of the writing. This may include initials, a typed name, a letterhead, a seal, perhaps a thumbprint, or other marks used for that purpose.

Question: What terms must a contract contain in order to satisfy the statute of frauds:

1. For sales of goods under the UCC?
2. For other contracts?

Answer:

1. Under the UCC, a writing must be signed, must indicate the existence of an agreement, and must include the quantity of goods involved.
2. Under the Restatement (Second) of Contracts, the writing must be signed, must indicate the subject matter of a contract, must indicate the existence of an agreement (or an offer by the party to be charged), and must specify the material terms of the unperformed promises.

Question: Can a writing signed by the party seeking to enforce the contract but not signed by the party to be charged satisfy the statute of frauds?

Answer: Yes, but only in very specific circumstances. In a contract for sales of goods, a writing between merchants sent within a reasonable time after contract formation will be treated as if the recipient had signed it if it would be sufficient against the sender, the other party actually received it, had reason to know of its contents, and did not object within 10 days of receipt. Aside from these limited circumstances, writings must be signed by the party to be charged.

Question: If a party begins performance under an agreement unenforceable because of the statute of frauds, does she have any remedy when the other party breaches?

Answer: Yes. Restitution will prevent unjust enrichment. If the other party has received a benefit from her performance and has not paid for that benefit, she will be required either to return the benefit or to pay its fair market value to the party who performed. Under some circumstances, a party may recover reliance expenditures even if the other party did not receive any benefit from these expenses. Usually, however, mere reliance, even if foreseeable by the other party, will not permit an expectation recovery if the statute makes the contract unenforceable.

Question: If a party has fully performed under a contract, can she later argue that the agreement was unenforceable because of the statute of frauds and seek to recover her performance or its value?

Answer: No. Even if she is the only party who has performed, her performance serves as ample evidence that she really had entered an agreement. Thus, courts generally recognize an exception that would preclude her from using the statute to undermine the contract. If the other party does not perform, the performing party might be able to elect restitution rather than expectation as the appropriate remedy for the breach. That issue is discussed later. See Chapter 23.

INTRODUCTION TO DEFENSES: FACTORS THAT INTERFERE WITH ARM'S-LENGTH BARGAINING

 CHAPTER OVERVIEW

The next few chapters address a range of defenses that a party can use to avoid liability for breach of contract. Each can be studied on its own. A few general points, however, apply to more than one defense. Those issues are raised here. They help put the defenses into a useful context. (The Uniform Commercial Code does not include provisions for most of the defenses in this chapter, with the notable exception of unconscionability. UCC §2-302. In most cases, however, the UCC explicitly incorporates the common-law approach to contract defenses. UCC §1-103.)

- Contract defenses can be asserted by a plaintiff seeking **rescission and restitution**. They are not limited to use as a defense in a breach-of-contract action.
- Most contract defenses make a contract **voidable, not void**. That is, a party may choose to waive the defense and enforce the contract.

A. FRAMEWORK OF DEFENSES

Bargains help us identify transfers that increase wealth — those where the parties value what they receive more than they value what they give up. The law relies on the parties themselves to decide how much they value the items exchanged. In some cases, however, the parties may be unable to make accurate assessments of the relative values of the items exchanged. Some impediments to accurate decisions have no legal effect. A party who makes a bad deal because she did not think carefully about the transaction has no one to blame but herself. Other impediments, however, are sufficiently general and severe that they undermine confidence that the deal in fact increases wealth. The defenses that follow generally reflect reasons the transaction may not deserve state intervention because we lack confidence that the transaction increases societal well-being.

B. PROCEDURAL FRAMEWORK

Contract defenses can arise in two ways — one distinctly offensive.

1. Breach and Defend

If a party recognizes the defense before she has fully performed, she may stop performing. If the other party sues for breach, she pleads the defense. If she proves the defense, the other party loses the breach of contract suit and collects nothing. Note: If the other party knows the defense is valid, she might not sue for breach, choosing instead to keep whatever she received and lay low.

2. Rescission and Restitution

A party may perform part or all of the contract before she recognizes the defense. If she wants that performance returned, she may need to sue the other party. She can sue for breach of contract if she wants the other party to perform as promised under the invalid contract. But if she wants her own performance back, she instead sues for rescission: a decree that the contract was not binding in the first place. After rescission, the normal remedy is restitution: re-creating, as nearly as possible, the situation that preceded the contract — usually, returning each party's performance to her.

3. Selecting the Remedy

Decisions in these cases involve a choice of remedy as much as a decision regarding liability. A decision to enforce the contract (because the defense was invalid) entitles one party to her expectation interest. A decision not to enforce the contract (because the defense is valid) entitles one party to restitution to prevent unjust enrichment. In either case, the court will award a remedy to one party unless, by chance, the performance to date has left the parties in the position the court's remedies would seek to create. (For example, if the court decides rescission is appropriate before either party began performing, there might be nothing to restore.)

C. TERMINOLOGY: VOID VERSUS VOIDABLE

1. Voidable

Most of the defenses in this section make a contract **voidable**. A voidable contract is valid until the aggrieved party elects to **avoid** or to **disaffirm** the agreement. If a contract proves beneficial to a person with a right to avoid the transaction, she may instead **ratify** the agreement, in effect **waiving** the defense.

 a. Rationale. The defenses below often make a contract voidable to protect one party from others who might take advantage of her. If the party the law seeks to protect does not want the law's protection, there is little reason to force it on her. For example, the victim of fraud should have the right to enforce an agreement if, once aware of the fraud, she still prefers what she will receive under the contract to what she will give up under the contract.

 b. Disaffirmance. A party who wants to cancel the deal and get her performance back may elect to disaffirm. This usually requires some notice to the other party.

  i. Manner of disaffirmance. Sometimes courts treat bringing an action for rescission or even breaching the contract as notice of the election. But express notice may be useful.

  ii. Timely disaffirmance. Some defenses require an aggrieved party to disaffirm promptly upon discovering the defense. Failure to disaffirm a contract within a reasonable time may waive the defense.

 c. Ratification. A party may elect to ratify a contract.

  i. Express ratification is possible but somewhat uncommon. A party who expressly states that she wants the contract enforced rarely sues for rescission thereafter.

  ii. Implied ratification (or waiver) is more common. A party who learns of her defense but does not assert it within a reasonable amount of time may waive the defense. Similarly, a party who continues to perform under the terms of a contract after learning of her defense implicitly indicates an intent to ratify the contract.

2. Void

A **void** contract is unenforceable from the beginning. The court will not enforce the contract **even if the parties both want the agreement enforced**. Similarly, third parties may challenge the enforceability of a void agreement. If a contract is void, disaffirmance is unnecessary and ratification impossible. Generally, the law makes contracts void only when a public policy is at stake. The defense involved does not protect the individual but the public interest. The individuals cannot waive the public's interest.

3. Avoiding Confusion

a. **Void versus avoided.**   Once a court holds that a party has established a defense that made the contract voidable, there is a temptation to refer to the contract as void. Resist that temptation. The voidable contract was **avoided**, but it did not change from voidable to void by virtue of the decree.

b. **Careful word choice.**   You can minimize confusion by keeping the terms straight. You don't want the professor to think you don't know the difference. You don't want a judge to start thinking about issues applicable to void contracts but not to voidable ones. In short, there are risks to using the terms imprecisely.

c. **Effects similar.**   The consequences for the parties, however, may be no different. Whether void or avoided, the court still refuses the enforce the agreement and, depending on the circumstances, may enter another remedy to prevent unjust enrichment. (For some void contracts, restitution may not be available, but the reasons relate to the public policies at issue, not to whether you call the contract void or avoided.) Thus, you will see cases in which courts are not careful about the distinction.

REVIEW QUESTIONS AND ANSWERS

Question: Chris, who was 17, bought a motorcycle from Pat. (Agreements by people under 18 are voidable for lack of the capacity.) After paying the full price and driving the cycle for three months, Chris discovered numerous problems with the vehicle. Can Chris return the vehicle to Pat and receive a refund on the ground that Chris lacked the capacity to enter the contract?

Answer: Yes. Chris need not wait for Pat to sue to raise incapacity as a defense. Because Pat has already been paid, Pat will never sue. Chris, however, can sue Pat for rescission, offering to return the motorcycle in exchange for a refund.

Question: Bobby persuaded Sean to buy Bobby's car by lying about the number of miles on the odometer. After delivering the car and receiving the payment, Bobby received a better offer for the car. Can Bobby raise fraud to rescind the contract and recover the car from Sean?

Answer: No. Once Bobby reveals the fraud to Sean, Sean may elect to rescind the contract. But if Sean decides to ratify the contract, Sean may keep the car. (Or, if Sean hears about this other buyer, sell the car to that person.) The defense makes the contract voidable at Sean's option. It is not void.

6 INCAPACITY

 ## CHAPTER OVERVIEW

If a party lacks the capacity to enter a contract, any agreement she makes is voidable (at best).

The four basic sources of incapacity are:

- Infancy;
- Mental illness or defect;
- Intoxication; and
- Guardianship.

Persons under the age of 18 lack the capacity to enter contracts, with some exceptions:

- A minor who misrepresents her age may be estopped to raise the defense;
- In some states, marriage removes the incapacity, regardless of age; and
- In some states, contracts to obtain the necessities of life are enforceable despite infancy.

Persons who enter contracts with minors generally can receive specific restitution of the thing they gave the minor but cannot recover restitution of the value of the item if the specific thing is not available.

Mental illness or defect makes a contract voidable if:

- A party cannot understand the nature and consequences of the transaction; or
- A party cannot act in a reasonable manner and the other party has reason to know of her inability.

Persons who enter contracts with the mentally ill can enforce the contract if:

- A party unaware of the illness or defect has relied on a contract that was made on fair terms; and
- In some states, the contract involves the necessities of life.

Persons who enter contracts with the mentally ill generally may use the full range of restitutionary recovery.

Intoxication makes a contract voidable if:

- The intoxicated person cannot understand the nature and consequences of the transaction; or
- The intoxicated person cannot act in a reasonable manner with regard to the transaction; and
- The other party has reason to know the intoxication is sufficiently severe to incapacitate the victim.

Once a guardian has been appointed for a person (generally based on mental condition), that person has no capacity to enter contracts; only the guardian may enter contracts on her behalf.

A. RATIONALE

If one party lacks the judgment or mental capacity to assess the relative values of the items exchanged, the transaction might leave that party with something she actually values less than what she gave up. The bargain itself does not carry its usual significance as an indicator of a mutually beneficial exchange. When the law cannot rely on the parties to make their own assessments of the values exchanged, the law refuses to enforce the transactions. Incapacity raises two difficult issues: defining who suffers an incapacity and balancing the interests of the other people in these transactions. Particularly when people do not realize they are dealing with someone with an incapacity, courts may need to protect the interests of both parties. Thus, the rules below involve two segments (which occasionally overlap): the rules defining the incapacity and the rules protecting parties dealing with the incapacitated person.

B. INFANCY

Until the day before a person's eighteenth birthday, any contract she enters is voidable. Restatement (Second) of Contracts §14. The actual age of majority generally is set by state statute. Some statutes use the birthday, not the day before. Eighteen is the most common age but is not universally adopted. In reading cases, remember that before the 1970s, infancy continued until age 21.

1. **An Infant's Power to Avoid a Contract**

   a. **Age, not appearance, defines infancy.** Infancy is defined objectively based on the party's age, not on how old she looks or acts. Thus, in an era of birth certificates and driver's licenses, disputes over whether a party really was an infant are generally easy to resolve.

   b. **In some states, marriage negates infancy.** This allows married people of any age the full power to enter contracts.

   c. **Ratification after reaching the age of majority waives the defense.**

   d. **Contracts for necessaries are not voidable.** A minor may need to enter contracts for the necessities of life, such as food, clothing, and shelter. If these contracts were not enforceable, vendors would be unwilling to deal with minors—particularly in states with the strictest rules on restitution noted in the next section. Thus, most states enforced contracts made by a minor for the purchase of necessaries. Some recent courts have expanded the definition of necessaries. (The term "necessaries" comes from the English "doctrine of necessaries," which held a husband liable for debts incurred by the wife if the purchases involved necessary expenses. Necessities, which rings better in the modern ear, sometimes will replace the term of art, necessaries.) For instance, one court enforced an employment contract on the ground that employment is necessary to obtain money for food, clothing, and shelter.

2. **Protection for Parties Unaware of Another's Infancy**

   a. **Exempt transactions.** Some statutes exempt specific transactions, such as payment of insurance premiums and withdrawals from a bank, from the defense.

   b. **Fraudulent representation of age. This action may negate the defense.** If an infant fraudulently states that she is 18 or older, the infant may be estopped to assert that she was less than 18. The equitable defense of unclean hands may account for this exception as easily as estoppel.

   c. **Limitations on restitution.** People who enter contracts with infants receive less in the way of restitution than allowable in most other defenses.

i. **Specific restitution is available.** When an infant asserts the defense, the other party is entitled to recover the item given in exchange for the infant's promise.

  (a) **Damage or use.** The property may not be in the same condition it was at the time of sale. A new car purchased by the infant will be a used car when returned — and may be a wrecked car, if disaffirmance occurs after a traffic accident.

  (b) **Adjustment for use.** In some states, a minor's recovery of amounts paid is reduced to account for the value of her use of the property for the time it was in her possession.

  - **Rental Value**. If a minor returns property in good condition, she may need to pay the fair rental value of the property for the period it was in her possession.
  - **Depreciation**. If a minor returns property that has depreciated, she may need to pay the difference between the value the property had when she received it and its value when she returned it. See, e.g., *Dodson v. Shrader*, 824 S.W.2d 545 (Tenn. 1992) (court ruled seller could recover depreciation while minor held truck where minor who knew of engine problem but did not repair it drove truck until engine blew up).
  - **Overreaching**. When a person overreaches while dealing with a minor — that is, takes advantage of the minor's poor judgment to make an unfair deal — courts generally do not apply these mitigating doctrines. Caveat vendor.

ii. **Restitution in money generally is unavailable.** An infant who cannot return the specific thing received often need not return anything to the other party.

  (a) **Proceeds of sale.** An infant who sold the thing received probably must return the proceeds of that sale to the other party.

  (b) **Not fair market value.** But most states do not require the infant to pay the fair market of nonreturnable items. Thus, contracts for the purchase of services (like flying lessons) or goods for consumption (restaurant meals) pose particular risks for people dealing with minors.

(c) **Statutes.**   Again, some states have adopted different rules by statute.

iii.   Possible rationales.

(a) **Caveat vendor.**   The law may expect merchants to protect themselves from dealing with infants. Infancy does have physical clues that can alert a party to verify the other's age. Age verification is relatively easy — at least compared with verifying other incapacities. When misrepresentations by the infant negate the defense, verification can be complete protection for others.

(b) **Restitution may negate rescission.**   Restitution can produce exactly the result that the defense seeks to avoid. When a contract was made on fair terms, which may be common, the fair market value of the goods and the contract price will be nearly identical. Allowing restitution, then, would equate with enforcing the contract, the result the defense is designed to prevent. If the law is serious about allowing minors to disaffirm their contracts, perhaps it should not allow restitution to undermine the defense. (Objective fairness of the exchange does not protect the minor. The issue is how much she values the items relative to what she gives up for them, not how much others value them. When the bargain is suspect, all enforcement is suspect.)

C.   MENTAL ILLNESS OR DEFECT

Defining mental illness is much more difficult than defining infancy. Objective or verifiable definitions of mental illness are elusive. Moreover, the cost of a poor definition is enormous. An overinclusive definition will deprive many people of the right to make contracts — perhaps including the right to hold a job or rent a home. The ability to rescind the contract may deter people from entering contracts with the mentally ill — and perhaps those suspected of mental illness. Any advantage the exchange might have for others would disappear upon disaffirmance, making it pointless to enter the exchange in the first place. Thus, the law faces more difficulty in both halves of the inquiry.

1.   The Mentally Ill Person's Power to Avoid a Contract

The law has recognized two types of incapacity that may interfere with the bargaining process: **cognitive** incapacity and **volitional** incapacity. Both types of **incapacity must stem from a mental illness or defect**. Poor education or lack of forethought do not constitute an incapacity.

a. **Cognitive incapacity.**   This exists if a person is "unable to understand the nature and consequences of the transaction." Restatement (Second) of Contracts §15(1)(a). This type of incapacity is what most people think of when they think of mental illness. The person does not understand what the transaction entails. Thus, her assent to it is not evidence that she valued what she received more than what she gave up.

b. **Volitional incapacity.**   This exists if (i) a person is "unable to act in a reasonable manner in relation to the transaction" and (ii) "the other party has reason to know of his condition." Restatement (Second) of Contracts §15(1)(b).

   i. **Understanding unaffected.**   Volitional incapacity may apply to someone who understands exactly what the transaction entails and who evinces that understanding by asking cogent and perceptive questions about the transaction. Nonetheless, if the disorder prevents her from exercising a free choice, she may later avoid the contract. The choice she manifests may or may not reflect the value she attaches to the items exchanged; her inability to control her own behavior in entering the transaction makes inferences regarding value impossible.

 # EXAMPLE AND ANALYSIS

Mrs. Ortolere suffered from involutional melancholia. At retirement, she elected to take a pension for the duration of her life "without option." This changed her earlier election of pension that would pay less per month but would allow her husband to collect any unpaid amount due to her if she died before exhausting her balance. She died two months after retiring. Her husband sought to revoke the election. The evidence indicated that she fully understood the choices. Some evidence suggested that her psychosis prevented her from acting in the manner she desired. There also was evidence that she felt she and her husband could not live on the smaller amount payable each month under the reserve option. The school system was aware of her illness. The court held that her new election was ineffective for lack of capacity and reinstated her original option. *Ortolere v. Teachers' Retirement Bd.*, 250 N.E.2d 460 (N.Y. 1969).

ii.   **Conceptual difficulties.** It is difficult to distinguish, even in theory, an offer a person could not refuse due to incapacity from an offer she did not refuse despite an ability to do so. Incapacity requires a separate determination for each transaction because an inability to conduct some transactions does not mean an inability to conduct any transactions. Without any conceptual guidance, a jury has very little hope of accurately deciding which category the specific transaction fits. Nonetheless, it is difficult to deny the defense of incapacity to those who suffer from volitional disorders as science improves our understanding the way mental illness works.

2.   **Protection for Parties Unaware of Another's Mental Illness**

a.   **Necessaries.** Some states enforce contracts that provide necessaries for the mentally ill. Thus, persons providing the mentally ill with a place to live, food, and most clothing can collect debts incurred as long as they do not take unfair advantage of the mentally ill.

b.   **Reason to know.** The "reason to know" requirement for volitional incapacity helps protect persons dealing with the mentally ill. Volitional incapacity may be harder to detect; the party's ability to understand the transaction means some warning signs of mental incapacity may not be present. The ability to enforce contracts when the other party had no reason to know of the condition protects their legitimate expectations when dealing with the mentally ill.

c.   **Exception for good faith.** When a party has dealt in good faith with a mentally ill person, courts may enforce contracts with the mentally ill to protect reliance. Restatement (Second) of Contracts §15(2). The Restatement does not use the word good faith, but the elements seem to add up to protection for honest dealings with the mentally ill.

i.   **Unaware of the mental illness or defect.** A person who knew of the mental illness could not reasonably rely on the enforceability of the contract. In addition, a person who did not know of the defect could not exploit that condition to negotiate a one-sided deal. Thus, protection seems more appropriate for those acting without knowledge of the defect.

(a)   **Reason to know?** Although the text of the Restatement (Second) refers to "knowledge," the comment refers to "reason to know." This implies that one who should have known of the illness or defect should not rely on the contract—or that injustice might not result from non-enforcement if the other party had an opportunity to prevent the situation by recognizing the illness and not entering the contract.

ii. **Detrimental reliance.** The power to disaffirm a contract remains intact as long as avoidance will not harm the other party. But after partial performance or other changes in circumstances, prejudice to the other party may be so great that avoidance would be unjust—particularly if restitution is unavailable or significantly limited.

iii. **Fair terms.** Courts will allow the mentally ill to disaffirm an unfair contract even after the other party has performed. The provision is not intended to enforce contracts, which may not benefit both parties, as much as to protect reliance.

iv. **Effect of the exception.**

(a) **Enforceable contract.** According to the Restatement (Second), these facts terminate the mentally ill person's power of disaffirmance. That makes the contract enforceable to the full extent of other contracts. In effect this makes expectation the normal remedy.

(b) **Limited relief.** Paradoxically, the Restatement (Second) states that the court "may grant relief as justice requires," language similar to that used in endorsing the reliance interest. *Compare* Restatement (Second) of Contracts §15(2) *with* Restatement (Second) of Contracts §90(1). Thus, some courts may seek to achieve justice by awarding restitution or compensating reliance rather than enforcing the contract.

D. INTOXICATION

Intoxication presents the weakest case for incapacity, perhaps because it frequently is a voluntary incapacity. Nonetheless, intoxication is legal. The law has no reason to punish intoxication by encouraging people to take advantage of drinkers. The balance between protecting intoxicants and protecting those who deal with them, however, shifts significantly in favor of the sober(er) party.

1. An Intoxicated Person's Power to Avoid a Contract

a. **Cognitive and volitional incapacity.** Intoxication includes both cognitive and volitional incapacity. That is, a person's intoxication may allow her to rescind a contract if the intoxication caused her to be:

- "Unable to understand in a reasonable manner the nature and consequences of the transaction," or
- "Unable to act in a reasonable manner in relation to the transaction." Restatement (Second) of Contracts §16.

b. Reason to know of incapacity. Intoxication allows disaffirmance only if the other party has reason to know of the **incapacity.**

i. Incapacity, not intoxication. Awareness of the intoxication probably is not enough. The other party must have reason to know that intoxication has left the person unable to understand the transaction or unable to act reasonably. But see Restatement (Second) of Contracts §16 comment b.

ii. Exception for inducement. A person who induces another's intoxication may be unable to obtain enforcement even if the intoxicated person cannot prove that person had reason to know that the intoxication was sufficiently severe to produce an incapacity. Having tried to get her drunk, the other party can hardly complain that she didn't know she had succeeded in getting her so drunk she could not think straight.

c. Nonalcoholic substances. The Restatement (Second) implies that intoxication rules may apply when intoxication results from the use of substances other than alcohol. Restatement (Second) of Contracts §16 comment a.

d. Other defenses. In some cases involving intoxication, defenses of fraud or unconscionability may arise from the conduct of the other party. Even if incapacity is not demonstrated, analyzing these other defenses may be useful.

2. Protection for Parties Unaware of Another's Intoxication

a. Reason to know. Most of the protection for the other party comes from the reason to know requirement. Contracts will not be voidable in the first place unless the other party had reason to know of the incapacity.

b. Timely disaffirmance. An intoxicated person must disaffirm a contract promptly after becoming sober. The definition of promptly will vary with the circumstances. A person who delays too long waives the defense.

c. Tender return of benefits. The intoxicated person (like others seeking restitution) must offer to return any consideration she received under the contract at the time she disaffirms the contract, unless the consideration was dissipated during the intoxication. That is, restitution rules appear to work normally except for items consumed immediately.

REVIEW QUESTIONS AND ANSWERS

Question: At 16, Jo bought a car from a dealer. Two years later, on Jo's eighteenth birthday, Jo returned the car to the dealer and asked for a refund of the purchase price. Can she succeed?

Answer: Yes, unless the state allows an offset for depreciation in the value of the car or for the fair rental value of the car. Jo disaffirmed the contract on the first day after becoming an adult—prompt enough by any standard. Dealers should protect themselves by not selling to children.

Question: True or false: If a merchant asks a person how old she is before entering the contract, the merchant can avoid any difficulty with incapacity based on infancy?

Answer: True. If the minor admits to being under age, the merchant can refuse to sell to the minor, thus preventing any problems down the road. If the minor lies about her age, the minor's misrepresentation usually estops her from later seeking to rescind the contract based on infancy. Note: If the merchant knew the customer was under age, it might not be reasonable to rely on the misrepresentation. But if the merchant knew the age, she can protect herself by refusing to deal with the minor.

Question: True or false: If a mental illness prevents a person from understanding the nature of a transaction, the contract still will be enforceable if the other party had no reason to know about the person's mental illness.

Answer: False. The reason to know requirement applies only to volitional mental disorders, not to cognitive mental disorders.

Question: True or false: If intoxication prevents a person from understanding the nature of a transaction, the contract still will be enforceable if the other party had no reason to know about the person's intoxication.

Answer: True. For intoxication, the reason to know requirement applies to both cognitive and volitional impairment.

Question: True or false: If intoxication prevents a person from understanding the nature of a transaction, the contract still will not be enforceable if the other party had reason to know about the person's mental illness.

Answer: False. Reason to know of the intoxication is not enough to make a contract voidable based on intoxication. The other party must also have reason to know that the intoxication prevented the person from understanding the nature of the transaction.

Question: True or false: If the terms of a contract are fair, courts will enforce the contract even if one party suffered from an incapacity based on mental illness or defect.

Answer: False. Courts will enforce fair contracts despite a mental illness, but only if the party was unaware of the mental illness at the time the contract was formed and has relied on the agreement in ways that make it unjust to refuse to enforce the contract. Fair terms alone will not justify enforcement.

7   IMPROPER PRESSURE

 ## CHAPTER OVERVIEW

When a person assents to a bargain because of improper pressure, the law lacks confidence that she actually values the return more than she values what she gave in exchange. Thus, the exchange lacks the indicia of importance that encourage the law to enforce contracts.

Improper pressure can take the form of **duress** or **undue influence**.

Duress involves three elements:

- An **improper threat**; that
- **Induces a party's assent** to the agreement; under circumstances where
- She had **no reasonable alternative** but to assent.

The following threats are always improper:

- A threat to commit a **crime or a tort**;
- A threat that itself would be a crime or a tort if the threatener obtained property as a result;
- A threat of **criminal prosecution**;
- A threat to use of **civil process in bad faith**; and
- A threat to breach an **obligation of good faith under a contract**;

The following threats are improper if the resulting contract is not on fair terms:

- The act threatened would harm the other party without significant benefit to the threatener;
- The effectiveness of the threat is enhanced by prior unfair dealing by the threatener; and
- The threatened act is a use of power for illegitimate ends.

A threat induces assent if it **substantially contributes** to the decision to agree to the terms.

A party who can refuse to assent and obtain protection from the consequences via other reasonable means cannot avoid the contract.

Undue influence exists is unfair persuasion of:

- A person under the domination of the persuader; or
- A person whose relation to the persuader justifies the assumption that the persuader will not act in manner contrary to the interests of the party being persuaded.

In deciding whether persuasion is unfair, several factors deserve consideration:

- Did the persuasion occur at an unusual time or place?
- Did the persuader insist on unusual haste?
- Did any other unusual feature reduce a party's ability to recognize or assess the merits of the transaction proposed?

A. DURESS

Duress involves the use of improper threats to induce assent. Although some refer to assent induced by duress as involuntary, this can be misleading. The threatened person may voluntarily choose the lesser of two evils: Faced with a choice between "your money or your life," most people voluntarily choose life and relinquish money. When the choice is to sign a contract or be killed, we know the person who signs values her life more than the things she relinquishes under the contract, but we do not know whether she values what she received in exchange more than she values what she gave up. The problem is not the voluntariness of the choice but the fact that the choice must be made at all. The evil is that a threat forces a person to choose between two things, when she is entitled to both.

1. Elements

See Restatement (Second) of Contracts §175.

a. **Threat.** Did the party seeking to enforce the agreement threaten the party seeking to avoid enforcement?

b. **Improper threat.** Was the threat improper?

c. **Inducement.** Did the threat induce the party seeking to avoid enforcement to assent to the agreement?

 d.   **Lack of reasonable alternatives.**   Did the threatened party have a reasonable alternative to assent?

2.   Threat

Generally, a party seeking to avoid enforcement will have little difficulty establishing a threat. Virtually any offer of an exchange can be characterized as a threat. For example, the offer "I will give you 10 calendars if you will give me $50" is also a threat: "Give me $50, or else I will not give you 10 calendars." This is not an improper threat, but it is a threat.

 a.   **Focus on propriety.**   Because every bargain includes an implicit threat, duress tends to focus on whether the threat was **improper**. Before you can assess the propriety of the threat, however, you must identify the content of the threat. Exactly what did the threatening party threaten to do?

 b.   **Implicit threat.**   **A threat need not be stated expressly.** Consider such comments as "That's a nice family you have. It would be a shame if anything should happen to them, like an accident, maybe." These remarks, common in B movies, could be menacing under some circumstances. The fact that no explicit threat to harm the family was expressed need not prevent a finder of fact from determining that a threat was made.

3.   Improper Threat

Some threats are proper. For example, the threat not to give away calendars unless paid the price you demand is not improper. People have no obligation either to give their calendars away or to accept a price less than the value they attach to them. Some threats, however, exceed the bounds of propriety. The Restatement (Second) of Contracts §176 has attempted to categorize these threats.

 a.   **Improper regardless of terms.**   A threat is always improper if:

  i.   **The threatened act is a crime or a tort.**   Threats of violence fit this category. So would a threat not to take reasonable precautions to prevent an accident.

  ii.   **The threatened act would be a crime or a tort if the threatening party obtained property as a result of the threat.**   Some acts, though perfectly legal in themselves, cannot legally be threatened to extort property. For example, it is legal to publish true but embarrassing information in the press. Laws against blackmail and extortion generally make it illegal to obtain payments from another by threatening to publish such information. Thus, the **threat** would be improper even if the **act threatened** (publishing information) is legal.

iii. **The threatened act is a criminal prosecution.** Criminal prosecutions serve a public purpose. It is improper for people to threaten them for private gain.

   (a) **Ethical implications.** This rule can pose difficulties for attorneys who discover criminal wrongdoing while investigating a civil case. Threatening to expose the crime might produce a better settlement of the civil suit. For example, a battery victim might threaten to swear out a criminal complaint unless the defendant settles the civil case on favorable terms. Such threats are improper.

   (b) **Explanation versus threat.** A good faith explanation of possible criminal consequences may not constitute a threat. *See* Restatement (Second) of Contracts §176 comment c. The line between good faith explanation and implicit threat is likely to be exceedingly fine and very difficult to predict.

iv. **The threatened act is the use of civil process in bad faith.** Generally, a threat to commence a civil suit is proper. But if a party knows or believes that she has no reasonable basis for such a suit, a threat to pursue a lawsuit may constitute bad faith. If so, the threat is improper. Similarly, a threat to defend against a suit may be improper if the party making the threat knows or believes that she has no valid basis on which to resist the other party's claim.

v. **The threatened act would breach an obligation of good faith and fair dealing under a contract with the threatened party.** This type of threat usually arises when one party seeks to modify an existing agreement. A threat to stop performing unless the other party agrees to modification can be proper. New circumstances may justify renegotiation and might even excuse nonperformance if they support a finding of mistake or impracticability. A threat made without any legitimate basis for seeking modification, however, would be improper. Similarly, a threat unrelated to the existing contract may be improper.

   (a) **Breach of good faith.** Not every threat to breach a contract threatens to breach an obligation of good faith and fair dealing. Some threatened breaches may be proper.

EXAMPLES AND ANALYSIS

1. A agrees to excavate a foundation on B's land for a fixed price. After work has begun, A discovers that the ground under B's land consists almost entirely of rock, which is much more expensive to excavate than the soil A anticipated would be there. A seeks to modify the contract in light of the unexpected costs. A's threat not to complete work unless B agrees to the modification is not improper. See *Watkins & Sons v. Carrig*, 21 A.2d 591 (N.H. 1941).

2. A agrees to build a store for B in one city. B later decides to build another new store in a nearby city. A threatens to stop work on the first store unless B awards A the construction contract for the new store. The threat is improper because the purpose of the threat does not relate to the contract to be breached.

Additional facts might alter this conclusion if they linked the two contracts in some significant way. For instance, if construction delays caused by B had made the first store unduly expensive to build, A might be permitted to threaten to walk off the first job unless B awarded the second job as a kind of compensation for the problems encountered in the original contract.

(b) **Not limited to express terms.** A threat might breach the duty of good faith and fair dealing even if it does not breach an express term of the contract.

 EXAMPLE AND ANALYSIS

A employs B under an agreement with no specified duration. A legally can discharge B at any time; discharge would not be breach. A threatens to fire B on grounds A knows to be false, unless B agrees to waive a claim for overtime pay against A. The threat might constitute bad faith even though discharge would not breach a contract. (This is another situation in which the act itself may be proper, but a threat to commit the act is improper.)

---

b. **Improper if terms unfair.** Some threats may be improper even though they do not fall within the categories described in the preceding section. An effort to catalogue every kind of improper threat inevitably would succumb to the ingenuity of people who invent new and imaginative ways to apply pressure to obtain their desires on unfair terms. Thus, some courts have found duress in cases in which the threat was not improper under these criteria. The Restatement (Second) attempts to classify the factors that courts relied on in deciding to call additional threats improper. These criteria are more open-ended and vague than the criteria noted earlier. Examples are fairly rare and often involve unusual situations. Nonetheless, familiarity with these criteria may help you argue that other threats are improper. (Because these situations are open-ended, they can make excellent exam questions.)

i.   **When a threat results in a contract not on fair terms, the threat is improper if:**

(a)   **The threatened act would harm the threatened party without significantly benefiting the threatening party.** In these situations, the only reason to fulfill the threat would be vindictive, because no advantage would accrue to the threatening party. The Restatement offers an example similar to blackmail: Publication of embarrassing information might harm the threatened party without benefit to the threatener.

EXAMPLE AND ANALYSIS

A and B are siblings. A inherited a family heirloom that B cherishes. A threatens to burn the heirloom, destroying any hope that B might obtain it later, unless B sells stock to A at an unreasonably low price. The threat seems improper even though A owns the heirloom and has every right to destroy it because destruction would not benefit A but would harm B.

(b)   **The threat has been made significantly more effective by prior unfair dealing by the threatening party.** Weakness increases susceptibility to a threat. When the threatener unfairly caused the weakness or susceptibility, prior unfair dealing may change the nature of an otherwise legitimate threat into an improper threat. For example, if A's unfair dealing with B drives B to the brink of insolvency, a threat by A not to pay money owed to B under a contract may be deemed improper even if the threat would not constitute a breach of good faith and fair dealing under the contract.

(c) **The threatened act is a use of power for illegitimate ends.** The legitimacy of the threatening party's ends does not offer a very clear standard for courts to apply. In effect, this catch-all provision exists to describe cases in which courts have done what they think justice requires despite the absence of precedent or any clearly delineated rule.

 ## EXAMPLE AND ANALYSIS

Consider *Dunham & Co. v. Kudra*, 131 A.2d 306 (N.J. 1957), upon which the Restatement based its illustration. Dunham owned a department store. Hurwitz operated a fur concession within the store. Hurwitz offered fur storage services to customers who purchased furs there. Hurwitz arranged to have Kudra, a competitor of Dunham, store the furs. Hurwitz became insolvent and unable to pay Kudra for storing the furs. Dunham offered to pay Kudra for the furs. Kudra refused to deliver the furs to Dunham unless it paid all the money Hurwitz owed Kudra, including money for "other furs." Dunham succumbed to the threat but sued to recover the amount paid for other furs. The court found the threat to withhold the furs improper and ordered Kudra to repay those amounts. The Restatement treats this as a use of power for illegitimate ends.

The case is somewhat more complex than the Restatement's version. The "other furs" involved were furs Hurwitz asked Kudra to store for Dunham's customers in previous years, not furs stored for people unrelated to Dunham. Nor does the court explain why Kudra had any obligation to give the furs to Dunham, which did not own the furs and had no contract with Kudra that entitled it to delivery of the furs (except the contract Dunham wanted to rescind). Although Kudra exercised power in its negotiations with Dunham, the end Kudra sought — payment for services that benefited Dunham's customers — could be deemed legitimate.

ii. **Application difficulties.** Threats that are improper only if the terms are not fair pose several difficulties. They attempt to capture the essence of a few odd cases by creating ill-defined categories that leave some room for unique situations that might arise. Because the rules are malleable, these criteria make interesting exam questions. But cases will be so fact-specific that any generalizations offered here are likely to be useless. We can only note a few of the difficulties involved.

(a) **Fair terms unascertainable.** No standard exists for determining whether the contract was "not on fair terms." Generally, contract law allows the parties to determine the fairness of terms. Because parties will not agree to pay more than the value they expect to receive, the law infers that terms are fair — unless the agreement is the product of duress (or another similar defense). To make duress depend on whether the terms are fair is circular. It implies an objective standard of fairness, divorced from the values these parties attach to the goods or services involved.

(b)   Standardless concepts.   The same subjectivity inheres in terms such as "illegitimate ends" and "prior unfair dealings." Neither "illegitimate" nor "unfair" conveys an objective standard that a neutral decision maker can apply. They invite courts and attorneys to identify the facts that make conduct seem acceptable or unacceptable, without providing any guidance for how to assess or weigh those facts.

(c)   Storytelling.   The best advice to be offered is to build a good story — an account of events that casts them in the light most favorable to your client, without omitting or unfairly stating any significant facts — and hope the account will be more persuasive than alternative stories.

4.   Inducement

If the party would have entered the agreement even if the other party had not made an improper threat, the threat should not permit her to change her mind later. Thus, the power to disaffirm the agreement depends on whether the threat induced the party's assent.

a.   Subjective standard.   At one time, courts assessed inducement based on an objective standard: Would the threat have overborne the will of a reasonably firm person. That rule no longer applies. Duress rules need to protect the weak, not merely the strong.

b.   Substantial contribution.   If the threat "substantially contributed to the manifestation of assent," the threat induced the assent. Restatement (Second) of Contracts §175 comment c; see also Restatement (Second) of Contracts §167 (fraud inducing assent). Thus, the threatened party need not prove that she would have rejected the offer if no threat had been made. As long as the threat contributed to the decision, the threatened party has satisfied her burden. But inducement does not exist if the other party can show that she would have entered the contract even if no threat had been made, because the threat could not have played a significant role. In effect, this rule allocates the risk of uncertainty to the party who made the threat.

5. Reasonable Alternatives

Sometimes the law expects a threatened party to "just say no." When the party has reasonable alternatives to succumbing to the threat, courts may reject efforts to disaffirm the contract.

    a.   Restoring an objective test. This requirement in part replaces the objective test of inducement. It prevents disaffirmance on the basis of threats that should have been resisted. A party satisfies the inducement requirement even if she succumbed to a relatively minor threat. But a party who should have resisted the threat anyway (by pursuing an alternative course of action) cannot disaffirm the contract. The focus of reasonableness shifts from the severity of the threat to the effectiveness of alternatives.

 # EXAMPLE AND ANALYSIS

When a person threatens to initiate an unjustified civil suit unless another agrees to a contract, the threatened party often can protect her interests by defending in the civil suit. She need not succumb to the threat and later bring an action for rescission. When the civil action would allow the threatening party to seize the threatened party's property or disrupt its sale, the exigencies may make the alternative of defending against the suit unreasonable.

 # EXAMPLE AND ANALYSIS

In *Dunham & Co. v. Kudra*, the plaintiff arguably could have sought replevin against the defendant to recover the coats. The court held this remedy inadequate because defendant could have precluded recovery of the coats by posting a bond for their value, thus preventing Dunham from recovering them in time to avoid the threatened harm.

6. Threats by Third Parties

In deciding whether the contract benefits society, it does not matter who makes the threat. If the threatened party does not value what she receives more than what she gives up, the exchange is not the type that society usually wants to enforce. But when the other party to the contract is not responsible for the threat, the law must balance the interests of two innocent parties.

a. **Good faith reliance.** Threats by a third party will make the contract voidable unless the other party to the contract relies materially on the agreement in good faith and without reason to know of the duress. Restatement (Second) of Contracts §175(2).

b. **Indirect threats.** A person who makes a threat at the behest of a party to the contract may be an agent of that party, not a third party.

 ## EXAMPLE AND ANALYSIS

In the movie *The Godfather*, an actor asked the Don to help him get a movie role. The Don, by implicit threats, persuaded the director to give the part to the actor. Even if the actor had no reason to know about the threats, the Don was acting at the actor's request, arguably acting as the actor's agent. Agent here does not mean a booking agent, customarily used by entertainers. Anyone acting with authority on behalf of another is that other's **agent**. The party who employs an agent is called the **principal**.

c. **Reason to know.** When a party to the contract has reason to know about the threat, reliance is unreasonable and, therefore, does not require judicial protection.

B. UNDUE INFLUENCE

Sometimes pressure may not arise from threats — or may arise from threats that are unintended or too subtle to identify. In these circumstances, the contract still may not deserve enforcement (i.e., it may not move property to those who value it more). Rules governing undue influence supplement rules governing duress to extend the protection to these other situations.

1. Elements

The elements of the defense are somewhat unhelpfully general: **undue influence** and **inducement**. If assent was induced by undue influence, the agreement is voidable.

2. Inducement

Inducement has been discussed above in relation to the duress. See 7.A.4. The substantial contribution test applies in this context, too.

3. Undue Influence

The root of undue influence is **unfair persuasion**. Unfair persuasion alone, however, will not justify avoiding a contract. Most people are expected to recognize and resist persuasive efforts by others. In two situations, however, unfair persuasion justifies rescission. Restatement (Second) of Contracts §177(1).

a. Domination. A person "under the **domination** of the party exercising the persuasion" has less ability to resist unfair persuasion. Thus, she may avoid the agreement after succumbing to the persuasion.

b. Relationship. Sometimes the relationship between two people makes it reasonable to believe that the other will help protect your interests. If, instead, that person employs unfair persuasion, a party may avoid the agreement.

4. Domination Difficult to Define

a. Dependency. Domination can arise when one party depends so heavily on another that she feels she cannot refuse the other's offer. In effect, the person under domination perceives a threat that refusal would cause the other party to withdraw the support on which she relies so heavily.

EXAMPLE AND ANALYSIS

Invalids or seniors often depend heavily on nurses or others, both for assistance and for emotional support or company. Promises made to these people may reflect genuine gratitude or affection. Sometimes, however, agreements may reflect fear that rejection would jeopardize the companionship or services of the person on whom they rely.

---

    b.   **Overbearing presence.**   Domination can result from transient contact when one party possesses power that the other cannot resist. Particularly when a physically larger person is present in another's home, assent to an offer may seem the only way to persuade them to leave.

 # EXAMPLE AND ANALYSIS

An elderly person awakened at home at 1:00 A.M. by a real estate broker who insisted she sign an agreement immediately may feel she is under that person's domination if she cannot make him depart without signing. See *Fyan v. McNutt*, 254 N.W. 146 (1934). One hospitalized and unable to move may be under the domination of a person who refuses to leave her hospital room until she signs a release. See, e.g., *Weger v. Rocha*, 32 P.2d 417 (Cal. Ct. App. 1934).

---

    c.   **Relationship.**   Domination also can result from a relationship of authority between the parties. Employers, by virtue of their authority over employees, may have a dominant presence regardless of dependency or physical size.

 # EXAMPLE AND ANALYSIS

Plaintiff was a teacher. After an arrest for criminal homosexual conduct, the principal and superintendent came to his home to persuade him to resign. They pointed out that resolving his employment quietly, rather than in public hearings about moral turpitude, would improve his opportunity to obtain employment elsewhere. Plaintiff had not slept for 40 hours and was distraught over the arrest and police interrogation. He signed a resignation, which he later sought to rescind. The court held that the allegations were sufficient to support a claim for undue influence. Two important public officials ganging up on one tired and distraught person, telling him there was no time to consult an attorney and otherwise pressuring immediate action may have overborne the plaintiff's will—a fact to be established at trial. *Odorizzi v. Bloomfield School Dist.*, 54 Cal. Rptr. 533 (1966).

The case combines elements of each aspect above. Teachers rely on principals—though probably not to an extent that would make this aspect sufficient to establish domination. Two people against one in the one's home suggests an overbearing presence. And the power implicit in the superintendent's relationship to the teacher may exacerbate the other factors.

5. Relationship

A relationship exists if the persuaded party is "justified in assuming that that person [exerting persuasion] would not act in a manner inconsistent [the persuaded party's] welfare." Restatement (Second) of Contracts §177(1).

a. **Nonfamilial relationships.** Relationship can arise without any family ties. A clergyman, physician, or lawyer may have a relationship to a party that justifies her believing the other would not act inconsistently with her welfare. Close friendship also may have that effect in some cases.

b. **Self-preservation preferred.** Parties must look out for their own interests. A party is not justified in believing that strangers, casual acquaintances, or those with whom she conducts business (even personal business) will look out for her. Some special aspect of the relationship must justify her decision to rely on the advice or decisions of others rather than make her own assessment of the value of the proposed contract.

 # EXAMPLE AND ANALYSIS

Recall *Odorizzi v. Bloomfield School Dist.*, 54 Cal. Rptr. 533 (1966). Plaintiff was a teacher persuaded to resign by the superintendent and principal. The court did not explicitly state that it relied on domination rather than a relationship in applying undue influence to the case. The relationship of employer and employee, however, probably would not satisfy the rule. Employers and employees generally bargain at arm's length. Each knows the other is looking out for her own interests and that those interests may not coincide.

6. Unfair Persuasion

Unfair persuasion defies precise definition. Basically, you need to identify forces that made it harder for a person to recognize or assess the merits of the deal being offered. Each case (or exam question) will require detailed analysis of its specific facts. The best that can be offered here are a few red flags that may make the issue worth addressing.

  a. **Time and place of assent.** When assent occurs in an unusual place or at an unusual time, consider why that happened. If one party selected the time and place to catch the other when her resistance would be lower than usual, that may be one component of unfair persuasion.

  b. **Rushed assent.** When one party insists on immediate assent, consider why. If haste seems unimportant, perhaps the pressure was intended to prevent the other party from reflecting carefully on the transaction. Particularly when a party might use time to consult others (e.g., an accountant or lawyer), the rush may be a component of unfair persuasion.

  c. **Fair persuasion.** Often, an immediate decision may be important —which may explain why one party sought the other at an unusual time or place. Contracts induced by fair persuasion must remain enforceable unless courts want to convert dependency or relationship into the equivalent of contractual incapacity. Be careful about undermining bona fide deals because the same tactics sometimes are abused.

7. Influence by Third Parties

In deciding whether the contract benefits society, it does not matter who exerts undue influence. If the influenced party does not value what she receives more than what she gives up, the exchange is not the type that society usually wants to enforce. But when the other party to the contract is not responsible for the undue influence, the law must balance the interests of two innocent parties. Thus, **undue influence by a third party will make the contract voidable unless the other party to the contract relies materially on the agreement in good faith and without reason to know of the undue influence.** Restatement (Second) of Contracts §177(3). See 7.A.6.

REVIEW QUESTIONS AND ANSWERS

Question: What are the elements of duress?
Answer:

  1. Improper threat; that
  2. Induced assent; where
  3. A party had no reasonable alternatives.

Question: What threats are always improper?
Answer:

1. A threat to commit a crime or a tort;
2. A threat that is a crime or a tort (or would be if it succeeded in extracting property from another);
3. A threat of criminal prosecution;
4. A threat to use civil process in bad faith; and
5. A threat to breach an obligation of good faith under a contract.

Question: What threats are improper only if the contract terms are unfair?
Answer:

1. The threatened act would injure the other party without significant benefit to the threatener;
2. Prior inequitable conduct increased the threat's effectiveness; and
3. A threat to use power for illegitimate ends.

Question: True or false: a contract is voidable for duress only if the party would not have agreed to it if no threat had been made?
Answer: False. A party can establish that the threat induced the assent by showing that the threat contributed substantially to the decision to assent. She need not prove she would not have agreed but for the threat. But if the other party can prove she would have agreed even without the threat, the threat could not have been a substantial factor.

Question: What are the elements of undue influence?
Answer:

1. Undue influence; that
2. Induced assent.

Question: What makes influence undue?
Answer:

1. Unfair persuasion; plus either
2. Domination of one party by the other; or
3. A relationship that justified a party in believing the other would not act inconsistently with the persuaded party's welfare.

8 MISREPRESENTATION

CHAPTER OVERVIEW

A contract is voidable for **misrepresentation** if a party's **assent is induced** by a **material** *or* a **fraudulent** misrepresentation on which the party was **justified in relying**.

- A misrepresentation is an **assertion not in accord with the facts**.
  — An assertion may be a statement of fact, a promise, or an opinion.
  — Silence can be an assertion.
- An assertion is **material** if:
  — It **would be likely to induce a reasonable person's assent** to the transaction; or
  — The speaker **knows it is likely to induce the other party's assent** to the transaction.
- An assertion is **fraudulent** if the speaker **intends for it to induce the other's assent** and:
  — The speaker **knows or believes** it is false; or
  — The speaker implies she is confident it is true when she **lacks that confidence**; or
  — The speaker implies she has a basis for the assertion when she **lacks that basis**.
- An assertion **induces assent** if it **substantially contributes** to the decision to assent.
- Generally, parties are **justified in relying** on another's assertions, particularly of fact.
  — Reliance is **justified** if the speaker **implies she has a factual basis** for an **opinion**.
  — Reliance on **pure** opinions is **not justified** unless a **relation of trust and confidence** exists between the parties, the deceived party reasonably be-

lieves the **speaker has special expertise**, or the **deceived party is particularly susceptible** to deception.
— A party cannot rely on assertions if she **knows they are false** or her
own **failure to act in good faith** prevents her from discovering the fal-
sity.

Nondisclosure or concealment of a fact is an **assertion that the fact does not exist**.

- **Concealment** is action intended or likely to prevent a party from discovering
  a fact.
- **Nondisclosure** is the failure to mention a known fact, but only if:
  — A **relation of trust or confidence** entitles the other party to disclosure;
  — The speaker knows disclosure is necessary **to prevent an earlier
    statement from misleading** another;
  — The speaker knows disclosure would correct the **other party's mistake
    concerning the character or essential terms of a writing**; or
  — The speaker knows disclosure would correct the **other party's mistake
    concerning a basic assumption** on which her assent is based **and** failure
    to disclose would breach an obligation of **good faith** and fair dealing.

An agreement is **void** if a **misrepresentation** concerning its **character or essential
terms** induces another to manifest assent **without knowledge or an opportunity to
discover** the character or essential terms of the writing.

A. RATIONALE

A party who is deceived about the substance of the transaction cannot make a
reasonable assessment of whether she prefers what she will receive to what she
gives up. This is the archetype of agreements where courts can have no confidence that the agreement moves goods to those who value them more. The
reasoning applies to any mistake about the underlying transaction, not merely
to those where the other party caused the deception. The rules below (and in
Chapter 9, Mistake) attempt to separate agreements in which mistakes undermine the rationale for enforcing the agreement from those in which the mistakes
do not have that effect — either because the mistakes did not influence the agreement or because the mistaken party should have prevented the mistake. The
rules of misrepresentation (in this section) naturally show more deference to the
mistaken party, as the other party caused the mistakes by false statements or
by misleading silence.

B. FRAUDULENT OR MATERIAL MISREPRESENTATION

The most common type of deception involves the characteristics of the things
exchanged. Misrepresentations of this sort may lead a party to attach an unrealistically high value to the things she expects to receive or an unrealistically
low value to the things she expects to give up. Other misrepresentations may

have similar effect, such as lies about a pertinent law (say, a zoning law where land is being sold) or lies about other people's intentions (say, other investors or banks whose behavior might affect the value of a company). Misrepresentations about the terms of the agreement itself generally are resolved under different rules. See 8.D. An agreement valid under those rules, however, may nonetheless be voidable under the rules provided here.

1. Elements

To establish that an agreement is voidable, the aggrieved party must establish four things:

- A **misrepresentation** was made;
- The misrepresentation was either **fraudulent or material**;
- The misrepresentation **induced** her manifestation of assent; and
- She was **justified in relying** on the misrepresentation.

2. Misrepresentation

A **misrepresentation** is "an assertion not in accord with the facts." Restatement (Second) of Contracts §159.

a. Implied assertions. Assertions need not be express. Sometimes, actions or silence can be assertions. Those situations are covered shortly. See 8.C. In general, the law treats actions or silence as if the person had stated aloud that the fact concealed was false.

b. Nonfactual assertions. Assertions are not limited to statements of fact. Statements of opinion, promises, and statements about the law all are assertions. To decide whether an assertion is in accord with the facts, some assertions are interpreted as assertions of fact.

    i. Promises. A promise implies that the party intends to perform as promised. The existence of that intention is an assertion of fact that may be true or false. The assertion is false (or not in accord with the facts) if the party does not have that intention at the time the promise is made.

    ii. Opinions. A statement opinion implies that the person actually holds that opinion — and may imply that the person has knowledge of some fact that justifies the opinion. Both implications are assertions of fact that can be true or false. The assertion is false if the party does not hold the opinion expressed or, in cases in which the opinion implies a basis, the basis does not exist.

    iii. Law. The law is a particular kind of fact. Assertions about the law can be true or false just as assertions about the time can be true or false. In situations where the law is uncertain, a statement about the law may be an opinion, subject to analysis under the preceding section.

3. Material

One way to establish an actionable misrepresentation is to show that it was material. When a misrepresentation was material, it does not matter whether the party making the assertion knew it was false — or even that she had no way to know it was false. The deceived party assessed the value of what she would receive based on the incorrect assertion. That being so, the law cannot assume enforcement of the contract would increase societal wealth unless the assertion played a relatively minor role in the decision to enter the agreement. Materiality is one of two ways the law assesses the role the representation played in the decision. (The other is inducement. See 8.B.5.)

a. Definition.   A misrepresentation is material if:

   i.   "It would be likely to induce a reasonable person to manifest" assent to the agreement; or

   ii. "The maker knows that it would be likely to induce" the other party to manifest assent to the agreement. Restatement (Second) of Contracts §162(2).

b. Objective test.   When a reasonable person would attach importance to the representation, the law finds materiality even if the other party did not attach importance to the statement. (Of course, if the other party did not attach importance to the statement, inducement will be absent.) Because people generally would attach importance to the assertion, a party should not make the assertion unless confident of its truth.

c. Subjective test.   When the maker knows the other party attaches importance to a particular fact, a misrepresentation will be material even if a reasonable person would not. Because the other party will attach importance to the assertion, a party should not make it unless confident of its validity.

d. Speaker's perspective.   Note that both portions of the definition take the perspective of the speaker. They identify situations in which the speaker should not have spoken unless confident of the truth of the assertion.

i. **Implicit fault.** Although never explicit in the Restatement (Second), this suggests a negligence standard. When the speaker had no reason to believe the words would have any significance to the transaction, the speaker can be excused for making the statement — unless she knew it was false. See 8.B.4.

ii. **Credibility test.** Alternatively, the rule may be an attempt to screen out implausible claims. When a party claims to have been induced to enter an agreement by assertions that most people would have found trivial, courts may wonder whether the party really attached importance to them or is grasping at any straw to avoid a contract that she now regrets for different reasons. (Misrepresentation arises in cases only if the deceived party regrets the deal; otherwise, she would ratify the contract instead of disaffirming it.) Although inducement could screen out these cases, the subjective standard employed there may be less effective than a requirement based on what the speaker knew or should have known.

iii. **Fraud distinguished.** When the assertion is fraudulent, neither concern arises. Fraud establishes culpability more effectively than negligence. And the possibility of minor points excusing contract performance is less significant where the deceiver thought the matter was important enough to lie about. The fact that she guessed, rather than knew, the assertion was important to the other party does not make the fraud any more acceptable. In addition, the intentional deceit raises questions about the credibility of the deceiver who claims she had no idea the assertion was important to the other party.

4. Fraudulent

Another way to establish an actionable misrepresentation is to show that it was fraudulently made. Even if the statement was immaterial, the deceiver's intent to defraud may make the contract voidable.

a. **Definition.** A misrepresentation is fraudulent if:

i. The party "intends [the] assertion to induce another party to manifest . . . assent to the agreement"; **and**

ii. One of the three following conditions applies:

(a) The speaker knows or believes the assertion is false; or

      (b)   The speaker "does not have the confidence [s]he states or implies in the truth of the assertion"; or

      (c)   The speaker "knows [s]he does not have the basis that [s]he states or implies for the assertion." Restatement (Second) of Contracts §162(1).

b. Intent to induce the other party's assent. An assertion made without the intent to induce the other party to enter the deal is not fraudulent. Most statements made in negotiations satisfy this requirement. Statements made before negotiations (e.g., if neighbors enter negotiation after years of conversations) or casual conversation during negotiations may not have been made with the requisite intent.

c. Known misleading. The catalogue of possible deceit should be general enough to capture most statements the speaker knows are misleading.

    i. Believed false. Assertions the maker thinks are false constitute classic fraudulent statements of fact.

    ii. Exaggerated confidence. A speaker who exaggerates her confidence in the truth of an assertion cannot hide behind the characterization of her statement as an opinion. She implied that she had confidence in the statement when she did not. The assertion of confidence is false.

    iii. Baseless opinions. Similarly, opinions that imply the speaker has a factual basis for her judgment will be false if the speaker does not have such a basis.

5. Inducement

"A misrepresentation induces a party's manifestation of assent if it substantially contributes to his decision to manifest his assent." Restatement (Second) of Contracts §167.

a. Subjective test. It does not matter whether a reasonable person would have been induced by the misrepresentation—except to question the victim's credibility. As long as the assertion played a substantial role in the deceived party's decision, the element is satisfied.

b. Multiple motivations. The assent may have been induced by several factors. The value of what she expected to receive may have been significant despite the misrepresentation. If the misrepresentation substantially contributed to the decision, the existence of other induce-ments is irrelevant.

i. **Not a "but for" test.** It is not necessary for the deceived party to demonstrate that she would have refused the offer if she had known the truth. If the other party can demonstrate that she would have entered the contract on the same terms even if she had known the truth, inducement is absent. The misrepresenta-tion did not contribute significantly (or at all) if the outcome would have been identical.

ii. **Contribution to the terms.** Often the misrepresentation does not make the things received valueless to the deceived party. She might have agreed to buy them anyway but might not have of-fered so much for them. That in itself establishes the substantial contribution of the misrepresentation to the decision to enter **this** contract.

c. **Materiality implies inducement.** If the fact was the type to which people generally attach importance, inducement may be presumed.

d. **Independent investigation.** When a party conducts her own inves-tigation into the truth of the assertion, this may (or may not) indicate that she did not rely on the misrepresentation. A misrepresentation may still contribute to the decision when the investigation is incom-plete or inconclusive. But an investigation may indicate that the party did not place any trust in the assertion and that her assent was induced only by her own determination of the facts.

6. Justified Reliance

Usually, a party is justified in relying on assertions by the other party. Problems primarily arise involving matters of opinion and situations in which the deceived party may have been at fault for her own deception.

a. **Opinions.** Generally, individuals are equally capable of forming their own opinions, making reliance on the opinions of others less justifi-able. But a party who shares her opinion and then urges that the other should have ignored it because opinions are inherently suspect does not present an appealing argument. Thus, courts have found ways to prevent deceit via opinions.

i. **Opinion as assertion.** As noted earlier, opinions can be asser-tions of fact. See 8.B.2.b.(2). To the extent that opinions assert facts (such as confidence in or a factual basis supporting the opinion), a party justifiably may rely on them. Restatement (Second) of Contracts §168.

ii. **Pure (nonassertive) opinions.** An opinion does not assert facts when a party does not imply that she knows any facts that support the opinion. **Reliance on a pure opinion generally is not justified.** In some circumstances, even reliance on a pure opinion will be justifiable. Restatement (Second) of Contracts §169.

(a) **Relationship.** A relation of trust and confidence between the speaker and the deceived party may make it reasonable for the deceived party to rely on the opinion. Relations of trust and confidence include attorney-client, physician-patient, trustee-beneficiary, and other similar relationships. Other relationships such as husband-wife (even during divorce proceedings) and businessman-consultant may justify reliance, though they do not fall within the traditional categories.

(b) **Special expertise.** When the deceived party reasonably believes that the other party has special skill, judgment, or objectivity that she herself does not possess, it may be reasonable to rely on the opinion. Thus, a consumer may be justified in relying on the opinions of a jeweler or a novice investor in relying on an experienced stockbroker.

(c) **Special susceptibility.** When the deceived party is particularly susceptible to misrepresentation via opinion, the court may find her reliance justifiable. This catch-all category has no justification but reflects the tendency of courts to "do the right thing" when faced with unusually gullible people who have been deceived.

b. **Deceived party's fault.** Usually, a deceived party is not blamed for having believed and relied on another's misrepresentation. If the deceived party's ignorance results from a "**failure to act in good faith** and in accordance with reasonable standards of fair dealing," reliance on the misrepresentation is **unjustified**. Restatement (Second) of Contracts §172.

i. **Known to be false.** A party cannot justifiably rely on an assertion she knows is false.

    ii.   **Obviously false.** Where a cursory examination will reveal the falsity of an assertion, a party cannot justifiably rely on the assertion. Good faith requires a party to use her powers of observation when considering an agreement.

    iii.   **Significant investigation.** When discovery of the truth would require significant effort, the party generally is entitled to rely on the misrepresentation. This is particularly true as the misrepresentation often will lead a party to conclude that investigation is unnecessary. Even if the reliance is objectively unreasonable, unless it amounts to bad faith, the law will protect the deceived and not the deceiver.

    iv.   **Actual investigation.** Actual investigation by the deceived party may suggest that she did not rely on the misrepresentation but does not change the requirements for justifiable reliance. That is, when a party could, in good faith, make no investigation, it would be perverse to hold that her justification for reliance disappeared when she made an investigation that should have revealed, but did not reveal, the truth. Such a rule would discourage investigation.

7. Misrepresentations by Third Parties

In deciding whether the contract benefits society, it does not matter who made the misrepresentation. If the deceived party does not value what she receives more than what she gives up, the exchange is not the type that society usually wants to enforce. But when the other party to the contract is not responsible for the misrepresentation, the law must balance the interests of two innocent parties. Thus, misrepresentation by a third party will make the contract voidable **unless** the other party to the contract relies materially on the agreement in good faith and without reason to know of the misrepresentation. Restatement (Second) of Contracts §164(2).

C. NONDISCLOSURE AND CONCEALMENT

Sometimes a party can deceive another without uttering a word. By remaining silent, a party can perpetuate mistakes that induce agreement. Sometimes silence will not suffice, but the party must act to prevent investigation to practice the fraud. In each case, however, courts have found occasion to find contracts voidable despite the lack of an express statement they could call a misrepresentation. The technique nonetheless requires an assertion. For purposes of analyzing the other elements, **silence is taken as an assertion that a fact does not exist**. If the fact does exist, that assertion is not in accord with the facts. This section addresses when courts will take silence as an assertion.

1. Concealment

This is the greater of the sins. It does not involve mere silence but active attempts to prevent the other party from discovering the true state of affairs. This interference comes closer to creating a mistake than to allowing a party to make her own mistakes.

    a. **Action as an assertion.** If a party intends or knows that her action "is likely to prevent another from learning a fact," the law treats the action as an assertion that the fact does not exist. Restatement (Second) of Contracts §160.

EXAMPLE AND ANALYSIS

If a homeowner papers over cracks in a wall to prevent potential buyers from noticing the defects, the action constitutes concealment. The owner has not merely remained silent. She has actively prevented another from discovering facts.

    b. **Remedial disclosure.** Disclosing the facts concealed will eliminate any risk of misrepresentation. The other party cannot rely on the mistaken state of affairs once informed of the truth.

EXAMPLE AND ANALYSIS

A homeowner put up wallpaper over cracks in a wall. Several years later, she decided to sell the house. Knowing buyers would attach importance to the existence of cracks, she fully discloses the existence and extent of cracks under the wallpaper. The act of papering the walls is not concealment.

Arguably, putting up wallpaper years before trying to sell the house is not concealment. The owner made a decorating decision for her own use of the property, not a conscious effort to deceive a potential buyer. This would be important if the owner forgot to mention the cracks. Because the owner knew, when papering the walls, that the paper would conceal the cracks, courts could find concealment even though she did not realize at the time she acted that the concealment would affect buyers as opposed to guests.

2. Nondisclosure as a Representation

When a party makes her own mistake, other parties generally are not required to correct them. Misrepresentation law aims primarily at mistakes a party induces, not mistakes the party does not prevent. When a party wants assurance that her assumptions are correct, she may ask the other party. The response will be an assertion, one way or the other, to which misrepresentation rules apply. Sometimes, however, parties who make mistaken assumptions about goods allege that the other party should have volunteered correct information even without an inquiry. Occasionally, the argument prevails: A party's failure to reveal a fact may equate to an assertion that the fact does not exist. When the fact does exist, the assertion will be a misrepresentation. (Courts sometimes refer to this as a duty to speak, though language of duty does not clarify the issues and probably should be avoided.)

a. **Correct prior assertions.** When a party **knows** that disclosure of a fact is necessary to prevent a prior assertion from being a misrepresentation or from being fraudulent or material, she must disclose the additional facts. Restatement (Second) of Contracts §161(a). Deceit by half-truths is still deceit. A party who begins to speak must speak fully enough to prevent deception or risk disaffirmance of the contract if she does not. But a party who does not know of the other's misinterpretation has no obligation to clarify the prior statements.

b. **Correct known mistake re content of writing.** When a party knows that disclosure of a fact would correct the other party's mistake as to the contents or effect of a writing embodying the agreement, she must disclose the additional facts. Restatement (Second) of Contracts §161(c). One cannot hold another to the terms in a writing if one knew at the time that the party did not understand what the writing said or the effect the writing would have. The rule here expresses the same concern for actual assent displayed in the next section. See 8.D.

c. **Relation of trust.** "Where the other person is entitled to know the fact because of a relation of trust and confidence between them," she must disclose the additional facts. Restatement (Second) of Contracts §161(d). Relationships of trust and confidence have always carried significant obligations of disclosure. Often these relationships rest on one party's greater expertise or access to information. The requirement of full disclosure is quite usual, even inevitable, in these situations.

d. **Good faith and known mistakes of basic assumption.** "Where [s]he knows that disclosure of the fact would correct a mistake of the other party as to a basic assumption on which that party is making the contract and if non-disclosure of the fact amounts to a failure to act in good faith and in accordance with reasonable standards of fair dealing," she must disclose the additional facts. Restatement (Second) of Contracts §161(b). This rather complex statement of the rule breaks down into several components.

   i. **Basic assumption.** The deceived party must be making a mistake about some fundamental aspect of the transaction. The language of mistake regarding a basic assumption comes from the next major defense. See Chapter 9. It will be explored more fully there.

  ii. **Known mistake.** The deceiver must know about the mistake. Reason to know plays no role here.

 iii. **Good faith.** The law does not require disclosure for every known mistake by the other party. Unless good faith or reasonable standards of fair dealing require disclosure, silence is not an assertion.

   (a) **Often overlooked.** Students tend to overlook the good faith issue. In fact, **the requirement of an obligation to act in good faith is the most critical aspect of the rule**. It is easy to excuse nondisclosure when one party made no mistake or when the other party did not know about it; few cases raise that issue.

   (b) **Not universal.** There is a temptation to assume that an obligation of good faith arises in all cases. A duty of good faith is implied in every contract. *See* Restatement (Second) of Contracts §205. But **no contract exists during negotiations**; it will exist only after the parties manifest their assent. When parties to an existing contract negotiate another deal, an obligation of good faith may arise. In other situations, however, you will need to explain why an obligation of good faith exists between parties dealing at arm's length.

   (c) **Context significant.** Disclosure required by good faith will vary with the setting. Some businesses may involve higher standards than others. For instance, used car sales may require little or no disclosure even between friends, whereas sales of medical appliances or drugs may require significant disclosure, even between strangers. Similarly, latent defects that the other cannot reasonably discover for herself may require disclosure, whereas patent defects may be left for the other to discover if she looks. No black-letter rules exist to guide the decision of when good faith requires disclosure.

D. MISREPRESENTATION CONCERNING THE CONTENT OF THE AGREEMENT

Some misrepresentations concern the actual terms of the agreement. For example, a person may sign a contract for the sale of her house because she was told the contract covered the sale of her car. We know she valued the price more than she valued the car, but we have no confidence that she valued the price more than she valued her house. The rationale, however, can be more technical. The person who told her the contract involved the sale of her car can have no reasonable belief that her assent involves the sale of her house, even if that is what the document says. Thus, the defrauded party never assented to the contract in the first place. The issue is not whether she can rescind her assent but whether she ever assented at all. Restatement (Second) of Contracts §163. (This issue should be discussed in connection with contract formation but seems to fit better with the other rules governing misrepresentation.)

1. Elements

To decide whether the deceived party's alleged manifestation of assent actually operates as a manifestation of assent, you must address the following questions:

a. **Misrepresentation.** Was the content of the writing misrepresented?

b. **Character or essential terms.** Did the misrepresentation involve the character or essential terms of the agreement?

c. **Reasonable opportunity to know the terms.** Did the other party know or have a reasonable opportunity to know the character and essential terms of the agreement?

d. **Inducement.** Did the misrepresentation induce the other party's manifestation of assent? Restatement (Second) of Contracts §163.

2. Preliminary Notes

a. **Written contracts.** Situations of this type almost always involve a writing. It is very difficult to obtain an oral agreement while misrepresenting the terms of the agreement. The oral statement of terms would **be** the agreement, not a representation about it. The manifestation of assent would be to the terms recited, not to some other terms concealed from one party. When a document is signed, however, oral statements may misrepresent the contents of the document.

b. Speaker irrelevant.   Because the issue involves assent, it does not matter who misrepresents the nature of the writing. The innocence or good faith of other parties does not alter the fact that one party never assented to enter the contract at all.

 ## EXAMPLE AND ANALYSIS

R sends an employment agreement to E. E's reading glasses are broken, so she asks her sister, S, to read the agreement to her. S omits several key provisions when reading the agreement to E. These provisions, if known to E, would have led her to negotiate further with R before signing the agreement. E signs the agreement. The fact that R made no misrepresentation does not matter; E did not assent to the agreement because she did not know what it said. (Issues concerning whether she had reasonable opportunity to know the essential terms could arise.)

3. Misrepresentation

The definition of misrepresentation, including misrepresentation by silence, has been discussed elsewhere. See 8.B.2, 8.C.2. The rules are identical here; only the subject matter of the misrepresentations differs, being limited to deception concerning the character or essential terms of the contract.

4. Character or Essential Terms

a. Character.   This refers to the nature of item under discussion. A party may lie about whether it is a contract at all, representing it to be a letter or some other kind of document in order to obtain a signature.

b. Essential terms.   This refers to the subject matter of the contract— such as the car/house example in the introduction to this section. Misrepresentations about minor terms do not fall within this rule. Only misrepresentations that go to the essence of the transaction destroy assent.

c. Reformation of minor terms.   Misrepresentations about minor terms may give rise to an action for reformation—a suit to amend the writing to conform to the terms actually agreed upon by the parties. Restatement (Second) of Contracts §166.

5. No Opportunity to Know

People should read what they sign before signing it. Courts do not excuse performance if a party who could have discovered the nature of the agreement failed to do so. Even the blind and the illiterate are expected to have someone read a contract to them before they sign it. Clever fraudfeasors, however, may obtain a signature without the other party having reason to know the contents, such as by switching writings after the party has read the agreement but before it is signed or by suborning the person reading the writing to another to read different terms than those the writing contains. When a writing differs from what the parties orally agreed, reformation under Restatement (Second) of Contracts §166 or rescission under Restatement (Second) of Contracts §164 may be available.

6. Void versus Voidable

The conclusion that the deceived party never assented to the agreement probably makes the agreement **void**, not merely voidable. The absence of assent means no contract ever existed.

a. Advantage: Timing. Calling the agreement void can benefit the deceived party. The failure to raise the objection promptly will not constitute a ratification when the contract is void.

b. Disadvantage: No election. Calling the agreement void may disadvantage the deceived party if the agreement proves favorable to her but unfavorable to the other party. (Thus, the other party would not assent to the agreement again if the original agreement is unenforceable.) Lack of assent can be raised by the deceiving party. Unless both parties assent, no contract exists.

REVIEW QUESTIONS AND ANSWERS

Question: What must a party prove to avoid a contract for misrepresentation?
Answer:

1. That a misrepresentation was made;
2. That the misrepresentation was fraudulent **or** material;
3. That the misrepresentation induced the deceived party's assent; and
4. That the deceived party was justified in relying on the misrepresentation.

Question: Are assertions of fact the only kinds of misrepresentations?
Answer: No. Promises and opinions can be misrepresentations. Usually, these statements are misrepresentations when they imply facts that are inaccurate (such as present intent to perform a promise or a factual basis for an opinion).

Question: When is a misrepresentation material?
Answer:

- If the assertion would substantially contribute to a reasonable person's decision to assent to the transaction.
- If the speaker knows the assertion would substantially contribute to the other party's decision to assent to the transaction.

Question: When is a misrepresentation fraudulent?
Answer: If the person making the assertion intends it to induce the other party to assent to the transaction **and**

- The speaker knows or believes the assertion is inaccurate;
- The speaker implies she has confidence in the accuracy of the assertion when she does not have such confidence; or
- The speaker implies she has a basis for the assertion when she does not have such a basis.

Question: When is it unjustified to rely on another party's misrepresentation?
Answer: If one already knows the truth, if one could discover the truth so easily that failure to do so would constitute bad faith, or, with some exceptions, if the assertion is a pure opinion (an opinion that does not imply the speaker possesses facts that support the opinion).

Question: When will silence be considered an assertion?
Answer:

- If a party knows that a prior assertion would mislead the other party unless she makes additional disclosure;
- If a party knows that disclosure will correct a mistake about the character or essential terms of a contract;
- If a relation of trust and confidence entitles a person to know the fact; or
- If a party knows that disclosure would correct a mistake of basic assumption and nondisclosure would breach an obligation of good faith and fair dealing.

Question: What is the difference between concealment and nondisclosure?
Answer: Concealment involves knowingly impeding another party from discovering a fact. Nondisclosure involves failing to reveal a fact to another — which is objectionable only if a duty would require disclosure.

Question: When will a misrepresentation make a contract void?

Answer: When a misrepresentation about the character or essential terms of the contract induces assent under circumstances in which the deceived party had neither knowledge nor a reasonable opportunity to know the character or essential terms of the contract.

9 MISTAKE OF BASIC ASSUMPTION

CHAPTER OVERVIEW

Any mistake by a party may undermine the conclusion that she values what she receives more than she values what she gives up. Even if the other party did not cause the mistake, the contract may not increase societal wealth. The law cannot protect people from all the mistakes they make. For instance, one who buys stock under the mistaken impression that the price of the stock will increase cannot expect to rescind the transaction when the price goes down. **Mistakes of judgment or mistaken predictions about future events are the risk of doing business.** (People who want protection from this kind of mistake should not enter contracts for future performance; they should wait until the day they want the item and buy it at its value at that time.) Courts, however, have identified some mistakes that seem to justify legal intervention. These mistakes are not easy to classify, but the Restatement (Second) identifies some of the common threads among these cases.

A contract is voidable for **mutual mistake** if both parties were mistaken and:

- The mistake involved facts **at the time the contract was formed**;
- The mistake concerned a **basic assumption** upon which the agreement was made;
- The mistake **materially** affected the agreed exchange; and
- The adversely affected party did not **bear the risk** of the mistake.

A party bears the risk of a mistake if:

- The **contract allocates the risk** to her; or
- She entered the contract even though **aware that she lacked information** concerning the mistaken assumption; and
- The **courts finds it reasonable** to allocate the risk to the party.

A contract is voidable for unilateral mistake if the elements of mutual mistake are satisfied and:

- Enforcement of the agreement would be unconscionable; or
- The party not mistaken caused the other party's mistake; or
- The party not mistaken had reason to know of the other party's mistake.

A. MUTUAL MISTAKE

In some cases, both parties share a mistaken belief. Cases refer to this as **mutual mistake**. (Cases in which only one party was mistaken, called **unilateral mistake**, are discussed below. See 9.B.)

1. Shared Mistake

For a mistake to be mutual, the parties must be mistaken about the same thing. If one party is mistaken about one thing and the other party mistaken about something different, no mutual mistake exists.

2. Elements

Although generalization is difficult, four elements seem to exist in the cases that grant rescission for mutual mistake.

    a. Mistake at formation. The mistake existed "at the time the contract was made."

    b. Basic assumption. The mistake involved "a basic assumption on which the contract was made."

    c. Material effect. The mistake had "a material effect on the agreed exchange of performances."

    d. Allocation of risk. The adversely affected party did not bear the risk of the mistake. Restatement (Second) of Contracts §152.

3. Present Mistakes

A mistaken prediction about future events does not fall within the scope of the rule. Contracts allocate the risk that future events will change in favor of one party or the other. In fact, that is the primary reason for making promises of future performance instead of making a contemporaneous exchange at a future date.

    a. Present mistake with future effects. Both parties may be mistaken about a condition that exists today but does not affect the value of the exchange until later. Almost every case of mutual mistake involves conditions discovered after the contract was made. When conditions are discovered before the contract was made, at least one party will not be mistaken about them.

EXAMPLE AND ANALYSIS

A septic system failed to comply with health laws at the time of the contract. Thus, land sold as a three-unit apartment in fact was not suitable for human habitation. Leaking did not reveal the problem until after the sale. The mistake concerned a condition that existed at the time of the contract, even though the condition was not discovered until later. *Lenawee County Bd. of Health v. Messerly*, 331 N.W.2d 203 (Mich. 1982).

    b.   Unclear distinction.   The line between present mistakes and future events is not always clear. This leaves room for some courts to stretch mistake to cover future events.

EXAMPLE AND ANALYSIS

The parties entered a long-range contract that included a formula for computing permissible price increases during the life of the contract. The formula proved inadequate in light of the energy crisis that developed in the mid-1970s. The court held that the formula was inadequate for its intended purpose even at the time the contract was made (because it failed to give sufficient weight to electricity costs, a major component of aluminum production costs). Thus, the parties were mistaken about a present fact—the adequacy of the formula—but discovered the mistake later, when future events produced inadequate price adjustments. The result is controversial, but the case settled before an appellate court could resolve the issue. *Aluminum Co. of America v. Essex Group*, 499 F. Supp. 53 (W.D. Pa. 1980).

    4.   Basic Assumption

        Peripheral mistakes will not justify rescission. A mistake must go to the heart of the deal in some way.

a. **Characteristics of the performance.** Mistakes usually affect the subject matter of the transaction. Mistakes about market conditions or about one party's solvency do not undermine the benefits of exchange. These are risks that parties to a contract should consider and allocate. A mistake about the condition of property, however, goes to the subject matter of the transaction.

b. **Unconscious mistakes.** The mistake need not be a conscious one. Often, parties do not focus on their assumptions. For example, in *Lenawee County*, 9.A.3.a, neither party may have considered the septic system explicitly. Yet both parties assumed the septic system was appropriate for the existing use of the property (as a three-unit rental building).

c. **Obsolete concerns: Identity versus value.** Courts once tried to distinguish mistakes about the identity of the performance from mistakes about the value of the performance. You may see that language, but it has little present effect.

 # EXAMPLE AND ANALYSIS

Buyer bought a cow that seller said was barren. In fact, the cow was with calf. When seller discovered the mistake, seller refused to deliver the cow. The court held that fertility not only made the cow more valuable but made it a different thing: a dairy cow as opposed to meat. *Sherwood v. Walker*, 33 N.W. 919 (Mich. 1887).

In *Lenawee County*, a subsequent Michigan case, the court rejected this distinction. Technically the court limited *Sherwood* to its facts rather than overruling it. But references to identity and value no longer accurately describe the law.

The result in *Sherwood* would be the same under the new rules. The cow's fertility (or lack thereof) was a basic assumption on which the cow was sold.

d. **Rule of thumb.** If you cannot tell who values the thing actually sold more, the mistake probably implicates a basic assumption.

EXAMPLE AND ANALYSIS

In *Sherwood*, 9.A.4.c, the court could not conclude that the buyer valued a fertile cow more than the seller valued a fertile cow, only that the buyer valued a barren cow more than the seller.

Similarly, in *Lenawee County*, 9.A.3.a, the sale showed the buyer valued an apartment building more than the seller did, but provided no evidence of the value each party attached to land that could not be used for human occupation.

5. Material Effect on Exchange

Only significant mistakes justify rescission. When a mistake has only minor effects on the exchange, no legal action seems appropriate. The risk of the mistaken assumption can fall where it may. But some mistakes alter the exchange dramatically from that to which the parties thought they had agreed. Material effect is particularly (but not exclusively) likely where each party is affected: **One gets more than she expected and the other gives more than she expected**.

 EXAMPLE AND ANALYSIS

When parties agree to the sale of a rock that turns out to be a valuable gem, the seller gives up much more than she thought and the buyer receives much more than she thought. Thus, the mistake has a material effect on the exchange.

6. Risk of Mistake

The risk of mistake is present in all contractual situations. Much of the law is designed to decide which party must bear the risk of mistake. For example, in *Lenawee County*, one party would end up with worthless land and the other would end up with money. The mistake doctrine helps decide which of two innocent parties should bear the loss. Restatement (Second) of Contracts §154.

    a. **Allocation by contract.** Often the agreement will contain provisions that expressly or implicitly impose the risk of some contingencies on one party.

EXAMPLE AND ANALYSIS

Lenawee County, 9.A.3.a. The contract contained a provision stating, "Purchaser has examined this property and agrees to accept it in its present condition." The court treated this language like an "as is" clause, indicating that the buyer agreed to assume the risk of latent defects.

    b. Conscious ignorance. A party who enters an agreement even though she knows she lacks information assumes the risk that the facts prove adverse to her. Restatement (Second) of Contracts §154(b).

EXAMPLE AND ANALYSIS

Plaintiff bought a 16-day-old bull calf from defendant. The calf later proved to be incurably sterile. Fertility cannot be determined until a calf is about a year old. The buyer knew fertility was unascertainable when it purchased the cow. By going forward in the face of that uncertainty, the buyer must have intended to accept the risk of sterility. *Backus v. McLaury*, 106 N.Y.S.2d 401 (N.Y. App. Div. 1951).

    i. Incentive to investigate. The rule may encourage people to obtain information before entering contracts instead of agreeing in haste and asking courts to save them from their mistakes. A party who knows she has not investigated sufficiently cannot take advantage of mistakes she should have discovered before entering the agreement.

    ii. Negligence insufficient. There is some tension between the rule regarding conscious ignorance and the rule regarding fault. "A mistaken party's fault in failing to know or discover the facts before making the contract does not bar him from avoidance or reformation . . . unless his fault amounts to a failure to act in good faith and in accordance with reasonable standards of fair dealing." Restatement (Second) of Contracts §157. Thus, mere negligence in failing to discover the mistake will not preclude rescission.

iii. **Implied term.** Conscious ignorance may be an effort to interpret the agreement between the parties. Even though no express term allocates the risk to either party, **one who proceeds in the face of a known risk (the risk that her information is inadequate) reveals, by her actions, her willingness to accept the risk of mistakes.** This implicit term allocates the risk between the parties as effectively as an express term found under §154(a). Fault plays no part in the reasoning. Even if the intentional action is not blameworthy or in bad faith, it does reflect a willingness to accept the risk of mistakes. When identifiable, the court can interpret this allocation of risk as part of the agreement.

c. **Judicial allocation.** The court may allocate the risk to the adversely affected party if that is reasonable under the circumstances. This catch-all provision recognizes that courts seek to accomplish fair results by taking into account many factors. For example:

i. **Ability to insure.** If one party is in a better position to insure against the loss, perhaps that party should bear the risk of the loss.

ii. **Availability of other relief.** If one party is in a better position to recover the loss from a wrongdoer, perhaps that party should bear the loss.

EXAMPLE AND ANALYSIS

Lenawee County, 9.A.3.a. A prior owner was responsible for the defects in the septic system and for the inability to repair them. The seller arguably could have pursued remedies up the chain of title to that wrongdoer. Because the court decided the contract allocated the risk to buyer, it did not consider whether this factor might justify assigning the risk to seller.

iii. **Ability to prevent mistake.** If one party was in a better position to have discovered the mistake, the court may allocate the risk to that party. For instance, a landowner generally has a better opportunity to learn of latent defects in the property or of latent assets (e.g., minerals) on the property. Perhaps she should bear the risk of a disadvantageous contract given her opportunity to avoid the mistake.

>   **iv.   Fault irrelevant.**   Fault is not a basis for denying rescission unless a party acted in bad faith. Factors that border on fault, like those in 9.A.6.c.iii, may not prevent reliance on the defense.

B.   UNILATERAL MISTAKE

In one sense, unilateral mistake is a harder defense to justify. At least one party knew the actual state of affairs and bargained with that in mind. The mistake defense would deprive this party of her expectations under the contract, even though we know she valued what she got more than what she gave. Yet, unilateral mistake also borders on misrepresentation or nondisclosure. One party knew the truth but did not share that information with the other. Arguably, the law should examine these transactions even more closely than cases involving mutual mistakes, to ensure that no party has overreached. The result is an uneasy balance.

1.   Elements

The **elements of unilateral mistake** are identical to those for mutual mistake, with the **addition** of one new hurdle: the party seeking rescission must demonstrate that:

- Enforcement would be **unconscionable**; or
- The other party **caused** the mistake; or
- The other party had **reason to know** of the mistake. Restatement (Second) of Contracts §153.

2.   Enforcement Would Be Unconscionable

As used here, unconscionability means the contract turned out to be significantly disadvantageous (but would have been advantageous but for the mistake). A mistake that simply makes the profit smaller than it would have been is not unconscionable. Similarly, a mistake that converts a small profit into a small loss does not seem unconscionable. Unlike the unconscionability defense discussed in Chapter 10, ''unconscionable'' here refers only to the substantive fairness of the resulting bargain, not the fairness of the bargaining which produced the contract.

3.   Other Party Caused Mistake

When the other party caused the mistake, the adversely affected party may avoid the contract even if the agreement is not unconscionable.

a. **Misrepresentation compared.** If the other party caused the mistake, a misrepresentation almost certainly exists. It is difficult to picture cases in which a party can cause a mistake without misrepresenting or concealing material facts — particularly as nondisclosure rules require a party to clarify any misleading remarks. See 8.C. Pleading mistake makes it unnecessary to prove the other party's duty to disclose the information.

b. **Allocation of risk.** Misrepresentation has strategic advantages, especially if the contract allocates the risk of a mistake to the adversely affected party. Misrepresentation permits rescission regardless of an "as is" clause, conscious ignorance, or other allocation-of-risk issues that defeat the unilateral mistake defense.

4. Other Party Had Reason to Know of the Mistake

If one party has reason to know the other is mistaken and enters the agreement without correcting that mistake, that party's entitlement to enforcement is somewhat tenuous. Courts may suspect that party really knew of the mistake and pretends ignorance to avoid rescission for nondisclosure.

a. **Too good to be true.** One may have reason to know of a mistake when a deal is "too good to be true." For example, construction contractors who receive bids far below all the other bids probably should know the bidder made a mistake.

b. **Misrepresentation compared.** Where the other party actually knows the other is mistaken, the failure to correct it may constitute nondisclosure (depending on the requirements of good faith). See 8.C.2. Where the other party merely has reason to know of the other's mistake, misrepresentation does not apply.

c. **Mistake narrower.** Unilateral mistake is limited by two factors that do not affect misrepresentation. First, the mistake must affect a basic assumption — a somewhat more stringent requirement than materiality in misrepresentation. Second, the mistaken party may bear the risk of the mistake, a factor that has no bearing on misrepresentation.

REVIEW QUESTIONS AND ANSWERS

Question: What are the elements of mutual mistake?
Answer: When both parties are mistaken about facts as they exist at the time the contract was made, the mistake involves a basic assumption on which the

agreement was made, the mistake has a material effect on the agreed exchange, and the party adversely affected by the mistake does not bear the risk.

Question: When does a party bear the risk of a mistake?

Answer: When the contract allocates the risk to one of the parties, when a party knows she lacks knowledge of the facts but decides to enter the contract anyway, or when the court decides it is reasonable to allocate the risk to a party.

Question: In entering a contract to perform in a motion picture, a star agrees to accept a lower guaranteed salary in exchange for a higher percentage of the gross receipts of the picture. Both the producer and the star thought the film would do well. Instead, it flopped. Can the star rescind the contract for mutual mistake?

Answer: No. The mistake involves a prediction of future events — the success of the film at the box office. That is not a mistake of facts as they exist at the time the contract was formed. Equally important, a clause giving a party a percentage of the proceeds is to allocate to her the risk that proceeds might not be very large. In fact, that is the primary effect of the clause. Thus, it seems likely that the star bore the risk of the mistake. Nor is it clear that the star is the adversely affected party. The poor performance hurt both the star and the producer.

Question: What must a party prove, in addition to the elements of mutual mistake, to avoid a contract based on a unilateral mistake?

Answer: That enforcement would be unconscionable, that the other party caused her mistake, or that the other party had reason to know of her mistake.

UNCONSCIONABILITY: EFFORTS TO AVOID UNFAIR CONTRACTS

10

CHAPTER OVERVIEW

When one party drafts a contract and refuses to deal unless the other agrees to those terms, the contract sometimes is called a **contract of adhesion**.

When a contract of adhesion produces results that a court finds unfair, courts sometimes seek ways to avoid the unjust results, including:

- **Interpreting** any ambiguities in the contract **against the party who drafted it**;
- Interpreting unambiguous terms in a manner consistent with the **reasonable expectations of the party who did not draft the contract**;
- Declaring certain terms of the contract **void because they violate public policy**.

These doctrines still exist but have receded as courts began to apply rules on unconscionability.

If a court determines that a contract term is **unconscionable**, it may:

- **Refuse to enforce the contract**; or
- Enforce the contract but **refuse to enforce the unconscionable term**; or
- **Limit the effect of the term** to prevent an unconscionable result.

Unconscionability is determined as of the **time the contract was made**. That is, a term that seemed reasonable at that time is not unconscionable, even though it may produce harsh results.

A term is unconscionable if:

- The term or its effect **unfairly surprises** the adversely affected party; and
- The effect of the term is **unreasonably favorable** to the other party.

Some courts consider other factors in deciding whether a term is unconscionable.

- If a term has **harsh or oppressive consequences**, some courts treat that as sufficient to find the term unconscionable — at least if the harshness existed at contract formation.
- If a party has **undue bargaining power** (can refuse to deal unless the other party accepts an unwanted term), some courts consider that power in evaluating unconscionability.

A.   UNCONSCIONABILITY IN CONTEXT

The rules on consideration allow parties to decide for themselves how much they value the performance they will receive. See 3.C.3. This freedom occasionally results in some extremely one-sided contracts, where it is difficult to understand how anyone could have agreed to give so much in exchange for so little. Inquiries into how such a one-sided bargain could be made often reveal defects in the bargaining process, such as fraud, duress, or incapacity. **Oppressive terms should raise a red flag, alerting you to consider whether these traditional defenses apply.** Sometimes, however, the proof does not establish a traditional defense to the contract. In these situations, courts intent on doing justice sometimes refuse to enforce the contracts or particular terms in them. Courts initially used several other doctrines to explain these results. Recently, the UCC authorized courts to act directly when agreements are unconscionable. UCC §2-302. The Restatement (Second) has acknowledged that unconscionability of a term explains the pattern of decisions better than the doctrinal facades courts had erected to explain the results.

B.   CONTRACTS OF ADHESION: THE ROLE OF FORM CONTRACTS

There is no separate defense for contracts of adhesion. A contract of adhesion may be voidable for other reasons. **Most adhesion contracts are enforceable.** Nonetheless, contracts courses tend to discuss contracts of adhesion as a separate topic, closely related to unconscionability. Thus, this outline takes up the issue here.

1.   Definition

"Contract of adhesion" refers to any agreement offered on a "take it or leave it" basis, where one party is completely unwilling to negotiate the terms. Usually, contracts of adhesion are standard forms prepared in advance by one party. To deal with this party, the other party must sign the standard form, manifesting assent to its terms. Sometimes one party cannot even see the contract terms until after the contract is made. Examples are numerous.

a. **Insurance contracts.** These are standard forms that cannot be negotiated — though some insurers offer a choice between several standard terms, such as differing coverage limits. Insurers often send the policy, which contains the terms, only after they have cashed the first premium.

b. **Leases.** These usually are standard forms. Some, however, are not contracts of adhesion. Landlords sometimes agree to insert new provisions. Some forms even include space for them.

c. **Credit card agreements and consumer mortgages.** These are contracts of adhesion. The lender specifies the terms. For credit cards, consumers typically don't see the terms at the time they apply for the card, though they can see the terms before they use or sign the back of the card. They can sign or not, as they wish. But they don't get the money unless they sign. Business loans, however, may be negotiable.

d. **Overnight delivery services.** Such services use standard forms and refuse to negotiate the terms. These are contracts of adhesion.

e. **Warranties.** Many products you purchase include standard forms inside the boxes that purport to limit the warranties or other terms of the agreement. Again, consumers typically cannot see them before the purchase.

2. Value of Form Contracts

Form contracts serve a number of useful functions that help keep the cost of consumer goods down.

a. **Drafting error.** Drafting each contract anew would risk inadvertently omitting terms that the parties intended to include. Form contracts allow the drafter to get it right once and not worry about later mistakes.

b. **Legal costs.** A drafter concerned about the legal effect of particular language may want to consult attorneys before entering an agreement. A form permits the drafter to consult the attorney once instead of paying new fees (and incurring new delays) every time a new contract is prepared. Deviation from the form, of course, would undermine this advantage.

c. **Consistency.** A drafter may want to keep its responsibilities standard under all similar contracts. For instance, a manufacturer may want the same warranty obligations to all customers. Otherwise, each time a warranty claim was made, an agent of the seller (probably with legal training) would need to evaluate the contract to determine seller's obligations under that particular warranty provision. Standardization allows the employer to train employees to handle warranty claims appropriately without going to law school.

    d. Transaction costs.   Individual negotiations with every buyer could absorb a lot of hours, raising the cost of the goods to cover the cost of the negotiations. The costs also affect the consumer. Just imagine haggling over every term in your lease as you and the landlord draft it from scratch. Would you rather spend those hours earning money, having fun, studying for an exam, or haggling with your landlord. (Even studying for an exam has some long-term benefits.)

3. Danger of Form Contracts

Form contracts involve costs as well as benefits.

    a. Inflexibility.   Standardized forms may make it harder, if not impossible, to find a party willing to offer the mix of terms that you prefer. Drafters choose the terms; consumers can only choose among drafters.

    b. Uniformity.   Sometimes, an entire industry uses the same standardized terms. For example, most homeowner's insurance policies offer the same terms, no matter who sells them. Many manufacturers include the same warranty disclaimers and limitations of remedy provisions. On the positive side, uniformity can help consumers compare products: They can evaluate differences in price or quality without worrying about differences in each manufacturer's fine print. Price and quality may be more important to many consumers than other terms.

    c. One-sided terms.   The net result is that standardization may produce terms that favor the drafter and disfavor the other party. The inability to negotiate over these terms may strike some as unfair in itself. When the term produces a harsh result, the unfairness of the term may become intolerable.

C. JUDICIAL TREATMENT OF FORM CONTRACTS

In situations in which unfavorable terms have produced harsh results, courts sometimes have tried to avoid or minimize the harshness. Several legal doctrines arose from these efforts. The most important of these doctrines today is the defense of **unconscionability**, discussed in the next section. See 10.D. Several other doctrines remain available to courts, although their primary interest is historical.

1. Interpretation against the Drafter

This technique originated in efforts to interpret insurance contracts to find coverage. When applied to obscure terms inserted specifically to allow an insurer to escape liability after collecting premiums, the device prevented a business practice tantamount to fraud. The expansion of the technique to other contexts and its perpetuation into today's highly regulated insurance industry are more controversial.

a. Modest version. Sometimes a contract drafted by one party contains ambiguities. A court normally tries to interpret ambiguous terms to give effect to the intentions of the parties at the time they entered the contract. See Chapter 12. When normal interpretive techniques fail, courts sometimes reject the interpretation advanced by the drafter on the ground that she could have drafted the contract more carefully and, thus, prevented the dilemma the court confronts. This rule is a last resort, a tie-breaker that resolves interpretation when all other techniques fail.

b. More active version. When a form contract threatens to produce an unjust result, courts sometimes find an ambiguity and resolve it against the drafter to avoid the harshness. The extreme version differs from the modest version in several ways.

    i. First versus last resort. Courts sometimes apply the rule as a first step, instead of attempting to interpret the clause. Although the usual interpretive techniques might reveal what the parties intended, that intent might not avoid the harshness of the term.

    ii. Phantom ambiguities. Courts may find ambiguities where none exist. To avoid injustice, they must apply the rule; to apply the rule, they must find an ambiguity. So, by god, an ambiguity they will find!

    iii. Fairness overshadowed. The rule often overlooks the justification for the provision. The interpretation against the drafter is mechanical; it does not necessarily involve a conclusion that the term was unfair, only that it disadvantaged the other party.

2. Reasonable Expectations of the Nondrafting Party

Courts sometimes will interpret the contract to embody the reasonable expectations of the nondrafting party—or of the insured, because these cases almost always involve insurance policies. Courts created this doctrine in part to avoid the disingenuousness of finding ambiguities in reasonably clear contract clauses. Under this doctrine, when the insured reasonably believes the policy covers a particular situation, the court interprets it that way despite clear language to the contrary in the policy. Often the cases involve sales material that describes broad coverage but policy provisions that limit the coverage in unexpected ways. Because the doctrine generally does not arise in first-year contract courses, no further discussion seems necessary here.

3. Public Policy

Some courts refused to enforce harsh clauses on the ground that the clauses violate public policy. This is a separate defense, discussed in detail below. See Chapter 11. Form contracts that imposed harsh terms often ran afoul of public policies announced by courts. Some vestiges of this approach remain in statutes that preclude enforcement of certain kinds of contract provisions, though the language today may invoke unconscionability. See, e.g., UCC §2-719(3) (declaring limitations of remedy unconscionable when applied to consumer goods that cause physical injury).

D. ELEMENTS OF UNCONSCIONABILITY

Unconscionability is one of the vaguest terms in all of contract law. The UCC and the Restatement (Second) announce that courts may refuse to enforce unconscionable contracts, **but they do not define unconscionable!** The comments to each offer illustrations and advice concerning factors to consider, but little more. Nonetheless, this outline attempts to set up a framework for analyzing unconscionability. The discussion will proceed in two steps: First I give you the best and most justifiable approach to unconscionability I can derive from the cases and other source material; then I discuss other factors that do not fit that approach and which I find hard to justify but which seem to play a role in some cases. The first explanation represents my personal preference. Before you employ this approach on an exam (or in practice), be sure to review the way your professor (or state courts) approach unconscionability. The area is one of the most controversial and ill-defined aspects of contract law. It undoubtedly will develop and change as courts grope for appropriate boundaries. A summary like this cannot offer **the** way to approach unconscionability but can only identify the alternatives.

1. Effect of Unconscionability

If a term is unconscionable at the time the contract is made, a court may:

- Refuse to enforce the contract;
- Enforce the contract without the unconscionable term; or
- Limit the effect of the term to prevent unconscionability.

2. Identifying Unconscionable Terms

There are two components to finding a contract term unconscionable.

a. **Unfair surprise.** When the term was not apparent to the party at the time the contract was made, her assent may not indicate that she valued the performance with the term more than she valued what she gave in exchange. See UCC §2-302 cmt.

b. **Unreasonably favorable terms.** When the surprising term unreasonably favors one party, courts wonder whether the disfavored party really would have assented if aware of the term. *Williams v. Walker-Thomas Furniture*, 350 F.2d 445 (D.C. Cir. 1965).

3. Extent of Unconscionability

Although the language used here refers to a contract term, courts can hold an entire contract unconscionable without isolating a particular term.

a. **Secondary terms.** Usually, the terms that produce unconscionable results are matters of secondary concern, such as warranty disclaimers, termination provisions, or other matters not central to the exchange.

b. **Salient terms.** Sometimes, however, courts have found obvious and salient terms unconscionable. For instance, even though the parties almost always consider the price when deciding whether to enter the contract, some courts have found price terms unconscionable.

4. Unfair Surprise

This helps explain how someone could agree to a term that produces such one-sided results: **The party did not know the term was there or did not know what effect the term would have.** Unfair surprise undermines our confidence that the party valued what she received more than she valued what she gave up. Some of the costs did not enter her deliberations because she was unaware of those costs. Just as with misrepresentation and mistake, her assent does not carry its usual significance.

a. **Lack of fair notice.** Surprise will be unfair when a party lacked fair notice that the agreement included the terms in question. They may be concealed in fine print, couched in language so confusing that few people can understand their import, or presented under circumstances that deprive a party of a fair opportunity to read them. This rule does not excuse people from their normal responsibility to read their contracts before signing them. It does **not** make every unread or misunderstood contract voidable. But it recognizes the existence of practices or circumstances that impede informed decisions. Particularly when the other party erects those impediments to informed choice, the law may recognize that what appears to be a bargain lacks the usual indicia of a beneficial exchange.

 # EXAMPLES AND ANALYSIS

1. Mrs. Williams purchased several items of furniture on credit from Walker-Thomas. The form contract included a cross-collateral clause that allowed the store to repossess nearly all the furniture they had sold her in the past if she failed to make payments on her most recent purchase (a stereo). The clause, part of the store's standard form contract, achieved this result indirectly by allocating payments among various items purchased such that no item was fully paid until all items were fully paid. Even if she read the form contract, Mrs. Williams may not have been able to understand the clause. Mrs. Williams defaulted after making payments that, but for the clause, would have satisfied her debt on all the furniture except the stereo. The store repossessed all the furniture they had sold Mrs. Williams. The court held that unconscionability was a valid contract defense and remanded for a factual determination of whether the clause was unconscionable. *Williams v. Walker-Thomas Furniture*, 350 F.2d 445 (D.C. Cir. 1965).

2. Plaintiff entered a franchise agreement with defendant. The agreement was terminable by either party on 90 days' notice, with no requirement of cause for termination after the first 12 months. After several years, defendant terminated the agreement but offered to negotiate a new agreement (on terms more favorable to it). The termination clause was not buried in fine print. It was clearly worded and expressly called to plaintiff's attention. Plaintiff was encouraged to consult an attorney but chose not to do so. The court concluded that the termination clause presented no unfair surprise. *Zapatha v. Dairy Mart*, 408 N.E.2d 1370 (Mass. 1980).

    b.   Dangerous incentives.   Parties often sign form contracts without reading or understanding them. A rule that treated every unnoticed or misunderstood provision as an unfair surprise probably would undermine too many contracts. It also would create a perverse incentive for people to ignore contracts instead of looking out for their own interests by reading them and refusing to sign them if they contained unfair terms. Form contracts offer significant advantages for society. A rule that undermined their usefulness would be very costly for everyone in the long run. **Thus, some surprises may not constitute unfair surprise.** In addition, unfair surprise alone will not establish unconscionability.

5. Unreasonably Favorable Terms

This portion of the rule embodies the requirement that the terms of the contract be harsh or oppressive. See UCC §2-302 comment 1. Not every harsh term will be unconscionable; only **unreasonably** harsh terms justify judicial intervention.

a. **Reasonably favorable terms.**   Some parties include opportunistic terms, designed to extract as much as they can from unsuspecting parties. But others include favorable terms to protect themselves from risks inherent in the transaction. These risks will be borne by one party or the other; there is nothing illegitimate about agreeing in advance who should bear the risks in a fair bargaining process. Courts should prevent exploitation or oppression, but **terms that serve legitimate commercial interests may deserve enforcement even when they produce harsh results.**

 ## Examples and Analysis

1. K.D. took the LSAT twice. The second time his scores improved dramatically but showed a striking resemblance to the answers of the person sitting next to him. Educational Testing Service invoked a contract provision that allowed them "to cancel any test score if, in our sole opinion, there is adequate reason to question its validity." K.D. argued that the clause was unconscionable. Canceling the test score effectively prevented him from pursuing his chosen profession, because every law school requires the LSAT. The court upheld the reasonableness of the provision. *K.D. v. Educational Testing Serv.*, 386 N.Y.S.2d 747 (N.Y. Sup. Ct. 1976).

2. The cross-collateral clause in *Williams v. Walker-Thomas Furniture*, 10.D.4.a, arguably served a legitimate commercial interest. The store made furniture available on credit to people who were too poor to get credit or furniture elsewhere. The risk of default was high. Yet the used goods repossessed often might not be worth as

much as the buyer still owed. Additional collateral allowed the store to cover its full loss. The alternatives to additional collateral may have been equally bad for people like Mrs. Williams.

The store could demand larger down payments to cover the depreciation in the first months of use. But their poor customers, like Mrs. Williams, might not be able to buy on those terms.

The store could charge higher interest rates so that its losses on default were covered by other customers who did not default. But this would force the people who did make payments to pay more to cover for those who defaulted. This might price some of them out of the market and, at best, would force them to buy less of something because more money went to furniture.

The store could loan to people who posed less risk of default. But that seems likely to deprive the poor of the only source of credit available to them.

The store's choice allowed more people to borrow, allowed them to borrow at a lower rate, and forced the defaulting party to cover the losses caused by the default — arguably a reasonable approach.

Cross-collateral clauses are now regulated by statute. The specific provision used by Walker-Thomas is now illegal. See Uniform Consumer Credit Code §§3.302-3.303.

3. Seller sold Jones a freezer for three times its market value, plus credit charges total twice the value of the freezer. The court held the price term unconscionable. It considered arguments that selling on credit to the poor required additional protection for the seller. The court believed that whatever additional protection the seller required did not justify such extreme disproportion between price and value. *Jones v. Star Credit*, 298 N.Y.S.2d 264 (N.Y. Sup. Ct. 1969).

Jones illustrates a secondary concern: Sometimes businesses that sell primarily to the poor on credit charge prices higher than those available at other stores. Because the poor cannot buy at other stores, competition does not keep their prices down. These higher prices may compensate the business for the risk of selling to the poor. To add other onerous terms may exact more compensation than is reasonable.

---

      b.   Specific analysis of each clause's purpose.   The issue of reasonableness cannot be brushed aside with superficial conclusions. To determine the reasonableness of a term, courts need evidence concerning why the term was included in the contract and whether those concerns justify the clause. That will require economic analysis of the business, not easy proclamations based on sympathy.

E.   ALTERNATIVE VIEWS

The approach listed previously cannot explain all the cases or even all the rhetoric in the cases that support it. The following approaches identify other views of unconscionability that may have considerable persuasive power when presented to some judges or professors.

1.   Unequal Bargaining Power

Some attribute unconscionability to unequal bargaining power. Big companies can force consumers (or small companies) to accept any terms the big companies wish to cram down their throats. Thus, consumers who agree to these terms should be allowed to escape from the consequences of these agreements if the terms later prove disadvantageous — or, at least, if they later prove harsh or oppressive.

   a.   UCC rejection.   The UCC emphatically disavows the bargaining power as a basis for unconscionability. "The principle is one of the prevention of oppression and unfair surprise and **not of disturbance of allocation of risks because of superior bargaining power**." UCC §2-302 comment 1 (citation omitted, emphasis added). The Restatement (Second) quotes this language.

   i.   Bargaining power not sinful.   Everyone tries to negotiate terms favorable to themselves. Some succeed. Success, however, is not a reason to avoid favorable contract terms.

   ii.   Bargaining power cannot compel a bad deal.   Large companies can refuse to deal with those who will not accept their terms. But they cannot compel people to deal with them if the terms are unacceptable. Assent shows people really value what they received more than what they gave up, including the undesirable term — even though they would rather have received it for less or without the unwanted clause.

   iii.   Unless terms are concealed.   When part of the cost is concealed in terms that unfairly surprise the consumer, the deal may cost more than it is worth to the consumer. But the imbalance has nothing to do with bargaining power, only with the ability to conceal important costs from the other party until after she has committed to the agreement.

   b.   Lack of reasonable choice.   Courts sometimes couch this problem in terms of the "absence of meaningful choice." Courts using the language imply that the inability to persuade the other party to alter the term produces an absence of meaningful choice. Because the party cannot choose between entering the contract with the objectionable term and entering the contract without the objectionable term, she has no meaningful choice. This overlooks other choices a party may have.

i.   **Just say no.**   A party who finds the cost of a term too high can refuse the deal altogether. Thus, if the value of the item received is less than the value of what she gives up (when the effect of the objectionable term is included), the other party can and should refuse to enter the transaction. This choice is meaningless when the existence of the term comes as an unfair surprise to the party. But when the term is known and understood, assent implies a decision that the cost of the term is less than the value of the other party's performance.

ii.   **Go to the competition.**   When one company imposes an onerous term, others may not. The choice to shop around or deal with others can be meaningful.

iii.   **Pay the price.**   When everyone imposes the same term, the term may serve a reasonable commercial purpose. If not, one would expect to see some company deleting the term and gaining against its competitors.

2.   Unconscionability Means Harshness

Some cases suggest that unfair terms, without any other factor, justify a finding of unconscionability.

 # EXAMPLE AND ANALYSIS

Toker v. Westerman, 274 A.2d 78 (N.J. Dist. Ct. 1970). Plaintiff sold refrigerator-freezers door to door. Defendant agreed to buy one for a price about two and a half times the amount charged in local stores selling similar goods. After making about half the payments, the defendant stopped making payments. Plaintiff sued for the balance due. The court found no unfair surprise or unfair bargaining power but denied enforcement of the contract on the ground that the outrageous price made the contract unconscionable. The court did not rescind the contract but simply held defendants did not have to make any more payments.

The buyers almost certainly considered the price and decided that they preferred the freezer to the money. They probably did not investigate other sellers, which would have sold an equivalent freezer for less. But unconscionability seems a poor substitute for comparison shopping.

Other circumstances might justify the decision. A price stated in an amount per month may have concealed the true total to be paid. Interest charges might have been difficult to understand. Modern credit disclosure laws may have corrected (or at least ameliorated) these problems.

---

a. **Unconscionability or duress?** Door-to-door sales have an implicitly coercive aspect. Someone in your home does not want to leave until you sign a contract. Again, recent legislation allowing consumers to rescind contracts entered in their home within three days of making them reduce this problem. (They also make it hard to get service from a plumber in less than 3 days.)

b. **Statutory reform.** Door-to-door sales of refrigerators and freezers at exorbitant prices has produced a substantial number of unconscionability cases. The decision to regulate these practices by statute instead of avoiding contracts only for those who sue and win may offer a more effective long-range solution for the victims of opportunistic sellers.

F. PUTTING THE RHETORIC IN CONTEXT: PROCEDURAL VERSUS SUBSTANTIVE UNCONSCIONABILITY

The concerns identified previously help you apply unconscionability on an exam. In class discussion, however, you may encounter discussions that break unconscionability down into two subcategories: substantive unconscionability and procedural unconscionability. This section will try to help you put the principles identified above into that framework. It does not present anything new and does not repeat the arguments above in detail. It does attempt to refocus the discussion in a way that may prove helpful in correlating your classroom discussions with the rules above.

1. Substantive Unconscionability

This term refers to the substance of the transaction—the fairness of the terms of the bargain. It corresponds most closely with the view that the courts should strike down any term that produces harsh results. See 10.E.2. Substantive unconscionability can include consideration for the reasonableness of the contract term in issue. A term that serves reasonable commercial purposes may not be unfair, even if harsh. Usually, however, substantive unconscionability focuses on the results of the transaction, not on the purpose the clause might serve.

2.   Procedural Unconscionability

This term refers to unfairness in the way the bargain is formed. It focuses on unfair surprise, because concealed costs prevent one party from making an informed choice about the relative costs and benefits of the transaction. See 10.D.4. When the parties can make an informed choice, however, courts should enforce any bargain, no matter how harsh the terms.

a.   **Bargaining power as procedural.**   Some people include concerns for unequal bargaining power in procedural unconscionability. The other party's bargaining power may impede choice, just as failure to recognize the costs impedes choice.

b.   **Bargaining power as sui generis.**   As noted earlier, bargaining power does not make bargaining unfair. See 10.E.1. Nor does unfair bargaining power produce substantive unfairness. In short, unfair bargaining power does not fit the procedural–substantive breakdown — perhaps because it does not belong in the law of unconscionability at all. See UCC §2-302 comment 1.

REVIEW QUESTIONS AND ANSWERS

Question: Before unconscionability, what techniques did courts use to avoid enforcing harsh or oppressive terms in an otherwise valid bargain?

Answer: Courts often found or created ambiguities in a contract and interpreted them against the party who drafted it (usually the party the term favored). In some cases, courts would decide that because a reasonable person in the place of the nondrafting party would expect the contract to include a particular term (or limitation on a harsh term), that contract should be interpreted to include that provision. Sometimes courts would declare that a term violated public policy, making it (and sometimes the entire contract) unenforceable.

Question: What are the elements of unconscionability?

Answer: Unfair surprise and unreasonably favorable terms. Some courts treat harshness or oppression as sufficient without regard to either surprise or the reasonableness of the terms. Others treat extreme bargaining power by one party as a surrogate for unfair surprise or as an additional factor supporting a finding of unconscionability.

Question: What is the remedy if a term is unconscionable?

Answer: The court may refuse to enforce the contract (rescission and restitution), may enforce the contract without the offending term, or may limit the effect of the term in order to avoid unconscionable results.

Question: How does unconscionability differ from other contract defenses?

Answer: Two significant differences are the grounds and the result. (1) Most other contract defenses focus on the bargaining process: If the process is flawed, the contract is unenforceable, regardless of the result. Unconscionability focuses heavily on the results, with some courts holding that flaws in the bargaining process are unnecessary. (2) Other contract defenses permit a party to avoid an entire contract but do not allow a party to enforce part of the contract while avoiding other parts. In effect, unconscionability allows courts to rewrite the contract. The court can carve out parts of the agreement and enforce others, even if the other party never would have agreed to the terms the court decides to enforce.

Question: True or false: If an unscrupulous seller persuades a buyer to pay ten times the fair value of an item, the outrageous price alone is sufficient to declare the contract unconscionable.

Answer: False—usually. The price term rarely is a surprise—though a clever drafter sometimes can obscure the price from an unwary buyer. Thus, it is likely the party agreed to that price up front. Courts generally expect people to do their comparison shopping before they buy, rejecting bad offers instead of trying to rescind them in court. Anything else amounts to reviewing the adequacy of the consideration, which courts say they will not do. Nonetheless, if a price term has been obscured—and perhaps sometimes when it has not—some courts have found an outrageous price sufficient to support unconscionability. The court then fixes a price—often the amount paid so far—and refuses to award the seller any more than that amount.

Question: Discuss the following statement: A party with extreme bargaining power sometimes can compel a party who wants something very much to pay more for it than the amount of value she expects to derive from it. Thus, extreme bargaining power is an important factor in determining unconscionability.

Answer: If a party really values her money more than she values the benefit she expects to receive from the promised performance, it is hard to explain how any amount of bargaining power could persuade her to enter the contract. In saying that she wants something very much, the statement implies that she expects to receive a great deal of benefit from the performance. But in most cases it is nonsense to suggest she will agree to pay more than the value she expects to receive. In effect, her decision to enter the contract tells us the minimum amount of benefit she expects: the amount she agrees to pay. Sometimes people get caught up in the heat of the moment and lose all sense of proportion—say, at an auction.

Here, the eagerness is not born of the other party's bargaining power but of her own excitement. A party with virtually no bargaining power could create the same excitement.

Disclaimer: This essay is my own reaction to the statement. The existence of judicial opinions relying on undue bargaining power suggest other reactions may be valid, as well.

11 PUBLIC POLICY LIMITS ON CONTRACTS

CHAPTER OVERVIEW

If a statute declares that a contract is unenforceable, courts will refuse to enforce the contract.

If a public policy against enforcement clearly outweighs the interest in enforcement, courts will refuse to enforce a contract.

- In assessing the interests in favor of enforcing contracts, courts consider:
    — The parties' justified expectations;
    — Any forfeiture if enforcement were denied; and
    — Any special public interest in enforcement.
- In assessing the public policy against enforcement of contracts, courts consider:
    — The strength or importance of the policy involved;
    — The likelihood that nonenforcement would advance the policy goal;
    — The seriousness of any misconduct;
    — The deliberateness of any misconduct; and
    — The directness of the connection between the contract term and the misconduct.

Public policy issues frequently arise in contracts involving family relationships.

- Express contracts among family members are enforceable if evinced by clear and convincing evidence. Courts are less inclined to enforce implied contracts.
- Contracts altering family status may violate public policy—though some willingness to allow parties to shape their rights within a family by agreement have eroded this policy.

- Contracts creating informal families (e.g., unmarried cohabitants) are increasingly enforceable, though with limits similar to those for other contracts within a family.

Contracts in restraint of trade are unenforceable, with some exceptions.

- A limited restraint of trade ancillary to a valid agreement is enforceable.
- To be reasonable, a restraint of trade must:
  — Apply for a reasonably limited amount of time;
  — Apply within a reasonably limited geographic area; and
  — Apply to a reasonably limited range of trade activities.

A.   IN GENERAL

Some agreements may be unenforceable even if both parties want them enforced. An agreement that violates public policy may make society worse off, even if it makes both individuals better off. To pose an extreme example, a contract of murder for hire might suit the interests of both parties. Yet the courts should not enforce such agreements because they are unlikely to benefit society. Although public policy offers a fairly broad basis upon which to negate contracts, courts usually show restraint in applying the doctrine.

1.   Elements

Courts will refuse to enforce a contract if:

- "Legislation provides that it is unenforceable"; or
- A public policy against enforcement clearly outweighs the interest in enforcement. Restatement (Second) of Contracts §178(1).

2.   Contracts Unenforceable by Statute

Some statutes, usually state statutes, declare that particular contract provisions are unenforceable. Although some examples will illustrate the point, you should always check local statutes, especially statutes regulating particular businesses or trades, to determine what restrictions may apply in your jurisdiction.

a.   Penalty clauses.   A contract term setting liquidated damages at an unreasonably high level is void. UCC §2-718(1); see Chapter 22. The parties cannot waive this provision by agreement.

b.   Some indemnities.   In some states, a contract provision that attempts to relieve one party of liability for her own negligence is unenforceable.

This is particularly important in construction contracts, where contractors often must indemnify owners for injuries during construction.

c. **Licensing statutes.** States that require licenses to practice a trade often pass laws making contracts entered by an unlicensed person unenforceable, at least by the unlicensed person. Thus, someone practicing that trade without a license could never sue to collect unpaid bills for her services.

3. Balancing Competing Public Policies

In most cases, the legislature has not enacted a provision specifically addressing the enforceability of contracts. For instance, few legislatures have thought it necessary to enact a separate law declaring that a contract for murder is unenforceable. The murder law itself is sufficient announcement of the public policy in this area. Of course, public policy also favors the performance of contracts and their enforcement when breached. Not every statute or public policy may outweigh the interests in enforcing contracts. For instance, if one party needed to park illegally to perform a contract, the contract still might be enforceable. Without a legislative enactment that explicitly draws the balance for them, courts balance the public interest in enforcing the contract term against the public interest in refusing to enforce the term. **The presumption lies with enforcement; unless the public policy clearly outweighs the interest in enforcement, the contract is enforceable.**

4. The Interest in Enforcing Promises

The benefits of exchange and of planning have been mentioned above. Courts consider several more specific factors when assessing the enforceability of a particular contract or term. These factors include:

a. **Parties' justified expectations.** Generally, the parties to a contract legitimately expect it to be enforceable. When the parties know the agreement requires illegal conduct, they may not expect enforcement and, if they do, they would not be justified. But in cases in which the parties had reason to believe the contract was legitimate, the court should not frustrate those expectations lightly. Restatement (Second) of Contracts §178(2)(a).

b. **Forfeiture.** When performance has begun, refusal to enforce the agreement may significantly disadvantage one party — especially if she cannot salvage the work already done, as when she has delivered the performance to the other party or when customized work has no value to others. In some situations, the other party may be unjustly enriched if allowed to keep the performance without paying for it. Forfeiture and unjust enrichment weigh in favor of enforcing the contract. Restatement (Second) of Contracts §178(2)(b).

    i.   **Restitution might prevent unjust enrichment.**   Restitution will not prevent forfeiture when reliance has not benefited the other party. When restitution is available, it could remedy the inequities between the parties, thus reducing the need to enforce a questionable contract.

    ii.   **Restitution is not available in most public policy cases.**   Generally, a court that refuses to enforce a contract on the grounds of public policy leaves the parties as it finds them. Because each party entered an invalid exchange, neither can invoke the court's power in her favor.

EXAMPLES AND ANALYSIS

1. Plaintiff and defendant were partners in holding up travelers on the highway. Plaintiff claimed defendant failed to share the profit in accord with their agreement. The chancellor dismissed the bill, leaving defendant with an unduly large share of the loot. *Highwayman's Case* (1725), reported in 9 L.Q.R. 197 (1893).

2. Defendant promised plaintiff $10,000 plus commissions if he obtained movie distribution rights for defendant's theaters. Defendant paid the $10,000 and plaintiff got the rights, but defendant refused to pay the commissions. When plaintiff sued, defendant alleged that plaintiff obtained the rights by using the $10,000 to pay a bribe. The court held that the public policy against bribery would support defendant's nonpayment and remanded the case for findings on whether plaintiff actually bribed anyone. The result could leave defendant with the movie rights it sought but with no obligation to pay for them. *McConnell v. Commonwealth Pictures*, 166 N.E.2d 494 (N.Y. 1960).

    iii.   **Exceptions.**   In two situations, courts have shown some willingness to allow a plaintiff to recover restitution.

        (a)   **Excusable ignorance.**   Restitution is available to a party who is excusably ignorant either of **facts** or of a **minor law** that made the promise unenforceable, unless the parties to the contract were "equally in the wrong." Restatement (Second) of Contracts §197.

    (b) Laudable regret. A party who has not engaged in **serious misconduct** may recover in restitution if (i) she **withdraws** from the contract before it achieves its improper purpose, or (ii) allowing the claim would **end a continuing violation** of public policy. Restatement (Second) of Contracts §198.

  c. Public interest in enforcement of a particular term. Sometimes a promise, even if made for a bad reason, will have a good result. When the promise will benefit the public, courts weigh that benefit in deciding whether to enforce it. Restatement (Second) of Contracts §178(2)(c).

5. The Policy against Enforcement

Usually the harm of enforcing the agreement will be fairly clear. Nonetheless, difficult cases can arise in which the following factors will help you work through the competing interests. *See* Restatement (Second) of Contracts §178(3).

  a. Strength of the policy. Policies may derive from either statutes or judicial decisions. But not all public policies are equal. Policies against felonies are strong, against misdemeanors less strong. Some regulations, particularly if antiquated, may present very little in the way of a public policy against enforcement.

  b. Advancing the policy goal. Some misconduct will not be deterred by a refusal to enforce the agreement. When the public policy is too ill-defined for people to know when they have violated it, refusal to enforce the agreements may not prevent people from entering similar contracts in the future. In other cases, contract rules will add nothing to other deterrents. For instance, sales of illegal narcotics will continue whether or not the courts enforce these contracts. If anything, a policy to enforce such contracts might draw some (stupid) criminals to reveal their criminal conduct by suing to enforce their contracts. See, e.g., Highwayman's Case (1725), reported in 9 L.Q.R. 197 (1893). **When refusal to enforce the agreement will not further the public policy at issue, the interests in enforcement of the contract may outweigh the policy against enforcement.**

  c. Severity of misconduct. When the contract involves serious misconduct, the policy against enforcement increases. The point is similar to the strength of the policy because the law will evaluate the seriousness of the misconduct in light of the importance of the policy of preventing it.

d.   Deliberateness of misconduct.   When misconduct was inadvertent, enforcement of the agreement may be appropriate. The parties' expectation of enforcement is more legitimate when misconduct was inadvertent. In addition, the parties' behavior seems both less reprehensible and harder to deter when the parties did not realize the conduct violated a public policy.

e.   Connection between the contract and the misconduct.   Sometimes a contract specifically calls for misconduct, as a contract for murder. But sometimes the connection is more tenuous. When the connection is remote, refusal to enforce the agreement seems less appropriate.

    i.   Agreements induced by illegal acts.   Some perfectly legal contracts are induced by illegal actions. For example, if S, a seller, bribes A, an agent of B Corp., to persuade B Corp. to buy S's goods, B Corp's promise to buy the goods is unenforceable. It was obtained by illegal acts.

    ii.   Agreements performed by illegal acts.   Sometimes a party to a contract that calls for perfectly legitimate conduct commits an illegal act in the course of performing the contract. The illegal act may be too minor to notice, as when a delivery person parks illegally to meet a deadline. But some illegal acts may be more serious. Thus, in *McConnell*, 11.A.4.b.(2), the agent could have obtained the movie rights by legitimate negotiation. Instead, he allegedly bribed someone to obtain the rights. The contract neither required nor encouraged illegal conduct, except to the extent that any contract encourages a party to perform by any means necessary. Thus, the dissenters urged that the connection was too remote to justify the defense.

    iii.   Contracts that tend to induce violations of public policy.   Even though not requiring an illegal act, a contract may create an incentive to violate public policy. Thus, some contracts involving married people have been declared unenforceable on the ground that the promise tended to encourage divorce. These promises would be unenforceable even if no divorce occurred. Their tendency to produce undesirable consequences violates public policy. Similarly, bribes tend to induce agents to breach fiduciary duties to their principals. This tendency makes the bribe unenforceable even if the agent does not commit the breach of fiduciary duty.

B. CONTRACTS WITHIN A FAMILY: STATUS VERSUS CONTRACT

Typically, the law governs relations among family members as a status (when it governs them at all). Status means your station in life, not your prestige. It refers to duties that arise from your relationship to others. Thus, parents have duties to children because they are parents, not because they made any promises to the children. The state imposes these duties by law, whether you agree to them or not—much the way the legislature imposes criminal law on all citizens, whether or not they consent to obey the law. As peoples' ideals for family life diverge, contract has become a way for people to shape their own duties, regardless of what the state might think appropriate for family members. When contracts run up against the duties that arise from status, the law may need to resolve conflicts.

1. Contracts between Family Members

Many contracts between members of a family will not conflict with their duties. For instance, you can pay your child to mow the lawn or hire your sibling as your accountant. These raise no issue of public policy. Two fears, however, have led to some reluctance to enforce even these innocuous contracts among family members: (a) the fear that no bargain was intended but that one party now seeks compensation for actions originally performed gratuitously, and (b) the fear that judicial intervention into the affairs of a family may cause more harm than good. The courts' uneasiness has produced doctrines that limit enforcement of contracts within the family more narrowly than agreements among strangers.

a. Express contracts. Family members are free, via express contracts, to take on additional duties to one another in bargained-for exchanges. Thus, in *Hamer v. Sidway*, 3.C.1.b, the uncle's promise to give the nephew $5,000 if he refrained from drinking, smoking, swearing, and gambling until he reached the age of 21 posed no public policy issues. Because the evidence clearly established the existence of a contract, the court enforced the bargain.

b. Not implied contracts. Only express contracts between family members will be enforced. Courts are reluctant to infer the existence of a bargain from the actions of family members. Family members often perform services for one another or convey property to one another out of love and affection, not out of an expectation that they will receive compensation for the services or property. Thus, performance may not indicate that an unstated bargain has been reached — or even that one party has been unjustly enriched. (There is no injustice in keeping a gift without paying for it.) Absent an express promise, courts do not enforce contractual duties among family members.

c. **Standard of proof.**   Courts sometimes impose a higher than usual burden of proof on a party seeking to establish the existence of an express oral contract. A written agreement presents few difficulties for courts. An oral agreement may present a harder case unless both parties admit the agreement (in which case litigation is unlikely). When one party denies an agreement or when one party cannot testify (perhaps because of death or disability), courts fear that the other party may attempt to recharacterize an essentially gratuitous transaction as an oral contract. (If enforced, one heir may receive a larger portion of an estate: part under the contract, part via inheritance.) To minimize this risk, some courts insist on more than a mere preponderance of the evidence, such as clear and convincing evidence, in this setting.

2. **Contracts Altering Status under the Law Governing Families**

Marriage is generally regarded as a status — though the changing nature of marriage in the last few decades may change that characterization before long. By statute, states regulate the terms of marriages, specifying the duties between spouses both during and after marriage. Although spouses are free to create their own relationship within a marriage, many of their legal duties (such as support, etc.) are not alterable. Contracts that undermine the state's regulation of marriage violate public policy. Some recurring situations are mentioned next.

a. **Unreasonable restraints on marriage are unenforceable.**   A contract whereby one party seeks to discourage the marriage of another is unenforceable as an unreasonable restraint on marriage. Some contracts, however, are enforceable even if the terms might tend to discourage marriage. For example, a promise to support a person until marriage is enforceable. These promises often do not purport to restrict remarriage. In fact, promises in separation agreements often include a promise of support until remarriage; at least one party has reason to hope that remarriage will occur soon. A contract that imposes too great a burden upon marriage, however, may be unenforceable even if it is not intended to restrict marriage. Restatement (Second) of Contracts §189.

b. **Do promises alter the essential terms of marriage?**   The public has an interest in some of the terms of the marriage contract, such as the obligation to support one's spouse. A contract that alters these obligations may be unenforceable. Restatement (Second) of Contracts §190. The sections that follow describe the common-law rule. A new uniform statute, adopted by many but not all states, alters many of these rules. The last subsection here describes the statute.

i. **When parties who have separated or who are about to separate enter such an agreement on fair terms, the agreement is enforceable.** The law does not compel separating couples to litigate the terms of their separation; they may amicably (or contentiously) agree to settle their affairs in any way they wish —as long as the terms are fair. The relation of trust and confidence that exists between spouses, even separating spouses, precludes arm's-length bargaining. Thus, the court will supervise the fairness of the agreement (a.k.a. the adequacy of the consideration).

ii. **An agreement that unreasonably tends to encourage divorce or separation is not enforceable.** The rule originated to prevent parties from defrauding a court into granting a divorce when no grounds for divorce existed. For example, one party's promise not to deny the allegations of adultery in the other's complaint would not be enforceable. The scope later expanded to include agreements made during or shortly before marriage that specified the terms of a separation, because favorable terms might encourage one party to seek a separation (though the same terms might discourage the other party from seeking separation).

iii. **Terms other than support can run afoul of these provisions.** In *Favrot v. Barnes*, 332 So. 2d 873 (La. Ct. App. 1976), a husband challenged an alimony award to his wife on the ground that she had violated their prenuptial agreement in which she agreed to limit intercourse to one time per week. The court refused to enforce the agreement, which changed an essential incident of marriage. The court did not explain the public interest in the frequency of intercourse between these people.

iv. **By statute, states have allowed prenuptial agreements to alter many of the terms of marriage.** See Uniform Premarital Agreement Act (UPAA). The statute allows prospective spouses to enter enforceable written agreements covering a broad array of subjects, including property rights, support obligations, and "any other matter, including their personal rights and obligations, not in violation of public policy or a statute imposing a criminal penalty." UPAA §3(a)(8). Agreements may be challenged on the ground of duress or fraud, but mere unfairness of the terms would not justify a refusal to enforce the agreement. UPAA §6.

c.   **An agreement affecting child custody or child support is not enforceable.**   The rights of a child cannot be bargained away between the parents without the approval of a court. **A court may decide that the agreement serves the best interests of the child but the agreement itself is not dispositive.** Restatement (Second) of Contracts §191; UPAA §3(b).

3. Contracts Creating Informal Families

Recently, people have shown increasing willingness to live together without taking the official step necessary to form a family — that is, without marrying. Some informal families take this route because the law will not permit them to marry. Homosexual couples and persons already married face this constraint. Others freely choose to form informal families. Contract law has little application to these informal families as long as they settle their disputes amicably. When families dissolve, however, contract law may present the only legal supervision available, because divorce is limited to those persons who actually marry. Before resolving contract disputes, however, the law must decide whether any promises made within informal families are enforceable.

a.   **Context.**   Agreements between the members of informal families vary. In most circumstances, however, one party alleges that the other promised to share income, property, or support for life in exchange for household services, companionship, giving up a career, and other similar sacrifices. When the couple separates, the party seeking property or support sues for breach of the agreement.

b.   **Analogues.**   The public policy against sexual intercourse out of wedlock poses the most significant obstacle to informal families. Two lines of precedent created long before the sexual revolution of the 1960s tend to shape the approach courts take to this issue.

   i.   **The prostitution model.**   A promise to exchange money or property for sexual intercourse is void as against public policy. Courts have not abandoned rules that prevent prostitutes from suing to collect their fees — at least in states that ban prostitution. Although informal families are not prostitution, an agreement that includes sexual relations as part of the consideration may fall within these rules.

ii.   **The domestic servant model.**   Two people do not lose the right to enter and to enforce agreements with one another merely because they also share a sexual relationship. For example, a cook seduced by the employer can still sue if the employer refuses to pay the promised wages. Similarly, an employer who hires her lover as a cook cannot escape the obligation to pay wages because of their relationship.

c.   **Implicit sex.**   When the agreement does not explicitly mention sexual relations as part of the consideration for the contract, the agreement is not void under public policy. The courts prefer to assume that the agreements made within informal families reflect payment for services independent of sexual relations. This assumption honors the distinction between informal families and prostitution while ignoring the distinction between informal families and employment of domestic servants.

i.   **Careful drafting.**   This rule will permit almost any plaintiff to present the case to a jury or other finder of fact. Most cases involve allegations of an oral agreement. The complaint, drafted by competent counsel, will not allege that the agreement included a sexual relationship.

ii.   **Blind eye.**   The approach seems somewhat unrealistic. Though not expressly mentioned, sexual relations often are a material aspect of these agreements. The parties often would not have entered into the other terms of the agreement if they were not also sharing a bed. This seems particularly likely when the other terms involve sharing income or property equally or providing support for life — terms uncommon in the employment of domestic servants.

EXAMPLE AND ANALYSIS

Actor Lee Marvin lived with Michelle Triola for seven years. After they broke up, she sued alleging that he had promised to support her for life and to share equally all property acquired while they lived together, in exchange for her services as "companion, homemaker, housekeeper and cook." The trial court dismissed the action on public policy grounds. *Marvin v. Marvin*, 557 P.2d 106 (Cal. 1976). The state supreme court held that the agreement did not violate public policy because it was not "explicitly founded on the consideration of meretricious sexual services."

The court refused to award the plaintiff the remedies provided in the California Family Law Act. The contract, not the marital status, governed the parties' obligations to one another.

The court held out the possibility that even if no express contract existed, an action for unjust enrichment might be available if the services plaintiff provided enriched defendant.

On remand, plaintiff received nothing. The court found no express contract and no unjust enrichment. The trial court awarded some money for rehabilitation, but the appellate court reversed that award because no ground for liability existed. *See Marvin v. Marvin*, 122 Cal. App. 3d 871 (1981).

---

     d.   **Traditional rule.** Other courts have remained steadfast in their refusal to enforce contracts among unmarried cohabitants. In *Hewitt v. Hewitt*, 394 N.E.2d 1204 (Ill. 1979), the court refused to follow *Marvin*. The court held that the public policy favoring marriage was so strong that no exception should be permitted.

     e.   **Middle course.** Other states enforce express agreements, but refuse to allow claims based on unjust enrichment. *See Morone v. Morone*, 413 N.E.2d 1154 (N.Y. 1980). From a public policy standpoint, this is odd. One might expect a refusal to enforce the contract mitigated by a willingness to allow recovery for unjust enrichment. From a practical standpoint, this may be a good compromise. Express agreements may be easier to prove or rebut, minimizing the chance that the court will impose obligations on parties who did not intend to create a legally enforceable relationship.

C.   CONTRACTS IN RESTRAINT OF TRADE

To a large extent, contracts in restraint of trade are now regulated by antitrust laws. See, e.g., Sherman Antitrust Act, codified at 15 USC §1 (1996). Naturally, you do want to study antitrust law as you prepare for your contracts exam. These laws originated as doctrines of contract law. The doctrines continue to have effect in a few situations, which are discussed here.

1.   Elements

     a.   **A promise is unenforceable if it would unreasonably restrain trade.** Restatement (Second) of Contracts §186(a).

     b.   **A promise restrains trade if performance would limit competition or restrict the promisor's ability to pursue her occupation.** Restatement (Second) of Contracts §186(b).

c. **A promise that restrains trade is unreasonable unless it is "ancillary to an otherwise valid transaction."** Restatement (Second) of Contracts §187.

d. **A promise that restrains trade may be unreasonable even if ancillary to an otherwise valid agreement if certain elements pertain.**

   i. **The restraint is greater than needed to protect the promisee's legitimate interests.**

   ii. **The harm to the promisor and the public outweighs the promisee's need for protection.** Restatement (Second) of Contracts, §188(1).

2. **Restraint of Trade**

These rules embody the assumption that competition is good. The more competition, the more choices consumers have, including choices of various levels of price and quality. Thus, decreased competition injures the public interest. The same is true of competition for jobs. If some people cannot compete for a job, the person who gets the job may not be the best person for the job. Equally important, a person may have difficulty earning a living if she cannot pursue the occupation for which she is best qualified. Although such individuals may not end up on the public dole, the public loses the benefit of the best use of the individual's talents.

3. **Ancillary Provisions**

Nonetheless, some restraints of trade serve useful purposes. Although they may reduce competition in some ways, these restraints may enable people to enter otherwise valid contracts on better terms than would be available if they could not include a promise not to compete. Agreements in restraint of trade normally arise in these types of settings.

a. **Purchase of a business.** One party may buy a business from another but seek assurance that the seller will not open a competing business that will draw away all the customers. Buyers will pay more for a business that has an established clientele. Thus, the seller has an interest in being able to persuade the buyer that the clientele is reasonably likely to remain with the business.

b. **Employment.** An employer may want to give an employee access to sensitive information or useful training. If the employee can take the information or training and go work for competitors, employers will be reluctant to provide these benefits — or will only provide them if the employees pay for them (perhaps via decreased salaries). Employees who want promotions or training have an interest in assuring employers that they will not jump ship once they have the benefits.

    c. Legitimate business interests.   The promisor can benefit substantially by making a credible promise not to compete with the promisee. The promise is not a penalty against the promisor but a means by which the promisor is able to bargain for a gain she otherwise might not get.

4. Reasonable Limitations on Scope of Restraints

Because a promise not to compete can have a serious effect on society, the law enforces these promises only when they are narrowly drawn to protect the legitimate interests of the promisee. This usually involves three concerns.

    a. Limited time.   A promise not to compete should cover only a period necessary to prevent harm to the promisee. For example, the purchaser of a business should be able to establish her own relationship with the preexisting clientele within, say, a year or two. (The length will vary from business to business.) A promise not to compete that lasted longer than reasonably necessary to allow that opportunity would be unreasonable.

    b. Limited space.   A promise not to compete should be limited to the geographic area appropriate to the promisee's interests. Thus, the sale of a shoe store might require a seller to promise not to open a shoe store in the same county but probably would not require a promise not to open a shoe store anywhere in the world. On the other hand, an employer who competes worldwide may need to prevent an employee with key information from working for a competitor anywhere in the world.

    c. Limited market.   A promise not to compete should be limited to the type of business or employment in question. Thus, the sale of a shoe store would not justify a promise not to open any business (even, say, a delicatessen) in the county. Similarly, a noncompetition clause in an employment agreement probably could not include a promise not to work for a company whose products do not compete with the employer's wares.

5. Balancing the Hardships of Restraints

Sometimes, even reasonable restraints will harm the promisor. For example, a computer programmer whose employer sells a broad range of products worldwide might be unable to work in her chosen profession at all for a year or two after she quit. This hardship may be very great, both to her (because her capacity to support herself is significantly diminished) and to the public (which loses the value of her best skills). These arguments may not outweigh the promisee's interests in any given case. But when they do, courts will not enforce even an otherwise reasonable restraint of trade.

REVIEW QUESTIONS AND ANSWERS

Question: Under what circumstances will a court enforce a contract even though a statute prohibits enforcement?

Answer: In theory, none. The rules on public policy provide no exception if the legislature has specifically passed a law making a contract unenforceable. But we have read some of the judicially created exceptions to statutes of frauds (making some unwritten contracts unenforceable). See 4.B.6, 4.B.8. Thus, there may be room to argue for enforcement, even here. For example, if a person who hired an unlicensed lawyer sued the lawyer for damages, perhaps the court would enforce the contract despite the public policy. This, in effect, treats the contract as voidable rather than void. Or it may have more to do with malpractice than with contract.

Question: If no statute prohibits enforcement, when will a court refuse to enforce a contract on grounds of public policy?

Answer: If the policy against enforcement clearly outweighs the interests in enforcing the contract.

Question: What factors will a court consider in balancing interests for and against enforcement?

Answer: Weighing for enforcement, the court will consider the parties' justified expectations, any forfeiture that would result from nonenforcement, and any particular public interest in enforcement. Weighing against enforcement are the strength of the policy, the likelihood that refusing enforcement will further the policy, the seriousness of the misconduct, the deliberateness of the misconduct, and the directness of the connection between the contract and any misconduct.

Question: When will contracts among family members be enforced if they do not implicate the duties imposed by their family status?

Answer: When the agreements are express and proven by clear and convincing evidence. Some states may not impose both limitations, but most are slow to order compensation for services that arguably were gratuitous.

Question: Will courts enforce an agreement between unmarried cohabitants to share all the earnings and property they accumulate while living together?

Answer: If the agreement is express and does not explicitly refer to sexual relations as part of the consideration, many courts will enforce the agreement.

Some states refuse to enforce any agreement seeking to create the equivalent of a marriage by contract. At least one will enforce even an implied agreement of this sort. (The justifications are harder to state than the results.)

Question: Jo sold his book store to Chris for $70,000. As part of the contract, Jo promised not to open or work for any other book store anywhere in the county for two years. Is this restraint of trade enforceable?

Answer: Probably. The restraint is ancillary to a legitimate contract — the sale of the store. The geographical area seems reasonably limited, as does the nature of the prohibited business activities. The reasonableness of precluding competition for two years could be argued, but no obvious overreaching appears on these limited facts.

Part 2 · WHEN SHOULD THE LAW INTERVENE?

Part 1 addressed which promises are enforceable. The law, however, does not intervene in the vast majority of enforceable promises: Parties usually perform their duties or work out their disputes without any need for assistance from the courts (or even from lawyers, in most cases). The law intervenes only when one party accuses the other of failing to perform. This section introduces the issues that surround the inquiry into whether a breach occurred.

INTERPRETATION

To decide whether a party has breached, courts first must decide what the contract required. Thus, this part begins with a chapter on contract interpretation. Interpretation is not an issue in itself. Interpretation is used to answer other questions that arise, such as:

1. **Was performance due?** Contracts may specify conditions that must occur before a party must perform. A breach cannot occur unless the conditions occurred, making performance due. Courts must interpret the words of a contract to determine whether they specified a promise or a condition (or both) and what exactly must occur before performance is due.

2. **Did the party perform?** Even when the parties do not dispute what each did, they may disagree about whether the actions satisfy the contractual obligations. Courts must interpret the contract to determine what duties each party owed the other and whether their conduct complied with those duties.

LIMITS ON ENFORCEMENT

Even after deciding a party has not performed, the law may not provide a remedy for the breaching party. Two other issues may prevent enforcement of the contract:

3. **Was performance excused?** Unforeseen events, such as war or natural disasters, may make performance completely unreasonable. The parties can

draft their agreement in a way that compels performance regardless of intervening events, but courts usually do not assume the parties intended to require performance when it would produce draconian consequences. Thus, sometimes the law excuses nonperformance—particularly if the parties probably would have agreed to an excuse if they had discussed the issue in advance.

4.   **Is enforcement timely?** If a party repudiates a contract before performance is due (anticipatory repudiation), an aggrieved party may sue immediately. But some plaintiffs jump the gun, suing because they fear a breach. Courts must decide whether suit was premature.

These are the key issues addressed in the chapters of this section. They focus on the second element of the cause of action for breach of contract. See 1.C.3.a.

INTERPRETATION: WHAT DOES THE CONTRACT REQUIRE?

 ## CHAPTER OVERVIEW

To decide whether either party has breached a contract, the court must decide what the contract required the party to do. Only then can it compare the party's actions to the requirements set by the contract. Deciding what the contract requires is called interpretation.

Start by finding the words the parties used—easier in a written than in an oral contract.

If the parties expressed agreement upon what the words meant, apply that meaning.

- Definitions in the contract may reveal their intended meaning.
- Statements during negotiation may reveal their intended meaning.
- Other clauses may reveal the meaning the parties intended.

Inferences about meaning may arise from usage at other times or by other parties.

- Usage of trade. Parties in a trade probably use words the same way others in the trade use them.
- Course of dealing. Parties who used words in prior dealings with one another probably used the words the same way this time.
- Course of performance. If a party has not objected to performance that met one meaning of the terms in the past, that may indicate she thought the performance satisfied the meaning of the term.
  - Express language is better than these inferences.
  - Course of performance is better than course of dealing or usage of trade.
  - Course of dealing is better than usage of trade.

Canons of construction offer some rules of thumb in interpreting language.

- An interpretation that would make a contract legal is better than one that would not.
- An interpretation consistent with all terms is better than one that makes terms inconsistent.
- An interpretation that gives all terms effect is better than one that makes some superfluous.
- When all else fails, courts sometimes interpret the contract against the drafting party.

Statutes and context may indicate that some promise was implied, even if not expressed.

- All contracts include an obligation of good faith.
- The UCC includes several default terms that fill in details the parties may have omitted.
- Express terms govern over default terms — though some statutory duties are not waivable.

IMPORTANT NOTE

Interpretation is not a separate issue that you can address on an exam. It is a tool you use in analyzing other issues. You will not write a separate section headed interpretation. But in discussing performance and breach — and some other issues, such as illusoriness — you may need to ascertain what the terms of an agreement actually mean. That is when you will resort to the tools mentioned here.

A.   GENERAL TECHNIQUES OF INTERPRETATION

The decision that a contract exists embodies an assumption that the parties assented to **the same** terms. The goal of interpretation is to decide what the parties intended the terms of the contract to mean. At the time of formation, the parties apparently shared common ground — they each had a reason to want to enter the transaction and they (usually) agreed on words that expressed that agreement. To the extent possible, interpretation seeks to identify and to give effect to that common ground. As always, secret intent plays no part in the interpretative process; words and actions are interpreted objectively.

1.   Express Language

Usually, the words the parties chose to express their agreement provide the best indication of what the parties intended. The express language of the contract, therefore, is the usual starting place for all interpretation.

a.   **Examination technique.**

   i.   **Identify exactly the word(s) you need to interpret.**   Most interpretation techniques are specific; they must be applied to particular language, not to the contract in general. Some sources of meaning allow you to interpret the contract without interpreting particular words. But others do not. Focus on particular words will prevent the development of sloppy habits that will obscure your exam answer—and are likely to produce problems in practice, as well.

   (a)   **Oral contracts.**   Such contracts may make it difficult to identify the exact words of an agreement. The first step may be to decide what words were agreed. Then you can interpret the agreed words.

   (b)   **Exams versus practice.**   Most exams will involve written contracts or oral contracts in which the conversation itself is not disputed. It is difficult for a professor to construct a problem that calls for you to investigate the facts and decide what each party actually said when the other alleges a different conversation. Thus, you generally will know the exact words to be interpreted.

   ii.   **Identify what meaning each party seeks to attach to those terms.**   Interpretation does not involve finding the one true meaning of particular words. It involves deciding which of the alternative interpretations is most plausible or best fits the context. Before arguing for one interpretation or another, identify each plausible interpretation a party might present.

   (a)   **No contest.**   Sometimes, all plausible interpretations favor the same party. When that happens, say so. You may not need to explore the meaning of a term in detail if, no matter what it means, the same party wins. [Some professors may want you to explore the meaning in depth anyway. Adapt accordingly.]

   (b)   **Be creative.**   Carefully consider whether other interpretations are possible that favor the other side. When testing interpretation, professors usually have in mind at least one interpretation that would favor each party. If you don't see it at first, consider what, if anything, a term would need to mean to favor the other party. If you come up with something plausible, rebut it.

(c)   **Keep moving.**   If all interpretations favor one party, consider two other possibilities: (i) interpretation is not one of the issues the professor wants you to write about on this exam, thus no ambiguity was placed in the terms; or (ii) some other term is ambiguous and requires interpretation. Don't waste too much time interpreting clear terms.

iii.   **Select appropriate techniques for interpreting the unclear terms.**   There is no reason to apply every technique to every term. Choose the techniques that you have facts to support or that provide the best indication of what the parties intended.

2.   Agreed Meaning

The first place to look for meaning is in the contract itself. Parties may define terms in the contract. When they do, that definition governs. The Restatement calls for the use of generally prevailing meaning "**unless a different intention is manifested.**" Restatement (Second) of Contracts §202(3). Thus, parties may define cotton to mean the fleece of an ovine creature (wool) or cash to mean checks or letters of credit (in addition to currency), as long as they express that definition in the agreement.

a.   **Oral definitions.**   An intention to use a word in an unconventional way must be manifest, but that does not necessarily require that it be written. In an oral agreement, all manifestations are oral. Oral statements may affect the interpretation of written agreements, too. The parol evidence rule may limit oral manifestations when a final integrated writing exists — but usually not if a term of the writing is ambiguous. *See* 14.E.2.

b.   **Written definitions.**   Careful practitioners include a section of definitions in written contracts. But not every ambiguity can be anticipated. Sometimes words the parties thought were perfectly clear turn out to be ambiguous. (Before you took a contracts course, would you have thought "chicken" was ambiguous? What about "dozen"? Even in a bakery?)

c.   **Manifestations not necessarily definitions.**   Sometimes, the terms of a contract make sense when interpreted one way but produce odd results if interpreted another. These indications of meaning are internal to the contract, arising from the parties' manifestations of assent. They can provide clues to meaning as easily as definitions.

 # EXAMPLE AND ANALYSIS

Plaintiff, a Swiss company, ordered frozen chickens from defendant, an American company. Plaintiff argued that the word "chicken" meant young chickens (broilers) as opposed to old chickens (stewing fowl). When defendant shipped old chickens, plaintiff sued. The court held that the plaintiff failed to satisfy its burden of proof to show chicken meant young chickens. *Frigaliment Importing v. B. N. S. Intl. Sales*, 190 F. Supp. 116 (S.D.N.Y. 1960).

During negotiations, defendant asked plaintiff's agent what kind of chicken it wanted and was told "any kind of chickens." The agent also used the German word *huhn*, which both parties agree included old chickens. This oral response supported plaintiff's contention that the parties intended the word chicken to include old chickens.

The contract called for chickens of two weights. Only young chickens came in the lighter weight. Plaintiff argued this meant the heavier weight also required young chickens, as the same word applied to each. This inconsistency is the kind of non-definitional argument that can shed light on meaning. The court rejected the argument. If "chicken" is a general word, covering both young and old chickens, it would not cease to be general simply because other terms (weight) limited it in one clause. Thus, the weight term did not manifest an intent to use the word "chicken" in some special way.

3. Plain Meaning

When parties have not specified a different meaning, words may be given their usual, or "generally prevailing," meaning. Restatement (Second) of Contracts §202(3). This rule allows courts to look at dictionaries and other customary reference sources.

4. Special Meaning

Some terms have technical or special meanings in some fields or localities. When used in a transaction within that field or locality, the word should be given its special meaning—unless another intent is manifest. Thus, in a bakery, dozen may mean 13, not 12.

B. INFERENCES

Efforts to discern the parties' intent are not limited to linguistic reference materials. Often, the parties' conduct will give rise to inferences concerning what they intended a word or phrase to mean. This is particularly true when the parties deal with one another repeatedly — either under a single contract or under a series of contracts using the same language.

1. Usage of Trade

Sometimes a practice becomes customary in a particular trade. Persons within the trade expect that the custom will apply to all transactions within the trade unless otherwise specified. When such a usage of trade exists, terms of a contract will be interpreted in light of that usage of trade.

   a. **Usage of trade may give special meaning to terms.** Parties may argue that a particular term has a special meaning when used in the trade. To this extent, the rule overlaps with the provision on special meaning noted above. *See* 12.A.4.

   b. **Usage of trade may provide an additional term the parties did not expressly write into the contract.** Courts may provide omitted terms when the parties clearly intended to make a contract. Restatement (Second) of Contracts §204. Usage of trade may help a court decide what term the parties intended to govern their conduct.

   c. **Usage of trade requires nearly universal understanding.** When trade practice is inconsistent, it is harder to infer that the parties' silence incorporated one particular approach.

   d. **Usage of trade may not apply to newcomers to the trade.** Newcomers will be governed by trade usage if they have actual knowledge of the usage or if the community outside the trade is so familiar with the usage that the newcomer's knowledge can be inferred. *Frigaliment Importing v. B. N. S. Intl. Sales*, 190 F. Supp. 116 (S.D.N.Y. 1960). Some jurisdictions may not be so solicitous to newcomers; they may hold them to usage of trade on a lesser showing, expecting newcomers to become familiar with the trade, rather than excusing their ignorance.

 # EXAMPLE AND ANALYSIS

Frigaliment also involved allegations that, within the poultry trade, "chicken" meant broiler or fryer, not stewing fowl. The court held that plaintiff failed to establish such a trade usage.

Actions speak louder than words. Some of the witnesses who testified that chicken meant young chickens carefully specified broilers or fowl when they entered contracts. Others asked the buyer to clarify the age during negotiations. The court held their practice suggested the understanding was not sufficiently general to constitute a usage of trade.

Several witnesses testified that chicken was a general term, requiring further specification. Their stature within the industry rebutted the existence of any consensus on the meaning of chicken.

2. Course of Dealing

Parties who have dealt with one another in the past may expect words in the current contract to have the same meaning that they had in other contracts. Thus, when the parties' conduct has established a meaning under prior contracts, courts may interpret the current contract in the same way.

 ## EXAMPLE AND ANALYSIS

Gulf promised to supply Eastern with all the aviation fuel it required at the Miami airport. An OPEC oil embargo made the contract disadvantageous for Gulf. It alleged (among other things) that Eastern breached its obligation of good faith and fair dealing by a practice called "fuel freighting." Basically, this involved filling at airports where the local contract made fuel cheaper so they could avoid refueling at cities where the local contract made fuel more expensive. The practice had been common throughout the 30 years Gulf and Eastern had done business under various contracts, without any objection from Gulf. The court interpreted the contract to permit fuel freighting based on this course of dealing and course of performance. Thus, fuel freighting was not a breach of good faith. *Eastern Air Lines v. Gulf Oil*, 415 F. Supp. 429 (S.D. Fla. 1975).

3. Course of Performance

Course of performance refers to the way the parties have performed in the past under the contract being interpreted. By definition, it can apply only if the contract involves multiple performances (e.g., repaying a loan or delivering goods in monthly installments).

a.   **Evidence of actual intent.**   If prior performance has been accepted without objection, that may indicate that the parties interpreted the terms such that the performance complied with the contract. Restatement (Second) of Contracts §202(4); UCC §2-208.

   i.   **Opportunity to object.**   Inferring a party's actual interpretation works only if she knew enough to realize the performance might not comply and had an opportunity to object to it. Silence explained by ignorance or a lack of opportunity to object offers little indication of the meaning attached by the parties.

   ii.   **Unchallenged performance.**   An objection to performance precludes an argument based on course of performance. In *Frigaliment* ("what is chicken?"), defendant alleged that plaintiff's acceptance of the first shipment of old chickens indicated that old chickens satisfied the contract. The court rejected this inference because plaintiff promptly protested upon discovering the first shipment involved old chickens.

b.   **Waiver or modification.**   A party might not object to performance even if she believed it did not comply with the requirements of the contract. She might prefer not to sue, at least for this one breach, in effect waiving the nonconformity. Waiver, however, is revocable (unless reliance creates an estoppel), at least under the UCC. *See* UCC §2-209(5). Alternatively, conduct may indicate the parties intended to modify the contract. Tender of the nonconforming performance could offer a modification; accepting it without objection could accept the modification.

   i.   **Intuitive appeal.**   Because course of performance involves conduct after formation of the contract, it is easier to view the lack of objection as changing what was originally agreed rather than evincing what was originally agreed.

   ii.   **Factual inquiry.**   A party may accept performance because it is within her understanding of what the contract required. The fact that others would interpret the contract differently is unimportant if the parties themselves intended the contract to allow this kind of performance. Thus, waiver and modification have no inherent advantage over using course of performance to interpret the agreement. The issue is factual.

4.   Priorities of Construction

When arguments point in different directions, a court may need to decide which factor deserves more weight. The following general guidelines help balance conflicting evidence. Generally, they give priority to arguments that relate most closely to what the individual parties actually said and did, with less weight to inferences drawn from words or actions more removed from their attention.

a.   **Specific language deserves more weight than general language.** Specific terms suggest the parties actually contemplated a particular type of situation. General terms are more abstract. The specific governs, even if it creates an exception to the general rule. Restatement (Second) of Contracts §203(c).

b.   **Negotiated terms deserve more weight than standardized terms.** Terms the parties added to a form received the parties' actual attention when they assented to the agreement. These terms may be exceptions to terms in the printed form. Restatement (Second) of Contracts §203(d).

c.   **Express terms deserve more weight than inferences from conduct.** Thus, course of dealing, course of performance, and usage of trade should not govern when the contract itself clearly expresses the performance required. Restatement (Second) of Contracts §203(b); UCC §2-208. (Course of performance, however, still might establish a waiver or a modification.)

d.   **Course of dealing and course of performance deserve more weight than usage of trade.** The parties' conduct may show they preferred to deal on unconventional terms. The parties' conduct deserves more weight than industry custom. Restatement (Second) of Contracts §203(b).

e.   **Course of performance deserves more weight than course of dealing.** More recent conduct should govern over past conduct. Restatement (Second) of Contracts §203(b).

C.   CANONS OF CONSTRUCTION

Courts have generated many guidelines that describe how people usually use language. The guidelines, or canons, offer an inference concerning what the parties meant by their words. Many canons are general; they will apply to interpreting statutes as well as to interpreting contracts. Some of these guidelines may help you in a contracts exam.

1.   Inferences, Not Rules

All these canons represent intuitions about how people usually use language. **They are subordinate to evidence that the parties actually intended**

to use language differently. They are rules of thumb for divining intent, not rules imposed upon parties who harbored a different intent.

2.   Government Regulations

When possible, interpret a contract to require performance that is consistent with the law (or public policy) rather than requiring illegal conduct. The parties probably intended to remain within the law. Rather than interpreting an agreement as illegal (and therefore unenforceable), courts usually give the parties the benefit of the doubt. Of course, where there is no doubt that the parties wanted an illegal performance, this canon cannot apply. Restatement (Second) of Contracts §203(a).

a.   Incorporation by reference.   Parties may, but need not, incorporate government regulations into their contracts. When the government has defined a term in a particular way, the parties also may intend to use the term that way. But that is a question of fact. The parties are not required to follow the usage of the government. They may use language in any way they like.

b.   Example (*Frigaliment*).   The defendant argued that USDA regulations defined chicken to include both young and old chickens. On its own, that fact is either irrelevant or relevant only in the context of whether a trade usage exists. But the parties' contract referred to the USDA regulations, at least to the grading system for chickens. The court took this as some evidence that the parties intended to make the government regulations their dictionary.

3.   Inconsistent Terms

When a term can be interpreted in a manner that is consistent with other terms in the contract, that interpretation is preferred. Sometimes a contract contains two terms that seem inconsistent — at least, they would be inconsistent if interpreted as one party proposes. Parties who included both terms probably thought they were consistent, not contradictory, at the time they wrote the agreement. Thus, interpreting the terms as consistent with one another probably comports with the parties' original intent. Restatement (Second) of Contracts §202(5).

 # EXAMPLE AND ANALYSIS

Trident borrowed money from the insurance company to build an office building. The loan documents prohibited prepayment in the first 12 years. The contract also provided that, if Trident defaulted during those years, the lender could accelerate the loan (demand immediate payment in full), including a 10% prepayment penalty. Interest rates fell and Trident wanted to prepay the loan. It argued that it had a right to prepay the loan by paying the 10% penalty. That interpretation would be inconsistent with the provision that prohibited prepayment. The court preferred to interpret the penalty provision as an option the lender, not Trident, could exercise—and that only if Trident defaulted. *Trident Ctr. v. Connecticut Gen. Life Ins.*, 847 F.2d 564 (9th Cir. 1988). (Issues under the parol evidence rule prevented the court from resolving the case until further evidence was taken on remand.)

---

    a. Reformation of truly inconsistent terms. Parties usually do not intend to include terms that irreconcilably contradict one another. If one clause was included by mistake, a court can correct the mistake by reforming the contract, deleting or amending the inadvertent term—as long as the evidence permits it to determine which term was included by mistake. See 13.B.

    b. Interpretation priorities. Sometimes courts can resolve inconsistencies by resorting to the priorities noted earlier—preferring a specific term over a general or a negotiated term over boilerplate. See 12.B.4.a through 12.B.4.b.

    c. Last resort. Rarely will these techniques fail to resolve the issue—in part because lawyers and judges show remarkable ingenuity in interpreting contracts. If unable to reform, reconcile, or interpret them appropriately, a court probably would refuse to enforce either of the inconsistent terms. The court might apply a gap filler or find no assent existed in the first place. The latter is unlikely; if the terms were sufficiently fundamental to undermine the entire agreement, the parties probably would have noticed and corrected the contradiction up front.

4. Superfluous Terms

When a term can be interpreted in a way that gives effect to all terms in the contract, that interpretation is preferred. Sometimes one interpretation of a term would make some other term of the contract superfluous. Parties who included both terms probably thought that both terms had some effect. Otherwise, they would have saved their time and ink by omitting the superfluous term. Thus, interpreting terms in a way that does not render other terms superfluous probably comports with the parties' original intent. Restatement (Second) of Contracts §203(a).

EXAMPLE AND ANALYSIS

A bond issue required the issuer (1) to pay interest to the bondholders (2) once the bonds matured. Another provision provided for interest when the bonds became "due and payable." The bonds became due and payable after I defaulted. I argued that it did not owe interest because the phrase "due and payable" meant "due and payable at maturity." (The bonds had not matured yet.) That interpretation would make the "due and payable" provision superfluous; there would be no need to include it at all because another provision already allowed interest at maturity. Thus, a court would interpret the phrase "due and payable" to include due and payable upon a default, giving that term some effect.

5.   Interpretation against Drafter

When a term is susceptible to equally plausible interpretations, the court may reject the interpretation offered by the party who drafted the contract in favor of the interpretation advanced by another party. Restatement (Second) of Contracts §206.

a.   Blaming the drafter.   This rule seems to blame the drafter for the ambiguity; if only she had chosen words more carefully, the court would not need to resolve doubt concerning the meaning of this term. That approach, however, would produce a very limited rule. It would apply only when fault existed. When the parties had no reason to know their language would prove ambiguous, neither should be penalized for the choice of words. And it would be a last resort. If other factors allowed a court to choose one interpretation as more reasonable than another, it need not break the tie by recourse to this canon.

b.   Unconscionability.   The rule originated to avoid unconscionable results. A drafter may have the power to draft terms more favorably to itself, especially when form contracts are involved. A drafter might include an ambiguous term intentionally, planning to decide later how she preferred the term to be interpreted. Before courts refused to enforce terms on grounds of unconscionability, they avoided harsh results by finding ambiguities in the terms and interpreting them against the drafter.

i.   Limited to imposition.   When neither party imposed a term on the other, courts are less likely to interpret the agreement against the drafter. Courts sometimes reason that they cannot tell which party selected the language, even if they know who prepared the draft, when the parties negotiated on fairly even footing. See *Joyner v. Adams*, 361 S.E.2d 902 (N.C. Ct. App. 1987) (lease of property for commercial development not construed against lessee who drafted it because record did not show the language in question "was actually chosen" by lessee).

     ii.   **Policy, not interpretation.** Used to fight unconscionability, the canon does not really involve interpretation. The court does not seek the parties' meaning but refuses to enforce an unfair provision even if the parties intended to agree to that term.

     iii.   **Diminishing importance.** Today courts can address unconscionability directly. See UCC §2-302. Thus, outside the insurance context, they resort to this canon less often.

  c.   **Legally required terms.** Only terms the parties create are susceptible to interpretation against the drafter. Some state statutes require that contracts of a particular type (especially insurance contracts) include specific terms. Those terms are interpreted to further the intent of the legislature. They will not be construed against the drafter, regardless of who wrote the contract. Nor will a court interpret them against the legislature, no matter how unclear, because that might undermine the policy the legislature sought to pursue.

D. FILLING GAPS IN THE AGREEMENT

As noted earlier, when the parties intend to make a contract, courts will enforce the contract even when the parties have not agreed on all the terms necessary to complete the transaction. This section addresses how courts fill these gaps in the negotiations. For a discussion of when courts fill in gaps (and when they do not), see 2.B through 2.H.

1. Terms Implied from Context

Often, terms the parties have agreed on will suggest other terms they intended to govern the transaction, even though those terms were not expressed. Careful reading of the agreement will allow inferences concerning the parties' mutual intent.

 # EXAMPLE AND ANALYSIS

Lucy gave Wood an exclusive right to place her endorsement on fashion items. Lucy promised Wood half the revenue from her endorsements. The written agreement, however, did not explicitly require Wood to make any efforts to place endorsements. With no return promise, Lucy arguably received no consideration and, thus, need not perform the unenforceable agreement. *Wood v. Lucy, Lady Duff-Gordon*, 118 N.E. 214 (N.Y. 1917).

The court identified several aspects of the agreement that implied the parties expected Wood to use his services to obtain endorsements. These provisions included Wood's promise to make monthly accounting of any profits; his promise to obtain necessary patents, copyrights, and trademarks; and the recital that Wood possessed a business organization suitable to obtaining endorsements. In context, the court decided that the agreement obligated Wood to make reasonable efforts to endorse products in Lucy's name. (Thus, Wood had made a promise, Lucy had received consideration, and Lucy had no excuse for failing to perform.)

---

2.   Terms Implied by Good Faith

Each party's obligation to act in good faith may lead a court to infer some duties or promises not expressly stated in the agreement.

a.   Obligation of good faith and fair dealing.   Every contract includes an obligation of good faith and fair dealing, either by common-law decision or by statute. See, e.g., UCC §1-203. Even if the contract does not mention good faith, courts will include it among each party's duties.

b.   Good faith defined.   Generally, good faith means "honesty in fact." UCC §1-201(19). For a merchant, good faith also requires "observance of reasonable commercial standards of fair dealing in the trade." UCC §2-103(1)(a).

c.   Implications of good faith.   The requirement of good faith may require a party to do things not specifically mentioned in the agreement. Failure to do them would not breach any express term, but would breach the obligation of good faith.

 EXAMPLE AND ANALYSIS

Recall *Mattei v. Hopper*, 330 P.2d 625 (Cal. 1958). Mattei promised to buy Hopper's land (for a shopping center) if his broker obtained satisfactory leases for the project. The writing did not explicitly require Mattei to seek leases. (Thus, Hopper argued she received no consideration.) The court determined that Mattei had an obligation to evaluate the satisfactoriness of leases obtained by the broker in good faith. Presumably, the court would also infer an obligation to make good faith efforts to obtain leases. Thus, Mattei could not simply change his mind, avoid seeking leases, and use the lack of satisfactory leases to avoid the contract.

---

d. **Sincerity versus pretense.** Honesty may be vague, but at a minimum it includes sincerity and excludes pretense. If Mattei obtained satisfactory leases but pretended they were not satisfactory, his pretense would not be honest and would breach the duty of good faith. If Mattei sincerely was dissatisfied with the leases, it would have been honest (and, thus, good faith) to say so — even if a reasonable person would have been satisfied with the leases.

e. **Good faith before contract formation.** Until the parties enter the contract, they are acting individually, for their own benefit. Once they agree, their mutual purposes may require cooperation beyond the text of their agreement. Until the parties have entered the agreement, however, they usually are not bound by duties of good faith. (Some provisions of the Restatement imply good faith may apply during negotiations. See, e.g., Restatement (Second) of Contracts §161. These provisions are exceptional.)

3. **Terms Implied by Statute: Default Rules or Gap Fillers**

The UCC provides a wealth of provisions that will govern unless the parties specify their own terms. These terms are gathered primarily in the sections that begin 2-3xx. A few examples are shown below.

a. **Right to contract around statutes.** Most of the terms provided by the UCC are not imposed upon the parties. Rather, they apply only if the parties fail to specify how they want particular situations to be handled. The parties retain the right to agree to any other term they prefer (within some limits).

b. **Obligation of good faith and fair dealing.** Every contract includes an obligation of good faith and fair dealing. See UCC §§1-203, 2-306(b). Unlike most other default rules, this rule is not prefaced with the words "unless otherwise agreed." Most states treat this obligation as unwaivable.

c. **Time for delivery.** Unless otherwise agreed, delivery must occur within a reasonable time after formation of the contract. UCC §2-309(a).

d.   Place of delivery.   With some exceptions, delivery is to be made at the seller's place of business (or residence, if seller is not a business) unless the parties agree otherwise. UCC §2-308.

e.   One lot or two?   Unless otherwise agreed, all goods must be delivered in a single delivery. UCC §2-307.

f.   Time and place for payment.   Unless otherwise agreed, payment is due at the time and place the buyer receives the goods (which, when goods are shipped, may not be the place of delivery).

g.   Price.   Unless otherwise agreed, the price is a reasonable price at the time for delivery. UCC §2-305.

4.   Implied Warranties

A number of UCC default provisions deal with **warranties**: assurances regarding the quality of goods. As with other default terms, the parties may exclude most warranties by agreement. The UCC often requires special notice to disclaim a warranty. The details, although important in upper-level courses on the UCC, will not be discussed here. The fundamentals of warranties, however, are outlined here.

a.   Terminology: Warranty versus guaranty.   In common usage, people sometimes refer to warranties as guaranties. In law, these terms are not synonymous. Guaranty is a term of art referring to a promise to pay another's debt if the debtor fails to pay it. (At one time, your parents may have agreed to guaranty your debts — cosigning a loan or a lease, for example.) Warranties are assurances regarding the quality of goods. In class and in practice, try to use each term precisely.

b.   Warranty of title.   Unless specifically disclaimed, every sale includes a warranty that the seller has title to the goods and that they are conveyed free of any liens. UCC §2-312.

c.   Warranty of merchantability.   Unless specifically disclaimed, every sale **by a merchant** includes a warranty that the goods are merchantable. Merchantable means that the goods would pass without objection in the trade; are of average quality, "are fit for the ordinary purposes for which such goods are used," are of roughly even quality, are adequately packaged, and conform to the label. UCC §2-314.

d.   Warranty of fitness for a specific purpose.   Unless specifically disclaimed, a contract includes a warranty that the goods are fit for the buyer's purpose if (1) the seller has reason to know the particular purpose for which buyer wants the goods, and (2) the seller knows the buyer is relying on the seller's skill to select suitable goods. UCC §2-315.

REVIEW QUESTIONS AND ANSWERS

Question: Define:

1.   Course of performance
2.   Course of dealing
3.   Usage of trade

Answer: Course of performance refers to performance under an existing contract that would be appropriate under one interpretation of the language and to which no objection was made.

Course of dealing refers to the interpretation parties applied to the same language when used in prior contracts between them.

Usage of trade refers to the meaning attached to a term by virtually everyone in particular business.

Question: A university cafeteria promised to buy 100 dozen bagels per week from a local bakery. The written contract specifically defines the word "dozen" to mean 12. In the bakery trade, however, dozen means 13. The first two weeks, the bakery sent 1,300 bagels and the university paid for 100 dozen. In the third week the bakery sent 1,200 bagels. The university objected that this was a breach of contract. How many bagels per week is the university entitled to receive?

Answer: The performance for the first two weeks establishes a course of performance, under which dozen would mean 13 and the university would be entitled to 1,300 bagels per week. Usage of trade in the bakery business also supports the university's right to 1,300 bagels per week. Express contract terms, however, supersede both course of performance and usage of trade. Thus, dozen means 12. The university is entitled to receive only 1,200 bagels per week.

Question: A customer saw a dog in a pet store and asked to buy "that Collie and two more like her." The store agreed to sell the Collie to the customer and to order two more Collies for her. The dog really was a Shelty (Shetland Sheepdog), which resembles a collie but is smaller. The store tendered two more Shelties. The customer refused to accept delivery because the two dogs were not Collies but kept the first dog, for which she had already paid. Does the contract require the store to provide Collies or Shelties?

Answer: Collie has a clear meaning, both in English and in the trade, and does not mean Shelty in either one. The parties, however, can define a word any way they like. From context, it appears that the parties defined "Collie" to mean "Shelty": The customer asked for Collies just like the one that she bought (i.e., a Shelty). That's idiosyncratic but not forbidden. If the customer had a particular reason for wanting a Collie, the first transaction may be voidable for mutual mistake. See Chapter 9. Because the customer found the first "Collie" acceptable, she may need to accept the other "Collies." Accepting the first dog could establish a course of performance. But express terms would govern over course of performance. Nor does an implicit modification work well here. The conduct that arguably modified the agreement was conduct at the time the agreement was made. Thus, the agreement seems to have called for Shelties from the start. It did not call for Collies the first day, then get changed to call for Shelties later.

Question: While browsing at a swap meet one morning, Pat saw an old car she just had to own. She spoke with Terry, the owner, and they agreed that Pat would pay $4,000 for the car. Pat offered a check, but Terry wanted cash. Pat said she needed to go to the bank, but that she definitely wanted the car. Pat jotted a quick note stating the price and identifying the car, which both of them signed. Pat then left to get the cash. She returned as the swap meet was closing, but Terry had already sold the car to another. Terry said that when Pat didn't return by 4 P.M., Terry assumed Pat had changed her mind. Has Terry breached the contract?

Answer: It depends on when payment was due. The facts do not specify whether the parties agreed on a particular time, so let's assume they did not. (If they did, the answer depends on whether Pat returned with the cash before that time.) The UCC provides that when a time for payment or delivery is not specified, it should occur within a reasonable time. How long is reasonable depends on the specific facts. The delay of only a few hours here seems reasonable — though one can imagine facts that would make it seem undue. (Perhaps Terry needed to sell the car before she left town the next day. If it was Saturday and the banks closed at noon, Terry reasonably might believe that Pat's failure to return for several hours after the banks closed indicated she could not raise the money.)

Note: The last few questions force you to put interpretation in the context of a contract dispute. That is inevitable. Interpretation helps you decide what the contract required on the way to deciding whether it was breached or performed. The interpretation step can be easy (within a reasonable time) or hard (Collie means Shelty?). But it is only one step of a process.

13 Effect of Parties' Mistakes on Interpretation: Misunderstanding and Mistake of Integration

 Chapter Overview

Manifestation of assent exists when the parties agree on the same words. Sometimes, however, the parties hold different views of what these words mean. Each believed she knew what the term required, but the meanings they attached differed, perhaps significantly. Misunderstanding and mistake of integration cover two ways the law addresses these differences.

If parties attached different meanings to a term at formation, a court may interpret the agreement to conform with one party's meaning if:

- That party had no knowledge of the other's meaning but the other knew of her meaning; or
- That party had no reason to know of the other's meaning but the other had reason to know of her meaning.

If parties attached different meanings to a term at formation, a court may decide that no assent exists if:

- Neither party knew or had reason to know of the other's meaning; or
- Each party knew or had reason to know of the other's meaning.

When a writing fails to reflect the agreement the parties reached, a court may **reform** the writing to accurately state the agreement.

- Reformation usually requires that the party's actually agreed on a term different from the one that appears in the writing.
- If one party knows a writing does not contain the terms the other thinks it contains, her failure to disclose the mistake, if fraudulent, would justify reformation.

Reformation usually requires clear and convincing evidence.

Reformation may be denied if it would affect the rights of third parties who had no notice that the terms of the writing were inaccurate.

A. MISUNDERSTANDING

Misunderstanding exists when parties enter an agreement, each believing that a term has a meaning different from the meaning the other party attaches to the term. Arguably, this means the parties never really assented: They may have manifested assent by signing the same written agreement, but they never agreed on the misunderstood term. **Courts are reluctant to hold that the parties never assented based on a misunderstanding.** That would make a party's secret intention regarding what the terms of an agreement meant an excuse for not performing. Secret intentions are difficult for courts to discern and easy for parties to make up after the fact. Giving them weight would undermine people's ability to rely on contracts. Thus, **courts prefer to interpret contracts**, rather than declare assent never existed.

1. Exam Tip: Misunderstanding versus Mutual Mistake of Basic Assumption

Usually, mistakes about the content of a contract, including the meaning of its terms, should be addressed under the rules described in this section. Treating a mistake about the content or meaning of a contract as a mistake of basic assumption can produce some very complex and unwieldy arguments. In theory, (unilateral) mistake of basic assumption or misrepresentation can serve as a fallback if the rules presented here do not produce a favorable outcome. In practice that theory may be worth exploring. On an exam, the time required to analyze linguistic errors under mistake-of-basic assumption rules probably will not increase your overall score much but may consume time better spent addressing other, more important issues.

2. Misunderstanding as an Aid to Interpretation

If parties claim they intended different meanings when they entered an agreement, courts first try to interpret the contract. A court may enforce one meaning even if a party did not realize the contract had that meaning at the time she entered the agreement, as long as each party objectively manifested assent to that meaning.

a. **Basic rule: Knew or should have known.** Misunderstandings may govern interpretation in two situations. Restatement (Second) of Contracts §201(2).

i. **Actual knowledge.** When one party knew the other attached a different meaning to a term, but the other party did not know the first attached a different meaning to the term, the contract will be interpreted in accordance with the meaning attached by the second (unaware) party.

 EXAMPLE AND ANALYSIS

O, a mall owner, leases a store to M, a merchant. In the lease, M promises not to sell "spirits" on the premises. M believes that "spirits" means only distilled spirits, but M knows O believes the term precludes the sale of any alcoholic beverage, including beer and wine. O does not know that M believes "spirits" is limited to distilled spirits. Upon this evidence, a court would interpret "spirits" to include beer and wine. Thus, the lease would prevent their sale by M.

ii. **Reason to know.** When one party had reason to know of the meaning attached by the other, but the other party had no reason to know the first attached a different meaning to a term, the contract will be interpreted in accordance with the meaning attached by the second party (the one with no reason to be aware).

 EXAMPLE AND ANALYSIS

O, a mall owner, leases a store to M, a merchant. In the lease, M promises not to sell "spirits" on the premises. O believes the term precludes the sale of any alcoholic beverage, including beer and wine. M believes that "spirits" means only distilled spirits, which is the meaning usually attached to the term in the dictionary and in the trade. O does not know that M believes "spirits" is limited to distilled spirits. But the common use, in the trade and the dictionary, may mean O had **reason to know** the term had a different meaning. On this evidence, a court probably would interpret "spirits" to exclude beer and wine. Thus, the lease would not prevent their sale by M.

b. **Plausible interpretations.**   Misunderstanding requires two plausible interpretations of the contract language. When a party proposes an implausible meaning for a term, courts need not rely on misunderstanding to interpret the agreement. A person arguably has reason to know an implausible meaning was not the meaning the other party intended. Alternatively, a court may find it incredible that the party actually believed the term had an implausible meaning, concluding that she is merely grasping at a straw to escape an agreement she intended to enter but now regrets.

3. **Misunderstanding as Negating Assent**

Sometimes, the interpretive process fails. Both meanings are plausible and neither party's awareness of multiple meanings allows the court to prefer the other's meaning. In these cases, courts may hold that the parties never assented to a contract.

a. **Elements.**   Misunderstanding prevents assent if "the parties attach materially different meanings to their manifestations and (a) neither party knows or has reason to know the meaning attached by the other; or (b) each party knows or has reason to know the meaning attached by the other." Restatement (Second) of Contracts §20.

 # EXAMPLE AND ANALYSIS

Plaintiff sold defendant cotton "to arrive ex Peerless" from Bombay. Several ships were named Peerless, including two that left Bombay carrying some cotton after the formation of this contract. Plaintiff tendered cotton from the second ship to leave. Defendant refused to accept it, claiming that it thought the agreement referred to the first ship to leave. *Raffles v. Wichelhaus*, 2 Hurl. & C. 906 (Ct. Exch. 1864). Held: for defendant. The agreement did not specify either Peerless and neither party had reason to know the other meant a different ship.

 # EXAMPLE AND ANALYSIS

Plaintiff agreed to buy defendant's Swiss coin collection. Plaintiff intended to buy all Swiss coins owned by defendant. Defendant intended to sell the coins in a group she called the "Swiss Coin Collection," but not the Swiss coins in her "Rarity Coin Collection." Defendant refused to deliver. *Oswald v. Allen*, 417 F.2d 43 (2d Cir. 1969). Held: for defendant. The parties never agreed on the coins to be sold and neither had reason to know of the other's meaning.

---

    b.   Rare. Cases appropriately employing this provision are extremely rare. Consider two interesting facets of these examples.

        i.   Names versus words. Both cases involve names, of a ship or of a collection. Most English words have meanings that a court can interpret using normal tools. Names, however, have significance only with relation to the thing named. They are inherently subjective. No dictionary (or other objective source) will help determine what the parties meant (or had reason to know) when they said "Peerless" or "Swiss Coin Collection."

        ii.   Objective manifestations may differ. *Oswald* involved an oral agreement. It was not clear whether the parties even used the same words: One may have said "all Swiss coins" while the other said "the Swiss Coin Collection." Thus, *Oswald* may involve a lack of objective assent to the words, not a misunderstanding of what the words meant. If the court believed both parties agreed to the sale of "all Swiss coins" in plaintiff's collection, seller probably would have reason to know the other party wanted to buy the Swiss coins in the Rarity Collection — which she had shown him during his visit. The decision that no contract existed suggests the court was not sure they used these words.

 # EXAMPLE AND ANALYSIS

In *Joyner v. Adams*, 361 S.E.2d 902 (N.C. Ct. App. 1987), the court appeared to apply misunderstanding, but ultimately balked at the result the rule would require. Joyner leased property to Brown. Rent increased each year according to a formula. The lease was amended to substitute Adams for Brown and to suspend the rent increases, provided Adams subdivided and developed each lot by a specified date. Failure to develop any lot would require retroactive payment of rent under the formula. Adams developed all lots but one on time. The last lot had been prepared for a building (graded, water and sewer lines, driveways and roads), but the building was not begun until two years later. Joyner sued to collect rent under the formula. Adams contended that the land was developed on time, because this required that the lot be **prepared for a building** rather than that a building be completed. This meaning was common among developers but unknown to Joyner (a real estate novice). The trial court interpreted the agreement against Adams (the drafter), without determining whether either party had reason to know of the other party's intended meaning. The appellate court remanded for findings on misunderstanding (holding interpretation against the drafter inappropriate; see 12.C.5.b).

On remand, the trial court found that neither party knew nor had reason to know of the other's interpretation. Thus, it refused to interpret the agreement according to Joyner's interpretation. The appellate court affirmed. 387 S.E.2d 235 (N.C. Ct. App. 1990).

The finding appears to require holding that the parties never assented to the amended lease. This suggests that a term other than a name can defeat assent under misunderstanding.

The court **did not** hold Joyner and Adams never assented to an effective agreement. Without assent to the amended lease, the formula that increased rent (in the original lease) would apply regardless of development! (In fact, Adams would have no rights at all to the property. Without the amendment, Brown, not Adams, would be the lessee.) The court enforced the lease amendment which gave Adams rights to collect rents on the buildings and required him to pay rent to Joyner. It simply refused to award retroactive back rent — in effect, adopting Adams's interpretation of the agreement rather than holding that no agreement existed.

An additional fact may explain this result. Negotiators for Joyner (her lawyer-husband and an accountant) suggested the amended lease require Adams to complete all buildings by the specified date, but Adams refused to agree to that term. Arguably, this gave Joyner (or her agents) reason to know Adams believed the language requiring developed lots did not require completed buildings. Joyner tried to convince a court to impose a term that she could negotiate for herself. Two warnings are important. First, this fact is reported in the last appellate court opinion, not the one in some casebooks. Second, the court did not hold that Joyner had reason to know of Adams's meaning. It found neither had reason to know of the other's intent — then enforced the amended lease (as interpreted by Adams) anyway!

B.   MISTAKE OF INTEGRATION AND REFORMATION

In reducing an agreement to writing, mistakes may be made. Zeros may be added or dropped from numbers. Warranties, definitions, or other provisions may be omitted inadvertently. Thus, the agreement the parties sign may differ from the agreement the parties thought they were signing. Mistakes about the content of the writing can be corrected via **reformation**.

1.   Note on Terminology: Contract versus Writing

The terms on which parties agree are the contract — not necessarily the terms in the writing they sign. The writing is evidence of the agreement, not the agreement itself. Often it is convenient to refer to the written document as the contract, but that shorthand can cause confusion in this context.

 ## EXAMPLE AND ANALYSIS

Sean agrees to sell a used car to Billy for $1,000. When typing the bill of sale, Sean inadvertently types $10,000. Both parties sign the bill of sale. Billy pays Sean $1,000. Sean later demands that Billy pay $9,000, the balance due. Billy can have the contract reformed to read $1,000, the price actually agreed. A mistake in the writing does not change the terms of the contract.

2.   Reformation Defined

Reformation is a court order effectively rewriting contract documents to correct mistakes. (The documents need not be literally rewritten. The court decree itself is sufficient.) A party can seek reformation in a separate proceeding, after she discovers the mistake. Often, a party suing for breach seeks reformation during that suit, alleging the writing inaccurately states the terms. (Note that reformation logically precedes interpretation. The court must interpret the parties' actual agreement, not the inaccurate expression of it.)

   a.   Clear and convincing evidence.   Reformation usually requires clear and convincing evidence. Litigation arises only if one party contends the writing **accurately** reflects the agreement. Courts are reluctant to reject the writing in favor of one party's recollection of what the writing was supposed to say.

   b.   Fault not an impediment.   A party may seek reformation even if the mistake was her fault, unless she failed to act in good faith. Restatement (Second) of Contracts §157. Thus, in the example above, Billy could seek reformation even if she mistyped the bill of sale.

   c.   Rights of third parties.   When third parties have relied on the written agreement, unaware of the inaccuracy, the court may limit or deny reformation.

EXAMPLE AND ANALYSIS

L loans B $20,000 at 10% interest. They sign documents that inaccurately state the interest rate as 12%. L, needing cash, later sells the note to C. C calculated the amount to pay for the note based on the 12% rate in the documents. To protect C, a court might deny reformation. B had a right to reformation against L, but reformation now would affect C, who was unaware of the mistake. (B may have a claim against L, probably in restitution.)

---

3. **Mistake as Grounds for Reformation**

   A mutual mistake about the accuracy of a writing can be corrected by reformation. Restatement (Second) of Contracts §155.

   a. **Original agreement necessary.**   Courts may enforce the agreement the parties actually made. Unless an actual agreement existed, which the writing failed to express accurately, reformation is unavailable. This is not a technique for changing the agreement to what a party wishes it had said.

   b. **Modification distinguished.**   If parties want to change the writing because they now wish they had agreed on different terms, they may modify the contract by agreement. Unlike reformation, modification does not require any action by the court — largely because it requires the assent of both parties, making litigation unnecessary.

4. **Misrepresentation as Grounds for Reformation**

   Reformation is not available for unilateral mistake. If one party knew the terms of the writing and intended that to be the agreement, the court usually cannot impose different terms upon her, terms to which she did not agree. Rescission, allowing the parties to negotiate from scratch, may be appropriate. Some unilateral mistakes, however, result from misrepresentations concerning the content or effect of a writing. In these situations, courts might reform the contract rather than rescind it.

   a. **Nondisclosure.**   A party who **knows** the writing does not accurately express the agreement must reveal that fact **if she knows the other party is unaware of the inaccuracy.** Restatement (Second) of Contracts §161(c). Failure to disclose is equivalent to saying that the writing accurately reflects the agreement, bringing the nondisclosure within the rules on misrepresentation.

i. **Actual knowledge of the inaccuracy.** A party who lacks actual knowledge of an inaccuracy has no duty to disclose the inaccuracy. Thus, reason to know of an inaccuracy plays no role in analyzing misrepresentation. In this situation, however, the mistake probably is mutual, falling under Restatement (Second) of Contracts §155.

ii. **Actual knowledge of the other's ignorance.** A party who does not know the other is unaware of the inaccuracy has no duty to inform her of the inaccuracy. This can arise, for example, when parties in different locations receive different copies of the same document for execution. Either might assume the other recognized the inaccuracy and, thus, was not mistaken. It also might happen when a party believes the writing is accurate. This suggests the parties had not reached prior agreement on the term, making reformation inapt.

b. **Fraud required.** Reformation is available only for fraudulent misrepresentations regarding content or effect of a writing. An innocent misrepresentation regarding the content of a writing will not justify reformation, even if material. Innocent misrepresentations may justify rescission but will not justify imposing terms to which a party did not assent.

c. **Justifiable reliance.** As with any misrepresentation, the deceived party must be justified in relying on the misrepresentation in order to establish a claim to reformation. Restatement (Second) of Contracts §166(a).

REVIEW QUESTIONS AND ANSWERS

Question: S, owner of a pet store, promised to sell B a Collie, to be delivered the day before a holiday on which B will give it as a gift. S knew that B thought the word "Collies" referred to "Shelties" (dogs that resemble Collies but are smaller). B did not know that Shelties and Collies were different breeds. At the prescribed time, S tendered a Collie to B. B refused because the dog was much bigger than anticipated. Did the contract require S to tender a Shelty?

Answer: Yes. S knew B meant a Shelty, even though B said Collie. B did not know that Collie might be interpreted either way. The agreement will be interpreted according to B's intended meaning.

Question: S, owner of a pet store, promised to sell B a Collie, to be delivered the day before a holiday on which B will give it as a gift. S had overheard B referring to a Dachshund as a Collie while B was browsing the puppies. Dachshunds are nothing like Collies. B, however, believed that Collies referred to the breed everyone else calls Dachshund. At the prescribed time, S tendered a Collie to B. B refused because the dog was nothing like a Dachshund. Did the contract require S to tender a Dachshund?

Answer: Probably not. The overheard comment might give S reason to know B thought Collie meant Dachshund. But S might have thought B was joking with someone, in which case the comment would offer no reason to know of B's misunderstanding. Even if S had reason to know B meant a Dachshund, the implausibility of using the word "Dachshund" to mean Collie might lead a court to reject that interpretation—perhaps because B had reason to know (from a dictionary, dog book, store labels, or common usage) that Collie did not mean Dachshund. Even here, however, a court could decide that S had enough reason to question B's intent to clarify the breed up front.

Question: At an antique store, B found an unidentified music manuscript that S told him was by Schuman. B, a collector of music manuscripts, agreed to buy it, believing it was a manuscript by Robert Schumann. In fact, it was a manuscript by William Schuman, a considerably less famous and more recent composer. When B discovered the error, he refused to perform the contract. Can either party sue the other for breach? If so, whose meaning prevails?

Answer: Probably neither party can recover, except in restitution seeking the return of any partial performance. Each believed a different Schuman(n) was the author. Neither had reason to know the other believed a different Schuman(n) was involved. Thus, no assent existed. There was no contract for either to enforce. **Arguably,** B could recover on the ground that S had reason to know B would believe Schuman(n) referred to the more famous Robert Schumann. Even then, however, S might argue that B, too, had reason to know of the other meaning. The age of the manuscript and the style of the music might give a collector reason to know of the discrepancy. Merely knowing that two Schuman(n)s exist—more likely for a collector than a store owner—might give B reason to know of the difference. If both parties had reason to know of the other's meaning, then no assent occurred.

Question: O sold land to D. In the contract, the land description erroneously referred to the parcel as the "NW quarter" when the land actually was in the NE quarter. Before the deed was conveyed, O changed his mind. D sued for specific performance. O defended on the ground that he did not own the parcel described in the contract. D requested the court to reform the contract to read "NE quarter." Is reformation available?

Answer: Yes, as long as clear and convincing evidence reveals that the parties really agreed to a sale of the parcel in the NE quarter.

PAROL EVIDENCE: LIMITATIONS ON INTERPRETATION AND GAP FILLING

 CHAPTER OVERVIEW

Parties sometimes put agreements into writing in order to collect all the terms in final form. This allows them to evaluate the deal as a whole before binding themselves to a contract. Sometimes, however, parties seek to prove that some promises were omitted from the writing. If successful, this argument undermines a party's ability to use a writing as protection from unintended promises. On the other hand, refusing to honor oral promises can allow a party to avoid performing a promise intentionally made. The parol evidence rule reflects the courts' efforts to balance these two concerns.

If an agreement is reduced to an **integrated writing**, parties may not introduce **extrinsic evidence** of **prior or contemporaneous** events to **vary, contradict**, or (in some cases) **supplement** the terms of the writing.

An integrated writing is one the parties intend to contain all of the terms of their agreement.

- An agreement is **completely integrated** if parties intend it to be the **complete and exclusive** agreement between them on this subject matter.
- An agreement is **partially integrated** if parties intend it to be the **complete** agreement of the terms it contains, without excluding the existence of other agreements they might have made.
- Extrinsic evidence is admissible to prove additional promises consistent with a partially integrated writing but not to vary or contradict its terms.

Extrinsic evidence refers to written or oral evidence of prior or contemporaneous events. Evidence of subsequent promises is unaffected.

Extrinsic evidence of prior or contemporaneous events may be introduced for purposes other than to vary, contradict, or supplement a writing, such as:

- To prove whether a writing is integrated;
- To prove whether a writing is partially or completely integrated;
- To show the meaning of a writing, at least if a term is ambiguous;
- To establish a contract defense, such as fraud or mistake;
- To establish whether a particular remedy is appropriate;
- To establish a condition of contract formation; and
- To establish a tort action.

When extrinsic evidence is offered to show the meaning of an integrated writing:

- Some courts refuse to admit the evidence if contract meaning is plain; and
- Some courts admit the evidence to show whether the term is ambiguous.

A.   RATIONALE

Oral contracts can present difficulties for courts, particularly with regard to interpretation. It is hard enough to decide what the parties meant when you can read exactly what they said. Oral contracts often involve more than one version of what was **said** before reaching arguments about what the words **meant**. Courts, therefore, prefer that the parties write out all the terms and sign them. Even then, however, parties sometimes allege that additional promises, usually oral, also deserve enforcement. Courts are reluctant to relinquish the relative security of a written document they can interpret.

1.   Danger of Enforcing Side Promises

A party who regrets a deal may fraudulently try to change it to something more favorable by fabricating side promises. Honest parties, too, may argue that tentative agreements reached during negotiations were part of the contract, even though not included in the writing. If accepted, either practice might bind the other party to an agreement she never intended to make and thought she had protected herself against by obtaining a signed writing stating the terms. To give the writing proper effect, courts created the **parol evidence rule**.

2.   Danger of Not Enforcing Side Promises

Like statutes of frauds, the parol evidence rule can cause injustice, too. The rule precludes evidence of an oral agreement even if that evidence is completely persuasive. A party lured into a transaction by side promises may find the court enforces a contract quite different from what she intended to make. To avoid these inequities, courts crafted numerous ways around the rule, discussed seriatim below.

B.   THE BASIC RULE

When parties have reduced their agreement to an **integrated writing**, the court will not allow extrinsic evidence of prior or contemporaneous discussions for the purpose of varying, contradicting, or (in some cases) supplementing the terms of the writing. Restatement (Second) of Contracts §215.

 ## EXAMPLES AND ANALYSIS

1. Plaintiff leased space in an office building and sold tobacco, candy, and soft drinks. The building was sold. The new owner offered a lease that prohibited the sale of tobacco. Plaintiff agreed (and paid more rent) because the owner orally promised that he would be the only person allowed to sell soft drinks in the building. The lease did not mention this exclusive right. The owner leased to a drugstore that sold soft drinks and plaintiff sued. *Gianni v. R. Russell & Co.*, 126 A. 791 (Pa. 1924). Held: for the owner.

An exclusive right naturally would be included in the lease — especially as the lease included the prohibition on tobacco sales, which allegedly was the consideration for the right. Its omission from the writing, therefore, precluded extrinsic evidence of the promise.

2. Libby bought Thompson's logs. Each signed a one-sentence letter stating the terms. The letter did not mention any warranty concerning the quality of the logs. Libby, however, alleged that Thompson orally promised the logs would be of a certain quality. The court held that because the promise was not in the writing, evidence of the oral warranty could not be admitted. *Thompson v. Libby*, 26 N.W. 1 (Minn. 1885).

Note: As summarized here, *Thompson* illustrates the workings of the parol evidence rule. Another part of the opinion, however, is not consistent with modern law. Before applying the parol evidence rule, a court must decide whether the parties intended the one-sentence letter as a completely integrated agreement. Today, most courts admit extrinsic evidence when determining whether the agreement was integrated. Restatement (Second) of Contracts §214(a). The *Thompson* court, however, refused to consider extrinsic evidence even for this limited purpose.

C.   INTEGRATED WRITINGS

The parol evidence rule applies only if **the parties intend their writing(s) to express the final term(s) of their agreement**. These are called integrated writings. Restatement (Second) of Contracts §209. This limitation spawns two ways around the parol evidence rule: argue the agreement was not integrated at all or argue it was partially integrated. Casebooks tend to focus on the latter.

1. Identifying Integrated Writings

a. **Integration clauses.** Parties commonly specify that a writing is the complete and final agreement between them. These provisions are called integration clauses—or, sometimes, merger clauses, because they have the effect of merging all prior discussions or agreements into a single, final writing.

i. **Clause not conclusive.** An integration clause is evidence of integration but is not conclusive. A court may hear oral evidence that the parties did not intend an integrated agreement despite the clause. This commonly occurs when a merchant uses a standard form when dealing with consumers.

ii. **Hidden provisions.** An integration clause concealed in a standard form may not be effective. **When the drafter of a standard form has reason to believe that the other party would not assent if she knew the writing contained a particular term, the term is not part of the agreement.** Restatement (Second) of Contracts §211(3). This rule is not limited to integration clauses, even though it appears in the section covering parol evidence.

iii. **Difficulty showing materiality.** Integration clauses may not meet the requirement that a party "would not have assented" if aware of the clause. Many people might attach little importance to a provision making the writing the final contract—or might approve of it, assuming the form included the oral promises. Note the language here seems to require more than the "substantial contribution" test used to assess the materiality of a misrepresentation. See 8.B.5.

b. **Completeness may imply integration.** Parties are less likely to intend brief notations to include all terms of their agreement. Completeness and specificity, on the other hand, make it more likely the parties included all terms in the writing. Faced with a fairly thorough document, courts will presume it is integrated until a party proves otherwise. Restatement (Second) of Contracts §209(3).

c. **Usage of trade.** Evidence relating to customs in the trade may reveal whether agreements of this type generally are intended as integrated agreements.

   d.   **Extrinsic evidence.** As noted previously, extrinsic evidence is admissible for purposes of determining whether a writing is an integrated agreement. Restatement (Second) of Contracts §214(a).

   e.   **Multiple documents.** The integrated writing need not be a single document; several writings may, taken together, constitute an integrated agreement.

2. Partially Integrated Writings

Parties may intend a writing to integrate only part of the agreement(s) between them — especially if they have several dealings at once. For example, if an employer sold a car to an employee, a bill of sale for the car, though integrated concerning that sale, might not include all the terms of their employment contract. Matters become more difficult when the two contracts are closely related.

   a.   **Completely integrated writings.** When the parties adopt the writing as **the complete and exclusive agreement** between them, it is a completely integrated agreement. Restatement (Second) of Contracts §210(1). In effect, this denies the existence of any side deals; the integrated writing covers all of their commitments to one another.

   b.   **Partially integrated writings.** Parties may adopt a writing as the complete agreement concerning the terms it contains but may not intend for it to be exclusive of other agreements they have made about other (perhaps related) subjects. In these situations, the agreement is partially integrated.

      i.   **Contradictory evidence inadmissible.** If an agreement is partially integrated, a party may not introduce extrinsic evidence to vary or contradict the terms of the writing.

      ii.   **Supplemental evidence admissible.** If an agreement is partially integrated, a party may introduce extrinsic evidence to show the parties agreed to additional terms that are consistent with the terms in the writing (i.e., do not contradict them). Restatement (Second) of Contracts §216.

      iii.   **Factors to consider.** Courts place weight on two factors in identifying partially integrated agreements.

         (a)   **Separate consideration.** If a party gave separate consideration for the consistent additional term, courts may hold the writing partially integrated. Separate consideration makes it plausible that the parties intended a side agreement, not included in the writing. If the consideration for the additional term is the same as the consideration for the written promises, it seems more likely the parties would have included it in the writing.

(b) Natural omission. Even when the consideration is the same, other circumstances may make it seem natural that the parties would omit the term from the writing. If so, the court may conclude that the agreement was only partially integrated. Restatement (Second) of Contracts §216(2).

(c) Credibility. These factors seem to relate to the credibility of the claim. Integration depends on whether the parties **intended** the writing to be integrated. Although a writing that seems complete may be presumed to be integrated, the parties may produce evidence to show their true intent. The naturalness of a decision to omit a term from the writing tends to make the claim that the parties intended a partial (rather than a complete) integration more credible. But even a term that naturally might have been included in the writing may have been excluded by these parties, with the intent that it be a collateral agreement. If that is their intent, courts should honor it.

 # EXAMPLES AND ANALYSIS

1. The Laths sold a farm to Mitchill. Before offering to buy the land, Mitchill commented on an ice house that she considered an eyesore. (It was owned by the Laths, but located on adjoining property.) The Laths promised to remove it if Mitchill bought the land. She did; they didn't. *Mitchill v. Lath*, 160 N.E. 646 (N.Y. 1928). Held: for the Laths.

The contract for the sale of the land was so complete in detailing each party's obligations that it could not be considered a partially integrated agreement. In effect, the court held that the duty to remove the ice house would not naturally be omitted from the sale contract. (The dissent urged that the contract was complete as to the conveyance of the farm but did not integrate the collateral agreement concerning the ice house on the adjoining parcel.)

2. Lee owned half of a liquor distributorship. His brother, who owned the other half, wanted out. Seagram promised Lee that if he would consent to the sale of the dis-

tributorship, Seagram would locate another (smaller) distributorship that Lee could buy. Lee voted his shares in favor of the sale and the company sold its assets to Seagram (which sold them to a new distributor). Lee sued Seagram when it did not locate a new distributorship for him. Seagram argued the parol evidence rule precluded proof of the side agreement because the written contract selling the distributorship to Seagram did not mention that side agreement. *Lee v. Joseph Seagram & Sons*, 552 F.2d 447 (2d Cir. 1977). Held: for Lee.

The sale of the business was between the distributorship and Seagram not between Lee and Seagram. Thus, that contract would not naturally include promises made to Lee individually. The court also noted the close 13-year relationship between Lee and Seagram's representative, which made a handshake seem a reasonable way to conclude the side agreement. The absence of an integration clause in the documents concerning the sale of the business may have influenced the court.

D. CONDITIONAL CONTRACTS

Sometimes parties create a writing on the understanding that the agreement will become effective only if a particular condition occurs. If the condition does not occur, no contract exists at all, despite the signed writing. It is good practice to put the condition into the writing. Sometimes parties neglect to do so.

1. Evidence of Condition Admissible

Parol evidence may be introduced to show that the parties intended no performance unless a condition occurred. Restatement (Second) of Contracts §217.

 # EXAMPLE AND ANALYSIS

Plaintiff (a bank) loaned money to a company. Defendants, officers of the company, guaranteed the loan (agreed to pay the bank from their personal funds if the company defaulted). Defendants argued that their obligation on the note was conditioned on the bank obtaining the signature of all five officers. The bank obtained only four signatures when it renewed the note (and did not sue the fifth officer). The bank won summary judgment; this court reversed. *Long Island Trust v. International Inst. for Packaging Educ.*, 344 N.E. 377 (N.Y. 1976). Oral evidence showing a condition upon formation may be introduced, making summary judgment inappropriate.

The court suggested that extrinsic evidence would not be admitted to show a condition that was inconsistent with the writing. If the writing had said it was unconditional, oral evidence contradicting that point would not be allowed. **The**

Restatement does not endorse this limitation. Evidence of a condition shows the agreement was not intended to be integrated or, at best, was partially integrated. Extrinsic evidence is always admissible on this point, even if it contradicts the terms of the writing. Picture it this way: The writing was meant to be unconditional once it took effect but would take effect only after a particular condition occurred. Thus, the parties made the writing unconditional even though it might not take effect unless a condition occurred.

E. INTERPRETATION

To decide whether extrinsic evidence varies or contradicts the written terms, the court must know what the written terms mean. Most of the previous examples (especially *Thompson v. Libby* and *Mitchill v. Lath*) involve cases in which a party claimed a prior **promise** or **agreement** was not included in the writing. A party claims she was promised more than the writing mentions. This implicitly (and sometimes explicitly) contradicts the terms of the writing. Sometimes, however, the party seeks to introduce prior negotiations to illuminate the **meaning** of the terms in the writing. This evidence arguably does not contradict the terms, but defines them.

Courts struggle with these cases. Often they involve interpretations that turn a term into something quite different from what the language itself seemed to provide. Thus, a broad exception for interpretation threatens to swallow the parol evidence rule. On the other hand, the terms mean what the parties intended for them to mean, at least if they shared that intent—even if they intended to use the words in a peculiar way. See Restatement (Second) of Contracts §201(1).

1. Traditional Hostility: The Plain Meaning Approach

When the terms of an integrated writing seem clear on their face, courts have invoked the parol evidence rule to preclude the admission of extrinsic evidence. No additional evidence seems necessary to interpret a clear term. Rather, a party offering evidence seeks to prove that plain words don't mean what they say, contradicting the terms of the contract. Concerns about fraud arise. Courts often excluded the evidence rather than allow a jury to be deceived by it.

 # EXAMPLE AND ANALYSIS

Whitelawn obtained a nonexclusive license to distribute Eskimo Pie ice cream products in the New York metropolitan area. The parties admitted the written agreements were integrated. Whitelawn argued the license was nonexclusive as to national marketers (such as Borden) but was exclusive as to other local marketers. The court (at a preliminary hearing *in limine* to decide the admissibility of extrinsic evidence) ruled that nonexclusive was plain on its face. The court, therefore, refused to hear any evidence to vary the interpretation of that term — except evidence regarding a usage of trade. *Eskimo Pie v. Whitelawn Dairies*, 284 F. Supp. 987 (S.D.N.Y. 1968).

---

    a. Exception for ambiguous terms. Extrinsic evidence is admissible to help interpret an ambiguous term, even under the most traditional approach to the parol evidence rule. These terms are not plain on their face; thus, extrinsic evidence does not contradict them.

    b. Exception for usage of trade. Extrinsic evidence is admissible to establish that people in a business attach a special meaning to a term, even under the plain meaning approach. That special meaning may have been plain to the parties, even if not to a court. Risk of fraud is limited; an industrywide usage is hard to falsify.

2. Modern Relaxation

Recently, courts have been less confident of their ability to divine a plain meaning in words. Thus, they tend to admit extrinsic evidence in more cases, largely by stating that the terms are ambiguous and, therefore, require clarification in light of extrinsic evidence.

    a. Extremes (*Pacific Gas & Electric*, 442 P.2d 641 (Cal. 1968)). This case offers two rules.

        i. Fairly susceptible test. When a contract term is "fairly susceptible" to either of the interpretations proposed, extrinsic evidence is admissible to support either interpretation.

        ii. Admit parol to determine ambiguity. Extrinsic evidence is admissible to show that a contract term is fairly susceptible to either of the interpretations proposed. When the court, after hearing the extrinsic evidence, decides the term is not fairly susceptible to one interpretation, the court may strike the evidence (or, if the jury has not yet heard it, refuse to admit it).

 # EXAMPLE AND ANALYSIS

Defendant (G. W. Thomas) agreed to perform work on a turbine owned by plaintiff (PG&E). The agreement included an indemnity clause: Defendant promised to pay for "all loss, damage, expense and liability" PG&E incurred "resulting from injury to property, arising out of" performance of the contract. Defendant dropped a cover on PG&E's turbine, damaging it. Defendant contended that the clause was intended to cover damage to the property of third parties, not damage to plaintiff's property. The trial court noted that language of this sort commonly is used in indemnity clauses covering losses to third parties, but the words here plainly covered damage to PG&E's property. The court refused to admit the extrinsic evidence. *Pacific Gas & Elec. v. G.W. Thomas Drayage & Rigging*, 442 P.2d 641 (Cal. 1968). Held: for defendant. Extrinsic evidence should have been admitted, at least to determine whether the provision was fairly susceptible to defendant's interpretation.

- **b. Consistent with interpretation rules.** Other rules governing interpretation make extrinsic evidence relevant to determining the meaning of a term, even if arguably plain.

  - **i. Parties' meaning central.** The parties' mutual understanding governs, even when peculiar. See Restatement (Second) of Contracts §201(1). Excluding evidence of that mutual understanding is odd.

  - **ii. Knowledge of other's meaning.** In some cases, one party's knowledge or reason to know of the meaning attached by the other affects interpretation. See Restatement (Second) of Contracts §201(2). Excluding evidence of negotiations that show the knowledge seems odd. When language really is plain, that may give the party asserting a peculiar interpretation reason to know the other intended the plain meaning. But that, too, requires reference to what was said during negotiations.

  - **iii. Plain meaning involves extrinsic components.** Plain meaning itself relies on extrinsic evidence: a dictionary, at best; the judge's linguistic education or prejudices, at worst. The parties' subjective understanding seems at least as useful as a judge's subjective understanding.

- **c. Frivolous claims.** The modern approach allows a party to present extrinsic evidence to support even an absurd interpretation. This makes it harder for courts to dispose of weak claims summarily.

EXAMPLE AND ANALYSIS

Plaintiff (Trident) borrowed money from defendant. The contract prohibited prepayment for 12 years. In case of default, however, the contract allowed defendant to accelerate the entire amount due and, if default occurred in the first 12 years of the loan, to assess a 10% prepayment fee. Trident did not default, but sought to prepay the loan (plus the 10% prepayment fee) after four years. It sued for a declaratory judgment that the contract allowed prepayment. The trial court, finding the contract language clear, dismissed the suit and sanctioned the Trident for filing a frivolous action. *Trident Center v. Connecticut Gen. Life Ins.*, 847 F.2d 564 (1988). Held: for Trident. Because California law governed the case, a reluctant court held that Trident deserved the right to introduce the extrinsic evidence before the court could conclude the language was not fairly susceptible to the meaning proposed.

---

       d.   The pendulum swings.   The opinion in *Trident* reflects hostility to extreme erosion of the parol evidence rule. It may signal a return of traditional hostility to extrinsic evidence. Watch for further developments.

F.   EXCEPTION FOR TORTS

Plaintiffs may evade the parol evidence rule by pleading fraud instead of breach of contract.

1.   Parol Evidence Rule Inapplicable in Tort

The parol evidence rule does not apply to torts. Thus, a promise not contained in the writing can be alleged as the basis of a fraud claim. This is true even if the promise is unenforceable under contract law.

2.   Promissory Fraud

But plaintiff might sue for fraud based on the oral promise by alleging that defendant did not intend to perform at the time she made the promise. A promise implies a present intent to perform. A promise made with no intention to perform misrepresents the promisor's intent. Assuming other elements of fraud are alleged, the written agreement will not prevent plaintiff from suing.

EXAMPLE AND ANALYSIS

Employer (Leonard) persuaded Lipsit to leave his old job and work for employer by promising Lipsit a chance to become part owner of the business—a promise reiterated when the annual contract was renewed. None of the written employment agreements contained an enforceable promise to this effect. (One included the promise in language too indefinite to enforce.) Leonard eventually offered Lipsit a chance to buy shares (after the business incorporated) on terms Lipsit could not afford. Leonard apparently fired Lipsit shortly thereafter. The trial court dismissed both the contract claim and the fraud claim. *Lipsit v. Leonard*, 315 A.2d 25 (N.J. 1974). Held: for plaintiff. The parol evidence rule does not preclude a fraud claim.

G. EXCEPTION FOR CONTRACT DEFENSES

The parol evidence rule does not preclude evidence introduced to prove a defense to the contract. Restatement (Second) of Contracts §214(d).

1. Rescission versus Contradiction

Extrinsic evidence is admissible to establish a right to rescind the agreement. Defenses seeking rescission of the contract do not really seek to vary the terms of the contract but to avoid agreement entirely. Thus, by its terms, the rule does not apply. (Another way to picture this: If the contract is voidable, so is the integration clause (whether express or implied). Thus, the parol evidence rule cannot apply to a voidable contract.)

2. Reformation

Extrinsic evidence may be admitted to establish reformation despite the parol evidence rule. Although the parties may have intended an integrated writing, they also intended the writing to include the terms to which they actually agreed. Thus, before the writing gains preclusive effect, it may need to be reformed to comport with the parties' agreement.

3. Remedial Discretion

Extrinsic evidence may be introduced to influence the court's equitable discretion. Remedies such as specific performance are not automatic but rest in the court's discretion. The court may admit extrinsic evidence that shows the parties may have intended something other than the written terms in deciding whether to deny specific performance, even though the damage remedy is based on the writing alone. Restatement (Second) of Contracts §214(e).

H. EXCEPTION FOR MODIFICATION

The final writing can integrate all provisions discussed up to that point. It cannot integrate all provisions to be discussed in the future. Thus, the parol evidence rule does not apply to modifications.

1. Potential Abuse

A party unable to introduce evidence that the original agreement differed from the writing may simply argue that the parties subsequently agreed to the different term. Requiring modifications to be in writing reduces the danger.

2. Requiring Written Modifications

Parties may try to constrain oral modifications via requiring modifications to be in writing — a topic addressed in connection with the statute of frauds. See 4.C.2; UCC §2-209.

3. Relaxation Possible

Courts may enforce requirements that modifications be in writing with the same vigor (or lack of it) they employ when enforcing the parol evidence rule or statutes of frauds. The same incentives for relaxation apply. Parties often amend agreements informally, despite merger clauses requiring written modification. (This is common in construction, where changes frequently are made in the field. Insisting on written modifications often impedes the work, leading parties to dispense with formalities a little more often than they should.) When the oral amendment really was requested and performed, courts may be tempted to find a way to give effect to the modification, despite the writing requirement. See UCC §2-209(4) (ineffective oral modification may serve as waiver).

REVIEW QUESTIONS AND ANSWERS

Question: How can you tell whether an agreement is integrated?
Answer: The agreement is integrated if the parties intend it to be their complete agreement. The best indication of that intent is an integration clause — though even that may not be dispositive. Without an integration, consider the thoroughness of the writing, whether similar agreements usually are embodied in integrated writings, and any extrinsic evidence concerning whether the parties intended the writing to be integrated.

Question: What is the difference between a partially integrated writing and a completely integrated writing?

Answer: The difference is **effect** in that a completely integrated writing precludes evidence of side agreements while a partially integrated writing precludes evidence of terms that contradict the writing but does not preclude evidence of other agreements between the parties. In deciding which kind of clause is present, the difference depends on **intent**. The language of an integration clause may reveal intent, as might the factors listed in the preceding answer. At root, ask yourself whether parties who had entered a side agreement really might decide not to record it in the writing. If you can't devise a plausible explanation for omitting it, that may indicate the parties intended a completely integrated agreement.

Question: S sold B a parcel of land for commercial development. The contract documents included a clause stating it was a completely integrating writing. B claims that after the sale, S promised to remove some debris from the land, including an old water tank. Can S use the parol evidence rule to preclude this evidence from being admitted?

Answer: No. The discussions occurred after the writing was signed. The writing can integrate all agreements up to that date, but cannot integrate agreements made after that date. If the contract also contains a provision requiring modifications to be in writing, the promise may not be an enforceable modification. But this involves preclusion under the contract, not under the parol evidence rule.

Question: When is extrinsic evidence of prior or contemporaneous discussions between the parties admissible?

Answer: Whenever the evidence is not offered to vary or contradict the terms of an integrated writing (or to supplement the terms of a completely integrated writing). For example, extrinsic evidence is admissible to establish:

> Whether a writing was integrated;
> Whether it was completely or partially integrated;
> Whether it was enforceable (i.e., whether contract defenses were valid);
> What the contract terms meant (unless the terms are plain, sometimes); and
> Whether a remedy is appropriate.

Question: When a term in an integrated writing appears to be plain, can evidence of course of dealing be introduced to show it is not plain?

Answer: Almost certainly. Even courts most inclined to refuse extrinsic evidence interpreting a plain term will allow usage of trade and course of dealing. That is particularly important when a term may seem plain to a judge but, in context, would have a special meaning for the parties. Judges wary of testimony on subjective intent accept testimony of objective facts, such as how the parties acted in prior dealings using the same language.

Question: When a term in an integrated writing appears to be plain, can evidence of the party's negotiations be introduced to show it is not plain?

Answer: In California, yes. Elsewhere, probably. The evidence lacks the objective verifiability of course of dealing. But courts often recognize that their own view of plain meaning may not match that of the parties to the contract. Thus, they may admit evidence that the term is ambiguous conditionally, striking the evidence later if it decides the term really was plain.

15 CONDITIONS: IS PERFORMANCE DUE?

CHAPTER OVERVIEW

A condition is an event that must occur before another's performance is due.

- If a condition does not occur, failure to perform is not breach because the performance was not due.
- A party protected by a condition may waive the condition.

A condition either occurs or does not; almost doesn't count.

If a condition does not occur, a party who has already performed may suffer forfeiture when the return performance is excused.

To reduce the risk or consequences of forfeiture, courts prefer to interpret terms as promises rather than conditions when the issue is close.

When a condition does not occur, performance may nonetheless be due if:

- A party waived the condition by promising to performing despite its non-occurrence; or
- A party is estopped to perform because another relied on her promise to perform despite the nonoccurrence of the condition; or
- The parties modified the contract by deleting the condition; or
- A court excuses the condition because it produces disproportionate forfeiture and was not material to the agreed exchange.

A. NONPERFORMANCE AND BREACH

As noted in the introduction to Part 2, not every nonperformance qualifies as a breach. Sometimes, performance does not occur because it is not yet due. Sometimes nonperformance is excused — either by the prior nonperformance of the other party or by other unanticipated contingencies. And sometimes non-performance will give rise to an immediate breach, even though performance was not yet due. This section takes up these issues in turn. Before beginning, however, a few basic principles deserve mention.

1.   Innocent Breach Is Still Breach

Unlike torts, which usually involves some element of fault, failure to perform can be a breach even if the breaching party did everything humanly possible to perform. If you promise a result, you must produce that result or pay damages for failure. The result has potential for harsh consequences. Some of the doctrines here represent efforts to minimize any harshness.

2.   Parties May Limit Promises to Avoid Innocent Breach

When a party knows she may not achieve a particular result, she can limit her promise appropriately to account for that risk. One method is to promise efforts rather than results. Doctors usually sell services, not cures. (To decide which was promised, you must **interpret** the agreement.) Another is to anticipate the events that might impede success and provide for them in the contract. Thus, if bad weather may postpone completion of a job (such as painting a house or building it), the parties can specify completion by a certain date, if the weather remains clement. Provisions of this sort limit the **conditions** under which a party is obligated to perform. Parties can limit their promises in any way they like (though limitations making a promise illusory destroy enforceability).

3.   Courts Assume Some Limitations

Even if the parties fail to provide for some contingencies, the law may take them into account. Some situations are so remote parties often fail to mention them in the contract. Nonetheless, compelling performance (or damages for nonperformance) when these circumstances prevent performance seems so harsh that courts presume the parties would have included appropriate conditions if they had adverted to these possibilities. Parties who want unconditional duties, even under extreme circumstances, must expressly provide for them. (Excuses do not quite reintroduce fault into the equation. The excuses involve rather rare events. A person who strives mightily to perform may nonetheless be liable for breach unless a fairly narrow class of excuses applies.)

B.   CONDITION DEFINED

A condition is "an event, not certain to occur, which must occur, unless its non-occurrence is excused, before performance under a contract becomes due." Restatement (Second) of Contracts §224.

1. Conditions versus Promises

You must identify whether language creates a condition or a promise because conditions and promises have different effects. Details are addressed below, but you need to understand the basic difference now.

a. Promises and breach. The failure to fulfill a promise is a breach of contract (unless excused). Thus, the nonbreaching party may bring an action for damages.

b. Conditions and discharge. The failure to fulfill a condition means performance does not become due. Thus, the failure to perform is not breach and no damage action arises.

c. Both promise and condition. Some language may create both a promise and a condition. If so, the party who promised the condition would occur may have breached that promise, in addition to the effect of the condition.

EXAMPLE AND ANALYSIS

S promises to deliver 100,000 bushels of wheat to B. In exchange, B promises to pay $300,000 to S 30 days after delivery of the wheat.

Delivery of the wheat is a condition of payment; B's duty to pay is not due until the wheat is delivered. Delivery of the wheat also is a promise — the primary promise S made. Thus, if S fails to deliver the wheat, S breaches the contract and B could sue for her damages.

2. Recognizing Conditions

You can recognize most conditions by the language used. Words such as "if" or "unless" generally introduce conditions.

EXAMPLES AND ANALYSIS

1. B promises to buy S's house for $85,000, **if** B can obtain a mortgage for $45,000 at an interest rate no higher than 8.5% for not less than 20 years. Obtaining the

mortgage is a condition of B's duty to buy the house. *See Luttinger v. Rosen*, 316 A.2d 757 (Conn. 1972). If B cannot find such a mortgage, she need not buy the house. S may sell it to someone else but has no action for breach against B.

2. S promises to close the sale of a house (deliver the deed and possession) on August 15, **if** S is able to obtain suitable substitute housing by August 1. Obtaining substitute housing is a condition of B's duty to deliver the house on August 15. If S cannot find suitable substitute housing by August 1, she need not deliver the house on August 15.

3. C issues an insurance policy on the home. B agrees to pay $650 annually in premiums and C agrees to pay the cost to repair or to rebuild the home **if** fire damages or destroys it. Fire damage is a condition of C's duty to pay B any money. If no fire damages the house, C need not pay any money to B.

---

    a.   **Form is not determinative.**   These words are clues (and very good ones). But using "if" does not change what is in substance a promise into a condition. Similarly, some items not without an "if" may be conditions. You need to analyze the substance of the transaction carefully.

    b.   **Substance involves the effect of the words.**   If the language allows a party to refuse to perform unless an event occurs, it is a condition.

    c.   **Promises can be found in words of condition.**   Words that seem to be conditions may be interpreted as promises.

 # EXAMPLE AND ANALYSIS

A general contractor promised to make final payment to a subcontractor "within 30 days after the completion of the work included in this subcontract, written acceptance by the Architect and full payment therefor by the Owner." This appears to make payment by the owner (inter alia) a condition upon the contractor's duty to pay the subs. Owner filed bankruptcy before paying for the work. The subcontractor sued the owner for payment. *Peacock Constr. v. Modern Air Conditioning*, 353 So. 2d 840 (Fla. 1977). Held: summary judgment for subcontractor affirmed. The risk that the owner will not pay the contractor is generally born by the contractor, not the subs. Parties wishing a different result must clearly specify it in the writing.

The court seems to rely on trade practice here, though it does not mention evidence to support a usage of trade. (The court cited other judicial decisions, but these establish how courts view the situation, not the meaning of these terms in the construction trade.) The court also calls this the fair result, suggesting it might be imposing the term it wishes the parties had written rather than interpreting the one they did write.

3. Conditions Are Events

The condition is the event that must occur, not the contract term that specifies the event. Nonetheless, people often refer to the clause as a condition.

4. Events after Formation but before Discharge

Implicitly, condition refers to events that occur after contract formation and before discharge. Events before formation either have or have not occurred: Their occurrence is certain, even if the parties are not aware of their occurrence. Once a contract has been discharged, no duties could fall due regardless of whether an event occurred.

C. EFFECT OF CONDITIONS

If a condition does not occur, performance does not become due. Thus, the failure to perform is not breach. Restatement (Second) of Contracts §225.

1. Conditions Limit Promises

Contract law enforces the promises people make but does not make them perform promises they did not make. A party who promises to perform *if* something occurs has made no promise to do anything if the condition does not occur.

 # EXAMPLE AND ANALYSIS

Consider the two previous examples involving the sale of a home. See 15.A.2, 15.B.3.b.ii.

In the first example, B never promised to buy the house without a mortgage — or without a mortgage at rates she could afford. She promised to buy the house only if she obtained a suitable mortgage. The law cannot force her to buy the house without a suitable mortgage because she never promised to do so.

In the second example, S never promised to deliver the house on August 15 if that meant living on the street (or, perhaps, in a hotel). She promised to deliver the house only if she found suitable substitute housing. The law cannot force her to deliver the house without a suitable substitute because she never promised to do so.

2.   Conditions Can Produce Harsh Effects

Excusing one party's performance may allow that party to keep what she received under the contract without paying the return she promised. When this happens, the consequences for the other party may seem harsh.

 ## EXAMPLE AND ANALYSIS

O, a homeowner, buys a fire insurance policy from R. The policy provided that R must pay for fire damage *if* O gives written notice of the loss within 30 days of the fire. After a fire, O gave R oral notice during the first 30 days and written notice 35 days after the fire. The condition did not occur. If a court treats the language as a condition, R has no obligation to perform; R never promised to pay unless timely notice was given.

a.   **Harshness is not inevitable.**   Sometimes enforcing conditions will not produce harsh results. In the examples discussed in 15.A.2, 15.B.3.b.ii, nonoccurrence of a condition probably would not damage either party (though it would prevent them from realizing the gains they expected under the contract).

   i.   **Housing examples.**   If B could not get a mortgage, S could sell the house to someone else. Similarly, if S could not find suitable housing by August 1, probably delivery would be delayed rather than canceled. At worst, B can buy a different house. Reliance expenses might be wasted, but probably would be modest.

   ii.   **Insurance example.**   If no fire occurred, the insurer could keep the premiums and pay nothing to the insured. This is not harsh; it is how insurance works. But it illustrates the way nonoccurrence of a condition can produce one-sided performance—and the danger of assuming every one-sided performance constitutes a forfeiture. That conclusion would make insurance impossible.

3. Promises Less Harsh

Interpreting the language as a promise would produce effects that are not quite as harsh as those of a condition. The nonoccurrence of the event would be a breach. (Interpreting the language as a promise means the party promised the event would occur.) Thus, the other party could collect damages. But the other party might not avoid performing her side of the bargain.

    a. Material breach.   As discussed in the next chapter, breach of a promise allows the other to **refuse to perform** the contract only if the breach is **material**. See Chapter 16. When a provision is relatively minor or the performance was close to what the provision required, a court may hold the breach was not material (or that performance was substantial —different words for the same conclusion). If so, the aggrieved party could collect damages but could not cancel the contract or refuse to perform.

 EXAMPLE AND ANALYSIS

O, a homeowner, buys a fire insurance policy from R. The policy provided that R must pay for fire damage *if* O gives written notice of the loss within 30 days of the fire. After a fire, O gave R oral notice during the first 30 days and written notice 35 days after the fire. The notice did not conform to the contract requirements. If a court treats the language as a promise, it may find O's breach was not material. If so, R must pay for fire damage to O's house.

Note: O has breached the contract and must pay R any damages R suffered because of late notice. R may have trouble proving its loss if late notice prevented it from investigating early and discovering what an early investigation might have revealed.

    b. Jargon.   You will hear it said that a condition must be strictly performed but a promise may be substantially performed. That is misleading.

        i. Substantial performance is breach.   Performance that does not strictly fulfill all of one's duties under the contract is a breach. The other party can recover damages caused by the breach, but she cannot **terminate** the contract if performance is substantial.

ii.   **Conditions are not performed.**   Conditions occur or do not occur—though sometimes, as in the notice provision, a party can cause a condition to occur. Anything short of the condition, no matter how close, means the condition did not occur.

 ## EXAMPLE AND ANALYSIS

B promises to buy S's house for $85,000, **if** B can obtain a mortgage for $45,000 at an interest rate no higher than 8.5% for not less than 20 years. B finds a 9% mortgage but cannot find an 8.5% mortgage. The condition did not occur. No matter how close, B need not buy the house because the condition did not occur.

4.   Interpretation as a Promise Preferred

If contract language is uncertain, courts prefer to interpret the language as creating a promise rather than a condition. Restatement (Second) of Contracts §227. This minimizes the number of cases with harsh results. This rule does not preclude the parties from creating a condition if they use clear language. This is a guide to interpretation, not a limitation on the parties' ability to create their own contract.

 ## EXAMPLES AND ANALYSIS

1. Defendant (FCIC) insured Howard's tobacco crop against weather damage. Rain allegedly damaged the crop. Before FCIC's inspector could examine the stalks to verify the cause of the damage, Howard destroyed the stalks by discing the fields in order to sow a cover crop (preventing soil erosion). The policy required that the stalks "shall not be destroyed until after the [FCIC] makes an inspection." *Howard v. Federal Crop Ins. Corp.*, 540 F.2d 695 (4th Cir. 1976). Held: summary judgment for FCIC reversed. Other language in the policy clearly stated conditions, although this passage did not use the language of conditions. Because the character was in doubt, summary judgment based on characterizing the provision as a condition was erroneous.

Note on usage: The court refers to warranties. In insurance contracts, conditions sometimes are called warranties. Warranty here does not mean a promise assuring quality, as in other contracts.

2. *Peacock Construction*, 15.A.2.c, may be another example of interpreting language in favor of a promise. The court did not announce a preference for promises over conditions. But its interpretive technique rather casually dismissed the parties' intent in favor of an ill-supported usage of trade argument.

---

5.   Role of Conditions

Conditions allow the parties to allocate the risk of uncertainty between themselves. Some events will have significant effects on the benefit of the transaction. Whenever a party wants to avoid or to limit a risk, she can make performance conditional on that risk (if the other party agrees).

a.   **Uncertainty regarding ability to perform.**   A party may fear she will be unable to perform if (or unless) certain events occur. For example, a home buyer often cannot afford to pay the price unless she obtains a loan — and may be unable to make the monthly payments on a loan unless the interest rate is low enough. If she unconditionally promises to buy a house, she may be forced to breach the contract if unable to find a suitable loan. Rather than become liable for the seller's expectation interest, she may make a conditional promise — assuming the seller will accept a conditional promise.

b.   **Uncertainty regarding the quality of the item.**   Some defects may not show up on casual inspection. A buyer might agree to purchase **if** the item passes a more detailed inspection. (Such inspections may be costly or intrusive, making inspection before an agreement is reached prohibitive.) For instance, houses may have termites, roof leaks, or other problems that a civil engineer could discover. Sales of business corporations often include such conditions. A detailed investigation and audit make sense only if you know an agreement can be reached. Thus, the sale is negotiated first but is conditioned on satisfactory verification of the company's worth.

c.   **Uncertainty regarding outside circumstances.**   Many events, especially market forces, may affect the value of a performance. A party unwilling to risk changes may include a condition covering those events. For example, in *Gray v. Gardner*, 17 Mass. 188 (1821), a buyer promised to buy whale oil at a specified price per barrel and agreed to pay a premium unless the quantity that arrived in port that season exceeded the quantity brought to port the preceding season. Higher supply would reduce the price of the oil. The condition allowed buyer to protect itself against that possibility while allowing seller the possibility of a higher price than buyer would pay without that protection. (**Note:** The dispute in this case did not involve the purpose of the condition but its application. Buyer wanted to count a ship that was approaching harbor on the last day of the period but did not anchor until after midnight. The court held the condition was not met because the oil had not arrived in the specified time. Thus, the buyer had to pay the premium.)

   d. Conditions affecting incentives.   Sometimes parties write conditions to encourage performance. When a condition is within the other party's power, either a promise or a condition will require the other party to perform. Specifying a promise invokes damage remedies, but specifying a condition excuses one's own performance. The latter may be a more powerful incentive if one's payment is substantial. On the other hand, no damages are available for failure of a condition. The strongest incentive comes from making a term both a promise and a condition.

EXAMPLE AND ANALYSIS

You probably have car insurance. Which result is more likely to encourage you to pay the premium on time: (1) knowing that if you are late, the insurer can charge you interest on the late payment; or (2) knowing that if you are late, the insurer can refuse to pay any losses you suffer in a traffic accident? The first represents damages for breach of contract, the second excusing performance for nonoccurrence of a condition.

6. Abuse of Conditions

Sometimes, parties invoke conditions because they have changed their minds for other reasons. The condition then becomes a convenient excuse for not going forward rather than a protection against a risk that materialized.

EXAMPLES AND ANALYSIS

1. The buyers received a loan at 8.75%, higher than the 8.5% specified in the contract. The seller offered to make up the difference, so that the buyers paid the equivalent of an 8.5% mortgage. Buyers refused the offer. The refusal may have been legitimate, based on concerns about sellers' reliability or other details of the offer. But it is possible buyers found a house they liked better and were using the condition as an excuse to allow them to back out of this contract and pursue the other home. *Luttinger v. Rosen* (see 15.A.2).

2. Buyer ordered 96,500 pockets of rice from seller at $8.25 per pocket to be delivered "F.A.S. [free alongside ship] Lake Charles and/or Houston" in "December, 1952" two weeks after buyer gave shipping instructions to the seller. Buyer gave instructions for 50,000 pockets to be delivered to St. Charles, which seller delivered by December 23. On December 17, buyer had not given instructions for deliveries to Houston. Because instructions given after December 17 would not allow delivery in December 1952 (two weeks would be January), seller refused to perform. The primary reason appears to be that the market price on December 17 ($9.75 per pocket) greatly exceeded the contract price. *Internatio-Rotterdam v. River Brand Rice Mills*, 259 F.2d 137 (2d Cir. 1958). Held: for seller. The time for delivery was "of the essence" in this contract. The contract did not require delivery in January 1953 and did not require delivery on less than two weeks' notice. No performance was due once the condition could not occur.

    a.   **Notes on *Internatio-Rotterdam*.**

        i.   **Practice question.**   What is the condition in this contract? (No "if" or "unless" tips it off.)

           Seller promised to deliver rice **if** shipping instructions were received at least two weeks before the end of December 1952. The court inferred the condition from the other terms. But the structure of the agreement makes it fairly clear that performance could become due only if shipping instructions were timely received. Seller "[obviously] could not deliver free alongside ship . . . until [buyer] identified its ship and its location."

        ii.   **Promise and condition.**   The court treated the language as both a promise and a condition. Buyer promised to give shipping instructions (by December 17). Performance of this promise was a condition of seller's duty to deliver—just as delivery was a condition of payment in the earlier example. See 15.A.1.c.

b.   Time of the essence.   In *Internatio-Rotterdam*, the court discussed whether time is of the essence in the contract. Many contracts expressly state "time is of the essence." The effect of this provision deserves some attention.

    i.   Material breach.   When parties say "time is of the essence," they mean that any breach of the time limits in the contract is a material breach and therefore justifies termination of the contract.

    ii.   No damages.   No action for damages arose in *Internatio-Rotterdam* because the seller lost nothing. The price went up, so seller benefited from buyer's breach of the promise to give delivery instructions.

    iii.   Recital inconclusive.   Saying doesn't make it so. Courts usually accept the parties' characterization of how important time is to them. But courts sometimes inquire into the substance of the transaction to determine whether the failure to perform on time was a material breach (or a condition).

7.   Satisfaction as a Condition

Some contracts specify that a party's duty to perform arises only if she is satisfied with the other party's performance. This is a strong incentive to perform well. But it also is a powerful opportunity for abuse.

 # EXAMPLE AND ANALYSIS

Plaintiff persuaded defendant to allow him to enlarge a photograph of the defendant's deceased daughter by stating that the defendant would owe nothing if he was not completely satisfied. Defendant was dissatisfied with the result and refused to pay. Plaintiff tried to correct the problems (which defendant had difficulty expressing), then sued. *Gibson v. Cranage*, 39 Mich. 49 (1878). Held: for defendant. Defendant is the only one who could assess his satisfaction. If that's what the parties agree, so be it.

a. **Pretext of dissatisfaction.** A condition requiring satisfactory performance does not authorize a party to back out of a deal even when the performance is satisfactory. That is, if she refuses to perform and pretends to have been dissatisfied, she has breached the contract and the other party may sue.

b. **Proving pretext.** To recover, the plaintiff must prove that the condition occurred — that is, that the performance really was satisfactory to the defendant. Courts apply two tests, depending on the kind of performance involved.

    i. **Reasonable dissatisfaction.** The quality of some performances can be assessed objectively. If a party claims that the wheat delivered was unsatisfactory, expert testimony can establish whether the wheat satisfied reasonable commercial standards in the trade. Absent unusual circumstances, satisfying reasonable commercial standards will establish the occurrence of the condition.

    ii. **Good faith dissatisfaction.** Some performance cannot easily be judged by commercial standards. Artistic merit depends on taste. Some performances may involve numerous interrelated factors that make judgment or taste more likely to vary. In these situations, the court still can assess whether the individual acted in **good faith**. If she really was dissatisfied by the performance, the condition did not occur. But a party would breach if she tried to use the condition as an excuse despite being satisfied with performance. As long as a court can discern the lack of good faith, it will hold that the condition occurred and that the defendant breached by failing to perform.

 # EXAMPLES AND ANALYSIS

1. Defendant agreed to buy chipping potatoes from plaintiff provided they chipped to buyer's satisfaction. The chips were satisfactory until the market price declined and buyer could get potatoes cheaper. *Neumiller Farms v. Cornett*, 368 So. 2d 272 (Ala. 1979). Judgment for plaintiff affirmed. See also *Devoine Co. v. International Co.*, 136 A. 37 (Md. 1927) (cherries were satisfactory until demand declined).

2. In dicta, the court announced that commercial leases involved so many variables

that a good faith test should apply to a satisfaction clause. *Mattei v. Hopper*, 330 P.2d 625 (Cal. 1958) (see 2.A.4.c.i).

---

    c.   **Satisfaction of a third party.**   Construction contracts frequently require satisfaction of a third-party arbiter, such as an engineer or architect. Contracts may purport to make the third party's discretion unreviewable concerning satisfaction with the work. Nonetheless, the architect generally is paid by the owner. A court is unlikely to allow an arbitrary or capricious refusal to certify satisfactory completion of the work to prevent the contractor from receiving payment from the owner.

 # EXAMPLE AND ANALYSIS

Regal promised to build a race track for Laurel. Final payment depended on the engineer's certifying that performance was complete and satisfactory. The engineer did not issue the certificate, Laurel did not pay, and Regal sued. *Laurel Race Course v. Regal Constr.*, 333 A.2d 319 (Md. 1975). The trial court held the parties equally responsible for the problems with the track and ordered payment to Regal. The appellate court reversed. The engineer's decision was not reviewable except for fraud or bad faith. Because the certificate had not issued, judgment for Regal was error. Although the court built a strong case for the finality of the certificate, it nonetheless left room for review of bad faith decisions.

D.   EXCUSING CONDITIONS: WAIVER, MODIFICATION, AND ESTOPPEL

Courts have found ways to minimize the harsh consequences of conditions even when the parties clearly intended to create a condition. These decisions are fact-dependent, driven by the equities of the situation as perceived by the court. Courts, however, often view the matter with 20-20 hindsight, depriving a party of the benefit conditions that, during negotiations, made perfectly good sense.

1.   Waiver

The party for whose benefit the condition was specified may waive it. This is not technically the waiver of a right (though one can think of it as waiving the right not to perform). Rather, the party excuses the nonoccurrence of the condition, in effect modifying the agreement to eliminate the condition.

EXAMPLE AND ANALYSIS

In *Luttinger v. Rosen* (see 15.A.2), the buyer received a loan at 8.75%, higher than the 8.5% specified in the contract. Buyer could have elected to waive the condition and to proceed with the sale. S cannot refuse to perform merely because B's mortgage rate is higher than expected.

a. **Promise to waive.** A promise to waive a condition usually is enforceable even if no consideration is given for the promise to waive the condition. Restatement (Second) of Contracts §84.

b. **Waiver revocable.** Waiver of a condition is revocable unless another has relied to her detriment on the waiver. Thus, §84 of the Restatement allows revocation if:

  i. The condition was in the control of the promisee (or a beneficiary)—that is, the promisee can cause the condition to occur or prevent it from occurring;

  ii. The waiver was made before the time for the occurrence of the condition;

  iii. Notice of revocation "is received while there is still a reasonable time to cause the condition to occur";

  iv. Reliance does not make revocation unjust; and

  v. The waiver was not enforceable for other reasons—such as consideration the promisee gave the waiving party in exchange for the waiver.

 EXAMPLE AND ANALYSIS

Borrower (Morgan) was consistently late with payments on his Porsche. After 14 months, the lender repossessed the car. Morgan sued for conversion. *Mercedes Benz Credit v. Morgan*, 850 S.W.2d 297 (Ark. 1993). Held: for borrower. The contract gave the lender the right to repossess unless Morgan made timely payments. But the lender, by accepting 13 late payments, had waived the right to insist on timely payments. It could reinstate that right (revoke the waiver) by notifying Morgan of its intent but did not give notice prior to repossessing the car. See also *Margolin v. Franklin*, 270 N.E.2d (Ill. App. 1971) (wrongful repossession of a Thunderbird; court unclear whether waiver, modification, or estoppel prevented lender from repossessing based on late payments).

2.   Modification

Parties may modify a contract to delete reference to the condition. The last provision of §84 notes the possibility that a waiver may become irrevocable if a party gives consideration for the waiver. In effect, this amounts to modifying the contract to make the promise unconditional. Assent to a modification usually involves words but can involve conduct. Modification, however, may require a writing, under either the statute of frauds or an integration clause.

3.   Estoppel

A party may be estopped to insist on a condition. In this context, estoppel usually involves a **waiver** on which other parties have **relied**. Reliance makes the waiver irrevocable. Otherwise, there is little difference between waiver and estoppel in this context.

4.   Disproportionate Forfeiture

When a condition produces "disproportionate forfeiture," courts may excuse the condition "unless its occurrence was a material part of the agreed exchange." Restatement (Second) of Contracts §229. This rule seeks to prevent injustice even in cases in which the parties clearly intended a condition.

a.   **Forfeiture.**   Forfeiture usually involves amounts a party has irretrievably invested before the condition excused the other party's performance. For instance, insurance premiums, installment payments, or other expenditures may be unrecoverable and, therefore, forfeited. Forfeiture does not refer to the benefits expected under the contract.

b.   **Disproportion.**   Disproportionate forfeiture requires that the loss to one party greatly exceed the benefit the other receives from the condition. [The benefits of conditions are discussed above. See 15.B.5.] For example, the benefit of timely notice to the insurer of (ability to investigate promptly) may be relatively small compared to the loss to the insured (in premiums paid or in the cost to rebuild without insurance). A slight imbalance, however, is unlikely to induce a court to ignore the condition.

c. **Materiality.** A condition may be a material part of the exchange. For instance, if no fire occurred, the insurer keeps the premiums and pays nothing to the insured. The court will not restructure the deal by excusing the condition. [Note: alternatively, the court could excuse the condition and require the insurer to pay the insured the cost to repair fire damage as promised — which is $0, if no fire occurred.]

E. CLASSIFYING CONDITIONS

Although you need to recognize conditions and their effect, you usually do not need to put conditions into a classification. In case you encounter cases that use these categories, they are defined here.

1. Express Conditions

Most conditions are specified by the parties in their agreement. These are **express conditions**.

2. Implied Conditions

Conditions can be imposed upon the parties by law, much as the court supplies any other term as a gap filler. Restatement (Second) of Contracts §226. These are called **implied conditions**. Two of the most noteworthy implied conditions are discussed below.

a. **Substantial performance by the other party.** Even if a contract does not say so, a party may refuse to perform when the other party's breach is material. This implied condition is the subject of the next chapter.

b. **Good faith and fair dealing.** The law imposes an obligation to act in good faith in every contract. UCC §1-203; Restatement (Second) of Contracts §205. Often the obligation is a promise, the breach of which may give rise to a cause of action for damages. But the other party's good faith can serve as a condition — or lack of good faith can excuse a condition.

3. Conditions Precedent

By definition, conditions are events that must occur before performance is due. The event must precede the performance.

4.   Conditions Subsequent

An event may end further obligation under a contract after performance had begun. For example, a contract may require a party to perform **until** an event occurs. **This is not a condition at all.** Performance is due, unconditionally, from the outset. The contract is **discharged** (i.e., performance is **complete**) when the event occurs. Discharge excuses further performance.

a.   Interpretation favors conditions precedent.   When contract language is unclear, courts will interpret terms as creating conditions, not as discharging duties that have already fallen due. See Restatement (Second) of Contracts §227(3).

b.   Avoid this terminology.   If you are tempted to call something a condition subsequent, try to reframe the issue in terms of discharge. Calling it a condition is more likely to confuse than enlighten.

REVIEW QUESTIONS AND ANSWERS

Question: How do promises and conditions differ?
Answer:

1.   **Differences in Effect.** The failure to perform a promise entitles the other party to sue you for damages caused by the breach. The nonoccurrence of a condition excuses the other party's performance but does not entitle her to any damages for breach. If a term is both a promise and a condition, nonoccurrence entitles the party not to perform and to sue for any damages.

2.   **Difference in Intent.** If the parties intend the nonoccurrence to give rise to an action for damages, it is a promise. If the parties intend it to excuse performance, it is a condition. Differences in form are clues to intent, not the test itself.

3.   **Differences in Form.** A condition usually begins with a word such as "if" or "unless." An event that will or will not occur without regard to how the parties act usually is a condition. (It is unusual for a person to promise something beyond her power to perform.) A commitment to achieve a particular event or result usually is a promise.

Question: How can you persuade a court to interpret language as a promise rather than a condition?
Answer: If the language is clearly a condition, you probably cannot persuade a court to interpret it as a promise. Thus, you must argue that the language fairly could be taken as a promise to produce an event rather than as a complete excuse to the other's performance if the event did not occur.

Courts generally interpret a doubtful term as a promise. Thus, establishing the plausibility of that interpretation should suffice.

Question: If a court decides language was a promise instead of a condition, will that prevent the other party from refusing to perform?

Answer: No. Material failure to perform a promise also can excuse the other party's performance. You gain the opportunity to argue that the nonoccurrence of the event was not material. If successful, the other party must perform, but can recover damages for the breach.

Question: Can a party who has waived a condition later refuse to perform if the condition does not occur?

Answer: Yes. Waiver is revocable by notice to the other party, unless the other party has relied on the waiver to her detriment. Reliance converts a waiver into an estoppel.

MATERIAL BREACH: DOES NONPERFORMANCE JUSTIFY TERMINATION?

CHAPTER OVERVIEW

A party's duty to perform is conditional on the absence of any earlier **uncured material** nonperformance by the other party (e.g., If the other guy doesn't deliver the goods, your duty to pay for them is suspended.). This implies several questions:

- Was the other party's performance required first or simultaneously?
- Was the other party's nonperformance **material**?
- Was the other party's nonperformance **cured** (by resuming performance) in time?

The order of performance, if not specified in the contract, is:

- Simultaneous performance, if possible.
- If only one party's performance requires time, she must perform first.

Material nonperformance depends on five factors, weighed in an indeterminate way.

- How much of the contract's benefit will the nonbreaching party lose because of the breach?
- Will damages adequately compensate for the benefit lost?
- How much will the breaching party **forfeit** if the contract is terminated?
- Is the breaching party likely to **cure**?
- Is the breaching party acting in **good faith**?

Material breach may not immediately **discharge** the nonbreaching party's remaining duties. Thus, time may exist within which the breach may be **cured**.

- Nonperformance immediately suspends the other's duty to perform.

- Nonperformance discharges the other's duty when the condition (absence of material nonperformance) cannot occur—that is, when cure is no longer possible.

The time for **cure** (between **breach** and **discharge**) depends on amorphous factors, including:

- The factors determining **materiality**;
- The extent to which delay will hinder **substitute arrangements** by the nonbreaching party;
- The extent to which the contract makes timely performance **essential**.

Forfeiture may be limited by treating the contract as **divisible**. **Divisibility** involves enforcing the portion of the contract already performed but **discharging** the remaining duties.

A contract is **divisible** if it includes **pairs of part performances** that are **agreed equivalents**.

A.   RATIONALE

Why allow termination for material breach? The party who performs first is at a disadvantage. The other party, by not performing, receives all the benefits of the contract but incurs none of the costs—unless the performing party sues. The cost of attorneys and the risk that a jury underestimate damages may deter suit or, at least, produce a settlement for less than the value of performance. Thus, a party who performs last has a strategic advantage. (Most parties perform rather than exploit this advantage. The rules here deal with those who do not perform.) As a result, **parties prefer not to perform unless the other party either has performed or is prepared to perform immediately.**

1.   Terminology: Dependent and Independent Promises

Sometimes courts refer to promises as dependent or independent. This language really represents a conclusion about whether one party's failure to perform a promise justifies the other party's refusal to perform in return. The terminology is not very useful, but you need to understand it if you encounter it.

    a.   **Independent promises.** Promises are **independent** if they must be performed even if the other party has not performed. At one time the law considered promises **independent**.

EXAMPLE AND ANALYSIS

Seller sold buyer a cow for 50 shillings. Seller sued for the price. Buyer defended that the cow had not been delivered (at least, delivery was not mentioned in the complaint, as it would need to be if delivery were a condition of the duty to pay). *Nichols v. Raynbred*, 80 Eng. Rep. 238 (K.B. 1615). Held: for seller. Even if the cow was not delivered, buyer can sue for damages.

Puzzling Motives. Why would seller refuse to deliver the cow but sue for the price? Perhaps damages for nondelivery were less than 50 shillings. When buyer sues (for breach of the promise to deliver the cow), she may recover the value of the cow. If the cow is worth more than 50 shillings, she profits. But if the cow is worth less than 50 shillings, she recovers less than the 50 shillings seller recovered.

b. **Dependent promises.** Promises are **dependent** if one party's duty to perform depends on whether the other party has performed.

c. **Invoking independent promises.** If one party's performance was substantial, the other must perform despite minor breaches. In effect, this means the promises were independent. But the issue turns on the nature of the performance, not the nature of the promises.

d. **Invoking dependent promises.** Allowing termination for material breach makes promises (to some extent) **dependent**: One party's duty to perform depends on the other party's performance of (at least) the most important duties under the contract. Again, however, the issue revolves around the extent of the breach (or performance), not the character of the promises.

e. **Note.** Dependent promises do not prevent the Alphonse–Gaston problem. ("After you." "No, after you." "No, I insist: after you." etc.). If neither party has performed, **dependent promises** mean **neither** party can recover; **independent promises** mean **either** party can recover.

2. **Opportunistic Termination of Contracts**

Dependent promises create opportunities for abuse similar to those noted for conditions. See 15.B.6. The right to refuse to perform because the other party breached will be invoked selectively. No one tries to terminate a good contract.

a.   **Advantageous contracts are enforced.**   A party who made a good deal often does not want her performance excused when the other party breaches, unless she can get the same benefits elsewhere. She may sue for specific performance or, at least, expectation damages.

b.   **Disadvantageous contracts are terminated.**   A party who made a bad deal wants out. She may be able to get the same goods for less elsewhere. Termination permits her to refuse to pay the higher price she promised under the contract. Or she may no longer want the goods, if (for example) the demand for them has diminished and she cannot resell them at a profit. In either event, the termination is motivated by other factors: Breach is not the reason for termination; it is the excuse that allows termination.

   i.   **Entire performance affected.**   Termination may affect the entire contract, not just future performance. For instance, suppose a shipment of 100 cartons of fruit is one carton short. If buyer can get fruit cheaper elsewhere, she might try to reject the whole shipment. See UCC §2-601. (In appropriate cases, courts can prevent this effect. See 16.G.)

   ii.   **Prior performance affected.**   Termination may alter the price for performance already rendered. For instance, suppose a contractor misses an essential deadline after the building is 70% complete. If termination is allowed, the contractor may be unable to recover the contract price for the work so far. (She can sue for restitution, but recovery would be limited to the fair market value of the services, not the contract price.) Because the owner will terminate only if the contract price is higher than the market price, this will create a bargain for the owner—not only when she hires a new contractor to finish the job but also when she settles the lawsuit with the first contractor.

c.   **Termination requires material breach.**   Requiring a material breach limits the opportunities for opportunism. Minor defaults may justify damages but will not justify termination.

3.   The Wages of Breach

Arguably, the breaching party deserves no protection from the consequences of her own breach. She can protect herself from termination simply by performing. Why not allow termination for every breach, even immaterial ones?

a. **Innocent breach.**   Avoiding breach is harder than it sounds.

   i. **Honest interpretations.**   Sometimes contracts are hard to interpret. Words that seemed clear during negotiations take on different meanings as problems arise. A party may believe it is performing until a court decides whose interpretation is correct.

   ii. **Unavoidable breach.**   Despite superhuman efforts, a party may be unable to perform every detail of the contract. Sanctions to encourage additional efforts may fail — or may produce precautions so extreme they are wasteful. Delays in performance are particularly easy to understand. Have you ever mailed a check really early that arrived late anyway?

 ## EXAMPLE AND ANALYSIS

Consider some of the ways termination might affect you. Should your insurer be able to cancel the policy every time payment is a day late? Should your landlord be entitled to evict you if your rent is late? (Only when rents are rising, of course. The landlord will excuse the breach if a new lease would involve lower rent.) Should a bank be allowed to cancel your credit card when payment is late or less than the minimum due?

b. **Wasteful opportunism.**   Opportunism involves costs, too.

   i. **Disproportionate costs.**   Termination may cost the breaching party far more than the harm caused by the breach.

 ## EXAMPLE AND ANALYSIS

A builder spent $77,000 building a house. For the plumbing, it used the wrong manufacturer's pipe. The owner refused to make the final payment unless the builder tore down the walls and inserted the specified pipe. It appeared the pipe used was as good as the pipe called for in the contract. The court allowed the builder to recover the payment — less any damages the owner could prove because of the substitution. *Jacob & Youngs v. Kent*, 129 N.E. 889 (N.Y. 1921).

    ii.   Exaggerated concerns.   Opportunistic parties may look for any excuse, no matter how minor, to justify termination of the contract. Breaches a party really doesn't care about may be raised as justifications for termination. Even with the requirement of material breach, small breaches may be blown out of proportion to justify termination and allow her to make a different, more profitable, deal.

4. The Danger of Termination

Refusing to perform because the other party breached first is perilous. If a court later decides the breach was not **material**, a party's refusal to perform is a breach (because her nonperformance was not excused). Instead of a nonbreaching party exercising rights against the breacher, she becomes the breaching party and must pay damages caused by her breach. Because termination usually arises in contracts that were bad for the terminating party and good for the other party, the damages the terminating party must pay may be substantial.

    a.   Uncertainty may deter opportunism.   The danger of terminating wrongfully may deter opportunistic terminations. But it also may deter appropriate terminations, forcing parties to continue to deal with unreliable breachers, even though they could receive much better terms from others who they can trust to perform rather than breach.

 # EXAMPLE AND ANALYSIS

Defendant (Harrison) operated a dry cleaning business. He leased a sign from plaintiff for the front of the business. (The lease was a sale, but title remained in plaintiff until the last lease payment was made.) Plaintiff agreed to maintain the sign "as often as [plaintiff] deemed necessary" during the lease period. A tomato and some rust soiled the sign, but plaintiff did not respond to repeated complaints by defendant. Defendant stopped making payments. Plaintiff sued for the entire amount due. *Walker & Co. v. Harrison*, 81 N.W.2d 352 (Mich. 1957). Held: for plaintiff. The failure to clean the sign was not a material breach. Thus, defendant's performance was due and failure to perform was breach. Defendant could have sued for damages resulting from plaintiff's nonperformance but had no right to terminate the contract and stop performing.

> **b. Law enhances uncertainty.** The consequences of terminating prematurely make it important to have fairly clear rules governing when termination is appropriate. Instead, we have a rule that is as vague as any you will study in this class. But see UCC §2-601 (offering a fairly clear rule for sales of goods); 16.F.2.d.

B. THE RULE

One party's substantial performance is a condition of the other party's obligation to perform. More precisely, a party need not perform if there is an earlier **uncured material nonperformance** by the other party. Restatement (Second) of Contracts §237. The rule sounds simple. The devil, as they say, is in the details.

1. Nonperformance When Due

The other party's performance must have been due earlier to excuse performance. Thus, the order of performance must be established.

2. Material Nonperformance

The other party's nonperformance must have been material. Deciding which breaches are important enough to justify nonperformance is more difficult than it sounds.

3. Uncured Nonperformance

The other party's nonperformance must be uncured. Unless time is crucial, a party may need to suspend performance and await cure before terminating the agreement and making other arrangements.

4. Nonperformance Need Not Be Breach

A failure to perform when due may excuse the other party's performance even if the nonperformance is excused, say, by impracticability or frustration. Nonetheless, this outline and most casebooks commonly use **material breach** as a shorthand for **material nonperformance**.

> **a. Condition versus excuse.** The rule will not come into play if the other party's performance does not become due because a condition does not occur. Only nonperformance "that was earlier **due**" brings this rule into play. Restatement (Second) of Contracts §237.

    b.   **Impracticability or frustration excuses one party.** For the other party to suspend performance, she must invoke this rule and demonstrate that the nonperformance was material.

C. THE ORDER OF PERFORMANCE

The law must decide who was required to perform first to decide whether one party's failure to perform excused the other's decision not to perform.

1. Contract Provisions

A contract may specify which party shall perform first. Courts do not question the parties' decision regarding which should go first. Either of them may extend credit to the other (by performing first and collecting later).

 # EXAMPLE AND ANALYSIS

S sells wheat to B. The contract requires payment within 30 days after delivery. S must perform first by delivering the wheat. S could not refuse to deliver on the ground that B had not paid yet.

2. Simultaneous Performance

When the contract is silent, the parties should perform simultaneously, if possible. Restatement (Second) of Contracts §234. Thus, neither party has a right to receive the other's performance unless she simultaneously performs her duties. For example, payment would be due at the time the buyer receives the goods. See UCC §2-310(a).

    a.   **Tender and breach.** Simultaneity does not prevent termination for material breach. Each party's duty to perform is conditioned on the other's **tender** of substantial performance. Restatement (Second) of Contracts §238.

    b.   **Tender defined.** Tender is an offer to perform immediately combined with a manifest ability to do so. For example, holding cash or a check (in the amount due) and offering it to the seller tenders performance of the duty to pay.

    c. Failure to tender. Upon tendering performance, a party need not complete performance unless the other tenders the return performance. The tendering party need not perform first and face the disadvantage of needing to sue if the other failed to perform. But if each tenders performance, each must immediately complete the transaction.

3. Prolonged Performance First

If one party's performance must be rendered over time, that performance is due first. In some situations, simultaneous performance is impossible.

    a. Employment. Employees earn pay by working for a period of time. Employers need not pay them every second (or minute or hour or day) as they perform. Rather, the employee must work first, then the employer pays for the work completed. The Friday paycheck usually covers the work completed that week; not the work to be done the following week.

    b. Construction. Construction is not instantaneous. The builder must work over time to complete the project. Unless the contract specifies otherwise, courts assume that the party whose performance takes time (the builder) must perform first; payment would be due upon completion.

    c. Practical note: Progress payments. Construction contracts almost always include a schedule of progress payments, allowing the builder to collect partial payments as work progresses. The contract often specifies payments less than the value of the work done, reserving about 10% of each payment until completion of all the work (as an incentive to speed things along and to get them right).

D. FACTORS AFFECTING MATERIALITY OF A BREACH

Restatement (Second) of Contracts §241 identifies five factors deemed significant in deciding whether a breach is material. These are not elements of a defense. The nonbreaching party need not prove all five. No one factor is determinative, though in any given case one factor might outweigh the others. Examples of how courts balance these factors are given below. See 16.F.

1. Amount of Benefit Lost

When the breach deprives the nonbreaching party of a substantial part of the benefit expected under the contract, it is more likely to be material.

Breaches that have a relatively modest impact on the overall benefit received are less likely to be material.

 ## EXAMPLE AND ANALYSIS

Plaintiff built a sign and leased it to defendant for the front of his business. Plaintiff agreed to maintain the sign. A tomato and some rust soiled the sign but plaintiff did not respond promptly to defendant's call for maintenance. Defendant stopped making payments and plaintiff sued. *Walker & Co. v. Harrison*, 81 N.W.2d 352 (Mich. 1957). Held: for plaintiff. The failure to clean the sign was a relatively small part of the benefit defendant received under the contract—the production of the sign being much more significant. This was one factor in deciding that the failure to clean the sign was not a material breach.

2. Adequacy of Compensation

When damages can compensate for the losses caused by the breach, the breach is less likely to be material. Compensation partially makes up for the benefits lost, reducing the weight of the first factor.

a. Damages for breach. When nonperformance is a breach, adequacy of compensation will depend on the remedies available. When damages are difficult to prove, compensation may not be adequate.

b. Restitution. When nonperformance is not a breach (because excused by, say, impracticability), damages will be unavailable. The adequacy of compensation then may depend on whether a cause of action exists at all, such as a claim for unjust enrichment. If a claim exists, the adequacy of the remedy also must be addressed.

c. Termination may prevent some losses. If the nonbreaching party can withhold payment, she will not need to recover that money in a lawsuit. Similarly if the nonbreaching party can stop work, she will sink less expense into the project and have less need to seek damages in a lawsuit. Termination and prompt cover might prevent consequential losses. If preventing loss is significantly better than compensating for it later, the court is more likely to find the breach material. (In fact, a plaintiff may not recover damages if she unreasonably failed to avoid them. See 22.E.1.)

3.   Amount of Forfeiture by the Breaching Party

When the breaching party has relied significantly on the contract, suspension or termination may produce significant waste. Wasted reliance makes a breach less likely to be material.

a.   **Forfeiture versus expectation.**   Forfeiture refers to wasted expense preparing to perform or performing prior to the breach. Forfeiture does **not** mean the breaching party will lose the benefit of the bargain. Unlike the nonbreaching party, a breaching party is not entitled to the benefit of the bargain at the other party's expense (even when the nonperformance is excused.)

 EXAMPLES AND ANALYSIS

1. A builder spent $77,000 building a house. For the plumbing, it used the wrong manufacturer's pipe. To cure, the builder would need to tear down most of the house and rebuild it; the expense of building it the first time would be wasted. A finding of material breach would produce forfeiture. *Jacob & Youngs v. Kent*, 129 N.E. 889 (N.Y. 1921).

2. Buyer ordered stationery from seller, to be engraved with buyer's logo and drawings. The shipment arrived a few days late. The goods could not be resold to anyone else. A finding of material breach would produce forfeiture. *Beck & Pauli Lithographing v. Colorado Milling & Elevator*, 52 Fed. 700 (8th Cir. 1892).

b.   **Resale or cover may prevent waste.**   Although the breaching party may not receive as much as promised under the original contract, the resale may cover all reliance expenses, eliminating forfeiture. This explains the normal rule for sales of goods that any nonconformity is a material breach. Because goods usually can be resold to others, no forfeiture occurs.

c.   **Net forfeiture.**   The amount of forfeiture is net of any payments received so far or other remedies available, such as restitution.

EXAMPLE AND ANALYSIS

C, a construction contractor, agrees to build a house for L, a landowner. After numerous delays, L seeks to cancel the contract. C can resell some materials not yet used on the project. The materials already attached to L's land, however, cannot be retrieved and resold by C. The cost of those materials (and the labor to erect them) would be a forfeiture. Any progress payments C has received for work already done would reduce the amount of the forfeiture. So would any recovery in restitution for work not yet compensated by progress payments. A small net forfeiture makes termination less harsh and, therefore, makes it more likely a court would find the breach material.

4. Likelihood of Cure

When cure is uncertain, the breach is more likely to be material. The non-breaching party has a greater need to seek substitute performance when cure is uncertain.

a. Cure obviates termination.   When cure is likely or certain, the non-breaching party will obtain much of what she expected, though late. She need not seek out substitute performance, especially if cure will be as quick as cover.

b. Cure may be insufficient.   Even if cure is certain, breach may be material — particularly when timely performance is crucial to the non-breaching party. Performance may be worthless by the time cure occurs. Alternatively, the nonbreaching party may be able to cover faster than the breaching party can cure. In either event, a finding of material breach may protect the nonbreaching party better than cure, even if cure is certain.

5. Breaching Party's Good Faith

A party's lack of good faith and fair dealing increases the likelihood of a finding of material breach. The nonbreaching party may need to seek performance from a trustworthy source. A party who breaches despite good faith efforts to perform poses less risk of future breaches. Similarly, courts show less complacence about imposing losses on a party who strove to perform than about imposing them on a party who breached willfully.

E.   SUSPENSION OR TERMINATION? TIME FOR CURE

If a breach is material, the nonbreaching party immediately may suspend performance until the other party cures. Eventually, the party may want to terminate the contract and make other arrangements for the performance (or even live without it). Determining whether termination is permissible requires an additional inquiry.

1.   The Rule

A party has no further obligation to perform once a condition of her performance "can no longer occur." Restatement (Second) of Contracts §225. Substantial performance by the other party is one such condition. If the breach would still be material even if the breaching party cured, the nonbreaching party need not wait any longer. Her performance is discharged and she may terminate the contract.

2.   Time for Cure

The time for cure is governed by a set of factors similar to those for determining materiality—and every bit as amorphous. Restatement (Second) of Contracts §242. All the factors for materiality are included in this list of factors. Again, no one factor is determinative. Again, in any given case, one factor might outweigh all the others.

    a.   Five factors governing materiality.   The factors for determining materiality will not be reiterated here. See 16.D. Loss of benefit weighs in favor of quicker discharge; compensation, forfeiture, cure, and good faith weigh against.

    b.   Amount of harm from delaying substitute arrangements.   When delay will prevent or hinder efforts to make substitute arrangements, such as cover, discharge will occur sooner.

        i.   Minimizing loss.   Substitute arrangements may prevent or minimize consequential losses. Remedial rules seek to encourage efforts to minimize the loss. See 22.E.1. This factor recognizes the usefulness of preventing losses rather than compensating them after the fact.

        ii.   Importance of promptness.   Cover is particularly important because damages for breach usually are measured on the day of the breach. See UCC §§2-708, 2-713. Subsequent fluctuations in price cannot be recovered. Thus, prompt cover may be vital.

c.   **Agreement that time is of the essence.**   The contract may require timely performance, either expressly or by implication. An agreement that timely performance is important makes immediate discharge more likely.

i.   **Late performance curable.**   Merely specifying a time for performance does not make timing essential. Cure is possible, even though the time for performance has passed and subsequent performance cannot be timely. Restatement (Second) of Contracts §242(c). Courts usually will allow some room for cure unless the agreement shows that timely performance is important. (Thus, paying rent a day late cures the materiality of the breach, even though it does not undo the breach.)

ii.   **Substance, not form.**   Stock phrases such as "time is of the essence" may not make timing essential. These words support the claim that time was important to the parties, but they are not determinative. If delay seems to cause little problem and damages for delay seem adequate, courts will allow time for cure.

iii.   **Timely performance as a condition.**   Parties can make timely performance an express condition. Because express conditions apply strictly, they make materiality irrelevant. Courts examine materiality for **promises** because the parties did not agree to make them conditions; the court imposes that result upon the parties. (If the parties make timely performance an express condition, the court could still excuse a condition that worked a disproportionate forfeiture. See 14.C.4.)

F.   EXAMPLES: BALANCING FORFEITURE WITH PARTIES' EXPECTATIONS

Some types of cases present recurring problems. These can be discussed most effectively by addressing each type of case independently, with examples. This section will not give you a formula for resolving the balance required under the Restatement. But it will give you some indication of how courts have applied these factors. That may help you apply them when a new situation appears before you at the exam.

1.   Construction Cases

When a building contractor breaches a contract after considerable work, courts often will find substantial performance. Several aspects of construction contracts support this result.

     a. **Forfeiture is extremely likely.** The materials have been attached to the nonbreaching party's land, so they cannot be salvaged. Labor, of course, cannot be salvaged; once the day is worked, it can never be spent on a different job. Thus, discharging the buyer's duty to pay almost inevitably works a forfeiture unless compensated. Finding substantial performance allows compensation under the contract (less the damages caused by the breach). Finding material breach relegates the builder to progress payments already made and restitution for the fair market value of the labor and materials.

     b. **Damages often compensate nonbreaching party.** Losses may be easy to calculate in construction cases. When the builder has made a mistake, even a serious one, cost to repair can be ascertained by getting bids on the work. Appraisal can estimate how much less the building is worth with the mistake than without it. (Value as is can be determined exactly by selling the property, though the owner may have good reasons not to sell.) Thus, damages often will compensate adequately for the harm.

     c. **Cover is difficult.** Substitute arrangements may require no more time than cure. In construction, the time to hire a new contractor frequently exceeds the time required for the original contractor to cure. Thus, immediate termination is less important as a means of preventing harm.

 # EXAMPLES AND ANALYSIS

1. A builder spent $77,000 building a house. For the plumbing, it used the wrong manufacturer's pipe. The pipe used may have been of equal quality, but the testimony was excluded. The error was discovered after the building was completed but before the final payment (about $3,500) was made. The builder sued to collect. If the breach was material, the duty to pay was not due until the breach was cured. Cure would require tearing down much of the house to replace pipe in the walls — a substantial forfeiture. But if the pipe used was equally good, the repairs would not make the house any more valuable. The court remanded for consideration of whether the breach was material, including evidence on the relative quality of the pipe and whether the house was worth less because it had the wrong pipe. *Jacob & Youngs v. Kent*, 129 N.E. 889 (N.Y. 1921).

Did the owner really want the right pipe or did she only want to keep the final payment? Some people have idiosyncratic tastes. Perhaps the owner's dream house was ruined because the wrong pipe was used, a fact that will haunt her every time she brushes her teeth. Probably these cases are rare. Most people care about the quality of the pipe. If the pipe is as good, who cares that it is from a different factory? Courts could try to allow recovery for people with idiosyncratic tastes. But idiosyncracies may be too easy to fake. Given a chance to keep a few thousand dollars, more people might develop a few idiosyncrasies (after the fact) — even inserting specific clauses they don't care about in contracts, hoping the other party will overlook them. By keeping the rules and the recoveries within reason, courts may deter abuse and posturing.

2. The builder did not quite finish the house, but sued for final payment. The builder agreed that owner could withhold $1,600, the cost to finish the job. Owner claimed damages for other mistakes in construction, including the removal and rebuilding of a wall one foot from its location. That would cost $4,000 but would not increase the value of the house at all. If that breach was material, the owner had no duty to pay. But moving the wall would waste the cost to build it originally, with no benefit to the owner. *Plante v. Jacobs*, 103 N.W.2d 296 (Wis. 1960). Held: the builder has substantially performed. The owner recovered the cost to complete and to repair all defects except moving the wall. The owner received the benefit she bargained for in that respect: a habitable house with a certain value.

3. Builder sued for payment. Church defended on the ground that the ceiling was two feet too low, the windows were too short, and the seats too narrow. If these defects were material, the church's duty to pay would not be due until the builder corrected the defects. The court held that the building was suitable as a church, thus giving the owner some benefit (substantial performance). Purporting to apply a restitution theory, the court allowed recovery of the contract price less the diminished value caused by the defects. *Planches v. Swedish Evangelical Lutheran Church*, 10 A. 264 (Conn. 1887).

Restitution is the appropriate remedy if the breach was material. Payment of the contract price would not be due, but the builder could recover the fair market value of the services in restitution. But the court actually awarded the contract price less damages for diminution in value! That is right only if the court found no material breach. The statement that the church was serviceable for its intended purpose sounds like a finding that the builder substantially performed.

---

    d.   **Beneficial performance.**   Note that all the cases involve buildings that were useful for their intended purpose — and often had almost the same value they would have had without the defect. Although the problems are hard to repair, they do not seem to deprive the nonbreaching party of the benefit of the bargain. The breaches seem to be annoying more than harmful.

2. Sales of Goods

Courts originally refused to recognize substantial performance in sales of goods. This was called the **perfect tender rule:** Unless the performance complied with the contract in every detail, the breach was material. The UCC perpetuates that basic rule but includes some exceptions that reduce its harshest impact.

a. **Forfeiture is rare.**   Most goods are fungible. If the buyer refuses to take them, they can be sold to someone else. Thus, allowing the buyer to cancel when tender was not perfect rarely worked a hardship.

b. **Compensation could be difficult.**   Although the value of the goods may be easy to determine, the consequential losses may be uncertain — or unrecoverable because unforeseeable. Thus, damages might not compensate for the full losses the buyer would suffer.

c. **Prompt cover may be important.**   Prompt cover can prevent or minimize consequential losses. Prompt cover also guards against fluctuations in price. The price of goods tends to fluctuate more rapidly than the price of land or other contract items. Thus, postponing cover to allow the seller to cure risks increasing the loss if prices change and cure is not forthcoming. Because damages are calculated on the date of the breach, the seller would not need to compensate the buyer for losses caused by subsequent changes in the price.

d. **The UCC.**   Without attempting to recite all UCC provisions relevant to tender and cure, the following provisions show both the codification and the softening of the perfect tender rule.

　　i. **Perfect tender.**   Any defect in the tender, no matter how slight, justifies rejection of the goods. UCC §2-601.

　　ii. **Timely cure.**   If the time for performance has not yet expired, seller may cure by tendering conforming goods. UCC §2-508(1).

　　iii. **Untimely cure.**   Even if the time for performance has expired, the seller is allowed a chance to cure within a reasonable time if she had reason to believe the goods tendered would be acceptable to the buyer. UCC §2-508(2).

iv. **Accepted goods.** If buyer accepts nonconforming goods, she may later revoke the acceptance only if "the non-conformity substantially impairs" the value of the goods. UCC §2-608.

v. **Multiple lots.**   If performance involves a series of installments, the buyer cannot reject future installments unless the nonconformity in the current installment "impairs the value of the whole contract." UCC §2-612.

 # Examples and Analysis

1. Buyer ordered 300 crates of onions from Australia, to be shipped in March 1918. Only one ship sailed from Australia to the United States in March. Seller was ready to load 300 crates but could only load 240 because the U.S. government commandeered the rest of the ship (during World War I) for wheat. Plaintiff (who had tried to cancel the order before shipment) rejected the onions. Seller sued. *Prescott & Co. v. Powles & Co.*, 193 P. 680 (Wash. 1920). Held: for buyer. Seller's nonperformance was excusable; buyer could not collect damages from seller. But tender was not perfect, so buyer's duty to perform did not become due.

2. Buyer ordered stationery from seller, to be engraved with buyer's logo and drawings. The shipment arrived a few days late. Buyer rejected the goods, which could not be resold to anyone else. Seller sued. *Beck & Pauli Lithographing v. Colorado Milling & Elevator*, 52 Fed. 700 (8th Cir. 1892). Held: for seller. The court noted the perfect tender rule applicable to sales goods. The court circumvented the rule by holding that the contract called for services (the manufacture of specially designed stationery), not the sale of goods. The court applied the rule for construction contracts (substantial performance).

The result is just, but would be hard to justify under the UCC. Stationery is a good. The court could not avoid the statute by pretending it was not. The facts illustrate that the general factors that make the perfect tender rule appropriate for sales of goods are not universally true. Today, seller might prevail under §2-612 — but probably would lose if §2-601 governed.

3. Plaintiff (Moulton) promised to produce 26 molds for production of salable innersoles and to deliver the molds within 5 weeks. After 10 weeks, plaintiff tendered molds that did not fit the machine and produced innersoles that were not salable due to flashing (a little excess plastic at the mold seam). Defendant rejected the molds and covered at a higher price. Plaintiff sued for the amount due under the contract (less an allowance for the flashing). The judge instructed the jury on substantial performance. The jury awarded plaintiff a little less than the contract price. *Moulton*

Cavity & Mold v. Lyn-Flex Indus., 396 A.2d 1024 (Me. 1979). Held: for buyer. If tender varies in any detail from the contract, the buyer may reject the goods. The court remanded the case for new trial, because the five-week provision was not in the written contract and the jury could decide how long was a reasonable time for plaintiff to perform.

Why does the time for performance matter? If the molds tendered would not produce salable innersoles, they were nonconforming even if timely. But UCC §2-508 allows a seller to cure if "the time for performance has not yet expired." Thus, if a reasonable time was longer than 10 weeks, there might still be time for seller to tender conforming molds.

3. Failure to Pay Money

Courts often find the failure to pay money material — for reasons that are not entirely clear.

a. **Benefit material.**   Money often is the entire benefit a party expects from a contract. Not receiving it destroys the benefit, which suggests breach is material.

b. **Compensation is easy.**   The amount of money owed usually is clear. Interest will compensate for late payment in most cases. Because termination is unnecessary, the breach seems immaterial.

c. **No forfeiture.**   The breaching party usually suffers no forfeiture. She has kept the money instead of paying it; it remains hers to use (pending the damage action). Because termination would not harm the breaching party, finding the breach material works no injustice.

d. **Substitute arrangements vary.**   The need to cover varies with the item sold. Prices of goods fluctuate rapidly, so promptly selling them to another may be important. Land values fluctuate more slowly, so time for cure may not harm efforts to minimize the loss.

 ## EXAMPLE AND ANALYSIS

Plaintiff (Spindler) owned a newspaper. Sackett agreed to buy the stock for $85,000, payable in three installments, the last of which was to be $60,000. Sackett paid the first two installments, but the check for the third installment bounced. Sackett several times assured Spindler that he would perform, but kept delaying performance. Eventually, Spindler sold his stock to another for about $21,000. He sued Sackett for the difference. *Sackett v. Spindler*, 56 Cal. Rptr. 435 (1967). Held: judgment for Spindler affirmed. Sackett's breach justified Spindler in refusing to perform and seeking damages for the breach. The delays made cure seem unlikely and the court questioned Sackett's good faith. Even though Spindler received part performance and money damages would compensate for the rest, Spindler could treat the contract as materially breached.

G.   DIVISIBILITY: MITIGATING THE HARSHNESS OF MATERIAL BREACH

Sometimes material breach occurs after the breaching party has performed part (or even most) of the contract. Compensation is required for benefits of part performance bestowed on the nonbreaching party. **The issue is whether to allow compensation under the contract or to limit the breaching party to a claim for restitution.** By allowing recovery under the contract, the court can reduce the difficulty of ascertaining the fair market value of the performance (as required under restitution) and minimize the advantage of opportunistic claims of material breach.

1.   Effect of Divisibility

If a breaching party has performed all duties of a divisible portion of a contract, the court will allow that party to recover the contract price (or other return performance) for that part of the contract — even though the party breached other portions of the divisible contract.

a.   Limits effect of material breach.   A nonbreaching party may not terminate a performed part of a divisible contract, even if the unperformed part would be material. A material breach would justify termination of the unperformed part but would not allow her to escape from the entire contract.

b.   Contract recovery by breaching party.   When a contract is divisible, the breaching party may have rendered full performance of a divisible portion. If so, she is entitled to recover full compensation under the contract for the divisible portion performed — even though her non-performance precludes recovery under the remainder of the contract.

EXAMPLE AND ANALYSIS

Defendant (Buyer) ordered gloves from plaintiff, a manufacturer. Plaintiff (Seller) never delivered part of the order (24 dozen gloves). Buyer did not pay for the gloves delivered, arguing perfect tender was a condition of her duty to pay. Seller sued for the price of the gloves delivered. *National Knitting v. Bouton & Germain*, 123 N.W. 624 (Wis. 1909). Held: for Seller.

i.   Why didn't Buyer sue first, seeking damages for the failure to deliver the remaining gloves? Three explanations are possible.

(a)   Buyer may have thought it could keep the gloves and not pay for them, which would make up for the losses it suffered from the breach. That is too naive to credit. Restitution for benefits received was common. Buyer must have known it would need to pay at least the fair market value of the gloves accepted.

(b)   Buyer may have been preparing to sue when Seller filed first. Buyer's claim would need to be brought as a counter-claim in Seller's action, which it was.

(c)   Buyer may not have been injured by the loss of the gloves. If prices were declining, Buyer could cover for less than the contract price. Thus, it had no loss.

ii.   Why did Buyer keep the gloves and refuse to pay? Why not reject the imperfect tender if receiving all the gloves was important?

(a)   Restitution is measured by the value of the gloves at the time and place of delivery. If the price of gloves declined after contract formation, Buyer could keep the gloves and pay less than the contract price.

(b)   Divisibility removes this advantage. Buyer must pay the contract price for any gloves she keeps, not just their restitution value.

Example and Analysis

Plaintiff (Gill) agreed to drive a specified quantity of defendant's logs downstream to its boom for an amount specified per 1,000 feet of logs delivered. Defendant drove some of the logs to the boom, but a dam burst washing away the rest of the logs. Plaintiff sued for payment at the contract rate. Defendant contended its performance was not due, because the plaintiff did not substantially perform the contract. *Gill v. Johnstown Lumber*, 25 A. 120 (Pa. 1892). Held: judgment for defendant reversed. Plaintiff could recover at the contract rate for the logs delivered. Plaintiff, however, could not recover for logs driven part way to the boom, only logs actually delivered.

Notes: (1) Without divisibility, plaintiff (the breaching party) could recover the fair market value of the services rendered, up to the contract rate. If the market value was less than the contract price, defendant would receive the services for less than she promised to pay. (2) In a normal case, defendant could recover damages for nonperformance of the rest of the contract. Here, the flood probably excused nonperformance. See 17.A.

2. **Identifying Divisible Contracts**

When the contract can be divided into **pairs of part performances that are agreed equivalents**, the court may treat the contract as if it was two or more contracts, each involving a pair of part performances. Restatement (Second) of Contracts §240.

   a. **Corresponding pairs of part performances.** Divisibility usually requires a contract that specifies a price for each part of performance. Prices per unit (e.g., $1 per ton) make divisibility easy. Sometimes a court will divide a total price that was calculated from per-unit prices. When the contract does not specify price, divisibility is common. A reasonable price supplied by a court (per UCC §2-305) may take into account the value of each part of the performance.

   b. **Agreed equivalents versus timing provisions.** Pairs of part performances must be agreed equivalents. When a price per unit is specified, the parties clearly intended the price as the compensation for each unit. Sometimes, however, a payment regulates the timing of performance. It may not reflect an intent that each payment compensates for the work done so far.

EXAMPLE AND ANALYSIS

The U.S. government entered an industrial preparedness contract with a company to ensure it would be ready to provide vital defense parts in case of emergency. The company completed and tested its preparedness to produce the part, thus becoming entitled to progress payments under the contract. The contract required the company to remain on call for six years. The company became insolvent and its creditors sued the United States for $45,000 in unpaid progress payments. The United States counterclaimed for a refund of payments made so far. *Pennsylvania Exch. Bank v. United States*, 170 F. Supp. 629 (Ct. Cl. 1959). Held: for the United States. The contract was not divisible. The United States had only one benefit: the readiness to produce the part in case of emergency. That benefit was not received. The timing of payments for that benefit did not create pairs of part performances that were **agreed equivalents**.

REVIEW QUESTIONS AND ANSWERS

Question: What factors will a court consider in deciding whether a breach is material?

Answer: The extent to which the nonbreaching party is deprived of the benefit of the bargain, the extent to which damages can compensate for the loss, the extent of any forfeiture by the breaching party, the likelihood of cure, and the good faith of the breaching party.

Question: If a breach is material, can a party immediately terminate the contract and seek substitute performance elsewhere?

Answer: Not always. The nonbreaching party may need to perform as promised if cure is reasonably prompt.

Question: What will a court consider in deciding whether termination was premature?

Answer: All the factors considered when assessing the materiality of the breach, plus the importance of promptly making substitute arrangements and the parties' expressed intent regarding the importance of timely performance.

Question: Will material breach allow a party to terminate the entire contract, including portions that have already been performed?

Answer: Yes, unless the contract is divisible. If the court decides to treat the contract as divisible, termination will not affect any divisible portion that has been performed.

Question: What makes a contract divisible?

Answer: The existence of corresponding pairs of part performances fairly seen as agreed equivalents. This usually requires some form of unit pricing, allowing the allocation of each party's performance as compensation for a part of the other's performance.

EXCUSABLE NONPERFORMANCE: DOES NONPERFORMANCE JUSTIFY DAMAGES?

17

CHAPTER OVERVIEW

Sometimes nonperformance results from unusual causes the breaching party could not have prevented. In these situations, it may seem unjust to require the defendant to pay damages for breach. Several doctrines identify the situations in which performance should be **excused**.

A party's failure to perform may be excused by subsequent **impracticability** if the party proves:

- The parties entered the contract on the **basic assumption** that an event would not occur;
- The event occurred;
- The event made **performance impracticable** (not merely more expensive);
- The party is **not at fault** for the impracticability (**note**: for sales of goods, fault is not mentioned, but **good faith** is always required); and
- The party did not agree to perform despite the occurrence of the event.

A party's failure to perform may be excused by subsequent **frustration** if the party proves:

- The parties entered the contract on the **basic assumption** that an event would not occur;
- The event occurred;
- The event **substantially frustrated** the party's **primary purpose** for entering the contract;
- The party is **not at fault** for the frustration; and
- The party did not agree to perform despite the occurrence of the event.

369

When a fact existing at the time of contract formation makes performance impracticable or frustrates the purpose of the contract, the same rules may prevent a duty from arising.

- If a party had reason to know of the existing fact, she may not rely on its existence to avoid the duty to perform.
- An existing fact may allow relief under the rules governing mistake.

Nonperformance due to impracticability or frustration may not excuse the other party's performance. Rules governing material nonperformance apply.

Temporary impracticability or frustration suspends the duty to perform, but does not automatically discharge it.

Partial impracticability does not discharge performance of other duties if:

- Substantial performance remains practicable; **or**
- The other party agrees to perform in full despite receiving only partial performance.

A.   IMPRACTICABILITY

Extreme events, such as fire, war, drought, disease, or changes in the law, may impede performance. Parties may make unconditional contracts that require performance no matter how extreme the obstacles. Today, however, courts are reluctant to assume that the parties intended to require performance under these circumstances. The doctrine of impracticability excuses performance when events of this type make performance extremely burdensome.

1.   Elements

When the nonoccurrence of an event is a basic assumption on which the contract was made, the occurrence of that event excuses a party's nonperformance if, without the nonperforming party's fault, the event makes performance impracticable—unless the contract or other circumstances indicate that the party agreed to perform despite the event. Restatement (Second) of Contracts §261; UCC §2-615.

a.   Defense for sellers.   The UCC expressly applies only to sellers. UCC §2-615. The Restatement in theory can apply to buyers. But the comments indicate that changes in ability to pay generally are not basic assumptions on which contracts are made. Frustration, however, protects buyers.

b. **Practicability is not a condition.** Cases sometimes call the nonoccurrence of the event a condition. This characterization helps explain the origin of the rule. It does not, however, comport with the Restatement's treatment of conditions. If practicability were a condition of a party's duty to perform, the rules on material nonperformance would not apply. (Because the party's duty to perform would not become due, nonperformance caused by impracticability would not fall within Restatement (Second) of Contracts §237, contrary to the Restatement's clear intent.) In any class taught heavily from the Restatement, avoid referring to impracticability as a constructive or implied condition.

2. Exam Tip: Identify the Event or Contingency

For clarity's sake, it usually is critical to begin your discussion of impracticability by identifying the contingency or event that caused the impracticability. This will make it easier to address whether its nonoccurrence was a basic assumption, whether it occurred without the party's fault, and whether the agreement allocated the risk that this event would occur to one of the parties.

3. Basic Assumption

Unless the nonoccurrence of an event was a basic assumption on which the contract was made, the occurrence of the event will not support a finding of impracticability.

a. **Death or incapacity.** If a particular person is critical to performance, parties usually assume that she will not die or suffer incapacity. Restatement (Second) of Contracts §262. For example, if a law school hired a professor, it could not sue the professor's estate if her death or incapacity prevented her from performing. See, e.g., *O'Neal v. Colton Consolidated School Dist.*, 557 P.2d 11 (Wash. App. 1976) (teacher's deteriorating eyesight excused nonperformance).

b. **Destruction of property.** If the existence of a particular thing is critical to performance, parties usually assume that it will not be destroyed, severely damaged, or prevented from coming into existence. Restatement (Second) of Contracts §263. For example, an agreement to install a floor in a specific warehouse is discharged if the warehouse is destroyed by fire. See *Carroll v. Bowersock*, 164 P.2d 143 (Kan. 1917).

c. **Destruction of identified goods.** The UCC makes special provision for the destruction of goods identified to the contract at the time of formation. See UCC §2-613. When the specific thing sold is destroyed, the duty to deliver is discharged. **Excuse under this section does not require analysis of other elements under §2-615.** (UCC §2-613 involves some details that usually do not arise in a first-year contracts course. If your professor expects detailed knowledge of this provision, read it rather than rely on this outline.)

    d.   Changes in the law.   Parties usually assume that performance is legal and will remain legal. Restatement (Second) of Contracts §264. For example, a brewery's contract to deliver beer would be discharged if the law changed to prohibit sales of alcoholic beverages.

4.   Performance Becomes Impracticable

Impracticability requires more than just reduced profitability or even losses under the contract. "Extreme and unreasonable difficulty, expense, injury or loss" is required. Restatement (Second) of Contracts §261 cmt. d. An increase in cost that "alters the essential nature of the performance" may constitute impracticability. See UCC §2-615 cmt. 4.

    a.   Flexible approach.   Impracticability, by its nature, involves unusual events, the effects of which are difficult to anticipate and to address in the contract. Hardship is not sufficient to justify escape from a disadvantageous contract. But courts do not define precisely how severe the effect must be in order to constitute impracticability.

    b.   Extreme effects versus extreme causes.   Requiring that nonoccurrence be a basic assumption limits excuse to cases where the causes are unusual. Impracticability logically adds a requirement that the effects be extreme. Some courts blend the discussion together. Comments about the extent of impracticability frequently refer to the source of the problem. Acts of God, such as fire, tornado, hurricane, drought, pestilence, flood, and earthquake, receive note. So do acts of third parties, such as war, embargo, and shutdown of supply sources. These illustrate the **events** the parties probably assumed would not occur; they do not illuminate how severe the effect must be to qualify as impracticability.

    c.   Case analysis vital.   Because the standard is flexible, the best way to get a feel for the extent of harm required is to study examples—especially those in your casebook, but a few will be offered here.

EXAMPLE AND ANALYSIS

The United States paid a shipowner to carry wheat from Texas to Iran. Egypt closed the Suez Canal, forcing the ship to travel around the Cape of Good Hope. This added 3,000 miles to a 10,000-mile trip and cost about $44,000 on a $305,000 contract. The court opined that the difference between expected cost and actual cost was not big enough to constitute impracticability. *Transatlantic Financing v. United States*, 363 F.2d 312 (D.C. Cir. 1966); *see also American Trading & Prod. v. Shell Intl. Marine*, 453 F.2d 939 (2d Cir. 1972) (ship diverted around Cape traveled 18,000 miles instead of 10,000 at a cost $132,000 greater than the $417,000 price, held not impracticable). **Both cases depend in part on the interpretation of the contract.**

If the contract **required** the use of Suez, its closure would make performance impracticable. The ship could not use the canal at any price. That would excuse performance and permit the ship to return to port without delivering the cargo. The parties could renegotiate in light of the change. Without a new agreement, the detour around the Cape might deserve compensation outside the contract (usually restitution for the value of services rendered).

Most contracts called for delivery at a specific port. The closure of the canal made performance more expensive but not impossible. Even if both parties assumed the canal would remain open, the increased cost must make performance impracticable, not just more expensive.

EXAMPLES AND ANALYSIS

1. Gulf promised to supply jet fuel to Eastern for five years. The price escalation clause failed to account for the dramatic increase in oil prices following the OPEC embargo in 1973. Gulf argued that the embargo made performance impracticable. The court found insufficient evidence that the price imposed hardship on Gulf. *Eastern Air Lines v. Gulf Oil*, 415 F. Supp. 429 (S.D. Fla. 1975).

The court's reasoning was suspect. The court lumped Gulf and its subsidiaries together and examined total profits rather than the profit or loss on **this contract**. Impracticability assesses the justice of enforcing this contract, given changed circumstances; the existence of other profitable contracts has no obvious bearing on the unexpectedness or severity of the hardship involved in this contract. When big companies claim hardship, courts may repeat this mistake.

2. Defendant was building a bridge near plaintiff's land. Defendant promised to take all the gravel necessary for construction from plaintiff's land and pay for it. After taking about half the gravel needed, defendant bought the remaining gravel elsewhere. The rest of the gravel on plaintiff's land was under water and would require a different, more expensive machine to remove and an expensive drying process before it could be used in the bridge. These measures would cost at least 10 times usual cost of gravel. *Mineral Park Land Co. v. Howard*, 156 P. 458 (Cal. 1916). Held: for defendant.

The court's language suggests that a thing necessary to the performance (enough dry or commercially available gravel) did not exist. The case arguably involves impracticability existing at the time of formation. This would not change the result because neither party had reason to know too little gravel was above the water table. The case also involves partial impracticability. Judgment for plaintiff was affirmed for the amount of gravel actually taken.

---

5.   Without a Party's Fault

When a party's own act makes performance impractical, her performance is not excused.

a.   **Sales of goods versus other contracts.**   Absence of fault is specified by the Restatement but not the UCC provision on impracticability. See UCC §2-615. But see UCC §2-613 (including a fault provision). The UCC's ubiquitous requirement of good faith and fair dealing probably disposes of some cases in which a party's own fault made performance impracticable. The good faith standard, however, probably would not preclude the excuse for negligence.

b.   **Fault caused event.**   A party at fault for causing the **event** to occur is not excused. For example, a party might negligently cause a fire that burns a factory or a crop. Intentional conduct, such as lobbying for a change in the law, might breach the obligation of good faith. Cf., e.g., *Seaman's Direct Buying Serv. v. Standard Oil*, 686 P.2d 1158 (Cal. 1984) (oil supplier who persuaded a federal agency to prohibit sales to buyer breached obligation of good faith).

c.   **Fault caused impracticability.**   A party at fault for causing the performance to be impracticable as a result of the event is not excused. For example, a farmer who negligently fails to protect a crop from pests may not be excused if pests destroy the crop. She did not cause the pestilence, but her negligence caused the pestilence to destroy the crop. See also UCC §2-613 (no excuse if a party is at fault).

EXAMPLE AND ANALYSIS

Dunbar promised to obtain molasses for plaintiff from a specific refinery. The refinery cut back production, making it impossible for seller to obtain the quantity required. Buyer sued. *Canadian Indus. Alcohol Co. v. Dunbar Molasses*, 179 N.E. 383 (N.Y. 1932). Held: for Buyer. If Dunbar had entered a contract with the refinery, it might not have reduced production. Dunbar's failure to take this precaution prevented excuse for impracticability.

> **d.** **Practice question.** Is a strike at a seller's plant an event that occurs without its fault?
>
> **i.** Seller could settle a strike instantaneously by acceding to all of the employees' demands. Its failure to do so is intentional, not merely negligent.
>
> **ii.** Should the issue depend on whether the seller's bargaining position is reasonable? That requires a court to second-guess the economic justification for the employer's position. Judges usually are not well trained to evaluate the business outlook for a particular company and assess how much it can afford to pay employees.
>
> **iii.** A seller's ability to negotiate with employees probably should not disappear because it has contractual commitments. The seller will feel pressure to fulfill the contracts even if they are excused. It earns money by fulfilling contracts, not by backing out of them. Thus, a strike might be the kind of event that produces impracticability.
>
> **iv.** Although fault may not preclude excuse for strikes, the issue of whether the nonoccurrence of a strike was a basic assumption of the parties still must be decided. An anticipated strike might be allocated by the parties in the contract, and sometimes is.

6. Agreements to Assume Greater Obligations

When parties can foresee events, they may provide for them in the contract. If a party agrees to perform in spite of an event that would make performance more burdensome, impracticability will not excuse nonperformance.

a. **Unqualified duty insufficient.** An unqualified duty does not automatically include the burden to perform despite events that make performance impracticable. If it did, the failure to include an impracticability clause (called a "force majeure" clause) in the contract would preclude the defense.

b. **Recognized risks.** An unqualified duty in the face of a recognized (or even foreseeable) risk may indicate that the parties intended performance even if the risk materialized. See, e.g., *Glidden Co. v. Hellenic Lines*, 275 F.2d 253 (2d Cir. 1960) (parties discussed closure of Suez and provided for transport around Cape or via Panama as an alternative).

c. **Explicit assumption preferable.** The courts can infer from circumstances that the parties intended an unqualified duty to be performed despite events making performance burdensome. Usually, however, a clause providing that performance must occur despite events producing impracticability should be explicit; courts seem unlikely to infer them very often.

7. Remedial Concerns

Impracticability may excuse performance when uneven partial performance makes it necessary to award a remedy to one party or the other. The usual tools are available. Restatement (Second) of Contracts §272.

a. **Divisibility.** If the contract is divisible, the portion performed so far may be compensated at the contract rate.

b. **Restitution.** This remedy for benefits bestowed remains available but may be offset by reliance expenditures.

8. Temporary Impracticability

Events may not make performance impracticable forever. The Suez Canal will reopen; the oil embargo will end.

a. **Duty suspended.** A party's duty to perform is **suspended** while the impracticability lasts but is not automatically discharged.

b. **Duty discharged.** Either party may seek to have the duty discharged even though the impracticability is temporary.

i. **Party facing impracticability.** If performance after the impracticability ends would be "materially more burdensome" than it was if the impracticability had not occurred, the duty is discharged. Restatement (Second) of Contracts §269.

ii. **Other party.** When impracticability delays performance, rules on material nonperformance govern the other party's ability to terminate the contract and make substitute arrangements. *See* 16.B.

c. **Temporary frustration.** These provisions apply equally to frustration. Restatement (Second) of Contracts §269.

9. Partial Impracticability

Events may reduce a party's ability to perform without preventing all performance. In these situations, a party's performance may not be excused.

a. **Under the UCC.** When events make full performance of all contracts impracticable, a seller must allocate its deliveries (in any fair and reasonable manner) among customers. UCC §2-615(b). The UCC also requires notice to customers of the reduction or elimination of deliveries. (The buyer's options in response to this excuse are specified in UCC §2-616.)

b. **Under the Restatement.** Under some circumstances, a party who can provide part performance must do so. The failure to perform the part that is practicable will be breach because it is not excused, even though the failure to complete performance will be excused. Restatement (Second) of Contracts §270.

i. **Substantial partial performance.** Part performance is not excused for impracticability if a party can still provide substantial performance under the contract.

ii. **Waiving full performance.** Part performance is not excused for impracticability if the other party agrees to render full performance in exchange for the part performance the party can deliver practicably. Thus, if part performance is so valuable to the other party that she will pay the full contract price for just the part that remains practicable, she is entitled to receive that performance.

10. Impossibility

Most casebooks begin excuses with older cases based on impossibility. **Impracticability has replaced impossibility**; you do not need to address both of them on an exam. Impossibility was narrower. The usual provisions of impossibility are expressly included into impracticability by Restatement (Second) of Contracts §§262-264. See 17.A.3. Anything excused by impossibility should also be excused by impracticability.

B.   FRUSTRATION

Buyers have trouble persuading courts that payment satisfies the requirements of impracticability. Nonetheless, events may deprive the buyer of the benefit of the bargain in much the same way that events make performance impracticable for sellers. Thus, the defense of frustration arose.

1.   Elements

When the nonoccurrence of an event is a basic assumption on which the contract was made, the occurrence of that event excuses a party's nonperformance if, without that party's fault, the event substantially frustrates the party's principal purpose — unless the contract or other circumstances indicate that the party agreed to perform despite the event. Restatement (Second) of Contracts §265.

a.   Sales of goods.   The UCC does not mention frustration. In that silence, "the principles of law and equity . . . supplement [the UCC's] provisions." UCC §1-103. Frustration probably is among the principles of law that this preserves.

b.   Impracticability similar.   Many of the elements of this excuse are identical to those for impracticability. That discussion is not repeated here. See 17.A.2-17.A.4, 17.A.6.

2.   Principal Purpose of the Contract

The frustration must effect the essence of the contract: an object "so completely the basis of the contract that, as both parties understand, without it the transaction would make little sense." Restatement (Second) of Contracts §265 cmt. a.

 ## EXAMPLES AND ANALYSIS

1. Defendant (Henry) rented plaintiff's flat for two days to see the coronation procession. The procession was delayed by the King's illness. Krell sued for the balance of the rent (£50 of the £75 promised). Henry counterclaimed for return of the £25 deposit but later withdrew the claim. *Krell v. Henry*, [1903] 2 K.B. 740 (Ct. App.

1903). Held: Judgment for Henry affirmed. Both parties were aware the coronation was the only reason Henry wanted the room, making that the essence of the contract.

2. Plaintiff sold lamb pelts to defendant. Buyer took possession in Toronto, for shipment to Philadelphia. After the first shipment, U.S. regulations changed, prohibiting import of these pelts. Buyer refused to accept delivery in Toronto. *Swift Canadian v. Banet*, 224 F.2d 36 (3d Cir. 1955). Held: for seller. The court's discussion of frustration is not direct. On one interpretation, the court did not believe import to the United States was buyer's principal purpose, even though specified in the contract. The buyer could change the destination at will once the pelts were delivered. (Alternatively, this may suggest that the destination or U.S. import rules were not a basic assumption of the contract, shared by both parties.)

3. Substantially Frustrated

Events that make the contract less valuable do not substantially frustrate the contract. The effect must be extreme, much the way the effect of impracticability must be extreme.

 # EXAMPLES AND ANALYSIS

1. In August 1941, defendant leased a lot from plaintiff. The lease limited it use to the sale (and service) of new cars (90% of defendant's business), gasoline (10%), and an occasional used car. War was declared in December. The government prohibited the sale of new cars except to military personnel. Plaintiff agreed to waive some restrictions in the lease, but defendant repudiated the lease. Plaintiff relet and sued for the difference in rent. *Lloyd v. Murphy*, 153 P.2d 47 (Cal. 1944). Held: for plaintiff. The regulations did not destroy the value of the property. Defendant continued to sell new cars at other locations and could sell them (to military personnel) and gasoline here.

2. Recall *Swift Canadian v. Banet*, 224 F.2d 36 (3d Cir. 1955) (lamb pelts delivered in Canada could not be imported to United States due to change of law, judgment for seller). See 17.B.2. The court appeared to hold that the buyer's ability to ship the goods anywhere in the world but the United States meant the purpose (to resell the pelts) was not substantially frustrated, merely limited, by laws foreclosing resale in the United States.

3. Defendant (Stoneway) leased plaintiff's land for nine years for strip mining. The parties expected to spend two years getting permits (as the rent reflected). After five

years with no permit, Stoneway repudiated the lease. Plaintiff sued for rent due. *Weyerhauser Real Estate v. Stoneway Concrete*, 637 P.2d 647 (Wash. 1981). Held: for Stoneway. The inability to mine deprived it of all benefit of the contract.

The real issue centered on the provisions of the contract. It allowed Stoneway to cancel on one year's notice if mining proved unprofitable. On the other hand, the rent was due regardless of whether Stoneway actually obtained any minerals from the land. The lower court held these provisions allocated the risk to Stoneway. The clauses in question allocate the risk of **unsuccessful** operations to Stoneway. But they do not seem to address the possibility that **no** operations would be possible.

---

4. **Exploring (*Chase Precast v. John J. Paonessa Co.*, 566 N.E.2d 603 (Mass. 1991))**   This case is fairly straightforward in itself, but offers several interesting twists that justify more extensive exploration — the kind of twists that might show up in an exam question.

   a. **The case.**   The state hired defendant (Paonessa) to repair a highway, including replacing a grass median with concrete barriers. Defendant ordered the concrete barriers from plaintiff (Chase). After public protest, the state decided to keep the grass median and canceled that part of the job (as the contract allowed). Defendant paid plaintiff for the barriers that had already been produced, but canceled the rest of the order. Plaintiff sued for profit lost on the canceled portion of the order. Held: for defendant.

   b. **Full excuse?**   Did the defendant need to pay for the part of the order already produced? Or could it reject all barriers?

      i. **Excuse.**   Arguably, frustration excused its remaining duties. Because any payment not already made was excused, it could refuse to make any further payment under the contract.

      ii. **Restitution.**   Restitution would not require payment unless defendant received a benefit. That seems to require delivery of the barriers, not merely their production.

      iii. **Reliance.**   The court, however, could compensate reliance if restitution recovery did not produce justice. Restatement (Second) of Contracts §272(2). Under that theory, the expense of producing the barriers might be compensable even if the contract was frustrated. Revenues plaintiff realized by reselling the barriers probably would offset recovery. (Plaintiff probably cannot use the lost-volume seller rules when the contract was excused by frustration.)

c. **Barriers received?**   Could defendant keep barriers it had already received without paying for them? No.

    i. **Return the goods.**   At the very least, it would need to return the barriers to plaintiff. That is specific restitution. Arguably, plaintiff is more likely to be able to resell them than defendant.

    ii. **Restitution.**   Any barriers it could not return (or chose not to return) it would need to pay for at their fair market value.

d. **Contract price or restitution?**   Could plaintiff collect the contract price for barriers already delivered?

    i. **Divisibility.**   The contract probably was divisible, allowing assessment of the contract price for the portion already delivered under Restatement (Second) of Contracts §240.

    ii. **Frustration unlimited.**   The entire contract was frustrated. Defendant had no use for the concrete barriers already delivered (except those already built into the road and, therefore, paid for by the state). Delivery arguably should not affect the analysis.

e. **Refund?**   Would that reasoning extend to barriers for which defendant had already paid? Could defendant get a refund from plaintiff? Probably not. Even in *Henry v. Krell*, the plaintiff kept the deposit but could not collect the balance. Courts tend to leave parties where they are — or where they should have been at the time the event occurred — without allowing either to collect from the other for any subsequent changes. This judicial intuition has no theoretical basis.

5.   Cautionary Note

The cases reveal some reluctance to find frustration. Courts often feel a party claiming frustration of contract simply means "I don't want it anymore." If changing one's mind became a defense, contract would virtually disappear. Thus, courts reserve the defense for the most extreme cases.

C.   MISTAKE, REPRISED

The element of "a basic assumption on which the contract was made" appears in mistake as well as impracticability and frustration. See Restatement (Second) of Contracts §§152, 153. Thus, these defenses may overlap.

1. **Mistake, Impracticability, and Frustration Compared**

   a. **Existing circumstances versus subsequent events.**   Frustration and impracticability include both subsequent events and circumstances that existed at the time the contract was made. Restatement (Second) of Contracts §266. In theory, mistakes concern circumstances only as they existed at the time the contract was made. Subsequent changes usually cannot be the subject of the mistake defense. But see *Aluminum Co. v. Essex Group*, 499 F. Supp. 53 (W.D. Pa. 1980) (construing the failure of a price escalator clause to keep up with electricity costs during the energy crisis as a mistake concerning circumstances at the time the contract was made).

   b. **Degree of hardship required.**   Mistake must have a "material effect on the agreed exchange of performances." This seems a much lower standard than either making performance impracticable or substantially frustrating the principal purpose of the contract. Thus, mistakes about existing facts may be easier to win.

   c. **Allocation of risks in the contract.**   All three arguments are subject to the provisions of the contract. If the parties allocate the risks among themselves, courts will not use these doctrines to reallocate the risks.

      i. **Express allocation.**   In impracticability and frustration, the contract may need to be much more explicit to persuade a court that the parties intended performance to proceed despite the event. The defenses arise because future events bring rather significant surprises which the contracting parties probably did not anticipate. The court will not easily infer that a clause allocated those risks.

      ii. **Implicit allocation.**   In mistake, the courts seem relatively willing to infer allocation of risk from contract terms. An "as is" clause allocates virtually every risk to the buyer, no matter how unanticipated the problem was by both parties. Courts also can allocate the risk to one party based on conscious ignorance or other factors not expressed in the agreement. See Restatement (Second) of Contracts §154.

   d. **Voidability versus excuse.**   Mistake affects the validity of contract formation; impracticability and frustration affect performance. Mistake makes a contract voidable by the adversely affected party. Mistake implies the contract never should have been formed. Thus, a party may rescind it—even after full performance. Impracticability and frustration are more moderate. The formation is valid, but performance (or part of it) is excused. There is no corresponding provision for partial mistake.

2. Mistakes regarding Future Contingencies

Courts occasionally treat mistakes about future contingencies under the mistake doctrine rather than impracticability or frustration.

a. **Circumstances (*Aluminum Co. v. Essex Group*, 499 F. Supp. 53 (W.D. Pa. 1980)).** ALCOA agreed to supply Essex with molten aluminum. This required Essex to build its factory adjacent to ALCOA's. Because Essex could not easily move the factory, a long-term contract was necessary. The contract included a formula governing price increases. The clause was intended to keep pace with ALCOA's cost of producing aluminum. The energy crisis of the 1970s forced electricity costs very high. Electricity is a major element in the production of aluminum. Unfortunately, electricity cost was not directly represented in the formula. As a result, the contract allowed Essex to buy aluminum for about half what it was worth. If compelled to live with the formula for the life of the contract, ALCOA would lose about $75 million.

b. **Result.** The court held that the parties made a mutual mistake about the ability of the formula to reflect the cost of producing aluminum. Although the mistake was not discovered until the energy crisis forced electricity prices up, the mistake existed at the time the contract was formed. Even at that time, the contract had no ability to reflect electricity costs adequately.

c. **Unusual remedy.** Instead of rescission, the normal remedy for mistake, the court ordered **reformation** to a term that it created. The price the court dictated gave Essex a discount but allowed ALCOA a profit of one cent per pound. The case settled before an appellate court could rule on this novel use of reformation.

REVIEW QUESTIONS AND ANSWERS

Question: What are the elements of impracticability?
Answer: A contingency, the nonoccurrence of which was a basic assumption, occurred, making performance impracticable, without the fault of the party pleading the excuse, unless the party promised to perform despite the occurrence of the contingency. Note: Under the UCC, absence of fault is not a component of impracticability, but a party's good faith remains essential.

Question: What are the elements of frustration?

Answer: A contingency, the nonoccurrence of which was a basic assumption of the contract, occurred, substantially frustrating a party's principle purpose, without her fault, unless the party promised to perform despite the occurrence of the contingency.

Question: Can a buyer claim impracticability?

Answer: Not in contracts for the sale of goods. The UCC provides impracticability only for sellers. In other contracts, a buyer theoretically could claim impracticability. But ability to pay is more likely to be a risk the parties intended buyer to face rather than a basic assumption the nonoccurrence of which was so remote that the parties could not have intended the contract to be enforceable under those circumstances.

Question: Does an event that makes performance expensive or unprofitable satisfy the requirement of impracticability?

Answer: Not without more. Mere expense is not enough. Extreme expense — particularly if it results from a change in the nature of the performance — may constitute impracticability. Minor expenses, even small losses, probably do not justify an excuse. The effect must be sufficiently extreme that the parties, if they had thought about it, probably would not have required the party to perform under the circumstances.

REPUDIATION: CAN BREACH OCCUR BEFORE PERFORMANCE IS DUE?

CHAPTER OVERVIEW

Sometimes a party, before the time for performance arrives, announces that it will not perform. Technically this is not breach: unexcused nonperformance **when due**. This chapter addressed problems associated with **repudiation** (or anticipatory repudiation, as it is sometimes called).

Repudiation gives rise to a claim for damages for total breach, even if no breach has yet occurred.

- An unequivocal statement that a party will commit a material breach is a repudiation.
- A voluntary affirmative act that leaves a party unable (or apparently unable) to perform is a repudiation.

A party may demand **adequate assurance of performance** when she has reasonable grounds to believe that the other party will commit a material breach.

- If reasonable, a party may suspend performance until she receives assurance.
- **But** a party may not suspend performance for which she has already received the agreed exchange.
- A failure to provide, within a reasonable time, adequate assurance that a party will perform when due is a repudiation.

Repudiation can be retracted by:

- Actual notice to the other party of a statement retracting the repudiation; or
- Actual notice to the other party that the events which made it seem the repudiating party could not perform no longer exist.

Repudiation cannot be retracted if, before actual notice of the retraction:

- The other party has changed her position in reliance on the repudiation; or
- The other party has indicated that she considers the repudiation final.

The rules governing the effectiveness of retraction apply even if the other party has urged the repudiator to perform or to retract.

A.   REPUDIATION

Once a party indicates that she no longer intends to perform under the contract, the other party needs to make alternative arrangements. Yet those other arrangements may be wasteful if the first party later changes her mind and decides to perform. The rules in this section attempt to minimize waste by giving parties a firm basis on which to decide whether to make alternative arrangements following repudiation.

1.   Introduction

Repudiation can consist of either a statement or actions. A statement constitutes **express repudiation**. Actions constitute **implied repudiation**. In either case, a repudiation exists only if the statement or action indicated that the party will commit a **material breach** — or "a breach that would of itself give the obligee a claim for damages for total breach under §243." Restatement (Second) of Contracts §250.

2.   Express Repudiation

  a.   Unequivocal.   A statement repudiating a contract must be unequivocal. Statements that a party either will not or cannot perform are repudiations. Statements of doubt about the ability to perform do not repudiate a contract.

  i.   Equivocal statements.   Statements of doubt may give rise to reasonable grounds for insecurity. See 18.B.

 # EXAMPLE AND ANALYSIS

Defendant (Johnston) promised the services of a stud horse for plaintiff's mares. After an implied repudiation and retraction (see 18.A.3, 18.C.1.b.ii), defendant's agents postponed stud service on plaintiff's mares until the season was nearly over, giving plaintiff the impression that they did not intend to provide the promised service. Plaintiff bred the mares with a different stud. *Taylor v. Johnston*, 539 P.2d 425

(Cal. 1975). Held: for defendant. Plaintiff's fears did not convert defendant's equivocal statements into a repudiation.

> ii. **New demands.** Statements that impose new requirements on a party's willingness to perform are repudiations. Insisting that the other party live up to the obligations of the contract is not a new demand, though parties cannot unilaterally rewrite the order in which they must perform.

> b. **To the other party.** Statements of repudiation must be made to an obligee (including a beneficiary or assignee). See Chapter 24. A party blowing off steam need not worry that words will become a repudiation unless she makes the statement to the other party to the contract.

3. Implied Repudiation

An action that leaves a party unable or apparently unable to perform is an implied repudiation.

 ## EXAMPLE AND ANALYSIS

Recall *Taylor v. Johnston* (see 18.A.2.a.i). Defendant (Johnston) promised the services of a stud horse for plaintiff's mares. Defendant sold the stud to a syndicate in another state. The sale made performance apparently impossible, thus repudiating the contract.

> a. **Action versus inaction.** Implied repudiations arise from voluntary affirmative acts. Inaction is not repudiation (except in response to a request for assurance of performance). Nor can one infer repudiation from events over which a party has no control.

> b. **Insecurity.** As with statements, actions that fall short of a repudiation may give rise to reasonable grounds for insecurity. See 18.B.

4. Total Breach

Total breach basically means material breach. The Restatement (Second) of Contracts gives a rather convoluted formulation of total breach — a formulation that gets circular when combined with the rules on repudiation.

We could walk through the complexities of this interaction, but if you had enough time for that, you would be reading the Restatement instead of an outline. Here, let's boil it down to its essence.

a. **Total equals discharge.** Total breach is a breach that discharges a party's remaining obligations under the contract. Restatement (Second) of Contracts §243(1).

b. **Discharge equals incurable and material.** A breach discharges obligations under a contract if it is **material** *and* if cure is no longer possible. *See* 16.E.1.

c. **Repudiation always curable?**   In theory, cure is always possible when the time for performance has not expired. This implicates a party's ability to retract the repudiation, discussed below. See 18.C. For deciding whether a breach is total, assume the repudiation is not retracted and the breach occurs as threatened. If that would discharge the contract, the threatened breach is total.

d. **Exception for payment.** When the only remaining duties are the breaching party's duty to pay in installments for performance already completed by the other, breach regarding one installment is not total breach. Restatement (Second) of Contracts §243(3). Institutional lenders often include in their contracts acceleration clauses that effectively make the failure to pay one installment a total breach.

e. **Role of the rule.**   A repudiation will not give you the right to suspend or terminate performance when the breach itself would not have given you the right to suspend or terminate performance. For example, telling the other party that you intend to take the curtains with you when you move may breach the contract to deliver the house with its fixtures, but is unlikely to be a repudiation.

B. REASONABLE GROUNDS FOR INSECURITY

Because some statements or actions are equivocal, they will not amount to repudiation. Nonetheless, the other party may fear that continued performance will increase her vulnerability to breach or her damages in case of breach. Recently, the law has provided an avenue for protecting people from these risks.

1. The Rule

When a party has reasonable grounds to believe that the other will commit a material breach, she may (a) demand adequate assurance of due performance; (b) if reasonable, suspend performance (except to the extent she has already received compensation for the performance); and (c) treat the failure to provide adequate assurance within a reasonable time as a repudiation of the contract. Restatement (Second) of Contracts §251; see UCC §2-609.

a. Written demand. The UCC requires that a demand of adequate assurance be made in writing.

b. 30-day limit. The UCC allows no more than 30 days to respond to a demand for adequate assurance. A faster response may be necessary, but "a reasonable time" cannot exceed 30 days.

c. No insecurity. The UCC treats the failure to give assurances as a repudiation only if the demand was justified. Although sensible on its face, it injects a level of uncertainty into the situation that may lead each party to believe the other has repudiated. (One because she has not received assurance; the other because the first stopped performing when she did not receive assurance.)

2. Adequate Assurances of Performance

Identifying what assurances are adequate under the circumstances can be difficult.

a. Unjustified demands. A party who refuses to perform unless she receives assurance may in fact be repudiating or breaching the contract if she has no right to the assurance demanded.

b. Good faith. A demand for assurance is limited by the obligation of good faith and fair dealing. Repeated and unjustified demands may breach this duty. Similarly, a demand for assurance that rewrites the contract may not be in good faith.

    i. Assurances that rewrite contract. When negotiating, parties may decide who should perform first and whether either should receive security against breach (such as a bond or collateral). Parties cannot use the fear of breach (when breach has not occurred) to justify a demand that the contract be changed.

    ii. Modification. The parties can agree to modify the contract. But a party's refusal to modify the contract is not a repudiation of the contract as written.

c. Equivocal assurances. Such assurances probably are insufficient. Statements such as "I'll try" or "I'll do my best" do little to reassure a party who legitimately fears the other may be unable or unwilling to perform.

d.   Insolvency.   When a party's insolvency produces insecurity, assurance may take the form of performance, an offer to perform, or security (collateral). Restatement (Second) of Contracts §252. This special provision identifying acceptable assurance only applies when a party has stopped paying his debts on time, cannot pay his debts on time, or is insolvent under federal bankruptcy law.

C.   EVENTS AFTER REPUDIATION: RETRACTION AND MITIGATION

1.   Responses by the Nonrepudiating Party

After a repudiation, a party may respond in several ways. She may accept the repudiation as final and proceed to make other arrangements. She may urge the other party to retract the repudiation and perform. She may do nothing and hope the other party performs. See also UCC §2-610 (characterizing the options slightly differently). Each has advantages. The law must sort out the consequences of each, particularly as they relate to the non-breaching party's responsibility to avoid losses if possible. See 22.E.1.

a.   Terminating the contract.   Repudiation discharges the other party's duty to perform under the contract. Restatement (Second) of Contracts §254. Thus, the other party may accept the repudiation as final and make substitute arrangements immediately.

i.   Suspend performance.   The party should suspend performance immediately. Damages will not be recoverable if the party could have avoided them by acting reasonably (e.g., by suspending performance). See UCC §2-610(3) & cmt. 1.

ii.   Notice.   The party should notify the repudiating party of her intent to take the repudiation as final. This will preclude the other party from reviving the obligation to perform by retracting the repudiation.

b.   Urging performance.   Often substitute arrangements will be unsatisfactory. For instance, other providers may not be as good or may require too much time to arrive. A party may wish to urge the other party to retract the repudiation and to perform.

i.   Suspend performance.   Even while urging retraction, a party should suspend performance. If continued performance causes damages to mount unreasonably, those damages may not be recoverable.

    ii.   **Substitute arrangements permissible.** Urging retraction does not affect one's rights later to make substitute arrangements — unless, of course, retraction occurs before the arrangements have been made.

 ## EXAMPLE AND ANALYSIS

Recall *Taylor v. Johnston* (see 18.A.2.a.i). After selling the stud to a syndicate in another state, defendant made arrangements for the stud to cover plaintiff's mares in that state. Plaintiff accepted these substitute arrangements and shipped the mares to Kentucky. The repudiation was retracted, the duty to provide stud service reinstated.

    c.   **Inertia.** Some parties do nothing. This is dangerous. Although it leaves the other party time to retract, it does not encourage retraction. Nor does it take steps to minimize losses by making substitute arrangements. In short, inertia runs all the risks of both alternatives, without the benefits of either.

2. Retraction by the Repudiating Party

As noted earlier, as the time for performance has not arrived, cure (by performing when due) is inherently possible. A rule that always allowed cure, however, might prejudice the other party. If she makes substitute arrangements based on the stated unwillingness to perform, she may find herself with too much performance if the repudiating party also cures. In the context of repudiation, rules governing retraction dictate the legal effect of efforts to cure.

    a.   **Actual notice required.** Retraction requires actual notice to the nonrepudiating party. The rules governing retraction require that notice "come to the attention of the injured party" or that she have "knowledge" that events no longer make performance impossible. Restatement (Second) of Contracts §256. The language encompasses notice from a third party, if sufficiently reliable.

    b.   **Timeliness.** Retraction must be timely. Retraction is too late if:

    i.   The other party has **relied** on the repudiation; or

   ii.   The other party has **indicated** to the repudiating party that **she considers the repudiation final**.

Part 3

How Should the Law Respond?

In Chapter 1, we introduced the various remedies available when a party breaches a contract. This section explores those remedies in detail.

EQUITABLE RELIEF

19

CHAPTER OVERVIEW

Specific performance is an **injunction** ordering a party to perform as promised under a contract.

- Like the expectation interest, specific performance seeks to place the plaintiff in the position she would have occupied if the contract had been performed —but by actually compelling defendant to perform, instead of trying to calculate the equivalent in money damages.

Injunctive relief (including specific performance) is available only if the **remedy at law is inadequate**.

A remedy at law is inadequate unless it is as **complete, practical, and efficient** as the equitable remedy.

- If you cannot use money damages to obtain exactly what you were promised, the remedy at law is inadequate. (This covers unique items or items in short supply.)
- If the amount of damages will be difficult to calculate or to prove, the remedy at law is inadequate.
- If the remedy at law will exclude recovery for losses that specific performance could prevent, the remedy at law is inadequate.
- If the other party cannot pay a judgment for money damages, the remedy at law is inadequate.

Courts may refuse to grant injunctive relief based on equitable discretion. Courts commonly use their equitable discretion to deny specific performance when:

- The performance will be impossible;
- The performance will require extensive judicial supervision;

- Compelling performance would violate public policy.
    - Courts generally do not order specific performance of personal service contracts; but
    - Courts sometimes grant specific performance against employers.

Courts may grant other injunctions even if they deny specific performance.

- Courts may order a breaching employee not to work for anyone else during the time she had promised to work for the employer.

A. SPECIFIC PERFORMANCE: COMPELLING THE BREACHING PARTY TO PERFORM

In Chapter 1, we noted that the basic remedy for breach of contract is the expectation interest, which seeks to place the nonbreaching party in the position she would have occupied if the breaching party had performed the contract. One way to achieve that result is to compel the breaching party to perform. In fact, sometimes this is the only way to protect the expectation interest. When a court issues an **injunction** that orders a party to perform as promised under the contract, that order is called **specific performance**.

1. Traditional Reluctance

Courts have been reluctant to grant specific performance, sometimes calling it an extraordinary remedy. Specific performance is more common than this statement suggests. Still, courts try not to use it unless necessary.

    a. Contempt of court. Violating an injunction is contempt of court. There are several strong sanctions for contempt.

        i. Civil compensatory contempt is the weakest sanction. It awards actual damages to the party injured by the contempt. That produces about the same result as if damages had been awarded instead of the injunction.

        ii. Civil coercive contempt involves putting a person in jail or fining her a certain amount per day until she removes the contempt. You've seen it on TV, when reporters or other witnesses are locked up until they agree to testify. They can leave at any time by removing the contempt. In contract, a court could lock someone up until she performed the contract (or agreed to perform it —she might need to be out to perform).

    iii. **Criminal contempt** involves fining or locking a person up as a punishment—not just until she removes the contempt but until she has served her time.

   b. **Severe sanctions.** These penalties are harsher than most contract remedies, which are limited to compensating the injured party. Contempt mobilizes much greater power to compel compensation and sometimes extracts more than compensation requires. In some cases that seems excessive. You may have recognized how debtor's prisons could exist: Under civil coercive contempt, a person who violated an order to pay money could be locked up until she paid it.

   c. **Damages preferred.** Because injunctions involve a serious use of the state's power to enforce a contract, judges prefer to invoke it only when necessary. When a damage remedy will suffice, courts deny injunctions. Today, courts find more and more cases where damages do not suffice.

2. Inadequate Remedy at Law (The Irreparable Injury Rule)

A court will deny an injunction if the remedy at law is adequate. (This is sometimes called the irreparable injury rule: An injury is irreparable if the remedy at law will not repair it.) A remedy at law is inadequate if it is not as complete, practical, and efficient as injunctive relief. That is, **unless damages are just as good as an injunction, the court will grant the injunction.** In several situations, damages are not as good as an injunction.

   a. **Uniqueness.** Most courts will grant specific performance if the promised performance is unique. A remedy at law is not as good as an injunction because you could not take the money and use it to buy a suitable substitute for performance. When the performance is unique, it is not available elsewhere.

      i. **Land generally is held to be unique.** No two pieces of land are located in exactly the same place. Money damages are not as good as an injunction because they will not permit the plaintiff to buy exactly what she was promised. Thus, specific performance is common in contracts involving land.

      ii. **Art often is unique.** So is any tangible item to which sentimental value might attach.

      iii. **People are unique.** Even those with no special skills are a unique assortment of attributes—at least as different as parcels of land in a modern subdivision. For reasons discussed shortly, courts usually do not order employees to complete their term of employment despite uniqueness.

    iv. **Money is not unique.** Rarely will a court order specific performance of a promise to pay money. Money damages are almost always just as good.

    v. **Goods usually are not unique.** Most of the goods we buy are fungible: There are others just like them available elsewhere. Custom-made goods may be unique.

b. **Shortage.** The ability to use money damages to buy the same performance elsewhere may be limited by scarcity. If there are few of the things available, money may not be as good as specific performance. The UCC recognizes scarcity as one of the "other proper circumstances" that justify specific performance. See UCC §2-716 cmt. 2 ("inability to cover is strong evidence of other proper circumstances").

EXAMPLE AND ANALYSIS

Defendant promised to sell plaintiff (Sedmak) a limited edition Corvette. (Only 6,000 were made, with varying options; and only one was sent to each dealer.) Defendant refused to deliver the car for the promised price, insisting that plaintiff bid on it. Plaintiff sued for specific performance. *Sedmak v. Charlie's Chevrolet*, 622 S.W.2d 694 (Mo. Ct. App. 1981). Held: for plaintiff. Although one of 6,000 is not strictly unique, the expense, delay, and inconvenience of cover (by finding one from another dealer or collector in another city, perhaps another country) made the remedy at law inadequate.

c. **Difficult damage remedies.** Sometimes damage remedies will be difficult to use. When this happens, preventing the loss by ordering specific performance may be more practical than relegating plaintiff to a damage action.

    i. **Damages may be difficult to prove.** Preventing the loss may provide plaintiff better, more accurate relief than hoping a jury will guess the right amount of damages to award — if the certainty doctrine does not preclude recovery. For example, when a breach of contract prevents a party from opening a new business, it will be difficult to ascertain how much profit (if any) the business would have generated if it had opened. Specific performance may avoid that problem by permitting the business to open and profit (or not) on its own.

   ii.   **Damages may be precluded for other reasons.**   Contract law usually does not compensate for emotional distress (among other things). If specific performance can prevent the distress, perhaps it is better than a damage action. (That's a big if. The distress of litigation may overshadow the distress of the breach.)

 d.   **Insolvency.**   A damage judgment against a party who cannot pay it is worse than inadequate; it is worthless. An injunction is much more practical.

3.   Other Limitations on Injunctions

Even when the remedy at law is inadequate, courts may deny injunctions for other reasons.

 a.   **Undue hardship.**   An injunction can cause serious hardship for the defendant. When the harm to the defendant greatly exceeds the benefit to the plaintiff, a court may decide to deny the injunction and award damages instead.

EXAMPLE AND ANALYSIS

Plaintiff leased space for a billboard on the side of building facing a tunnel into Manhattan. Defendant bought the building and the rest of the block, planning to redevelop it. Defendant canceled the lease (a breach). The court refused an injunction because the cost of holding up redevelopment of the block would greatly exceed the cost to plaintiff of finding a other places for billboards—especially as defendant would pay that cost as damages. *Van Wagner Advertising v. S&M Enterprises*, 492 N.E.2d 756 (N.Y. 1986).

The court said the remedy at law was adequate. Don't be misled. There is probably no land more unique than a billboard facing a tunnel into Manhattan. Also note that denying the injunction merely relegated plaintiff an action for damages. It did not let defendant off the hook. Finally, consider whether an injunction really would have precluded redevelopment. Defendant probably would have bought plaintiff off. An injunction just would have given plaintiff more bargaining power than the damage remedy.

---

     b. Excessive judicial supervision.   Courts will deny injunctions when the burdens of enforcement exceed the benefits an injunction has over the damage remedy. Injunctions are not self-executing; defendant may not automatically perform. In complex contracts, courts may need to resolve a series of disputes about what the contract (or an injunction) required and whether the defendant complied. Rather than become embroiled in the minutiae of a contract, a court may deny the injunction.

 # EXAMPLE AND ANALYSIS

Plaintiff hired defendant to renovate a steel plant. During part of the work, the contract seemed to require defendant to operate two shifts to minimize the time the plant was shut down. Defendant was behind schedule and was operating only one shift. Plaintiff sued seeking an injunction ordering plaintiff to add a second shift of 300 people. *Northern Delaware Indus. Dev. v. Bliss Co.*, 245 A.2d 431 (Del. Ch. 1968). Held: for defendant. The court refused to supervise the construction details of the project. The court mentioned concerns that qualified workers were not available and that additional workers might impede rather than hasten progress on the project — concerns the defendant contractor was better able to address than the court.

---

     c. Compelling individuals to perform personal services.

        i. A peculiar institution.   Ordering an individual to perform personal services looks a bit like returning a slave to a master. The analogy breaks down. But the image remains. As a result, courts usually refuse to grant specific performance of personal service contracts.

        ii. The problem of supervision.   An employee can be ordered to perform. Ordering her to perform well poses difficulties. Allegations that an employee failed to perform in good faith could arise in contempt proceedings. A court may have trouble deciding whether the opera singer missed a note accidentally or because she wasn't really trying. Thus, the problems of supervision noted above impede the use of specific performance in this context.

iii. **Strained relationships.** Once a breach or threatened breach occurs, the relationship between employee and employer inevitably changes, usually for the worse. Rather than compel either party to live with those changes, courts avoid specific performance.

iv. **Modern exception: specific performance against employers.** Until recently, these policies worked both directions. An employer would not be ordered to accept the services of an employee she no longer wanted. Recent statutes, however, began to limit the employer's ability to discharge employees, particularly for invidious reasons such as discrimination. Under these statutes, courts can order employers to hire, reinstate, or even promote people who they would not choose.

d. **Exam note: Personal services versus services.** Not all services fall within the restraint. Employment contracts are contracts for personal services. But construction contracts are not. A promise by an individual that she, personally, will do something is a personal service contract—unless she can delegate the duty to perform to another. A promise by a company usually is not a personal service contract. The company can tell any employee to perform its duties. Thus, an injunction ordering a contractor to complete work on a construction job is not against public policy.

B. ENFORCING NEGATIVE COVENANTS

A promise to work for one employer implicitly includes a promise not to work for any other employer at the time you are working for this employer. (You can moonlight, but you can't work two 9-to-5 jobs.) Part of this promise—not to work for others—can be specifically enforced. Employees who cannot be ordered to work for one employer can be forbidden to work for any other.

1. Enjoining Alternatives to Performance

In each of the following cases, the court determined that the individual's services were unique. See *Dallas Cowboys Football Club v. Harris*, 348 S.W.2d 37 (Tex. Civ. App. 1961) (unique does not mean one-of-a-kind, only that it would be difficult to locate someone as good).

EXAMPLES AND ANALYSIS

1. Wagner agreed to sing at Lumley's opera house. The agreement included a promise not to sing at any other opera house during the same period. Before starting, Wagner entered a new contract with Lumley's competitor to sing at a different opera house instead of Lumley's. Lumley sought an injunction ordering Wagner not to sing at the competing opera house during the time she had promised to sing at his. *Lumley v. Wagner*, 42 Eng. Rep. 687 (Ch. Div. 1852). Held: for Lumley.

2. Lillian Russell agreed to perform in plaintiff's operas for two seasons, seven performances per week, excluding Sundays. In the middle of the second season, she promised to perform for Duff's competitor. Duff sued to enjoin her performance elsewhere. *Duff v. Russell*, 14 N.Y.S. 134 (1891). Held: for Duff. Although the contract did not include an express covenant not to work for others, that was fairly implied from the requirement of seven performances a week.

2.   Enforcement beyond the Contract Term

Some promises not to work for others continue after the employment relationship ends. This can help protect trade secrets or prevent a person from competing with the employer who taught her the ropes (for a limited time, anyway). Courts are reluctant to limit employment after the contract period without an express clause in the contract.

 ## EXAMPLE AND ANALYSIS

Wolf was a sportscaster for ABC. Their contract required Wolf to bargain in good faith on a renewal during the last 90 days of the contract and not to bargain with anyone else during the first 45 days of this period. Wolf also agreed not to accept a job with anyone else during the first 90 days after expiration without giving ABC a right of first refusal (a chance to employ Wolf on the same terms as the competing offer). Wolf signed with CBS before the agreement expired, thus breaching the obligation to negotiate in good faith with ABC during that period. ABC sought specific performance of its right of first refusal and to enjoin Wolf from broadcasting for CBS. *ABC v. Wolf*, 420 N.E.2d 363 (N.Y. 1981). Held: for Wolf. The right of first refusal applied to offers accepted after the contract expired; Wolf accepted this offer before the first contract expired. Because the contract contained no negative covenant not to work for others after the contract expired, ABC could not receive such an injunction.

---

3. Relation to Public Policy

The public policy concerns noted previously do not impede enforcing negative covenants. But other concerns arise.

a. No involuntariness. No person is compelled to work for another. The strained relationship is not perpetuated.

b. Supervision uncomplicated. The performance need not be supervised. It will be clear whether a party works for another. Quality is not an issue.

c. Restraint of competition. Injunctions of this sort can limit competition. These issues are discussed above. See 11.C.2.

d. Earning a living. A broad injunction may prevent a person from earning a living. Most employees must work to eat. Thus, courts need to tailor their injunctions narrowly to protect the employer without starving the employee.

REVIEW QUESTIONS AND ANSWERS

Question: What factors may lead a court to deny specific performance?
Answer: The most important is the availability of an adequate remedy at law. If damages will give the plaintiff a remedy as good as specific performance, courts prefer to award damages. Other factors include concern for the difficulty of supervising compliance with the injunction and public policy concerns, such as those forbidding specific performance of personal service contracts.
Question: Would you agree with the following statement of the law: A court will grant specific performance "(1) Where there is no adequate remedy at law; (2) Where the specific articles or property are of peculiar, sentimental or unique value; and (3) Where due to scarcity the chattel is not readily obtainable"?
Answer: Yes. But it makes one rule into three. A remedy at law is inadequate when you cannot use money to buy the thing you were promised from another. The second two parts of the rule simply specify reasons a party might be unable to use money to buy the promised performance. When the thing promised has unique, sentimental value, one can buy something like it, but not the thing

with sentimental value. When the thing is scarce and unobtainable, one cannot use damages to buy it.

Question: Is specific performance available where damages would be difficult to calculate or difficult to collect?

Answer: Yes. A remedy at law is inadequate unless it is as complete, practical, and efficient as the injunction. If damages may be inaccurately assessed or uncollectable, the damages are not as complete or as practical as the injunction. Other factors may preclude injunctive relief, but the irreparable injury rule will not.

Question: Can any injunctive relief be granted in personal service contracts?

Answer: Yes. Specific performance against an employee violates public policy. An injunction ordering an employee not to work for others during the time she promised to work for the plaintiff does not violate public policy — with the possible exception of an injunction so broad that it precludes the employee from earning a living. More recently, some courts have granted specific performance to employees, ordering employers to perform as promised. Injunctions against employers, however, usually arise from statutory violations, such as illegal discrimination, not from breach of contract.

EXPECTATION INTEREST: THE NORMAL RECOVERY RULES

CHAPTER OVERVIEW

Courts generally calculate damages according to the **expectation interest**.

- The expectation interest awards the nonbreaching party (plaintiff) an amount of money equivalent to what **she would have received if the breaching party had performed**.
  - The **value** of things promised but not delivered is the central component of damage calculations. Value can be measured by the **cover price** actually paid for substitute performance or by estimating its **market price**.
  - If, to obtain substitute performance, the plaintiff incurs additional costs, these **incidental costs** are recoverable.
  - If breach prevents the plaintiff from using the performance in a profitable way, these **consequential costs** are recoverable.
- Damages should not put plaintiff in a better position than she would have occupied if the contract had been performed. Thus:
  - If plaintiff would have incurred additional costs to obtain performance but **avoided those costs** due to the breach, the savings offset the amount of damages.
  - If plaintiff would have incurred losses if defendant had performed but **avoided those losses** due to the breach, the savings offset the amount of damages.

In awarding damages, courts do **not** include:

- Losses the **plaintiff could have avoided** by reasonable efforts, even if she did not actually avoid those losses;
- Losses the **defendant had no reason to foresee** at the time the contract was made;
- Losses the plaintiff cannot establish with **reasonable certainty**;

- **Attorney's fees** incurred to collect the damages;
- Damages for **emotional distress**, with few exceptions; and
- **Punitive damages**, with few exceptions.

When the expectation interest cannot be established with reasonable certainty — and in a few other instances — a court may calculate damages according to the **reliance interest**. Reliance is covered in the next chapter.

A.   BASIC PRINCIPLE: THE FINANCIAL EQUIVALENT OF PERFORMANCE

The expectation interest seeks to place the nonbreaching plaintiff in the position she would have occupied if the breaching defendant had performed the contract. Unless specific performance is available, the expectation interest requires the court to calculate the amount of money that is equivalent to performance. How much money will it take to allow the plaintiff to receive all the benefits of the contract? The question is simple. Difficulties may arise if the facts are complicated. Complications often involve the exceptions, not the rule.

1.   Fundamentals

To calculate expectation, you need two numbers:

- How much wealth (money or property) **should** the plaintiff have received? (That is, how much would she have if defendant had performed?)
- How much **did** she receive? (That is, how much does she have despite the breach?)

Subtract the second from the first. That is the expectation interest.

2.   Formulas

You will see many different formulas for calculating expectation. Most include more than two elements. All of them boil down to these two numbers. Although detailed formulas are not necessary, they may help in two ways.

a.   Identifying components.   Detailed formulas may help you focus on the various components that go into calculating the amount a party should have received or did receive. For example, the amount the plaintiff would have received might include both the amount it will cost her to buy the property from someone else and the amount she would have gained by reselling it to another. The amount she did receive might include both partial payments and any gains from selling materials for scrap.

    b. **Adapting to context.** Detailed formulas may help you adapt the principle to different contexts. For example, construction contracts may involve overhead in ways that do not explicitly arise in sales of goods. Thus, a formula derived from the UCC may look a little different from a formula derived from a case involving a construction contract.

    c. **Principle unchanged.** If you can apply effectively the fundamental approach, you need not memorize different, more detailed formulas for each context. The examples that follow illustrate some of the formulas.

3. Math Phobia

Relax. Most professors chose law over an MBA, too. Calculating remedies involves addition and subtraction. (You might have to multiply or divide in cases involving a price per unit, but not often.) You learned that in elementary school and practice it every time you count your change. Contract class is just as simple—and usually involves very simple numbers. They just have a few zeros on the end to make litigation seem worthwhile.

B.   VALUE OF THE PROMISED PERFORMANCE

The central component of all damage calculations is the value of the thing promised. Many different things can be promised: goods, land, services, intangibles (stock or insurance), or money. They all have a price. Failure to deliver the thing promised is the equivalent of failure to deliver the price of that thing. Basically, the law assigns value to a performance in one of two ways: market value or an actual substitute transaction (cover).

1. Market Value

When a performance is available in the market, the price set by the market is the value of that performance. Presumably, awarding the plaintiff this amount of money will allow her to go into the market and buy the same performance from another supplier. Thus, she receives the equivalent of what she was promised.

    a. **Where?** Market value is measured at the place performance was to occur.

    b. **When?** Market value is measured at the time the plaintiff learns of the breach. See, e.g., UCC §§2-713 (buyer's remedies), 2-708 (seller's remedies).

i.   **Time of performance.**   If breach occurred by repudiation, market value is measured at the time performance was to occur.

ii.   **Time breach discovered.**   If, following repudiation, the case is tried before the time for performance arrives, market value is measured at the time the buyer learned of the repudiation. UCC §2-723.

c.   **Lack of a market.**   Market value is hard to ascertain when the promised performance is unique—that is, suitable substitutes are not available from other suppliers. Experts often can testify about how much an item would fetch in a market. But when the performance is unique, specific performance may be available. See, e.g., UCC §2-716.

2. Cover Price or Resale Price

Sometimes a plaintiff will make her own arrangements for substitute performance: She will sell the performance to a different buyer or buy a substitute from another seller. The law may look to the actual transaction instead of trying to identify a hypothetical market price among the many different prices charged in the market.

a.   **Plaintiff's option.**   The UCC allows the plaintiff to recover based on an actual transaction at her option. See UCC §§2-706, 2-712. In other contexts (e.g., sales of land), courts sometimes prefer market prices over actual substitute transactions.

b.   **Cover more accurate.**   That actual transaction may offer a more accurate indication of the loss for several reasons.

i.   **Subjective value.**   It may indicate the subjective value of the performance to the plaintiff. If she was willing to pay more than the contract price, she probably valued the performance that much—though she might expect to collect damages and, therefore, not care how much substitute performance costs.

ii.   **Better evidence.**   An actual market transaction is good evidence of market price. Unless the plaintiff entered into a bogus or unreasonable transaction, the actual price charged probably is the market price—or, within the range of prices actually charged within the market.

c.   **Commercially reasonable transactions.**   Only commercially reasonable transactions (sometimes called bona fide arm's-length transactions) can substitute for market price. Paying more (or accepting less) than a reasonable buyer (or seller) would have paid (or demanded) deprives the cover (or resale) transaction of its validity as a proxy for market price (or even of subjective value). Thus, a plaintiff who covers by buying from a relative and paying twice the market price will be limited to a recovery based on market price, not on the actual substitute transaction.

d.   Examples.   The following examples illustrate the basic approach. The next section revisits them with a few additional details.

 # EXAMPLES AND ANALYSIS

1. B agrees to buy S's used car for $2,000. B changes her mind without excuse. S, after reasonable efforts, sells the car to T for $1,750, the highest bid she received. S should have received $2,000, but only received $1,750. S may recover $250 from B.

2. B agrees to buy S's used car for $2,000. S changes her mind without excuse. B, after reasonable efforts, locates a similar car and buys it for $2,500. B should have received a car for $2,000, but instead received a car for $2,500. B can recover $500 from S.

3. In trying to sell her used car to B, S warrants that the odometer reading (95,000 miles) is accurate. B agrees to buy the car for $2,000, the fair market value of a car with that mileage. After delivery, B discovers that S had altered the odometer. Because the true mileage of the car cannot be determined, the car was worth only $1,300 when delivered. B should have received a car worth $2,000 but instead received a car worth only $1,300. If B decides to keep the car (rather than return it to S for a refund), B may recover $700.

4. O hires C to build a home on land owned by O, promising to pay $100,000 for the work. C builds the house, incurring costs of $84,000. C receives progress payments totaling $80,000. O, without excuse, refuses to pay the rest of the price. C should have received $100,000 but actually received only $80,000. C may recover $20,000 from O.

5. O hires C to build a home on land owned by O, promising to pay $100,000 for the work. C builds half the house and receives progress payments totaling $45,000. C, without excuse, refuses to finish the job. O hires T to finish the job. T charges $60,000, a reasonable price for the remaining work. O should have received the house

for $100,000 but actually paid $105,000 for the house ($45,000 to C and $60,000 to T). O may recover $5,000 from C.

C. AVOIDING UNDERCOMPENSATION: INCIDENTAL LOSSES, CONSEQUENTIAL LOSSES, AND PREJUDGMENT INTEREST

Sometimes breach involves more costs than just the loss of the promised performance. Plaintiff may incur some expenses in making arrangements to replace the promised performance. If substitute arrangements are not possible, the plaintiff may lose not only the performance but the benefit of whatever use she would have made of that performance. In either case, if the contract had been performed, the nonbreaching party would not have faced these losses. To place the plaintiff to the position she should occupy, contract remedies must take these costs into account.

1. Definitions

To facilitate discussion of these costs, it is convenient to name them. You need to recognize those names: **incidental** and **consequential** losses. Naming does not change them. Incidental and consequential losses are part of the expectation interest. They merit separate discussion because sometimes people overlook them — and because consequential losses in particular raise some additional issues addressed below. The losses a party suffers from breach generally fall into one of three categories: the value of promised performance (see 22.B), incidental losses, and consequential losses.

a. Incidental losses. These involve additional costs incurred because the deal fell through. The cost to advertise goods when seeking a new buyer; the cost to insure, store, or protect the property pending resale; and commissions paid to find a new buyer all are examples of incidental losses. *See* UCC §2-710. Similarly, costs a buyer incurs to obtain substitute goods — commissions, phone expenses, transportation costs, etc. — are incidental losses. See UCC §2-715.

 # EXAMPLES AND ANALYSIS

---

1. After B refuses to buy S's car, S spends $10 per week to run an ad in the paper for two weeks before finding another buyer (who paid $250 less than B promised). In addition to the $250 difference in price, S may recover $20 in incidental losses.

2. After S refuses to sell the car to B, S spends $30 for gas to visit other possible sellers before finding a similar car (for which B paid $500 more than S's price). (Parking costs and depreciation could also apply.) In addition to the $500, difference in price, B may recover the $30 for gas as an incidental loss.

---

  b.   Consequential losses.   These are at least one step removed from the lost performance. Usually, they involve the way the plaintiff intended to use the performance. A plaintiff who intended to resell property or use it in her business might lose profits on the resale or on the business when the property is not delivered. Lost profits are the most common consequential loss — so common that few people discuss other consequential losses. As a general rule, any argument that runs "If you had performed, then I could have . . ." identifies a consequential loss.

 # EXAMPLE AND ANALYSIS

Before buying S's car, B had arranged to sell it to T, a collector, for $2,300. When the odometer reading proved inaccurate, T justifiably refused to accept the car and canceled the contract with B. If S had performed (delivered a car with only 95,000 miles on it), B would have received $2,300 — not just the $2,000 fair market value of the car. Assuming the loss was foreseeable (see 22.E.3), B may recover both the $700 in lost value and the $300 in consequential losses for the lost resale.

Note: Arguably, T's willingness to pay $2,300 for the car means the fair market value of the car was $2,300, not $2,000. If so, the base damage formula (see 22.B.2.d) would produce the same result: B was entitled to a car worth $2,300; she received a car worth only $1,300. Thus, she is entitled to the $1,000 difference. (This could make a difference if foreseeability is at issue.)

---

  c.   Prejudgment interest.   This is a special example of consequential (or, in some cases, incidental) losses, but one that is considerably simpler to understand. When a breach delays the date on which plaintiff receives money (or property she could sell to obtain money), the plaintiff loses the use of that money (or property) for that period. She could have invested the money and earned interest (a consequential loss). Or she may need to borrow the money and pay interest on the loan (an incidental loss). Either way, the delay causes a loss. Interest compensates for that loss.

   i.   Statutory.   Interest rates usually are set by statute.

   ii.   Imprecise.   Consequential damages for the failure to pay money almost always are **limited to interest**. Interest may not accurately reflect the real loss plaintiff suffered. She could have bet the money on a horse that paid 50:1 or bought a winning lottery ticket. More plausible cases arise where plaintiff alleges she needed the money to take advantage of a stock option. Nonetheless, courts rarely award more than interest.

 # EXAMPLE AND ANALYSIS

When O refused to pay C (see 22.B.2.d), the only credible loss was interest on the money. C had already completed performance and had no more to do. Sometimes businesses try to claim they went bankrupt and lost years of profits because one payment was late, but this is the kind of claim that the limitation to interest is intended to avoid.

2.   Differentiating Incidental and Consequential Losses

Both incidental and consequential losses are one step removed from the breach. They involve losses that occur because of the breach but losses that involve additional actions more remote from the failure to perform. Thus, it can be hard to distinguish the two. Usually, that is not important. But under the UCC, some limitations on damages apply to consequential losses only, not to incidental losses. The following guidelines are imprecise, but should help distinguish the two.

a.   Incidental damages.   Incidental losses usually involve **direct expenditures**. Thus, advertising costs or transportation costs are incidental. In addition, incidental costs usually are **closely linked** to the failure to deliver the goods. They are almost inevitable results rather than remote consequences.

b.   Consequential losses.   Consequential losses often take the form of lost gains rather than direct expenditures. The opportunity to use the performance profitably disappeared. In addition, these losses tend to be more remote. The chain of causal events linking the breach to the loss involves more steps or more tenuous steps than with incidental losses.

 ## EXAMPLE AND ANALYSIS

After C refused to complete construction (see 22.B.2.d), O's architect charged an additional $2,000 for the work involved in finding and negotiating with T and briefing T on the work that had already been done. In addition, O's construction loan fell due during the delay. O had to pay a $5,000 in fees and additional interest to obtain bridge financing to pay the construction lender. In addition, B justifiably refused to buy the home from O because it was not ready on time. O paid a broker a $12,000 commission to find a new buyer. O also lost $10,000 in profits because the best offer the broker obtained was $10,000 lower than the price B had agreed to pay.

Okay, it isn't always simple. Sometimes, more than one cost figures in the same problem. In addition to the $5,000 extra T charged for finishing the work, O should recover $19,000 as incidental damages: $2,000 to find a new builder, $5,000 to obtain interim financing, and $12,000 to find a new buyer. O also might recover the $10,000 lost profits as consequential damages if foreseeability poses no obstacle. You could argue the new loan and the broker fees were consequential, not incidental, but it probably doesn't matter.

3. Exam Technique

When the facts of an exam question include references to side expenses, you know you need to discuss whether they are recoverable as incidental or consequential losses. But what if the question is more straightforward, including no such facts? In shorter questions, omitting this discussion should be fine. But in longer questions, you might score an extra point by asking whether your client incurred additional expenses that weren't mentioned originally. Don't take a lot of time with this: If the professor wanted a full discussion, she would have given you facts to work with. But a sentence raising the issue of whether other expenses might exist and suggesting that further investigation is in order might give you one point that others don't score. Every little bit helps.

D. AVOIDING OVERCOMPENSATION: REASONABLE COVER, LOSSES AVOIDED, AND COSTS AVOIDED

Just as the simple examples can conceal some costs the plaintiff incurred because of the breach, they can conceal some gains the plaintiff received because of the breach. If the plaintiff can keep these gains and still collect all costs from the defendant, she may end up better off following the breach than she would have if defendant had performed. The expectation interest seeks to avoid over-compensation just as much as (or perhaps more than) it seeks to avoid under-compensation.

1.   Substitute Goods of Superior Quality

When a seller fails to deliver goods, a buyer is entitled to obtain substitute goods and recover the difference in price. The UCC refers to this as "cover," a term useful even when land or services are at issue. See UCC §2-712. When goods of equal quality are available, the buyer cannot substitute higher-quality goods and expect that seller to make up the difference. The buyer should have received goods of a particular quality. If buyer must spend extra money to obtain goods of that quality, the seller caused the loss. But the seller never deprived the buyer of better-quality goods because she never promised to provide such goods.

 # EXAMPLE AND ANALYSIS

Thorne agreed to repair White's roof for $225. The job involved putting a four-ply roof on top of White's existing roof. When Thorne breached, White hired another to install a five-ply after removing the existing roof. The cost for that work was $582.26. The trial court awarded the full difference in price ($357.26). The appellate court reversed and remanded for a new trial on damages. If the contract had been performed, plaintiff would have received a four-ply roof, not a five-ply roof. To give him a five-ply roof for $225 would put him in a better position than he would have occupied if the contract had been performed. *Thorne v. White*, 103 A.2d 579 (D.C. Mun. Ct. App. 1954).

a.   **Equivalent goods.**   In the previous examples (see 22.B.2.d) consider the possibilities hidden in the sentence "B, after reasonable efforts, locates a similar car and buys it for $2,500." Was it the same year, make, model, mileage, color, appearance, and condition as the car S had promised? Although some facts might be less relevant to value (e.g., color), care should be taken not to charge S for B's decision to buy a better car than the one S promised.

b.   **Substitute goods at a better price.**   Few cases exist in which a party received substitute goods at a better price. Having saved money because of the breach, the nonbreaching party is unlikely to hire a lawyer to sue the breaching party. This is the legal equivalent of "no harm, no foul." When the remedy calculation comes up zero (or less), the plaintiff recovers nothing.

    c.   **Reasonable cover.**   In some cases, a buyer may need to acquire substitute goods to avoid significant consequential losses. If goods of equivalent quality are unavailable, it may be reasonable to cover with goods better goods. When cover is reasonable, the difference between cover price and contract price is recoverable.

2. Costs Avoided

Sometimes a breach will occur before the plaintiff has rendered her full performance. After the breach, she may be able to stop performing, at least if the breach was material. If she stops performing, she saves some of the costs she would have incurred. Those savings offset the recovery of damages.

 ## EXAMPLE AND ANALYSIS

O hires C to build a house for $100,000. C performs about half the work, incurring costs of $42,000 (half the total expenses of the job). O, without excuse, fires C and orders her off the property. C obeys, thus saving $42,000 in expenses she would have spent to complete the job. C is entitled to the $100,000 promised, minus the $42,000 saved, for a total recovery of $58,000. (To award her the $100,000 without the offset would leave her better off than if O had performed, because if O had performed, C would have incurred the additional expenditures.)

    a.   **Losing contracts.**   Sometimes costs avoided will **exceed the value of the performance**. For instance, suppose C misjudged the cost to build the house: It promised to complete work for $100,000, but the total cost will be $120,000, not $84,000 as it thought when it entered the contract. C can recover $22,000: the $100,000 promised minus the $78,000 in costs avoided. C ends up losing $20,000 (it has spent $42,000 but only recovered $22,000). But that is exactly what would have happened if the contract had been performed by all parties. (C would have spent $120,000 but only recovered $100,000.) Thus, C is in exactly the position she would have occupied if O had performed.

EXAMPLES AND ANALYSIS

1. B promises to buy S's car for $2,000. S, without excuse, refuses to deliver the car. The fair market value of the car is $2,500. B is entitled to the value of the promised performance ($2,500) minus the cost avoided (the $2,000 she would have paid if S had delivered the car), for a total recovery of $500. The result is the same if B actually purchases a similar car for $2,500.

2. B promises to buy S's car for $2,000. B, without excuse, refuses to perform before S delivers the car. The market value of the car is $1,750. S is entitled to the promised $2,000, **minus** the $1,750 value of the car because S avoided the cost of giving up the car. (Allowing her to recover the $2,000 and keep the car would make her better off than if B had performed, because if B had paid for the car S would have had to deliver the car to B.) The result is the same if S actually resells the car to another for $1,750.

3.   Losses Avoided

Some losses can be avoided by shifting resources that would have been used in one contract to another profitable use. Although the cost of these resources has already been incurred (and thus, the cost has not been avoided), part of the cost may be recovered in other ways. When losses are avoided, allowing the plaintiff to recover the cost without an offset for the losses avoided would make her better off than if the contract had been performed (because she could not have avoided the loss if she had completed performance of the contract).

 EXAMPLES AND ANALYSIS

1. In the building contract between C and O, some of the $42,000 in costs incurred so far might be for materials that have not yet been used in the construction of the house. If C sells these goods to another contractor for $5,000, the price collected for the goods reduces the total loss the contractor suffers. C not only avoids the $42,000 in expenses not yet incurred but also avoids losing $5,000 of the money already spent (by reselling the materials). The result is the same if C uses them to build another building. She would have had to buy these materials if they had not been shifted from the job with O. C effectively reduced the loss on the O contract by the amount she would have had to pay for the materials to perform the other contract.

2. R, an employer, promises E, an employee, $1,000 a week for a one-year contract. After 32 weeks, R fires E without excuse. E immediately finds another job that pays $900 per week. E is entitled to the promised performance ($20,000, because 20 weeks remain in the contract year), minus the amount of loss avoided by taking a different job ($18,000), for a total recovery of $2,000.

---

a. **Distinction insignificant.** The difference between cost avoided and loss avoided is not important. You can treat the time the employee saved as a cost avoided, like the car the seller retained. Or you can treat the car the seller resold as a loss avoided, like the time the employee resold. Either way, the savings offset the recovery. You will reach the same result no matter which category you put it in. No rules affect one differently than the other — as long as you are dealing with amounts **actually** avoided. (Rules governing avoidable losses are discussed shortly. See 22.E.1.) The key is to identify **how much to subtract**, not what to call it when you subtract it.

4. **Losses Not Really Avoided: The Lost-Volume Seller**

Sometimes a party can enter more than one contract, earning profits on each. The fact that the party earned a profit on a second contract, then, does not necessarily mean that she has avoided the loss of profit on the contract defendant breached. Before treating losses as avoided, consider whether plaintiff could have entered both contracts.

 EXAMPLES AND ANALYSIS

1. D is a new car dealer. B promises to pay $20,000 for a new car on the lot. B breaches. The next day, D sells the car to T for $20,000. Can D recover any damages from B?

Probably. If B had performed, D probably could have obtained another car just like the one B bought and sold that car to T. If so, D would have earned the profit on the sale of two cars, not just the sale to T. D has lost the profit she would have made on one of those sales. As such, the loss of profit caused by B's breach was not avoided. *Neri v. Retail Marine*, 285 N.E.2d 311 (N.Y. 1974), illustrates the same point but with a boat.

2. If you represented B, could you argue that the sale to T really did avoid the loss of profit?

You might prove that if B had performed, T would not have bought a car from D. Thus, D could have sold that car to B or to T but could not have sold two cars. This may be true but depends on several factors:

1.   T must have been in a hurry and bought the car only because it was present on the lot. If T would have waited for D to order one just like it, D could have sold two cars.
2.   T must have wanted exactly that car. If T would have bought a similar car on the lot had B's car been unavailable, then D could have sold two cars.

3. S is an individual trying to sell her used car. B promises to pay $2,000 for the car. B breaches. The next day, S agrees to sell the car to T for $2,000. Can S recover any damages from B?

Probably not. The sale to T avoided any loss because T gave S the full price S was entitled to receive. S might have incidental damages if she paid for a new ad because of the breach or incurred additional costs for gas to allow T a test drive. Basically, however, she received exactly what she expected: $2,000 for the car.

4. E is employed by R as an office worker from 9 A.M. to 5 P.M. R fires E without excuse. E takes a job driving a cab from 6 P.M. to midnight. Should the court offset the amount E earns driving a cab against the lost wages she can recover from R?

No (probably). E could have worked both jobs. If so, she would have both the wages from R and the earnings from driving a cab. The new earnings do not avoid the loss of the old.

5. If you represent R, could you argue that E's earnings as a cab driver really did avoid the loss of wages?

E probably would not have taken the job driving a cab if she continued to work for R. Thus, if the contract had been performed, E would have received only one set of earnings, not both. The fact that she decided to work nights instead of days does not change the fact that she still only works one job, preferring to keep the rest of the day free for sleep and leisure. To allow her to recover two salaries for working one job would make her better off than if R had performed. (This argument is correct, assuming E would not have worked both jobs. Some courts may hold that because E **could** have worked both jobs, R cannot **prove** that she would not have worked both.)

a.   **Clues.**   The lost-volume rule applies to people with plenty to sell. Thus, you should look for this issue when plaintiff is a manufacturer or large-scale seller. Its application to individuals is more rare.

    b. **Approach.** The issue only arises when plaintiff resold the contract performance to another. That makes it appear she avoided the loss. Lost volume is a response to defendant's claim that the resale eliminated or reduced plaintiff's loss. Unless defendant can make that claim, you need not discuss this rule.

E. LIMITATIONS ON EXPECTATION RECOVERIES

Sometimes courts have been reluctant to award the full amount the expectation interest prescribes. Several well-established exceptions or limitations on recovery exist. Some are in transition; you should watch for developments. But at least between now and the examination, you can rely on needing to take into account the following limitations.

1. Avoidable Consequences (or Mitigation of Damages)

Sometimes plaintiffs do not avoid costs following the breach, even though they should have avoided them. Courts subtract the costs a plaintiff **should have avoided** anyway, just as if the plaintiff actually had avoided them.

    a. **Preventing losses.** Plaintiff cannot recover for any loss that she could have avoided without undue risk, burden, or humiliation. Restatement (Second) of Contracts §350. The phrase "undue risk, burden, or humiliation" identifies efforts that it is unreasonable to expect a plaintiff to take to minimize the loss. If, by reasonable efforts, a plaintiff can prevent losses from mounting, the court will not allow recovery for those preventable losses even if plaintiff did not take the necessary steps.

        i. **Inaction.** Reasonable efforts often involve inaction: Plaintiff should stop work when the defendant notifies plaintiff of the breach.

EXAMPLE AND ANALYSIS

G, a county government, hires C, a contractor, to build a bridge. G decides not to build the road to the bridge and, without excuse, cancels the contract with C. C finishes the bridge anyway and sues for the price promised. C cannot recover for any expense incurred after G notified C of the breach because it could have avoided those costs by reasonable conduct (stopping work). See *Rockingham County v. Luten Bridge*, 35 F.2d 301 (4th Cir. 1929).

ii.   **Action.**   Reasonable efforts may require positive steps. A discharged employee must seek other work. A buyer must seek substitute sources before claiming lost profits.

 # EXAMPLES AND ANALYSIS

1. W, a wholesaler, promises to sell R, a retailer, 1,000 cases of aspirin for $20,000. W breaches. R would have resold the cases to customers for $25,000. R could have obtained identical aspirin for the same price from another supplier and resold it to consumers. R did not order any substitute aspirin and lost the sales to consumers. R may not recover the $5,000 in lost profits because by reasonable efforts she could have avoided all lost sales. See UCC §2-715.

2. R, an employer, hired E, an employee, for one year at a salary of $1,000 per week. After 32 weeks, R fires E without excuse. E could have immediately taken a similar job with another company for the same salary but decided not to take the job. E may not recover the $1,000 per week in lost salary because she could have avoided the loss by taking the other job.

b.   **Defendant's burden.**   The defendant must prove the amount that could have been avoided by reasonable efforts. That burden can be broken down into three parts.

i.   **Identify reasonable efforts.**   Defendant must state how plaintiff could have minimized the loss. Courts cannot evaluate the reasonableness or effectiveness of the measures until they have been specifically identified.

ii.   **Establish plaintiff's unreasonableness.**   Defendant must show plaintiff was unreasonable in failing to make these efforts. Showing that defendant's proposed efforts were reasonable is not enough. If plaintiff made other reasonable efforts to minimize the loss, courts will not reduce her recovery merely because she did not choose the method defendant preferred. Restatement (Second) of Contracts §350(2).

iii.   **Establish amount of loss avoidable.**   Defendant must establish how much of the loss plaintiff could have avoided by taking reasonable efforts. That may be difficult; if the plaintiff did **not** take reasonable efforts, we have to estimate what would have happened if she had.

c. **Plaintiff's reasonableness precludes reduction.** Some defendants, with 20-20 hindsight, spot other things the plaintiff could have done that would have reduced damages even more than the efforts plaintiff actually took. A defendant who wants to control the ways to minimize the loss may either take those steps for the plaintiff or negotiate with plaintiff to encourage those steps. A defendant who breaches, however, must accept the results of any reasonable efforts the plaintiff decides to make. As long as plaintiff's efforts to minimize the loss are reasonable, damages will not be reduced by amounts that could have been avoided by other methods.

d. **Unreasonable efforts not required.** Sometimes defendants identify steps that would have reduced the losses but at some cost to the plaintiff. If these steps involved **undue burden, risk, or humiliation**, plaintiff need not take them no matter how effective they might have been. Particularly in the employment context, some types of unreasonable steps have hardened into rules. Although some of these rules seem more appropriate to the nineteenth century than the twentieth, for now they cling to life.

   i. **Change of career.** A discharged employee need not take work in a different field to minimize the loss. In other words, executives need not flip burgers or push a broom to reduce the amount of lost earnings. This rule may reflect the humiliation of other work. It may also be reasonable to spend time looking for more lucrative work rather than accept the first job that comes along.

   ii. **Relocation.** A discharged employee need not take work in a different locale to minimize the loss. It may be unreasonable for an employee to change homes or commute long distances, at substantial cost, simply to minimize the loss the defendant would need to pay in lost wages. This is an undue burden argument —one employers should approve, because the alternative rule would make the cost of moving an incidental loss they would pay as damages!

   iii. **Same employer.** A discharged employee need not take work with the same employer on inferior terms. This holding, too, may involve humiliation. It also may be reasonable to refuse to work for employers who have already demonstrated they cannot be trusted to keep their agreements with employees. The rule also may deter employers from attempting to coerce employees into accepting modifications to their contracts. (Such modifications might be held enforceable, making it important for the employee to reject them.)

 # EXAMPLE AND ANALYSIS

A film company breached a contract with Shirley MacLaine (Parker) to make a musical in California but offered her the same salary to make a western in Australia. The offer omitted clauses that allowed Parker to veto script changes and choice of director for the musical. The court did not reduce the award by the amount that she could have earned on the western because it was different or inferior to the original job. *Parker v. Twentieth Century Fox Film*, 474 P.2d 689 (Cal. 1970).

The film required work in a different location. Movie stars often must work away from home to make a movie. Perhaps it would be reasonable for Parker to take such a job to minimize the loss — even though it might be unreasonable to reduce the award of a factory worker who did not move.

The film was a western, not a musical. Parker was noted for her work in musical comedy. Starring in a western, however, is not exactly a different career. Cf. *Two Mules for Sister Sara.*

The substitute offer from the same employer included inferior terms in that Parker lost the right to veto script changes and the choice of director. This is not exactly the kind of coercion typical in employment contracts ("Take a pay cut or you're fired.") No bad faith or coercion is evident here. But if these terms were sufficiently important to Parker, they might affect the value of the consideration she received. Working without them could involve humiliation; some stars have egos, after all. Perhaps the change made it reasonable for Parker to reject the offer.

---

e.   **Unavoidable losses.**   Amounts that could not be avoided are recoverable. Substitute measures may reduce but not eliminate the loss. The portion of the loss that cannot be avoided is recoverable.

i.   **Treat avoided and avoidable alike.**   Results under the avoidable consequences doctrine can be reached by treating amounts that should have been avoided as if they actually were avoided in calculating damages. You will still need to decide whether the plaintiff should have avoided the loss (i.e., that the efforts to minimize the loss were reasonable). But once you do, just plug the amount that could have been avoided into the equation as if it really had been avoided. No further calculation is needed.

 ## EXAMPLE AND ANALYSIS

R hired E for one year at a salary of $1,000 per week. After 32 weeks, R fires E without excuse. E makes no effort to find new work until the end of the year. R proves that there were many jobs available for people with E's qualifications. Thus, with a reasonable search E could have found work earning at least $900 per week after two weeks of looking. Instead of recovering $20,000, E may recover $3,800: $2,000 for the two weeks it would have taken to find another job, plus $1,800 for the 18 weeks she would have earned only $900 instead of the $1,000 promised by R.

     ii.   **Futile efforts.** If reasonable efforts to avoid the loss would be futile, a plaintiff may recover the full loss even if she made no efforts at all to minimize the loss. (If she had made reasonable efforts, the amount of loss avoided would be zero; thus, courts will subtract zero from the award.)

 ## EXAMPLE AND ANALYSIS

R hired E for one year. After 32 weeks, R fired E without excuse. E made no effort to find new work until the end of the year. R cannot prove any jobs in E's field were available. (Or perhaps E can prove there were none.) E may recover $20,000. Although a job search would have been reasonable, E need not make futile efforts merely to protect her right to recover damages against R.

    f.   **Costs of minimization recoverable.** Some efforts to minimize the loss are costly. If defendant had performed, the plaintiff would not have needed to incur those costs. Thus, any costs incurred to pursue reasonable efforts to minimize the loss are recoverable from the defendant — normally as an element of incidental damages. Note, however, that high cost may make it unreasonable to expect a plaintiff to take such measures at all — particularly if the damages will be small or the plaintiff has limited means.

 # EXAMPLES AND ANALYSIS

1. S promised to sell B 1,000 cases of aspirin at $20,000. S breached. To avoid lost profits on resale, B called every supplier in the state before finding someone who could supply her need for aspirin on time. If S had delivered the goods, B would have resold them at a profit without calling all over the state looking for a new supplier. These incidental costs are part of the damage recovery.

2. R hired E on a one year contract. After 32 weeks, R fired E without excuse. To find substitute employment, E printed up her resume and paid for transportation to interviews. If R had not fired E, she would have received her salary without incurring these costs. They are recoverable as incidental damages.

3. In the preceding example, E could not find suitable work locally. R proves that she could have found suitable substitute employment in a neighboring state. The expense of moving to that state may be so great that E reasonably could refuse to take that job without any reduction in damages for the amount she could have earned if she had elected to take the job.

The cost of relocation is generally so great that some courts treat this as a rule: An employee need not seek work in a different city; only damages avoidable by obtaining work locally will reduce the award.

If E actually does take a job in a different city, earnings from that employment will be a loss actually avoided that will reduce the award. Similarly, the cost of the move arguably would be recoverable as incidental damages. Few cases arise in which the employee did not have other reasons (unrelated to the discharge) for moving. If such cases do arise, courts might deny unreasonably large moving costs.

2.   Cost to Repair versus Diminution in Value

Sometimes there are two ways to compensate the expectation interest. One is to award plaintiff enough money to allow her to repair the inadequate performance to comply with the contract. The other is to award her the difference in value between what she was promised and what she received.

When these two values differ significantly, the court must decide which to allow. **Typically, the smaller amount is recoverable**.

EXAMPLE AND ANALYSIS

Recall *Jacob & Youngs v. Kent*, 16.A.3.b.i. A builder used the wrong manufacturer's pipe in building a house. The owner refused to pay unless the builder replaced the pipe, even though that would require the builder to tear down the walls and rebuild them. We noted that termination was not allowed because the breach was not material. The issue here is how much should be allowed as damages: the cost the owner would incur to repair the performance by replacing the pipe or the difference between the value the house would have had with the promised pipe and the value it did have with the pipe used?

a.   **Both remedies compensate for expectation.**   Both remedies provide the plaintiff with an expectation recovery. But they take a different view of what the plaintiff was promised.

  i.   **The thing promised.**   The cost of repair permits plaintiff to obtain the thing promised by using the money to repair any defects in performance.

  ii.   **The value promised.**   The diminution in value will not give plaintiff the thing promised but gives her the same value as the thing promised. Thus, in the previous example, the plaintiff would receive a house worth a little less than the promised house, plus money to make up the difference. Plaintiff's wealth is exactly the same as it would have been had the entire value been delivered in the form of the house.

b.   **Relation to avoidable consequences.**   Most cases of this sort can be resolved by asking whether plaintiff acted reasonably to minimize the loss.

  i.   **Repair reasonable to avoid large diminution in value.**   If cost of repair is less than the diminution in value, cost of repair is the typical remedy. It would be unreasonable for plaintiff to fail to repair when that would avoid a large diminution in value. Although plaintiff might not have the money to repair until after damages are awarded, damages will be calculated by the cost of repair.

ii.   Repair unreasonable to avoid small diminution in value.   If repairs will cost more than the benefit they create, it is unreasonable to make the repairs. For example, few people spend $10,000 to repair a car that would be worth $500 after the repairs were completed. Just as a plaintiff must stop work to keep losses from mounting during continued performance, a plaintiff would need to stop (or not start) repairs if their cost would increase the amount of loss rather than reduce it.

iii.   Subjective value.   Most cases involve costs to repair that exceed diminution in value. They raise the possibility that the plaintiff attaches a subjective value to the thing promised that exceeds value attached by the market. If so, the decision to repair might be reasonable for the plaintiff, even though other buyers would not pay more for the repaired property.

 # EXAMPLE AND ANALYSIS

Plaintiff leased their property to a coal company for strip mining after negotiating a clause in which the company promised to restore the land to its original condition after mining. The coal company breached. Restoring the land to its original condition would have cost about $29,000 but would have increased the value by only $500. *Peevyhouse v. Garland Coal & Mining*, 382 P.2d 109 (Okla. 1962). Held: for defendant. Plaintiff could recover only $500.

Plaintiffs may have attached a very high subjective value to the restored land. The fact that others would pay little more for it if repaired may not reflect its value to them as part of their home. Thus, they may have valued the restored land more than they valued $29,000—just as Kent may have really attached huge value to a specific manufacturer's pipe in his dream home.

iv.   Objective value preferred.   Because courts cannot easily verify claims of subjective value, they tend to award the lesser amount rather than attempt to determine, on a case-by-case basis, whether subjective value actually requires a larger recovery.

c.   **Risk of undercompensation or overcompensation.**   When cost of repair exceeds diminution in value, dangers of incorrect remedies exist.

   i.   **Overcompensation.**   Awarding cost of repair risks overcompensation. A plaintiff might decide not to repair the property and pocket the excess. If so, her wealth is greater than it would have been if the defendant had performed. She has property worth a little less than promised plus money worth much more than the difference.

   ii.   **Undercompensation.**   Awarding diminution in value will undercompensate plaintiff if she in fact attaches a subjective value to the repaired property that the market does not reflect.

d.   **Relation to specific performance.**   Recall the undue hardship defense to orders for specific performance. If an injunction will harm the defendant much more than it will benefit the plaintiff, a court will deny the injunction and relegate plaintiff to an action for damages.

   i.   **Cost of repair like an injunction.**   Ordering the defendant to pay the cost of repair, when that exceeds diminution in value, is like ordering specific performance. When repairs would benefit the plaintiff (by increasing her wealth) less than it would harm the defendant (by paying for them), the same imbalance suggests the remedy is inappropriate.

   ii.   **Cost of repair as a liquidated injunction.**   When specific performance would be allowed, cost of repair is no different. It simply allows the plaintiff to select a different person to perform the repairs instead of ordering defendant to perform them.

3.   Foreseeability

The cases on foreseeability in the casebooks can be confusing, but the rule is easy, and applying it isn't as hard as it sounds. Let's start with the easy stuff.

a.   **Rule.**   A plaintiff can recover damages if either (i) the loss flows naturally from the breach or (ii) the defendant, at the time the contract was made, had reason to know that losses of this type probably would form a breach. When the consequences of breach are unusual, the only way defendant will have reason to know about them is if plaintiff tells her about the likely consequences of breach.

i.   **Consequential losses.**   Foreseeability problems usually involve consequential damages. Consequential damages involve the ways the plaintiff planned to use the defendant's performance, which frequently are unknown to the defendant. Thus, she may have no idea the type and size of losses the plaintiff faces in the event of breach.

ii.   **Terminology.**   Courts sometimes divide damages into general and special damages. General damages are the losses that flow naturally from the breach. These tend to include lost value and incidental damages. Special damages relate to unusual circumstances, which may require notice to the other party. This could be equated with consequential damages but should not prevent you from arguing (when appropriate) that consequential damages flowed naturally from the breach. On the whole, terms such as "general" and "specific" damages are more confusing than helpful, particularly because their meaning in tort is almost the reverse of their meaning in contract.

iii.   **Incentive to share information.**   Foreseeability forces the party who knows how disastrous breach would be (the plaintiff) to tell the party who needs to take precautions to avoid the breach (the defendant). Sometimes, breach can be avoided, but the cost to avoid breach exceeds the benefit of avoiding the breach. In those cases, it makes sense to breach and pay damages. To make that calculation, defendant estimates the likely costs of breach. Although the defendant can include the natural consequences and those she can foresee, she cannot include unusual consequences — unless the plaintiff warns her about the unusual possibilities. Thus, the rule requires a plaintiff who has unusually important reasons for seeking the defendant's performance to either reveal those reasons (so defendant can take the appropriate amount of precaution to prevent breach) or forego damages for the loss of those unusual possibilities.

iv.   **Advance mitigation.**   The plaintiff, by warning the defendant, might minimize the loss by discouraging defendant from breaching. If she does not warn the defendant about the possible consequences of breach, plaintiff cannot recover for those unforeseeable losses.

b.   **Buyer's losses.**   Foreseeability problems usually involve buyers seeking damages from sellers. The seller, in most cases, lost money. The consequences of losing money are losing interest on that money — or so the law assumes to avoid plaintiffs claiming they would have invested the money and made millions that defendant should now pay. Buyers, however, would use what they receive in a variety of different ways. This makes the consequences harder to foresee and, thus, more likely to arise as a problem on an exam. In fact, the UCC does not have a provision applying foreseeability to seller's losses (or, for that matter, a provision for consequential damages for sellers — everything is wrapped into §2-710, the provision on seller's incidental damages).

c. **Common errors.**

i. **Reason to know versus knew.** Foreseeability requires reason to know, not actual knowledge. Defendants cannot plead subjective ignorance. If they had reason to know of the type of loss, their failure to know will not limit damages.

ii. **Amount versus type of loss.** Foreseeability, at least in theory, does not require that defendant have reason to know how much the damages will be, only the type of damages that will result. In fact, the UCC seems to require only that defendant be aware of the plaintiff's "general or particular requirements or needs." UCC §2-715(2)(a). Courts, however, rarely allow recovery when the seller knows buyer needs something unusual but does not have reason to know why or what type of consequences will result if the need is not met.

iii. **Tacit agreement.** Except in a few states, foreseeability does not depend on a tacit agreement to accept responsibility for damages. Oliver Wendell Holmes thought the foreseeability rule was too generous to plaintiffs. He argued that mere foreseeability was not enough; unless the facts show that the defendant agreed (perhaps by silence) to be responsible for unusual damages, plaintiff could not recover them. Some states still follow this approach; most do not. The UCC, adopted in almost every state, rejects the tacit agreement test for sales of goods.

iv. **Foreseeability differs in tort.** In tort almost everything seems to be foreseeable — especially in hindsight, as courts and juries tend to look at things. Tort tends to treat possible consequences as foreseeable. In contract, foreseeability refers to consequences that are almost inevitable — that any reasonable person should have recognized as consequences of a breach. Try not to mix these different approaches.

    d.   Actual notice.   Foreseeability can arise without actual notification by the buyer to the seller.

4.   Certainty

Plaintiff cannot recover damages unless she can prove them with reasonable certainty. Restatement (Second) of Contracts §352. This maxim is ancient, but its strictness has eroded over the years. Today, the emphasis is on "reasonable," not on "certainty."

    a.   Consequential losses.   Uncertainty applies to all damages but is most important for consequential damages, such as lost profits. The rule is general. But market value, cover transactions, incidental expenses, and so on, usually are easy to prove. Thus, the issue tends to arise when the plaintiff claims that she would have earned profits by using defendant's performance in a particular way: For example, if defendant had delivered the leather, I could have made belts and sold them for a profit.

    b.   Existence of loss.   The plaintiff must show that she suffered a loss from the breach. When the breach may not have caused any loss at all, courts typically refuse any recovery. These cases, however, are quite rare. They can exist only if the plaintiff had not begun to rely on the promise. If the plaintiff had incurred any expenditures in preparation to perform, some loss is demonstrable, at least until met with rebuttal evidence.

    c.   Amount of loss.   If the **existence** of a loss is certain, the jury may make a reasonable estimate of the **amount** of the loss. The jury is not allowed to speculate, particularly if it is possible that no losses resulted from the breach. Thus, some evidence must be introduced to support a jury verdict. But testimony by an expert predicting the amount of the loss is sufficient basis for allowing the jury to estimate the amount of loss caused by the breach.

        i.   History.   Established businesses frequently have a history of profitability from which a jury (with help from an expert witness) can estimate the profits that would have been earned if defendant had performed.

        ii.   Comparable business.   New businesses may be able to identify similar businesses whose profitability support the inference that this venture also would have been profitable.

iii. **New businesses.**   However, new businesses may have trouble showing sufficient similarities between themselves and other businesses to justify these inferences. Other businesses run by **other people** do not mean that these plaintiffs could run a business as successfully. Other businesses in **other places** or other industries may not mean that a business in this industry and place would have been successful. But some similarities may support the award. For example, a new McDonald's franchise probably could use the profitability of other similar new McDonald's franchises as a basis for projections. The franchisor's reputation (or the training it provides franchisees) may be more important than the plaintiff's own business sense in generating profits.

d. **Reliance interest.**   Lack of reasonable certainty frequently produces recourse to the reliance interest. Frequently, plaintiff can prove she incurred expenses but cannot prove she would have made a profit if defendant had performed. She might have run a loss. If so, the expectation interest will not allow recovery amounts that will make the loss smaller than it would have been if the contract had been performed.

EXAMPLE AND ANALYSIS

R, a restaurateur, rents a building, buys kitchen equipment, and hires C, a unique famous chef. After R pays $1 million for the building and equipment, the chef breaches the contract, making it pointless to proceed with the restaurant project. R can show an expenditure of $1 million.

The loss might be less than $1 million. If revenues the restaurant would have earned (minus additional expenses avoided) would have been less than $1 million (say, $700,000), the **loss caused by the breach** will be less than $1 million (say, $300,000).

The loss might be zero. If revenues minus costs avoided equals zero, the entire $1 million would have been lost even if defendant had performed.

The loss might be negative — that is, the breach might have prevented R from losing even more money. If future costs (now avoided) would have exceeded revenues, R would not have recouped any of the $1 million and would have lost even more money by proceeding.

Rather than deny all recovery, courts frequently allow recovery of the reliance interest. See Chapter 21. In this example, R could recover the $1 million already spent but could not recover more unless she could prove profits with reasonable certainty.

In effect, this assumes that the project would have broken even: that total revenues would have equaled total expenses, including the expenses already incurred.

---

    i.   **Plaintiff's burden.** To recover profits, plaintiff must prove with reasonable certainty that revenues would have exceeded total expenses. But plaintiff may recover expenditures without proving the venture would have broken even.

    ii.   **Defendant's burden.** To avoid paying expenditures, defendant must prove the venture would not have broken even — that expenses would have exceeded revenues. But defendant — whose breach prevented the plaintiff from obtaining evidence of what profits would have been — cannot rely on the uncertainty doctrine to avoid paying costs already incurred.

    iii.   **Default position.** The presumption effectively allocates the risk of uncertainty between the parties. It presumes profits will be zero. A party who wants to recover more or pay less has the burden to prove that profits would have been greater than or less than zero.

5. Emotional Distress

Contract law primarily governs business transactions, where the distress of not receiving the promised performance is simply part of the stress of doing business. Thus, **damages for emotional distress usually are not recoverable in contract actions**. Two exceptions exist and have been growing in recent years.

a.   **Physical harm.** When a breach of contract causes physical injury, emotional distress or pain and suffering are part of the recovery. Thus, a plaintiff injured by a defective product may recover much the same damages whether she decides to sue in contract for breach of warranty or in tort for strict products liability.

b.   **Emotional contracts.** When a contract or a breach is particularly likely to cause severe emotional disturbance, damages for distress may be recoverable.

    i.   **Burials.** This line of cases began with funeral homes: dropped caskets, empty caskets, caskets containing the wrong body, etc., all caused considerable distress that courts proved willing to remedy in contract actions.

ii. **Insurance.** It expanded to insurance cases: an insurer's refusal to pay a person who has just suffered a tragedy (a fitting description of many insured events, such as fire, death, disability, or severe illness) naturally causes some distress as well as economic hardship. Recovery for emotional distress has been allowed in some cases — though often by calling breach of an insurance contract a tort, making emotional distress a normal component of recovery.

iii. **Vacations.** Breaches that destroy vacations may cause distress.

 # EXAMPLE AND ANALYSIS

Defendant sold plaintiff a tour package in Switzerland based on a brochure including some rather inflated claims. Instead of a group, plaintiff was the only person on the tour for one of the two weeks. Skiing was inconveniently located; the rental equipment was in odd sizes. The hosts could not speak English. The bar was closed during his stay. Altogether, the vacation was a bust. The appellate court awarded recovery for the lost enjoyment — about twice the price paid for the vacation. *Jarvis v. Swans Tours*, [1973] 1 Q.B. 233 (Ct. App., Civ. Div. 1973).

iv. **Joy versus distress.** Absence of joy and presence of distress are not identical but two sides of the same coin. The willingness to take into account not only the pecuniary values but the psychological benefits suggests some willingness to expand the cases in which emotional factors play into the damage award.

c. **Probing the rule.** The Restatement (Second) of Contracts §353 states the second exception rather broadly: Emotional distress will be excluded unless "the contract or the breach is of such a kind that serious emotional disturbance was a particularly likely result."

i. **Foreseeability test.** This seems to be a foreseeability rule. Although some concerns with emotional losses deal with uncertainty — the inability to attach realistic values to the distress involved — the Restatement seems unconcerned with this rationale for denying distress.

ii. **But different.** The foreseeability test seems both narrower and broader than the normal foreseeability rule discussed previously. The requirement that disturbance be "particularly likely" seems to demand more than just reason to know disturbance might occur. This may narrow the foreseeability test in this context. The idea that the "breach" might make disturbance particularly likely suggests that disturbance need only be foreseeable at the time of the breach. This would make it possibile to show foreseeability in far more cases than under the normal rule.

iii. **Severity.** Note the rule is limited to cases in which "severe" emotional disturbance is particularly likely. Normal distress — perhaps even including dissatisfaction over a vacation package — may not rise to the level envisioned by the Restatement. The words, however, leave some room for courts to expand recoveries without changing the rule at all.

6. **Attorney's Fees**

Attorney's fees usually are not recoverable as an element of damages in a contract action. There are exceptions.

a. **Express contract.** When the contract provides for the recovery of attorney's fees as part of the damages, that provision of the contract usually is enforceable. See Chapter 22.

b. **Collateral litigation.** When defendant's breach of a contract forces the plaintiff to incur attorney's fees in litigation against third parties, those fees are recoverable as consequential damages.

 ## EXAMPLE AND ANALYSIS

O sells land to B, promising to deliver clear title to the land. T sues B, claiming that T really owns the land. If B incurs attorney's fees defending the suit by T, those fees would be recoverable consequential damages in a suit against O (assuming, of course, that O has breached the promise to deliver clear title). If T wins the suit, O might also recover the fair value of the land as damages.

EXAMPLE AND ANALYSIS

A, an attorney, promises to represent C, a client, in a lawsuit for a flat fee of $5,000. A, without excuse, refuses to perform. C pays L, another lawyer, $7,000 in fees to perform the services A had promised. A may recover $2,000 from C. The fact that cover here involves hiring an attorney will not prevent recovery of the excess fees.

c.   **Statutes.**   Some statutes permit a prevailing plaintiff to recover attorney's fees. Most involve public wrongs, such as employment discrimination. Some contract disputes may fall within consumer protection statutes prohibiting unfair business practices. These statutes sometimes allow fees. Litigation reform efforts may produce additional state statutes allowing recovery of fees in some contract actions.

d.   **Costs of litigation.**   American law generally deals with attorney's fees as an element of litigation costs, covered by civil procedure rules. As a result, damage rules often do not address attorney's fees, at all. Arguably, these fees are like any other consequential damages: If defendant had performed, plaintiff would not have incurred these costs. But that is not the rule.

7.   Punitive Damages

Punitive damages are not recoverable in contract actions. As usual, however, there are some exceptions. Following the examples, some general notes about claims for punitive damages should help you analyze an exam question if it raises a novel claims for punitive damages.

a.   **Breach of promise to marry.**   Such a breach traditionally allowed recovery of punitive damages. Punitive damage may have been a means to compensate for emotional distress. Because most jurisdictions have abolished the action for breach of promise to marry, this exception is not very important.

b.   **Insurance contracts.**   When a large insurer wrongfully refuses to pay an individual — especially an individual who just suffered a tragedy that insurance usually covers — some courts award punitive damages. Typically, courts have treated these breaches of contract as a tort.

c.   **Employment contracts.**   Like insurers, employers have considerably more power than employees. When they wrongfully discharge an employee, some courts have awarded the employee punitive damages. It is important to recognize three distinct types of employment claims.

    i.   **Retaliatory discharge.**   When an employer fires an employee in retaliation for legitimate conduct, courts treat the discharge as a tort. Thus, an employee who refused to commit perjury for an employer received punitive damages. Similarly, employees fired for filing a worker's compensation claim have recovered punitive damages. The motivation for the discharge is critical. Unless a public policy is at stake, retaliatory discharge is unlikely to succeed.

    ii.   **Breach of the obligation of good faith and fair dealing.**   Some courts have interpreted open-ended employment contracts to include an implied promise to use good faith in deciding whether to discharge employees, especially long-term employees. An employer who does not use good faith — who, for example, fires a long-term employee with an excellent record to hire a relative — may breach that obligation. Although some courts have flirted with the idea of awarding punitive damages for these breaches, most courts apply normal contract remedies. That is, most courts deny punitive damages in this setting.

    iii.   **Breach of a duration term.**   Some contracts include a duration term — typically one year. Discharge before that time is a breach (unless excused). These situations tend to be straightforward contract cases. Absent bad motives that implicate good faith or retaliation, courts have not shown any inclination to award punitive damages.

  d. **Other commercial contexts.**   Sporadically, courts have awarded punitive damages in other commercial contexts. Usually these efforts have been overturned. This, however, is one area in which the law is in flux. The tort reform attack on punitive damages may prevent expansion into contract. Because denying attorney's fees makes contract remedies undercompensatory, litigants will continue to look for ways to get punitive damages in contract cases.

  e. **Bad faith: Necessary but not sufficient.**   Aside from promises to marry, all courts that have awarded punitive damages for breach of contract have found bad faith by the defendant. But many courts have refused to allow punitive damages despite a defendant's bad faith. Thus, bad faith is necessary, but is not sufficient to obtain a judgment for punitive damages.

f.   The meaning of bad faith.   Courts requiring bad faith have applied that requirement in various ways. If a defendant knows she has no justifiable defense to damages for breach of contract but still refuses to perform or to pay the damages, bad faith seems clear. Pleading a defense that she knows is fallacious does not constitute "honesty in fact." This verges on a tort: If malicious prosecution is tortious for plaintiffs, malicious defense should be tortious for defendants. Some courts, however, seem to suggest that unreasonable defenses constitute bad faith. Thus, even if the defendant honestly believes she does not owe any money to plaintiff, refusing to pay may give rise to a judgment for punitive damages in addition to compensatory damages.

REVIEW QUESTIONS AND ANSWERS

Question: What is the goal of the expectation interest?

Answer: To put the nonbreaching party (plaintiff) in the position she would have occupied if the breaching party had performed the contract.

Question: At its most basic level, how do courts calculate expectation damages?

Answer: They determine what the plaintiff would have received if the contract had been performed and subtract from that any savings plaintiff enjoyed by not having to complete her own performance.

Question: If a plaintiff suffered emotional distress as a result of the breach, will courts compensate for that loss?

Answer: Usually not. In cases in which severe distress is particularly likely, courts may allow recovery for distress. Most courts apply this exception to a very limited range of cases.

Question: If a plaintiff would have suffered losses had defendant performed, can she recover anything?

Answer: Maybe. If her actual losses are greater than the losses she would have suffered if defendant had performed, she may recover the difference. But if her losses are smaller than they would have been from performance (e.g., because she has saved money she otherwise would have needed to pay the other party), any recovery would leave her better off than if the contract had been performed.

Question: What are the three primary limitations on recovery of the expectation interest?

Answer: The avoidable consequences doctrine, foreseeability, and the requirement of reasonable certainty.

Question: What must a defendant prove to reduce a damage award under the avoidable consequences doctrine?

Answer: That the plaintiff's efforts to minimize the loss were unreasonable, that other measures were reasonable, and that those measures would have avoided part of the plaintiff's loss.

Question: What must a plaintiff establish to show her losses were foreseeable?

Answer: Show that the defendant, at the time the contract was made, had reason to know that loss of this sort probably would occur if she breached. Courts identify two ways to meet this requirement: (1) show that the losses were a natural consequence of the breach—the kind of loss that almost inevitably flows from a breach of this sort; or (2) show that defendant had special notice of plaintiff's probable losses at the time the contract was made.

THE RELIANCE INTEREST

21

CHAPTER OVERVIEW

The reliance interest seeks to put the plaintiff in the position she would have occupied if the defendant had not made the promise.

Courts may resort to the reliance interest when:

- Expectation damages cannot be proven with sufficient certainty;
- Expectation damages cannot be awarded because the promise is unenforceable, but the restitution interest provides inadequate compensation; and
- Expectation damages would provide disproportionate compensation.

Usually, the reliance interest involves compensating plaintiff for expenditures that she would not have incurred if the promise had not been made.

- When a plaintiff gives up clearly identifiable potential gains to enter the contract with defendant, those lost opportunities may be included in the reliance interest.
- Usually, lost opportunities are too difficult to prove with sufficient certainty.

The reliance interest cannot exceed the expectation interest.

- Plaintiff cannot recover expenditures that would have become losses even if defendant had performed.
- Defendant must prove the extent of losses plaintiff would have incurred to limit reliance recovery under this rule.

Most limitations on expectation (such as certainty and foreseeability) apply to reliance, but in cases in which courts resort to the reliance interest, reliance damages usually satisfy the requirements.

A.   APPROPRIATE CASES FOR THE RELIANCE INTEREST

As noted in the introductory chapter, contract scholars identify three interests that could be used to measure recovery. Courts almost always start with the expectation interest when a contract has been breached. Courts rarely look further unless expectation fails to produce an appropriate remedy. In appropriate cases, however, courts will resort to other remedial interests. These cases fall into four basic categories.

1.   Reliance Damages Are Available When Expectation Damages Are Uncertain

As noted earlier, the most common use for reliance damages is to allow some compensation when a breach is clear but when the expectation interest cannot be proven with sufficient certainty. See 20.E.4.

2.   Reliance Damages May Be Available When a Contract Is Unenforceable, but Restitution Provides an Inadequate Remedy

In some cases, promises are made that cannot be enforced for various reasons. In these cases, restitution will allow plaintiff to recover any benefits bestowed upon the defendant. When that recovery is inadequate, however, courts sometimes allow recovery of the reliance interest.

a.   Undermines contract defenses.   Each exception of this nature involves a rule that reduces the force of substantive contract defenses. That is, a defendant who establishes one of these defenses may find that instead of being free from any obligation under the promise, the obligation is merely reduced from the amount of the plaintiff's expectation interest to the amount of the reliance interest.

i.   Restitution.   This is not unique. Restitution, too, remains recoverable despite the absence of a contract — and is available in all the situations discussed below if defendant received benefits that she should not be allowed to retain. A cause of action for unjust enrichment may exist without any promise. Thus, the existence of an unenforceable promise does not preclude recovery in restitution.

ii.   Tort.   Similarly, recovery for tort is not precluded simply because a contract is unenforceable. Tort duties exist independent of a promise. (You may be liable for battery or negligence even if you never promised not to commit battery or negligence.) In some ways, promises that produce reliance are treated as if they are torts: The promise is not enforced but damages caused by making the promise are assessed against the party who made the promise.

b. **Statute of frauds.** When the statute of frauds precludes recovery because no writing supports the contract, courts sometimes award reliance as a way to prevent injustice. The rule is discussed above as an exception to the statute of frauds. See 4.B.8. It involves the typical elements of reliance: a promise the promisor reasonably should expect to cause reliance, which does cause reliance, and injustice can be avoided only by enforcement. Restatement (Second) of Contracts §139.

c. **Mistake.** When a mistake (mutual or unilateral) allows rescission of a contract, courts sometimes allow the plaintiff to recover reliance expenses incurred before the mistake was discovered. Restatement (Second) of Contracts §158(2).

d. **Consideration.** When lack of consideration precludes enforcement of a promise, courts sometimes rule the promise enforceable anyway on grounds that action in reliance makes it unjust to allow the promisor to refuse to perform. In these situations, courts can limit recovery to the reliance interest if they so choose. See, e.g., Restatement (Second) of Contracts §90.

 i. **Expectation common.** Most courts do not limit recovery to reliance in these situations. Instead, they either enforce the promise or refuse to enforce it, treating reliance as an exception to the substantive rule requiring consideration.

 ii. **Disproportionate recovery.** When courts do limit recovery, this resembles a conclusion that expectation would produce an unduly large recovery. This principle is discussed below.

e. **Incapacity.** Some cases involving defendant's mental incapacity, if plaintiff was unaware of it, may justify recovery of the reliance interest. The substance of the rule is discussed above. See 6.C.2.c.i(b). Again, the general rule is that the promises are enforceable — a rule allowing expectation recoveries. The rule, however, permits courts to limit recovery to the reliance interest if the interests of justice so require. Restatement (Second) of Contracts §15(2).

3. Disproportionate Recovery

Some cases exist in which a court concluded that the full expectation interest simply allowed too great a recovery in proportion to the wrong committed. In these rare cases, some courts have balked at awarding the full expectation recovery. But because defendant has breached an enforceable promise, some recovery was required. Reliance seemed a suitable compromise.

a.   Related to foreseeability.   The Restatement buried the rule allowing this limitation in the provisions governing foreseeability. See Restatement (Second) of Contracts §351(3). The rule, however, relates to damages that **are** foreseeable.

b.   Indications.   The comments to the Restatement suggest that it should be invoked when the informality of the transaction or the very small price charged imply the defendant did not intend to assume the duty to pay very large damages in the event of breach. The comment suggests that courts tend to stretch foreseeability doctrine or apply it unsoundly to deny recovery in these cases. The rule is designed to allow courts to deny recovery without warping rules governing foreseeability.

c.   Defect in title.   I know of only one class of cases in which the result has been achieved: **defect of title in sales of land.** O promised to sell the land to B, but O did not own the land. The expectation interest would require O to pay the full difference between the market value of the land and the contract price. If O acted innocently, believing in good faith that she owned the land, and the problem was discovered before the sale was concluded, some courts have limited recovery to any expenses B incurred in preparation to conclude the sale. (If O acted fraudulently, the full expectation recovery may be entirely appropriate —and tort or contract law would permit it.)

B.   CALCULATING RELIANCE RECOVERIES

The reliance interest seeks to put the plaintiff in the position she would have occupied if the defendant had not made the promise.

1.   Expenditures Incurred

Reliance primarily involves reimbursing the plaintiff for any expenditures made in reliance on defendant's promise.

a.   Partial performance.   Expenditures include down payments or other partial performance conveyed to defendant. For example, a buyer of goods may recover any amounts paid to the seller, even if other remedies are unavailable. Similarly, a builder may recover the cost of any construction completed before breach.

b. **Preparations.** Expenditures include collateral costs in preparation for performance.

EXAMPLES AND ANALYSIS

1. Defendant sold plaintiff machines for reclaiming used rubber. Plaintiff built a foundation on which the machines would be placed. Defendant breached. Plaintiff recovered the cost of building the foundation. *L. Albert & Son v. Armstrong Rubber*, 178 F.2d 182 (2d Cir. 1949).

2. Plaintiff rented an iron mill from defendant. In reliance, plaintiff purchased iron (or iron ore) to be milled. Defendant breached. Plaintiff recovered the amount spent on iron (ore). *Nurse v. Barns*, Sir T. Raym. 77 (K.B. 1664).

3. Defendant hired plaintiff as a sales manager in a car dealership. Plaintiff moved from California to Hawaii to take the job. Defendant fired plaintiff before the contract term ended. The contract was unenforceable because it was not in writing. The court, however, allowed the expense incurred in moving from California in reliance on the contract. *McIntosh v. Murphy*, 469 P.2d 177 (Haw. 1970). (Note: the amount recovered looks strangely like the amount of salary for the rest of the contract period. The court, in affirming the jury verdict, may not have been too careful about how the reliance interest was measured.)

c. **Entire venture.** When defendant's performance is part of a larger venture, expenditures include other expenses incurred to pursue that venture.

EXAMPLES AND ANALYSIS

1. Plaintiff intended to make a television play. They rented a location and incurred fees for the director, designer, stage manager, and others. They also hired Robert Reed to play the lead. Reed breached the contract just before filming was to begin. Plaintiff could not locate a suitable replacement

on short notice, so the project was canceled. Plaintiff recovered all expenses incurred in connection with the film because defendant's breach caused those expenses to be wasted. *Anglia Television v. Reed*, [1971] All E.R. 690 (Ct. App. Civ. Div. 1971).

2. Plaintiff planned to promote an effort to break the world record for flagpole sitting. To finance the venture, it needed to sell shares to the public. It hired defendant (an attorney) to help it incorporate and offer the shares for sale. Plaintiff sold stock and incurred substantial liabilities, including construction of a suitable flagpole (including amenities such as a toilet), hiring public relations specialists to help promote the venture, and borrowing money from a bank. Plaintiff then learned that defendant had not complied with legal restrictions on sales of stock. Thus, no more stock could be sold and the amount already received needed to be placed in escrow for shareholders. The venture collapsed because plaintiff could not afford either the escrow or a securities specialist to straighten matters out. Plaintiff recovered the costs incurred before the venture collapsed, not just the money paid to the defendant. *Wartzman v. Hightower Prodns.*, 456 A.2d 82 (Md. Ct. Spec. App. 1983).

2.   Lost Opportunities

In theory, the reliance interest also requires the defendant to compensate plaintiff for any opportunities lost as a result of the promise, such as the opportunity to enter a similar contract with a different promisor.

   a.   Application problematic.   Because courts have difficulty identifying and evaluating lost opportunities, this element frequently is omitted from reliance interest calculations. Frequently, a person who accepts one contract stops looking for others. Thus, she cannot easily identify the terms of the other contract she would have entered if the defendant had not made the promise. Thus, courts are reluctant to speculate as to what benefits that contract might have included for plaintiff. Instead, they limit recovery to expenditures.

   b.   Next best offer.   This rule seems to apply even where the next best offer is fairly identifiable. For instance, when contracts are based on a bidding process, the next best bid may be ascertainable. Nonetheless, courts are reluctant to award reliance remedies that exceed expenditures.

   c.   Employees.   An exception exists for employees who leave one job to take another. Here, unlike possible other contracts, plaintiff was involved in an actual contract. The earnings she could have made by staying in that job will be recoverable as a reliance cost. But the earnings she could have made by taking the next best job offer she had usually will not be allowed.

C. THE RELIANCE INTEREST CANNOT EXCEED THE EXPECTATION INTEREST

1. In Losing Contracts, Reliance Will Exceed Expectation

The reliance interest, by allowing recovery of all expenditures, allows the plaintiff to break even on any contract: She will not recover any profit but will not suffer any loss either. If the plaintiff would have lost money if the contract had been performed, the expectation interest would not allow the plaintiff to recover all expenditures. Instead, however much she would have lost from performance will be unrecoverable. In these cases reliance will exceed expectation.

 EXAMPLE AND ANALYSIS

O hires C to build a house for $100,000. After C has spent $50,000, O breaches. C calculates that she would have needed to spend another $60,000 to complete the job.

1. The expectation interest is $40,000: $100,000 price expected minus $60,000 cost avoided. Thus, C would lose $10,000 on the contract (having spent $50,000 but recovered only $40,000), exactly as she would have lost $10,000 if the contract had been performed (having spent $110,000 and received $100,000).
2. The reliance interest normally would be $50,000: the expenses incurred in reliance on the promise. If the contract had not been made, plaintiff would not have incurred any of those expenses. Thus, C will break even on the contract, even though she would have lost $10,000 if the defendant had performed.

   a. **Exam tip.** Don't fight the numbers. If the question tells you how much it will cost to finish the job, take it as a given. In practice, the amount of future expenditures may be uncertain. Plaintiff may be able to show ways to economize so that she could finish the job under budget. If so, she might recover profits on the deal. But often enough, plaintiff will know only too well that she would have lost her shirt if defendant had performed—and in precisely those cases, she will present no evidence of the cost to finish the work, hoping that uncertainty will allow her to recover reliance instead. In any event, don't rewrite the exam question to allow a recovery you want to give. Take the facts as you find them.

2. Expectation Cap on Recovery

If reliance damages exceed expectation damages, recovery will be limited to the expectation interest. If the defendant can prove plaintiff would have suffered a loss even if defendant had performed, plaintiff can recover expenditures that exceed the amount she would have lost but cannot recover any more. Restatement (Second) of Contracts §349.

 # EXAMPLE AND ANALYSIS

In the previous illustration, C may recover $40,000. She may recover expenditures only to the extent that they exceed the $10,000 she would have lost if O had performed. Because expenditures ($50,000) exceed the amount of the loss ($10,000) by $40,000, that is how much she can recover. (The Restatement phrases the calculation in reverse: C may recover all expenditures minus any losses O can prove. The calculation is the same—$50,000 − $10,000 = $40,000.)

Rationale:

1. Bumper sticker version. Courts will not make a better contract for the plaintiff than the one she made for herself. If plaintiff negotiated a deal that produced a $10,000 loss, courts will not make a better deal for her.

2. A-paper version. Reliance is primarily a compromise measure of damages: It does not allow the plaintiff the full expectation interest, but it does not limit the plaintiff to recovering benefits bestowed on the defendant, as restitution does. This is reflected in the situations in which reliance is used —cases in which, usually, the court wants to grant less than the expectation interest would allow. If the reliance interest produces a recovery greater than the expectation interest, this compromise is not served.

3. Genius version. The reliance interest does not really exist. We're just coming as close as possible to the expectation interest. When profits are uncertain, we still allow expenditures because we assume (until defendant proves otherwise) that plaintiff would have broken even. See Kelly, *The Phantom Reliance Interest in Contract Remedies*, 1992 Wis. L. Rev. 1755. **Caveat:** Not everyone agrees that this is the work of a genius.

a.   **Losing contracts.**   In many losing contract cases, plaintiffs seek recovery on a restitution theory. Unlike reliance, restitution recoveries can exceed the expectation interest—at least under the current law.

3.   Allocating Burden of Proof

The defendant bears the burden to prove the amount of any losses plaintiff avoided due to the breach—just as plaintiff bears the burden to prove the amount of any profits. If neither establishes a different result, courts will award expenditures, in effect assuming the plaintiff would have broken even if defendant had performed.

a.   **Eases plaintiff's burden.**   To some extent, this reverses the rule that plaintiff must prove the loss with reasonable certainty. Unless plaintiff can show that she would not have incurred any losses if defendant had performed, she cannot show with certainty that she is entitled to damages under the reliance interest. If uncertainty is resolved against the plaintiff, the plaintiff cannot recover.

  i.   **Certainty required.**   The rule of certainty applies to the reliance interest. The certainty rule also explains why plaintiff usually cannot recover for lost opportunities. Similarly, a plaintiff cannot recover expenditures unless she can prove them with reasonable certainty. Expenditures usually are readily ascertainable, posing no difficulty for plaintiff to prove.

  ii.   **Strict application undermines goal.**   Strict application of the certainty rule would preclude recovery unless plaintiff could demonstrate she would not have incurred even greater losses if defendant had performed. The reliance interest's most important application comes in cases in which the plaintiff cannot establish lost profits with reasonable certainty—that is, she cannot prove that she would at least have broken even. Thus, she may have difficulty proving that she would not have incurred serious losses if defendant had performed.

  iii.   **Cause of uncertainty.**   The strict application seems unjust because **defendant's breach caused the uncertainty**. If defendant had performed, we would know whether plaintiff would have profited or lost from performance. The breach thus creates the need for damages but also undermines their ascertainability and, therefore, would prevent their recovery.

b.   **Risk of uncertainty shared.**   The reliance interest allocates the burden to prove profitability of the venture between the parties.

    i.   **Proof of expenses.**   Plaintiff can prove her expenses, which usually will be certain. If she also can prove profits with reasonable certainty, she may recover them; otherwise she will recover only expenses.

    ii.   **Proof of losses.**   Defendant may prove plaintiff's losses. If she cannot prove the amount of the loss with reasonable certainty, courts will not reduce the recovery of expenses to offset the award.

    iii.   **Zero profit presumed.**   In effect, the court will presume that the plaintiff's venture would have broken even: no profit, no loss. If either party wants a different recovery, she must prove it with reasonable certainty.

EXAMPLES AND ANALYSIS

1. Plaintiff intended to make a television play. It rented a location and incurred fees for the director, designer, stage manager, and others. Later, plaintiff hired Robert Reed to play the lead. Reed breached the contract just before filming was to begin. Plaintiff could not locate a suitable replacement on short notice, so the project was canceled. Plaintiff recovered all expenses incurred in connection with the film because defendant's breach caused those expenses to be wasted. *Anglia Television v. Reed*, [1971] All E.R. 690 (Ct. App. Civ. Div. 1971).

   Anglia is an unusual case because plaintiff hired Reed **after** incurring most of the expenses. It is odd to say that the plaintiff relied on Reed's (so far unmade) promise when incurring those expenses. But it is not at all odd to say that plaintiff expected to recoup all of those expenses from selling the finished television play. This suggests the court really was awarding the expectation interest but assuming profits would be zero—that plaintiff would recoup its expenses but not earn any profit.

2. Plaintiff promised Jack Dempsey money to fight Harry Wills. Dempsey breached the contract. Plaintiff could not prove how much profit the fight would have generated. Most of plaintiff's expenses were incurred before Dempsey signed. The court refused to award these precontract expenses under the reliance interest. But see *Chicago Coliseum Club v. Dempsey*, 265 Ill. App. 542 (1932).

REVIEW QUESTIONS AND ANSWERS

Question: What is the goal of the reliance interest?

Answer: To place the nonbreaching party (plaintiff) in the position she would have occupied if the contract had not been made.

Question: If plaintiff's reliance interest exceeds expectation, will the court allow recovery of the full expenses incurred in reliance?

Answer: Not intentionally. Plaintiff may recover all of her expenses, minus any amount the defendant can prove plaintiff would have lost if the contract had been performed. If defendant cannot prove that the amount of loss that would have followed performance, plaintiff may recover her full expenses. But a court that **knows** (because defendant proves) plaintiff would have suffered losses from performance will reduce damages by the amount of those losses, leaving plaintiff in the position she would have occupied if the contract had been performed.

Question: When will a court allow recovery of the reliance interest?

Answer: If plaintiff cannot prove the expectation interest with sufficient certainty, if the promise is unenforceable and the court determines that restitution will not provide an adequate recovery, or (in theory) if expectation damages would provide disproportionate compensation.

Question: How are reliance losses calculated?

Answer: Usually by totaling the expenditures plaintiff incurred in pursuance of the contract—and subtracting any losses defendant can prove plaintiff would have suffered if the contract had been performed. In rare cases, courts may also award the value of any opportunities plaintiff could have pursued if she had not entered the contract with defendant. This may permit an employee who left a job to work for defendant to recover the salary she would have made on the previous job. Other applications have yet to emerge.

22   REMEDIES AGREED ON BY THE PARTIES

CHAPTER OVERVIEW

The remedial rules discussed previously are default rules, rules that will apply if the parties do not agree on a different approach. If parties want to prescribe a different approach to remedies, they may do so by agreeing to those terms in the contract.

Agreements about remedies typically take one of four forms:

- Agreements that provide an exclusive remedy, such as repair or a refund;
- Agreements that exclude recovery for certain elements of damages;
- Agreements that specify the amount of damages recoverable; or
- Agreements that specify who shall assess remedies, often removing issues from the courts.

The parties may augment, exclude, or limit the remedies available to the plaintiff.

- A limitation that is unconscionable will not be enforced.
- A limitation that fails of its essential purpose will not be enforced.
- When a limitation is unenforceable, the default rules govern the remedies available.

The parties may agree on a **liquidated damages clause**: a term specifying the amount recoverable in case of breach.

- Liquidated damage clauses are enforceable if they provide a **reasonable estimate** in light of the **actual or anticipated loss** and **difficulty of proving** the amount of loss.
- The parties may **not** agree to impose damages as a **penalty** for breach.
- Unless otherwise specified, remedial provisions will be **optional rather than exclusive**.

451

The parties may agree on how disputes will be resolved, including:

- Specifying the **forum** where suit may be filed;
- Specifying which state's **law** applies when a suit is filed; and
- Specifying that disputes must be submitted to **arbitration** instead of filed in court.

If an agreement requires arbitration, courts will stay proceedings until arbitration is completed.

If one party challenges the results of arbitration, courts will defer to the arbitrator unless:

- The arbitrator decided issues **outside the scope of her authority**;
- The arbitrator was guilty of **misconduct**, such as accepting a bribe;
- The arbitrator's decision was **completely irrational**; and
- The arbitrator's decision violated **public policy**.

Within these limits, an arbitrator **need not apply contract law** the way courts would.

A. TYPES OF AGREED REMEDIES

Several types of agreements concerning the amount of damages or the way remedies are determined have become common. Before discussing each in detail, this section identifies and describes them.

1. Agreements Expanding the Recovery Available

The parties may agree to allow recovery of elements of damage not usually allowed by the courts.

a. Attorney's fees.   Commercial contracts frequently allow a plaintiff to recover attorney's fees incurred to enforce the contract. These provisions are uniformly enforceable.

i. Avoid undercompensation.   The inability to recover attorney's fees frequently leaves the plaintiff undercompensated. Although she may recover all her losses on the contract, she may need to spend thousands of dollars (or hundreds of thousands) on attorneys in the process. If those fees are not recoverable, plaintiff's net position is much worse than if the defendant had performed. Thus, parties with significant bargaining power may provide that attorney's fees are recoverable.

ii. Uncertainty limits scope.   Parties often prefer not to include a provision for attorney's fees. When entering a contract, parties may not know whether they will be the breaching party or the nonbreaching party. Thus, they cannot tell whether the term will aid or harm them.

iii. **Loans.** Lenders (such as banks) typically include these provisions in their loan documents. Once the lender delivers the loan proceeds, almost all breaches will come from the borrower. Thus, the bank is unlikely to ever be liable for the borrower's attorney's fees.

iv. **One-way clauses.** Sometimes a bank can draft the clause in such a way that it allows the bank to recover fees but does not allow the borrower to recover fees if she sues the bank. Landlords, too, find the provision useful when drafted in this way.

v. **Mutuality.** Some states statutes make attorney's fees clauses mutual, regardless of how they are drafted: If one party can recover fees when she sues for breach, either party can recover attorney's fees.

b. **Other losses.** Few other types of losses have been litigated. For example, the parties, at least in theory, could provide for recovery of emotional distress. Neither the Restatement nor the UCC indicates a policy against awarding distress if the parties so choose. In practice, however, these clauses rarely appear. The people most likely to want them (consumers) are also the people least likely to think about adding them to a contract. Thus, a legal test of this possibility may never arise.

c. **Unconscionability.** Clauses expanding the remedies available may be unenforceable for unconscionability. There is nothing inherently unconscionable about the provisions, which are commonly enforced. But like any other legitimate promise, if extracted improperly, it might be unenforceable.

2. Agreements Excluding Recovery of Consequential Damages

Many sellers seek to exclude liability for consequential losses directly. A contract explicitly may disclaim any liability for consequential damages. These disclaimers do not limit liability for loss in value but prevent potentially large consequential damages from being assessed. See 22.B.

3. Agreements Providing an Exclusive Remedy

Many sellers seek to exclude potentially large recoveries by providing alternative remedies. Some limit remedies to repair or replacement of the item sold. Others limit the remedy to returning the product for a refund. Either approach necessarily excludes any consequential loss. Both probably prevent the buyer from holding the seller responsible if cover requires substantially more money than the contract price. Thus, damages are kept to a manageable level. See 22.C.

4. Liquidated Damage Clauses

Sometimes parties wish to avoid the expense of litigating over the amount of damages—particularly when each might need to employ expensive expert witnesses to testify concerning the amount of the loss. In these cases, parties may estimate the amount of damages likely to result and provide that the plaintiff may recover that amount in the event of breach. See 22.D.

a. Formula. Liquidated damage clauses often employ a formula rather than a flat amount, allowing the amount recoverable to vary with the magnitude of the breach. For instance, leases provide for an amount of damages per day that a tenant who holds over after the lease expires must pay. Construction contracts may estimate the amount of loss per day that results when a building is not finished on time.

b. Bad estimates. Accurate estimates of the amount of loss pose no problem. Courts have more trouble when the clause does not accurately reflect the amount actually lost.

i. Underliquidation as a limit on recovery. Some liquidated damage clauses really serve as limitations on the amount recoverable, effectively precluding the plaintiff from seeking a higher amount even if greater losses are provable.

ii. Overliquidation as a penalty. On the other hand, liquidated damages can overestimate the amount of the loss, effectively producing a penalty for breach.

5. Arbitration and Similar Procedural Clauses

The parties may seek to specify the way in which disputes are resolved. Sometimes this involves specifying a particular court in which suit must be brought in case of a dispute. At other times, parties will specify the state law that governs the dispute, regardless of where the suit may be filed. Other clauses provide that disputes should not be brought in court at all, but should be submitted to arbitration. See 22.E, 22.F.

B. AGREEMENTS EXCLUDING CONSEQUENTIAL DAMAGES

As the previous discussion of foreseeability may have revealed, courts are suspicious of claims for consequential damages. Their potential to greatly exceed the price of the performance rendered frightens some sellers. Thus, sellers frequently seek to exclude liability for consequential losses. In effect, they say, "I'll give you the product, but what you do with it is your own business. If you can't make a profit using it, that's your business not mine. I'll give you the value of the product I promised, but I will not guaranty your profits on the venture, which is out of my control."

1. Generally Enforceable

The parties can negotiate over who should bear the risk of consequential losses. The price of the product can reflect the risk. The law has no particular reason to insist that either party bear that risk — at least when the parties' contract clearly specifies which of them accepts the risk.

2. Unless Unconscionable

Contracts of adhesion often contain limitations on the remedy. A consumer opens a box after taking a product home, only to find that it contains a card purporting to limit remedies available for breach. The surprise involved here may implicate the rules against unconscionability. See 10.D. The UCC makes two express provisions concerning unconscionable limitations.

a. **Personal injuries.**   A clause excluding consequential damages for personal injuries caused by consumer goods is prima facie unconscionable. UCC §2-719(3). Although the seller may attempt to establish that, under the circumstances, the provision was fair, the presumption is against that conclusion.

b. **Commercial loss.**   A clause excluding consequential damages when the loss is commercial is not prima facie unconscionable. UCC §2-719(3). Parties seeking to establish the unconscionability of limitations on commercial consequential damages will need to establish the defense without the benefits of any presumption. (Note: the language of the UCC could be read to declare that these limitations are not unconscionable, rather than not prima facie unconscionable. That interpretation seems unpersuasive in context.)

c. **Exam note.**   Unconscionability is the only contract defense that is likely to be helpful to plaintiffs in combatting limitations on remedies. Plaintiff usually wants to **enforce** the contract but wants to avoid the application of one clause of an otherwise valid contract. Defenses such as duress, mistake, or misrepresentation will allow plaintiff to avoid the entire contract — that is, she escapes from her obligation to perform and receives her money back. But these defenses will not allow her to avoid a single clause while enforcing the rest of the contract. Only unconscionability allows the court the flexibility to refuse to enforce the offensive clause while enforcing the rest of the contract. *See* UCC §2-302. (Some courts may invoke public policy in this way. Usually, however, contracts that contravene public policy are unenforceable, not enforceable in part.)

C. AGREEMENTS SPECIFYING AN EXCLUSIVE REMEDY

Many parties, particularly sellers, are concerned about the possible size of damages in case of breach. Consequential damages in particular can greatly exceed the price the seller received for the product. Sellers frequently attempt to avoid excessive liability by providing remedies that exclude consequential damages. By limiting their obligation to repairing or replacing the defective product, sellers reduce the risk of enormous damages. Most cars are sold on these terms. Other sellers limit the remedy to a refund. This is particularly common for inexpensive goods.

1. Generally Enforceable

Parties legitimately may provide for an exclusive remedy. Such agreements may keep the price paid lower than it would be without the limitation. Courts, however, limit the ability to use disclaimers to produce unjust results.

    a. Repair or replace. Automobile warranties frequently provide that the buyer's only recourse is to have the car repaired at the seller's expense or replaced by the seller if the car cannot be repaired. This excludes claims for a refund. It also excludes claims to buy a substitute car and charge the seller for the difference in price.

    b. Refund. Some manufacturers promise a full refund if you are not completely satisfied with their product. Depending on the language, these words may limit your remedy. For example, if a carpet cleaner changed the color of your rug unevenly, the contract might allow you to collect your money back, but preclude you from claiming damages (say, for replacing the carpet).

 # EXAMPLE AND ANALYSIS

Defendant sold plaintiff a burglar alarm and monitoring services. The contract limited damages to $50 but suggested plaintiff could negotiate for a higher limit in exchange for larger monthly fees. In responding to a call, defendant's agent failed to notice that the alarm line had been cut. Thus, when a second break-in occurred, no alarm sounded and thieves escaped with more than $90,000 in merchandise. The court found the limitation of damages enforceable. Seller did not become an insurer against theft. The parties agreed that the risk of consequential losses would remain with plaintiff. *Fretwell v. Protection Alarm*, 764 P.2d 149 (Okla. 1988).

The clause in *Fretwell* was drafted as a liquidated damages provision. The court, however, treated it as a limitation on the amount recoverable because it did not purport to estimate the actual losses but set a maximum on the amount recoverable.

The Fretwells sued in tort for negligence. Because the defendant's duty arose out of the contract, the court held that any enforceable limitation contained in the contract would limit the damages recoverable in tort as well.

---

2. Optional versus Exclusive Remedies

A remedial provision in a contract is optional **unless the contract specifies that the remedy is exclusive**. Language that offers a refund or repairs may not preclude plaintiff from seeking other remedies. The right to repairs could be treated as an additional option for the plaintiff, not as the exclusive remedy. See UCC §2-719(1)(b). If the language does not explicitly state that the specified remedy is exclusive, buyer, at her option, may seek either the specified remedy or any other remedy allowed by the law.

a. Liquidated damages. The same rule probably applies to liquidated damage provisions. A liquidated remedy allows the plaintiff the option to seek damages specified in the contract. But unless the contract states that liquidated damages are the exclusive remedy, the plaintiff has the option to seek damages under other remedial rules.

b. Contrary authority. Some courts treat liquidated damage provisions as exclusive even if the language does not specify exclusivity. This probably conforms to the intent of most parties who include a liquidated damage clauses. But it does not fit the statutory language very well. The intricate techniques courts use to evade the statute rarely arise in this course.

3. Remedy That Fails Its Purpose

If an exclusive remedy fails of its principal purpose, the plaintiff may resort to other remedies allowed by law despite the clause excluding or limiting recourse to those remedies. Limitations of remedy specify how a breach should be remedied; they need not deprive the nonbreaching party of any effective remedy. When a limitation destroys relief from the breach, courts will not deprive the plaintiff of access to alternative remedies.

a. **Failure versus undercompensation.** A limitation that prevents complete relief does not fail of its essential purpose merely because the law would provide additional compensation that the limited remedy excludes. All limitations will prevent recourse to some options that the law would have allowed. (That arguably is the principal purpose of the limitation.) Thus, mere undercompensation does not equate with failure of its principal purpose.

b. **Worthless remedy.** When a limited remedy cannot be implemented, it becomes worthless. For example, when an item cannot be repaired or replaced, a clause limiting the remedy to repair or replacement fails to provide any relief at all. In these situations, the remedy fails of its essential purposes. Recourse to other remedies is essential.

c. **Independent limitations.** Some contracts contain multiple limitations. For example, a contract may limit the remedy exclusively to the obligation to repair or replace **and** explicitly disclaim any liability for consequential damages. When the first remedy fails of its essential purpose, the plaintiff obtains the right to sue for damages. But the second limitation — excluding consequential damages — may be enforceable.

 # EXAMPLE AND ANALYSIS

Defendant (Smith) custom-designed and built a tunnel-boring machine for plaintiff (Wilson) in exchange for $550,000. The machine never worked properly and repeated efforts to repair it failed. Plaintiff sued for consequential damages. *S. M. Wilson & Co. v. Smith Intl.*, 587 F.2d 1363 (9th Cir. 1978). The court held that the exclusive remedy (repair or replacement) failed of its essential purpose. Thus, plaintiff could sue for damages. But the clause precluding recover of consequential damages was enforceable. Plaintiff still could have recovered lost value of the promised performance. Plaintiff recovered nothing because it had stipulated that it did not suffer any damages for lost value, but only consequential damages.

1. The court denied recovery for consequential damages because the clause excluding those damages was not unconscionable. Plaintiff had not argued that it was unconscionable, but appeared to assume that if the exclusive remedy failed of its essential purpose, the exclusion of consequential damages would automatically fail as well.

2. If you represented the plaintiff, would you stipulate that plaintiff suffered no damages for lost value? If not, how would you argue that the plaintiff had suffered damages for the lost value of the machine?

Cover — purchasing a similar machine from another manufacturer — is not very practical. But the formula for breach of warranty would apply: the value the machine would have had if it had been delivered as warranted (i.e., working properly) minus the value it had as actually delivered. Presumably, the value of a machine that worked properly would be about the contract price ($550,000). The value of a machine that did not work would be considerably lower. Thus, some damage for lost value of the machine seems appropriate. The stipulation was ill-advised.

3. Is there any basis for arguing that the failure of the repairs negated not only the exclusive repair remedy but also the separate exclusion of consequential damages?

If defendant committed a material breach of contract, plaintiff would have the right to suspend his performance and eventually cancel the contract. This would permit rescission and restitution. Rescission, however, permits a refund ($550,000), far less than the $1.8 million in consequential damages the plaintiff sought. Thus, material breach would win the battle (knocking out the limitation on consequential damages), but not the war (recovering the consequential damages).

---

d. **Exam note.** The last two example and analysis questions required you to integrate knowledge of other remedies to see the weakness of various arguments against the limitations and to plot the best course for a client. That is typical of both practice and exam questions. Issues often cannot be isolated effectively. Be prepared to discuss the way remedial options interrelate.

D. LIQUIDATED DAMAGES AND PENALTIES

Litigation over damages can be expensive, especially when damages are difficult to assess and may require expert testimony to establish with reasonable certainty. Liquidated damage clauses can obviate those litigation costs. Liquidated damages also can facilitate planning, both when deciding whether to litigate or settle and, in some cases, when deciding whether to perform or breach. Knowing the amount of loss the other side deserves brings some predictability to these decisions. These advantages, however, accrue only if liquidated damage clauses are enforceable. For reasons discussed below, courts have been less than enthusiastic about enforcing these provisions.

1. Basic Rule

Courts enforce liquidated damage clauses but refuse to enforce penalties. Courts prefer to keep exclusive control over the use of penalties. Thus, parties cannot compel a court to employ a punitive measure simply by agreeing to one in the contract. There are sound reasons for avoiding the use of punitive sanctions for breach of contract, at least when the court imposes them on the parties. But litigation designed to distinguish an unenforceable penalty from an enforceable liquidated damages provision can reduce or destroy the advantages gained by agreeing upon the amount of damage recoverable.

2. Reasonable Estimate of the Loss

Parties may agree on any amount of damages that is reasonable in light of the anticipated **or** actual loss caused by the breach and the difficulty of proving the loss. UCC §2-718(1); Restatement (Second) of Contracts §356.

   a. **Actual loss: Result versus intent.** The enforceability of the remedy turns on the reasonableness of the result, not the intent of the parties. Thus, a clause intended as a penalty may be enforceable if, by chance, it produces a reasonable approximation of the actual damages. A clause intended as an estimate of the losses will not be enforceable if it is unreasonable.

   b. **Anticipated loss: Foresight versus hindsight.** Agreement on an amount that is reasonable at contract formation is enforceable. The fact that actual damages differ significantly from the anticipated damages will not deprive the parties' reasonable estimate of its enforceability — under the rules stated. Courts sometimes stretch to deny recovery when the liquidated amount greatly exceeds the actual loss, no matter how reasonable the clause may have seemed when the contract was formed.

   c. **Difficulty of proving the loss.** Reasonableness may depend on how hard it would be to assess damages after the fact. When damages will be relatively easy to establish, the advantages of a liquidated damage clause will be smaller. Thus, even small deviations from actual damages may make the estimate seem unreasonable.

   d. **Caveat.** These conclusions logically flow from the language of the UCC and the Restatement (Second) of Contracts. But courts reluctant to relinquish their power over damages may not employ the rules as predicted.

      i. **Hypothetical breaches.** Some courts evaluate the reasonableness of the clause in reference to breaches that did not occur. If the clause would have been **unreasonable for those breaches,** the court concludes it must have been **intended as a penalty**. Thus, the court disallows recovery, no matter how reasonable the provision is with regard to actual losses.

 # EXAMPLE AND ANALYSIS

Defendant, a comedian, quit in the second year of a four-year contract that liquidated damages at £1,000 for any breach by either party. Because the clause literally would have applied if the theater had been a day late paying the comedian or the comedian had missed a single show, the court held the clause punitive and refused to enforce it, despite the significant breach by the defendant. *Kemble v. Farren*, 130 Eng. Rep. 1234 (Ct. Common Pleas 1829).

     ii.   **Uncertainty required.** Some courts treat difficulty in ascertaining actual damages as a threshold requirement. If actual damages are relatively easy to prove, the liquidated damage clause will be unenforceable no matter how reasonable it is. If damages are difficult to prove, the court will consider the reasonableness of the provision. See *Layton Mfg. v. Dulien Steel*, 560 P.2d 1058 (Or. 1976).

    iii.   **Lowest plausible award.** Some courts seem to allow recovery of the actual damages or the liquidated amount, whichever is smaller. This precludes penalties. It also suggests that a plaintiff must bear the risk of undercompensation without any prospect of benefit if the liquidated damage provision would be generous. This converts liquidated damages from an effort to economize on the cost of litigation into an effort to minimize the damages a plaintiff can recover. Someone must prove the actual damages to establish which remedy to apply, eliminating any savings. And the plaintiff always recovers the least amount, eliminating any hope of full compensation for losses. See, e.g., *Layton Mfg. v. Dulien Steel*, 560 P.2d 1058 (Or. 1976) (Lent, J., concurring).

  e. **Enforce penalties?** Judicial misapplication has led some scholars and courts to suggest that all liquidated damage clauses should be enforceable even if they provide a penalty. Be alert for changes in this area in the future.

3.   Penalty or Bonus?

Parties intent on including penalties may discover ways around the rules. For example, including a bonus for early performance can have the same effect as including a penalty for late performance — if the price and date are adjusted accordingly. Although the effect can be the same as a penalty, existing law may not reach this tactic.

a.   Not liquidated damages.   A bonus technically promises additional compensation. It is not invoked upon breach but upon good performance. Thus, it is not a damage provision at all. Rules regulating liquidated damages do not, by their terms, apply to bonuses.

b.   Not a penalty.   A bonus does not deprive a party of anything promised in the contract. Rather, it promises additional compensation. The failure to earn the bonus is hard to characterize as a penalty.

 ## EXAMPLES AND ANALYSIS

1. A baseball player signs a contract that includes a bonus of $50,000 if he hits 35 home runs and another $100,000 if he hits 100 RBIs (runs batted in). The player fails to achieve either goal. It is difficult to say the player has been penalized for breach. Failing to hit homers or RBIs is not a breach. And failing to get extra money (not promised as part of the basic contract) is not a typical penalty.

2. O hired C to build a house. The contract, drafted by O, required C to complete construction by April 20 at a price of $90,000 but promised a bonus of $1,000 per day (up to a maximum of $10,000) if construction was completed early. C testified that during negotiations with O, C offered to complete the house by April 10 for a price of $100,000, with a $1,000-per-day penalty (up to a maximum of $10,000). O drafted the contract this way and C signed it because it had the same effect as her offer. C completed work on April 20. O paid her $90,000. Can C collect an additional $10,000?

If O had drafted the contract as described in C's offer, the $1,000-per-day penalty probably would be unenforceable. It seems unlikely that an owner will suffer anything near $1,000 per day as damages for late delivery of a $90,000 home. Achieving the same effect via a bonus circumvents the rule (with C's consent — but all liquidated damage clauses involve the consent of both parties). But as drafted, C loses nothing it was entitled to receive; O never promised to pay $100,000 for the house. Even a court looking at the substance rather than the form might find it difficult to characterize the term as a penalty—especially if it contained an integration clause, discharging any earlier discussions (under the parol evidence rule).

---

c. **Unreasonable bonuses.**   Neither the UCC nor the Restatement limits bonus payments. Thus, unlike a liquidated damage provision, no reasonableness limit applies. Parties can agree to an unreasonably large or unreasonably small bonus without judicial review.

E. AGREED REMEDIAL PROCEDURES: CHOICE OF LAW AND FORUM SELECTION

Parties frequently find it useful to specify the way their disputes should be resolved. The possibilities range from avoiding court altogether to specifying which court or which state's law should resolve the matter. These agreements serve different purposes, but each is generally enforceable.

1. Choice of Law

Every state has its own body of rules governing contracts. When parties are silent, state law often fills in the terms that state thinks the parties would have (or should have) wanted. When negotiating a contract, it can be useful to specify which state's law a court should employ when selecting the default rule—or when evaluating the enforceability of terms on which the parties have agreed. Knowing which state's law applies can help parties predict how the contract will be interpreted and, thus, what they should include in the contract or what they must do in order to comply with the contract.

a. **Generally enforceable.**   Although a choice-of-law provision could be stricken as unconscionable, it is difficult for a court to say that the law of a sister state is so severely flawed that applying that law would produce injustice. This would be conceivable only if the parties chose the law of a state with no connection to any party or to the performance.

b. **Default rules.**   There are default rules deciding which state's law applies, too. Most schools offer an entire course on this subject. The rules vary greatly. When in doubt, try the traditional rule: Disputes are governed by the law of the **state in which the contract was made**. A contract was made where the acceptance was uttered.

2. Forum Selection

Some parties do business in many places. This may subject them to suit all over the country. For their own convenience (and to keep costs down), they may wish to consolidate litigation in one convenient forum. A contract provision that requires suits against the party to be filed in a particular state can achieve this goal. (It also makes the choice of law more predictable.)

a. Generally enforceable.

A forum selection clause usually is enforceable as long as the forum chosen has some connection to at least one party or to the dispute.

b. Unconscionability.

Some parties choose a forum to make it harder for opponents to sue them. The inconvenience of a forum may make it unconscionable to require a party to bring suit in that jurisdiction.

i. Harshness and unfair surprise.

The inconvenience of the forum may suggest the term is harsh. Unfair surprise, however, may not be present. Parties who freely negotiate a forum selection clause cannot easily complain about the inconvenience of the result. Because these clauses frequently appear in contracts of adhesion, unconscionability may be found in some cases.

ii. Remoteness.

Unconscionability seems particularly likely when the party choosing the forum has no connection with the jurisdiction chosen. Inconvenience then seems like the purpose of the provision rather than simply an unavoidable side effect of choosing to consolidate litigation in a place convenient for one party but not the other.

F. ARBITRATION

Parties may prefer not to have a court decide their case at all. As full-fledged litigation grows more expensive and takes longer, arbitration becomes a more attractive alternative. Courts initially resisted being supplanted by private decision makers. By statute or decision, however, most American jurisdictions now recognize arbitration as a legitimate method to reduce the burden on courts and shift the cost of litigation from the taxpayers (who pay judges) to the parties (who pay arbitrators). Nonetheless, arbitrators have not official power to enforce their judgments. Thus, arbitration awards still come to court.

1. Agreement to Arbitrate Enforceable

This section discusses only arbitration agreed on by the parties to a contract. Although some jurisdictions try to require parties to arbitrate before coming to court, the issues there are somewhat different and will be discussed, if at all, in a course on civil procedure or alternative dispute resolution.

a. Original contract. Parties usually agree to arbitration at the time they enter the contract. Parties can agree after the breach to submit the dispute to arbitration. At that point, however, one party usually prefers judicial proceedings while the other prefers arbitration. (One prefers delay, the other speed; one prefers application of legal rules, the other ad hoc justice.)

b. Fighting arbitration. Despite an agreement to arbitrate, a party may seek to avoid arbitration in one of two ways.

  i. File suit. A party may file suit in court instead of initiating arbitration, even though she agreed to submit the dispute to arbitration.

  ii. Contest an award. A party might ask a court to set aside an arbitration award after it has been made.

2. Suits Stayed Pending Arbitration

If one party sues in court instead of initiating arbitration, the court usually will stay proceedings pending the outcome of arbitration — if the other party requests a stay.

a. Waiver. The defendant can waive the arbitration clause by simply defending in court instead of requesting arbitration.

b. Scope of the arbitration clause. The court must ascertain that the dispute involved is within the scope of the arbitration clause before staying proceedings. Although many arbitration clauses are broad, covering all disputes arising under the contract, some are more limited. If the dispute is not one the parties agreed to submit to arbitration, the court will proceed with the case.

3. Review after Arbitration

If one party objects to the arbitration award, a court may review it and, in an appropriate case, set it aside. The grounds for setting aside the decision of an arbitrator are fairly narrow.

a. Exceeded authority. As mentioned earlier, the parties may agree to submit only some disputes to arbitration. If the arbitrator decides a matter that the parties have not agreed to allow her to decide, the court cannot bind a party to the arbitrator's decision on that point.

    i.   **Unintentional waiver.**   A party who litigates an issue before the arbitrator may be held to have agreed to allow the arbitrator to decide that issue. Even though it was outside the scope of the original arbitration clause, failing to object when the arbitrator considers that issue may waive the limitation or implicitly modify the contract.

    b.   **Serious misconduct.**   A court will not defer to arbitration proceedings infected by fraud, bribery, corruption, or other difficulties that undermine the fairness of the hearing. The same rule would apply to judges or juries tainted by bribery, corruption, or prejudice. Nonetheless, the court will insist on proof of the taint before vacating an arbitration award. Moreover, some concerns — for instance, a conflict of interest on the part of the arbitrator — may be waived by the parties if they proceed with the arbitration after discovering the alleged impropriety.

    c.   **Complete irrationality.**   A court will not enforce a decision that falls outside the realm of any reasonable result.

    i.   **Arbitrators not bound by law.**   An arbitrator need not apply the law the way a court would. Arbitrators are not bound by judicial rules and precedent. They may do justice as they see fit, even if courts would apply different rules and produce a different result. Thus, a party cannot establish complete irrationality merely by claiming the result is not in accord with the law.

 # EXAMPLES AND ANALYSIS

A partnership agreement required disputes to be submitted to arbitration. The agreement also specified that, upon dissolution, the partnership assets should be divided equally. The arbitrator took account of the partner's unequal original contributions, allowing those who contributed more a larger share of the partnership's assets to compensate for the inequality. The court held that this decision was not completely irrational. *Lentine v. Fundaro*, 278 N.E.2d 633 (N.Y. 1972).

    d.   **Public policy.**   The bounds of this requirement are not well defined. Certainly an arbitrator who attempted to impose capital punishment upon a contract defendant would find the court unwilling simply to defer to that decision. Capital punishment is a penalty reserved to the state, not delegable to an arbitrator even by agreement of the parties. Punitive damages pose a more interesting question.

4. Arbitration and Punitive Damages

Because arbitrators are not bound by the substantive rules that govern courts, they arguably could ignore the rule against punitive damages in contract actions. The rule against penalty clauses, however, is based on a public policy against penalizing breach of contract. These two concerns conflict. Unsurprisingly, courts have disagreed about the best result.

a. **Punitive Damages Forbidden (*Garrity v. Lyle Stuart*).** Some states forbid arbitrators to award punitive damages. The scope of the prohibition is not entirely clear, in part because the rationale is not entirely clear.

   i. **The case.** Plaintiff, an author, sued her publisher for fraud and harassment. While that action was pending, defendant allegedly refused to pay royalties due plaintiff. Her claim seeking payment of those royalties was submitted to arbitration. The arbitrator awarded plaintiff $45,000 in compensatory damages and $7,500 in punitive damages. The court refused to enforce the award of punitive damages. *Garrity v. Lyle Stuart, Inc.*, 353 N.E.2d 793 (N.Y. 1976).

   ii. **The rationale.** The decision mentioned several possible rationales. Some of those rationales might allow arbitrators to award punitive damages under different circumstances.

      (a) **Public official versus private party.** The court stated that punitive damages are a public power that cannot be wielded by private parties such as arbitrators. This suggests that only state officials (such as judges or juries) may assess punitive damages. Under this rationale, courts would never affirm an arbitrator's award of punitive damages.

      (b) **Public wrong versus private wrong.** The court stated that punitive damages are assessed for wrongs against society, not merely for private wrongs. This suggests that a private party (an arbitrator) could award punitive damages if the wrong committed were a violation of a duty to the public (say, a tort duty, imposed by society) instead of a duty to another individual (such as contract duty, imposed only by agreement).

  (c) Scope of authority. The contract in *Garrity* did not expressly allow the arbitrator to grant punitive damages. The court distinguished precedent where it had affirmed an arbitration award of treble liquidated damages (a clear penalty) specified in the contract. See *In re Associated Gen. Contrs.*, 335 N.E.2d 859 (N.Y. 1975). Elsewhere in the opinion, however, the *Garrity* court expressly stated that it would not enforce punitive damages awarded by an arbitrator even if the contract authorized the award. The court did not reconcile these two statements.

b. Punitive damages allowed. Other courts have enforced arbitration awards that included punitive damages.

  i. Public wrongs. Many of the cases involve tort claims. These claims almost always involve a contract because the arbitration clause is contractual. But some contracts border on tort. For example, a patient retaining a doctor enters a contract even though a malpractice claim is a tort. Similarly, claims for fraud arising out of contractual settings may be submitted to arbitration. This rationale is consistent with the prohibiting punitive damages for breach of contract.

  ii. Assent to authority. When parties agree that an arbitrator may assess punitive damages, courts may enforce such an award.

  (a) Implicit consent. Some courts have found consent in conduct of the arbitration even if the contract does not mention penalties. Typically, one party asks for punitive damages in an arbitration proceeding and the other party does not object to that request during the arbitration. Courts infer the parties implicitly agreed to allow the arbitrator to grant punitive damages.

  (b) Unclear extent. Many of the tacit consent cases also involve torts. A simple breach of contract may produce more resistance to punitive damages by an arbitrator.

c. Stay tuned. At the risk of stating the obvious, this issue remains unsettled. Keep your eyes open in practice—and in class—for the latest details in this emerging issue.

REVIEW QUESTIONS AND ANSWERS

Question: When is a contractual provision excluding consequential damages enforceable?

Answer: Always, unless it is unconscionable. A clause preventing consequential damages in cases involving personal injury is per se unconscionable. A clause preventing consequential damages for commercial losses is presumptively valid.

Question: When is a provision limiting the remedy to repair or replacement by the seller enforceable?

Answer: Always, unless it fails of its essential purpose — or, arguably, if it was unconscionable. The UCC does not specifically discuss unconscionability of a limited remedy, but UCC §2-302 (on unconscionability) does not exempt remedial limitations from its general rule on unconscionability.

Question: When can a plaintiff choose to forego a contractual remedy of repair or replacement and sue for expectation damages instead?

Answer: If the clause providing the repair or replacement remedy does not specify that it is the exclusive remedy, it is optional. In that situation, plaintiff may sue for expectation losses without regard to the alternative of seeking repair or replacement. Otherwise, she must seek repair or replacement until (and unless) that remedy fails of its essential purpose.

Question: When are liquidated damage provisions unenforceable?

Answer: An unreasonably large amount of liquidated damages is void as a penalty. If the clause provides a reasonable estimate in light of the actual or anticipated loss and the difficulty of proving the amount of loss, it is enforceable.

Question: Under what circumstances will a court refuse to enforce an arbitration award?

Answer: If the arbitrator decided issues outside the scope of her authority, if the arbitrator committed serious misconduct, if the decision was completely irrational, or if the decision violated public policy.

Question: Will a court even enforce an arbitrator's award of punitive damages in a contract action?

Answer: Yes, if the amount of the punitive damages is included in the contract itself, as the treble liquidated damage provision approved in New York before *Garrity*. Although other situations may emerge, no clear rule exists specifying exactly when arbitrators may award punitive damages today.

23 RESTITUTION AND UNJUST ENRICHMENT

 CHAPTER OVERVIEW

Restitution is a remedy designed to prevent **unjust enrichment**. It seeks to place the **defendant** in the position she would have occupied if the contract had not been made (or if plaintiff had not performed the beneficial service). Usually this means taking away any benefit defendant received from the plaintiff.

In a contracts class, restitution usually arises in one of three different contexts:

- When no enforceable contract exists but plaintiff has performed services that benefit defendant—often, but not always, in the belief that an enforceable contract existed.
- When defendant breaches an enforceable contract and plaintiff elects to seek recovery in restitution instead of pursuing damages for breach of contract.
- When plaintiff breaches an enforceable contract and sues to recover the value of her performance so far.

When no enforceable contract exists, either party may claim that partial performance under the unenforceable contract unjustly enriched the other.

- Unjust enrichment exists if defendant has **received a benefit** which she **cannot in fairness keep** without compensating the plaintiff.
- Recovery for unjust enrichment is measured by the **amount of the benefit**.
- Each party may have claims against the other for unjust enrichment, requiring offsets or action by each to return benefits received.

Restitution for breach of an enforceable contract is measured in one of two ways:

- If plaintiff's performance (or partial performance) increased defendant's wealth, defendant must refund the amount of the **increase in her wealth**.

471

- If plaintiff's performance (or partial performance) saved defendant the need to hire another to provide that performance, defendant must pay the amount **another party would have charged to provide that performance.**

If defendant breached an enforceable contract:

- Plaintiff usually may elect the larger of the two measures of restitution.
- Restitution may exceed the amount that could be recovered under the interest.
- If plaintiff has fully performed and defendant's only remaining duty is to pay money, plaintiff cannot recover in restitution but may sue on the contract for the price owed.

If plaintiff breached an enforceable contract:

- The court usually awards the smaller of the two measures of restitution.
- Restitution may not exceed a pro rata share of the contract price.
- Restitution is available only if the value of plaintiff's performance exceeds the amount of damages to which the nonbreaching defendant is entitled.

A.   TERMINOLOGY

Unjust enrichment appears under many different names. Some are left over from the English forms of action. The **common counts** included actions for **quantum meruit** (the value of services rendered), **quantum valebant** (the value of goods delivered), and money had and received (sorry, no Latin equivalent survives). These actions have been grouped together and called actions in **quasi contract**. Sometimes **quasi contract** is referred to as contracts implied in law. There are two important facts to recognize here.

1.   Restitutionary

All these names refer to restitution (or, more properly, unjust enrichment). The various names describe different circumstances that made restitution seem appropriate. Today, they can be gathered under one title. But you must recognize references to the older names when you encounter them.

2.   Not Contractual

None of these actions really involves a contract. The contracts are **quasi** or **implied in law** because, in fact, recovery does not depend on finding an enforceable agreement between the parties. The court requires one party to pay another even if no promise to pay was ever made. (This differentiates contracts **implied in law** from contracts **implied in fact**, where a party's actions indicate she really did make a promise, even though she may not have expressed that promise in words.)

3. Exceptions Exist

In some jurisdictions, you can allege the common counts even if a contract existed. Plaintiff's performance may entitle her to compensation whether rendered under a contract or without any agreement. A contract is unnecessary to recovery but is not always an impediment to recovery. In other jurisdictions, courts require a plaintiff to elect between the common counts and an action for breach. They will dismiss a complaint that tries to plead both or that pleads the wrong one. These complications rarely arise in class.

B. RESTITUTION WHEN THE CONTRACT WAS NOT ENFORCEABLE

Unjust enrichment is a separate cause of action, fully equal to breach of contract and the various torts. A separate Restatement of Restitution exists. Thus, even when conduct does not breach a contract or commit a tort, recovery may be justified to prevent unjust enrichment. The subject is vast, perhaps justifying an entire course. Probably, however, contracts is the only course that will address it in any detail. Thus, it requires some attention here.

1. Elements of an Action for Unjust Enrichment

To establish entitlement to recover for unjust enrichment, a plaintiff must prove two things: that the defendant received a benefit from the plaintiff's (partial) performance and that it would be unfair to allow the defendant to retain that benefit without compensating the plaintiff. These elements are not terribly well defined. They leave plenty of room for interpretation.

    a. Benefit received. Restitution seeks to deprive the defendant of benefits she cannot, in fairness, retain. That principle limits unjust enrichment to situations in which defendant really has received a benefit. Expenditures made by a plaintiff that did not benefit the defendant do not give rise to a cause of action for restitution.

 ## EXAMPLES AND ANALYSIS

1. R hires E to work in her factory. E turns out to be a minor who elects to avoid the contract after working for a week but before receiving any pay. Can E recover for the work performed so far?

Yes. (The amount may not be the contract wages. See discussion of calculating restitution at 23.D.) R received the benefit of E's services and cannot return that benefit to E. Thus, R must compensate E for the benefit.

2. B orders a machine from S. In preparation for S's performance, B constructs a foundation for the machine. S refuses to perform. B cannot recover for breach of contract because she failed to obtain a writing signed by S, as required by the statute of frauds. Can B recover for the cost of the foundation?

No. The foundation was an expense to B, but was not a benefit to S. S must refund any down payment she received. But B's expenditures in reliance are not necessarily included within a restitution recovery.

3. O hires A, an architect, to design a building for her. After A has worked on the plans for a week, she learns that O suffers from a mental incapacity and has elected to avoid the contract. Can A recover for the work done so far?

Probably not. Again, the work done is a cost to A, but has no benefit to O, especially if she (or her representative) does not want the building at all.

Some courts have allowed recovery in these situations. They reason that because O requested the work, the work must have been a benefit to her even if no plans have been delivered and she no longer wants the building. The unfairness to A may lead courts to stretch the law a little, treating A's reliance as if it is a benefit to O. It is more realistic to recognize reliance recoveries directly — as is possible in this example under Restatement (Second) of Contracts §15(2). See 21.A.2.e.

> **b.   Injustice.**   People may give benefits that others have no obligation to return. Gifts are one example. Vounteers and officious intermeddlers also have no claim to compensation for their unrequested services. Only when circumstances make it unjust to allow the defendant to keep the benefit without compensating the plaintiff will an action for unjust enrichment lie.

 # EXAMPLES AND ANALYSIS

---

1. D has an account with bank B. D makes a deposit of $200. B inadvertently credits two deposits of $200 to D's account. Can B recover the extra $200 from D's account?

Yes. D has no right to the extra $200. It was not a gift from B but an error that B now seeks to correct. It would be unjust to allow D to keep the money. (If your neighbor parks her car in your driveway, the car does not become yours.)

2. M gave W a necklace that had belonged to M's mother. Three weeks later W broke up with M. Can M recover the necklace?

Probably not. It is not unjust to keep gifts. By definition, gifts are not part of an exchange, where the failure to provide compensation makes it unjust to keep the gift.

3. M asked W to marry him and gave W a diamond ring. W agreed to marry M. Three weeks later, W broke up with M. Can M recover the ring?

Probably. Some gifts are conditional even though no compensation is bargained for. An engagement ring typically is considered a conditional gift: a gift that becomes final upon marriage. Because the condition upon which the gift would become W's property did not occur, the property remains M's and he may recover it in an action for restitution.

---

2. Situations Requiring Restitution

Often parties discover that a contract is unenforceable after performance has already begun. Because the contract is unenforceable, the party cannot reclaim her performance (or its value) by suing for breach of the contract. In some cases, the contract may be unenforceable because of a tort (e.g., fraud or duress). In others, however, no tort will permit recovery of the partial performance (e.g., incapacity or mutual mistake). To recover the partial performance already rendered, the party must resort to unjust enrichment in order to obtain relief.

a. **In general.**   Any reason a contract might become unenforceable may require a cause of action for unjust enrichment. Some situations, however, are more common than others. At the risk of stating the obvious, the following sections briefly identify the most common situations.

b. **Statute of frauds.**   When no writing exists to support an agreement that falls within the statute of frauds, courts cannot enforce the contract. If one party has performed, even in part, it is unjust to allow the other to keep the benefit of that performance without compensating the performing party. Thus, restitution is available following a holding that the statute of frauds makes a contract unenforceable.

c. **Duress, undue influence, and misrepresentation.**   A party may rescind a contract when the other person coerced or deceived them into accepting the deal. That right is useless unless the coerced or deceived party also can recover any performance she has already given under the alleged contract. Less obvious, even **the party who committed the**

fraud or duress is entitled to recover anything she performed under the contract. A party committing fraud or duress is likely to extract more than she gives up, making a net recovery in favor of the victim more common. But the victim cannot both recover what she gave up and keep what she received from the perpetrator.

d.   Mistake.   In mistake, often neither party is blameworthy for the unenforceability of the contract. In these situations, it is clearer that both parties are entitled to recover any benefits they bestowed on the other party.

e.   Lack of consideration.   Consideration poses an odd problem. Performance makes a promise enforceable even without consideration.

i.   Delivered gifts.   Once delivered, a gift is final. The donee, not the donor, owns the property. Courts will not order donees to return the gift even though no consideration was given in exchange for it.

ii.   Unintended gifts.   When a party intends to enter a contract, not to make a gift, no donative intent exists. If the contract later proves unenforceable due to lack of consideration, performance should not convert her attempted exchange into a gift.

iii.   Reliance.   Action in reliance may make promises enforceable in most situations like this, making recovery in restitution unnecessary. Restatement (Second) of Contracts §90.

f.   Incapacity.   Incapacity also poses a problem. Obviously, the person under the incapacity is entitled to restitution of her performance upon electing to rescind the contract. But the person who bestowed benefits on the incapacitated party faces an obstacle.

i.   Specific restitution available.   If the incapacitated person can return the performance, specific restitution is allowed. Specific restitution requires returning exactly the thing defendant received, as opposed to its money value (much as specific performance is an order to perform as promised rather than pay the financial equivalent of performance).

ii.   Money restitution limited.   Sometimes the incapacitated person cannot return the other's performance. She may have consumed it or it may have been services. In these cases, restitution usually calls for payment of the value of the performance. Monetary restitution, however, may equal enforcing the contract—making the right to rescind the contract worthless even if the incapacitated person had no use for the services in the first place.

iii. **Vary by context.** Limits on monetary restitution tend to vary with the specific incapacity. Many states limit restitution against minors unless the minor lied about her age. Thus, a merchant may have no remedy against a minor who cannot return the item purchased. Apparently, people are expected to recognize and avoid dealing with minors. In other situations, monetary restitution is more common. The chapter on incapacity addresses some of these variations. See Chapter 6.

3. Public Policy

Restitution generally is not available when a contract is declared void because of public policy. Courts prefer to leave the parties where they are, ordering neither to pay the other. This is understandable when one thief sues another for her share of the loot. Exceptions for more sympathetic situations were discussed in some detail earlier. See 11.A.4.b.iii.

C. RESTITUTION AS A REMEDY FOR BREACH OF CONTRACT

"Give me my money back!" may be the most intuitive response to a breach of contract. Essentially, that is a restitution recovery: The defendant must return any benefit she received under the contract. Because other contract remedies (e.g., expectation) usually are more generous than a refund, restitution is not the most commonly requested remedy—at least, not once suit is brought. Nonetheless, restitution remains a plausible alternative to the expectation interest.

1. Motivation to Seek Restitution

Most plaintiffs seek restitution when they wish they had made a better contract. Getting their money back allows them to go out and make a better deal elsewhere—or, in the case of losing contracts, to avoid the losses they would have suffered if they had needed to complete performance.

a. **Example (*Bush v. Canfield*, 2 Conn. 485 (Conn. 1818)).** Plaintiff (Bush) ordered flour from defendant to be delivered in New Orleans at the price of $14,000. Bush paid $5,000 down. Defendant never delivered. At the time the flour was due, Bush could have covered for only $11,000. Bush sued for a refund.

i.   **Expectation.**   Under the expectation interest, Bush could recover only $2,000. Bush would have needed to spend $11,000 to cover, but would have avoided the $9,000 balance due under the contract, a net loss of $2,000.

ii.   **Reliance.**   Reliance damages also would be limited to $2,000. Bush could show $5,000 spent in reliance on the contract but defendant could show Bush would have lost $3,000 if the contract had been performed. (Bush would have paid $14,000 for the flour but could not resell it for more than $11,000, the market value of the flour.)

iii.   **Restitution.**   The court allowed recovery of the full $5,000. Defendant cannot keep $3,000 in exchange for doing nothing simply because Bush miscalculated the market. It would be unjust to allow defendant to retain the down payment; it must be returned to Bush.

b.   **Restitution can exceed expectation.**   Plaintiffs request restitution precisely because it is better than expectation. It avoids any losses they would have suffered or allows them to make a better deal. Unlike reliance, which is limited to no more than the expectation interest, a party can recover more than expectation in restitution.

EXAMPLE AND ANALYSIS

Defendant hired plaintiff (Coastal Steel) as a subcontractor on a construction job. Defendant refused to pay some of the bills plaintiff submitted. This was a material breach of the contract. After completing 28% of the work, plaintiff refused to continue. Defendant completed the job with another subcontractor. The amount owed plaintiff for work done prior to the breach was $37,000. However, if plaintiff had completed the job, plaintiff would have lost more than $37,000 on the contract. *United States ex rel. Coastal Steel Erectors v. Algernon Blair*, 479 F.2d 638 (4th Cir. 1973).

The trial court awarded nothing, a proper application of the expectation interest. Plaintiff actually had lost $37,000 but had avoided more than $37,000 in losses, leaving no net recovery available. The appellate court reversed, allowing recovery in restitution. Defendant received the services. If plaintiff had not provided them, defendant would have needed to pay another to provide those services. Thus, by keeping the services, defendant saves the cost of hiring another to do the work — a saving it cannot in fairness retain without compensating plaintiff for the value of the services.

---

2.   **Problems with Restitution That Exceeds Expectation**

The result in *Algernon Blair* is controversial. It is not followed in all states.

    a.   Injustice hard to identify.   Unjust enrichment has trouble explaining restitution for breach of contract. Plaintiff promised to perform for a price. As long as defendant pays the promised price, there is nothing unjust about allowing her to keep the performance she received. The expectation interest determines how much, if any, more defendant must pay as the price of the performance. If the expectation interest produces no recovery, plaintiff received as much of the price as she was entitled to receive. Thus, there was no injustice in allowing defendant to keep the services; it had paid for them.

    b.   Strategic behavior.   Restitution in excess of expectation can encourage strategic behavior. Because plaintiff would be better off if defendant breached, plaintiff may try to goad defendant into breaching — perhaps by committing minor breaches itself in the hope that defendant will commit a material breach in response.

    c.   Measurement problems.   Restitution can be more difficult to measure than expectation. Expectation looks at the actual contract. Restitution must assess what the deal would have been if a different party at a different time had promised to provide the same performance. This hypothetical inquiry introduces opportunities for error. Thus, assessments of restitution may be less accurate and, therefore, less just, than assessments of expectation.

    d.   Intuitive justice.   The result in *Bush v. Canfield*, however, is not very controversial. Defendant had done nothing and, thus, had not earned any portion of the price. Nor is calculation of restitution at all difficult: Giving the money back is among the easiest remedies to calculate.

    e.   Limiting restitutionary remedies.   Restitution in excess of expectation seems most useful **when performance has not begun or has barely begun.** At that point, the parties' affairs can be sorted out easily and each returned to her precontract position. The further performance progresses, the more likely it is that strategic behavior (goading a breach) or difficulties in ascertaining remedies will make restitution less accurate and less fair.

D. CALCULATING THE BENEFIT BESTOWED

If it would be unjust for defendant to keep the benefit without compensating the plaintiff, courts must decide how to calculate the amount of compensation required. **Restitution seeks to restore the defendant to the position she would have occupied if the contract had not been made**.

1. Reliance Distinguished

Both restitution and reliance seek to recreate the situation that would have existed if the contract had not been made — or, in cases where performance occurred without a contract, if no performance had occurred. Reliance focuses on the **plaintiff's position**: What did she expend or lose in pursuance of the contract? Restitution focuses on the **defendant's position**: What did she receive or gain from the plaintiff's performance? Thus, reliance seeks to compensate for harm to the plaintiff; restitution seeks to recover any benefit to the defendant. Although the two can be similar, they are not always identical.

2. Specific Restitution

The easiest cases involve specific restitution: returning to plaintiff exactly what she gave the defendant.

a. Common. Specific restitution is more common that the casebooks make it appear. When plaintiff seeks to rescind the sale of her land based on fraud, duress, or mistake, defendant can simply sign the deed over to plaintiff. When a teen claims incapacity to avoid paying for a motorcycle, the dealer can recover the motorcycle. When someone asks for a refund of their money, it is easy to calculate how much money should be returned.

b. Complications. Specific restitution can involve complications, particularly when the condition of the property has changed. When defendant has improved the property or damaged it, some adjustment may be necessary to achieve restitution. These cases involve a combination of specific restitution and monetary restitution for the value bestowed.

EXAMPLES AND ANALYSIS

1. F, by fraud, persuades V to sell her house. After conveyance, F builds an addition to the house. V, upon discovering the fraud, sues to rescind the contract and recover the house.

F must return the house to V and V must return any payments to F. F probably is entitled to an offset for cost of the improvement. It is unjust to allow F to retain the house as conveyed by V, but it is not unjust to allow F to retain the value of the addition she purchased. (Viewed the other way, V did not bestow the value of the addition on F, so V has no claim to have the addition restored to her.)

2. B purchases a used car from S on the mistaken impression that the odometer reading is accurate. B uses the car for several months before discovering someone had tampered with the odometer. B sues for rescission, seeking her money back.

B is entitled to her money back and must return the car. S may be allowed to deduct the fair rental value for the use of the car during the months it was in B's possession from the amount of money S returns to B. (If B had wrecked the car, S might be allowed to deduct the cost of repairs.)

3. B purchases a used car from S on the mistaken impression that the odometer reading is accurate. B pays for significant repairs to the car and uses it for several months before discovering someone had tampered with the odometer. B sues for rescission, seeking her money back.

B is entitled to receive her money back and S is entitled to receive the car. In addition, if the repairs increased the value of the car, B may be entitled to the amount of increase in the value of the car attributable to the repairs.

---

3. Cost to Obtain Similar Performance

When an item cannot be returned specifically, its value can be measured by deciding how much it would have cost to obtain that performance from another party. The plaintiff is entitled to recover the **amount that a third party would have charged to perform the same services** at the time the plaintiff performed the services. Restatement (Second) of Contracts §371(a). The rules here frequently speak of services because services typically cannot be returned specifically: The time, once spent, is gone. The rules also apply when goods cannot be returned.

a. Defendant's savings.

The plaintiff, by performing services, saved the defendant the money she would have spent to hire someone else to do those services. Thus, the market value of those services — the amount defendant would have needed to spend to obtain them from another — is one way to measure the value of the services to the defendant.

b. Not contract price.   The contract price is not the measure of restitution. Maybe other persons would have charged the same amount specified in the contract. But this must be proven. The contract price itself is relevant only if it helps establish what other people would have charged.

c. Time of performance, not time of formation.   The relevant time is the time the performance was rendered. Neither the time of contract formation nor the time of breach is determinative of the value of the services at the time they were performed. The contract price may have been negotiated considerably before the performance. Breach may have occurred after values changed. Thus, neither other bids received when deciding whom to hire nor the cover price a party paid to complete work determines the value of the services.

4. Value to Recipient

Sometimes services will increase the value of defendant's assets. The plaintiff is entitled to recover **the amount by which the defendant's property increased in value** because of the services rendered. Restatement (Second) of Contracts §371(b). For instance, building a fence around plaintiff's home may make the property worth more than it was worth without the fence. When the increase in value can be measured, plaintiff is entitled to recover that amount: Without plaintiff's services, defendant would not have possession of that value.

a. In theory.   The increase in defendant's wealth will exceed the price of the services. Defendant will not promise to pay more than the benefit she expects to receive from the services.

b. In fact.   Many improvements do not increase the market value of property as much as they cost. Others may not value the improvements as much as the defendant. For example, a house with a swimming pool may be worth more than a house without one, but often the increase is less than the cost to install the pool. People buy pools to enjoy them, not merely to increase the value of their land.

c. Partially finished improvements.   When a beneficial improvement has been partially finished, it is treated as if the defendant intends to complete it. Property with a building on it usually is worth more than property with no building on it. But property with part of a building on it may be worth less, at least to anyone who does not intend to finish the building; the partial building is useless and the property is uglier than in its natural state. However, to anyone who wants to finish the building, property with a partially finished building is worth more than the property with no building because she will need to spend less to finish the work than she would to build from scratch. Thus, for purposes of assessing the benefit of services, it is sometimes necessary to overlook esthetics and value the property for its function — assuming the project will be completed.

d.   **Measurement difficulties.**   Measuring the increase in wealth can be difficult. An expert appraiser may be needed to decide how much the property was worth before and after the improvements. This is particularly true with partially finished services because few people buy and sell land with half-finished houses.

E.   RESTITUTION TO THE BREACHING PARTY

Because unjust enrichment is a separate cause of action, the plaintiff, to recover, need not prove that the defendant breached a contract. (In fact, unjust enrichment can arise when no enforceable contract existed at all.) Thus, a party who breaches a contract can seek restitution against a party who did not breach the contract. The law is not generous in such cases, but courts have recognized situations in which the breaching party is entitled to some recovery.

1.   Not a Contract Action

An action for breach of contract can be maintained only if the defendant breached. Sometimes, however, a party who breached a contract seeks to recover against a party who did not breach the contract. Obviously, the suit is not about the defendant's breach. Only a tort or unjust enrichment could permit a breaching party to recover from a nonbreaching party.

2.   When Breaching Parties May Recover in Restitution

Sometimes one party (A) must perform first. The other party (B) receives the benefit of her performance before paying for it. If for any reason A does not complete performance, B retains a benefit. B may be entitled to keep that benefit as damages for the A's breach of contract. But sometimes the benefit she receives is larger than the damages she suffers. In these situations, A may claim restitution for any benefit B received in excess to the damages to which B was entitled.

EXAMPLES AND ANALYSIS

1. Plaintiff agreed to work for defendant for one year in exchange for $120, payable at the end of the year. After working for nine and a half months, plaintiff quit without excuse. Plaintiff sued seeking restitution for the value of the services. The court affirmed a jury verdict for plaintiff awarding him $95. Defendant had received substantial services. Although he need not pay under the contract, he could not retain the value of the services without compensating the plaintiff for them. *Britton v. Turner*, 6 N.H. 481 (1834).

2. Plaintiff (Neri) paid $4,250 down on a boat. Later, he canceled the order, a breach of contract. Neri sued to recover the down payment. The court allowed Neri to recover $997: the down payment minus seller's damages from Neri's breach ($3,253). *Neri v. Retail Marine*, 285 N.E.2d 311 (N.Y. 1972).

3.   **Limitations on Remedies to the Breaching Party**

Unsurprisingly, the breaching party does not receive as much sympathy as a plaintiff who sues a breaching defendant. The remedies available to the breaching plaintiff are limited in several ways to avoid encouraging breach.

a.   **Pro rata share of the contract price.**   A party who breaches can never recover more than she would have received if she had performed the contract. Otherwise, breach might be more profitable than performance. Thus, the most a breaching plaintiff can recover is a percentage of defendant's performance equal to the percentage of performance actually rendered by the plaintiff. Because the plaintiff usually renders services for which defendant promised to pay, this limitation frequently is expressed as limiting plaintiff to a pro rata share of the contract price.

 EXAMPLE AND ANALYSIS

Consider *Britton v. Turner*, 23.E.2. Plaintiff agreed to work for one year at $120 but quit after nine and a half months. Plaintiff alleged that the work he did before he quit was worth $100. Assuming this is true, can plaintiff recover $100 in restitution?

No. Plaintiff agreed to accept $120 per year under the contract. Having worked about 79% of the year, plaintiff could recover no more than 79% of the contract price: about $95, the amount the court awarded. Had he performed, plaintiff could not have received $100 for the first nine and a half months of the year, no matter how beneficial his services were to the defendant. The defendant bargained for the additional benefit—his profit on the transaction. Plaintiff, by breaching, cannot claim defendant's profit for himself.

---

    b.   **Defendant's damages for breach of the contract.**   A breaching party may owe the other damages caused by the breach. Courts will not use restitution to deprive the nonbreaching party of the benefit of the bargain. Thus, a breaching party may recover restitution only if the benefit bestowed exceeds the amount of damages she owes the other party. *Neri v. Retail Marine* illustrates the way this works. See 23.E.2.

REVIEW QUESTIONS AND ANSWERS

Question: What are the elements of a cause of action for unjust enrichment?
Answer: Plaintiff bestowed a benefit on the defendant; it would be unjust for defendant to retain that benefit without compensating plaintiff for it.
Question: What are the two ways that a court may measure the amount of restitution?
Answer: The fair market value of the services (the amount that the defendant saved by not having to pay someone else to provide the services) and the amount of increased in the value of defendant's wealth or property.
Question: Can plaintiff elect which measure of restitution she prefers?
Answer: A nonbreaching plaintiff usually may elect the more favorable of the two remedies—with some exceptions, such as when plaintiff saved defendant's life. A breaching party seeking restitution usually is limited to the less favorable of the two measures.
Question: When a breaching party seeks restitution, can she recover more than she could have obtained by performing under the contract?
Answer: No. The breaching plaintiff is limited to a pro rata share of contract price. She can recover that only if her services really were that valuable. And she may recover less, particularly if her breach damaged the other party.
Question: Will a court award restitution even though it will make the plaintiff better off than if the contract had been performed?
Answer: Yes, in some circumstances. A nonbreaching party is entitled to recover the full value of her services (or payments) even if she would have suffered a loss had the defendant performed. This result can be controversial.

Question: S, an artist, promised to paint a portrait of B for $5,000. After making a $1,000 down payment, B took the painting home. B has refused to pay the balance. Can S seek restitution for the fair market value of the painting? (Assume the value would be greater than the $4,000 balance due on the agreement.)

Answer: No. Plaintiff has fully performed and merely awaits the payment of money. Courts will not engage in the difficult process of evaluating the painting or the services when a simple and fair measure of the amount due (the contract price) is available. It is not unjust for defendant to retain the painting as long as she pays the balance (plus interest from the date due).

PART 4 # WHO CAN INVOKE THE LAW? RIGHTS AND OBLIGATIONS OF THIRD PARTIES

ASSIGNMENT, DELEGATION, AND THIRD-PARTY BENEFICIARIES

24

 CHAPTER OVERVIEW

Third parties can acquire rights under a contract in three ways:

- Both parties may intend to give the third-party benefits under the contract.
- One party may assign her rights under the contract to a third party.
- One party may delegate her duties under the contract to a third party.
- A combination of these devices may occur together in some cases.

When both parties intend to give a third-party rights under the contract, that party may sue in order to enforce those rights.

- Incidental benefits to a party do not create a right to enforce the contract.
- The rights of third parties are subject to any defenses to the contract.

A party freely may assign her rights under a contract to another person, unless:

- Assignment violates public policy;
- The contract validly prohibits assignment;
- Assignment would change materially the duty of the other party;
- Assignment would increase materially the burden on the other party;
- Assignment would increase materially the risk to the other party; or
- Assignment would materially reduce the value of the performance received by the other party.

A party freely may delegate her duties under a contract to another person, unless:

- Delegation violates public policy;
- The contract validly prohibits delegation; or

- The other party has a substantial interest in having the original person perform the duties.

A party who delegates duties remains liable for their performance unless a novation occurs.

- The nonbreaching party may sue either the original promisor or the party to whom she delegated the duties if the duties are not performed.
- The original party may sue the party to whom she delegated the duties for indemnification.
- The party delegating duties may end her liability under the contract by obtaining a release from the other party to the contract.

A.   THIRD-PARTY BENEFICIARIES

Some contracts include promises that benefit third parties — that is, people other than those who actually enter the contract. In Chapter 3, we noted that consideration can be given by a third person or to a third person. When a party promises to perform in a way that benefits a third person, that person **may** acquire rights under the contract — including the right to sue if the performance is not received as promised.

1.   Simple Illustrations

It may be easier to approach third-party beneficiary contracts if we first consider a few simple examples.

a.   Loan.   L loans $300 to B. In exchange, B promises to pay $300 to T, a person to whom L owes $300. If B fails to pay T, T may sue B. Even though T has no contract with B, T is a third-party beneficiary of the contract between L and B. See *Lawrence v. Fox*, 20 N.Y. 268 (1859).

b.   Gift.   P promises D, a car dealer, $20,000 in exchange for delivering a car to C, P's child, as a wedding gift. If D fails to perform, C may sue D. Even though C has no contract with D, C is a third-party beneficiary of the contract between P and D.

c.   Terminology.   In reading the Restatement and other accounts of these rules, it will be helpful to keep three terms clear. The **promisor** is a party to the contract whose performance would benefit the third party. The **promisee** is the other party to the contract, the one who apparently requested that the promisor give the benefit to the third party. The **beneficiary** or **third-party beneficiary** is someone who is not a party to the contract but who will receive a benefit if the contract is performed.

 EXAMPLE AND ANALYSIS

In the two examples above, who are the promisors? B and D. Who are the promisees? L and P. Who are the beneficiaries? T and C.

2. Rationale

It would be entirely plausible to deny third-party beneficiaries the right to sue under a contract. Their rights to performance would not disappear. But suit would need to be brought by a party to the contract. Nonetheless, rules governing third-party beneficiaries serve to streamline the litigation process.

a. Avoid multiple litigation.   Allowing a third party to sue can reduce the amount of litigation. In the first example above (see 24.A.1.a), B's breach would not keep T from recovering her $300. She could always sue L, who owed her the money in the first place. L then could sue B for breach of the promise to pay T. (L's damages for that breach are at least $300 because L would not have had to pay that amount to T if B had performed.) Allowing B to sue T accomplishes the same result with only one lawsuit.

    i.   Joinder of parties.   Modern joinder rules may permit the same result even without rules governing third-party beneficiaries. If T sued L, L might be able to implead B, allowing a court to decide the issues in a single case. See Fed. R. Civ. P. 14. Nonetheless, the case would involve three parties instead of two, perhaps making it longer and more complex than necessary.

    ii.   Donees.   Multiple litigation is less likely when the beneficiary is a donee rather than a creditor. In the second example above (see 24.A.1.b), C may not have any claim against P for the car (an undelivered gift). C may persuade P to sue D for breach but cannot compel the suit or enforce a claim against P. Thus, litigation would require only one suit regardless of the rule: Either C can sue D (as a third-party beneficiary) or P can sue D (as a party to the contract).

b. Avoid strategic behavior. Allowing the beneficiary to sue also avoids strategic behavior. The party who promised to provide the benefit cannot insulate itself from liability merely by dealing with the party to the contract. This is of greater concern to donees than to creditors because creditors can sue the original party to the contract even if the promisor need not pay.

  i. Compromising the beneficiary's rights. Because the donor, not the beneficiary controls the litigation, the donor could make decisions that are not in the beneficiary's best interests. The donor might accept a settlement that the donee would have rejected. Making the litigation rough for the donor might encourage this, particularly if she still intends to convey the recovery to the donee. The donor might choose to keep the settlement or judgment.

  ii. Beneficiary's control. The right to sue directly protects the third-party beneficiary. It places her in control of the litigation. She can decide when litigation becomes too costly to pursue (and she must bear the costs of the litigation). She may decide whether a settlement is acceptable.

  iii. Control. In some cases, the original parties to a contract can modify their agreement in ways that affect the rights of the third-party beneficiary. Thus, some room for strategic behavior remains. Phrased more positively, the original parties to the contract retain some control over the content and consequences of their agreement.

3. Intended Beneficiaries

Intended beneficiaries may obtain rights under a contract even though they are not parties to the contract. Incidental beneficiaries gain no such rights. Unless the parties to the contract **intend to give another person the right to sue to enforce the contract**, that person is not an intended beneficiary.

a. Incidental beneficiaries. Contracts may benefit many people who are not parties. In entering these contracts, however, the parties frequently have no intention to provide others with a right to sue under the contract. Allowing all beneficiaries to enforce the contract would unduly limit the contract rights of the parties — particularly the right to waive breaches of the contract.

EXAMPLES AND ANALYSIS

1. M, a manufacturer, promises to sell C, a contractor, a quantity of cement. C cancels the order, in breach of the contract. M decides not to sue C, a valued customer whom M expects to place more orders in the future. Because of the cancellation, M has more inventory on hand than necessary and closes the plant for a few days, laying off the workers. E, an employee of M, sues C for breach. E claims she is a beneficiary of the contract because the sale to C provided E with work. She claims lost income as damages for C's breach of the contract with M. E is not an intended beneficiary, even though the contract incidentally would have benefited E.

2. O hires L to landscape the grounds of her house. L fails to comply with many requirements of the contract, producing a much less attractive yard. O decides not to sue. N, a neighbor of O, sues L as a third-party beneficiary. N claims that her property would have had a higher value if L had produced an attractive yard as required by the contract. N is not an intended beneficiary even though the contract incidentally would have benefited N.

---

    b. Identifying intended beneficiaries. Three things must be true for a person to assert claims as a third-party beneficiary. Restatement (Second) of Contracts §302.

        i. Benefit. She must be a beneficiary of the contract. That is, she must be able to identify some benefit that would have flowed to her if the contract had been performed. This will be the easiest requirement to meet. Most of the rule is designed to limit which beneficiaries may make claims. But sometimes you may find it useful to argue that the contract in fact bestowed no benefit at all upon a person, negating any possibility that she was an intended beneficiary, and

        ii. Intent. Recognition of rights must be appropriate to effectuate the intention of the parties. The agreement must reveal the intention to allow the third person to enforce the agreement. Intention here requires a purpose to benefit another, not merely knowledge that another would be benefited if the contract is performed, and

        iii. Debt. The promisee owes money to the beneficiary and performance will satisfy that debt. A debt other than money might work if it is a liquid asset, such as bonds. Other debts, although they may motivate an effort to benefit a third party, may be analyzed under the next alternative, or

    iv.   **Gift.**   The promisee intends to give the benefit of the contract to the third party. In effect, this allows the donee of a gift to recover under a contract. The gift, however, need not be motivated by altruism or generosity. The desire to give a gift, regardless of the reasons for it, will suffice — as it would for any delivered gift.

c.   **Creditor and donee beneficiaries.**   The Restatement (Second) of Contracts abandoned the original Restatement's references to creditor beneficiaries and donee beneficiaries. The language had caused some confusion in the courts. Nonetheless, the Restatement (Second) defined "intended beneficiary" in a manner reminiscent of the older categories.

d.   **Identity immaterial.**   Sometimes the promise will identify by name the persons the parties intended to benefit. This is not required. As long as she can be identified with some certainty at the time they seek to enforce the contract. It does not matter that a beneficiary is not specifically identified in the contract.

4. Effect of Defenses

When sued by a beneficiary, the promisor may seek to plead various defenses to performance under the contract. Because some defenses may involve conduct of the promisee, not the beneficiary, rules have evolved governing which defenses a promisor may assert against a beneficiary.

a.   **Promisor's defenses against promisee.**   Defenses against the promisee often undermine the enforceability of the contract itself. If the contract was unenforceable, the promisor's duty to perform cannot be binding even though the beneficiary rather than the promisee seeks to enforce the agreement. **Thus, most defenses against the promisee are fully effective when asserted against a third-party beneficiary.** Restatement (Second) of Contracts §309.

    i.   **Void.**   A beneficiary cannot recover on a contract that was not formed (say, because it lacked consideration or assent).

    ii.   **Voidable.**   A beneficiary cannot recover on a contract that was voidable or unenforceable, provided that the promisor has standing to avoid the agreement. Thus, duress by the promisee would permit the promisor to rescind the contract, defeating any claim by the beneficiary. Duress by the promisor, however, would make the contract voidable at the option of the promisee. The promisor could not assert her own acts of coercion as grounds for denying recovery by the beneficiary.

iii.   **Discharge or excuse.**   A beneficiary may not recover on a contract if the promisor's duty to perform has been discharged or excused by events occurring after formation. Thus, impracticability, frustration, nonoccurrence of a condition, material breach by the promisee, or repudiation by the promisee may prevent recovery by a beneficiary.

iv.   **Other defenses.**   Other defenses against the promisee may not be asserted by the promisor against the beneficiary. Few contract defenses remain, so you may not encounter this situation on an exam. But other defenses could arise. For instance, after forming the contract, the promisee might incur a new debt to the promisor. The promisor could not refuse to pay the promisee in order to apply the money to the promisee's new debt.

b.   **Promisor's defenses against beneficiary.**   Any defense that arises from the conduct of the beneficiary may be asserted by the promisor. For example:

i.   **Offset.**   If the beneficiary owes the promisor money, the promisor may be able to offset any amount promised to the beneficiary under the contract against that debt.

ii.   **Beneficiary's misconduct.**   If the beneficiary, without the knowledge of the promisee, coerced the promisor into entering the contract, the promisor could assert that defense against the beneficiary, even though it might not be a defense against the promisee. Other similar misconduct also would apply.

c.   **Promisee's defenses against beneficiary.**   The promisor cannot avoid liability to the beneficiary by arguing that the promisee could have refused to provide the benefits.

i.   **Promisee's choice.**   The promisee, not the promisor, may choose whether to assert or to waive any right to avoid paying the beneficiary. The promisor may not invoke the promisee's defenses.

ii. **Especially for gifts.** A promisee is entitled to make a gift to the beneficiary by way of the contract. The fact that the promisee could have elected not to make that gift does not excuse the promisor — who received consideration for the promise — from performing by delivering the gift.

d. **Promisee's power to vary beneficiary's rights.** Sometimes the promisor and promisee may wish to modify the contract in ways that alter (or even eliminate) the beneficiary's rights. Having made promises they had no obligation to make, these parties arguably should retain the power to alter or extinguish these promises. Nonetheless, the possibility that others (particularly the beneficiary) might rely on the promises limits their power.

i. **Contractual limitations.** A contract provision prohibiting the promisor and promisee from altering the beneficiary's right is enforceable. Thus, beneficiary may enforce the contract even if the parties attempt to modify the contract or discharge it in other ways.

ii. **Permissible modification.** When the contract does not preclude the parties from altering the beneficiary's rights, the parties may modify or discharge the contract before the beneficiary relies on it.

iii. **Notice.** For modification or discharge to be effective, the parties must notify the beneficiary of the changes before she:

(a) Justifiably **relies** on the promise; or

(b) **Sues** to enforce the promise; or

(c) **Manifests assent** to the agreement at the request of one of the parties to the contract.

e. **Obscure details.** Third-party beneficiaries are governed by some additional rules that rarely appear in a first-year survey of contract law. If your professor devoted more than a few days to third parties, you may wish to review the Restatement (Second) of Contracts in more detail.

5.   Special Problems with Intent: Government Contracts

Almost every government contract seeks some benefit for the citizens. Sometimes these contracts provide a direct benefit to an identifiable subgroup of citizens. Usually, the government intends to retain the right to assert or waive the contract provisions as it sees fit, without empowering the citizens to sue directly. Nonetheless, the rules governing third-party beneficiaries might allow the citizens to enforce these contracts directly. Thus, some courts have developed special rules applicable to government contracts. Restatement (Second) of Contracts §313.

a.   **Rule.**   A beneficiary cannot assert rights against a promisor who made a contract with the government unless:

    i.   The contract **expressly** provides for liability to third parties; or

    ii.   The **government could be sued by the beneficiary** for failing to provide the benefit and a direct action against the promisor is consistent with both the terms of the contract and the law authorizing the contract.

EXAMPLE AND ANALYSIS

The U.S. government agreed to pay defendant (Socoma) $950,000 to convert an abandoned jail in a low-income neighborhood into a manufacturing facility and hire 650 disadvantaged residents for at least one year. Socoma collected most of the money ($712,000) and converted the facility but only hired 186 residents and wrongfully fired 139 of them in less than a year. G did not sue under the contract. Disadvantaged residents eligible for the jobs sued C as third-party beneficiaries of the contract. The court affirmed dismissal of the judgments. Although it is fairly clear that the parties intended to benefit these residents, the contract did not mention a right for them to sue to enforce the contract. Nor could they sue the government for failing to provide them with employment opportunities. Thus, there was no economy to be gained by allowing them to sue Socoma directly. *Martinez v. Socoma Cos.*, 521 P.2d 841 (Cal. 1974).

    iii.   **Parties retain control.**   The *Martinez* case is another example of the parties to the contract seeking to retain the authority to decide when to enforce the rights they have created and when to waive them.

 # EXAMPLE AND ANALYSIS

On the facts of *Martinez*, assume that the government had expressly released Socoma from any further obligations under the contract. Would that release preclude the plaintiffs from enforcing the contract?

The release does not fit the categories of defenses that excuse performance by promisors under Restatement (Second) of Contracts §309. The rule governing defenses based on subsequent events lists particular types of defenses, none of which include a release by the promisee. Rather, this defense seems to fall within the catch-all provision declaring that other defenses promisor might raise against the promisee do not preclude recovery by the beneficiary.

The release, however, modifies or discharges the promisor's duties. Under Restatement (Second) of Contracts §311, the promisee retains the right to discharge the obligation until the promisee relies, unless the contract forbids such changes. Nothing in the facts indicates that the contract contains such a provision, though we would need to examine the contract more closely before rejecting this possibility. The residents will have trouble establishing that they justifiably relied on the promise in any material way. It probably would not have been justifiable for them to refuse other employment in the hope that they might be among the few chosen for jobs with Socoma. If, however, the residents brought suit under the contract before the government released Socoma, that might terminate the government's power to modify the contract.

Note: I do not want to suggest that the case would come out differently if the plaintiffs sued more quickly. The analysis here assumes the residents were intended beneficiaries under the contract. Under Restatement (Second) of Contracts §313, the parties probably were not intended beneficiaries in the first place. The facts provide an interesting opportunity to discuss Restatement (Second) of Contracts §§309 and 311 in more detail. On an exam, you might find it useful to explore this line of reasoning, just in case your conclusion regarding intended beneficiaries was wrong. It was not important to the outcome of the *Martinez* case.

B.   ASSIGNMENT OF RIGHTS

A right to receive performance under a contract is a valuable thing to possess. Sometimes parties seek to realize this value before the other party has performed by selling the right to receive that performance (or giving it away). Thus, when someone buys a business, they buy the right to receive money from customers who owe the business money, the right to receive services from employees who have promised to work for the business, and the right to receive goods from those who have promised to supply the business with its needs. Assignment of the right to receive performance is so commonplace that many people barely notice it. But occasions can arise where assignment poses legal difficulties.

1. The Meaning of Assignment

a.   Assignor relinquishes rights.   Assignment occurs when one party (the assignor) relinquishes her right to receive performance in favor of another (the assignee). The assignor retains no right to receive performance from the obligor (the party who must perform.)

b.   Rights versus duties.   Assignment involves the right to receive another's performance, not necessarily the duty to perform any consideration promised in return. A right can be assigned even though the duty to perform is not delegated. For example, B purchases a stereo from S, a store, on credit, signing a note pledging to pay in monthly installments. S assigns the note to F, a finance company (in exchange for an immediate payment by F). F now has the right to receive payments from B. S, however, has not delegated any remaining duties under the contract — for instance, the duty to make repairs under warranty.

c.   Agency distinguished.   Sometimes parties designate agents to receive performance for them. Paying to the agent is the same as paying the principal (the person whom the agent serves).

 EXAMPLE AND ANALYSIS

A owes B money. B tells A to give the money to C, B's son. A gives the money to C. A has discharged the debt to B. Even if C does not give the money to B, A has delivered the money to the person B designated to receive payment. If B's agent fails to give the money to B, then B can sue the agent.

i.   Assignment differs.   Note the difference between naming an agent and assigning a right. If B told A that he had assigned the right to the money to C, paying C would still discharge A. But after an assignment, B would have no right to sue C for the money. C was not B's agent but the rightful owner of the debt owed by A. (B, of course, could seek payment in exchange for the assignment up front. B may sell the right to collect from A instead of giving it away.)

    ii. **Agency common.** You have probably been a party to similar transactions. Hospital forms frequently authorize them to receive payments from your health insurer. These forms can involve an assignment of your right to claim benefits under the policy or they may simply declare that you will treat payments made to the hospital as if they were made to you. Thus, if you sued the insurer, the insurer could treat any amounts paid to the hospital as if they had been paid to you because you designated the hospital as your agent for purposes of receiving payment.

2. Limitations on Assignment

Not all assignments are innocuous. An obligor may wish to prevent the assignment of rights under the contract. The obligor can accomplish this in several ways.

    a. **Imposed by contract.** A contract may limit the ability of the parties to assign their rights under the contract. Because assignment generally is favored, courts make it somewhat difficult for parties to prevent assignment.

        i. **Delegation only.** A clause that prevents assignment of the contract may be interpreted to preclude only delegation of duties. See UCC §2-210(3); Restatement (Second) of Contracts §322(1).

            (a) **Rationale.** Delegation usually poses more problems than assignment. A party may have a significant interest in who will perform the duties she is to receive but has much less concern who will receive the duties she is to perform. Thus, whether she ships the goods or the check to one address or another may make little difference. For this reason, the law generally assumes that clauses prohibiting assignment really mean to prohibit delegation.

            (b) **Exceptions.** Circumstances may indicate that the clause was intended to prohibit both assignment and delegation. If so, courts will so interpret it. On the whole, however, parties who want to prohibit assignment of rights should do so explicitly. It is dangerous to rely on courts to look past the statutory presumption here.

ii. **Assignment of damages.** A clause prohibiting assignment does not preclude assignment of a right to damages for total breach. *See* UCC §2-210(2); Restatement (Second) of Contracts §322(2)(a). Once the other party has breached the contract materially, she has no right to control who sues for damages. Thus, a party freely may assign the right to sue for damages even if the contract prohibits assignment.

iii. **No specific enforcement.** A clause prohibiting assignment may only give rise to an action for damages. Restatement (Second) of Contracts §322(2)(b). That is, the obligor may have to perform for the assignee, just as if the assignment were effective despite the prohibition. The obligor can sue the assignor for damages, if any, caused by the assignment. In effect, this rule prevents specific enforcement of the promise not to assign contract rights, limiting the plaintiff to damages.

iv. **Waiver.** The obligor can waive the clause that precludes assignment. Restatement (Second) of Contracts §322(2)(c). That is, the obligor can elect to render performance to the assignee. The assignor cannot complain that the contract was not assignable and sue to receive the performance.

v. **Consent provisions.** Sometimes the obligor must waive the right to preclude assignment. Some contracts, instead of prohibiting all assignments, prohibit assignment without the obligor's consent. When an obligor withholds consent, litigation may erupt over the reasons for withholding consent.

(a) **Arbitrariness.** Arguably, the obligor may withhold consent for any reason, even an arbitrary one. While many courts accept this position, it seems to undermine the requirement that parties to a contract act in good faith.

(b) **Good faith.** Some courts uphold any objection the obligor makes in good faith. Thus, an unreasonable concern with the assignment would preclude the assignment, as long as the obligor honestly believed that reason was sufficient. Litigation here tends to focus on whether the obligor really acted in good faith or merely asserted the unreasonable concern as a pretext for an arbitrary decision.

       (c)   **Commercial reasonableness.**   At least one court has gone even further, requiring a commercially reasonable reason for the refusal to accept the assignment.

 EXAMPLE AND ANALYSIS

Kendall tried to sell his business, the lease on the business premises (an airport hangar) contained a clause prohibiting assignment without defendant lessor's permission. Defendant withheld permission, apparently in an attempt to extract a much larger rental payment from the business. The court held that unless the defendant had a commercially reasonable objection to the assignment, the clause did not prevent assignment. Thus, the court reversed dismissal of the action and allowed plaintiffs' suit to proceed. *Kendall v. Ernest Pestana*, 709 P.2d 837 (Cal. 1985).

    b.   **Imposed by public policy.**   A few express statutes preclude assignment of rights under a contract. Absent an express statute, courts may weigh policies contravened by the assignment with the policy favoring its enforcement, as discussed in connection with Restatement (Second) of Contracts §178. See 11.A.3.

        i.   **Wages.**   Statutes commonly prohibit or limit assignments of wages due under employment contracts. People have to eat. Allowing them to assign their entire salary to a creditor could impose serious hardship. Thus, by law, assignments of wages often are limited to 10% or 25% of any given paycheck.

        ii.   **Pensions.**   Assignment of rights to receive pension benefits may be ineffective for the same reasons.

        iii.   **Nonstatutory policies problematic.**   Public policies against assignment of rights may be fairly difficult to sustain. As the rules in the preceding section indicate, clauses prohibiting assignment are difficult to enforce. In property class you have discussed the public policy against restraints on alienation. That policy may apply to clauses preventing the alienation of contract rights, at least to some degree. This would explain, at least in part, the hostility courts have shown to some prohibitions of assignment. If assignment is difficult to prevent when the contract prohibits assignment, it must be even more difficult to prevent assignment when the contract does not contain such a clause, leaving the lawyer to argue only public policy.

c. **Imposed by contract law.** Although assignments generally are favored, contract law recognizes that some assignments may impose hardship on the obligor. Restatement (Second) of Contracts §317(2). In these situations, the law refuses to enforce assignments. In effect, these rules identify situations in which the obligor's assent to perform for the assignor cannot be read as assent to performance for the assignee. The requirements below may overlap but are discussed separately as much as possible.

    i. **Duty changed materially.** An assignment that materially changes the duty of the obligor is not valid. Often assignment has little effect on the obligor's duty. A buyer can mail the check to one address as easily as another. A seller can put the goods on a railroad car without much care for who picks them up. But some performances may vary with the identity of the assignee. For example, if the seller promised to pay the shipping costs, assignment to a person in a very different place could significantly change the obligation — perhaps requiring shipment overseas instead of by rail. Similarly, a promise to support a person for as long as she lived might change the duty of the promisor — not only because one party might require more support, but also because the person supported would be different.

    ii. **Burden increased materially.** An assignment that materially increases the burden on the obligor is not valid. If the assignment materially increases the cost of performance, the burden to the obligor is clear. To some extent, the examples in the preceding paragraph involve increased burdens as much as changes in the duty. Shipping overseas poses problems in part because it is more expensive. Changing the identity of the person supported for life may increase the length of the support (e.g., if the assignee is younger — unless the contract is interpreted to cut off support when the assignor dies). Although minor increases in the burden may be tolerable, the obligor is entitled to decide for herself whether she wishes to assent to substantial changes in the burden of performance under the contract. (In fact, the law might allow the obligor the right to assent to any change in duty but for the fear of strategic or arbitrary decisions, such as those discussed earlier in connection with *Kendall*. See 24.B.2.a.v.(c).)

  iii.   **Risk increased materially.** An assignment that materially increases the risk to the obligor is not valid. This provision seems broad enough to encompass another oft-stated limitation: when the assignment materially impairs the obligor's chance of obtaining return performance. See UCC §2-210(2); Restatement (Second) of Contracts §316(2)(a). This seems just one of the risks that an assignment might materially affect.

    (a)   **Delegation.** Often, the risks involved change because the assignment includes a delegation of duties to the assignee. The assignee may be less reliable, increasing the risk that the obligor will not receive that to which the contract entitles her.

    (b)   **Assignment.** Sometimes, an assignment that does not include a delegation may increase the risk of default. If the assignor no longer has the right to receive the obligor's performance, perhaps she will be less diligent in performing her own duties.

 # EXAMPLE AND ANALYSIS

S sold a stereo to B on credit. S assigned the note to F, a finance company. (Thus, the store has received all the money it will ever get; F suffers if B stops paying.) B seeks warranty service from S. Might S's incentive to perform warranty work be lower? The buyer cannot obtain any leverage against the store by withholding payments because the payments go to F, not S.

Caveat: I am not familiar with any case negating assignment of a note on this ground. Assignment of notes is fairly common and a very useful commercial practice. Courts may not want to hinder it by taking this approach. Consumer protection statutes, however, may address this issue.

  iv.   **Value materially decreased.** An assignment that materially reduces the value of the return performance to the obligor is not valid. Because an assignment, standing alone, does not usually affect the type of performance the obligor will receive, it is difficult to imagine situations in which the value of return performance will decline unless assignment is accompanied by a delegation. But let's imagine one in the next **Example and Analysis.**

EXAMPLE AND ANALYSIS

U, a university, admits two students, A and B, to the entering class. U awards a scholarship to A, but none to B. A assigns her right to the scholarship to B.

The nature of U's duties does not change. It must pay money. The account to which it credits the money is immaterial.

The burden on U does not change. The scholarship is for a fixed amount of money no matter who receives it.

Might the risk to U increase materially? If A needed the scholarship, A might drop out of school, decreasing the amount of tuition U collects. Alternatively, A might get a job to support herself. Although U would collect the same amount of money, it would receive less of A's academic potential (or athletic potential) because her time would be occupied in other pursuits. (Did U bargain for academic efforts or only tuition? Could it sue A for breach if A devoted too little time to studies [or athletics]?)

Might the value of A's performance be materially lower? U may award scholarships to students whose class participation would edify other students in the class. Might A's outside work deprive U of that value? Of course, A might have been silent in class anyway. But is that a risk U should be allowed to assess for itself? (Note the crossover back to the risk factor.)

C. DELEGATION OF DUTIES

Delegation of duties often accompanies an assignment of rights but poses more problems. With an assignment, the obligor continues to receive exactly what she expected and must give exactly what she expected, she simply gives it to a different person than she anticipated. Delegation, however, involves receiving what she expected from a different person — a fact more likely to change significantly the value of the performance.

1. Terminology

A delegation again involves three persons. The **delegating party** is an **obligor**, one who owes duties under a contract with an **obligee**, who is entitled to receive the performance. Instead of performing those duties personally, the **delegating party** agrees with a **delegated party** that the **delegated party** will perform them. Thus, the **obligee**, without being consulted, may receive performance from the **delegating party**, someone with whom she has no contract.

a.   **Clarification.**   In assignment, the **obligor** was the odd person out: She was not a party to the assignment, the dealings between the assignor and assignee. In delegation, the **obligee** is the odd person out: She was not a party to the delegation, the dealings between the delegating party and the delegated party. The different names (obligor and obligee) can refer to the same party. In an exchange, each party is **both** an obligor and an obligee (a promisor and a promisee); each will have some duty to perform and some benefit to receive. That is the essence of consideration.

 # EXAMPLE AND ANALYSIS

T owns an airplane repair business. L owns a hangar that she leases to T for use in the business. T wants to sell the business to B. To sell the business, T would need to assign her rights to occupy L's building under the lease with L (the obligor) to B. T also would like to delegate her duty to pay rent to L (the obligee) to B. L is an obligor for purposes of analyzing the assignment and an obligee for purposes of analyzing the delegation.

2.   **Delegation Permissible**

Generally, delegation is allowed. That is, a person who owes a duty may perform that duty personally or via an agent. See UCC §2-210(1); Restatement (Second) of Contracts §318(1). The exceptions are discussed in the next section.

a.   **Harmless delegation.**   Often delegation will make no difference. For instance, your credit card company does not care whether you fill out the check and mail it or whether someone else performs those tasks for you (as long as the check arrives on time and clears). Similarly, a retailer may not care whether the broker ships goods from her warehouse or asks the factory to ship them directly to the retailer (as long as the goods arrive when promised).

b. Problematic delegation.   Sometimes delegation will pose more problems. If your law school hired Ruth Bader Ginsburg as a professor but Ms. Ginsburg attempted to delegate the duty to teach classes to a third-year law student, your school might object to the delegation.

3. Limitations on Delegation

Delegation is not permitted if the contract prohibits delegation, delegation contravenes public policy, or the obligee has a substantial interest in having the delegating party perform or control the performance of the duties. See Restatement (Second) of Contracts §318(1); UCC §2-210(1). (The UCC does not explicitly mention delegations that violate public policy, but it is unlikely that a court would interpret this silence to endorse enforcement of a delegation that violated public policy.)

a. Imposed by contract.   A contract validly can prohibit delegation of duties. In fact, a contract clause that prohibits assignment will be interpreted as prohibiting delegation of duties but allowing assignment of rights. See UCC §2-210(3); Restatement (Second) of Contracts §322(1).

  i. Courts sympathetic.   Contract clauses prohibiting delegation do not encounter as much resistance as contract clauses prohibiting assignment. Courts seem to recognize that the interest in having a particular party perform may be significant, even when the interest in having a particular party receive your performance is not.

  ii. Courts watchful.   Clauses prohibiting delegation may be interpreted to limit the obligee's right to prevent delegation. The power to prevent delegation might be employed arbitrarily to prevent legitimate business dealings or extract undeserved concessions.

EXAMPLE AND ANALYSIS

Recall the discussion of *Kendall v. Ernest Pestana*, 709 P.2d 837 (Cal. 1985), in connection with assignment of rights. See 24.B.2.a.v.(c). Kendall tried to sell his airplane repair business. The lease on the business premises (an airport hangar) contained a clause prohibiting assignment without defendant lessor's permission. Defendant withheld permission, apparently in an attempt to extract a much larger rental payment from the business.

The clause prohibiting assignment arguably prohibited only delegation of the duty to pay rent—though contract language or other circumstances in the case may have indicated an intent to bar both assignment and delegation.

If permitted to block the delegation, defendant can prevent the owner of the business from ever selling it. The business is useless without its location. (Some businesses can relocate without much loss. Others may depend heavily on location. An airplane repair business needs to stay at the airport, where the supply of hangars is limited.) Thus, the landlord can extort a portion of the value of the business from the owner in exchange for permission to delegate duties under the lease. Although a portion of the business's value undoubtedly stems from the use of the landlord's building, the landlord is compensated by rent. Her claim to a portion of the value of the business is relatively weak.

To preserve the alienability of the business, the court needed to limit the landord's ability to prevent delegation. The clause prohibited delegation without the landlord's consent. The court held it would breach the obligation of good faith and fair dealing to withhold consent without a commercially reasonable objection to the delegation. Thus, the landlord could prevent delegation to an unsuitable tenant but could not preclude delegation to a reasonable substitute. This protects legitimate concerns for delegation without allowing abuse of power. (A good faith test might serve better than a commercial reasonableness standard. That issue, however, I will leave to your classroom discussion.)

b. **Imposed by public policy.** As with assignment, public policy might prevent delegation.

   i. **Alienability favored.** To some extent, public policy is more likely to favor delegation. Limiting delegation limits the alienability of property. Public policy generally opposes unreasonable restraints on alienability.

   ii. **Duties to the government.** Delegation of duties owed to the government probably violates public policy. For example, if the government drafted an individual into the military, could that person delegate the duties to another? During the War Between the States, such delegations were legal and common. During the conflict in Vietnam, delegation was not permitted.

   iii. **Government employment.** The same result seems likely of any government employment. FBI agents (or Supreme Court clerks) probably cannot delegate their duties to others, though the prohibition against delegation may be included in their employment contracts rather than decreed as a matter of public policy.

c.   **Imposed by contract law.**   When the obligee has a substantial interest in having the obligor (delegating party) perform or control the performance, the delegation is forbidden by contract law, even if neither the contract nor public policy is at stake. In fact, the need to invoke contract language or public policy may reveal that no substantial interest can be identified: If it could, the obligee would not need to resort to these other elements of the law.

   i.   **Personal services.**   A substantial interest almost always exists in personal service contracts. Thus, a person hired to teach school (including law school) could not delegate the duties to another. The school, not the individual, has the authority to choose who may represent the school in the classroom.

   ii.   **Other services.**   Some service contracts are not personal service contracts. A person who enters a contract with a business entity rather than an individual may not have a substantial interest in having the work performed or supervised by any individual.

   (a)   **Construction.**   When a landowner hires a construction company to erect a building, she has no control over who the company hires to perform the work. The company provides services but is free to delegate the work—and even the supervision of the work—to employees. The owner hired the company, not an individual.

   (b)   **Law firms.**   When a partner promises to perform work for a client, she may delegate the performance of some duties to associates, law clerks, or paralegals. The client generally hires the firm, not the individual. (Of course, some clients may see things differently. If they insist that the partner do the work, prudence suggests that the partner will do so rather than lose the client.)

   iii.   **Corporations.**   Even when a company, rather than an individual, is hired to perform services, a court may find a substantial interest in having that company (or its key personnel) perform or supervise the services.

EXAMPLE AND ANALYSIS

Defendant (Nexxus) manufactured hair care products marketed only through salons. It engaged a company (Best Barber & Beauty Supply) to distribute these products in

Texas. Best merged with defendant (Sally). Sally was owned by Alberto Culver, a company that produced hair care products distributed through retail stores (grocery stores and pharmacies). Nexxus refused to deliver goods to Sally. Sally sued. *Sally Beauty Co. v. Nexxus Prod.*, 801 F.2d 1001 (1986).

The majority held that Nexxus had a substantial interest in having Best perform the services. The court placed importance on the trust Nexxus placed in Best's president, who apparently did not work for Sally after the merger. The court also attached significance to the fact that Sally was owned by a competing manufacturer.

The rationale presents difficulties. If the president of Best had quit or been replaced, Nexxus could not have refused to perform. The contract was with Best, not with the president. Thus, no delegation would exist that would excuse nonperformance. Similarly, if Alberto bought all of the shares of Best but no merger had occurred, Nexxus would have no right to refuse performance. Again, the company would continue to exist without any delegation of duties. Even taken together, purchase of the stock and a new president would not be a delegation or give Nexxus any excuse for refusing to perform. Thus, whatever interest Nexxus may have had in who supervised performance, it could not protect that interest under the contract it entered.

The merger looms large in the analysis. Because the merged company was called Sally instead of Best, it appears that Best ceased to exist and its duties were delegated to Sally. Arguably, Best continued to exist, it just got bigger and changed its name. At the least, attaching significance to the merger exalts the form of the transaction over the substance (because a different form, such as purchase of stock without a merger, would not produce a delegation).

Note that the analysis here focuses on whether a delegation occurred at all. If a delegation occurred, it seems plausible to claim that Nexxus had an interest in dealing with one company rather than another. However, if Nexxus's real fear was that Sally would breach the contract—either by selling to retail stores or by failing to make good faith efforts to promote Nexxus products—perhaps Nexxus should request adequate assurance of performance (see UCC §2-609) rather than assume Sally will breach.

---

4. Effects of Delegation

Delegation does not alter the underlying contract; it simply changes the identity of the person who must perform certain duties. Thus, issues surrounding performance and breach remain unaffected. The existence of the delegation, however, changes slightly the relationship between the obligee and the delegating party.

a. Sue the delegating party. If the delegated party does not perform, the obligee may sue the delegating party. See UCC §2-210(1); Restatement (Second) of Contracts §318(3). The delegated party is an agent of the delegating party. The performance by the delegated party may give the obligee everything to which she is entitled, in which case the contract is discharged by full performance. Delegation, however, does not destroy the contract between the obligee and the delegating party. Unless the obligee releases the delegating party from her obligations, the delegating party remains liable for any breach by the delegated party.

b. Sue the delegated party.   If the delegated party does not perform, the obligee may sue the delegated party. See UCC §2-210(4). The obligee has no contract with the delegated party. The obligee, however, is a third-party beneficiary of the contract between the delegating party and the delegated party. Thus, if the delegated party fails to perform, the obligee may sue the delegated party directly.

c. Request assurance of performance.   The obligee may treat the delegation as reasonable grounds for insecurity and demand adequate assurances of performance from the delegated party. See UCC §2-210(5). Any change in the identity of the party who will perform gives the obligee this right — even if she does not have sufficient interest in the identity of the performing party to prevent the delegation. In fact, the rule is most useful when the interest in preventing delegation is insufficient. In those cases, delegation is legitimate. Only by demanding assurances of performance can an obligee satisfy fears about the new performing party (and, perhaps, claim a repudiation if the party does not provide adequate assurance).

5. Novation: Obligee's Agreement to Excuse Delegating Party

The delegating party may want to eliminate its liability to the obligee. The obligee may agree to release the delegating party and look only to the delegated party for performance. Such a release is called a **novation**. In effect, the obligee agrees to rescind the contract with the original (delegating) party and replace it with a new (usually identical) contract with the new (delegated) party.

a. Release versus acquiescence.   Agreeing to accept performance from the delegated party does not establish a novation. The essence of a novation is a release of the delegating party. Simply agreeing to accept performance from the delegated party does not establish such a release. It indicates that the obligee will not oppose the delegation; that is, that she will accept performance as discharge of the duty. But without more it does not waive any rights upon breach.

b.   **Discharge of delegating party.**   A novation ends any liability of the delegating party. If the obligee releases the delegating party, her only recourse in the event of breach is against the delegated party. In effect, a new contract, involving only the obligee and the delegated party, replaces the original contract. The delegating party is not a party to the new contract and, thus, cannot be sued for its breach.

REVIEW QUESTIONS AND ANSWERS

Question: Terry agreed to pay Flora $100 to deliver two dozen roses to Pat at her home. Who is the promisor? Who is the promisee? Who is the beneficiary?

Answer: Flora is the promisor. Terry is the promisee. Pat is the beneficiary.

Question: Sidney owns a stereo store. She sold a stereo to Chris on credit. Banco paid Sidney $2,500 for the note signed by Chris, thus obtaining the right to receive payments from Chris. Who is the assignor? Who is the assignee? Who is the obligor?

Answer: Sidney is the assignor. Banco is the assignee. Chris is the obligor.

Question: Lester owns a liquor distributorship. He has a long-term contract with Billy's Bar to provide them with all the kegs of beer they require at a set price per keg. Lester sells the business, including all contracts, to Ralph. Who is the delegating party? Who is the delegated party? Who is the obligee?

Answer: Lester is the delegating party. Ralph is the delegated party. Billy's Bar is the obligee.

Question: When can a third party sue a promisor to enforce a contract?

Answer: If she is an intended beneficiary under the contract.

Question: When a third party sues a promisor under a contract, can the promisor argue that the other party to the contract (the promisee) did not really owe the beneficiary any money, thus excusing the promisor's failure to perform?

Answer: No. The promisee may raise or waive that claim as she wishes. She is permitted to enter a contract that benefits the third party as a gift, even if she owes nothing to the third party.

Question: Under what circumstances is an assignment of contractual rights unenforceable?

Answer: If assignment is forbidden by contract (with some exceptions), if assignment violates a public policy, if assignment materially changes the other party's (obligor's) duty, if assignment materially increases the burden on the obligor, if it materially increases the risk to the obligor, if it materially impairs the obligor's chance of obtaining return performance, and/or if assignment materially reduces the value of return performance.

Question: How do courts limit the power of parties to forbid assignment by contract?

Answer: Courts interpret a clause prohibiting assignment as prohibiting only delegation of duties, not assignment of rights, unless the clause or context clearly indicates the contrary. Courts refuse to enforce clauses prohibiting assignment of a right to collect damages for breach of contract. And courts refuse to grant specific performance of the clause prohibiting assignment. Thus, the assignment remains effective. The aggrieved party is limited to damages for breach of the promise not to assign the rights.

Question: Under what circumstances is a delegation of duties under a contract unenforceable?

Answer: If the contract prohibits delegation, if delegation contravenes public policy, or if the other party (obligee) has a substantial interest in having a particular person (the delegated party) perform or control performance of the duties.

Question: After an effective delegation of contractual duties, can the delegating party still be sued if the party to whom she delegated the duties fails to perform them?

Answer: Yes, unless there was a novation. If the obligee agreed to release the delegating party and look only to the delegated party for performance, she has waived any right to sue the delegating party if the delegated party breaches.

SAMPLE EXAM QUESTIONS

INTRODUCTORY ADVICE

After review or exam questions, I frequently inject a comment or two about the question or the answer. The comments will explore some alternative ways to approach a question—alternatives that some professors may prefer. Before raising a specific question, however, it may be useful to identify a few basic differences among professors' preferences. You may need to ask your professor what she thinks is important. Beware, however, of relying on students from prior years. Some students did not prepare good answers; relying on their assessment of what the professor wants is risky. Some good students may misjudge what made their answers good. Others may know what made the answer good, but communicate it imprecisely. You may do better by making your own decisions about how to structure your exam. Your own intelligence and judgment got you this far. Trust yourself now —as you must after graduation. (Examples to illustrate these introductory points are drawn from Question 1 (Trader Tom's) below. You may want to tackle it first, then read these remarks.)

Context or Salience. An answer should begin by putting the issue in context, explaining why the issue is worth discussing. Usually, it is pointless to simply mention a legal rule without stating why that rule has something to do with the exam question. Thus, the first answer begins, "Unless the flier is an offer, Bonnie's statement could not create a binding contract." Some professors might prefer an even more basic opening: "A contract requires mutual assent. Mutual assent requires an offer and an acceptance. For Bonnie's statement to be an acceptance, Tom's must be an offer." Others want you to get to the meat of the answer as quickly as possible, without spending too much time clearing your throat.

State the Rule Up Front. Answers should state the rule explicitly before applying it to the facts. This not only shows that you know the rule, it helps you keep the facts mentioned in the rest of the paragraph organized. It is easier to relate facts to the rule once you have stated the rule (e.g., "An offer is a statement manifesting willingness to enter a deal made in a manner that justifies the other party in believing her assent was invited and would conclude the transaction.").

No Citations. You need to apply the rule, not necessarily cite it. If you misstate the rule, a citation will not make the statement right. If you state the rule correctly, a citation adds little to the force of your argument (on an exam). Some professors, however, may want you to cite authority for any rule stated in the answer—here, Restatement (Second) of Contracts §§24, 26, 41 and the *Lefkowitz* case. And sometimes, if you are applying an obscure rule (say, one not mentioned in class), the professor may wonder where you came up with it. A citation there may help the professor appreciate your insight or figure out where you went astray. In my exams, however, citations are superfluous.

Conclusion Indecisive. Some professors want a definite conclusion. Others don't care about the conclusion at all as long as you can apply the law to the facts intelligently. My answer hedges. Personally, I think the concluding paragraph to Question 1 (Trader Tom's) is a waste of time. But if a question clearly has a right answer, every professor may be a little chagrined if you miss or hedge the conclusion. Look for clues in the call of the question. "Advise Bonnie" leaves room for hedging. "What result and why?" seems to ask you to commit yourself to a specific outcome. Note: If possible, commit yourself in the topic sentence, not at the end of the paragraph or paper. It will help you keep your answer focused on the goal.

Matter outside the Question. Some professors may not want you to bring up extraneous matters. Others want you to rely on your life experience, at least when it is pertinent to the issue (as it frequently will be when "reasonableness" is the standard). Still others may want you to identify facts that should be clarified—say, by asking the client for more information—and to explain how the additional facts might affect the outcome of the case. In the first answer, the facts about newspaper ads appear nowhere in the question. But they improve the answer.

Address Contingent Issues. In many questions, a court confronted by the case would address one dispositive issue and stop. For instance, once a court decided the ad was not an offer, everything else in the first answer would be superfluous. Some professors may want you to do the same thing. Many, however, want you to address all the issues raised by a fact pattern or, at least, to consider how the case would come out if you are wrong about the first issue. Thus, the answer here concludes there was no offer but goes on to consider how the case would be decided if the court disagrees with that conclusion.

Avoid Impertinent Issues. Questions usually do not ask you to tell the professor everything you know about contract law. For instance, you probably would get no additional points if your answer discussed the possibility that Tom (or Bonnie) was jesting. Some issues are too far afield to be worth mentioning. Sometimes, the call will be close.

Keep the Goal Clear. In most essay exams, professors want to know how you would **argue the case as an attorney**, not how you would decide it as a judge. The arguments, not the answer, are where you score points. If you treat the question as if the purpose is to get the right answer, you may follow some very bad tactics.

Missed Issues. Some students overlook pertinent arguments that deserve discussion. They can get to the right answer without discussing them, so why bother? Because the professor cares more about how well you argue the issues than what answer you reach. And the professor may care about your knowledge of several issues raised by the question, not just the one you find dispositive. If you keep your eye focused on your role as an attorney, you are more likely to include all the issues that might arise in the course of a case. An attorney must address them all, even if a judge can pick the most important one.

Conclusory Presentation. Some students list a fact that supports a conclusion and neglect others that might add support to the result. Once the right answer has been supported, why bother to pile on unnecessary additional support? Because the professor may want to see how well you argue, not just whether you got the right answer. Judges sometimes decree which facts are important and which not. But the attorney cannot always tell which facts or arguments the judge will find persuasive. Thus, the attorney must address them all. (And even judges must persuade an appellate court not to reverse.)

Overlooked Opposition. Some students support their conclusion thoroughly but neglect the responses the opposition might make. This is really just another form of giving a conclusory treatment to the problem. An attorney needs to consider how the opposition will respond and explain why the response is unpersuasive. That will add quality and depth to your exam answers.

Exceptions. Some exam questions may have a right answer. On multiple choice, true-false, or short-answer questions, professors frequently want to know the result. Getting it right and moving on may be the best strategy. Even some essays may be written with a definite outcome—but even then, a thorough explanation of the correctness of the result usually is better than a conclusory essay or one that addresses only one of several issues. The point is not to ignore answers but to recognize that there is more to an answer than a result.

CHAPTER 2   FORMATION

Question 1:   Trader Tom's, a specialty food and wine store, mailed a flier to all residents in the city announcing that it would sell one pound of its private-label coffee for $6 per pound. The flier extolled the virtues of the coffee but did not specify any other terms of sale or an expiration date. Two weeks later, Bonnie Byer appeared at Trader Tom's and stated that she wanted 20 pounds of the private-label coffee. When Trader Tom's tried to charge her $7 per pound, she refused to pay, stating that Tom's had an obligation to sell the coffee for $6 per pound, as announced in the flier. Advise Bonnie concerning her prospects if she sues Trader Tom's for breach of contract.

Answer: **Offer**. Unless the flier is an offer, Bonnie's statement could not create a binding contract. An offer is a statement manifesting willingness to enter a deal made in a manner that justifies the other party in believing her assent was invited and would conclude the transaction. Bonnie could not reasonably understand that her assent would conclude the transaction. The flier is an advertisement. Most advertisements are not offers but merely invite customers to make an offer the vendor can either accept or reject. An advertisement can be an offer when it is so complete, definite, and explicit that nothing is left to negotiate. The flier did not contain as many details as the cases that have found offers. For instance, no mention of quantity is made, potentially subjecting the vendor to orders greater than the supply available. This suggests that Tom's probably did not intend to be bound until it made some further expression of acceptance—the definition of preliminary negotiations.

Acceptance. Even if the flier is an offer, it may have expired before Bonnie accepted the offer. An offer that does not specify when it expires terminates a reasonable time after the offer is made. A reasonable time may have expired less than two weeks after the flier was distributed. This may depend on how long the parties reasonably would expect the offer in the flier to remain open. Fliers in newspapers, for instance, commonly expire in one week. Stores make new ads each week. If mailed fliers are like newspaper fliers, Bonnie probably should have known that two weeks was too long to wait before accepting. Mailed fliers may remain open longer, however, because mail (unlike newspapers) does not arrive the same day the store sends it. The price of most goods, like coffee, is not particularly volatile from week to week. Thus, a court might decide two weeks was not an unreasonable time for the offer to remain open.

Conclusion. The flier probably was not an offer, so Tom's probably is not bound by a contract to sell coffee to Bonnie. If a court decides the flier was an offer, Bonnie's acceptance probably was timely — though Tom's may persuade a court to hold that a reasonable time to accept the offer had already expired.

Question 2: In question 1, would Bonnie's reliance on the offer by coming to the store create an option?

Answer: No Option Existed. An option may be created by (a) giving consideration for a promise to keep an offer open for a particular period; or (b) a statute making an offer irrevocable; or (c) beginning performance in reliance on an offer that could be accepted only by performance; or (d) substantially changing position in reliance on an offer if the offeror should have expected reliance before an acceptance and failure to prevent revocation of the offer will produce injustice. The facts reveal neither a promise to keep the offer open nor consideration for such a promise. Without such a promise, the firm offer provision of the UCC would not make the offer irrevocable. The offer does not specify that only performance is a valid acceptance. When ambiguous, courts usually hold that an offer can be accepted either by a promise or by performance. Because beginning performance does not create an option when an offer can be accepted by a promise, no option arose under this rule. (In addition, the act of going to the store and asking for 20 pounds of coffee would not begin performance. At best, Bonnie prepared to perform.) Arguably, Tom's should have expected people who read the flier to prepare to perform by coming to the store with sufficient funds to purchase coffee without calling in advance to accept the offer. But that kind of reliance does not seem substantial. Although the gasoline or bus fare (and time) used to get to the store have some value, this does not seem to be a significant enough loss to create an injustice if the offer is considered revocable. Thus, no option was created.

Comments. Should you have addressed options in response to the first question? I think not. Option, like jest, is on the fringe of the question. Consider the following argument:

Assuming the flier was an offer and Bonnie's words an acceptance, it does not matter whether an option existed. An option prevents an offeror from revoking an offer before a certain time. Since Trader Tom's did not revoke the offer before Bonnie accepted it, it does not matter whether Trader Tom's had a right to revoke the offer. Either the offer was still open when Bonnie accepted it (because a reasonable time had not expired and Trader Tom's had not revoked it) or the offer had expired because a reasonable time had lapsed. In either case, discussing an option would not add anything to the resolution of the case. (The option, if it existed, would only keep the offer open as long as Trader Tom's promised it would stay open—or, since no promise existed, a reasonable time. Unless "a reasonable time" means something different when an implied option is at stake, the offer would expire at the same time with or without an option.)

Option may be sufficiently close to the edge of question 1 that some professors would want you to include a paragraph addressing it. If you included it in your answer to question 1, you may have made the right choice.

In response to question 2, some professors might want you to cut directly to the most plausible argument: the fourth one, an implied option based on reliance under Restatement (Second) of Contracts §87(2). The other three ways to create an option don't pertain to this fact situation. Explaining why is easy, like blowing over a house made of straw. Some professors, however, reward thoroughness. Because question 2 specifically asks about options, the full answer may be best.

Question 3:   On October 1, Rancher Roy promised to sell Butte Beef all the cattle on the "South 40" (a specific parcel of range land owned by Roy) on March 1 for $2 per pound. The parties did not specify the number of cattle because neither was sure how many of the 300 head then on the parcel would survive the winter. By February 15, a shortage of beef cattle had increased the market price to $3 per pound. Between February 15 and March 1, Roy moved 250 head of cattle from the South 40 to the East 60, a different pasture also owned by Roy. That left no cattle on the South 40. Butte Beef sued for breach of contract, alleging Roy had a duty to sell 250 head of cattle. What result and why?

Answer: **Roy's Promise Seems Illusory**. A promise is illusory if the promisor retains complete discretion to withdraw from the contract if she changes her mind about the deal. The contract did not limit Roy's discretion to move cattle among his two pastures. Thus, Roy had the power, at whim, to move all the cattle to the East 60 and, thus, deliver no cattle to Butte Beef. In effect, Roy promised to deliver cattle "unless I change my mind"—an illusory promise.

Implied Obligation of Good Faith Prevents Illusoriness. A court may interpret the agreement to include an implied obligation to act in good faith. Good faith would require Roy to behave honestly. Because Roy is a merchant of cattle, good faith also would require Roy to act in accord with reasonable commercial standards. This obligation would limit Roy's discretion to withdraw from the deal. If Roy moved the cattle to the East 60 in bad faith, that would breach the implied promise. Thus, the promise would not be illusory; Roy could not withdraw at whim. Here, it appears that the parties really intended to form a binding contract. The open quantity term was a hedge against lost cattle, not a hedge against changes in the price of cattle. Thus, the court might interpret the agreement to include a duty to act in good faith, making the promise enforceable.

Roy Breached the Obligation to Act in Good Faith. The issue here is close — and involves some factors discussed in later chapters. Roy appears to have moved the cattle simply to take advantage of the higher price for beef cattle he can get if he sells them at the new market price instead of delivering them to Butte Beef. But Roy may have a legitimate reason for moving the cattle — for instance, maybe the South 40 was overgrazed and the cattle could not find enough food there any longer. If so, Roy did not act in bad faith and, arguably, did not breach the contract by moving the cattle, even though no cattle remained on the South 40. If so, Butte would not be entitled to any cattle because no cattle met the condition specified in the contract.

Question 4: Tex Griller owns a popular steakhouse. A sign at the entrance announces that dessert will be complimentary for anyone who can finish the special 40 oz. "Cholesterol King" steak plate. Marnie, a petite young customer, asked Tex if the sign was for real or just decoration. Tex replied, "Of course, it's serious. I never say anything I don't mean." Marnie then ordered the Cholesterol King. Tex laughed and said, "Little lady, if you can eat all that, you can have my truck," and pointed to a new truck parked in the front. Marnie finished the entire steak, without leaving a scrap. After a free dessert, Marnie asked Tex for the keys and title to the truck. Tex refused. Advise Marnie about her prospects for success if she sued Tex for breach of contract.

Answer: **Offer**. A promise is a manifestation of intent to perform made in a manner that justifies another in understanding that a commitment has been made. If Marnie knew or should have known that Tex was joking about the promise to give her the truck, Tex made no promise, and a court will not enforce the undertaking. Under most circumstances, a reasonable person would understand that Tex did not seriously intend to commit to giving Marnie the truck. He used hyperbole to express disbelief in a manner he thought humorous—and that others should recognize as an attempt at humor. The case is harder because Tex preceded the offer by stating, "I never say anything I don't mean," words that indicated any offer he made could be taken seriously. The statement was specifically about the free dessert, but used the word "never," literally extending it to the offer to give away the truck. In light of those words, a reasonable person might have believed that the offer of the truck was serious.

Acceptance. Marnie could not accept an offer of which she was unaware. She ordered the steak before Tex offered her the truck. Thus, ordering the steak could not accept the offer. But one who learns of a promise after beginning performance may accept the offer by finishing performance. Finishing the steak (not ordering it) was the acceptance here. In fact, Marnie did not even begin to perform until after Tex made the offer (because eating, not ordering, the steak, was the acceptance). Marnie's performance accepted the offer. The promise to give her the truck is enforceable (pending discussion of consideration).

Comments. You could go on to discuss definiteness and consideration. We'll postpone consideration until that chapter. Definiteness poses no problem. A court can identify what constitutes performance or breach and an appropriate remedy. Pointing to the truck identified the vehicle involved. Details such as the time and place of delivery are easy for a court to fill in, especially given the default terms in the UCC. (Trucks are goods.)

Question 5: In the previous question, when Marnie was nearly finished, she told Tex to get the title ready. Tex, regretting his blunder, said, "That truck isn't for sale." Marnie finished the steak and requested the keys and title. Do the additional facts give Tex grounds to keep the truck?

Answer: Revocation. The statement that the truck was not for sale arguably revoked the offer to give Marnie the truck in exchange for eating the steak. When an offer can be accepted only by performance, an offeree who begins performance creates an option that precludes revocation by the offeror until the offeree has a fair opportunity to complete performance. Tex's offer invites acceptance only by performance. Tex had no apparent interest in a promise to finish the steak—or in suing a customer for breach of a promise to finish the steak. Thus, a promise by Marnie could not accept Tex's offer. Marnie began performance when she started eating the steak. Tex could not revoke the offer until Marnie had a fair opportunity to finish the steak. Thus, Tex's revocation had no effect. When Marnie completed her performance, she accepted the offer in the manner specified by Tex, forming a contract (unless jest negates the deal).

Question 6.   In question 4 in this section, when Marnie was nearly finished, she told Tex to get the title ready. Tex, regretting his blunder, said, "That truck isn't for sale, but if you finish, I'll not only give you a free dessert, but a free dessert for all your friends, too." Marnie finished the steak and called for the free desserts. Tex served them up. When finished, Marnie asked for the keys and title to the truck. Tex refused. Do the new facts change Marnie's prospects for success if she sued Tex for breach of contract?

Answer: **Offer.** Tex's offer to give free desserts to the entire table proposes a modification of the contract: If Marnie will give up her claim to Tex's truck, Tex will give free desserts to her friends. He did not phrase the offer in that way. He announced that he would not convey the truck, then made a conciliatory offer of free desserts. Nonetheless, in context it seems clear that Tex proposed a bargain: He would give the desserts **instead** of the truck, not in addition to it. A reasonable person in Marnie's position should have understood that meaning—and could reasonably believe that her assent was invited and would conclude the modification.

Acceptance. Tex cannot modify the contract alone; Marnie must assent to the changes. Assuming Tex's words were an offer, Marnie seems to have accepted the offer by her conduct. She called for the free desserts, which she knew (or should have known) were offered instead of the truck. This implicitly assented to waive her right to the truck. She may not have **intended** to assent to the modification. But her conduct would have led a reasonable person to believe she had assented. By manifesting assent, the modification was accepted, even if her state of mind differed from what her conduct implied.

Acceptance by Silence. Arguably, Marnie did not express an assent. She never said "Okay, you can keep the truck." Her failure to object to Tex's offer will constitute acceptance under some circumstances: if she accepted services from Tex, if she intended assent, if prior dealings mean Tex reasonably could believe her failure to object signified acceptance, or if she exercised dominion over Tex's property. The facts say nothing about Marnie's intent or any prior dealings. The desserts were goods, not services (though, because they cannot be returned, the same principles might apply). But Marnie treated the property as her own (by eating it and inviting her friends to eat it), even though she knew that Tex intended that property to become hers only if she waived any right to the truck. Thus, unless the offer was manifestly unreasonable, her silence accepted the offer.

Unequal Exchange. Problems of unequal exchanges are discussed in other chapters. See Chapter 10. The difference in value between a new truck and a few desserts (even terrific desserts) may make the offer seem outrageous. But Marnie did not give up a new truck in exchange for the desserts; she gave up a questionable contract right to receive the truck. Her ability to receive the truck depended on defeating Tex's defenses based on jest and revocation. Even if her chances were good, the expense of litigation would be significant. A 100% chance at hot fudge may be worth as much as a chance at a new truck minus the attorney's fees necessary to collect it. Thus, the offer might not be manifestly unreasonable, making Marnie's assent by silence effective.

Question 7:   Nester Nerd read the following ad in a computer magazine:

FREE GAME SOFTWARE!
MICRO-PLAYER'S
GALACTIC EMPEROR

You can receive the hottest new computer strategy game FREE weeks before it appears in the stores. The first 50 people who respond by e-mail will receive this revolutionary game FREE. In addition, your comments on the game may appear in future issues of this magazine. Games will be shipped immediately upon receipt of your e-mail message if you are one of the first 50 people who respond. Be sure to include your address in the message.

Nester immediately signed on to U.S.-Net, an online service, and sent an e-mail message to the specified address containing all the information Micro-Player requested. After sending the message, Nester opened new mail in his e-mail inbox and discovered a message from Micro-Player retracting the advertisement. The message had been sent to all persons who subscribed to any gaming forum of an online service, including Nester. (Micro-Play had taken other measures to notify people who might have seen the ad, including submitting magazine ads for upcoming issues of the magazines in which the original ad appeared, postings on electronic bulletin boards, online discussion groups, Micro-Player's web page, etc.) Micro-Player's message stated that the advertisement had been based on projected completion date but that complications had made it impossible to finish the game in time. The delay made it necessary to release the game to stores immediately upon completion, eliminating the value of distributing the game earlier to a few people free. Assuming Nester was among the first 50 people to respond, advise Nester concerning his chances to prevail if he sues Micro-Play for breach of contract.

Answer: **Offer**. Usually, advertisements are not offers. This offer, however, seems to leave nothing open for negotiation, specifying exactly who may accept (the first 50 people who respond), what will be shipped, when, the price, etc. This seems sufficiently complete, definite, and explicit that a court may decide a reasonable person would be justified in believing her assent was invited and would conclude the deal. Thus, this ad may be an offer.

Acceptance. Nester's e-mail responded in the way Micro-Player specified and provided all the requested information. It is a sufficient acceptance **if** the offer remained open at the time Nester sent the e-mail message. Nester's e-mail message probably was effective at the time he sent it, even if Micro-Player did not receive it immediately. Micro-Player invited acceptance by e-mail. Once sent, the e-mail message left Nester's control and passed into the control of U.S.-Net. (Nester may have been able to retrieve the message from U.S.-Net, but this is true of U.S. Postal Service regulations, also, and has not changed the general rule that an acceptance is effective when sent.) In fact, e-mail is nearly instantaneous: Once Nester sent it, it arrived within seconds in a box designated by Micro-Player. Thus, it may not matter whether acceptance occurred at the time the message was sent or the time it was received.

General Revocation. Micro-Player can revoke a general offer by giving the revocation as much exposure as the offer had received. The revocation via magazine ads was not yet effective because the issues in which the revocation would appear had not yet been published. The revocation by electronic postings may not suffice because it may reach a different audience than the magazine ad reached. Probably, however, it will reach many of the people who could accept the ad. Only people with the ability to send e-mail could accept the offer; these people seem most likely to be reached by the electronic postings.

Specific Revocation. Even if the ad was not revoked for others, Micro-Player's e-mail message to Nester might effectively revoke the offer to him. A revocation is effective upon receipt. Receipt occurs when a message is deposited with a person or in a place the recipient has designated for his messages. The e-mail box on U.S.-Net is a place arguably designated by Nester to receive his messages—just as putting a message in his mailbox would constitute receipt even if he had not opened the letter and read it yet. Thus, the revocation may have been effective even though Nester did not read it until after he had sent his acceptance. Presumably, the message will reveal the time it was received, allowing a definite determination of whether it arrived before Nester sent his acceptance.

Comments. The answer may not need to discuss the rule for revocation of a general offer. That rule does not contribute to the outcome of the case because the message to Nester (and other subscribers) probably revoked the offer to him regardless of whether the publicity was sufficient to revoke the offer to people who did not receive an individual message. But the question contains facts about the efforts Micro-Player took to revoke the offer generally. The inclusion of these facts suggests that the professor wants you to discuss the rule governing revocation of general offers. Of course, the facts could be distractors designed to see whether you recognize which revocation is more important. If you only have time to discuss one revocation, go for the one that matters: here, the e-mail message to Nester.

CHAPTER 3   CONSIDERATION

Question 1:   After a clothing purchase at a department store called Maystromock, the sales clerk invited the customer, Phil O'Blarney, to a party at the store to watch the Kentucky Derby on May 4. The store promised to hold a drawing and give away a sport coat (winner's choice from stock). Customers needed to be present at the party to enter the drawing but the winner would be notified by phone if not present when the drawing occurred. The clerk, acting on her own suggestion, arranged for alterations on Phil's purchases to be completed by May 4 (one day earlier than originally discussed) so he could pick up the suit on Derby day. Phil arrived early on May 4. While munching on the store's refreshments and waiting for the race, he made a few more clothing purchases. After the race, Phil's name was chosen at the drawing. He selected a sport coat and the store's tailor marked it for alterations. The store told Phil the alterations would be complete on May 11. Phil returned to the store on May 11 but the store refused to deliver the sport coat, claiming the store had no obligation to award the prize. Advise Phil whether a suit against Maystromock for breach of contract is likely to succeed.

Answer: **Purchases Not Consideration**. Consideration exists if the promisor seeks something in exchange for its promise and the promisee gives that something in exchange for the promise. Phil made two sets of purchases at the store: one before May 4, one on May 4. Neither set of purchases was consideration for the promise to hold a drawing or to give him a sport coat. The first purchases were made before he learned of the party. Phil could not have made those purchases in exchange for a promise of which he was not yet aware. In addition, the store did not request either set of purchases in exchange for the drawing. The store wanted Phil to make lots of purchases — it sought them. But it did not seek them **in exchange** for the drawing. Presence, not a purchase, was required to enter. Because neither set of purchases was sought by the store in exchange for the drawing, they could not be consideration for the store's promise.

Presence Was Consideration. The store may have intended to give away a sport coat with nothing sought in exchange. But the store seems to have sought the presence of customers at the Derby race in exchange for its promise to give away a sport coat. It required people to be present to enter. This could be a condition of the gift rather than something sought in exchange. But the store could have taken entries at any time instead of requiring a return trip on May 4. And as a condition, presence to collect the gift (rather than to enter) makes more sense. In addition, the store seemed likely to benefit from getting the customers back into the store for the Derby party. Customer presence increased the chance that they would make purchases and enabled the staff to make a sales pitch. The store called the event a party, perhaps hoping to generate goodwill and a mood that would induce purchases. Phil gave what the store sought — his presence at the party. Thus, there was consideration for the store's promise to give away a sport coat.

Reliance. Even if the store did not seek the presence of others, their promise may be enforceable on the ground of reliance. If the store reasonably should have expected others would rely on the promise and others did rely to their detriment on the promise, the court may enforce the promise if necessary to avoid injustice. Here, the store should have known that customers might come to the party in reliance on the promise to give away a sport coat. It is not clear whether Phil did rely. He needed to come to the store again to pick up his altered clothing anyway. He might not have come during the Derby party. If he came **during the party** in reliance on the promise, he actually relied. Phil might not have just picked up his clothing and left at any other time. This may explain why the clerk accelerated the alterations on his original purchases to get Phil in on May 4. The additional purchases while waiting for the race may have been made in reliance on the promise to hold a drawing. That is, perhaps he would not have made those purchases but for the goodwill generated by the gift promise. The last element (injustice or detriment) poses a closer question. It is hard to see how Phil was harmed by attending the party. He got free food, got new clothing that he wanted at a price he thought was fair, and had good company for watching the Derby. Phil, however, might have preferred to spend his time (and money) in other ways if the store had not promised a drawing. He lost that time in reliance on the promise. The store cannot return the time to him. Thus, perhaps it would be unjust to allow them to refuse to perform the promise.

Note on Remedies. A court could decide not to award Phil the coat (or the cost to obtain a similar coat elsewhere) if it decided the case on reliance grounds. Phil lost some time and (maybe) purchased some clothing he would not have purchased but for the store's promise. Allowing Phil to return the clothing for a refund and giving him compensation (perhaps at minimum wage) for the time spent in the store would compensate for any harm Phil suffered. That may turn out to be less costly to the store than giving him the coat. Even based on reliance, many courts simply enforce the promise (by awarding the coat or its value). If the court bases its holding on consideration, it almost certainly will award the coat or its value.

Comments. The first paragraph of this answer may be unnecessary. Your time may be better spent discussing the most promising approach to consideration, instead of ruling out an unpromising argument. Again, some professors reward thoroughness. If you have time to do both (without making each one superficial), you may edge past people who only do one. If you are sure the question is intended to address consideration, you also might omit the fourth paragraph. But discussions of reliance almost always include discussions of the possibility of limiting the remedy to the reliance interest. Thus, caution suggests including some comment about the remedial choice.

Question 2: Remember Tex Griller and Marnie? Tex owns a steakhouse that offered a complimentary dessert to anyone who can finish the special 40 oz. "Cholesterol King" steak plate. When petite Marnie ordered the Cholesterol King, Tex laughed and said, "Little lady, if you can eat all that, you can have my truck," pointing to a new truck parked in the front. Marnie finished the steak and called for the title and keys to the truck. Tex refused. Advise Marnie about her prospects for success if she sued Tex for breach of contract.

Answer: **Assent**. The assent issues are still present but have been discussed above. *See* Question 4 in the section on Chapter 2. In this section, let's focus on consideration.

Consideration: Sought in Exchange. Consideration exists if Tex sought something in exchange for the promise of a truck and Marnie gave that something in exchange for Tex's promise. Tex sought something in exchange for the promise of a free dessert. That promise might induce people to come to the restaurant and might induce some to order a bigger (and perhaps more expensive) steak than they really wanted. But Tex did not publish the promise of his truck. And Marnie had ordered the steak before Tex made the promise—thus, she did not give her **order** in exchange for the promise of a truck. Perhaps Tex sought Marnie's services in eating the steak—but it is hard to see why Tex would **seek** such a thing. More realistically, the promise may be like a reward or a prize for accomplishing a difficult feat (such as finding a dog or winning a golf tournament). Rewards or prizes are offered to **induce** a person to perform the feat. Regardless of benefit to the promisor, one who performs has done what the promisor specified—what the promisor sought. Thus, it seems fair to conclude Tex sought Marnie's performance.

Consideration: Given in Exchange. Marnie arguably did not give her performance in exchange for the promise. Doing exactly what one would have done even if no promise had been made does not give anything **in exchange**. She ordered the steak, presumably intending to finish it, before Tex offered the truck (based on the offer of a free dessert). Thus, she would have tried to finish the steak even if Tex had not promised the truck. But her conduct manifested an intent to give the performance in exchange for the promised truck. It does not matter whether the promise actually induced her to perform. Once Tex offered the truck, it formed part of the reason she performed—or would so appear to an objective observer. Thus, even if Marnie, subjectively, would not have stopped short if only a dessert was offered—or if no dessert had been offered—her conduct indicated she was finishing the steak in exchange for the offer. Consideration exists.

Question 3. Reconsider the modification in question 6 in the section on Chapter 2. When Marnie was nearly finished, she told Tex to get the title ready. Tex, regretting his blunder, said, "That truck isn't for sale, but if you finish, I'll not only give you a free dessert, but a free dessert for all your friends, too." Marnie finished the steak and called for the free desserts. Tex served them up. When finished, Marnie asked for the keys and title to the truck. Tex refused. Do the new facts change Marnie's prospects for success if she sued Tex for breach of contract?

Answer: **Assent** to the modification has been discussed previously.

Consideration for the Modification: first version. Both the truck and the dessert are goods. A modification of a contract for the sale of goods is enforceable regardless of consideration for the change, as long as the modification is made in good faith. (Consideration need not be discussed at all: The existence of consideration will not rescue a modification made in bad faith; absence of consideration will not undermine a modification made in good faith.) Good faith requires honesty in fact. (For merchants, good faith also requires compliance with reasonable commercial standards of the trade. Tex is a merchant of food but not a merchant **of trucks**. The contract modified involves the sale of a **truck**. Neither party is breaching the sale of the steak for the menu price.) Tex's conduct does not seem dishonest. He got caught running his mouth and seeks a way to compromise a troubling situation. The offer is not coercive; Marnie could always reject it and sue for the truck. See 7.A. This kind of compromise — particularly in a situation in which jest rather than a bargain may have produced the promises — should be legal.

Consideration for the Modification: second version. Marnie, not Tex, wants to object to the enforceability of the modification. She implicitly promised to waive any claim to the truck. The promise will be enforceable if she sought something in exchange for it and Tex gave that something in exchange for the promise. Arguably Marnie did not seek the desserts at all. Tex proposed the deal; Marnie didn't **seek** anything. On that interpretation, however, offerees never receive consideration; the offeror proposes the deal. Marnie's assent negates a willingness to relinquish her claim without the desserts; the desserts were at least part of the inducement for her promise. She sought the desserts in exchange for her waiver. Similarly, Tex gave the desserts in exchange for her waiver.

Adequacy of Consideration. Courts do not question the adequacy of consideration. As long as Marnie decided the desserts were worth giving up her claim to the truck, she may make a legally enforceable agreement on those terms. In addition, the terms are not entirely lopsided: The desserts were a relatively sure thing, the truck a risky proposition. Thus, she may have received as much as she gave up.

Comments. The problem arises under the UCC, so the first discussion of consideration is definitely the better choice. The second shows how the discussion might proceed if Tex had promised to sweep her floors for a month instead of promising his truck. In that case, not governed by the UCC, consideration, not good faith would be the first issue.

The second approach to consideration does not discuss the preexisting duty rule because it has no application here. Both parties' duties changed. Tex gave something he did not have a preexisting duty to give (dessert for others at the table). Marnie gave something she did not have a preexisting duty to give (her rights to the truck).

The last paragraph may be unnecessary. Because the law does not question adequacy of consideration, it is barely worth mentioning—unless an issue of unconscionability arises.

This question has been broken up into several shorter questions. Some professors will give only part of the question, allowing you to focus on a single issue. Others, however, may give the whole fact pattern. If so, your answer would need to address jest, assent to the original deal, consideration for the original deal, assent to the modification, and consideration for the modification—and perhaps duress, unconscionability, and remedies, depending on how the professor dressed up the facts. In preparing for exams, don't assume all questions have short answers. Be ready to pick out all the important issues—preferably, without picking out irrelevant issues, too.

Question 4: While crossing the Brooklyn Bridge, Sam Harrigan saw someone about to jump off. He raced to the rescue and caught the man in the act of leaping. The man struggled to get free and even offered Sam $50,000 if he would let go. Instead, Sam hauled the man to safety and waited with him until peace officers arrived to deter a repeat attempt. The delay caused Sam to be late for work (for the umpteenth time). He was fired on the spot. The next day, Sam received a call from Rhea Lative. Ms. Lative is the mother of the (adult) man Sam had saved. She expressed gratitude for his efforts and remorse for the way Sam's boss had acted. Ms. Lative promised to pay Sam $1,000 per week (his normal salary) until he could find new work. Sam warned her that with his employment record, it might take a long time to find someone willing to hire him. Ms. Lative stated that her wealth, like her gratitude, was effectively unlimited and that she did not mind paying him for as long as necessary. Two years later, Ms. Lative stopped making payments. During the entire time, Sam had made diligent efforts to find new work but was unsuccessful. Can Sam recover the amounts promised in a suit for breach of contract?

Answer: No Consideration. Rhea's promise was not part of a bargained-for exchange. A bargain exists when the promisor seeks something in exchange for her promise and the promisee gives that something in exchange for the promise. Rhea did not seek Sam's services (as a rescuer) in exchange for her payments. Sam already had performed the services; Rhea did not need to induce Sam to perform them. In addition, Sam did not give the services in exchange for the promise. He performed before the promise was made; the promise could not have been any part of the reason he acted. Thus, there was no consideration for the promise.

Moral Obligation: first version. A promise made by someone who received a benefit from the promisee may be enforceable despite the absence of consideration, if necessary to avoid injustice. Arguably, Sam's services benefitted Rhea by saving the life of her son. She appears to have considered this a benefit. She expressed gratitude and made a generous promise to Sam, when she could have said and done nothing. The benefit came from Sam. It is not clear whether injustice would result from refusing to enforce the promise. Sam lost his job because of the rescue. But his employment record suggests he might have lost the job anyway. His record is so cloudy that the employer fired him immediately and no one else would hire him for two years. It seems likely that he would have lost the job anyway before long. In addition, justice does not require compensation for people who act gratuitously, whether as donors or intermeddlers. Nonetheless, a rescuer may not fall within either category.

Moral Obligation: second version. This case falls between *Mills v. Wyman* and *Webb v. McGowin*, sharing some features with each. In *Mills*, the court refused to enforce a father's promise to pay for health care services given to his adult son during the son's final days. In *Webb*, the court enforced a promise by a man who was rescued from a falling object to make payments to the rescuer, who suffered a disability because of the rescue. This case looks like *Mills* in that the services were performed for the son, not the mother. The *Webb* court enforced the promise **because** the rescued person, not a relative, made the promise. But the services here differ from *Mills* in that Sam **saved** the son; the care given by Mills may have comforted the son's final days but failed to save his life. That is closer to *Webb*, where the rescue also was successful. In addition, the emergency nature of the rescues here and in *Webb* made negotiation in advance impossible. In *Mills*, it might have been possible for the promisee to bargain with the father sooner, before the services were completed. Unlike *Webb*, however, Sam lost a job; he did not suffer a physical disability. The need to compensate one who can work but does not have a job may be less than the need to compensate one who cannot work because he sacrificed his body to save another. Finally, the promisor in *Webb* never reneged on the promise; he paid until his death, when the executor of the estate stopped payments. Here, it seems that Rhea herself regrets the promise, more like *Mills*.

The differences make the case hard to predict. The benefit to Rhea, although less than the benefit to the man rescued, seems significant enough to justify enforcement if direct benefit is the important question. In addition, the promise suggests that Rhea would have been willing to make the same deal if there had been time to negotiate in advance. The accident that negotiation occurred after the rescue rather than before does not seem to deserve much weight. Rhea, at the time she made the promise, felt she was better off with the services she received than with the money she promised to pay for them. That is the kind of promise the law likes to enforce. Nor does it seem to matter who decided to stop payments. If a promise is enforceable, it is enforceable from the beginning. That does not vary with who changed her mind or when. Finally, the type of injury suffered by the rescuer does not seem to make any difference. Both physical and financial injuries hurt the rescuer. Unless Sam's job search has been a sham, his inability to make a living is no less severe (to him, at least) than the rescuer in *Webb*.

Comments. The second approach to moral obligation shows a different method of writing an exam—a method some professors may prefer. Most answers here take a rule, usually from the UCC or the second Restatement, and apply it. Common-law courts, however, work with precedent and try to infer rules from those prior cases and the justifications for them. The second answer works with those materials, rather than simply accepting the rule the Restatement derived from the cases.

The first paragraph (on consideration) may be optional. It usually makes sense to explore the issue of consideration before trying to apply an exception to the rule. But sometimes consideration obviously is absent and does not require discussion. Arguably, this is such a case.

The answer did not discuss reliance but could have. Sam is unlikely to prevail on this issue because he did not really rely on the promise

—or, at least, the facts do not identify any reliance. His search for a new job was not made in reliance on the promise. He would have searched for work just as hard (maybe harder) if Rhea was not supporting him. (A decision not to look for work would have been detrimental reliance—but might breach an obligation of good faith under the contract, making Sam a villain rather than a hero.)

Question 5:   In question 4 in the section on Chapter 3, Sam called Rhea when the payments stopped. Rhea explained that her husband had died leaving all the liquid assets to their children. She had a house and a trust to cover all household expenses but very little money for personal expenses—not enough to keep paying Sam $1,000 a week. She stated that if Sam would take the job of assistant chauffeur, she could continue to make the payments because that would be covered by the trust for household expenses. After learning the only duties would be driving if an emergency arose on the chauffeur's day off, he accepted the position. He continued to search diligently for other work in his profession but without success. Two years later, Rhea fired Sam without explanation or justification. Sam asks whether he can sue for breach of contract—and if so, which one?

Answer: Consideration. If the original contract was **un**enforceable, there is consideration for the employment agreement. Rhea seeks Sam's services as assistant chauffeur in exchange for $1,000 a week, and Sam gives those services in exchange. Because the original promise to pay $1,000 was not enforceable, Rhea had no preexisting duty to make those payments. Thus, the payments are new consideration in exchange for Sam's new promise to serve as a driver.

Consideration for the Modification. If the original contract was enforceable, the employment agreement was a modification. Because Rhea had a preexisting duty to pay $1,000 a week, Sam arguably received no consideration for his promise to give services in exchange for that payment. The issue, however, is whether Rhea received consideration for her promise; she, not Sam, is trying to avoid performing. Rhea sought services in exchange for her promise; Sam gave the services in exchange for the promise. The promise is enforceable against Rhea.

Alternative Question: What if Sam wants to quit and still collect the $1,000 a week?

CHAPTER 4   WRITING REQUIREMENTS

Question 1:   Terry had always admired a car owned by Sean, Terry's cousin. Sean told Terry that if Terry could go an entire year without smoking, Sean would give Terry the car. Terry immediately threw down her cigarette and declared that was her last one (for at least a year, anyway). The following year, Terry claimed the car from Sean. Sean refused to sign it over. Can Terry recover the car (or its value) in an action for breach of contract?

Answer: **Formation.** There are issues of assent and consideration here. Was the offer acceptable by promise or only by performance? Was throwing down the cigarette a promise to perform? Was giving up cigarettes consideration and, if not, would it satisfy the exception for action in reliance? None of those issues should prevent recovery. On an exam, you would address them in detail. Here, let's focus on the statute of frauds.

Sales of Goods. A car is a good, but the UCC requires a writing only if the price is $500 or more. There was no monetary price agreed here, which arguably places the contract outside the scope of the UCC's statute of frauds. Even if we could consider the value of the consideration (rather than just its price), the value to the seller is hard to assess when the buyer is the one who quits smoking.

Performable within a Year. A contract that, by its terms, cannot be performed within a year of formation is unenforceable without a writing. This might make it critical to determine whether the offer was unilateral or bilateral. A unilateral offer is accepted on the date performance is complete. Thus, formation would not occur until Terry had finished the year of abstinence — making performance simultaneous with formation, almost by definition. So let's assume the offer was accepted by a promise on the date it was made. If Terry could complete performance within a year, the statute of frauds does not govern the contract. If she starts immediately, performance will be completed one year from the date of formation. (If you want to get technical and count seconds, she will finish performance seconds after the year expires. But the law ignores parts of a day. If she can finish before the anniversary of the contract ends — before midnight starts the next day — she has completed performance within a year.) The statute would not apply even if Terry did not start immediately. She **could** start immediately, so she **could** finish within a year, so a writing is unnecessary.

Question 2: Sam agreed to lease a store at 145 Main Street to Chris for five years. The agreement was oral; both parties expected to sign a lease later. Before the lease was signed, Sam wrote Chris a letter which said: "Despite our agreement last week, I will not be able to lease the store at 145 Main to you. A five-year lease at the

$1,500 per month rent is far below the value of the property. I have decided to rent the property to another who is willing to pay its real worth." Can Chris recover for breach of contract?

Answer: The Statute of Frauds Applies. A five-year lease cannot be performed within a year. In addition, an interest in land requires a writing. The possible exception for leases of less than a year would not apply here.

The Statute Is Satisfied. To satisfy the statute, a writing must be signed by the party to be charged (Sam), must identify the subject matter of the contract (the store at 145 Main), must indicate that an agreement had been made, and must include the essential terms of the unperformed promises. The letter sent and signed by Sam mentions that they had reached an agreement, identifies the property, and notes the duration and the rent—the most important terms of the lease. This letter appears to be sufficient writing to justify enforcement of the contract. The only reservation is whether a court might feel that other terms of a lease were "essential." If so, the writing might fall just short of sufficient.

Comment. Writings don't need to be contemporaneous with the agreement or intended to document an agreement. This writing, designed to recant an agreement, made an unenforceable contract enforceable. Some professors love the irony of an agreement that was unenforceable until a party wrote a letter repudiating it. Be alert for this trick.

Question 3:   Mario runs a photocopy shop. On Thursday, October 1, he realized that the supply of toner was very low. He called Zorex and ordered 1,000 cartons of toner. Zorex's sales person quoted a price of $35,000, to which Mario agreed. Zorex promised delivery by Tuesday, October 20. On Monday, October 5, Mario prepared and mailed a purchase order on his usual form, which contained the company logo at the top. Mario kept one copy of the triplicate form and sent two copies to Zorex. The form mentioned the quantity, price, and delivery terms. The form contained a line for Zorex to sign and requested that Zorex return one signed copy to confirm the order. Typically, Zorex and other suppliers ignored this aspect of the purchase order, preferring to acknowledge the sale on their own forms, often included with the goods when shipped.

On October 20, the toner did not arrive. Mario called Zorex. The shipping department said they had no record of his order. Mario does not know the name of the sales person who took the phone order, nor does he know what happened to the purchase order he sent confirming the phone order. To continue operations, Mario urgently required toner. Due to a price increase after October 1 and his need for overnight delivery, Mario had to pay $41,000 to obtain toner from another source. Can Mario recover the $6,000 in damages from Zorex.

Answer: Statute of Frauds. If Mario sues, Zorex is likely to raise the statute of frauds as a defense. Under the UCC, a sale of goods for $500 is unenforceable without a writing signed by the party to be charged. Toner is a good (movable thing) and the price was well over $500. We should ask Mario whether he received any writing at all from Zorex. That seems unlikely. The order apparently got lost in Zorex's office, presumably without any writing signed by them. We can ask (during discovery). Even a note pad on which the person who took the order made notes might suffice (if initialed or on letterhead). But we should consider alternatives, in case.

Imputed Writing. Under the UCC, a writing signed by one party may be imputed to the other if, between merchants, a writing sufficient against the sender is sent within a reasonable time after formation, is received by the other party, the other party has reason to know of its contents, and the other party does not object within 10 days. Both Mario and Zorex are merchants: Zorex sells toner and Mario is an experienced buyer and user of toner. Mario sent a purchase order to Zorex four days after the phone conversation—and two of those days were a weekend. This seems reasonably prompt. The order was sent well before Mario knew Zorex would breach, so it seems unlikely Mario wrote the letter as a self-serving litigation position. The purchase order seems sufficient against Mario. It mentions quantity, the only essential term, as well as price and delivery date. Mario did not say he signed it. We should examine his copy to see. In any case, the business letterhead was placed on the order form to identify the buyer and to authenticate the writing as coming from Mario's business. That may suffice under the relatively loose definition of signed in the UCC. We must investigate to find out whether Zorex received it. It may have been lost in the mail. But it seems equally likely that Zorex received it and misplaced it. Perhaps the hardest element is to show Zorex had reason to know of its contents. The purchase order form announced the nature of its contents. Mario did not hide contractual language in some unusual document that someone at Zorex might overlook (and, thus, not realize the need to object promptly). Zorex, thus, had reason to know the contents, even if they unreasonably lost or failed to open the order. Finally, no objection has been given. The 10-day limit starts on the date

Zorex received the order. We do not know exactly what day that was—or if it occurred at all. But it seems likely that the mail would have taken it to Zorex by October 10 (five days after posting). If so, Zorex's failure to object **in writing** by October 20 would allow the order to serve as if Zorex had signed it.

CHAPTERS 5–11   CONTRACT DEFENSES

Question 1:   Charlie, a middle-level executive, was being considered for a terrific job with a much bigger company on the opposite side of the country. He discussed the possibility with Kim, a colleague, as the two watched Monday Night Football at a bar. By the fourth quarter, each had consumed a good deal of beer. Kim offered to buy Charlie's house because he wouldn't need it once he got the new job. Charlie agreed. Charlie was speaking slowly and slurring his words. He could not remember the score and at one point seemed to think San Francisco was ahead even though that was not one of the teams playing. On a napkin, Charlie wrote out a promise to sell the house to Kim for $250,000 on January 1 (the date the new job would start). The writing was legible if not neat and all the words were spelled correctly. The next day, Charlie regretted agreeing to sell the house and told her the deal was off. Kim insisted that the agreement was binding. Can Charlie avoid the agreement?

Answer: **Intoxication** is the hardest incapacity to establish. Charlie acted promptly to reject the agreement, so any right to avoid the deal is preserved. But Charlie would need to prove he was so drunk that he either did not understand the nature of the transaction or he could not control himself, and that Kim knew he was that drunk. The facts make it clear that Charlie was drunk and that Kim had reason to know Charlie was drunk. But it is not entirely clear that Charlie was unable to understand that he was selling his house or unable to control himself or whether Kim was aware that Charlie's drunken state had proceeded that far. This seems as good a case as any to argue intoxication, but the issue may hinge on expert testimony and on which party the jury finds more sympathetic.

Comment. Intoxication, like any incapacity, can be difficult to resolve without more facts than conveniently fit an exam question—and sometimes requires more expertise in psychology than it is fair to expect law students to have acquired while undergraduates. For this reason, intoxication and mental incapacity rarely appear on exam questions. When they do appear, professors often include dead giveaways in the question: Either they state facts that show the party had the capacity to enter the contract or they tell you point blank that a party could not understand the consequences and (perhaps) that the other party knew this. You should be prepared to argue from a sparse record, but you may not be asked to do so very often.

Question 2: The York Street Post (YSP) has a long-term contract with Bonded Sawdust (BS) to provide all the newsprint YSP requires for the publication of its daily newspaper at $200 per roll. On Thursday, October 17, Chris (YSP's buyer) realized that the supply of newsprint was so low that the Sunday paper could not be printed unless more paper was obtained immediately. Chris immediately called Terry (BS's account manager) and asked for delivery of 500 rolls on Saturday, October 19 ($100,000 at contract price). Terry indicated that Saturday delivery should be no problem. Chris heaved a sigh of relief and let slip that Sunday's paper would not appear without the delivery. Terry then paused and told Chris that BS could not deliver by Saturday unless it canceled other deliveries, which might get expensive if other customers complained about breach of contract. Chris recognized this as a request to offer a bonus and asked how much it would take to get Saturday delivery. After another pause, Terry said an extra $30,000 ($60 per roll) should cover any complaints by other customers. Chris agreed to pay the higher price. BS delivered the paper on Saturday. YSP put out its Sunday paper. Chris now wants to refuse to pay the $30,000 bonus. Chris feels that Terry recognized YSP's desperation and took advantage of it to extract a premium to which it was not entitled under the contract. The market value of newsprint on October 17 was only $250 per roll, $10 per roll less than BS demanded but $50 per roll more than the contract price.

Answer: **Duress**. Arguably, Chris made the promise to pay more for the paper under duress. Duress requires a showing of an improper threat that induced assent under circumstances in which a party had no reasonable alternatives. Terry implicitly threatened not to deliver the paper by Saturday unless YSP promised more money for the delivery. That threat would be improper if it threatens to breach an obligation of good faith under a contract. We need to know whether the long-term contract between BS and YSP required immediate deliveries at YSP's whim or required YSP to provide reasonable notice to BS (an interpretation issue). Assuming that BS was obligated to deliver by Saturday, failure to deliver would be a breach of contract. But it might not be a breach of good faith under a contract. Good faith requires honesty in fact. If Terry honestly reported that rush delivery would require breaching other contracts, perhaps the request for compensation was made in good faith. But Terry first indicated that Saturday delivery would be no problem, discovering the other contracts only after Chris mentioned how desperate YSP was to receive the paper. If Terry was not honest about the delivery problem, the threat probably breaches an obligation of good faith under the long-term contract. (Note: it would also be plausible to discuss the use of power for illegitimate ends to extract a contract on unfair terms, another ground for arguing the threat was improper.) The threat obviously induced the promise to pay the extra $30,000. Having a right to receive the paper for $100,000, no reason exists to promise an additional $30,000 except the threat not to deliver on time. Chris could have explored alternatives, such as buying the paper elsewhere or volunteering to send YSP's trucks over to pick up the paper. The first seems unreasonable. The exclusive contract may have required YSP to deal with BS — though if BS was unable to fulfill its part of the deal, perhaps that would excuse breach by YSP. In addition, other suppliers might be unable to provide prompt delivery. Taking BS (a sure thing) might be reasonable given the uncertainty of seeking other suppliers. The alternative of offering to pick up the paper might be reasonable. It shifts the cost of delivery from BS to YSP. Perhaps those costs would be recoverable if BS breached a duty to deliver.

Modification. In addition to the interpretation issue noted in the discussion of duress, this question also could raise issues of modification and the preexisting duty rule. Because the UCC recognizes any modification made in good faith, regardless of new consideration, the issue is less important than duress. A demonstration of bad faith on BS's part, however, might end the inquiry. Even without duress, the modification would not be enforceable.

Question 3:   Pat breeds poodles. Her prize poodle, LeRoi, is considered the best poodle in the world today. She received an offer from Sean, another breeder, to breed LeRoi with Sean's prize-winning dog, Bitsy. She agreed to provide LeRoi's services in exchange for $10,000 plus pick of the litter, provided Sean's poodle was of prize caliber. Sean assured Pat that Sean's poodle was a winner. When Pat took LeRoi to meet Sean and Bitsy, Pat discovered that Bitsy was a dachshund, not a poodle. Sean believed the cross will produce a very popular new breed. Pat has absolutely no interest in the pick of the litter of this monstrous cross. Sean in fact owned a prize-winning poodle, but that was not the breeding partner intended for LeRoi. Pat refused to provide LeRoi's services unless Sean promised $15,000. Sean refused. Can Pat avoid the contract?

Answer: Nondisclosure. A failure to reveal facts is the equivalent of stating that the facts do not exist if: disclosure is necessary to prevent other statements from being misleading, the party knows disclosure will correct the other party's mistake of basic understanding and silence would breach an obligation of good faith and fair dealing, or two other situations not pertinent here. When Pat's terms indicated the quality of Sean's poodle was important to her price, Sean almost certainly knew that Pat thought Bitsy was Sean's poodle. Knowing of Pat's mistake — which is basic to the contract because part of the price will be paid with a puppy — Sean probably should have corrected it. Sean and Pat, however, were strangers dealing at arm's length, with no duty to prevent the other from making a mistake. It is not clear how an obligation of good faith and fair dealing would arise between these parties, at least not until the contract was formed. But it may be worth a try.

Misrepresentation. If Sean had an obligation to reveal that Bitsy was not a poodle, silence was equivalent to stating that Bitsy was a poodle. That assertion is not in accord with the facts. Thus, Pat may rescind the agreement for misrepresentation if the assertion was material or fraudulent and induced Pat's assent, and Pat was justified in relying on it. An assertion is material if it would be likely to induce (contribute substantially to) assent by a reasonable person. The breed of the dog is likely to contribute to the assent of any person, particularly one who will be paid with a puppy. Moreover, it seems likely that Sean knew the breed was important to Pat; Pat asked specifically about the quality of the poodle, indicating not only the importance of the breed but the fact that not just any poodle would suffice. Thus, Sean may have known the fact was likely to induce Pat's assent. The fact probably did induce Pat's assent. The breed not only contributed to her decision; she never would have agreed to breed LeRoi to Bitsy if she had known Bitsy's breed. Generally, it is justifiable to rely on the other party's statements of fact — especially facts peculiarly within their knowledge, such as the breed of their dog.

Unilateral Mistake. If Sean did not actually know of Pat's mistake, or if Sean had no obligation of good faith to speak up, Pat may need to resort to unilateral mistake. To prevail, Pat must show a mistake of basic assumption with a material effect upon the agreed exchange, that she did not bear the risk of the mistake, and that Sean had reason to know of the mistake, caused the mistake, or that enforcement would be unconscionable. The mistake as to breed seems fundamental to Pat. She agreed to take a puppy because she thought Bitsy was a prize poodle. Forcing her to accept a poohund instead would materially reduce the value of what she receives under the contract. Arguably, however, Sean receives no more than what Sean expected—the litter of poohunds less one. Arguably, the effect being one way undercuts materiality. The contract does not explicitly allocate the risk of mistake as to breed to either party. Pat was not conscious of her ignorance regarding Bitsy's breed. In fact, she thought she had inquired about Bitsy by asking about the quality of Sean's poodle. Thus, unless the court finds reason to allocate the risk to Pat, the mistake defense seems sound. Finally, Sean both caused the mistake and had reason to know of it. His response to the question about his poodle undoubtedly contributed to Pat's belief that Bitsy was a poodle. The question clearly assumed that the poodle would be the parent of the puppy received in payment as pick of the litter. At the very least, the comment gave Sean reason to know of Pat's mistake. Thus, unilateral mistake makes the contract voidable by Pat.

Question 4:   The law firm of Korn & Pone (KP) decided to hire a prominent attorney in the field of insurance law. They entered negotiations with Gail, a successful attorney with a private practice. Eventually, Gail agreed to work for KP for $230,000 per year. The contract included several guaranties, including Gail's right to smoke a pipe in the office. Unknown to the parties, the city had recently passed a law making it illegal to smoke in any place of employment within the city. Employers would be fined $100 per smoker per day for violations of the ban. Upon discovering the law, KP notified Gail that, under the law, it could not permit Gail to smoke in the office. Gail threatened to sue for breach of contract. Is the contract enforceable?

Answer: **Public Policy**. The statute did not expressly state that contracts permitting smoking were unenforceable. Thus, the issue involves whether the public policy favoring enforcement of contracts outweighs the public policy against smoking in the workplace. Gail clearly expected to be allowed to smoke in the office. That expectation seemed justified but only because the ordinance was new and unknown. Parties cannot justifiably expect to be allowed to violate the law. It is not clear whether any forfeiture is involved. Perhaps the private practice office would not be considered a workplace—though this seems unlikely if Gail had a secretary working there. Nor is there any public interest in an individual's ability to smoke. On the other hand, the policies against smoking may not be very strong. The fine is low; $36,500 per year is less than 15% of the salary paid to Gail. The strength of the policy might depend on whether the city believed it was protecting workers from annoying stench or from a dangerous health hazard—facts that will also affect the seriousness of the misconduct (allowing Gail to continue smoking). In either case, refusing to enforce the term will further the policy. The misconduct (allowing smoking) will be deliberate now that the ordinance is known. And the contract clause would directly cause KP's decision to allow smoking (if enforceable). In short, although the severity of the harm may be small, the factors favoring enforcement may be even smaller.

Impracticability. The case could as easily (perhaps more easily) be addressed by discussing whether the law made it impracticable for KP to perform. That issue is addressed below.

CHAPTERS 12–14 INTERPRETATION, MISUNDERSTANDING, AND PAROL EVIDENCE

Question 1: Bonnie opened a small computer store, offering both sales and service. She hired Julie, a computer geek, to come into the store "every day at nine" to update the store's home page on the World Wide Web. Bonnie advertised that customers could see a web page produced and updated if they came to the store any day at 9 A.M. On opening day, Julie did not show up at 9 A.M., leaving Bonnie to apologize to a few disgruntled customers. At 9 P.M., Julie showed up to find the store locked and no way to get in to do her work. Julie assumed that 9 must mean 9 P.M. because all her jobs of this sort occur at night, when there are no customers around to get in the way. Has either Julie or Bonnie breached her contract?

Answer: **Interpretation.** If the contract required Julie to come at 9 A.M., Julie is in breach. (If it required her to come at 9 P.M., Bonnie can avoid breach by paying Julie for days when Julie appeared at 9 and was locked out.) "Nine" can plausibly mean either A.M. or P.M. There is little a court can do to interpret the word in favor of either party. Perhaps a court could interpret it against the drafter (or, in this case, speaker) on the theory that the speaker should have been more specific. On the whole, however, techniques of interpretation seem useless.

Misunderstanding. Each attached a different meaning to the word. If either knew or had reason to know of the other's meaning, we interpret the agreement to include the meaning of the party who had no such notice. There does not appear to be any reason either should have known the other's intent unless perhaps, if they had dealt before—or dealt with others who had similar preferences. Bonnie is new to the business, so prior dealings are unlikely to be helpful. All of Julie's jobs are at night—though perhaps she has dealt with others who wanted day services in the past. More likely, however, neither knew and neither had reason to know of the other's interpretation of "nine." Thus, it appears they never assented to a contract.

Question 2:   Al, a professor, was under consideration for a permanent appointment at a highly prestigious university in a different state. Jessie, a colleague of Al, offered to buy Al's house (which Jessie had always admired). Al pointed out that he might not get the job. Jessie offered to make the sale contingent upon Al's getting the job. Al agreed and they signed a one-paragraph contract, written by Al:

> Al Thierry promises to sell and Jessie Gerlac promises to buy the house and land located at 122 Tittle Place for $250,000, if Al Thierry moves from the state of California within one year.

Al did not get the appointment he sought. However, Al did receive a visiting offer from another major university in a different state. Al accepted that post. When Al told Jessie, she put her house on the market and began seeking a loan to help her buy Al's house. When Al found out about the preparations, Al stated he did not intend to sell the house because the visiting position might not become a permanent offer and, thus, he might be moving back to California within a year. Does the contract require Al to sell the house to Jessie?

Answer: **Meaning of "Move."** Al agreed to sell if he "moves from the state of California within one year." If leaving the state to take the job as a visiting professor satisfies this condition, Al's performance will be due and failure to perform would breach the agreement. Arguably, leaving the state temporarily is not a move from California. Although one year is longer than most vacations, it still appears to be a temporary move—at least pending further developments. Thus, if Al can persuade the court that "move" means "move permanently" or "move without an intent to return," the condition has not occurred and he need not sell the house (yet).

"Move" Means Permanently. The dictionary undoubtedly includes several definitions of move—from lifting a finger to changing residence permanently. Common usage also includes both meanings, depending on context. In context of the negotiations, a permanent move seems to square with the parties' intentions. They agreed at a time when Al was being considered for a permanent appointment. The word "move" was chosen with that in mind. In addition, the negotiations suggest that getting the permanent job was the condition, not merely moving from California. At the least, this suggests a permanent change was implied by the term move.

Parol Evidence. Jessie may seek to prevent any evidence of the negotiations from being admitted. If the writing is integrated, evidence intended to vary the terms of the writing would be inadmissible. The writing, however, does not seem to be integrated. It has no integration clause. It has barely enough terms to satisfy the statute of frauds. The parties easily may have intended additional terms (inspection, warranties on the deed, etc.) and probably did not intend this writing to be the complete agreement between them. Thus, the parol evidence rule would not apply. Even if it did, the term "move" is not plain on its face. It is fairly susceptible to both meanings (temporary or permanent move). Parol evidence could be introduced to help interpret the ambiguous term in an integrated writing.

Reformation. The negotiations suggest that Jessie would buy the house if Al got the permanent job then under consideration. Perhaps that is the real agreement and the writing erroneously recorded it. If so, the condition did not occur and Al has no obligation to sell the house. If Jessie admits that was their agreement, the court could reform the document. If Jessie contends that the parties changed the term from the one discussed to the one written, reformation seems unlikely. Al may have been mistaken about the content of the condition. But Jessie contends the written condition is exactly what she intended. If she fraudulently failed to disclose the change to Al, a court could reform over her objection. But Al wrote the contract. Although not dispositive in itself—Al can still claim to be mistaken—it makes it hard to say Jessie committed fraud. She may not have known Al was unaware of the change he made when writing the agreement. If so, her failure to mention the change was not an assertion at all, let alone a fraudulent one. Nor is it clear that Al can justifiably rely on Jessie's failure to tell Al that Al had changed the language. In short, reformation seems unlikely.

Comment. This question shows the interrelationship between interpretation and parol evidence. Almost every parol evidence issue will arise in the context of trying to decide what a clause in the contract means—and, if unfavorable, whether the clause was not really what the parties agreed.

CHAPTERS 15–16   CONDITIONS AND MATERIAL BREACH

Question 1: The law firm of Korn & Pone (KP) decided to hire a prominent attorney in the field of insurance law. The firm entered negotiations with Gail, a successful attorney with a private practice. Eventually, Gail agreed to work for KP for $230,000 per year. The contract included several guaranties, including Gail's right to smoke a pipe in the office. Unknown to the parties, the city had recently passed a law making it illegal to smoke in any place of employment within the city. Employers would be fined $100 per smoker per day for violations of the ban. Upon discovering the law, KP notified Gail that, under the law, it could not permit Gail to smoke in the office. Gail refused to work for KP resumed private practice (where smoking in the office was either legal or did not attract any attention from authorities). Has Gail breached the contract?

Answer: Material Breach. KP's failure to perform, if material, might permit Gail to terminate the contract. Materiality is assessed by considering several factors, including the extent to which Gail will be deprived of the expected benefit of the contract, the extent to which Gail can be adequately compensated for the loss, the extent of any forfeiture KP will suffer, the likelihood of cure, and KP's good faith. The last two factors are easily assessed. KP acted in good faith obedience to a city law. Thus, there is no reason to penalize KP's nonperformance by allowing termination. On the other hand, cure is unlikely. KP probably will continue to obey the law and there is no indication the city intends to repeal it. Thus, there is little hope that KP will resume performance of its promise to allow Gail to smoke. The more important issues focus on Gail's loss and forfeiture to KP. KP's nonperformance did not deprive Gail of her salary or any other benefits of the contract. The right to smoke in the office seems relatively small by comparison. We cannot tell whether Gail thought it was very significant or whether Gail had other reasons to want out of the deal and used this default as an excuse. Damages, on the other hand, are unlikely to compensate for the loss. KP's nonperformance probably is excused by impracticability, so damages are unavailable. Even if KP is liable, the opportunity to smoke is not something Gail can use money to buy. The loss seems largely emotional, not pecuniary, and emotional losses generally are not recoverable in contract. Thus, compensation is not practical. Forfeiture by KP also seems relatively small. The problem was discovered relatively early in the life of the contract. Thus, KP may have little invested in Gail other than the cost of negotiating the contract. Allowing Gail to terminate the contract and seek other employment would not produce much waste. Even if KP had paid Gail for a month, presumably KP also received a month of labor for it.

Balancing Factors. Combining these factors to reach a conclusion is difficult. Gail lost something that seems important, at least to Gail. Damages will not compensate for that loss. Cure is unlikely. Thus, the only way to protect Gail's right to smoke is to allow termination so Gail can practice in a private setting. KP's loss from allowing termination is relatively small. But KP acted in good faith. The firm faces some forfeiture of negotiation costs and perhaps preparations. And the loss to Gail is such a small part of the contract that it seems odd to magnify it this way. The issue probably turns on a factor not mentioned in the law: Gail's good faith. If she in fact values smoking in the office very strongly, termination seems the only way to protect that right. But if Gail seems to be using the smoking clause as an excuse for other reasons to terminate the contract, a court probably will find the breach not material.

Suspend or Terminate? In most cases of material breach, you will want to address a second step: Must the party await cure before terminating the contract? On these facts, that seems pointless. Cure is so unlikely that awaiting cure would be futile. There might be no harm in asking Gail to await cure. There is no great need to find substitute work because KP has not breached the duty to pay wages. And nothing in the contract makes time essential. These points make the answer more complete. But without any reason to expect cure, time might be used to better advantage elsewhere.

CHAPTER 17   IMPRACTICABILITY AND FRUSTRATION

Question 1:   The law firm of Korn & Pone (KP) decided to hire a prominent attorney in the field of insurance law. The firm entered negotiations with Gail, a successful attorney with a private practice. Eventually, Gail agreed to work for KP for $230,000 per year. The contract included several guaranties, including Gail's right to smoke a pipe in the office. Unknown to the parties, the city had recently passed a law making it illegal to smoke in any place of employment within the city. Employers would be fined $100 per smoker per day for violations of the ban. Upon discovering the law, KP notified Gail that, under the law, it could not permit Gail to smoke in the office. Gail threatened to sue for breach of contract. Is the contract enforceable?

Answer: Impracticability. If a party's performance is impracticable without her fault because an event occurred contrary to the parties' basic assumption that it would not occur, the party's performance is excused unless she agreed to perform despite the occurrence. A law that prohibits performance contravenes a basic assumption of the parties that performance would be legal. Although the law was a basic assumption of the contract, it may not have made performance impracticable. The fine for allowing Gail to smoke is relatively low. It will cost KP only $36,500. That is a cost, but mere expense does not make performance impracticable. In the context of a law firm that values Gail's services more than $230,000, perhaps price is not so great that performance must be excused. If the cost does make performance impracticable, performance probably will be excused. No facts suggest KP was at fault for the law's passage. Had the contract required KP to allow smoking regardless of changes in the law, it would have agreed to a greater obligation than necessary and impracticability would not excuse performance. But merely mentioning smoking does not assume an obligation to perform even if smoking becomes illegal.

Question 2:   Trauma, Inc., is a three-person medical software company based in Boston. It sold a 100 copies of a diagnostic program to St. Bernard Hospital in Cleveland for $1,000 each. The contract required Milton Trauma, the inventor of the program, to train St. Bernard's personnel in the use of the program. The software was delivered on time. Milton Trauma was seriously injured in a plane crash on the way to Cleveland. Although recovery is possible, for now he cannot move his arms and damage to his throat makes it difficult for him to speak for more than a few minutes each day. Is performance by Trauma, Inc., excused?

Answer: Impracticability. Unless parties have assumed a greater obligation, no breach occurs if "performance has been made impracticable by the occurrence of a contingency the nonoccurrence of which was a basic assumption on which the contract was made." UCC §2-615. The contingency was Milton suffering a disability. The parties almost certainly assumed that would not occur, but it did. Whether performance has become impracticable may depend on whether others can substitute for Milton. St. Bernard may have wanted Milton specifically, so that substituting another may not satisfy the contract. Alternatively, Trauma, Inc., being small, may not have other employees who could conduct the training even if St. Bernard would accept them as substitutes. Although Trauma, Inc., must make good faith efforts to provide the required training, if it cannot do so, its performance probably is excused.

Question 3:   In the preceding question, assume that Milton was the only person at Trauma, Inc., familiar with the diagnostic program. Trauma, Inc., could hire a team of outside specialists to study the program on an emergency basis and provide the training to St. Bernard. The study will require round the clock work for two weeks, plus the cost of sending the team to Cleveland to conduct the training. These efforts would cost about $50,000 more than it would have cost to have Milton perform the training. As a result, the total cost to perform the contract would be $120,000 instead of $70,000. Has performance been made impracticable by the increase in cost of performance?

Answer: A mere increase in cost does not make performance impracticable unless it changes the essential nature of the performance. The final stage of performance — training St. Bernard's employees — remains unchanged. The intermediate steps are substantially different. Instead of sending the inventor, who already knows the program, Trauma would need to send a team of people — and would need to pay the team to learn the program before they could do the training, all on an expedited basis. Those steps are dramatically different from what the contract seemed to require at the outset. These significant changes may qualify as a change in the essential nature of performance, thus making the increase in expense sufficiently important to render the performance impracticable.

Question 4:   In 1996, Pat led the National League in home runs and RBIs. In the off season, he became a free agent. The San Diego Padres offered Pat a four-year contract with a guaranteed salary of $30 million plus bonuses for performance. Pat accepted. In December 1996, Pat suffered a severe intestinal disorder that required the removal of 80% of his bowels. As a result, Pat cannot digest much of the food he eats. He has lost 70 pounds and has little prospect of regaining either the weight or the muscle mass lost as a result. In February 1997, Pat reported to the Padres' spring training camp. The Padres, concerned that the loss of muscle may prevent Pat from performing at the major-league level, ask whether they can terminate the contract. Assuming performance in spring training confirms the team's fears, what advice would you give the Padres?

Answer: Frustration. When a party's principal purpose is substantially frustrated without her fault by the occurrence of an event the nonoccurrence of which was a basic assumption, the performance is excused unless the contract or circumstances indicate she assumed a greater obligation. The event was the illness that disabled Pat. The parties probably assumed no such illness would occur. This is not entirely clear in the context of baseball. But the Restatement suggests that disability is per se an event the nonoccurrence of which was a basic assumption of the contract, at least when the issue involves impracticability. There is little reason to believe disability is less basic when frustration rather than impracticability is at issue. (But we will discuss whether the contract may require performance despite the disability.) The occurrence of the disability probably has substantially frustrated the principal purpose of the contract. Although Pat remains physically able to swing a bat, the contract was entered with a strong, unparalleled athlete, one with home-run power. Pat may no longer have those traits. If one views the principal purpose generally—to have a person on the team—Pat may still fill that purpose. But viewed realistically, the purpose of hiring a star player has been undermined almost entirely by the disease. No fault attaches to the Padres here—at least, none indicated in the facts. But a contract with a baseball player for a guaranteed salary may assume an obligation to pay the player regardless of factors that impede the player's performance. I need to read the contract itself before offering any firm conclusion. But injured players normally do not lose their right to compensation under a guaranteed contract (unless they are to blame for their injuries). Similarly, players whose performance does not measure up to expectations or hopes do not lose their right to a guaranteed salary. Arguably, Pat fits these categories: He can play, but not well, and that because of an injury for which he is not responsible. Although courts should beware undermining contracts by players suffering normal injuries or bad years, one wonders whether the changes Pat has suffered are so different—in degree if not in kind—that they require excusing performance even though the more normal injuries or performance differences would not. Although the Padres assumed the risk of injury—which usually means a temporary inability—and poor performance (also usually temporary), the team may not have assumed the risk of such complete changes in the physical person they hired that permanently impair his ability to perform. A close case, but one that might be worth arguing in court.

CHAPTER 18   REPUDIATION

Question 1:   In March 1995, Jan purchased four season tickets to the 1995-1996 season of the Santiago Symphony Orchestra. She was particularly excited about this season because the famous pianist Vladimir Van Richter was scheduled to perform Brahms's first piano concerto. As the time for performance neared, the symphony encountered financial difficulty. It announced that it might need to cancel its contracts with some of the more expensive soloists, including Van Richter, to continue to perform the season (unless contributions increased dramatically). Jan is upset that the orchestra would even consider going back on its promise to present Van Richter in concert. She seeks your advice concerning whether she can take legal action to prevent this breach.

Answer: Repudiation. If a party's words unequivocally indicate it intends to commit a material breach of the contract, that repudiation constitutes an immediate breach. Thus, if this is a repudiation, Jan can sue immediately to try to prevent the cancellation. Two problems arise. First, the words do not reveal an unequivocal intent to breach. The orchestra said it might have to cancel the concert, not that it would cancel it. It held out the possibility that contributions would allow it to present Van Richter as promised. Thus, no express repudiation exists. (No facts suggest an implied repudiation — actions that make it seem impossible for the party to perform.) Second, the breach may not be material. The orchestra intends to perform a concert, just not with that soloist. Although the soloist was very important to Jan (and perhaps others), the orchestra may provide enough performance that a court would not find the breach material. If so, even unequivocal refusal to perform would not be a repudiation. (Note: this section is devoted to Repudiation, so a detailed discussion of materiality is omitted. On an exam, you probably would go through the factors and try to resolve the materiality issue.)

Adequate Assurance of Performance. When a party has reasonable ground for insecurity — the possibility that the other party will commit a material breach — she may request adequate assurances that the other party will perform. If the other party does not provide reasonable assurance, that would constitute a repudiation, allowing Jan to seek relief immediately. Here, the announcement certainly gives rise to insecurity. The orchestra revealed the possibility, perhaps even the probability, that it would breach. Again, however, unless the breach will be material, Jan is not entitled to assurances and would not be entitled to treat the failure to give assurance as an immediate breach.

Other Issues. On an exam, you would address what Jan could accomplish by suing now. That part of the answer is in the next section. In addition, you might address whether misrepresentation or mistake would allow Jan to rescind the contract. That may not be very helpful. Jan wants performance, not cancellation. For that reason, it also would not be useful to discuss whether material breach excused her performance of the rest of the contract — in part because she probably has already paid for the tickets, but primarily because she does not want out of the deal. Oh, and you might want to read the orchestra's advertising to see if it included a statement such as "subject to change without notice." That kind of disclaimer means the orchestra did not really promise to present Van Richter; it simply announced a present intention to do so if possible. Lawyers make orchestra managements include those disclaimers, even if exam questions do not.

CHAPTERS 19–23   REMEDIES

Question 1:   In July, Green Grocery ordered 1,000 bushels of apples from Red Orchards at a price of $30 per bushel. Red promised delivery by October 15. On October 15, the apples did not arrive. Green's inquiries revealed that Red had overestimated the size of the harvest and did not have any apples to deliver to Green. Green immediately sought substitute apples. After an employee spent two full days calling other orchards and wholesalers, Green finally located substitute apples that could arrive by October 20. Green had to pay $40 per bushel, in part to expedite delivery and in part because the price of apples had increased between July and October. Between October 15 and October 20, Green had no apples to sell. During October, Green usually sold about two bushels a day, with a profit margin of about $15 per bushel. Green eventually sold all of the apples it received on October 20.

Answer: Basic Damages. Green was entitled to receive apples for $30,000. It actually had to pay $40,000 for the apples. It is entitled to recover $10,000. (In the terms of the UCC, cover price minus contract price.)

Incidental Damages. An employee who could have been doing other productive work had to spend two full days replacing the apples. The incidental cost of finding substitute apples approximately equals two days' wages for the employee — plus the phone bill that was run up. Although the employee might have been paid for those two days anyway, the employer would have received valuable services during those two days. Instead, the employer paid for services that it would not have paid for if the contract had been performed. Thus, the wages arguably should be included as incidental damages. (Some courts disagree.)

Lost Profits. The store did not sell any apples during the five-day hiatus. Normally it would have sold 10 bushels (2 per day) at a profit of $150 ($15 per bushel). But the store may not really have lost any profit. It eventually sold all 1,000 bushels of apples. It earned a profit on all 1,000 bushels. Arguably, Green is a lost-volume seller. If it had apples on October 15, it would have earned profit on those five days. If that meant its 1,000 bushels ran out five days sooner, it would have obtained more apples five days sooner and still earned the profit on them. Unless the shortage of apples would have prevented Green from obtaining more than 1,000 bushels this season, Green probably has lost five days of sales it could have made. [Note: Green probably did not earn less profit per bushel because it paid more for the apples. If it charged exactly the same price it would have for apples obtained at $30 per bushel (call it $45, to reflect a $15-per-bushel profit, ignoring overhead), it received exactly the same profit it deserves. It only earned $5 per bushel upon selling the apples ($45 − $40). But once it recovers $10 per bushel difference from Red, it nets $15 per bushel ($45 + $10 − $40). Green effectively paid only $30 per bushel for the apples; Red paid the $10 excess. Thus, Green's bottom line on the substitute apples as no lower than on the original apples. If Green charged more for the substitute apples than it would have for the original apples, its profits may be higher because of the breach.]

Foreseeability. If, at the time of contract formation, Red had no reason to know that a breach probably would cause Green to suffer lost profits, Red may not be liable to cover those consequential losses. If Red knew Green Grocery was in the business of selling apples, it must have known that failure to deliver the apples would prevent resale and, thus, produce lost profits. Even if Red expected Green to cover, it could foresee that cover might not be immediate, producing at least interim lost sales. This kind of loss flows naturally from the breach of a promise to sell to someone whom you know plans to resell the goods. Thus, foreseeability probably is satisfied even if Green never explicitly told Red that a breach would prevent it from reselling the apples at a profit.

Question 2:   In March 1995, Jan purchased four season tickets to the 1995-1996 season of the Santiago Symphony Orchestra. She was particularly excited about this season because the famous pianist

Vladimir Van Richter was scheduled to perform Brahms's first piano concerto. As the time for performance neared, the symphony encountered financial difficulty. It announced that it might need to cancel its contracts with some of the more expensive soloists, including Van Richter, to continue to perform the season (unless contributions increased dramatically). What remedies could Jan obtain if she brings suit for breach of contract?

Answer: Specific Performance. Van Richter, like any other artist, probably is unique. So is the Santiago Symphony Orchestra. Unless money damages would permit Jan to buy a ticket to hear Van Richter play with the Santiago Symphony, the remedy at law would be inadequate. Arguably, this is a personal service contract that cannot be enforced via specific performance. But neither Van Richter nor the orchestra musicians seem unwilling to perform. Rather, orchestra management is unwilling (or unable) to pay Van Richter. There is nothing terribly intrusive about ordering the orchestra to pay Van Richter. None of the policies concerning personal service contracts seem to apply here. An injunction seems no more intrusive than awarding money damages. But an injunction might not be practical here. Depending on the orchestra's financial plight, it might be unable to comply with the injunction. Courts generally do not order people to do the impossible (and will not punish them for contempt of court if they fail to do the impossible). Moreover, if paying Van Richter would prevent the orchestra from performing the rest of the season (e.g., if it would be unable to pay the orchestra musicians), the harm to the orchestra (and to the public) might greatly exceed the harm to Jan and other avid Van Richter fans.

Warranty Damages. If this were a sale of goods and Jan had accepted delivery of nonconforming goods, Jan could recover the value of the goods as promised minus the value of the goods as delivered. Here, if the ticket to a concert without Van Richter is worth less than a ticket to the concert with Van Richter, Jan can recover the difference. That is unlikely to satisfy Jan because she expected great joy from the concert. The UCC would allow any consequential damages. Loss of joy, however, may not be a consequential loss. The difference in joy is exactly what the difference in value of the tickets measures: People pay less for one ticket than the other because they expect less joy from the performance. The problem is that the market may not attach as much value to the performance as Jan did. Thus, her subjective loss may be greater than the loss measured by objective market values.

Cover Damages. Jan could try a different approach, but one a court may balk at. If the concert had been held, Jan would have heard Van Richter perform the Brahms concerto with a symphony orchestra of some quality. Jan could seek the amount of money it would require for Jan to hear Van Richter perform the Brahms (or a work of equal quality?) with another orchestra comparable to Santiago's. In effect, this rejects the nonconforming goods (Jan could return the tickets for a refund, then subtract the refund from the cost of cover, or the value of the tickets could be credited against the damages). Jan may also claim any increase in the cost of transportation to the concert—for instance, if the concert is in another city. This increase in cost may include hotel fare if Jan cannot return home the same night after the concert. It could even include lost wages if transportation to the other city requires Jan to miss work. Incidental damages—the cost to find such a performance, arrange for the ticket and transportation, etc.—would be included.

Avoidable Consequences. The cost of cover will be subject to limits of reasonableness. In effect, cover seeks to minimize the loss of enjoyment suffered by not hearing Van Richter. It may be unreasonable to incur costs that exceed the value Jan would receive from the concert. When the cost to repair a breach greatly exceeds the value of repairing the breach, courts award the smaller amount (the lost value). In this case, however, the lost value may be impossible to calculate or recompense. The joy of hearing a concert is primarily an emotional benefit. That makes it difficult to assess whether the cost of cover is in fact greater than the value of hearing the concert. Because defendant must prove that plaintiff's efforts to minimize the loss were unreasonable, the avoidable consequences doctrine may not limit recovery here. In addition, contract law usually does not compensate for emotional loss—unless the breach makes severe emotional disturbance particularly likely or the breach causes physical injury. The loss of joy is not exactly severe emotional disturbance. Although courts have allowed recovery against travel agents for botched vacation plans, the decision could be based on the distress of a bad vacation rather than the loss of joy anticipated during the vacation. Perhaps Jan can claim distress under the vacation cases, but the joy of hearing the concert seems unrecoverable. Relegating Jan to the lost value of performance may effectively preclude any remedy rather than preventing an unreasonably large recovery.

Consequential Losses and Foreseeability. If cover by seeing a concert in a different city were a consequential loss, it would be compensable only if foreseeable. In fact, the cost to see Van Richter perform elsewhere is the lost value of performance, not a consequential loss. To replace exactly what Jan had been promised,

Jan incurs the cost of a ticket elsewhere, with all the associated costs of attending that concert. Loss of joy, too, is just the loss of the value promised. But even if foreseeability applied to this element, it seems an inevitable consequence of canceling Van Richter that ticket holders will lose the joy of hearing Van Richter. Consequential losses could arise — if Jan had planned to entertain important business clients at this concert and the breach caused business losses. But the orchestra seems unlikely to have had any reason to know those losses would result from canceling Van Richter's appearance.

Question 3: On being chosen dean, Kohl commissions a portrait suitable for hanging with those of illustrious past deans. Ella Greco, a very talented but as yet unknown artist, accepts the commission. Kohl pays the full $2,000 price in advance to allow purchase of supplies and rent on Greco's studio. After three sittings, Greco becomes incensed at Kohl (a way of life for deans), throws Kohl from the studio, and warns Kohl never to return. Assume Greco's breach is not excused (despite what you know about deans). Greco has no income or assets. What remedies can Kohl receive.

Answer: **Injunctive Relief.** Greco's services may be unique. Her talents are subjectively unique — no other artist would be quite the same. Even for the purpose of creating a realistic portrait, creativity plays a role. Moreover, Greco's inability to pay damages makes the remedy at law inadequate, even if money could be used to hire an equally capable artist. Thus, an injunction ordinarily would be appropriate. Public policy, however, precludes specific enforcement of personal service contracts. If we treat this as the sale of a portrait, Greco could delegate the duty to complete the task to another artist (at Greco's expense) and then deliver the finished product. But Kohl probably has an interest in having the work done by Greco, which would preclude delegation. (Sorry. Sometimes the issues just don't segregate the way the chapters do.) Therefore, the contract really does involve personal services and specific performance is unavailable. A negative injunction ordering her not to work for others during the time she would have devoted to finishing Kohl's portrait is plausible but not very useful. A court might deny it because the contract probably does not identify exactly which times Kohl would sit for Greco, making it difficult to assess exactly which times Greco should be precluded from painting other works. Nor is such an injunction likely to have any effect. Greco does not seem to be working every spare minute. She has the flexibility to schedule other work around the injunction with virtually no inconvenience — and no particular benefit to Kohl. Finally, the only way Greco ever will be able to pay a judgment for damages—the only remedy that actually might help Kohl—is if she does work for others. Thus, an injunction would be counterproductive even if available.

Damages. The facts do not permit any numerical assessment of damages, but the manner of computation can be addressed. Kohl can recover the full $2,000. If Kohl must pay more than $2,000 to another artist to produce a portrait, Kohl also may recover the added cost. If the portrait by the other artist is not as good as the one Greco would have produced, Kohl theoretically is entitled to any difference in value of the two portraits. It seems unlikely that the value or quality of the portrait Greco would have produced can ever be assessed for comparison to the value or quality of the portrait actually produced by another. Thus, Kohl seems unlikely to be able to prove these consequential losses with sufficient certainty to allow their recovery. Any incidental costs—the time spent finding or auditioning substitute artists—also are recoverable. So might be the value of time spent in wasted sittings—at least to the extent that the new artist requires duplicative sittings, increasing the total amount of time posing above what it would have been if Greco had finished the portrait.

Question 4: Della, a developer, hires Connie, a construction contractor, to build homes on several lots D owns. The price for completion was to be $1 million. About halfway through the work, the real estate market goes into a depression and D calls off the project. C has already incurred about $600,000 in expenses. C can recoup $40,000 by salvaging materials on other jobs. But she cannot cancel equipment leases and other commitments that were made for the entire period of the expected construction. Even though she had spent $600,000 to complete half the work, C believes that she could have completed the work for another $350,000—in part because some expenses for the second half of the work were already included in the $600,000 figure and in part because work got more efficient after a few setbacks in the beginning stages of the project. How much can C recover as damages, assuming no progress payments have been made so far?

Answer: Where would she be if she completed the project? She would have $1 million in hand, but she would have spent $950,000 to get it. Thus, the target is to put her up $50,000. Where is she now? Down $560,000. She has spent $600,000, but she'll recover $40,000 of that by reselling or reusing materials. To move her from $560,000 in the hole to $50,000 ahead, we need to award

$610,000. (We can get there by other formulas, too. On an exam, you probably only need to use one.)

Revenues Less Savings. She would have received $1 million. From that we need to subtract any amounts she has saved because of the breach. C saved the $350,000 in additional expenses she would have incurred to complete the job and the $40,000. Thus, she can collect $610,000.

Costs So Far Plus Profit. We could reach the same result by adding the expected profit to the costs incurred so far. Her expected profit was $50,000: revenues of $1 million minus the $950,000 she would have spent to complete the job ($600,000 so far plus $350,000 to finish). She has spent $560,000 so far: gross expenditures of $600,000, but she'll get $40,000 of it back by salvaging materials. Thus, recovery will be $610,000: $560,000 + $50,000.

Question 5: In the preceding question, how much could C recover if the cost to complete would have required an additional $600,000?

Answer: She would have received $1 million, but would have spent $1.2 million to get it. She would be down $200,000. She is already down $560,000. To move from $560,000 down to only $200,000 requires an award of $360,000. Alternative approach: She would have received $1 million. But she has saved $640,000 ($40,000 by salvage and $600,000 in expenses she would have made to complete work). $1 million − $640,000 = $360,000.

Question 6: In the preceding problem, is there any way for C to recover more than $360,000?

Answer: **Reliance**. C could try to recover her reliance losses. She can prove her expenditures so far: $560,000 after the $40,000 of salvage. D then must prove any loss she would have suffered from the contract. On the facts shown, the loss would have been $200,000. But if D cannot prove the amount of the loss with reasonable certainty, C will be entitled to the full $560,000. If the numbers are as clear as posited here, D is likely to be able to prove the loss unless C commits perjury.

Restitution. C could claim the value of the benefit bestowed on D. The value can be measured by either the amount of increase in the value of D's property or the fair market value of C's services. The first measure is unfavorable to C. The value of real estate has declined, which is why D wants to stop work. Thus, the houses C has built probably have not increased the value of

D's land by as much as the cost to build them. (If they had, D would still be able to sell them at a profit and would not have breached.) The fair market value of C's services, however, might be higher than the contract price. Presumably, C was the lowest bid; others would have charged more. And the cost to C of providing these services exceeds the contract price. Unless C is inefficient, the value of the services probably is somewhere near the cost of the services — and usually a little higher than the cost. As a result, C might recover about $560,000 as the fair market value of the services in restitution.

Question 7: In the preceding question, what if C walked off the job without excuse? Could she recover anything? If so, how much?

Answer: The breaching party cannot recover against the nonbreaching party for damages caused by the nonbreaching party's nonbreach. But a breaching party can recover in restitution. Usually, courts limit the breaching party to the fair market value of the services or the increase in the value of defendant's property, whichever is less. In the preceding case — where real estate values declined — the increase in the value of defendant's property is likely to be lower than the fair market value of the services. No facts were given to allow computation of just how much value the partially finished construction added to the property.

CHAPTER 24 BENEFICIARIES, ASSIGNMENT, AND DELEGATION

Question 1: Good friends Sean and Pat will graduate from college in two weeks. Both want to go to law school. Each had a 3.7 grade point average. Sean, however, had significantly better LSAT scores. Each applied to UC-Berkeley and Stanford but to no other law schools. Each school offered Sean a place in the entering class; each rejected Pat's application. Sean accepted admission both to Berkeley and to Stanford and paid the deposit each requested. Sean and Pat then assigned the right to attend Stanford to Pat. Their contract made clear that all contractual duties owed to Stanford would remain Sean's obligation; Pat received only Sean's right to receive Stanford's performance. In exchange, Pat agreed to pay any expense Sean incurred in meeting those contractual obligations to Stanford, plus a 1% fee for incidental costs and time spent. Pat agreed to fulfill any obligations associated with attending Stanford that are not part of the contract between Stanford and Sean. Sean gave Stanford written notice that the right to a place in the entering class had been assigned to Pat. If Stanford refuses to admit Pat, will it breach a contract?

Answer: **Assignment.** Pat has a right to Stanford's performance only if the assignment from Sean is valid. Assignments are valid unless they are forbidden by contract, are contrary to public policy, or materially change the obligor's duty, materially increase the burden or risk on the obligor, or materially impair the chance of obtaining return performance or the value of that performance.

Contract. We need to review everything Stanford sent to Sean to see if it contains a provision precluding assignment of the right to attend classes. The application, the bulletin, any brochures, and the acceptance letter might include such a provision. Even if we find one, however, a court may interpret the word assignment to mean delegation. The law favors assignment and, unless the contract or circumstances indicate otherwise, will assume the parties meant to preclude delegation but not assignment. If the contract is explicit, Stanford may prevail. The factors that may lead a court to interpret the contract as barring assignment without an express clause probably are the same as the factors that might lead a court to find a public policy against assignment.

Materially Change Stanford's Duty. The contract allowed Pat to sit in class instead of Sean. Stanford's duty—to hold classes, administer tests, grant diplomas—did not change at all. Only the recipient changed, and that only if Pat succeeds in school. This factor does not seem to justify rejecting the assignment.

Materially Increase the Burden on Stanford. The burden on Stanford of having Pat in class instead of Sean does not seem materially different. Professors need not be paid any more, classrooms need be no larger, and so on. If Pat is harder to teach than Sean would have been, professors may face more difficulty. It is not clear that the difference is material. Moreover, Stanford itself does not face the burden, only employees, who probably have no claim to be allowed students of a particular caliber.

Materially Increase the Risk. Stanford may allege that it sought more than just tuition. Its admissions consider the probable success of its student body and the probable generosity they will have in sharing that success via contributions. Pat poses considerably more risk of lower success or lower generosity than Sean—in part because Stanford rejected Pat and in part because Pat's indicators predict less success. Although indicators are imperfect, they do identify risk. The issue may turn on how material the risk is: How much less likely (than Sean) Pat is to succeed or to be generous.

Materially Reduce the Value of Return Performance. If return performance is tuition, the value to Stanford is identical regardless of how it is received or from whom.

Materially Reduce the Likelihood of Obtaining Return Performance. Because Sean will not receive the benefit of education at Stanford, Sean may be less likely to make the tuition payments or to make them timely. On the other hand, because Sean will not want to jeopardize the right to receive a 1% bonus from Pat, Sean may be even more fastidious about timely payments. If the risk is any different, the difference may not be material.

Public Policy. Either of two public policies might support a university's right to refuse admission to assignees of those actually accepted for admission. First, the public policy of making opportunities available to those best qualified for them may preclude assignment. If Sean could assign the right to Pat, other applicants with records better than Pat's might be denied a place in the class despite their superior ability to benefit from the education provided. Public policy may support leaving the power to select the next best qualified person in the hands of the school—subject always to limitations imposed by antidiscrimination laws, etc. Second, public policy may support the creation of a diverse student body at universities. But assignment prevents a school from knowing whether the person who actually appears for classes will bring any diversity to the class—or, for that matter, the characteristics of the class as a whole. Because each place might be assigned by the person accepted, the school would be helpless to achieve any diversity goal. Only by allowing the school to select the individual who will fill a place—and that individual's replacement if she elects not to come—can a school pursue diversity in its student body.

Delegation. Sean did not delegate the duty to pay Stanford to Pat, so rules dealing with delegation are less likely to help. Stanford could argue that a student has a duty to attend class. A university could write its materials in a way that allowed it to hold a student in breach if she paid tuition but skipped classes. Absent express provisions, however, attending classes intuitively seems the students' right rather than their duty. They have a duty to pay tuition in exchange for the right to receive an education. Limited to a duty to pay, Stanford has little or no interest in who signs the check—and, in any event, the person signing the check was Sean.

NO CLUES

Question 1: On October 1, Rancher Roy promised to sell Butte Beef all the cattle on the "South 40" on March 1 for $3 per pound. The parties did not specify the number of cattle because neither was sure how many of the 300 head then on the parcel would survive the winter. By February 15, a surplus of beef cattle had decreased the market price to $2 per pound. Between February 15 and March 1, Roy moved 250 head of cattle from the South 40 to the East 60 because the South 40 had been overgrazed and could not support the herd any longer. Roy tendered the 250 cattle moved from the South 40 to Butte Beef on March 1. Butte refused to accept the cattle. Advise Roy whether to sue Butte for breach of contract.

Answer: **Promise**. Butte Beef promised to buy the cattle on the South 40 on March 1. No cattle were on the South 40 on March 1. Thus, there are no cattle that Butte promised to buy. Butte's promise might be enforceable, but Butte did not breach its promise by refusing the cattle on the East 60 — even those who had been on the South 40 until recently.

Good Faith. Courts will interpret a contract to include a promise to act in good faith. But a promise to take the cattle from the South 40 is hard to interpret as a promise to take cattle from the East 60. This is not a case in which Butte Beef dishonestly manipulated events so that a condition did not occur. The condition (location of the cattle) was in Roy's control, not Butte's. Butte accepted all the cattle it promised to accept. Because of Roy's conduct, that quantity turned out to be zero.

Illusoriness. If Roy's promise was illusory, Butte received no consideration for its promise to buy cattle. Without consideration, Butte's promise to buy cattle would not be enforceable. You could argue that Roy's promise was (or was not) illusory by the reasoning in Question 3 relating to Chapter 2. But what does that add? Until someone shows that the promise to buy cattle from the South 40 on March 1 really meant a promise to buy cattle that were on the South 40 February 15, there was no breach.

Glossary

Acceptance. A promise to perform on the terms specified in an offer.

Accord. An agreement to discharge one party's obligations under a contract in exchange for a performance different (usually less) than originally promised. Discharge occurs upon performance (satisfaction) of the accord. *See also* Executory Accord, Substitute Contract, Accord and Satisfaction.

Accord and satisfaction. A defense to a claim of breach of contract. The defense requires proof that the other party agreed to accept a different performance in place of the duty allegedly breached and that the different performance was delivered (the accord was satisfied).

Adequacy of consideration. A phrase used to question the fairness of the bargain. Usually, adequacy of consideration is not required. Parties are free to make their own decisions about how much a performance is worth.

Anticipatory repudiation. An unequivocal indication, given before performance is due, that a party does not intend to perform a contract when performance becomes due. *See also* Repudiation.

Arbitration. Submitting a dispute for resolution by a person selected in a manner specified by the parties, usually instead of filing suit in courts of law for resolution of the dispute.

Arbitrator. The person to whom a contract dispute is submitted under an arbitration clause.

Assent. The conclusion that all parties to the contract have committed themselves to perform according to its terms. *See also* Offer, Acceptance.

Assignee. A party who receives a right to performance under a contract to which she was not originally a party.

Assignment. A transfer of a right to receive performance under a contact from one party to another, leaving the assignor no right to receive that performance.

Assignor. A party who assigns a right to receive performance under a contract.

Bargain. An agreement to exchange values. Something is bargained for if it is sought by a promisor in exchange for a promise and given by a promisee in exchange for that promise.

Beneficiary. A party entitled to receive benefits under a contract. A third-party beneficiary is a person who is not a party to a contract but who will be benefitted by performance of the contract. If she is an intended beneficiary, she also may gain the right to sue to enforce the contract if it is not performed.

Breach. Unexcused nonperformance when performance is due.

Certainty. The requirement that the existence of damages be proven with reasonable certainty before allowing a finder of fact to assess the amount of damages. Sometimes used to refer to definiteness.

Coercion. Another name for duress.

Concealment. Action that a person knows or believes will prevent another from learning a fact.

Condition. An event, not certain to occur, that must occur before performance is due, unless occurrence is excused.

Contract. A promise the performance of which the law recognizes as a duty — usually by providing a remedy for breach of the promise to the nonbreaching party.

Counteroffer. A response to an offer indicating willingness to enter a contract on terms different, albeit trivially, from the terms of the offer. A counteroffer is a rejection.

Course of dealing. The actions of parties over a series of prior contracts. Usually refers to interpreting a term in a current contract by looking to how the parties' conduct suggests they interpreted it when used in prior contracts.

Course of performance. The actions of parties over a series of performances of an executory contract. Usually refers to interpreting a term in an agreement by looking to how the parties' conduct on prior occasions for performance of the agreement suggests they interpreted it when that performance occurred.

Cover. Technically, a buyer's act of obtaining from another party goods promised but not delivered by a seller. The term sometimes is loosely used to refer to any substitute performance obtained by the nonbreaching party.

Cure. The act of correcting any defects in performance. Often refers to cure after a breach occurs but can refer to cure before the time for performance has ended.

Definiteness. The requirement that a contract be sufficiently clear to allow the court to ascertain whether a promise has been performed and to determine a reasonable basis for a remedy.

Delegated party. A person to whom duties under a contract are delegated by a party to the contract.

Delegating party. A person who delegates her duties under a contract to another.

Delegation. The act of designating another person to perform one's duties under a contract.

Disaffirmance. A decision by a person with a right to rescind a contract based on a defense to formation to exercise that right and request a return of any performance rendered so far (including the obligation to return any performance she has received so far).

Duress. A defense to formation of a contract alleging that the party was compelled to assent. An improper threat that induces a party to assent to a contract when she had no reasonable alternative but to assent.

Expectation interest. An amount necessary to move the nonbreaching party from the position she now occupies to the position she would have occupied if the contract had been performed.

Foreseeability. A limitation on the recovery of damages that precludes recovery of losses if, at the time of contract formation, the breaching party had no reason to know those losses would be a probable result of a breach.

Frustration. A defense similar to impracticability but aimed at buyers. Performance is excused because unanticipated circumstances make the other party's performance so valueless that a party should not be compelled to accept it and perform the return duties.

Good faith. Honesty in fact. Even unreasonable conduct can comply with good faith, as long as a party acts in accord with honestly held beliefs. For merchants, good faith also includes the obligation to comply with reasonable commercial standards of fair dealing in the trade.

Goods. Things that are movable, including crops, but excluding currency and intangibles (e.g., stock or insurance policies).

Illusory promise. Words that are not a promise at all because a condition negates commitment, usually by permitting the party who uttered the words to refuse to perform if for any reason she changes her mind.

Impossibility. An older and less forgiving version of the impracticability defense, under which performance was excused only if performance was impossible.

Impracticability. A defense that arises when unanticipated circumstances make performance so onerous that a court concludes performance under the contract should be excused—usually under the guise that the parties themselves never intended for the contract to apply under these circumstances.

Incapacity. A legal conclusion expressing reservations about the individual's ability to protect herself from disadvantageous bargains. Contracts made by persons suffering an incapacity usually are voidable by that person.

Incidental beneficiary. A person who thought she would benefit from performance of the contract, but who was not a person on whom the parties intended to bestow the right to sue to enforce the contract.

Integrated writing. A writing that the parties intended to be the final statement of their agreement. When the parties intend the writing to be the exclusive statement of their dealings, it is **completely integrated**. If they intend it to be the final statement of the terms it contains, but do not intend for it to contain all of the agreements between the parties, it is **partially integrated**.

Intended beneficiary. A person, not a party to a contract, whom the parties intended to benefit from the contract and who, thereby, gains the right to sue to enforce the contract.

Interpretation. The effort to ascertain what the terms of a contract mean, particularly what the contract required each party to do to fulfill her obligations under the contract.

Irreparable injury rule. Rule that courts will deny injunctive relief, such as specific performance, if the remedy at law (usually damages) is adequate. A remedy at law is adequate if it is as completely practical and efficient as an injunction.

Liquidated damages. A provision in a contract specifying the amount or, more often, a formula used to calculate the amount of damages a nonbreaching party may recover as compensation for a breach.

Mailbox rule. Holding that an acceptance is effective once it leaves the possession of the offeree and enters the possession of a third party (such as the post office). The rule applies only if the manner of acceptance is reasonable.

Manifest. Observable, usually to a reasonable third person hypothetically present.

Material breach. The legal conclusion that a breach of contract was sufficiently significant to justify a party in suspending her own performance and, ultimately, terminating the contract.

Mirror-image rule. Requirement that an acceptance agree exactly with the terms of the offer. Any change or addition, however trivial, is not an acceptance under this approach. Courts have backed away from this requirement.

Misrepresentation. (1) An assertion not in accord with the facts; (2) a defense to contract formation alleging that the party entered the contract because she was deceived, usually about a material fact, but sometimes about the content or effect of the terms of the agreement.

Mistake. A term that can be applied to a number of different reasons a party regrets entering a contract. Legally significant mistakes include mistake of **integration** (an error in reducing the parties' agreement to writing), mistake of **basic assumption** (an erroneous belief about the nature of a thing exchanged), and **misunderstanding** (a belief that a term used in the contract means something other than what the other party believes it means).

Mitigation. An unfortunate term used to describe efforts by a nonbreaching party to minimize the loss caused by the breach. Minimization is a better choice. The avoidable consequences doctrine is better still.

Modification. An agreement by all parties to a contract to amend the terms of a contract.

Moral obligation or consideration. A phrase used to describe the situation in which a promise is made in gratitude for (or a sense of obligation arising from) a prior performance by the promisee. Technically, no bargain exists, but some courts will enforce promises made in response to a moral obligation to compensate another for benefits already bestowed.

Mutual mistake. The situation when both parties are mistaken about the same thing (usually a basic assumption), neither being aware of the actual state of affairs.

Nondisclosure. The failure to reveal facts to a person when circumstances require one to reveal those facts.

Novation. A release of an obligor, usually combined with the delegation of the obligor's duties to another.

Obligee. A party to whom another owes an obligation or duty.

Obligor. A party who owes an obligation or duty to another.

Offer. The first step in finding assent. An expression of willingness to enter a contract made in a manner that justifies another in believing that her assent is invited and will conclude the transaction.

Option. A contract in which one party promises to keep an offer open for a period of time in exchange for consideration. Some options are created without consideration, usually by reliance or by statute.

Parol evidence. Literally, oral evidence. Today it more accurately refers to any evidence other than a written contract and usage of trade.

Parol evidence rule. A rule that precludes admitting extrinsic evidence of prior or contemporaneous negotiations, discussions, or agreements if intended to vary, to contradict, or (if completely integrated) to supplement the terms of an integrated writing.

Past consideration. A term used to describe the situation in which a promise is given in (arguably) exchange for a performance the promisor has already received. Past consideration is not technically a bargain but sometimes will support enforcement of a promise.

Penalty clause. A contract provision specifying a remedy that exceeds a reasonable estimate of the actual or anticipated amount of the loss.

Preliminary negotiations. A legal conclusion that discussions had not yet produced assent.

Promise. A manifestation of an intention to act in a particular way, made in a manner that justifies another in believing that a commitment has been made.

Promisee. One to whom a promise is made.

Promisor. One who makes a promise.

Ratification. The decision by a person who has a right to disaffirm a contract (based on a defense to contract formation) not to exercise that right but to proceed with performance of the contract.

Rejection. (1) A response to an offer indicating unwillingness to enter a contract on those terms. (2) A refusal to accept nonconforming goods.

Reliance. Action or forebearance by a promisee that she would not have taken if no promise had been made. When reliance is detrimental and the promisor reasonably should have expected the reliance, courts may treat a promise differently than they would have if no reliance had occurred.

Reliance interest. The amount necessary to move the plaintiff from the position she now occupies to the position she would have occupied if no promise had been made. Usually this involves compensating for any costs incurred in preparation to perform or in partial performance of the promise.

Repudiation. An unequivocal indication that a party is unable or unwilling to perform contractual duties. Repudiation usually raises an issue only when it occurs before performance is due. This is sometimes referred to as anticipatory repudiation.

Rescission. A decree that a contract is not binding. Once rescission has been granted, a contract is rescinded.

Restitution interest. An amount necessary to move the defendant from the position she now occupies to the position she would have occupied if the contract had not been made (or, if no contract existed, if performance by the other party had not been started). Usually this involves refunding any benefit she received by the other party's performance.

Revocation. Notice to an offeree that the offeror no longer is willing to enter a contract on the terms stated in the offer.

Specific performance. An injunction ordering a party to perform a promise.

Statute of frauds. A statute forbidding courts to enforce certain promises unless evinced by a writing signed by the party to be charged.

Substantial performance. The opposite of material breach. The legal conclusion that performance was sufficiently complete to require the other party to accept it and continue performing her own side of the deal. Performance that is substantial, but not complete, is still a breach and still permits an action for damages for the breach.

Substitute contract. A new agreement which a party accepts in replacement of a prior obligation, without retaining any recourse to seek enforcement of the prior contract. Unlike accord and satisfaction, the making of the substitute promise discharges the original duty, not the performance of the promise.

Suretyship. A promise to pay the debts of another, usually contingent upon the other's failure to pay the debt when due.

Tender. An expression of willingness to perform a contract immediately combined with a manifest ability to perform immediately.

Unconscionable. A legal conclusion that a term in a contract is so onerous that it cannot fairly be enforced.

Undue hardship. A defense to injunctive relief and sometimes to damages when the remedy would harm the defendant much more than it would benefit the plaintiff.

Undue influence. (1) A defense to breach of contract based on pressure to agree; (2) unfair persuasion by a person exercised against one who either is under the domination of the persuader or who has a relationship with the persuaded that permits her to assume the persuader would not act in a manner inconsistent with the persuaded party's best interests.

Unilateral mistake. A mistake, usually a basic assumption, made by only one of the parties (or, in multiparty transactions, less than all the parties) to a contract.

Void. A legal conclusion that the agreement had no binding effect on any person at any time.

Voidable. A legal conclusion that one party could elect to disaffirm a contract and recover in restitution for any performance already rendered under the agreement.

Warranty. A promise that performance will be of a particular quality. Often supported by a promise to repair any performance that is not of appropriate quality.

Table of Cases

Table of Statutes

Table of Restatement (Second) of Contracts Provisions

Table of Uniform Commercial Code Provisions

Index